CW01213504

STRIKE UP, STRIKE SURE

The Pipes and Drums of the London Scottish Regiment

Duncan de Silva

*Simon
Told you I'd finish it...
...eventually!

Duncan*

Helion & Company

Helion & Company Limited
Unit 8 Amherst Business Centre
Budbrooke Road
Warwick
CV34 5WE
England
Tel. 01926 499 619
Email: info@helion.co.uk
Website: www.helion.co.uk
Twitter: @helionbooks
Visit our blog at blog.helion.co.uk

Published by Helion & Company 2022
Designed and typeset by Mach 3 Solutions Ltd (www.mach3solutions.co.uk)
Cover designed by Paul Hewitt, Battlefield Design (www.battlefield-design.co.uk)

Text © Duncan de Silva 2022
Images © as individually credited

Every reasonable effort has been made to trace copyright holders and to obtain their permission for the use of copyright material. The author and publisher apologize for any errors or omissions in this work and would be grateful if notified of any corrections that should be incorporated in future reprints or editions of this book.

ISBN 978-1-804512-53-1

British Library Cataloguing-in-Publication Data.
A catalogue record for this book is available from the British Library.

All rights reserved. No part of this publication may be reproduced, stored in a retrieval system, or transmitted, in any form, or by any means, electronic, mechanical, photocopying, recording or otherwise, without the express written consent of Helion & Company Limited.

For details of other military history titles published by Helion & Company Limited contact the above address or visit our website: http://www.helion.co.uk.

We always welcome receipt of book proposals from prospective authors.

Dedication

"Is that all?"

It was the voice of a small, slight, slender flapper in the crowd at Charing Cross yesterday, after the swift passing of the handful of men who represent all that is left of the brave battalion of those London Scottish, the first of the Territorial units to go out in the early days of the war. The speaker would have been but a small child five years ago, and for that reason her words carried no sting. But for many in the packed crowd that surged and broke out of line in their eagerness to welcome home this handful of heroes, the procession was full of poignancy.

The sons of London's great middle-class, not always of Scots descent, were once part of The London Scottish: many of them wore their khaki and blue long before the stern call came: many of them have so long ceased to wear it that mothers have laid aside their mourning garb, and keep their sadness hidden.

Great days have come and gone since we had that early picture of the ragged remnants of The London Scottish answering the roll-call after the first gallant work. Small wonder that, for some of the youngsters looking on, the group of fifty officers and men who passed out of the station, headed by half as many pipers, had no meaning at all. But for the rest of us it was a ghostly hour, in which we saw through tears the faces of the lads we loved in days when war was undreamed of, and our hearts were burdened with no more anxieties than the dread lest our own young hopeful, newly entered on a business career, and developing a blatant taste in socks and ties, should be led astray by that zest of life which helped to make him doubly precious to our eyes.

Very different lads they were from the men who came back. We dreaded once lest they should be facing life too frivolously. How could we dream that such a glory of pride and suffering should be their immortal legacy?

The bronzed group came, passed, and was lost to view in the following crowd within the space of a minute. If one were sight-seeing, it was little enough. It was only a few men looking gallant and happy, 'weel pleased' with London's shouting tribute, glad to be home and accounted among the 'lucky ones' in that they were able to march without fatigue on a hot day through Cockspur Street and Piccadilly, down Grosvenor Place and along Victoria Street to their yellow-flagged headquarters in Buckingham Gate.

"What went ye out for to see?"

A very frail, elderly lady, as slightly built as the little flapper whose voice one first heard, stood at the edge of the pavement clasping the arm of an elderly man, markedly erect and stern. The group of soldiers went past the couple: and, as the pipes skirled on ahead, the lady raised her face, quivering like a reed shaken with the wind, towards that of her husband, who gazed at unseen things far off and dim, but moved no muscle. And one saw, rather than heard, on her lips the faintest of whispers, "Oh, my boy, my boy!"

That was all.

The *Daily Graphic*, 17 May 1919 on the final return of the 1st Battalion London Scottish.

This volume is dedicated to all officers and men of the London Scottish Regiment, with special remembrance to those who gave their lives on Active Service, of whom the following served as Pipers or Drummers:

First World War:

Piper	**Archibald Angus**	01/11/14	Age 17
L/Cpl. Piper	**James Carey**	01/11/14	Age 31
L/Cpl. Piper	**Eric Glenn Chapman**	01/11/14	Age 22
Piper	**Douglas Roberts Parkyn**	01/11/14	Age 21
Piper	**John Forbes Bennie**	09/11/14	Unknown
L/Cpl. Piper	**Harry Gould Latham**	16/11/14	Age 29
Cpl. (Drummer)	**Frank Wilkins**	09/10/15	Age 20
2nd Lt. (Piper)	**Walter MacKenzie Wallace**	21/10/15	Unknown
2nd Lt. (Piper)	**Charles William Donaldson Mackay**	17/08/16	Unknown
Drummer	**Frank Albert Gosling**	28/08/16	Age 27
Piper	**Henry James Robert Woodcock**	09/09/16	Age 21
2nd Lt. (Piper)	**Alfred Cairns Wilson M.C.**	25/09/16	Age 40
Piper	**Alexander Allan Connell**	29/09/16	Age 25
Piper	**Simon Campbell**	13/05/17	Age 19
Piper	**Andrew Buchanan Paton**	13/05/17	Age 26
Drummer	**Alexander James Macpherson**	28/03/18	Age 19

Second World War:

Sgt. Air Gunner (Drummer)	**Douglas Borthwick Cowie**	15/08/40	Age 19
Cpl. Drummer	**John Alexander Bryden**	18/07/43	Age 35
Gnr. Piper	**William Turnbull**	09/08/43	Age 26
L/Sgt. (Drummer)	**William Ian Hamilton**	11/01/44	Age 23
Cpl. Piper	**William Kilgour McDougall**	21/01/44	Age 25
Cpl. Drummer	**Thomas Arnold Robson**	27/02/44	Age 29
Capt. (Piper)	**Donald Ross Spence**	27/08/44	Age 30
Capt. (Drummer)	**James Charles Hollebone**	05/09/44	Age 31

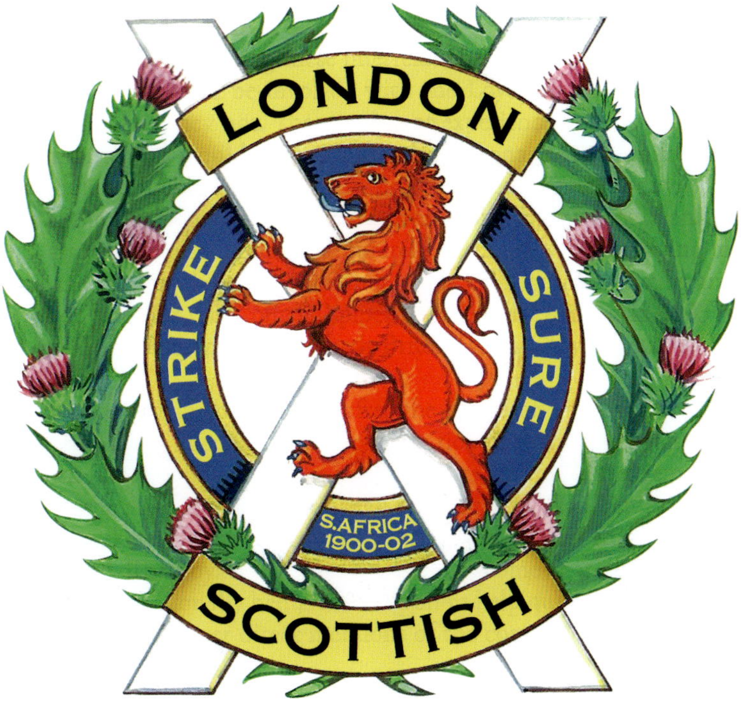
LONDON
STRIKE
SURE
S.AFRICA
1900-02
SCOTTISH

Contents

Foreword by His Royal Highness, Prince Edward, The Earl of Wessex	ix
Foreword by Major Gordon Rowan, Director, Army School of Bagpipe Music and Highland Drumming	x
Preface & Acknowledgements	xi
Genealogy of the London Scottish Regiment	xiii
1 Birth of a Tradition 1798-1814	15
2 The Early Years 1859-1880	40
3 Coming of Age 1881-1913	71
4 The Pipes and Drums at War 1914-1919	108
5 The Inter-War Years 1919-1939	175
6 The Second World War 1939-1946	203
7 The Post-War Years at 59 Buckingham Gate, 1946-1985	256
8 95 Horseferry Road to the London Guards 1986-2022	303
Appendices	
I Pipe Majors of The London Scottish Regiment	362
II Drum Majors of The London Scottish Regiment	364
Bibliography	365
Index	373

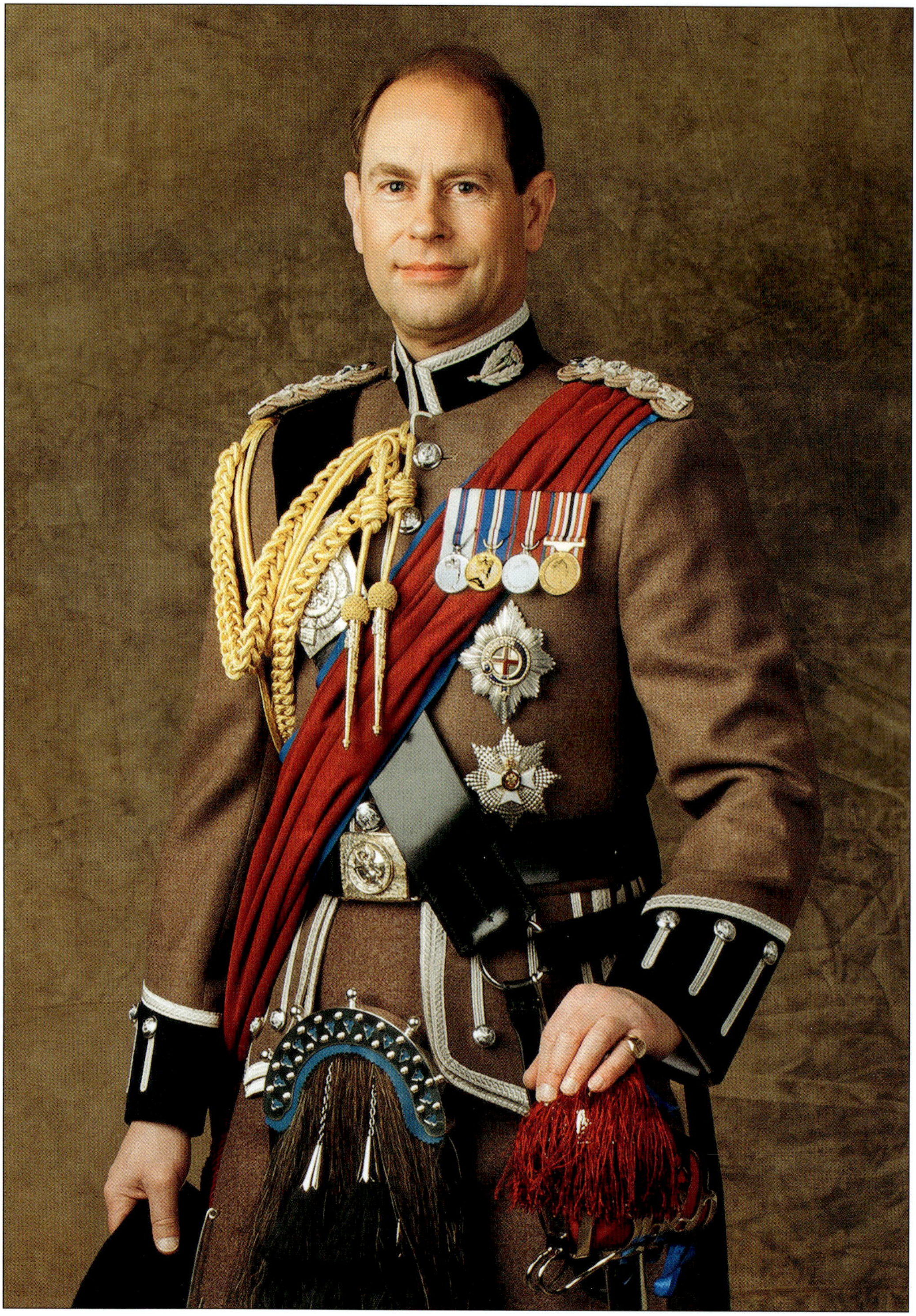

BAGSHOT PARK

From the outset, it is probably important to clarify certain facts about the London Scottish Pipes and Drums. First and foremost, they have nothing to do with a rugby club, although they are occasionally seen there, equally at home on the pitch or in the bar. No, this band takes its name from the London Scottish Regiment, although its formation actually pre-dates the Regiment by some 60 years. Given that the Pipes and Drums have been in existence for some 225 years, are one of the very oldest pipe bands in the world and their antecedents lay solid claim to have been at the very birth of pipe band evolution, are good reasons for penning their history in their own right.

During that time, the Pipes and Drums have achieved an astonishing number of 'firsts'; including the first recorded bagpipe music, the first broadcast on radio and, later, the first aired on television. The band has participated in many historically important ceremonial duties, from a leading role in Queen Victoria's Diamond Jubilee Parade in 1897, to joining the Massed Bands of the Guards Division for 'The Sword and the Crown' in 2021; the first military public event following the national lockdowns during the global Covid pandemic.

The current band are all volunteers and continue the story both here and abroad. They are much sought after and very distinctive in their Hodden Grey kilts and plaid. I've seen them Beating Retreat on Horse Guards Parade, at the British Military Tournament at Earl's Court and at a service commemorating the 100th Anniversary of the First World War at The Royal Hospital, Chelsea, to name but a few occasions.

There is one little known fact about the Pipes and Drums which I ought to let you know about. It concerns my grandmother, Her Majesty Queen Elizabeth, The Queen Mother, who was Honorary Colonel of the London Scottish Regiment from 1935 to 2002. During that time six successive Pipe Majors served as Her Majesty's Personal Piper. This rarely comes up in conversation and is just a footnote in their illustrious history, in fact I would be surprised if you can find much on the subject in this book . . . which is the only reason I raise it here.

All credit must go to Duncan de Silva for the extraordinary effort he has put into the research for this book. It is evident that since he took over responsibility for compiling the band notes for the Regimental magazine, he has warmed to the task. So much so, that he has found the pages of the magazine too restrictive and that obviously he needed greater scope for his new found talent. This book is testament to that.

All of us who know and appreciate the music produced by the present pipers and drummers are both impressed by what Duncan has achieved and grateful to him for documenting such a distinguished history. I very much hope that you will enjoy exploring the pages, photographs, memorabilia, anecdotes, and traditions.

One of those traditions is that the Pipe Major of the London Scottish serves as the Royal Honorary Colonel's Personal Piper. This tradition was started by HM Queen Elizabeth, The Queen Mother. Just saying, in case no one mentions it.

HRH The Earl of Wessex and Forfar, KG, GCVO, ADC
Royal Honorary Colonel

THE ARMY SCHOOL OF BAGPIPE MUSIC and HIGHLAND DRUMMING
Inchdrewer House, 299 Colinton Road,
EDINBURGH EH13 0LA

"Strike Up, Strike Sure: The History of the Pipes and Drums of the London Scottish Regiment"

As Director of Army Bagpipe Music and Highland Drumming I was delighted to be asked to write this foreword. As a piper I was delighted to read it. The Army School of Piping exists to train pipers, drummers and buglers and to maintain excellence in musicianship. The School also co-ordinates individual piping across the Army and supports individual players and pipe bands, for both regular soldiers and reservists.

The London Scottish have a unique history since 1859, having always been a volunteer Regiment and flying the flag south of the border, maintaining Scottish traditions. This history recounts how important the Pipes and Drums were to Regimental identity to the exiled Scots community in London and how important it was for those pipers and drummers to be a London Scot.

It tells the story of a small but vital part of a storied regiment and like many military histories it reflects the core values of the British Army, courage; discipline; respect for others; integrity; loyalty and selfless commitment. Focusing on the Pipes and Drums is entirely in step with the Army School's dual role in the promotion and education of our military piping and drumming heritage and as custodian of the history of piping and pipe bands in the British Army.

This book contributes to what we know about the London Scottish, specifically, and military piping, drumming and pipe bands generally. There is something universal in the stories related here about the London Scottish that will be familiar to anyone who has played in or been around a pipe band.

Gordon Rowan
Major
DABM

Preface & Acknowledgements

The seed of the idea which would eventually become this book was sown back in 2010 as the London Scottish Pipes and Drums celebrated their 150th anniversary. I was writing the Band Notes section for the *Regimental Gazette* at the time and was asked to put together a short speech on the history of the band, to be given at the anniversary band supper. After spending some time in the regimental archives, it soon became clear that the information I was beginning to uncover was hugely significant, in terms of regimental, military, pipe band and Scottish history. The more I looked, the more significant information I found, and it became apparent that the Pipes and Drums of this well-thought-of and slightly eccentric regiment had been punching above its weight for nearly 225 years. I gave the speech at band supper and decided to quietly continue my research. I did not consider that it would ever turn into a project of quite this magnitude.

My focus expanded outside of the regimental archives, as I began to trawl through thousands of newspaper articles, museum records and artifacts dating back to 1798 at the Scots Guards archives, Gordon Highlanders Museum, National Army Museum, Museum of Scotland, British Library and National Library of Scotland, amongst others. The influence of the band seemed never ending and the list of historical 'firsts' grew and grew. Back at London Scottish Headquarters at 95 Horseferry Road, I found a plethora of virtually untouched war diaries from both the First and Second World Wars and then the greatest gem; an archive of photographs and documents bequeathed to the regiment that was only partially catalogued. With the help of successive museum curators Clem Webb, John Wren and Andrew Parsons, I was entrusted and given free rein to search through boxes of untouched material, take down paintings throughout the building to photograph and scan hundreds of photos, documents and images. Regimental Secretaries Bob Harman and Stuart Young actively encouraged my endeavours and Laura Truman was forever obliging in assisting me with access.

The hours of academic research were subsequently joined by hours of scanning, cataloguing, cleaning and digitally repairing photographs and other images from as far back as 1859, whilst I also built my own collection of artifacts relating to the London Scottish Pipes and Drums. These, along with all my notes and scans are now in the care of the London Scottish Regimental Museum. Encouragement grew from various quarters to turn what I was uncovering into a book. Ex Drummer Charles Redman, Piper Gordon Skilling, Pipe Major John Spoore, Drummer Steve Hill, Piper Stuart Nicholson and David Hillman (among others) shared their photographic archives, and pipe band historians including Adam Sanderson, Keith Sanger, Jeannie Campbell, Rob MacDonald, Aad Boode and others on the *bobdunsire.com* online pipe band forum provided information. Regimental Colonel David Rankin Hunt facilitated access to unpublished paintings and images from the Royal Collection and Piper Rob Blackledge helped with initial ideas for layout and design. Ex Pipe Majors John Spoore and Chris Macpherson offered invaluable insights, as did ex Drum Majors Micky Powell and Bryan Alderson, either via interviews and/or extensive correspondence. Ex tenor Drummer Pat King provided information, photos, notes, DVDs from his Highland Classics collection, and agreed to be interviewed.

Turning an idea into an actuality, however, could not have happened without my incredible 'editorial board,' without whose considerable assistance, this book would never have been published. 'Editor in chief,' Drummer Nick Gair provided his extensive knowledge, wisdom and advise, in addition to meticulously editing each chapter. Corporal Piper Andrew Parsons not only extended his expertise in military and regimental history but was extremely generous in sharing his own personal research, especially concerning the First World War. He also spotted a couple of complete howlers which would have been particularly embarrassing had they gone uncovered. Drummer Andy Withers did a remarkable and thorough job of proof reading and correcting my terrible grammar and Piper Iain Barrett helped ensure that my writing style was accessible. Huge thanks extend also to ex Band President, Colonel Peter McLelland and to the current incumbent, Colonel Geoffrey Strickland, who proved top cover and access to people and places unobtainable to a lowly drummer. Piper Major Jim McLucas and Drum Major Nobby Foulis are also deserving of special thanks, not only for the assistance they have provided in the writing of this work but for their skill and dedicated leadership which has allowed the Pipes and Drums to grow and flourish.

Despite the best efforts of all those who have assisted me, there may well be mistakes and inaccuracies in this book. While I have tried my best to be as exacting as possible in my research and writing, I may have inadvertently made errors in writing up my findings. All such mistakes are mine and mine alone and can hopefully be corrected in the second edition!

Thanks also go to Helion, the publishers, for creating such an excellent product and special acknowledgement must go to the Swires Group, whose wide-wide operations are based at 59 Buckingham Gate, the former headquarters of the London Scottish Regiment, and who provided a substantial charitable grant that was the final piece in the jigsaw. All proceeds from the sale of this book are being donated directly to the London Scottish Regiment and to the Pipes and Drums. It has been a labour of love and I am thrilled to see it, at last, in print.

I would especially like to thank my family. My parents, Dawn and Michael de Silva, for making me who I am and for the constant reminders that you only ever truly regret the things you fail to attempt. To Amy, and to my children Isabel, Cora and Molly who I adore and who grew up with me talking about this elusive book! And to my incredibly supportive and understanding partner, Elisha, who could not possibly be more wonderful.

Finally, it would be remiss of me not to thank all the pipers and drummers of the London Scottish Regiment Pipes and Drums whose company I have shared over the last 20 years on practise nights, parades and tours and whose barrack-room humour and self-effacing attitude I value so highly. Your support and friendship has been, and remains, extremely gratifying.

Yours Aye and Strike Sure
Duncan de Silva

Genealogy of the London Scottish Regiment

1798: The Highland Armed Association
1799: The Royal Highland Volunteers
1803: The Loyal North Britons
1859: The London Scottish Rifle Volunteers
1860: The 15th Middlesex (London Scottish) Rifle Volunteers
1881: The 7th Middlesex (London Scottish) Rifle Volunteers
1908: The 14th (County of London) Battalion, The London Regiment (London Scottish)
1914: The 1st, 2nd, 3rd, 14th (County of London) Battalion, The London Regiment (London Scottish)
1916: Affiliated to corps of the Gordon Highlanders without change of title
1920: The 14th (County of London) Battalion, The London Regiment (London Scottish)
1922: The 14th London Regiment (London Scottish)
1937: The London Scottish, The Gordon Highlanders
1939: The 1st, 2nd Battalion, The London Scottish, The Gordon Highlanders
1941: The 3rd Battalion, 97th (London Scottish) Heavy Anti-Aircraft Regiment, Royal Artillery
1947: The London Scottish, The Gordon Highlanders
1967: TAVR II, 'G' (London Scottish) Company, The 51st Highland Volunteers
TAVR III, 'C' (London Scottish) Company, The London Yeomanry and Territorials
1972: 'G' (London Scottish) Company, 1st Battalion, The 51st Highland Volunteers
1993: 'A' (London Scottish) Company, The London Regiment, Queens Division
2006: 'A' (London Scottish) Company, The London Regiment, Household Division
2022: 'G' (Messines) Company, Scots Guards, 1st Battalion, The London Guards

1
Birth of a Tradition 1798-1814

All Regimental histories serve a double purpose. They are a last honour paid to the memory of brave men and old comrades who have gone before us. They perform also a most useful work by helping to keep alive among all ranks a proper pride in the achievements and good name of the Regiment to which they belong.[1]

Field Marshal, The Earl Haig
Honorary Colonel, The London Scottish Regiment
17 March 1925

The history of the London Scottish and of the regimental Pipes and Drums extends back much further than the official formation of the regiment in 1859. The genealogy of the London Scottish reaches historically and in the most general of terms, to the earliest Scottish soldiers stationed in London who were the unofficial 'Guardians of the Stone of Scone'. A more specific lineage leads directly to the antecedents of the regiment and the founding of the Scottish volunteer military tradition in London, and its musical accompaniment, which began to take shape in 1798.

This volunteer tradition began as a direct consequence of the wars of the French Revolution which had been in progress since 1793, when the new French Republic declared war on Britain. The summer of 1797 saw France defeat the First Coalition[2] and this success for Napoleon's armies allowed increasingly larger military forces to be stationed facing England in their Channel ports. As a consequence, fears of a possible French invasion increased substantially within the British population. At the end of May 1798, rebellion broke out in Ireland and with the threat of French support for this insurgency, which eventually materialised in August of that year when Napoleon's troops landed in County Mayo, danger appeared to be lurking on all sides.

With the country in panic, voluntary military societies, or armed associations, were authorised by the 1798 Defence of the Realm Act and raised around Britain, strictly for the purpose of homeland security.[3] London, naturally, was a centre for such volunteer activity and a number of meetings took place amongst influential Scots in the city with the idea of forming a specifically Scottish armed association, separate and distinct from others being raised (mostly on a geographical basis) within the capital. The proposal for such was first put forward at a meeting of the Highland Society of London on 14 June 1798, with a motion from William Ogilvie calling for a general meeting to discuss the 'forming of a Corps of Highlanders in the Highland Uniform from the Highlanders and other natives of Scotland resident in London under the patronage and direction

---

1 J.H. Lindsey (ed.), *The London Scottish in the Great War*, (London: London Scottish Regiment Press, 1926), p. xv
2 Austria, Prussia, The Netherlands, Spain, Portugal and Great Britain.
3 As such, the new volunteer associations fell within the jurisdiction of the Home Office, rather than the War Office.

of the Society.[4] A subsequent meeting took place at the Shakespeare Tavern, Covent Garden on 2 July 1798, where Captain Lawrence Dundas Campbell stated:

> In a short Speech, the purpose of the meeting, pointing out the necessity of extraordinary exertions in defense [sic] of the Country at this critical juncture, and that Scotchmen[5] would best promote the grand object in view, and more effectually contribute their assistance to the general security of the Empire, by joining themselves into a Separate Armed Association.[6]

It was agreed that the corps would be composed of 'Highlanders, and Persons Born in Scotland, as well as the Sons of Scotchmen and Highlanders, and Members of the Highland Society' that the corps would 'serve without pay, provide their own Clothing, Accoutrements, etc. and Arms' and that the uniform of the corps would be 'Tartain [sic] Plaid, Kilt, Bonnet and Hose.'[7] Volunteers were charged one guinea to join (a considerable amount of money at that time) and books were opened at the Shakespeare Tavern and at Lloyd's Coffee House for 'the Signatures of such Gentlemen as wish to serve.'[8] These founding structures set many of the conventions followed by volunteer units in future generations.

Later that month, Captain Dundas Campbell wrote to William Cavendish-Bentinck-Scott, the Marquis of Titchfield, who held the position of Lord Lieutenant of Middlesex, to formally propose the formation of a 'separate Corps, denominated Highlanders, and distinguished by the national dress and music.'[9] Even in this initial formal declaration, the role of traditional Scottish music is highlighted as being of major significance and fundamental to the composition of the corps.

The historical importance of Highland music is further echoed in the original standing orders set out on 30 July 1798 which, amongst other matters, proposed the following regulations:

> 6: The Battalion to consist of 800 rank and file ... eight companies each having ... two drummers.
> 12: That there be three pipers attached to the Corps.
> 13: That the pipers and drummers be paid from the fund of the (Highland) Society.
> 14: Dress – 42nd Regiment Plaid and Kilt.[10]

Thus music, and more specifically the involvement of pipes and drums, was an integral part of the organising philosophy of the Scottish volunteer tradition in London from its very birth. It would play an increasingly important role over the next century. It is interesting to note that the pipers and drummers are mentioned together here and that both were to be paid for by the Highland Society of London. The Society was to play an integral role in both the foundation of all of London's Scottish volunteer corps over the next 60 years, as well as securing the survival and increased popularity of Highland culture.

Highland dress was an important component of this revival, but it was not cheap. The extravagance and expense of the uniform, a concern when it came to recruitment, is best appreciated by the following contemporary description of the agreed upon uniform:

---

4 Extract from minutes of *Committee Meeting*, Highland Society, 14 June 1798.
5 The term 'Scotch' rather than 'Scots' was of common usage during this period.
6 *The Times*, 5 July 1798, p.2.
7 *The Times*, 5 July 1798, p.2.
8 *The Times*, 5 July 1798, p.2.
9 Public Records Office (P.R.O.), Home Office (H.O.), 50/43.
10 *Standing Regulations of the Highland Armed Association*, London, 30 July 1798.

A scarlet Jacket with yellow Facings; silver lace on the Button-holes; Button white, with Crown and Thistle; a belted Plaid and hose; a Highland Bonnet, smartly mounted with Ostrich Feathers; a green hackle Feather fixed under the Cockade with silver loop over it, and Button of the Corps; an ornamental hair Purse in front of the kilt; the Shoe to be tied with a Leather Latchet; the Plaid to be made of the Tarten [sic], similar to that worn by the 42nd Regiment.[11]

Such opulence, then, marks an organisation founded by the privileged and to be composed of Gentlemen.

On 7 August 1798, Lord Titchfield replied to Captain Dundas Campbell stating that he had 'laid the proposal of the Highland Association before the King, and that His Majesty has been graciously pleased to accept their Loyal offer.'[12] The name of this corps would be the Highland Armed Association, and Lieutenant Colonel R. MacFarlane (late Lieutenant Colonel of the 77th Foot) was gazetted as commanding officer. Somewhat confusingly, the Highland Armed Association was, from 1799 onwards, also to be officially known as the Royal Highland Volunteers. Quite how this name came about, and from where it obtained a 'Royal' designation, seems to be a mystery but *The London Gazette* of 24 September 1799 clearly states that Captain L.D. Campbell, who had been second in command of the Highland Armed Association, was granted the same rank of captain in the Royal Highland Volunteers.[13] The Volunteer List for 1800 names the corps simply as the 'Royal Highland.'[14] The various titles would be used and confused for the remainder of the corps' short existence.

Grand plans were in place, then, for a grand regiment but like so many grandiose ideas, the reality did not quite match up to initial expectations. Despite the advantages of joining volunteer associations conceded by the Exemption Act of 1799, which excused volunteers from forced conscription via the Militia Ballot, the Highland Armed Association struggled to attract recruits. It may have been the selective 'Highland' designation that excluded many Scots, or maybe the prohibitive cost of uniforms and membership subscriptions but, for whatever reason:

The high hopes of raising a corps of 800 men, commanded by a full colonel with sharpshooters, pipers, supernumerary ranks, and a large committee, all ended in a Corps which, at its greatest strength, was just over 100 commanded by a captain.[15]

The Highland Armed Association/Royal Highland Volunteers did, at least, have pipers. How many cannot be said for sure, but there are contemporary accounts which certainly confirm their existence. The *Aberdeen Journal* reports of a 'Grand Review' of 'most of the volunteer corps of London', some 4,500 rank and file, who paraded for the Prince of Wales and the Duke of York on Saturday, 23 July 1801.[16] The report misnames the corps as the 'Royal Highland Association', an incorrect combination of its two official titles, but there can be no doubt as to who was on parade that day as there was only ever one Highland volunteer corps in London

---

11 Thomas Rowlandson, *The Illuminated School of Mars or Review of the Loyal Volunteer Corps of London and its Vicinity* (London: Rudolph Ackerman, 1798-9), plate LXX.
12 P.R.O., H.O., 50/47.
13 *The London Gazette*, Issue 15187, 24-28 September 1799, p.982.
14 P.R.O., H.O., 50/48.
15 R.O. Robson, *London Scots of the Napoleonic Era* (Ipswich: Hadden, Best and Co, 1970), p.4.
16 *Aberdeen Journal*, 5 August 1801, Issue 2795.

Thomas Rowlandson, Officer of the Highland Association, Plate No. 70, *Loyal Volunteers of London and Environs, Infantry and Cavalry in their Respective Uniforms*, 1799. (LSMA (London Scottish Museum Archives), used with permission)

Peter Edward Stroeghling, Augustus Frederick, Duke of Sussex, later Prince of Wales c. 1805-10, in uniform of Royal Colonel, Loyal North Britons. (The Royal Collection © 2022 Her Majesty Queen Elizabeth II)

during this period.[17] A detailed report of the same Royal Review appears in the *Morning Post* of July 25th:

> Soon after twelve the whole line passed the Prince in open column … and marched off the ground in quick time. The Highlanders retired with the bagpipes, playing *Maggy Lauder*. They were dressed in their proper uniform – a tartan plain and filibeg, broad sword and dirk. They are fine men. The novelty pleased and attracted the crowd, who recollected the Highlanders of the 42nd.[18]

This may well have been the first time that military pipers had led troops on the march through London since the Highland Company of the 3rd Regiment of Foot (later to become the Scots Guards) arrived from Scotland for their disbandment in 1713, some 90 years previously. There is nothing in any of the numerous reports of this event to suggest that the pipes played with the drums (there is no contemporary evidence for the formation of pipe bands at this time) but the language within the report does suggest that there were multiple pipers on parade. Unfortunately, there seems to be no record of who those pipers were or how many they numbered.

We do not know if the Highland Society of London produced the funds for the three pipers and two per company drummers, as laid down in the original standing regulations. Iain MacInnes undertook exhaustive research of contemporary correspondence and accounts regarding the Highland Society of London for his influential 1988 Master's degree thesis[19] but makes no mention of such payments.[20] As many of the Society's records were lost in a fire in 1877, it will probably never be known for certain.

While we have documentary evidence to prove that pipers existed in the corps, we can only guess as to the situation regarding drummers. However, it would have been impossible for a military body at that time to function without drummers, and it is likely that a corps strength of around 100 rank and file would have included at least four drummers to perform the necessary duties, as laid down in the standing orders. A letter written in July 1800 from Philip Codd, Adjutant to the Highland Armed Association, to William Huskison, Under-Secretary of State for War, alludes to possible Government payment to adjutants, NCOs and drummers[21] but that is as far as the evidence extends. The Highland Society had agreed to pay for these drummers but whether their contribution actually stretched this far cannot, unfortunately, be confirmed.

Generally, however, the Highland Society's influence over, and involvement with, the Highland Armed Association was enormous, as indeed it would remain with all the subsequent Scottish volunteer forces in London prior to the formation of the London Scottish Regiment. It could almost be stated that these pre-1859 organisations functioned as the 'military wing' of the Highland Society. The Society had been founded in 1778 and among its original objectives were:

2: The preservation of the Ancient Music of the Highlands.

---

17 *The Times*, reporting on the same event lists the corps simply as 'Highlanders' but makes no mention of the pipes. See *The Times*, 23 July 1801, p.3.
18 *Morning Post*, London, 25 July 1801, p.2.
19 Iain I. MacInnes, 'The Highland Bagpipe: The Impact of The Highland Societies of London and Edinburgh 1781-1844', M. Litt Thesis, University of Edinburgh, 1988.
20 In personal correspondence, Keith Sanger stated that he also has no recollection of evidence of such payments from his own research in the Highland Society of London archives at the National Library of Scotland.
21 Codd was attempting to convince Huskisson that he should be paid for his services as Adjutant. See P.R.O, H.O., 50/48. However, it was not until the Volunteer Act of 1804 that such payments became standard.

7: The keeping of the Martial Spirit; and rewarding the Gallant achievements of the Highland Corps.[22]

It seems likely, then, that the Highland Society would have taken every opportunity to advance these aims and to combine them in the Highland corps over which it held most influence.

The Highland Society itself employed an 'official' piper and paid 'extra' pipers for various events and duties each year. It is probable that these pipers would have been involved with the Highland Armed Association. For example, John MacGregor of Fortingall was one of the 'extra' pipers who played for the Highland Society during this time. He arrived in London in 1799 and was paid by the Society from 1800 to 1804 in the role of 'extra' piper.[23] He was later to undertake the dual roles of official piper to the Highland Society of London and piper, possibly 'Pipe Major', to the Loyal North Britons. John MacGregor and his involvement with the Loyal North Britons will be discussed in more detail later in this chapter but it is conceivable that he was already playing with the Highland Armed Association as far back as 1799.

All reasonable conjecture, but what we can be sure about is that the peace treaty of Amiens in 1802 provided the perfect opportunity for the underachieving Highland Armed Association/ Royal Highland Volunteer corps to quietly dissolve. While this first attempt to provide a Scottish influenced volunteer force in London never, in truth, came close to reaching its potential, it did provide a blueprint for similar future endeavours which would prove to be increasingly successful on each subsequent occasion. Between 1798 and 1802, then, the groundwork for this prospective achievement had been laid. Of equal importance to the laying of such foundations is the fact that this accomplishment helped pave the way for the lasting influence of military pipe music, and the birth and subsequent development of the pipe band, in the capital of the British Empire.

The second opportunity to build a successful and enduring Scottish volunteer force in London came hard on the heels of the first. On 18 May 1803, after a year of nervous peace, Britain again declared war on France. For two years Britain stood alone against Napoleon, during which time the French general crowned himself Emperor and returned to his invasion scheme of 1798 but this time on a much grander scale. Around 2,000 craft and over 180,000 men of *L'Armée de l'Angleterre* gathered in ports up and down the French coast waiting for the perfect opportunity to invade and conquer Britain. Once more, watchtowers were manned along England's south and east coasts and a panicked British population prepared themselves, yet again, for invasion.[24]

The fear was very real. In a letter to his sister in July 1803, Robert Norris, who joined the newly formed Loyal North Britons at the age of 16, states that 'It is the opinion of most people here that he (Bonaparte) will be over with us in the course of 2 or 3 months at least.'[25] A passage from a subsequent letter in November the same year sums up the mood of the country at the time. Norris states that in the event of an invasion the French would receive 'a True British Reception with Balls and Bayonet.'[26]

This national resolve, in conjunction with the experiences and lessons learnt from 1798 to 1802, held the volunteer movement in good stead and in a matter of weeks during 1803, over 380,000

---

22 John Sinclair, *An Account of the Highland Society of London: From its Establishment in May 1778 to the Commencement of the Year 1813* (London, 1813), p.5.
23 MacInnes, 'The Highland Bagpipe', p.129.
24 To do so, the French needed to remove the threat of the Royal Navy. The actions of the French fleet in this regard represent the opening moves in a chess game that ultimately led to the Battle of Trafalgar in 1805.
25 Letter to Miss Nancy Morris, Scotland, from her brother Robert, London, 17 July 1803. National Army Museum Archives, 1988-09-71-1.
26 Letter to Miss Nancy Morris, Scotland, from her brother Robert, London, 26 November 1803. National Army Museum Archives, 1988-09-71-2.

men joined volunteer corps across the nation under the auspices of the hastily passed 1803 Volunteer, Billeting and Exemption Acts. On May 30th, barely two weeks after war was declared, the Highland Society and former members of the Highland Armed Association and Royal Highland Volunteers met once more at the Shakespeare Tavern in Covent Garden and proposed a new corps. They would, sensibly, take into consideration various factors that had hamstrung their efforts the first time around. It was realised that including the term 'Highland' in their corps title was too exclusive. It was also understood that uniforms had to be more affordable and at the expense of fashion, stating that they should cost no more than 10 guineas.[27] Most importantly, they realised that to be an effective organisational and fighting force, established numbers needed to be initially set much lower than battalion strength. A renewed offer of service from the freshly established 'Loyal North Britons' was duly sent to the Home office on 29 June 1803.[28]

The huge number of volunteers who came forward in England, Scotland and Wales caused something of a problem for the British Government. Many volunteer units were relatively small in establishment while others were rather disorganised. It took real effort to ensure that at least some semblance of military discipline was imposed on such a large and, to some extent, unwieldy force. The Government decided, therefore, that the number of volunteers would be capped at six times that of the Militia to ensure there were still enough men of military age eligible for conscription via the Militia Ballot. The Militia was of much greater use to the authorities as their service, although still bound to deployment within the British Isles, came on much more flexible terms than that of volunteers who agreed only to defend their local area or take over garrison duty within a radius of ten miles.[29]

It was not a forgone conclusion, then, that the Loyal North Britons would be recognised at all. However, 'their services were accepted on 15th July, 1803, and this was communicated to them in a letter from the Lord Lieutenant dated 19th July.'[30] Thus, the Loyal North Britons was born, dressed in a more traditional, cheaper and practical uniform of redcoats and trousers and initially established at a corps strength of four companies of 50 men. The corps was commanded by Eric Mackay, the 7th Lord Reay, who had been President of the Highland Society in 1798 and on whose lands in Scotland the Reay Fencible Highlanders (1794-1802) had been raised.[31] Despite their intended establishment of 200 men, and as proof that they had got it right this time, the Loyal North Britons were already over 350 strong by October 1803.[32] In fact, enrolment was so strong that Lord Reay wrote to Lord Titchfield on 2 August 1803 asking for the establishment to be raised to 600.[33]

A contingent of the 350 who enrolled in the corps were definitely pipers and drummers. Exactly how many may never be accurately known but there are clear contemporary reports which prove beyond doubt that not only were they in existence but that they were playing together, as the earliest recorded example of a pipe band.

It should be noted that the present notion of a pipe band; pipers and drummers playing together exclusive of any other instruments, did not come into existence until at least the end of the

---

27 P.R.O., H.O., 50/78.
28 P.R.O., H.O., 50/79.
29 Except in the event of actual invasion, in which case they would revert to full military control.
30 Robson, *London Scots of the Napoleonic Era*, p.5.
31 The Reay Fencibles, raised at the time of the 6th Lord Reay, who died in 1797, played a significant role in quelling rebellion in Ireland during the years of its formation. The 7th Lord Reay, however, was not a military man in any sense and struggled with the responsibility of commanding the Loyal North Britons.
32 The *Returns of the Volunteers of the United Kingdom*, ordered to be printed by the House of Commons, 9th and 13th December 1803, p.44, which was 50 over the Loyal North Britons' establishment of six companies of 50 men.
33 Permission was, however, denied.

Crimean War in the mid-1850s. Even at that point, it was far from common practice. Prior to that time, pipers played very much as solo performers without accompaniment from any other instrument. In *The Pipes in War and Peace*, C.A. Malcolm states that, 'In the eighteenth and first half of the nineteenth century, pipers played without any drum accompaniment' and that, on parade, 'each company marched or doubled past the saluting base to the marching or charging time of the battalion played by the piper of the company.'[34] Over time, regimental pipers would be formed up together to play each company past and this may well have constituted the primary evolutionary step from solo to massed pipers in the military. The subsequent step was to add drummers and although there is little supporting documentary evidence, it is generally agreed that the 1854 formation and deployment of the Highland Brigade in the Crimea brought together large numbers of pipers and drummers from the composite regiments within the brigade for the first time, creating the initial catalyst for massed pipes and drums playing together. The first example of this may have been in 1854 when the pipers and drummers of the 42nd (Black Watch), 79th (Cameron Highlanders) and 93rd (Sutherland Highlanders) Regiments, who were camped together at Kamara outside of Balaclava, joined together to play Long Reveille.[35]

In addition, the modern concept of pipers and drummers playing for troops in step and on the march also did not yet exist in 1803, primarily because the generally poor quality of roads prior to Macadam's new road construction techniques of the 1820s made it difficult to march in time over long distances. In addition, military drill books from 1792 through to at least 1811 stated the following:

> The use of music or drums to regulate the march is absolutely forbid, as incompatible with the just and combined movements of any considerable body, and giving a false aid to the very smallest.
> They never persevere in the ordered time or in any other, are constantly changing measure, create noise, derange the equality of step and counteract the very end they are supposed to promote.
> On occasions of parade or show, and when troops are halted, they are properly used, and when circumstances do not forbid it, may be sometimes permitted as inspiring in column of march, where unity of step is not so critically required.[36]

Documented instances of pipers and drummers performing together prior to the Crimean War and playing on the march are, therefore, almost non-existent. To find an example outside of the confines of the regular Highland regiments, and some 50 years prior, would be even rarer still.

Drummers have played an important role in military life for millennia and by the beginning of the nineteenth century were integral to every British regiment, including those from Scotland. Fife and drum corps had also long been a regular part of the British military and drummers played the calls which outlined a soldier's day (Reveille, Troop, Inspection, Drill, Meals, etc. through to Retreat and Tattoo) and provided the all-important command calls on the field of battle. This situation remained the custom until around 1815 when bugle calls, which could be heard over much longer distances than drums, began to take over. Until this time, fife and drum corps were also the norm in Scottish regiments, where the idea of pipers playing with drummers was yet to exist.[37]

---

34 C.A. Malcolm, The *Piper in Peace and War* (London: John Murray, 1927), p.20.
35 See David Murray, *Music of the Scottish Regiments* (Edinburgh: Mercat Press, 2001), p.234.
36 Duncan Tovey, 'Some Old Drill Books', *London Scottish Regimental Gazette*, 1910, p.115.
37 For more detail see Murray, *Music of the Scottish Regiments*, pp.3-9.

Highland Volunteers Recruiting Leaflet c. 1800. (LSMA, used with permission)

HIGHLAND VOLUNTEERS.

ALL Young Men, desirous of gaining *Reputation* in the Service of their KING and COUNTRY, in the *Honourable Regiment* of HIGHLAND VOLUNTEERS, commanded by Colonel JOHN CAMPBELL, and in Captain DAVID WEDDERBURN's own Company, are desired, without Loss of Time, to apply to Captain WEDDERBURN.

Such Young Men of Spirit as chuse to enlist in Captain WEDDERBURN's Company, shall receive great *Bounty Money*; shall enlist for any Term of Years they please; shall be compleatly cloathed in the *Highland Dress*; and shall be armed with short light *Fusees*, making on Purpose for this Regiment.

N. B. Any Person who brings a Man to Captain WEDDERBURN that shall be approved of, shall receive Half a Guinea for his Trouble.

William Henry Payne, Highland Regiment Piper, Plate No. 60, *The Costumes of Great Britain*, 1805. (LSMA, used with permission)

BIRTH OF A TRADITION 1798-1814 25

N. D. Finart, Drummer of a Highland Regiment, c. 1810-15. (The Royal Collection © 2022 Her Majesty Queen Elizabeth II)

Andrew Robertson, H.R.H. The Duke of Sussex, K.G. in Highland costume (uniform of Royal Colonel, Loyal North Britons), 1806. (LSMA, used with permission)

Pipers, by contrast, had no official recognition within the British military system and whilst drummers and the position of drum major were well established and even treated preferentially,[38] pipers were not on the establishment[39] and so had to either be paid for directly by sponsoring officers or hidden on the establishment as active 'supernumeraries' or even as drummers.[40] The association of the bagpipes with the 1745 Jacobite risings[41] made the playing of the bagpipes, which had long been designated as 'instruments of war' in the British Army a matter of real contention that lasted well into the 1880s.[42] After 'the '45', pipers in general became a limited commodity and finding willing pipers to recruit to Scottish regiments rarer still. This situation would continue until the middle of the nineteenth century[43] and it was a stated aim of the Highland Society of London to help resolve this dilemma.

With all these factors in mind, then, the notion that the earliest documented report of military pipers and drummers performing together would be found in 1803, in London, within a newly formed volunteer corps, a full 50 years before the practice began in the regular army's Highland regiments is, at first glance, quite astounding. The involvement of the Highland Society of London with the Loyal North Britons makes this slightly more understandable, but it remains a matter of some considerable revelation.

The first major parade of the Loyal North Britons took place a scant three months after their formation. The authorities had decided that a Royal Review of the new volunteer force was in order and King George III was asked to take the salute at two London parades arranged to take place on 26 and 28 October 1803, during the very peak of the invasion scare[44]. Over 27,000 volunteers would take part in each parade with upwards of 500,000 onlookers turning out on each day to witness the events. The Loyal North Britons, therefore, had a huge stage on which to make their debut and this small corps would make sure they stood out from the crowd by marching on parade to the innovative sounds of the pipes and drums.

The review itself was, by all accounts, quite an occasion. *The Times* correspondent reported that 'notwithstanding the many splendid scenes which have from time to time been witnessed in Hyde Park, perhaps that of yesterday has never been exceeded on any occasion.'[45] 33 corps assembled in the streets around Hyde Park, many with their own military bands, and began to make their way through the fog and into the park. Then it was the turn of the 286 assembled officers and men of the Loyal North Britons.

---

38   Drummers were deemed so important that they were paid the same rate as sergeants.
39   Murray, *Music of the Scottish Regiments* p.49 highlights one exception, the 1st Battalion, Royal Regiment which '…was authorized to hold a piper on its strength throughout the eighteenth century, a unique privilege extended to no other regiment, Highland or Lowland.'
40   John G. Gibson makes the case that the commonly held view of most pipers being listed as drummers at this time is incorrect, stating that '… although it may have happened here and there it is by no means established as a general practice.' See John G. Gibson, *Traditional Gaelic Bagpiping: 1745-1945* (Quebec: McGill-Queen's University Press, 1998), p.76.
41   Despite the association of bagpipes with the Jacobite cause, there were many pipers in the ranks of the Government-supporting clans and in the British army in 1745. It would not be until after the defeat of the Jacobites that Highland traditions, in all their forms, would be suppressed. The notion of the 'rebel piper" then, is purely a Victorian creation that survives today because of its romanticised image.
42   It should be noted here that playing the pipes was never outlawed by the 1746 Disarming Act (see UNITED KINGDOM, STATUTES, 19 Geo. 2, cap.39, 1746, 587-602) or the Amendment to it of 1748, despite the current, popularly held belief to the contrary.
43   See Malcolm, The *Piper in Peace and War*, p.28 regarding recruiting problems in 1794.
44   There was no official system of review and inspection until the Volunteer Consolidation Act of 1804 (44 Geo. III. Cap.54; 5 June 1804).
45   'Second Review in Hyde Park', *The Times*, 29 October 1803, p.3.

> At a quarter before nine the Duke of York … entered Hyde Park at Cumberland-gate, immediately after the corps of Loyal North Britons, who preceded him with bagpipes and kettle-drums, playing the old and celebrated Scotch tune, 'Over the hills and far awa.'[46]

Keith Sanger, in his 2003 article for the *Piping Times*,[47] makes a strong claim for this to be, by far, the earliest example of pipers and drummers performing together as a band. The fact that they were performing together at such a prestigious spectacle is even more remarkable. The effect of this ensemble on the watching crowd is not recorded but hearing bagpipes in London at this time would have been a novelty to the watching spectators. Hearing them played with the accompaniment of drums would have sounded even more innovative to the assembled royals, officers, men, musicians and spectators on parade that day.

There is evidence to demonstrate that the Loyal North Britons had 12 military side drummers on establishment at this time.[48] Specialist kettle drummers could possibly have been drafted in for the occasion, but it is probable that the reporter for *The Times* misnamed the drums as being kettle drums. It is much more likely that they would have been regular side drums or perhaps even a combination of side and kettledrums. There is no contemporary record of the Loyal North Britons having a military band which may have included marching kettle drummers and, as the tenor drum of their day, kettle drums would not have been played in any other context.[49] Therefore, kettle drummers would not have been on the establishment and it seems likely that, if such drums were indeed present, they would have needed to be brought in specifically to perform for the occasion. It is, therefore, much more likely that the drummers who performed with the pipers were the side drummers already on the establishment.

Military side drummers from the Loyal North Britons' 'Corps of Drums' would have been fully conversant with the tune mentioned in the report. *Over the Hills and Far Away* was a popular tune of the period, dating back to the seventeenth century and commonly played by fife and drum corps. The choice of this standard tune would have made the musical arrangement for pipes and drums very straightforward. There are contemporary reports that the Loyal North Britons had fifers as well as pipers and drummers by 1804, although they did not have fifers in 1803 at the time of the Royal Review, just a few months after the regiment's formation. It may be that this lack of fifers was also instrumental in stimulating the innovative use of pipers in their place.

There is also a question regarding how many pipers played on the day. While there is evidence to estimate the number of drummers there is no straightforward answer regarding the number of pipers but any less than three or four would have been miniscule for such an important occasion, both audibly and visually. It is also possible that the influence of the Highland Society could have helped to draft in supernumerary pipers to play for the corps on the occasion but, unfortunately,

---

46 'Second Review in Hyde Park', *The Times*, 29 October 1803, p.3.
47 'Newspaper Report Could Be the Earliest Evidence of Pipe Band Origins', *Piping Times*, Vol. 56, Number 3, December 2003, p.39. Sanger quotes from the *Edinburgh Evening Courant* of 3 November 1803 but it is clearly the same *Times* report reissued in a regional paper. The *Times* report also appears many years earlier in Robson, *London Scots of the Napoleonic Era*, p.12, but Robson does not make Sanger's connection with pipe band origins.
48 'The Returns of the Loyal North Britons', London, October 1803, P.R.O, H.O., 50/79.
49 I have been unable to find any contemporary instances of kettle drums being played exclusively with a lead instrument, except for the use of trumpets and large, mounted kettledrums played by cavalry bands such as the 1st Regiment of Life Guards. These instruments were strongly associated with royalty and royal occasions. Marching kettle drums, as used by infantry regiment bands, however, were much smaller, sometimes played in pairs of different sizes and used much as tenor and/or bass drums are used today.

there is no satisfactory evidence to make genuine claims regarding absolute numbers.[50] That some, if not all, of these pipers were enlisted members of the Loyal North Britons is, however, supported by the Volunteer Returns for October 1803. At the bottom of the Returns is a sentence stating that all ranks of the Loyal North Britons 'agree to serve without pay except for Adjutant, Sergeants and Music.'[51] The use of the word 'Music' rather than just 'Drummers' as would normally have been the case, suggests strongly that pipers were also enlisted in, and were an expenditure of, the corps.[52]

We must presume that the band of pipers and drummers who performed at the Royal Review also played other tunes during the day, as the Order of Review clearly states that each band was to play on at least two further occasions. The first time would be as King George III passed each corps on his arrival. Then later, during the March Past, orders stated that 'whatever music first passes his MAJESTY will wheel out to the left, and remain playing until relieved by the next band, and so of the others.'[53] Other selected tunes would have probably followed the same format as *Over the Hills and Far Away*, being popular standards familiar to, and playable on, both the fife and pipes, permitting straightforward musical arrangement.

With this evidence in mind, it seems highly likely that the Royal Review would not have been the first time that Loyal North Briton pipers and drummers played together. Rehearsal for such a prestigious event would have been needed, and we know that the corps assembled on Wednesday 19 October 1803 at their drill field at Winkworth's Building on the City Road[54] and then again on Saturday 22 October for inspection by Lord Harrington.[55]

The *Morning Chronicle* reports that, at the first assembly on 19 October, the corps was to march to the Scots Church, London Wall for a service on what had been proclaimed a National Fast Day by the Crown because of the fear of imminent invasion by Napoleon's forces. The report goes on to state that:

> The regiment will assemble on their parade in the City Road, and march to the bagpipes to the place of worship; and the singularity of the sight will, doubtless, assemble many spectators.[56]

We know that the event itself took place,[57] but have no confirmation that the pipes performed, let alone whether or not they had accompaniment from the drums. However, it is highly likely, considering the *Morning Chronicle* report, that the pipers did play. It remains a possibility, especially as the parade was so close in date to the Royal Review, that they also played with drums but it is equally possible that a performance this innovative would have been saved for the Royal Review itself in order to guarantee the biggest effect for such a momentous occasion.

---

50 In private correspondence, Keith Sanger stated that he believes it is possible that there could even have been only one piper playing but the pomp and ceremony associated with an event of this nature makes that possibility unlikely.
51 'Returns of the Loyal North Britons', October 1803, P.R.O, H.O., 50/79.
52 They were certainly not being paid for by Government funds, as letters between Reay and Titchfield in November and December 1803 make clear. See P.R.O., H.O., 50/79.
53 'Order of Review', from Adjutant General Harry Calvert, Horse Guards, 22 Oct 1803, as published in *The Times*, 25 October 1803, p.3.
54 *The Times*, 20 October 1803, p.2.
55 Harrington was Colonel of the 1st Regiment of Life Guards and Reviewing Officer for the London 'Brigade' of volunteers.
56 *Morning Chronicle*, London, 15 October 1803, Issue 10734.
57 *The Times*, 20 October 1803, p.2.

On the second occasion, the corps met on Saturday 22 October to practice the drill required of them at the Royal Review. Then, having performed the various manoeuvres to Lord Harrington's standards:

> At half-past nine o'clock, the corps marched off the field, accompanied by the bag-pipes, their ancient Scottish music, the novelty of which attracted the notice of the surrounding crowd.[58]

There is every reason to believe, based on the evidence at hand, that the drummers would also have been involved in such a full-scale dress-rehearsal. If so, this puts our earliest date for pipes and drums playing together further back by several days.

Prior to this date there is evidence from two dates in September 1803 of the Loyal North Britons undertaking marching drill to the tunes of the bagpipes. On 2 September, 300 men mustered at Archer's Field, Gower Street, although only 50 were in uniform by this point.

> After the corps had marched two or three times around the field, to the sound of their beloved music of the bagpipes, they were formed into a circle.[59]

A few weeks later, on 27 September, 250 members were:

> Put through the different manoeuvres in the platoon exercise, marching round the field to the sound of the bagpipes.[60]

An auspicious start then, both for the Loyal North Britons as a corps and for the establishment of piping and drumming in London.

Unfortunately, the historical record becomes muted after such promising beginnings and there is little contemporary information regarding the involvement of pipers and drummers within the corps from this point onwards. In fact, there is little definitive proof that they ever played together as pipes and drums again. The availability of such specific information is hampered by the existence of limited historical records for the Loyal North Britons in general after 1805.[61] However, the scant information that is available allows us to draw some useful conclusions.

The strongest evidence prior to 1805 is provided by the December 1803 and February 1804 Volunteer Returns. These returns, which were very ad-hoc in the early days, were sent to the Home Office by every volunteer corps to provide up to date information about their numbers. The format for the returns often changed, making it difficult to draw comparisons, but the returns for December 1803, under the heading 'Drummers', state clearly that the Loyal North Britons had six drummers on establishment.[62] In the returns for February 1804, however, the heading has changed to 'Drummers, Fifers and Pipers' and gives the combined number on establishment as 14.[63] Unfortunately, this figure is not broken down. The document goes on to state that expenses

---

58 *The Times*, 24 October 1803, p.3.
59 *Kentish Weekly Post*, 6 September 1803, p.3.
60 *Morning Post*, 29 September 1803, p.2.
61 This is mainly a consequence of Nelson's victory at the Battle of Trafalgar on 21 October that year, which removed any further threat of a French invasion, and resulted in a general decline in interest regarding the volunteer movement.
62 *Volunteers of the United Kingdom, Ordered by the House of Commons to be Printed 9th and 13th December 1803*, London, 1803, p.44.
63 'State of Present Establishment and Proposed Establishment of the Corps of Loyal North Britons', February 1804, P.R.O., H.O., 50/112.

included one drummer per company, totalling six drummers at one penny per day each. If the figure of six drummers is taken at face value, that leaves eight fifers and/or pipers within the corps.

To complicate matters, the October 1803 returns had listed 12 drummers on establishment, but there may be any number of reasons why the figures swing so dramatically, with the surreptitious inclusion of pipers under the heading of drummers, the most probable answer. Unfortunately, the February 1804 returns are the only ones to list pipers in any format and, thus, further direct comparison cannot be made. However, this document is incredibly important in proving that the pipers were an established part of the corps and not just brought in from outside for special occasions.

Enormous prestige came to the Loyal North Britons in 1805 when Prince Augustus Frederick, the first Duke of Sussex and sixth son of King George III, took command after the 'resignation' of the young and ineffectual Lord Reay. In a letter from the Right Honourable Charles Yorke to Lord Lieutenant Titchfield in April 1804, Yorke states:

> Lord Reay stated to me, that not only is he not a military man, but that his mercantile concerns were such as to prevent him from devoting so much of his time as he could wish to the regiment under his command.[64]

While this was certainly true, it was also the case that Reay was caught up in a huge society scandal that would require him to withdraw from public life and it is likely that Lord Reay was 'encouraged' to resign. He led a profligate lifestyle way beyond his means and it is ironic that this ex-President of the Highland Society of London, whose aims were to preserve the Highland way of life, would play such a large role in its destruction when, in 1829, he sold all the Mackay lands to the Countess of Sutherland and the Marquis of Stafford (later first Duke of Sutherland) for the huge sum of £300,000 to pay off his gambling debts. Acquiring the funds to pay off a degenerate London lifestyle led directly to the Highland Clearances and cost Clan Mackay all their ancestral lands.[65] What caused Lord Reay's downfall and removal from public life in 1805, however, was his involvement in a business scandal relating to investments in the West Indian slave trade and the swindling of a partner who then went public about the entire affair.[66]

Lord Reay resigned on 18 September 1805 and the Duke of Sussex officially accepted command the very same day. Often, such Royal patronage was questionable in its motives, but the corps became much more to the duke than a mere royal plaything, with contemporary reports depicting Augustus Frederick as an astute and assiduous commanding officer, very much involved in the activities of his troops.[67]

He confirmed as much on his very first parade with the regiment on 23 October, where he wore the uniform of the Loyal North Britons for the first time. Having received a Royal Salute, he had the regiment form into a circle and the Articles of War read out. Immediately after:

---

64 P.R.O., H.O. 50/112, 3 April 1804.
65 See Angus Mackay, *The Book of Mackay* (Edinburgh: Norman MacLeod, 1906), pp.232-3.
66 See George Baillie, *Narrative of the Mercantile Transactions of the Concerns of George Baillie and Co's Houses. From the Year 1793 to 1805 Inclusive* (London: 1805).
67 For example: 'He (The D. of S.) is always at his post with us when there is any appearance of commotion. During Sir Francis Burdett's riots, he was with us every night till four and five in the morning. On the night of Mr. Percival's murder, he came as usual and put himself under the police, and did not depart until they dismissed us.' Letter from Captain Andrew Robertson, London, to John Ewen, Aberdeen, 25 May 1812, National Army Museum.

> The record of the proceedings of a Court Martial, recently appointed to try the drummers and fifers of the corps for disobedience of orders, was read. It appeared that they had refused to return to parade with the corps, after receiving orders to that effect …. In several other instances they had also disobeyed orders … and being found guilty, the ringleader of them was sentenced to receive 100 lashes, others 50 lashes, etc in proportion to the shares they had taken in the offense.[68]

The Duke of Sussex reminded the offenders that had they been regular soldiers, they would have been shot and called them forward, 'uncovered' to receive their punishment. Having held the corps in suspense, the duke then summarily forgave the musicians and offered a new start.

> After his Royal Highness had expressed his clemency, the corps wheeled into line, and finally passed in review order, with their band playing, and deposited their arms in the orderly-room.[69]

On 4 December 1805, the corps marched to the Scots Church, London Wall with the Duke of Sussex at their head to give thanksgiving for the success of the Battle of Trafalgar. The Duke also joined his men lining the streets on The Strand before attending the funeral of Lord Nelson at St Paul's Cathedral on 9 January 1806.[70] There is no mention of pipers or drummers at these parades, nor is there further mention of their activity from this point until the dissolution of the corps in 1814.

Rank and file membership of the Loyal North Britons had reached over 350 by February 1804 and stood at a respectable 324 in March 1806. The Volunteers Returns to Parliament in 1806 state that that there were 12 drummers accounted for that year.[71] On taking command in 1805, the Duke of Sussex had initially wanted to expand the corps to 600[72] and then on to full battalion strength at 1,000 but, from 1807 onwards, enrolments levelled off and remained in the 200s. The number of drummers in the corps stayed relatively steady and generally reflected a two per company establishment. Robson furnishes a list of 22 individual drummers and their service dates[73] which, when recalculated, provides the following average yearly numbers:

Year:	1805	1806	1807	1808	1809	1810	1811	1812	1813	1814
Drummers:	10	10	6	11	6	6	7	7	8	8

The situation regarding pipers is much less clear. Records of drummers remain only because the Volunteer Act of 1804[74] allowed each volunteer corps to receive compensation for the costs of a corps adjutant in addition to a drill sergeant and a drummer for each company of 50 men on establishment. These costs needed to be reported and so thus can be traced. As already stated, pipers

---

68 *Public Ledger*, London, 25 October 1805, p.2.
69 *Public Ledger*, London, 25 October 1805, p.2.
70 See respectively, *The Times*, 5 December 1805, p.3 and *The Scots Magazine and Edinburgh Literary Miscellany*, Vol. 68, 1806, p.70.
71 *Returns, Presented to the House of Commons, of the Volunteer Corps of Cavalry, Infantry, and Artillery in Great Britain*, London, 26 March 1806, p.68.
72 *Morning Chronicle*, 10 October 1805, Issue 11356.
73 Robson, *London Scots of the Napoleonic Era*, Appendix, 'List of Drummers in the Pay Lists and Returns of the Loyal North Britons from 4th October 1803 – 24th June 1814, taken from P.R.O/W.O.13/4456.'
74 44 Geo.3 c.54.

F.C. Lewis (aquatint) after James Green, A Private of the Loyal North Britons, 1804. (LSMA, used with permission)

William Skelton (engraving) after Sir William Beechey, His Royal Highness, Augustus Frederick, Duke of Sussex, Colonel of the Loyal North Britons, 1816. (LSMA, used with permission)

J. Young (aquatint) after W. Owen, Henry Erskine Johnston, in the uniform of a private, Loyal North Britons 1804. (LSMA, used with permission)

Rosenburgh (aquatint) after J.F. Manskirch, The Highland Piper George Clarke, 1816. (LSMA, used with permission)

had no such official status and so had to be found and paid for from alternative revenue streams or smuggled onto the books. The search for an alternate source returns us, once again, to the aims and influence of the Highland Society.

In contrast to the formation of the Highland Armed Association, there are no records that state either how many pipers would be associated with the Loyal North Britons or how they would be paid for. There was no written commitment from the Highland Society at the corps' formation to cover the cost of pipers, regardless of whether or not such funding was actually forthcoming the first time around. Therefore, it is much more likely that the cost was covered either from general corps funds or by the time-honoured regimental tradition of officers themselves footing the bill for an associated piper who would carry their banner. Officers, under the unwritten rules of the Scottish Clan system,[75] were deemed to be leaders of men (the equivalent of *fir-tacsa* or Tacksmen[76]) and were, thus, permitted not only to have an associated piper but to provide that piper with a banner, embroidered with the officer's family crest on one side and the badge of the regiment in which he served on the other.[77] Alternatively, it is also possible that the pipers of the Loyal North Britons were purely volunteers, as were all other ranks except drummers, performing on the pipes as their 'unofficial' duties with officers providing uniforms and payment. However, they were organised, there is ample evidence of strong, direct, influence from the Highland Society.

From its inception, a large proportion of the Highland Society's membership came from those in the military. The Duke of Gordon and the Earl of Seaforth were original members, amongst several others who already had, or would in the future, raised Highland regiments of their own. As previously noted, the military incentive was clearly outlined in the society's founding objectives and ties in closely with the additional intention of ensuring the survival of piping and wider Highland traditions. Highland regiments played a huge part in furthering those objectives and the bonds between these regiments and the Highland Society were obvious and self-serving. In fact, writing in 1813, Sir John Sinclair states that:

> Had it not been for the exertion of the Society, the army would not have been supplied with Highland pipers, so rapidly was that species of music sinking into oblivion.[78]

It is important, therefore, to review available documentation for evidence that suggests that these aspirations were also played out within the Loyal North Britons.

In 1781, three years after its formation, the Highland Society instigated a prestigious piping competition. It was a concern of the society that pipers at this time were becoming a dying breed and those pipers willing to join Highland regiments, rarer still. The Highland Society wanted, and the Highland regiments required, more pipers. Thus, as MacInnes states:

> It seems a strong likelihood that the supplying of this need, through the financial encouragement of piping, was a major incentive in the HSL's inauguration of the piping competition.[79]

---

75 Gibson observed, 'The highland regiment itself was, until long after the removal of the heritable jurisdiction in 1747, a basically Gaelic institution, reflecting the stratified Gaelic social system, the subtlety of Gaelic discipline based on appeal to honour and the duties of kinship, and its unique war music.' Gibson, *Traditional Gaelic Bagpiping,* p.73.
76 Meaning literally, 'supporting man' the Tacksman was the tenant of a 'Tack' of land that he could then sublet and was an intermediary class between the laird and the crofters.
77 A tradition that remains in existence, to some degree, today.
78 John Sinclair, *An Account of the Highland Society of London* (London, 1813), p.14.
79 MacInnes, 'The Highland Bagpipe', p.28.

The role of the Highland Society in this and other regards has become embroiled in some valid debate concerning motives and outcomes, but such discussions remain far beyond the scope of this book.[80] What is of interest, however, is that these piping competitions took place, that they were prestigious, and that they provided a further connection between accomplished pipers, the Highland Society and the Loyal North Britons.

There is every reason to believe that such links would have been particularly robust during the era of the Loyal North Britons, because:

> The competition during the war years (pre-1815), was used by the organisers as an opportunity to extol the virtues of army life, and the value of the bagpipe as a military instrument.[81]

It seems highly probable, therefore, that the Highland Society would have used its influence to promote a military role for those pipers competing in its competitions and/or otherwise associated with the society and its aspirations. The society could best influence these endeavors from within the Loyal North Britons; a corps with whom they were so directly associated and who were located in the same city. There is evidence of this influence for at least two pipers who were both intimately connected with the Highland Society, its prize competition and the Loyal North Britons.

As mentioned earlier in this chapter, the only Loyal North Briton piper for whom we have *bona fide* contemporary documentation is John MacGregor (born 1782, died 1822). John was the son of Peter MacGregor who won the first Highland Society prize pipe in 1781[82] and who became the Highland Society's 'official' piper from 1782 to 1790. John's grandfather was the first famous piping John MacGregor (there were at least four of the same name during this period which causes some confusion), believed by many to have been personal piper to Prince Charles Edward and present at the Battle of Culloden in 1746. The younger John MacGregor, however, is an incredibly important figure in the world of piping in his own right as he was responsible for producing one of the earliest piping transcriptions using staff notation and the transpositional key of D when he was tasked by The Highland Society, in the spring of 1820, to set down 30 pieces of piobaireachd played on the practice chanter by the premier piper of his day, Angus MacArthur of Skye.[83]

John MacGregor was a prestigious piper from an early age, winning third prize in the Highland Society competition in 1792, aged just ten[84] and second prize in 1798. John's future was to change considerably when his father relocated the entire family to London in 1799. MacInnes states that, after moving to London, John attended most Highland Society meetings from 1800 to 1804, performing as an 'extra' piper[85] in accompaniment to Charles MacArthur, who was the society's 'official' piper until 1805. Receipts show that John's father, Peter MacGregor was also paid to perform this 'extra' piper role for the society in 1799 and 1800. John subsequently took over the

---

80 See, for example, Gibson, *Traditional Gaelic Bagpiping,* and *Old and New World Highland Bagpiping* (Quebec: McGill-Queen's University Press, 2002) or Kenneth McNeil, *Scotland, Britain, Empire: Writing the Highlands, 1760-1860* (Columbus: Ohio State University Press, 2007). More fervent, if somewhat frenzied, denouncement can be found in Alistair Keith Campsie, *The MacCrimmon Legend or The Madness of Angus MacKay* (Edinburgh: Cannongate, 1980).
81 MacInnes, 'The Highland Bagpipe', p.116.
82 *The Edinburgh Magazine and Literary Miscellany,* Volume 89, Edinburgh, March 1822, p.418.
83 For further details see A. Wright, R. Cannon and F. Buis, *The MacArthur MacGregor Manuscripts of Piobaireachd,* Music of Scotland Series Vol. I (Glasgow: Universities of Glasgow and Aberdeen Press, 2001).
84 Which may also be supporting evidence regarding the rarity of high-quality pipers during this period.
85 MacInnes, 'The Highland Bagpipe', p.137.

prestigious position of 'official' piper directly from MacArthur in 1805[86] and his regular 'extra' piper was Malcolm MacGregor, a London-based pipe maker, who fulfilled that role from 1805 to at least 1815. Malcolm MacGregor himself won the Highland Society Prize Pipes in 1804 and later made the prize pipes presented by the society to its competition winner in 1815.[87] John and Malcolm MacGregor, then, are two pipers very strongly associated with the Highland Society and its piping competition. They both also had direct involvement with the Loyal North Britons.

John MacGregor went on to win the Highland Society Prize Pipes himself in early August 1806, and the *Caledonian Mercury*, reporting his success, stated that:

> The First Prize, being a Handsome Pipe, properly mounted and adorned with a Silver Plate … together with 40 merks Scots money, was adjudged to John McGregor, a Piper to the Highland Society of London and to the Loyal North Britons.[88]

The association here is clear. Archibald Campbell states that not only was John MacGregor a piper with the Loyal North Britons, but that he was also their pipe major,[89] a position that MacInnes states was 'a distinct possibility given that this volunteer regiment was raised by the Society itself.'[90] There are, however, no historical records to confirm that this was the case, or that the rank of pipe major even existed in the regiment, although there is evidence proving that MacGregor did hold the rank of sergeant.

MacGregor, though, was unquestionably a piper with the corps and so, it seems, was Malcolm. The Pay Lists and Returns of the Loyal North Britons held in the Public Records Office show both John and Malcolm MacGregor listed as Sergeants in the corps; John from 1805 to 1814 and Malcolm from 1805 to 1808.[91] As appointed pipe major, John would have held the official rank of sergeant and Malcolm's own appearance in the sergeants list provides evidence of a senior role which, in turn, suggests the possibility of lower ranked pipers in the corps. Either that or the Loyal North Britons had found a novel way to recompense at least two pipers on establishment, by paying them in the guise of drill sergeants.

It is distinctly possible that both John and Malcolm rose to the rank of sergeant (rather than being assigned the rank through their position as pipers), with the implication that they joined the corps several years previously. This hypothesis, supported by contemporary records, means they would have been with the Loyal North Britons since its inception, and both could conceivably have played at the Royal Review in 1803 and been an integral part of the earliest documented origin of the combined pipes and drums. In addition, either or both could have played for the Highland Armed Association as far back as 1799. John arrived in London that year and began

---

86   Another 'extra' piper employed by the Highland Society at this time was John Buchanan, Pipe Major of the Black Watch, who famously played his 1802 Edinburgh prize-winning pipes on the battlefield at Waterloo.
87   'First prize, being a handsome pipe of superior tone and workmanship, constructed by Malcolm MacGregor, of London, pipemaker, and one of the pipers to the Highland Society there….' *The Scots Magazine and Edinburgh Literary Miscellany*, Volume 77, August 1815, p.634.
88   *Caledonian Mercury*, 7 August 1806, Issue 13197.
89   Archibald Campbell of Kilberry, 'The MacGregor Pipers of Clann an Sgeulaiche', *Piping Times*, Glasgow, July/Aug/Sept 1950.
90   MacInnes, 'The Highland Bagpipe', p.137.
91   'List of Serjeants and Drummers in the Pay Lists and Returns of the Loyal North Britons from 4th October, 1803 – 24th June, 1814', Public Records Office, W.O. 13/4456 as cited in Robson, *London Scots of the Napoleonic Era*, p.16.

playing with the Highland Society in 1800 whilst Malcolm, who was a respected and innovative pipe-maker, had been making pipes in London from at least 1798.

There are other examples which illustrate the close connections and interrelationship between the Highland Society and the Loyal North Britons with regard to piping. For instance, the Duke of Sussex took command of the corps in 1805, the same year that John MacGregor became official piper to the Highland Society of London and, possibly, pipe major of the Loyal North Britons. The following year, the Duke of Sussex was appointed President of the Highland Society of London and around the same time, John MacGregor, completing this circle of interconnections, was duly appointed personal piper to the Duke of Sussex.[92]

With further consideration regarding these interrelationships, it is logical that pipers associated with the Highland Society would be involved with the Loyal North Britons. In fact, it would have been extraordinary had they not. The number of experienced pipers in London at the time would have been minimal, as would opportunities for patronage. The limited size of the piping community in London would have automatically brought about connections with possible patrons and the influence of the Highland Society on the Loyal North Britons could only have aided this. While other such associations are harder to accurately document, it is satisfying to speculate that the reason behind the Highland Society spending nearly eight guineas (a substantial sum at that time) on a new set of pipes for their 'official' piper, Charles MacArthur, in 1803[93] was so that he could play them while leading the Loyal North Britons at the Royal Review. That is, however, purely conjecture.

The threat of invasion diminished greatly after the Battle of Trafalgar on 21 October 1805, and the wave of nationalism that had ridden on this tide of fear also began to subside. Britain remained at war with France throughout the next ten years, but hostilities remained at a distance; on the High Seas, in the Americas, the Caribbean and in the Iberian Peninsula. The significance of the volunteer forces likewise ebbed during this period and interest from government, populace and press slowly receded. The Loyal North Britons seem to somewhat disappear from public view during this time despite occasionally being called upon to help quell 'The Mob'[94] and, from 1806 onwards, there are fewer and fewer direct mentions of the corps in the press until their eventual disbandment in 1814.

Interestingly, the few mentions there are in the press mostly relate directly to the corps' musicians. The *Morning Advertiser* of 5 December 1807 publicised notice of a reward of two guineas over the 'usual' amount for the capture of 'Faustin Jeffrey, aged 18' who 'did act as a drummer in the Volunteer Corps of Loyal North Britons'[95] and who deserted on 26 November that year. The next reference to the corps doesn't come until 1814 when the *Morning Chronicle* and *Public Ledger* both report on the case of John Smith, a bugler in the regiment who was charged with robbing the regimental stores and making off with various items belonging to the Duke of Sussex and other officers, including 'silver pocket watches, silver lace epaulettes, silver buckles, silk sashes, ostrich feathers, musical instruments and other valuables.'[96] In court, Smith and another band member, John Stewart, faced deportation to a penal colony but the Duke of Sussex let it be known, via Captain Hamilton who spoke directly to the magistrate, that if the defendants agreed to join the Royal Navy and immediately take ship, that the matter would be taken no further.[97] It seems that

---

92 *The Edinburgh Magazine and Literary Miscellany*, p.418.
93 MacInnes, 'The Highland Bagpipe', p.136.
94 Robson, *London Scots of the Napoleonic Era*, p.12.
95 *Morning Advertiser*, London, 5 December 1807, p.1.
96 *Morning Chronicle*, London, 1 March 1814, p.3.
97 See also, *Public Ledger and Daily Advertiser*, London, 1 and 14 March 1014, p.3 and p.4 respectively.

musicians in the corps, of various sorts, provided more than their fair share of entertainment. Only the pipers remained untarnished by the exploits of their musical brethren.

Other contemporary mentions of the Loyal North Britons between 1806 and 1814 relate almost exclusively to the social arrangements of the corps' officers, which not only highlights the nature of the corps during this period, but also reflects the nation's lack of concern about any further invasion threat from France. A relevant example, including mention of the original Lieutenant Colonel, Lord Reay, is given in the *Morning Post* of 5 September 1810:

> We are highly gratified to understand that there will be this evening, at the Crown and Anchor Tavern, Strand, a very enlivening entertainment of Scotch, Irish and English music, for the benefit of renowned GEORGE CLARK, Piper to the 71st Highland Regiment, who, at the Battle of Vimiera [*sic*], and after he was severely wounded, continued to animate the courage of his fellow warriors, with the martial airs of ancient Caledonia, till he was removed from the field of action. And we are happy to find that his Royal Highness the Duke of Sussex, Lord REAY, and the Officers of the Loyal North Britons … intend to honour the assembly with their presence.[98]

This position of relative national calm was to remain until the conclusion of the War of the Sixth Coalition that resulted in British victory and Napoleon's abdication on 6 April 1814. To celebrate this victory, a grand review took place in Hyde Park on 20 June, attended by the Prince Regent, the Emperor of Russia and the King of Prussia which 'comprised most of the volunteer corps still existing in the Metropolis'[99] alongside a large number of regular cavalry units. George Cruikshank observed:

> Our Regiment, the Loyal North Britons, being commanded by a Royal Duke … had the post of honour next to the Royal troops …. I can assure my friends that we made a very respectable military appearance. But when we marched in review past the Prince Regent, his imperial visitors and the crowd of general officers, I remember feeling a considerable degree of chagrin at the paltry appearance we made in point of numbers and wished most heartily that these foreigners could have seen the 'mobs' of volunteers as they had mustered in that park in 1803.[100]

The very parade that saw the birth of pipe band history, when the Loyal North Britons marched before a pipe band for the first time.

This parade, however, proved to be the last for the Loyal North Britons. Volunteer units across the country were ordered to disband and the last regimental orders were issued by the Duke of Sussex on 23 June 1814, with arrangements made for the colours of the corps to be laid up in the new Gaelic Church at Hatton Garden, just yards from the corps' depot in nearby Kirby Street. The chapel was, of course, a project of the Highland Society and built, naturally, under the patronage of the Duke of Sussex. The laying up of the colours was probably the last time the pipers of the Loyal North Britons were ever heard in public.

The corps did make an official offer to reform after Napoleon's escape from Elba and landing in France in March 1815, but this proposal was rejected by the Lord Lieutenant of Middlesex. Ultimately, the Battle of Waterloo on June 18th that year, and the subsequent terms of the Congress

---

98 *Morning Post*, London, 5 September 1810, p.3.
99 *The Times*, 21 June 1814, p.2.
100 Jerrold Blanchard, *The Life of George Cruikshank: In Two Epochs, Vol. One* (London: Chatto and Windus, 1882)

of Vienna, subdued any call for a return of the volunteer movement and the ensuing era of peace with France meant that this situation would remain relatively unchanged for the next 40 years.

In the interim, a great many changes took place regarding the responsibility and execution of military music in the British Armed Forces. In general, it can be stated that the role of music in relation to morale, *esprit de corps* and military presence was taken much more seriously. The number of musicians allowed on establishment began to grow and the idea of musicians as functioning soldiers, rather than supernumeraries, started to take form.[101] By the time the London Scottish Rifle Volunteers were formed in 1859, military music and musicians had become an integral and essential part of military life and the establishment of pipers and drummers within this new corps would thus become a matter of priority.

The evidence is clear then that the London Scottish Regiment and their Pipes and Drums did not spring from a vacuum. A structure and tradition had been put in place 60 years prior to 1859 which prepared the ground and set the bar for a truly successful and permanent Scottish-influenced volunteer military and musical presence in London. The London Scottish Pipes and Drums can, with certainty and pride, trace their antecedence to those ground-breaking pipers and drummers of the Highland Armed Association, the Royal Highland Volunteers and the Loyal North Britons.

How direct the nature of that evolution may be is, in some respects, a matter of opinion. Speaking in 1863, Lord Elcho, Commanding Officer of the London Scottish Rifle Volunteers, declared that the 1859 founding of the regiment was, in fact a 're-establishment of the London Scottish Rifle Volunteers.' He goes on to state, 'I say re-establishment because the London Scottish Corps existed in 1803, when something like a million Volunteers stood forth.'[102] Such direct claims to ancestry would have been important for what was, in 1863, still a fledgling regiment. Duncan Tovey, writing just prior to the First World War, also states that the Loyal North Britons were 'a corps absolutely corresponding to the London Scottish, and one from who we may justly claim lineal descent.'[103] However, the following statement by Robson in *The London Scots of the Napoleonic Era* may also be appropriate:

> Although not claiming direct descent from the Loyal North Britons, London Scots of the present day consider it their privilege and duty to preserve as far as possible the meaning and traditions of their predecessors.[104]

Without their volunteer predecessors in the Highland Armed Association, the Royal Highland Volunteers and the Loyal North Britons, and without the close involvement of the Highland Society, the London Scottish Regiment and its famous Pipes and Drums would have had a much more laborious birth and much less assurance of longevity. The importance of the established history, traditions, and music of these early Scottish volunteer corps in London cannot be overemphasised, providing as they do, a precedent for what was to follow. Their experiences, successes, and innovative forays into pipe band music allowed the London Scottish Regiment, from the very moment of its birth, to march confidently behind their Pipes and Drums into British military history; a history that has continued successfully for over 160 years.

---

101 For further details see Henry G. Farmer, *The Rise and Development of Military Music* (London: W.M. Reeves, 1912); Murray, *The Music of the Scottish Regiments* and *The British Brass Band – A Musical and Social History*, ed. by Trevor Herbert (London: Oxford University Press, 2000).
102 After Dinner Speech of Lord Elcho, 1863, as quoted in Duncan Tovey, 'The History of the London Scottish Rifles', *London Scottish Regimental Gazette*, 1921, p.8.
103 Tovey, 'The History of the London Scottish Rifles', p.7.
104 Robson, *London Scots of the Napoleonic Era*, p.13.

2

The Early Years 1859-1880

There is a sound of thunder afar,
Storm in the south that darkens the day,
Storm of battle and thunder of war,
Well, if it do not roll our way.
Form! form! Riflemen form!
Ready, be ready to meet the storm!
Riflemen, riflemen, riflemen form!

Be not deaf to the sound that warns!
Be not gull'd by a despot's plea!
Are figs of thistles or grapes of thorns?
How should a despot set men free?
Form! form! Riflemen form!
Ready, be ready to meet the storm!
Riflemen, riflemen, riflemen form!

Let your Reforms for a moment go,
Look to your butts and make good aims.
Better a rotten borough or so,
Than a rotten fleet or a city of flames!
Form! form! Riflemen form!
Ready, be ready to meet the storm!
Riflemen, riflemen, riflemen form!

Form, be ready to do or die!
Form in freedom's name and the Queen's!
True, that we have a faithful ally,
But only the devil knows what he means!
Form! form! Riflemen form!
Ready, be ready to meet the storm!
Riflemen, riflemen, riflemen form!

Alfred, Lord Tennyson[1]
Poet Laureate

---

1   'The War', *The Times*, 9 May 1859, p.10. This poem, submitted for publication under the pseudonym 'T', was issued as a rallying call for recruits to the new volunteer rifle companies being set up across the country at this time.

A relative peace reigned between Great Britain and France in the decades after the Battle of Waterloo in 1815, with the Royal Navy's mastery of the seas and the *Pax Britannica* ensuring that Britain remained Europe's dominant economic force and 'Policeman of the World'. However, Britain's over-reliance on the Royal Navy to enforce this supremacy, and the associated detrimental management of the Army, became increasingly apparent during the Crimean War (1853-1856). It was soon obvious that British land forces were not adequate to mount a major campaign while, at the same time, being tasked with defending the 'mother country' and her empire. British tactical and logistical immaturity added to this burden, as did the outdated system of the sale of military commissions. The War Office was compelled to send at least ten battalions of Militia overseas during the Crimean War to take over garrison duties from regular Army regiments which were required for frontline fighting. Further militia units were again sent out during the Indian Mutiny in 1857. The British Army then, was at full stretch and without the necessary resources for homeland security. An invasion scare, similar to those in 1797 and 1803, would have the capacity to bring panic to the country once again.

Such a scare came in 1859, brought about by Napoleon III's empire-building in Habsburg-influenced Italy. Distrust of France had been gathering pace since this latest Napoleon, nephew of Napoleon I, staged a *coup d'état* in 1851, followed closely by his coronation as Emperor on 2 December 1852; the anniversary of his uncle's crowning 48 years previously. An emperor requires an empire, and Napoleon's attempts to unite the Italian peninsula, while conveniently annexing Nice and Savoy, along with a well-funded programme of naval expansion, was construed by the British populace as a direct threat to national security. These events came hot on the heels of a failed assassination attempt on Napoleon the previous year, which had been planned and armed in Britain,[2] and which had led to a small number of hot-headed French military commanders publicly declaring their zeal for an invasion across the channel. Napoleon's public statements regarding friendship and *Entante Cordiale* with Britain fell mainly on deaf and disbelieving ears.[3] Invasion fears grew and the clamour for a volunteer movement to ensure national defence was reborn.

The embryo of this volunteer movement began to form in January 1852 as a reaction to Napoleon's initial coup, with the formation of the first rifle club set up with the express intention of repelling French aggression.[4] Rifle Associations were to play an important part in the new volunteer movement, with their core ideal being the training of every British man to be capable with a rifle in defence of the nation, much like the Medieval and Tudor approach to universal male proficiency with the longbow.

Despite the British and French alliance in the Crimea, distrust of French ambitions continued to grow until critical mass was reached in 1859 when, on 12 May, the Secretary of State for War, General Jonathan Peel, citing the authority of the 1804 Volunteer Consolidation Act, sent a circular letter to the Queen's Lord Lieutenants of the Counties sanctioning the formation of volunteer rifle corps. The uptake was instantaneous and tremendous. Within a matter of weeks, over 100,000 men across the country had joined volunteer corps and a new and lasting military organisation had taken its first steps.

It did not take Scots in Britain's capital long to organise, and on 21 May a meeting of the Highland Society of London, held at 8 Davis Street (the home of Robert Hepburn, one of the

---

2   The three bombs used in the attempt had been designed and built in Birmingham.
3   Napoleon III had lived in Britain in the 1840s prior to the 1848 revolution and, paradoxically, this 'enemy of the state' was to die in Britain in 1873 after arriving in exile, having been deposed by the Paris mob in 1870.
4   This Rifle Club was set up by the poet Coventry Patmore and several his friends with the express aim of gaining government sanction and spreading such societies across the country.

founders and ex-presidents of the Caledonian Society), provided a forum for the various proposals that had been circulating amongst the Scottish community in London as how best to take up where the Loyal North Britons had left off. Discussions continued until a formal meeting, held under the joint auspices of the Highland Society of London and the Caledonian Society, was called for 4 July at The Freemason's Tavern, Covent Garden, which Lord Elcho, MP was asked to chair. Elcho was a prominent proponent of the volunteer movement and keen to play an active part in its development. Association with a specifically Scottish corps offered Lord Elcho the perfect opportunity to further his aims.

The meeting began with a speech from Elcho in which he laid out his argument regarding the necessity for such a movement. Referring to the earlier invasion scares of 1798 and 1803, Elcho stated that there should be an end to these 'periodic panics' and in order to do so, 'Our Fleet … must not be our sole reliance.' Britain required, he argued, 'a second and impregnable line of defense. [*sic*]'[5] This second line would be made of volunteer corps of riflemen who, 'if properly organised, may be made a most important and valuable element of national defense. [*sic*]'[6] Directly addressing the main criticism of the 1798-1814 volunteer movement, Elcho went on to state:

> We must, in fact, look upon the establishment of these volunteer rifle corps, not as a mere childish playing at soldiers, but as a sound and lasting element of national strength.[7]

Lord Elcho was quite clear on his views regarding a possible invasion. 'It is, unquestionably, not one of immediate, nor even threatened danger' he stated, before going on to conclude:

> Now I do not wish to be misunderstood: I do not think it is probable that we shall be invaded, but the question is too vital to be allowed to rest on probabilities, we ought to render a successful invasion an impossibility.[8]

This volunteer movement, then, was not being built in a panicked rush in response to any clear and present danger, as had been the situation during the earlier Napoleonic Wars. It was, rather, being developed with longevity in mind and this basic organisational difference would prove to be central to the movement's success.

Lord Elcho went on to discuss other matters, including those of dress, putting forward both his advocacy for the use of grey cloth in uniforms rather than red or green, as well as his preference for 'knickerbockers' rather than the kilt, questioning 'its merits as a costume for skirmishing amongst the hedgerows of Kent or Surrey.'[9] Further discussion took place on specifics and concluded with the following resolutions:

1. Moved by Sir John Heron Maxwell, Baronet, and seconded by Sir Charles Forbes, Baronet:
    'That, as the present condition of affairs on the Continent of Europe may lead to complications that will render it impossible for Great Britain, with due regard to her material

---

5   Lord Elcho, *Speech of Lord Elcho M.P. at The Freemason's Tavern, July 4th* (London: J. Ridgway, 1859), p.13.
6   Lord Elcho, *Speech of Lord Elcho*, p.9.
7   Lord Elcho, *Speech of Lord Elcho*, p.10.
8   Lord Elcho, *Speech of Lord Elcho*, p.13.
9   Lord Elcho, *Speech of Lord Elcho*, p.22.

interests and high station among the nations, to maintain a position of neutrality, it is expedient that Scottish residents in London and its neighbourhood be invited to participate in strengthening the defensive resources of the country, by forming a Volunteer Rifle Corps, to be designated the 'London Scottish Volunteer Rifles'.

2. Moved by Sir Charles Forbes, Baronet, and seconded by Cosmo Gordon, Esq, Fyvie: That for the purpose of more effectually carrying out the object contemplated by the first resolution, a Subscription List be formed for originating a fund from which Arms and Accoutrements can be supplied to such volunteers as may be unable to defray the necessary expenses from their own funds, as well as for meeting the incidental expenses of the Corps.[10]

This second resolution was to prove to be especially important when it came to eventual recruitment with 340 of the original 600 recruits classified as 'artisans,' or those paying no membership fees and who were outfitted from corps funds. The inclusion of those less privileged was in marked contrast to the efforts of 1798 and 1803 and opened the door to many Scots in the capital who would otherwise have been unable to enlist. That being said, large numbers of recruits still came from the social elites and an additional founding premise that all potential officers would have to work their way through the ranks created the remarkable social condition of lords rubbing shoulders with labourers.

No matter their social standing, however, membership would be restricted to those 'connected with Scotland by birth, marriage or property,'[11] while each member was to 'pay for his own uniform and accoutrements' with the uniform to have 'some distinctive mark of nationality.'[12] This was unequivocally an organisation for Scots, though specifically not just directed at Highlanders. It was, however, distinctly Scottish in nature with proof of national eligibility a required for enlistment.

In distinct contrast to the founding of its antecedent corps, the Highland Armed Association and Loyal North Britons, there was no initial mention or provision at the formation of the London Scottish for either pipers or drummers. The distinctive 'Highland' regimental ideal, with which the pipes were associated, was not as explicit with the formation of the London Scottish, despite the influence of the Highland Society, and Lord Elcho initially envisaged this new corps very much along the lines of a regular rifle battalion, with bugles and a military brass band.[13] It was to be several months before the idea of a pipe band took hold.

It should be remembered that while pipers had been supernumeraries in some Highland regiments for centuries, they had only been officially admitted to the establishment of the five kilted Highland regiments a few years previously in 1854.[14] Since that point, only the Scots Fusilier Guards, in 1856, had obtained additional official approval for the same provision of a pipe major

---

10 Lord Elcho, *Speech of Lord Elcho*, p.27.
11 Lord Elcho, *Speech of Lord Elcho*, p.27.
12 Lord Elcho, *Speech of Lord Elcho*, p.28.
13 The first bugler of the London Scottish, nominated as such on 18 January 1860 was John MacGregor (of 'Rob Roy' fame) who would later become captain of the second kilted company. The first official London Scottish bugle call was played in Westminster Hall a few days later, on 21 January. See Duncan Tovey, 'The History of the London Scottish Regiment', London *Scottish Regimental Gazette* (1921), p.36.
14 A Pipe Major and five pipers were assigned to each battalion. One piper for each of the six companies (from the ten companies each battalion held in total) that would be routinely sent overseas.

Henry Joseph Fleuss, Lord Elcho, M.P., Lieut-Colonel Commandant of the London Scottish V.R.C., 1860, with ranks of London Scottish pipers to the right. (LSMA, used with permission)

Drawn by W. Smart for Dr A. Halley, 'My design sketch for uniform for Highland or Scottish Volunteer London Regiment,' 2nd June 1859. (LSMA, used with permission)

Members of Highland Company, 1861. (LSMA, used with permission)

Unknown artist, The Royal Review of Volunteer Corps, Hyde Park, 23 June 1860, with the London Scottish front centre. (LSMA, used with permission)

and five pipers per battalion.[15] The entire notion of a pipe band, not just outside the confines of a Highland regiment but also outside the borders of Scotland, was still very much a novelty and subject to ridicule. Despite the Duke of Cambridge's success as Commanding Officer of the Scots Fusilier Guards in establishing the pipes in 1856, there was still considerable pressure from numerous fellow Guards officers for the pipes to be withdrawn. The regimental pipers had been burlesqued by John Leech in cartoons in *Punch* magazine in 1856 after their return to Windsor Castle from the Crimea.[16] As late as 1868, the Colonel of the regiment, with assistance from the Colonel of the Coldstream Guards, wrote to Queen Victoria recommending that:

> The pipers in my Regiment may be discontinued, that they may return to the ranks from which they were enlisted, and that the pipe-majors may revert to the rank of sergeants, to be absorbed as vacancies occur.[17]

It would be an audacious move then, to instigate a volunteer pipe band in this environment, in London, only five years after the initial authorisation for pipers and before all but one regular non-Highland Scottish regiment had been granted such permission.

Before there could be a pipe band, however, there had to be formal recognition for the regiment. In October 1859, an official offer of service by the London Scottish was duly made to government, recruitment opened, and drill nights began at various places around the city. The offer of service was formally accepted by the War Office and the London Scottish Volunteer Rifles officially came into being on 2 November 1859 with Lord Elcho gazetted as Colonel of the regiment on 10 February 1860. The initial establishment was 600 men, divided into six companies, each of which would have their own headquarters building. This establishment was quickly filled. Number One Company was designated 'The Highland Company,' which was based at 10 Pall Mall East and was distinct from the other five in wearing the kilt. The other companies followed Lord Elcho's wishes and wore knickerbockers.

All six companies did, however, conform with Elcho's suggestion of incorporating the 'Hodden Grey' as their uniform colour and, for the first time since 1746, troops in Britain paraded in kilts the colour of the homespun cloth weaved by the common people of Scotland. Not only did this avoid any inter-clan rivalry but it also represented an early understanding of the importance of camouflage in battle. Lord Elcho stated that 'a soldier is a man hunter, neither more nor less; as a deer stalker chooses the least visible colours, so ought a soldier to be clad.'[18] Elcho believed strongly that dressing soldiers in scarlet jackets and white cross belts made them attractive targets on the battlefield whilst tight fitting white trousers were uncomfortable and unsuitable for modern warfare. Hodden Grey cloth had the additional advantage of being cheap to produce and less liable to wear and tear compared to more traditional tartan.

Regular drill nights in civilian dress took place at each company's headquarters twice a week and, after various alternative venues had been offered and rejected, a uniformed general muster

---

15 'Seven battalions Foot Guards, each…17 drummers, including drum-major…and an addition of 1 pipe-major and 5 pipers to each battalion of the Scots Fusileer [sic] Guards'. In 'Reduction in the Army, Horse Guards, Sept. 5th', *Colburn's United Service Magazine*, Vol. 82 (1856), p.299.
16 John Leech, 'Piping Time of Peace', *Punch*, 5 April 1856. The caption reads, 'Melancholy fate of an officer in the Fusilier Guards, who after passing through all the perils of the Crimea, is put hors-de-combat, by six bag-pipers going off at once.'
17 As quoted in John Malcolm Bulloch, 'Making Scots Regiments More Scots: The Case of the Scots Guards', *London Scottish Regimental Gazette* (1935), p.65.
18 From a letter by Elcho quoted by J.O. Robson, *The Uniforms of The London Scottish 1859-1959* (London: Hadden, Best, 1960), p.7.

took place each Saturday in the prestigious surroundings of Westminster Hall at the Houses of Parliament. In December 1859, drill was being performed 'under the guidance of (six) drill sergeants of the Coldstream Guards, who appear to relish the aptitude and steadiness on parade of the intelligent volunteer.'[19] Recruitment remained strong, particularly to the kilted Highland Company, and in January 1860, the London Scottish were formally recognised as a battalion and given the official title of the 15th Middlesex (The London Scottish) Regiment.

From the very beginning, links with the Scots Fusilier Guards, who would later become the present-day Scots Guards, were particularly strong. This was especially the case regarding pipers and drummers. Whilst the London Scottish had been able to pay to take on a brass band of German musicians who were not enlisted members of the regiment,[20] there had not yet been the time or inclination to train and organise pipers and drummers from amongst the volunteers. In the first few months, pipers and drummers from the prestigious Scots Fusilier Guards regiment helped to provide musical accompaniment and to install an increased sense of Scottish national pride and regimental spirit. Contemporary reports of a drill on 30 May 1860 state that 'Four companies of the corps marched to the Regent's Park on Wednesday, with the Highland Company in front, wearing the kilt ... and the pipers of the Scots Fusiliers cheerily leading.'[21] *The City Press* reported that, 'The national music of Scotland sounded through all the din of the crowded streets as the pipers of the Fusilier Guards marched at the head of these volunteers.'[22] These pipers, and their drummer counterparts, would play an integral role in helping to build the original London Scottish Pipes and Drums.

In an almost exact repetition of the early history of both the Highland Armed Association and the Loyal North Britons, the first major parade for the London Scottish was a full-scale Royal Review of London's volunteer corps in Hyde Park. On 23 June 1860, Queen Victoria, Prince Albert, the King of the Belgians and many other dignitaries attended this grand parade which saw over 20,000 volunteers march through Hyde Park as they had last done in 1803. *The Times* reported that through the 'distant clash of many different bands ... some of the best known companies were cheered as they passed.'[23] The first of these 'best known companies' to be mentioned in the article was 'Lord Elcho and the Highland Company'[24] who led the 4th Brigade, to which Lord Elcho had been designated Commanding Officer. The London Scottish had a brass band on parade and as they passed Queen Victoria, 'Her Majesty stood up in her carriage and as the band struck up our Quick Step she marked the time with her programme and seemed greatly pleased.'[25] Unfortunately, this 'distant clash' of bands did not include pipes and drums representing the London Scottish; but it may well have acted as an additional catalyst for their introduction.[26]

Lord Elcho was a strong advocate for bands and the role of music in military life; in particular, that of the volunteer. In a House of Commons committee debate on government aid for volunteer regiments, for which he had tabled the motion, Elcho stated that:

---

19 *The Morning Chronicle*, 13 December 1859, p.5.
20 Lord Elcho stated that, while this was one of the biggest expenses for the regiment, it was of the highest imperative. *Bell's Weekly Messenger*, 3 August 1861, p.2.
21 *The Morning Advertiser*, London, 1 June 1860, p.5.
22 *The City Press*, London, 2 June 1860, p.6.
23 *The Times*, 25 June 1860, p.9.
24 *The Times*, 25 June 1860, p.9.
25 E. Bowers, *London Scottish Regimental Gazette* (1910), p.232.
26 Page six of the *Carlisle Patriot*, 30 June 1860 contains a fascinating article on the Royal Review, within which the London Scottish are given much prominence.

> The expenses of a Volunteer Corps were not confined to the mere uniform, accoutrements, and drill-sergeants. They had to provide themselves with drill and musketry instruction, drill-grounds, ranges, targets, armouries, armourers, head-quarters, and then came advertising, printing, postage, stationary, travelling expenses, and bands. The committee might smile at this last item, but it was very dull work, and the men could with difficulty be got together without bands (hear, hear); and although he admitted that they led to a considerable expenditure, bands were really a sine quâ non (hear, hear).[27]

It seems likely then, that the lack of any pipe band musical accompaniment for the London Scottish at the Hyde Park Royal Review in June 1860 brought the official formation of a pipes and drums to the fore. Pipers would have almost certainly been present in the London Scottish at this time, but it is unlikely that they were organised in any authorised capacity. Such official recognition, however, was not long in coming.

The earliest recorded evidence of London Scottish pipers is an unorthodox one. On Tuesday 6 November 1860 a 'division' of London Scottish soldiers marched to Wimbledon Common to level a hill that was obscuring the regiment's new 600-yard rifle range. This initial group worked all day whilst a second gang was organised and marched to the common to relieve them and continued working through the night to complete the job. This relief 'division' was accompanied on the march to Wimbledon by pipers, duly arriving after sunset and into a somewhat dream-like scene lit by torches and firelight. It was reported that 'The second division marched down in the dark, and their pipers sounded wildly across the heath.'[28] Bonfires were built up and a large crowd gathered, despite the late hour, 'Meanwhile the resting parties began to dance Highland reels to the piper's strains.'[29] This episode must have been quite something to behold.

It is almost certain that these pipes were played by an authorised accompaniment of London Scottish volunteers in uniform as official sanction had already been given for pipers by the regiment. Four days after the Wimbledon event, The *Volunteer Service Gazette* reported that:

> About ten members of the corps are being prepared as bagpipers, so that those who like this Northern symphony (and those who don't) will hear soon enough of it in the Strand.[30]

There is little likelihood, however, that these London Scottish pipers would initially have been accompanied by London Scottish drummers. Drummers were not on establishment in rifle corps, who were instead assigned 1 bugle major and 16 buglers, and contemporary records mention drummers from the Guards being involved with the London Scottish at this time. It would not, however, be long before this too was to change.

On Saturday 17 November, one week after the above-mentioned report from the *Volunteer Service Gazette*, the corps met at Westminster Hall to hear Lord Elcho announce that, as the strength of the regiment had now reached nearly 900, four new companies were to be formed. Despite his continued misgivings about the kilt, it was also announced that one of these new companies would be designated as a second Highland Company. The pretence for this being that a 'symmetrical appearance might be maintained in line by having two kilted companies as each flank',[31] but it is much more likely that weight of recruiting numbers for the over-subscribed

---

27 *Hansard*, 21 June 1861, Series 3, Vol. 163 c.1464.
28 *The Leeds Mercury*, 10 November 1860, Issue 7185.
29 'London Scottish Sappers and Miners: A Recollection', *London Scottish Regimental Gazette* (1908), p.117.
30 *The Volunteer Service Gazette Vol. II* (London: William John Johnson, 1861), p.34.
31 *The Times*, 20 November 1860, p.10.

first Highland Company was the deciding factor. It is worth stating here that, with only five kilted regiments in the British Army prior to 1881 (Black Watch, Ross-shire Buffs, Cameron Highlanders, Gordon Highlanders and Sutherland Highlanders), the idea of kilted volunteers in London in 1860 was audacious, but it was exactly this innovation which ensured that the uniform of the London Scottish Pipes and Drums would be Highland in nature.

As further evidence that musical accompaniment for London Scottish troops on the march had become an important consideration, the 17 November gathering also marked the first performance of the regiment's 'marching chorus,' made up of over 70 members. However, this idea never really took hold and the chorus were not much heard of again.[32] Lord Elcho, with much chagrin, would later admit to their demise in an address to the regiment in July 1861.[33] What men on the march really wanted to hear were military brass bands and pipe bands and, thankfully, preparation was being made for both.

In the same address, 'Volunteer pipers, Volunteer bandsmen, and Volunteer pioneers were asked for.'[34] Amongst these would be volunteer drummers who would be tasked to perform with both brass band and pipers. Further particulars regarding the fledgling pipe corps and future military band were detailed by Lord Elcho, as reported in *The Volunteer Service Gazette*:

> His Lordship then announced that five or six Volunteer pipers were in the course of training under a pipe-major, who would instruct them thoroughly, and that a brass band would be provided, which would form the nucleus for the practise of Volunteer bandsmen, as they come forward gradually for instruction.[35]

The original 'about ten' members being trained on the pipes had contracted to a nucleus of six. The 'pipe major' providing instruction was Piper John MacKenzie of the 2nd Battalion, Scots Fusilier Guards and the six original London Scottish pipers under his tuition were Alexander 'Sandy' Campbell, Peter McDonald, Davie Henry, Jim Coutts, Maule Bately and Wood.[36]

This list of names, specifying the very founding fathers of the London Scottish Pipes and Drums in 1860, comes from an informative article by C.N. McIntyre North which was published in the *London Scottish Regimental Gazette* in May 1897.[37] The article was penned in response to two earlier pieces, written by ex-Pipe Major Ronald Halley, that had appeared in the March and April 1897 issues of the *Gazette*,[38] claiming that there had been no pipers or drummers back in 1860 and that no pipe band existed in the London Scottish until 1873. Halley stated that:

> For parades, and marches out the pipers were obtained from, and by permission of the Colonel of the Scots Guards, or Scots Fusilier Guards as they were then designated.[39]

---

32 Although there is a reference in April 1861 to marching London Scottish troops 'being enlivened by members singing sundry national airs.' *Volunteer Service Gazette*, 13 April 1861, p.386.
33 *The Morning Post*, 30 July 1861, p.6.
34 *The Times*, 20 November 1860, p.10.
35 *The Volunteer Service Gazette*, 24 November 1861, p.66.
36 Unfortunately, Piper Woods' first name is unknown.
37 C.N. McIntyre North, 'The Early Days of the London Scottish R.V.', *London Scottish Regimental Gazette* (1897), p.77.
38 See Ronald Halley, 'The Pipes and Drums of the London Scottish', *London Scottish Regimental Gazette* (1897), p.43 and p.57.
39 Halley, 'The Pipes and Drums of the London Scottish', p.43.

Halley is, indeed, correct in that the Scots Fusilier Guards did provide pipers to assist the London Scottish volunteers on the march in the very earliest days of the regiment. We have seen that on 30 May 1860, for example, the pipers of the Scots Fusilier Guards led the four companies on the march to Regents Park. However, one of these pipers would have been John MacKenzie and there is ample contemporary evidence to show that he took on the role of Pipe Major with the London Scottish and, with some prestigious assistance, began training pipers from 1860.

Halley himself did not join the London Scottish until 1875 and did not play with the Pipes and Drums until 1876. Thus, his evidence was based on regimental memory which can be notoriously misleading and imprecise.[40] Thankfully, there is an abundance of contemporary evidence to refute his claim, including McIntyre North's article. Whilst Halley's statement, though rather confused, does retain some element of fact in that Scots Fusilier Guards pipers and drummers certainly did parade with the London Scottish on various occasions in the early years, it is categorically erroneous to suggest that there were no London Scottish pipers and drummers before the early 1870s.

McIntyre North[41] goes on in his article to explain that the first pipers practised in a local pub, the St Martin's Tavern on Duke Street (now John Adam Street) just across Trafalgar Square from the Highland Company headquarters in Pall Mall East and close to the new regimental headquarters building on Adelphi Terrace.[42] He reports that John MacKenzie instructed the pipers there until the summer of 1861 when the 2nd Battalion, Scots Fusilier Guards were sent to Canada to strengthen the border during the American Civil War.[43] The battalion did not return to Britain until 1864. After their homecoming, John MacKenzie promptly recommenced his role as instructor, 'wearing the uniform of the LSRV by permission of his Commanding Officer,'[44] a position he held until leaving the regular army later that decade. He would again take up the role of instructor in 1881 and was still in this position until ill-health forced him to retire in 1904.[45] This permission for MacKenzie to wear the London Scottish uniform was already in place prior to his departure for Canada in 1861 and, therefore, it was almost certainly Mackenzie who 'as pipe major enlivened the proceedings by an occasional pibroch from the gallery'[46] at the London Scottish School of Arms meeting at St James' Street in February 1861.

MacKenzie was a notable and important piper in his own right, having an accomplished solo piping career alongside his military achievements. He went on to win the prestigious Highland Society of London first place Prize Pipes in 1874 and he also won the Gold Medal and Dirk at the 1876 Northern Meeting. As the nephew of the great John Ban McKenzie (known as 'The King of the Pipers'), he came from a strong piping family and was one of the three most eminent pipers in London during his lifetime.

---

40   Halley's articles are, however, valuable and accurate when relating to developments after his enlistment.
41   McIntyre North joined the London Scottish soon after its founding and became a sergeant and an adept Highland dancer. An obituary for him in 1899 states that 'As a graceful dancer he was always in the front rank, and he took great interest in the original Pipe-Band, on which instrument he was no mean adept himself.' *London Scottish Regimental Gazette*, London, 1899, p.103. He emigrated in 1872.
42   This pub, first licensed in 1690, rebuilt in 1959 and now called the Theodore Bullfrog, still exists. The publican at the time, one John Brownleg, must have been very accommodating!
43   While the 2nd Battalion did not actually embark at Southampton until 19 December 1861 they were mobilised in the summer and were, thus, unable to continue assisting the London Scottish.
44   McIntyre North, 'The Early Days of the London Scottish R.V.', p.77.
45   Pipe Major Robert Reith makes request for contributions to a fund for John MacKenzie's healthcare in a letter published in the *London Scottish Regimental Gazette* (1904), p.29.
46   *Volunteer Service Gazette*, 2 February 1861, p.226.

What, then, of the earliest drummers? As a rifle regiment with no drummers on establishment, it is most likely that their derivation was associated with the military band being formed in autumn 1860. During this period, it was common practise in regular rifle regiments for the military band to lead any parade, with fife and drums to the centre or rear and buglers following behind. In Highland infantry regiments, pipers replaced the buglers in this procession. The band and pipers played turn and turn-about with the drummers providing the rhythmical accompaniment for both. This frequently created tension between the bandsmen, the drummers, and the pipers, all of whom fought to take the lead on any important parade or march past. It was not until 1871 that Queen Victoria settled the matter permanently by stating that any regiment with pipers should on all occasions march past to the pipes and that when marching past, the pipers should fall in *before* the band. This rearrangement necessitated drummers between the pipers and the brass band, forming the first notions of a modern pipe band and opening the possibility for the construction of drumming patterns specific to pipe band composition.[47] Until this time, drummers and drumming were more associated with military brass bands (as was the case initially with the London Scottish) or with fife and drum corps, which the London Scottish never formed, despite repeated requests on various occasions in their history to do so.

The only details regarding the initial, professional, brass band of the London Scottish can be found in a letter from Edward Peacock, an original member of the regiment, published in the *London Scottish Regimental Gazette* in 1902. In it, Peacock says of this first band:

> I may say they were 'made in Germany', the band at that time consisting of about 16 Germans. The bass and side-drummers were Guardsmen, and little or no Scotch music was played. The strains of the so-called music had a rather depressing effect, instead of an enlivening and invigorating one, as the present band of pipes and buglers do.[48]

Taking this statement as fact, the presumption would be that these drummers also came from the 2nd Battalion, Scots Fusilier Guards, as this regiment already provided the instructor for the pipers and had provided pipers for the London Scottish in their first year of formation. Scots Fusilier Guards drummers, unlike others in the Brigade of Guards, would have been experienced at playing with pipers and so would have been the natural choice. A close bond obviously already existed between the two units if the commanding officer was prepared to allow Piper John MacKenzie to wear the London Scottish uniform when performing with them. Whether the Scots Fusilier Guard drummers also wore London Scottish uniform when playing with the band is open to question, but it is certainly plausible. It is also probable that Scots Fusilier drummers, wearing their own uniforms, played on the march with their piper colleagues during the earliest days of the London Scottish.

Therefore, with only buglers on establishment in 1860, it seems highly credible that the first drummers to play with the London Scottish Pipes and Drums came from the Scots Fusilier Guards. This situation would have remained in place for the first few months of the band's existence while London Scottish drummers were trained as part of the volunteer band being put together at the time. In February 1861, the *Volunteer Service Gazette* reports that 'The volunteer band of this corps has commenced instruction under Mr Whitterbottom, of the Royal Marines.'[49]

---

47 It also led, by common usage, to the notion of 'Pipes and Drums' rather than the militarily correct, 'Drums and Pipes.' Drums have military seniority over the pipes through date of establishment but only the Gordon Highlanders referred to their band as 'The Drums and Pipes.'
48 *London Scottish Regimental Gazette* (1902), p.178.
49 *Volunteer Service Gazette*, 23 February 1861, p.274.

This is almost certainly a misquote, that should correctly refer to John Winterbottom who was, at the time, Bandmaster of the Royal Marine Artillery based in Portsmouth and who would soon become Senior Director of Music for the Brigade of Guards. The drummers from the Guards may well have remained with the London Scottish until they were posted overseas in summer 1861, by which time the volunteer drummers were trained and ready to take their place completely. No more is heard regarding John Winterbottom after this date and no more is heard of the volunteer band, which does not seem to have taken off. The professional band continued but now with the addition of volunteer drummers drawn from the ranks of the London Scottish to support them and, more importantly, the volunteer pipers.

John MacKenzie must have performed commendably as instructor to the pipers, as they were deemed ready to perform as a group in June 1861. Unfortunately, MacKenzie had already been mobilised for his posting to Canada and so was not on hand to see and hear the fruits of his labour. His place as piping instructor was taken over, informally, by Pipe Major William Ross, Sovereign's Piper to Queen Victoria. A grand event was organised to take place at Westminster Hall on Wednesday 19 June for this first major performance of the pipers. Lady Elcho and other Scottish ladies resident in London had collected a large sum of money in order to purchase six sets of high-quality pipes, along with a pipe banner for the pipe major. The pipes were purchased in Aberdeen from John MacKenzie's uncle, the great 'King of the Pipers' John Ban MacKenzie, piper and pipe-maker to the Marquis of Breadalbane.[50] They were mounted in silver and cost over £100.

The Pipe Major's pipes bore the following inscription:

> Presented with five other sets of bagpipes, a banner, and a donation of money in addition for the band, to the London Scottish Rifle Volunteers, by Scottish Ladies resident in London, June 1861.
>
> *Cuidich in rhi* (Help the King)

The pipe banner carried a crest of the regiment as used on officers' cross belts at the time, presumably because it was more elaborate than the silver thistle which was then the official regimental cap badge. The pipe-bags were covered in Government, better known as Black Watch, tartan. This tartan was chosen for two very good reasons. Firstly, this was the same tartan as used on the bagpipes of the 2nd Battalion Scots Fusilier Guards, whose first Pipe Major, Donald MacPherson, had transferred from the 42nd Regiment (The Black Watch) to take charge of their fledgling pipe corps in 1856. Secondly, Pipe Major Ross, who was aiding the instruction of the pipers, was also originally a piper in the Black Watch. By taking this tartan, rather than using the regimental Hodden Grey or Royal Stuart, the London Scottish Regiment and their pipers paid homage to those that had helped bring the pipe band into existence.

---

50   John Bàn Mackenzie (1796-1864), piper, composer and pipemaker, was born in Achilty, Contin, Strathpeffer and was taught piping by Donald Mòr MacLennan, John Beag MacRae and John Mackay of Raasay. He was awarded the special gold medal for former winners of the Highland Society Prize pipes when first issued in 1835 and after styled 'King of Pipers' or Rìgh nam Piobairean. He is a key figure in the transmission of traditional piobaireachd or 'classical' bagpipe music from the MacCrimmons to the present day; John Mackay of Raasay having been taught by Iain Dubh and Domhnall Ruadh, the last of the MacCrimmons of Skye. As a professional piper of the nineteenth century, he was successively piper to Mackenzie of Allangrange, Davidson of Tulloch and the Marquis of Breadalbane with whom he remained for 28 years. He earned a place in piping tradition, not only for his skills and achievements, but also for turning down an invitation to join the Royal Household and becoming Queen Victoria's Piper (*National Museum of Scotland*).

A copy of the programme from this event still survives and on the front page is an excellent illustration of a bearded London Scottish piper, with his pipes carrying the new banner. This image represents the earliest identified depiction of a London Scottish piper. It is not known who this piper is modelled on, but it is fair to assume that, as the pipe banner is present, this is a representation of Alexander 'Sandy' Campbell who was appointed to the position of pipe major for the occasion, becoming the first piper from among the ranks of the London Scottish to be given this appointment.

The event itself was a huge society affair and was widely reported in the press all around the country. Present in Westminster Hall, along with Lord and Lady Elcho, were the Duke and Duchess of Sutherland, the Countess's of Lichfield and Warwick, the Marquis of Abercorn (son of the Duke of Athol), General Sir Duncan MacGregor, the Speaker of the House of Commons,[51] Lieutenant Colonel Charteris,[52] as well as many of the Scottish ladies who had donated money for the pipes, and a large, invited crowd that packed the ancient hall.

The pipes and banner, supported by stacked rifles, were displayed at the end of the hall with troops lining three sides and facing the stage. From there, the presentation was made by Lady Elcho to Captain MacKenzie of the first Highland Company. Lady Elcho's presentation speech contained the following lines which have remained relevant to the role of the pipes in the London Scottish ever since:

> It is especially gratifying to us to present you with this national instrument. We are proud of our national corps, and well pleased to add in this way to the outward marks of your nationality. The wild notes of the pipes are, I am sure, dear to every Scotch heart; they awaken pleasant memories of home and country; they are associated with the gallant deeds of our heroic countrymen in all parts of the world, and we are not without hope too, that these pipes may in some degree do the work of the recruiting sergeant and that, attracted by the stirring sounds, many a good Scottish heart and arm may be gathered to our ranks.[53]

Captain MacKenzie replied to Lady Elcho's speech on behalf of the regiment and concluded by asking for three cheers for the Scottish ladies:

> Immediately afterwards the corps formed in order on either side of the hall, and the first notes of the new bagpipes resounded to the popular tune of *The Highland Laddie,* followed by *The Campbells are Coming,* etc., which was received with thunderous applause. The pipers were Messrs. Ross (the Queen's piper), Campbell (pipe-major), Wilson (piper to the Caledonian Asylum), McDonald, Coutts and Wood. The performance gave universal satisfaction, and at its conclusion the corps marched round the hall, headed by the pipers, and the proceedings terminated.[54]

---

51 John Evelyn Denison, later 1st Viscount Ossington.
52 Lord Elcho's younger brother and a member of the personal staff of Queen Victoria.
53 *Presentation of Bagpipes to the London Scottish Rifle Volunteers in Westminster Hall, Wednesday 19th June, 1861* (London: Day and Son, 1861), p.2.
54 'Presentation of Pipes to the London Scottish Rifle Volunteers', *Volunteer Service Gazette*, 22 June 1861, p.550.

54   STRIKE UP, STRIKE SURE

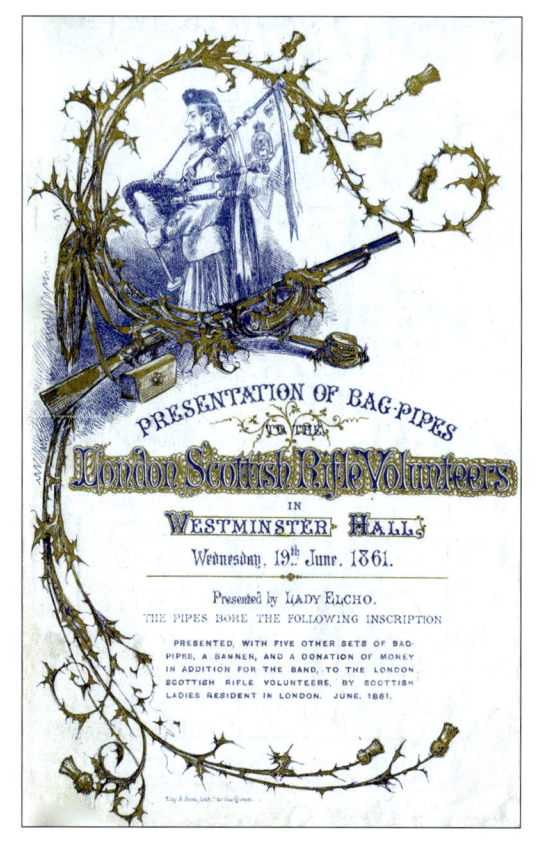

W. Thomas, 'The London Scottish Volunteers in Westminster Hall,' Houses of Parliament, *Illustrated London News*, 1860, with London Scottish piper to far right. (LSMA, used with permission)

Programme Cover, *Presentation of Bag-pipes to the London Scottish Rifle Volunteers in Westminster Hall*, Wednesday 19 June 1861, with illustration of London Scottish piper with pipe banner. (LSMA, used with permission)

Kenneth Macleay, Portrait of Queen Victoria's Sovereign Piper, Pipe Major William Ross, c. 1866. (The Royal Collection © 2022 Her Majesty Queen Elizabeth II)

It is apt that the first tune played on London Scottish pipes, *Gillie Gaidhealach*, was the tune that remains the regimental march, while the second tune played, Baile Inearaoradh,[55] represents the perfect tribute to Alexander Campbell's appointment as pipe major.

The presence of both Pipe Major William Ross, Sovereign's Piper to Queen Victoria, and Wilson, the official piper of the Caledonian Asylum, is also of interest. With John MacKenzie now overseas, a new permanent instructor for the pipe corps was needed, and Ross and Wilson were both involved in assisting Pipe Major Campbell.[56] Pipe Major Ross[57] was certainly closely involved with the Pipes and Drums and performed frequently with the London Scottish over the next few years, assisting greatly with the progress of the pipers during this period. The involvement of the sovereign's piper with the new pipe corps was a major coup and, alongside the association with the Scots Fusilier Guards, suitably illustrates the influence of the London Scottish Regiment from the time of its earliest development.

Pipe Major Ross paraded with the Pipes and Drums of the London Scottish on Saturday 23 June 1861 in Regent's Park for their first major outing after the presentation of the pipes, where 'an immense concourse of spectators assembled to witness the spectacle.'[58] The London Scottish were reviewed by their Honorary Colonel, Field Marshal Colin Campbell, The Lord Clyde, who himself wore the Hodden Grey.[59] Over 500 men, in eight companies, marched to the park from Wellington Barracks, 'proceeded by their band and pipers, among whom Ross, Her Majesty's Piper, was conspicuous'[60] and where the 'pipes recently presented by Lady Elcho were brought into effective requisition.'[61] As the inspection took place, the regiment 'marched past in quick time, in companies in open column, to the music of the band and pipes.'[62]

The Pipes and Drums of the London Scottish Regiment were now fully formed and had taken part in their first full scale parade. The presence of Pipe Major Ross implies that they were not quite ready to parade on their own, and he would parade with them again on Saturday 13 July 1861 when Prince George, Duke of Cambridge and Commander-in-Chief of the British Army, presented prizes at the National Rifle Association meeting at the London Scottish butts on Wimbledon Common. On this occasion there was a march past of bands from the different volunteer corps who had arrived to be reviewed later that day, during which 'the London Scottish

---

55 These are the Gaelic names for *Highland Laddie* and *The Campbells are Coming*.
56 As piper to the Caledonian Asylum, Wilson would have had many links with the London Scottish. The Caledonian Asylum, later known as the Royal Caledonian School, was founded by the Highland Society of London in 1815 to house and educate poor children of Scottish decent and those who found themselves orphaned after the Napoleonic Wars. It was first housed in Hatton Gardens, next to the Scots Church and the Headquarters of the Loyal North Britons. The Royal Caledonian School would be a prominent source of pipers for the London Scottish regiment over the next 100 years and the Royal Caledonian Schools Trust still provides assistance to children of Scots who have served or are serving in the Armed Forces and those from poor backgrounds.
57 Ross enlisted with the 42nd Regiment, Royal Highlanders (Black Watch) in 1839 as a piper and later became Pipe Major. He succeeded Angus Mackay as Sovereign's Piper on 10 May 1854 and retained the position for 37 years until his death on 10 June 1891, aged 68.
58 *Volunteer Service Gazette*, 29 June 1861, p.562.
59 A native of Glasgow, Campbell was one of Britain's most respected military figures, having been Officer Commanding the Highland Brigade, who won glory at the Battle of Alma and who's 'thin red line' famously held back the Russian advance at Balaklava during the Crimean War. He later became Commander-in-Chief of British Forces in India during the Indian Mutiny, presiding over the relief of Lucknow.
60 *Portsmouth Times and Naval Gazette*, 29 June 1861, p.3.
61 *Volunteer Service Gazette*, 29 June 1861, p.562.
62 *The Times*, 24 June 1861, p.7.

on their appearance with the pipes, were loudly cheered.'[63] A soldier of the London Scottish, writing in the *Inverness Courier*, sums up the importance of music on such an occasion:

> When we began to move round to the saluting post, we were loudly applauded; and, as we marched past, the band playing 'Highland Laddie,' cheer after cheer broke forth, while cries of 'Bravo the Scotch' made our hearts beat with pleasure to think we belonged to the land 'of the mountain and the flood.' We then left the ground, Ross, the Queens,' and our own pipers leading the way to the station. We got into town about 10 o'clock, highly delighted with the day.[64]

By mid-1861, the volunteer movement was entering its third year and issues of finance and long-term planning were beginning to become more acute. Volunteer rifle regiments were still very much self-supporting, with little money coming from government, and internal structures that had very often been cobbled together in the short-term were now being reappraised. This situation would continue for the next few years with regiments attempting to maintain levels of membership as the initial euphoria subsided. Such issues certainly confronted the London Scottish, with one of the largest expenses at the time being the professional brass band. This band of Germans, led by their German bandmaster, did not always live up to expectations and their knowledge of Scottish tunes was rather limited.

At the second annual meeting of the London Scottish on Tuesday 29 July 1861, Lord Elcho voiced his concerns on this matter stating that, while a large amount was being spent on the band:

> This charge was not sufficient to enable them to procure such a band as he felt assured they all desired [hear], and such a one as would be in keeping with the nationality of their corps [hear, hear].[65]

The German band was thus let go and a debate took place over the next six to nine months to decide whether or not it should be replaced. Lord Elcho also hoped that more volunteer pipers could be trained from the nearly 700 efficient soldiers within the regiment and promised that 'next year they never should march out without their national music' and that 'he would answer for this upon his own responsibility.'[66]

The debate surrounding the future of the volunteer movement continued to grow until Parliament set up a Royal Commission, chaired by Viscount Eversley, to enquire into the conditions of the volunteer force in Great Britain.[67] Lord Elcho sat on this commission and called a number of London Scots as witnesses, including the Adjutant, Captain S. Flood, who was questioned about the necessity and expense of bands. Captain Flood highlighted the importance of

---

63 *Lloyds Weekly Newspaper*, 14 July 1861, Issue 973.
64 *The Inverness Courier*, 25 July 1861, p.6.
65 'London Scottish Rifles', *Morning Chronicle*, 30 July 1861, Issue 29502.
66 'London Scottish Rifles', *Morning Chronicle*, 30 July 1861, Issue 29502.
67 The recommendations of the Royal Commission led to the passing of the Volunteer Act 1863 (26 & 27 Vict. C.65), that replaced the 1804 legislation. Amongst other things, it allowed for permanent staff members (Adjutant and Sergeant Instructors) and set up a system of annual inspections, efficiency standards and regulations for the Force. Volunteer regiments still came under the control of the Home Office (this would change in 1872) and Part II of the Act dealt specifically with conditions for actual military service, should the need arise.

military music by stating that 'I think it would be impossible to keep the corps together without a band,'[68] even though he estimated the cost being around £200 per annum.[69]

Importantly, Flood also stated that:

> We have in addition to the band, six pipers … but the pipers, with the exception of the pipe-major, to whom we pay 25l. a year, are voluntary. But having six pipers we never muster more than four on parade, and very often two, and sometimes we go out without one.[70]

It appears then, that Elcho's promise for the regiment not to march out without the national music was proving hard to fulfil and the formation of a pipe band without support from a military band, as would be recognised today, was still some way off. Flood's statement, however, is proof that a new band had been retained. On 11 January 1862, Lord Elcho stated the following:

> Upon the question of a band, he wished to tell them that a book had been opened at headquarters for subscriptions, and if £200 per year were collected they would have a band, but if not the corps would have to contend themselves with their national pipes. The volunteer pipers were getting on extremely well, and the warm thanks of the corps were due to them for their excursions.[71]

The £200 was raised and this new band, with Bandmaster Macfarlane, a Scot, in control, would allow better integration with the Pipes and Drums.

On 19 April 1862 the London Scottish pipers and drummers, along with the new military band, accompanied the rest of the regiment to the Volunteer Review at Brighton, where 20,000 troops were inspected by Lord Clyde. With their Honorary Colonel as reviewing officer, the London Scottish needed to ensure they gave an impeccable display. On the march past, 'the London Scottish Corps, was enthusiastically cheered, the band playing *Where ha' you been a' the day*,'[72] which would have certainly amused Lord Clyde. The review was followed by the mother of all mock battles and on completion of these activities:

> As this was the finish of the day's proceedings, the London Scottish defiled off the ground in fours, headed by their excellent band, which, along with their bagpipes and drums alternatively played them off the ground[73]

Importantly, this is the first mention of the Pipes and Drums as a unit. They were now teamed with an excellent band, under a Scottish bandmaster, which played predominantly Scottish music and that between them, began to forge a lasting reputation.

Much of this success can be credited to Pipe Major 'Sandy' Campbell who had taken the reigns after the posting of John MacKenzie to Canada. The pipers were obviously impressed by Campbell's lead, as they organised a dinner for him on Wednesday 26 March that year and

---

68 'To Enquire Into the Condition of the Volunteer Force in Great Britain. Tuesday 3rd June 1862', *Report from Commissioners, Sessions 6th February – 7th August 1862*, London Great Britain Parliament, House of Commons, 1862, p.54.
69 Other evidence given to the Committee showed that volunteer regiments were paying between £60 and £600 per year for their bands.
70 'To Enquire Into the Condition of the Volunteer Force in Great Britain', p.56.
71 *The Edinburgh Evening Courant*, 17 January 1862, p.3.
72 'The Grand Volunteer Field Day at Brighton', *Trewman's Exeter Flying Post*, 23 April 1862, Issue 5009.
73 'The Volunteer Review at Brighton', *Glasgow Herald*, 24 April 1862, Issue 6953.

presented him with a gold watch, worth 15 guineas as a thank you for teaching them the national music.[74] Senior Piper P. McDonald was in the chair and during the presentation, Piper Coutts stated that:

> Had any one a few years ago had the temerity to predict that a band of Volunteer Pipers would be formed at the present time marching at the head of a body of Scottish Riflemen in London, he most unquestionably would have been considered an ignoramus or a fit candidate for Hanwell.[75]

In August of the same year, the pipers of the London Scottish also inaugurated their first piping competition during a two-day regimental meeting of shooting and athletics at Wimbledon. This forerunner of the famous McLeod Medal was recorded at the time as follows:

> The competition among the pipers was carried on with great spirit during the firing, the judges being Sir Euan MacKenzie and Mr Wilson, piper of the Caledonian Asylum. The first prize was won by Mr MacDonald, a chanter mounted in silver, presented by Mr Brown; the second, by Mr Maule, a 'Skeen-Dhur' (so the *Southron* reported) presented by Captain MacKenzie; the third, by Mr MacKintosh, presented by Captain MacGregor; the fourth, by Mr Coutts, a book of music, presented by Pipe-Major Campbell, and Mr Henry, with a 'blank,' piped no less cheerily than the rest as the whole party marched back over the heath.[76]

This report includes the name of a new addition to the piping ranks in Mr MacKintosh, taking the total number of London Scottish pipers at this time to seven (six pipers and the pipe major). He was obviously a relatively strong piper, having taken third place in the competition. The existence of such a piping competition with substantial prizes, only two years into their existence, suggests a high degree of organisation and erudition within the pipe corps that would stand them in good stead for the future.

Further consolidation took place in 1863 and by 1864 the Pipes and Drums were increasingly well-known in London and beyond to the point of already becoming synonymous with the London Scottish Regiment. Good natured jokes about them began to appear in the press, in a similar manner to the following report from the National Rifle Association camp at Wimbledon in 1864:

> Last evening a sudden and violent illness seized the members of the Victoria Camp and caused great anxiety to their worthy and much respected surgeon. On mature inquiry, it was found to arise from the effects of the playing of the bagpipes in the Scottish camp; on the cessation of the noise the symptoms of the illness decreased, and the members gradually recovered.[77]

---

74 *Morning Chronicle*, 31 March 1862, Issue 29703.
75 McIntyre North, 'The Early Days of the London Scottish R.V.', p.77.
76 Quoted by Duncan Tovey, 'The History of the London Scottish', *London Scottish Regimental Gazette* (1921), p.94. I have been unable to trace the original source.
77 *MacMillan's Magazine*, ed. by D. Masson, G. Cravee, Marley and M. Morris (London: Macmillan and Co., 1867), Vol. 16, p.186.

Front cover of *The Illustrated London News*, 24 July 1869, with London Scottish piper bottom right. (LSMA, used with permission)

'The band of bagpipes was heard in the distance, and as these drew near it was perceived that the pipers headed a regular procession.' C.A. Ferrier, *The Leisure Hour*, July 1870. (LSMA, used with permission)

'Amusements in the Camp of the London Scottish,' Wimbledon, *The Illustrated London News*, 15 July 1871, with London Scottish piper to right. (LSMA, used with permission)

Officers and Senior NCOs of the 1st Battalion, Scots Fusilier Guards, with Pipe Major Robert MacKenzie, piping instructor to the London Scottish, seated second from right, Dublin 1883. (LSMA, used with permission)

Lord Elcho responded to such gentle ribbing about the pipes by stating in a speech to the regiment that 'he could only conclude that the people of this country who failed to appreciate its charms must be in a melancholy state of mind. (Laughter and cheers).'[78]

The pipes, particularly, appeared wherever the London Scottish went, playing at dinners, presentations and camps, and supplying accompaniment for the dancing of reels and flings that provided the evening entertainment. Lady Elcho, remembered fondly for supplying the pipers with pipes, and other female guests would be especially well looked after at camp. At the end of an evening, when they wished to retire, a procession would form with men carrying lamps and a piper at the head to conduct each lady to her temporary home.[79] The role of the Pipes and Drums had, then, already become embroiled in every aspect of regimental life.

By 1865, the Pipes and Drums, the London Scottish Regiment and the volunteer movement in general appeared to be going from strength to strength. Regarding the latter, it began to be said that the volunteer 'movement' was 'now a thing of the past, and a Volunteer Force may be safely regarded as part of our military establishment.'[80] Political unease in Europe, which would soon lead to the Austro-Prussian War of 1866 and the Franco-Prussian War of 1870-71, ensured that volunteer rifle regiments continued to attract large numbers of recruits. The London Scottish were now a fixture of military and social life in London, with the Pipes and Drums much less of a novelty and more of a defining feature.

They certainly helped to garner attention to the regiment from all quarters. On Saturday 13 May 1865, the London Scottish held their annual review in Hyde Park, which was to famously turn into an accidental 'Royal Review.' The regiment formed up at Wellington Barracks and then 'marched by Constitution Hill to Knightsbridge, headed by its band, together with its seven fine-looking pipers'[81] before entering the Guards drill-ground in Hyde Park. The sound of the Pipes and Drums attracted the attention of the Prince and Princess of Wales and the Crown Prince of Denmark, who happened to be in the park at the time and who decided to play their part in the review by taking the salute. 'The battalion ... wheeled into open column right in front, and marched past in quick time to their usual quick step, *Highland Laddie*.'[82]

Despite these successes, or maybe because of them, it is reported that issues began to arise for the Pipes and Drums. McIntyre North, writing over 30 years later, stated that:

> The Volunteer Pipers did yeoman service on the march and in camp until July, 1865, when at the camp, Campbell took umbrage at some remarks made by the Quartermaster, and, fully conscious that a Piper is a gentleman by rank as well as a skilled musician, he resigned, and the others, following his example, the Corps for years had to depend on the good offices of the Pipers of the 1st and 2nd Battalion of the Scots Guards.[83]

McIntyre goes on to state that the drummers continued, quoting a receipt for 'Tenor Drums for Pipes' from 30 November 1867.[84] Tovey agrees that the unfortunate disagreement between the pipe major and quartermaster did take place, but that it happened the following year in 1866. He states that there were no pipers at the prize distribution in 1866 and that there were none at

---

78 'Presentation of Prizes, Westminster Hall', *Reynolds Newspaper*, 4 December 1864, Issue 747.
79 *MacMillan's Magazine* (1867), p.186.
80 *Volunteer Service Gazette*, 1863-1864, p.691.
81 *Volunteer Service Gazette*, 1864-1865, p.391.
82 *Volunteer Service Gazette*, 1864-1865, p.391.
83 McIntyre North, 'The Early Days of the London Scottish R.V.', p.78.
84 McIntyre North, 'The Early Days of the London Scottish R.V.', p.78.

the annual inspection in 1867.[85] These comments would then, lend certain weight to Halley's claim that there was no pipe band until 1873 when 'men in the Regiment who played pipes got permission from the Colonel to form a band.'[86] However, there is an abundance of contemporary evidence, both literal and visual, to refute these claims. While it is probable that such an argument took place and that it influenced the function of the Pipes and Drums in some manner, London Scottish regimental pipers and drummers wearing Hodden Grey uniform are reported throughout the period 1865 to 1872; the very period they were alleged to be extinct.

On 17 March 1866, the regiment gave a dinner for their new Honorary Colonel, Lieutenant General Sir Hope Grant at St James's Hall, during which the 'fine band of the regiment played and the bagpipers played *The Prince's Salute*.'[87] Not itself conclusive evidence that these were London Scottish pipers, but on May 19th that year Hope Grant reviewed the regiment for their annual inspection at Wellington Barracks.[88] The field state of the regiment was reported as 'exclusive of the band and pipers: Officers 21; sergeants, 26; rank and file, 249.'[89] The pipers are specifically mentioned here as being of the regiment and we know from reports in the *Clerkenwell News* and *London Times* that the brass band and the pipers paraded.[90]

Interestingly, two months later, the *Daily News* reported on the National Rifle Association meeting at Wimbledon and the presentation of prizes by the Prince and Princess of Wales, the Duke of Edinburgh and the Duke of Cambridge. The London Scottish supplied the guard of honour and 'the drums of the London Scottish played the National Anthem.'[91] No mention here of the pipes, but quite how the National Anthem was played on the drums alone is open to conjecture. Was it perhaps at this camp that the pipers had taken offense and left the drummers to it, as Duncan Tovey suggests?

October 1866 gives us the earliest contemporary evidence of the celebration of Hallowe'en by the regiment.[92] It is often erroneously believed that the traditional Hallowe'en dinner observed by the London Scottish Regiment came about because of their role in the famous Battle of Messines of 31 October 1914, but Hallowe'en had always been a cause for celebration in Scotland. 31 October also happened to be the final day of the volunteer force year and so was the perfect occasion to report on and celebrate regimental accomplishments of the previous 12 months. The report of the Hallowe'en celebrations in 1866 mentions reels and sword dances performed to the accompaniment of pipes and, while this is not conclusive proof that these were London Scottish pipers, it does help to portray the continued role of the pipes within the regiment.

Stronger, irrefutable evidence, however, can be found in 1867. In April, the Volunteer Easter Review took place at Dover and all volunteers were mandated to attend church parade on Easter Sunday at Dover Castle chapel. 'The volunteers were accompanied on their march to and from the Castle by the band of the City of London and the pipers of the London Scottish Corps.'[93] A month later, the *Penny Illustrated Paper* reported on the athletics meeting of the London Scottish that took place in May at the Middlesex County Cricket Ground, Caledonian Road. The paper

---

85 See Tovey, Duncan, 'The History of the London Scottish', 1921, p.137.
86 Halley, 'The Pipers and Drummers of the London Scottish', p.43.
87 *Volunteer Service Gazette,* 1865-1866, p.240.
88 It was at this inspection that General Hope Grant pushed for the entire regiment to take up wearing the kilt.
89 *Volunteer Service Gazette,* 1865-1866, p.391.
90 'The regiment marched, headed by the brass band and the bagpipes, to Hyde-park….' *Clerkenwell News and London Times,* 15 May 1866, p.3.
91 'The National Rifle Association, Distribution of Prizes and Volunteer Review', *Daily News,* 23 July 1866, Issue 6307.
92 Volunteer Service Gazette, 1865-66, p.767.
93 'The Volunteer Review', *Daily News,* 22 April 1867, Issue 6541.

explained that 'the proceedings were greatly enhanced by the presence of the pipers and excellent band of the regiment.'[94] In June, a volunteer field day and sham-fight was organised at the Earl of Cowper's estate at Panshanger, attended by Colonel Erskine, the Inspector General of Volunteers. At the end of the day, all those involved, including the London Scottish, marched past Earl Cowper and Colonel Erskine with 'the bands of the various corps and the pipers of the London Scottish contributing greatly to the enjoyment.'[95] All three of these examples make specific reference to the pipers being of the London Scottish Regiment.

The most concrete of evidence, however, comes from 1868. On Saturday 25 January, the regiment paraded at Westminster Hall for their winter review and prize giving. General Hope Grant was, as usual, present for the inspection and to present the prizes where the 'regimental band and pipers played alternatively in the intervals of the proceedings.'[96] Lord Elcho was unable to attend as he was in Paris visiting a sick relative and so it fell to General Hope Grant to make the customary final speech. He praised the regiment for their turn out and for their impressive display the previous year at the Dover review. The general went on to say that 'he was glad see [sic] that the kilts increased and that the bagpipes flourished, and he hoped that both would continue to prosper.'[97] A prospering, flourishing pipe corps is some distance from one alleged to be extinct. Hope Grant continued in his speech by referring to a piper who, having had his legs shot off in battle, continued to play his pipes,[98] stating that 'He had no doubt the pipers would be equally stimulating to the London Scottish.'[99] At the end of his speech, the 'pipers then struck up, and the ceremony was at an end.'[100]

On Saturday 16 May 1868, the London Scottish practised modern drill movements that they had devised and which would later be taken up by the entire British Army. In the evening, at the end of this parade, 'the men fell-in and marched to the station, band and pipers playing alternately.'[101] Two weeks later, on Whit Monday, the regiment returned by train to Panshanger for a field day where, 'After a pleasant march of little more than a mile, enlivened by the band and the pipes and drums performing alternatively, the gates of Lord de L'Isle's park was reached.'[102] This last contemporary report even goes so far as to confirm that the pipes and drums were performing as one unit. Such reports are rare, as focus is usually reserved in contemporary newspaper reports for the pipers alone.

The most compelling evidence, however, comes from an incident that took place at the National Rifle Association meeting at Wimbledon in July 1868. The report from *The Times* on 15 July is corroborated by an engraving of the event that appeared independently in the *Leisure Hour*,[103] which clearly shows a rank of four London Scottish pipers in what is undoubtably Hodden Grey uniforms. The detailing is very exact and can only have been produced first-hand. *The Times* report, though somewhat protracted, is worth reproducing in its entirety as, in addition

---

94 'Athletic Sports of the London Scottish Volunteers', *Penny Illustrated Paper*, 4 May 1867, Issue 292.
95 *Pall Mall Gazette*, 11 June 1867, Issue 725.
96 'London Scottish Rifle Volunteers', *Daily News*, 27 January 1868, Issue 6781.
97 'London Scottish Rifle Volunteers', *Daily News*, 27 January 1868, Issue 6781.
98 It is most likely that he was referring to Piper McLaughlin of the 74th Regiment (Campbell's Highlanders) who had his legs shot off by a cannonball at the Battle of Vittoria on 21 June 1813. Piper McLaughlin famously asked for his pipes to be returned to him and continued to play his regiment forwards until his death.
99 'London Scottish Rifle Volunteers,' *Daily News*, 27 January 1868, Issue 6781.
100 *Volunteer Service Gazette*, 1867-1868, p.129.
101 *Volunteer Service Gazette*, 1867-1868, p.387.
102 *Volunteer Service Gazette*, 1867-1868, p.423.
103 Cartoon engraving by C.A. Ferrier, *The Leisure Hour*, London, July 1870.

to describing the involvement of the pipers and giving context to the picture, also provides an example of the humorous side of volunteer life at the time:

> The London Scottish surprised and amused the whole camp yesterday by a proceeding, apparently solemn, deliberate, and national in its character, which set everybody wondering what it could possibly mean. Between 6 and 7 o'clock, before the evening gun was fired … the band of bagpipes was heard in the distance, and as these drew near it was perceived that the pipers headed a regular procession. After the musicians walked some of the officers and non-commissioned officers of the London Scottish, four abreast, then a guard with shouldered rifles, and next a cart drawn by donkeys …, in which were placed, under proper military guard, two or three gigantic thistle-plants, in highly ornamented flower pots. A second cart, in all respects similarly filled, drawn and attended, followed the first, members of the escort being placed not only in the carts, but beside each wheel. Continuous peals of laughter at this most triumphal procession rang from every side, but the Scotchmen preserved their gravity unmoved, and marched strictly on at 'attention', as if carrying treasure to the Tower.[104]

Another humorous piece can be found in *The Tomahawk* magazine from April 1869. *The Tomahawk* was a satirical magazine in the style of *Punch*, or the more modern *Private Eye*, and produced a piece supposedly involving a French spy, named Jules Canard, who attended the Volunteer Review in Dover on 30 March that year. His report reads as follows:

> As I walked along, I saw some men in ballet girl uniforms, making a very hideous noise with some sticks and a bag.
> 'Who are those?' I asked.
> 'They are the pipers of the London Scottish' was the reply, 'They are always just in front of the regiment, to frighten away the enemy.'[105]

Similar reports from regimental parades, prize-givings, inspections, Volunteer Reviews and National Rifle Association camps at Wimbledon from 1869 through to 1872 continue to mention the pipers, drummers and band of the London Scottish regiment. For instance, in 1872, the National Rifle Association's prestigious Queen's Prize was won by Sergeant Michie of the London Scottish. When his victory was announced:

> The band of the Victorias, playing *See the conquering hero comes*, and that of the London Scottish, sounding the pibroch to the tune of *The Campbells are coming*, soon approached the victor and champion shot of the year. He was raised upon the shoulders of two comrades and was thus borne in triumph to the council tent, where he was presented to Earl Ducie, and his rifle examined. After this he was carried up to the camp of the London Scottish and was received with joyful exultation.[106]

There can be little question then, that the Pipes and Drums of the regiment continued in significant manner from 1865 to 1873. The evidence is sound, multifarious, and unequivocal in date and detail throughout every year of the disputed period.

---

104 *The Times*, 15 July 1868, p.5.
105 *The Tomahawk*, Vol. 4-5, London, 10 April 1869, p.166.
106 *Illustrated London News*, 27 July 1872, p.90.

In addition, there is evidence that John MacKenzie continued in his role as instructor to the pipers upon his return from overseas duty until 1869, when he retired from the Army. It is plausible that, after his retirement and until a new instructor was appointed in 1873, that the pipe band did begin to drift. MacKenzie played with the London Scottish pipers and band, under new Bandmaster Louis Beck, on Burns Night 1869 at a dinner of the Caledonian Society, which may well have been the last occasion he performed in the uniform of the London Scottish.[107] He held the rank of sergeant piper at this time and it may have been MacKenzie that, again, led the pipe corps after Pipe Major Campbell's possible resignation in 1865/6. If his resignation took place, it is certainly plausible that, during this difficult time, the pipe corps again recruited pipers from the 2nd Battalion, Scots Fusilier Guards as they had in the early days; but there is no specific evidence to corroborate such a hypothesis. Regardless of their origins, all pipers were regarded as London Scottish; they wore the Hodden Grey and, therefore, were regimental pipers in every sense.

Fresh impetus certainly came in 1873 with a concerted attempt to re-invigorate the Pipes and Drums. In the previous year, all companies of the regiment had finally heeded General Hope Grant's request and begun wearing the kilt, instigating a renewed vigour for all things Highland, including the pipes. A new piping instructor was necessary and members of the regiment approached the Regimental Colonel to see what could be done. Advances were made to the 1st Battalion, Scots Fusilier Guards and Pipe Major Robert MacKenzie was given permission to take on the role of instructor and acting pipe major, again with permission to wear the Hodden Grey. Halley states that the 11 pipers under MacKenzie's instruction at this point were

Lord Elcho and the London Scottish Volunteers, Regimental Dinner, *The Graphic*, 13 March 1880, with two London Scottish pipers, top right. (LSMA, used with permission)

---

107 *The Times*, 26 January 1869, p.5.

THE EARLY YEARS 1859-1880

'Tent Pitching: The Encampment of the London Scottish,' Wimbledon, *The Pictorial World*, 11 July 1874, with set of bagpipes on barrel, middle bottom. (LSMA, used with permission)

'Property of the Corps in possession of the Pipes and Drums,' 24 December 1878. (LSMA, used with permission)

J.D. Mill, MacIvor, J. Valentine, R. Hamilton, J. Gow, N. Macglashan, W.B. Inglis, Stevenson, D. MacKenzie, J. Murray and J. Farquhar.[108] These 11 pipers were assisted initially by four or five drummers with side drums and one tenor drummer. Their total number soon rose to eight but, unfortunately, Halley does not provide the names of the drummers. Practise took place at the headquarters building in Adelphi Terrace, in an underground room known as the 'coal cellar' which had a low, arched roof. Halley states that, considering their practise facilities 'it is surprising that we were not rendered stone deaf.'[109]

The practise was worth the pain, as *The Morning Post* report of the winter inspection that took place at Westminster Hall on 9 February 1875, states:

> At intervals the band of the regiment, under Mr W.F. Beck, the bandmaster, and the pipers, led by Pipe-Major MacKenzie, played some Scotch airs in excellent style.[110]

Halley joined the band himself in June of 1876, and it seems that Pipe Major MacKenzie had been keeping the pipes on a close leash during the three years of his instruction up until that point. In fact, it was not until July 1876 that MacKenzie allowed the London Scottish pipers to parade without him at their head. This parade was a review of the 'Grey Brigade'[111] held at Wellington Barracks, from where the London Scottish then marched, via Battersea Park, to Wimbledon Common. On this march, Brevet Colonel Lord Abinger, Commanding Officer of the Scots Fusilier Guards, 'honoured the "Scottish" by sending the Pipers of both battalions of his regiment to play at their head.'[112] MacKenzie, as pipe major of two of these three bands, would have marched with the 1st Battalion, Scots Fusilier Guards for this parade, which may have forced his hand. It is likely that J.D. Mill was designated acting pipe major on this occasion, as he was soon after to be officially appointed pipe major, in the early months of 1877. The day seemingly passed without problem and the London Scottish Pipes and Drums were back on course.

Robert MacKenzie continued in his role as instructor until being posted to Dublin with his regiment in 1881,[113] at which point, John MacKenzie agreed to return in a version of his previous role. He would continue to hold this position until 1904. Halley states that J.D. Mill relinquished his role as pipe major in 1881 and was replaced by Neil Macglashan,[114] however a contemporary handwritten inventory of Pipe Band equipment and supplies states that Macglashan was 'in charge of Pipe Band' as early as December 1878,[115] and he most likely became pipe major in early 1879.[116] Regardless of the exact date, this changeover of pipe majors initiated an uninterrupted lineage of succession which continues to the present day.

---

108 Halley, 'The Pipes and Drums of the London Scottish', p.43.
109 Halley, 'The Pipes and Drums of the London Scottish', p.57.
110 *The Morning Post*, 15 February 1875, p.3.
111 The 'Grey Brigade,' or the 1st Brigade of the 2nd Division of the First Army Corps as they were officially designated, were formed in 1869 for manoeuvre and training purposes and drilled regularly with the Scots Fusilier Guards at Wimbledon and Hyde Park. The Brigade consisted of, amongst others, The London Scottish, The Kensingtons and the Queen's Westminster Rifles and was known as the Grey Brigade as all constituent regiments wore grey uniforms.
112 *London Scottish Regimental Gazette* (1908), p.101.
113 Which had been redesignated the 1st Battalion Scots Guards by Queen Victoria in 1877.
114 Macglashan was a founding member and keen supporter of the London Scottish Rugby Club.
115 'Property of the Corps in Possession of the Pipers and Drummers', 24 December 1878, single sheet stocktake document, London Scottish Museum Archives.
116 See, A.F. Ferguson, 'Fifty Years Ago – Recollections of a Former London Scottish Piper', *London Scottish Regimental Gazette* (1935), p.91.

The 1878 inventory mentioned above is invaluable as it provides a real contemporary insight into the pipe band as it was assembled at that time. It provides the names of all the pipers and, for the first time, the names of the drummers. Corporal Drummer Larue played the tenor drum (the introduction of a bass drum was still some years off) and Privates Blake, Bishop, Bothwell and Payne, played the expensive brass side drums which, due to the close relationship with the Scots Fusilier Guards, were probably Guards regulation pattern drums. The pipe major's banner, which had been presented back in 1861, remained in use and no other banners had yet been made. Ribbons, hemp, boxes of reeds and 'Sundry copies of tunes' are all listed, along with seven spare drumsticks. Interestingly, four of the seven pipers, including Macglashan, were serving back in 1873, but none of the original six who formed the band back in 1860 were still involved with the regiment. Along with Sergeant Macglashan, the pipers named are Privates Brown, Houghton, Murray, Farquhar, Kennedy and Gow.

Pipe Major Macglashan was fundamental in instigating changes within the drum corps that would see the Pipes and Drums become a fully autonomous entity again. In a speech to the regiment during the annual distribution of prizes parade in 1878, Major Lumsden is quoted as saying:

> Most of the Bandsmen ... are now attested members of the corps, in accordance with War Office regulations. Our pipers have long been so, and our Pipe Major, has now in training a set of drummers to beat with them, which, under his instruction, will soon render his pipers entirely independent of the regular band.[117]

The Pipes and Drums of the London Scottish were, then, taking further steps towards becoming a pipe band in the modern sense. This allowed them the opportunity to practise and perform together exclusively and proceed in a different direction to the military brass band. This must have come as a relief to the drummers, who would now only be responsible for accompanying the pipers on the march. Halley was to give special praise to these hard-working drummers, stating that:

> I have never known one of them to fall out on the longest march, no matter what the weather was. They were always regular in their attendance at practise, and smart on parade and I am sure all ranks will agree with me that they are a most useful body and do credit to the Corps.[118]

Unfortunately, this respite for the drummers would prove to be shorted lived, as it would not be long before a bugle band was added to the regiments repertoire and the hard-working drummers would be responsible, once again, for supporting two bands. It did mean, however, that the pipe band drummers could begin to focus on the composition of beatings constructed specifically to compliment the music of the pipes.[119]

The earliest years of the Pipes and Drums of the London Scottish Regiment were not, then, without drama and difficulty. It is inconceivable to expect anything less. The fact that the band existed at all in London during this period is nothing short of astonishing. That they were able

---

117 Tovey, 'The History of the London Scottish', *London Scottish Regimental Gazette* (1923), p.101.
118 Halley, 'The Pipes and Drums of the London Scottish', p.57.
119 This style of drumming would become more distinct and complex over the ensuing decades until it later evolved into a totally separate drumming tradition that would necessitate the construction of specialist pipe band drums.

to overcome the difficulties they faced and emerge in a position of strength and security speaks volumes for their importance to, and position in, the regiment to which they belonged. These volunteer pipers and drummers forged links and held their own with royal pipers and the pipers and drummers of both battalions of the Scots Fusilier Guards, who were regular, professional, career musicians belonging to one of the most prestigious regiments in the British Army and with whom the London Scottish performed on many important occasions.

The London Scottish Pipes and Drums played on parade, on the march and in concert with some of the finest military bands in the country. They proudly led the London Scottish at royal reviews in front of tens of thousands of spectators, fellow volunteers and regular soldiers, and helped construct social and military traditions for the regiment that still retain their importance over 160 years later. This platform of success would provide later generations of pipers and drummers with a firm base on which to build a structure that would be integral to regimental pride, recruitment, morale, fitness, and *esprit de corps*; all of which would be vital to the increasingly important and demanding roles asked of London Scottish soldiers in the decades to come.

3

Coming of Age 1881-1913

When the Battalion is worried, or tired, or angry, it longs for its pipers, longs ardently for them, sir and … isn't happy till it gets them.

You can do anything with the Battalion through the Pipers. The man who rules the Pipers can twist the Corps round his little finger. Bullyrag the men, give them contradictory orders, turn them this way and that till they don't know where their front is or what section they belong to, spur them up to a double over the stiffest ploughed field when they are panting for breath – the first three beats on the muckle drum that ushers in the Pipers justifies everything.

'A Man in the Ranks'(1898)[1]

1881 would prove to be a momentous year for the entire British Army, the London Scottish, and their Regimental Pipes and Drums. The controversial Childers Reforms became law, much to the annoyance of the Army's 'Top Brass', setting in place a massive programme of reorganisation for Britain's armed forces. Pushed through Parliament by Hugh Childers, the Secretary of State for War, the Childers Reforms were a reinforcement and expansion of the Cardwell Reforms of 1868-1874 which had sought to learn the lessons of the Crimean War and to build a modern fighting force which could be efficient in the defence of Great Britain and the burgeoning empire. Childers' plans meant a total reorganisation of the Army, including the volunteer rifle regiments.

The basic building blocks of this new force would be dual-battalion regiments which were linked to geographical areas of the country for recruitment and had associated battalions of militia, yeomanry, and volunteers. Many single battalion regiments were merged, and each new regiment was assigned battalions of volunteers with whom they would coordinate instruction and training. The two regular battalions of each regiment would recruit equally and were to alternate overseas and home service, with much shorter tours of duty. The Highland regiments were particularly affected by the Childers programme, with many regiments losing their individuality, title and tradition. The new Black Watch (Royal Highlanders) Regiment was formed from the old 42nd (Royal Highland) and the 73rd (Perthshire) Regiments of Foot, while the 91st (Argyll) and 93rd (Sutherland) merged to form the Argyll and Sutherland Highlanders. In addition, the Seaforth Highlanders were formed from the 72nd (Duke of Albany's Own) and the 78th (Ross-shire Buffs), and likewise the Gordon Highlanders from the 92nd (Gordon) and the 75th (Stirlingshire) Highland Regiments.[2]

The geographical basis for such mergers and associations was particularly problematic in relation to London-based volunteer regiments. The capital had always been wary of raising and billeting regular soldiers but it had a large number of volunteer corps, spread throughout the metropolis.

---

1   'The Night March', *London Scottish Regimental Gazette* (1898), p.27.
2   Only the Queens Own Cameron Highlanders were left as a single battalion unit, gaining a 2nd Battalion in 1897.

All volunteer regiments were technically designated 'rifles' and so a number, including the London Scottish, who would be reclassified as the 7th Middlesex (London Scottish) Rifle Volunteers during the process, became affiliated with the new Prince Consort's Own (Rifle Brigade).[3] It was obvious, even at the time, that this situation was somewhat of a fudge, with a contemporary article in *The Times* stating of the London Scottish:

> This fine corps is now attached to the Rifle Brigade, with which it has no real connexion, it being connected with the Guards. It would be a gracious act were Her Majesty to cause the London Scottish to be made the Volunteer battalion of the Scots Guards.[4]

It would be another 125 and 140 years respectively before this wish would, to some degree at least, come to fruition.[5]

The enforced association with the Rifle Brigade appears, however, to have had little real impact on the London Scottish. As part of the Childers Reforms, each volunteer corps was to be provided with an adjutant from the 'mother' regiment, although somehow the London Scottish managed to secure the services of Major John Scott Napier from the Gordon Highlanders.[6] This appointment provided the foundation for what would become an extremely close relationship between the Gordons and the London Scottish over the next 100 years. Quite how and why this association came into being is lost in the mists of time[7] but, by establishing it, the London Scottish managed to strengthen their direct links with Scotland and the Highland regiments, keep alive their relevance as a kilted regiment and avoid being swallowed up by the immensity of the Rifle Brigade. These developments were all of particular importance to the future of the Pipes and Drums.

To commemorate the changes brought about by the Childers Reforms, several large-scale reviews were organised throughout the year, with the first that involved the London Scottish taking place in April at the annual Easter volunteer camp in Brighton. The usual mock battles were undertaken on the last day of camp, followed by a Royal Review received by the Duke of Cambridge, Generals Monck and Clive, and the French Military Attaché. The regiment was 'much cheered' and 'The London Scottish, a fine body of men, with a smart and soldier like bearing, went by to the tune of 'Highland Laddie' played by their pipes.'[8]

---

3   Another anomaly, which had four battalions rather than two and recruited throughout the United Kingdom.
4   'Easter Monday Operations', *The Times*, 18 April 1885, p.8.
5   In May 2006, the London Regiment joined the Household Division, becoming the T.A. regiment of the Foot Guards. 'A' (London Scottish) Company was associated with the Scots Guards, from whom their SPSI and Mortar PSI were drawn. In April 2022, they would go a step further and become 'G' (Messines) Company, Scots Guards, 1st Battalion, London Guards
6   Napier would be strongly associated with the regiment and wear Hodden Grey until 1908. It was Napier that was instrumental in raising the funds and organising the building, in 1886, of 59 Buckingham Gate – the first headquarters building that could house all eight companies of the regiment. His importance to the regiment cannot be overstated.
7   There is no reference in either the London Scottish or Gordon Highlanders archives as to how this appointment was originally conceived. However, Colonel Lumsden, Commanding Officer of the London Scottish at the time, may well have been the conduit, having previously served as a captain in the Royal Aberdeenshire Highlanders Militia, that became the 3rd Gordon Highlanders Militia Battalion in 1881. Whether the Scots Guards were initially approached is also unknown but seems unlikely.
8   'The Brighton Review', *The Times*, 4 April 1881, p.7

It was at this same camp that the London Scottish began a programme of route marches that would prove to be an incredible boon to them and their war-readiness in the coming decades. It was decided that long distance marching and fresh air would be beneficial to physical fitness, especially as more and more working-class men, who lived in the smoke and fog of central London, were joining the ranks. Earlier marches had been organised since 1877 by Sergeant Major Mackay and involved around 20 to 25 men with 'McGlashan and Farquahar as Pipers'[9] but, from 1881 onwards, official sanction was given for larger numbers to march together. This would eventually lead to full company and, in turn, full regimental marches taking place over weekends and then weeks at a time with full involvement from the Pipes and Drums. 'The enjoyment of these marches was all the greater as we always had the services of willing pipers, drummers and buglers.'[10] The Pipes and Drums would become an increasingly regular sight at the front of marching London Scottish troops, and the importance of their role in this regard would become self-evident on the veldt in South Africa during the Boer War and later through Europe's mud and in the deserts of the Middle East during the First World War.

The biggest parade of the year was a Royal Review that took place before Queen Victoria at Windsor on 9 July 1881. Over 60,000 volunteers from England and Wales paraded before The Queen, with the London Scottish and the Grey Brigade forming the 1st Brigade, 2nd Division of the 1st Army Corps and with the Pipes and Drums again in attendance. This review, however, was somewhat overshadowed by a second Royal Review, this time of Scottish troops,[11] that took place in Edinburgh on 25 August, in some of the worst parade conditions imaginable. The parade would forever after be remembered, with a hint of understatement, as the 'Wet Review.'

The London Scottish, which was the only regiment to be invited to both Royal Reviews, arrived in Edinburgh by train, having been played off by the regimental military band at King's Cross. They arrived to a huge reception, and a large crowd followed them as 'the pipe band played us through dark streets to our quarters – Summerhall Brewery – on the side of the Meadows, in whose lofts, redolent of malt, we ... slept two nights on adorable straw paliasses.'[12] It rained consistently for 24 hours prior to the parade and 'the square space in front of the Grand Stand, bare of grass, was one sea of mud, which irresistibly recalled ... the plateau of Sebastopol in the winter of 1855.'[13] Over 41,000 volunteers would march through this mire while Queen Victoria and the Dukes of Edinburgh, Cambridge and Connaught sat for three hours in the rain to see the troops past. As the review commenced, an absolute deluge of rain began to fall but this did not seem to affect the tens of thousands of spectators who had turned out for the parade and whose 'hearty cheer announced the approach of the London Scottish, and to the music of the pipes, they came in view, marching along with all the ease for which they have gained a truly just reputation.'[14] Despite having to march through a 'perfect sea of mud', the London Scottish 'went by with mingled dash and precision.'[15] After it was finished, and despite the conditions for both men and instruments, 'the Regiment marched through the Canongate, with pipes playing, to the station',[16] for the return journey to London. A truly memorable experience that would remain foremost in the minds of all those London Scots who attended.

---

9   H.G. Baker, 'Letter from an Old Comrade', *London Scottish Regimental Gazette* (1927), p.57.
10 James Alexander, 'Reminiscences', *London Scottish Regimental Gazette* (1913), p.203.
11 The London Scottish were the only regiment invited to attend both Royal Reviews.
12 Neil Munro, 'The '81 Review: a Reminiscence', *London Scottish Regimental Gazette* (1905), p.167.
13 'The Edinburgh Volunteer Review', *The Times*, 26 August 1881, p.5.
14 'Scottish Volunteer Review Edinburgh', *The Belfast News-Letter*, 26 August 1881, Issue 20664.
15 'The Edinburgh Volunteer Review', *The Times*, 26 August 1881, p.5.
16 Alex F. Ferguson, 'Fifty Years Ago: Recollections of a Former London Scottish Piper', *London Scottish Regimental Gazette* (1935), p.91.

The London Scottish arriving in Edinburgh for the 'Wet Review', *The Graphic*, 3 September 1881, with pipers bottom left. (LSMA, used with permission)

London Scottish Christmas Card, c. 1885, with Pipes and Drums top right. (LSMA, used with permission)

Earliest known photograph of a London Scottish Piper, Possibly Piper Cox, c.1883. (LSMA, used with permission)

Earliest known image of the London Scottish Pipes and Drums parading as a full band, Harry Payne, 'Easter Camp, 1884', *The Illustrated Sporting and Dramatic News*, 19 April 1884. (LSMA, used with permission)

Neil Macglashan was pipe major throughout these memorable events but, when he departed for South Africa on 1 November 1881, his appointment was passed to his second in command, John Farquhar, who would hold the position until the same month in 1885. In 1882, under Pipe Major Farquhar, the piper's uniform became distinguishable from that of a regular private, with the introduction of claymore broadswords, spats and, through the generosity of Piper A. Cox and his associates, rather splendid piper's dirks. Further embellishments of doublets, cross-belts, diced hose and full plaids with lion-rampant plaid brooches would be introduced the following year; completing a uniform little changed in the Pipes and Drums until the present day; and, uniquely, worn by both pipers and drummers.

Annual Easter camp of 1882 was at Petersfield, near Portsmouth, where the London Scottish:

> Had the honour of being played to quarters by the Royal Highlanders and the 3rd Hants Volunteers, in addition to their own band, the local corps having taken the opportunity of reciprocating some little courtesy which they had received from the Londoners during the Windsor Review.[17]

At the close of one day's exercise, the London Scottish returned to camp, headed by the Pipes and Drums and were met just outside of the town by the drummers, pipers and band of the Gordon Highlanders. This was the first time that the two pipe bands played together and the London Scottish are said to have held their own 'and more, with the warriors who had marched from Cabul to Candahar, and of whom a goodly number had fought on Majuba's fateful hill.'[18]

Links with the Gordon Highlanders Drums and Pipes[19] were strengthened further in 1884 when Pipe Major Farquhar was aided by the arrival of John Morrison as drumming instructor. Morrison, like piping instructor John MacKenzie, would go on to become an institution at the London Scottish and would hold the post of instructor for the next 23 years, marching regularly with the band and wearing the Hodden Grey. He had enlisted as a drummer and bugler in the 92nd (Gordon) Highlanders in 1860 and went to India with them in 1868, serving throughout the Afghan Campaign of 1878 to 1880 and then in South Africa for the momentous Majuba Hill Campaign of 1881. After returning to Great Britain in 1882, he was discharged from the Army the following year and came to London, employed as a messenger in the War Office.

Soon after arriving at the London Scottish, Morrison introduced the bass drum to the pipe band, taking the place of the oversized tenor drum that was typical of the times.[20] A mighty man was needed to beat this new heavy weapon and Tommy Hodgson, a member of the tug o' war team and trainee side drummer, took on the role of 'Muckle' Drummer. Then, in 1885, Morrison turned his attention to the side drums, which were of 'the old pattern' and 'not suitable to the pipes, being too sharp in tone.'[21] The new pipe major, Ronald Halley, who had taken over earlier that year, spoke to the commanding officer on the drummer's behalf. Colonel Lumsden, however, had legitimate concerns regarding costs, as the drummers wanted to purchase the newly designed, and expensive, Guards' pattern drums. The Pipes and Drums decided to raise the money themselves

---

17 'Volunteer Manoeuvres', *The Times*, 10 April 1882, p.5.
18 Robert S. Darling, Letter in *London Scottish Regimental Gazette* (1913), p.246.
19 The Gordons were the only British regiment to recognise that drums have military seniority over the pipes and, thus, should be recognised as Drums and Pipes not Pipes and Drums.
20 This old tenor drum was stored away and many years later rehabilitated, rechristened 'the old Presbyterian' and made famous on the London Scottish marches through Scotland.
21 Ronald Halley, 'The Pipes and Drums of the London Scottish', *London Scottish Regimental Gazette* (1897), p.57.

and put on a 'smoking concert', which was strongly supported by Colonel Lumsden and the regimental family; and the funds were duly raised. The drummers now had the necessary equipment to raise their status beyond that of mere 'pipers' labourers' and the band had a new and successful means of raising funds.

Both were important. The professional brass band had been stood down in November 1883, amid concerns regarding costs, and a volunteer band had taken its place the following year. This was not a particularly successful endeavour, although the volunteer band held on for the next nine years and provided a place, playing the sousaphone, for one Private Alfred Goodman, more of whom later. The position of the Pipes and Drums, therefore, became even more prominent, as they took over most of the regiment's musical duties. More buglers were added, and the drummers began to attain the lofty heights of regimental regard that had previously been reserved only for the pipers. Until this time, buglers and drummers had tended to stick together, with the pipers remaining more aloof. In fact, one ex-drummer, writing in 1905 stated:

> I don't know if Pipers fancy themselves as they did a quarter of a century ago. Pipers generally do; it is in their blood; but in those days they were beings apart and being allowed to join their band was almost like an invitation to dinner at Marlborough House. (The portrait of R_____d H____y as he appeared in the show case of Mackenzie, the photographer, at Birnam, was a thing to be remembered).[22]

Unfortunately, no photographs of Pipe Major Ronald Halley survive but he further inflated the profile, and chests, of the pipers in the autumn of 1886 by arranging two further smoking concerts that raised a total of £75 to fund the purchase of a pipe banner for every piper.

With the pipers and drummers thus suitably attired, it was decided that the band needed the final ceremonial touch, and the position of Drum Major was duly introduced the same year. Major Alexander, who was due to retire the following year, paid for a magnificent drum major's mace which he presented to the corps. Initially, it was hoped that the titanic Private Alfred Goodman would take the position of drum major, but he was intent on remaining within the volunteer military band, where he was about to be promoted to corporal, and so the opportunity was offered to Private A.J. Bertram, who become the first Drum Major of the London Scottish Regiment. Bertram's success in the role is undocumented but he was to resign from the regiment in November 1887, by which time Goodman had been persuaded to take up the appointment.

One look at a photograph of Drum Major Goodman will explain why he was so in demand for the role. At six feet three inches and over 20 stone, Goodman made for an incredible sight on the march and his commanding presence helped make the London Scottish Pipes and Drums world famous. Despite his size, he was returned efficient 21 years in a row and was undoubtedly extremely fit.[23] However, in 1887, he was new to the post and it would take another ten years for his fame to really blossom; by which time he was one of the most famous figures in Victorian London to the extent that, on at least one occasion, he almost upstaged Queen Victoria herself.

1887 marked the 50th anniversary of Queen Victoria's ascension to the throne and saw the beginning of the 'high point' of the British Empire and its military and economic power around the globe. London was the heart of this dominion which, at its zenith, covered a quarter of the world's

---

22 'Auld Memories', *London Scottish Regimental Gazette* (1905), p.8.
23 Goodman was an extraordinarily strong swimmer, swimming in the Thames every day. During one major flood he 'stripped into a bathing costume, rowed a boat up the swollen river from Molesey to Helliford, left the boat with a stricken friend and swam the four miles back to Moseley in the flooded river.' *London Scottish Regimental Gazette* (1915), p.65.

land surface and held sway over one fifth of the world's population. Vast wealth was on display in the empire's capital, inter-meshed with all the pomp and ceremony at the court of the world's most powerful ever empress. The festivities commemorating Queen Victoria's Golden Jubilee would follow this mould and boast a grandeur unrivalled until her Diamond Jubilee ten years later. The London Scottish would play their part in all the major military celebrations throughout the year, with the Pipes and Drums featuring quite prominently and gaining much national attention in the press. These events clustered around the summer months of June, July and August in the hopes of beating the worst of the British weather.

In April, before these series of high-profile events began, the London Scottish, headed by the Pipes and Drums, made their first church parade through the streets of London from Buckingham Gate to St Columba's Church in Knightsbridge. This Church of Scotland Kirk had been completed three years earlier and, during that time, had become the Regimental Church of the London Scottish. This association has endured with only slight interruption ever since.

The first of the jubilee events, and a warm-up for the bigger proceedings to come, was a Scottish-themed Jubilee and Highland Bazaar held at St James's Church from 16 to 18 June 1887 and attended by the 'great and the good.'[24] The pipers and drummers of the London Scottish performed at this extravagant event alongside the bands of the Scots Guards, Scots Greys and the King's Own Scottish Borderers, supported by the pipers of the Royal Caledonian Asylum. Two days later, Queen Victoria held a banquet at Buckingham Palace, to which 50 kings and princes from around the world were invited. These assorted royals had arrived in Great Britain in order to attend the main event of the celebrations, a service of thanksgiving, in honour of Queen Victoria which would take place the following day, 21 June, at Westminster Abbey.

Hundreds of thousands of spectators turned out for this occasion, lining the processional route from Buckingham Palace, down The Mall, through Trafalgar Square, along Northumberland Avenue to the Embankment, Parliament Square and finally, Westminster Abbey.[25] Troops of regulars and volunteers were assigned to guard the route and hold back the crowds, with the London Scottish positioned prominently on Northumberland Avenue. The procession was not due to proceed until 1115 hours but, by 0900 hours, the crowds were already enormous, particularly around Buckingham Palace and Trafalgar Square.

Just prior to 0900 hours, the London Scottish left their newly opened headquarters at 59 Buckingham Gate and marched to their parade position, which was reported on by various newspaper journalists along the route. At Buckingham Palace, at this early hour, 'the police alone had arrived, but shortly afterwards the London Scottish, headed by their pipers playing a Scotch air, marched past the Palace, and along the route which they would line.'[26] At Trafalgar Square, the 'picturesque costume and soldier-like bearing of the London Scottish R.V. who marched to the "skirl of the bagpipes" into Northumberland Avenue, was greatly admired.'[27]

On reaching their positions, the troops spread out to line the route, ready to control the crowds over the next few hours until the royal procession arrived. 'Then came a longer wait, unrelieved by striking incident ... and the pipers of the London Scottish varied the proceedings at fitful intervals.'[28] The procession itself was late arriving but when it did, it must have been quite a spectacle. Carriage after carriage, accompanied by troops of infantry and cavalry, paraded past while the Pipes and Drums played. Samuel Langhorne Clemens (better known as author Mark

---

24 See 'Amusements and Notices', *The Graphic*, 4 June 1887, Issue 914.
25 10 miles of terraced benches made of scaffolding had been erected along the route to house the crowds.
26 *Aberdeen Weekly Journal*, 22 June 1887, Issue 10090.
27 *Birmingham Daily Post*, 22 June 1882, Issue 9043.
28 *Freemans' Journal and Daily Commercial Advertiser*, 22 June 1887.

Twain) reported that the procession 'stretched to the limit of sight in both directions',[29] with Queen Victoria in her gilded state landau drawn by six cream-coloured horses, at the epicentre. The London Scottish troops had done their job holding back an enormous crowd, which had burst through the lines at other places on the route, with the Pipes and Drums playing their part by keeping the masses entertained.

The London Scottish were back at Buckingham Palace two weeks later for the Royal Review of the Home District Volunteers that took place on Saturday 2 July 1887. This was another enormous jubilee event with 24,000 volunteer soldiers marching past Queen Victoria, the Prince of Wales, the King of Denmark, the Duke of Cambridge, the Duke of Connaught and many other notables. Lord Wemyss, wearing the uniform of the London Scottish, was with the royal party, attired as a Queen's aide-de-camp. Volunteer bands were not on parade, with the music being supplied by the bands of the Grenadier, Coldstream and Scots Guards (with their drum majors in full state uniform) and the Royal Artillery. However, the London Scottish, again, managed to obtain a unique and special status.

The volunteer corps were organised into six brigades, with the London Scottish one of the last regiments on parade and provided a signal honour:

> As the 'Scottish' with their splendid swinging stride approached the Royal stand they received a most welcome surprise. The music hitherto had been supplied by the splendid massed bands of the foot guards and Royal Artillery, but now up struck the 'Highland Laddie' by the combined pipers of the Scots Guards and London Scottish, and to such strains what could the march past of a Scottish regiment be but good? And that it was so seemed to be the opinion of Her Majesty and the various members of the Royal Family beside her, if smiles of approval have any meaning.[30]

Of the 53 volunteer regiments on parade that day, the London Scottish were the only one given permission to march past to the accompaniment of their own musicians. It is no wonder that this 'splendid kilted corps … swept by Her Majesty with gallant bearing – every man looking as proud as a piper – and splendid order, amid the plaudits of the onlookers'[31] and that the 'usual round of cheering greeted the corps … and accompanied it all along the route.'[32]

A similar honour was bestowed upon them a week later, when on Saturday 9 July, after spending the intervening week at camp in Wimbledon, the London Scottish joined 58,000 other troops, both regulars and volunteers, for the premier event of the year, the Jubilee Military Review at Aldershot. A 50-gun salute started proceedings, after which the Duke of Cambridge, as Commander-in-Chief of the British Army, read the following message:

> Your Majesty's Army, including the Reserve Forces, humbly approaches the Throne, and offers its respectful homage and congratulations upon the completion of the 50th year of your Majesty's reign, and begs your Majesty's gracious acceptance of an offering to commemorate that happy event, and as a tribute of its love and devotion.[33]

---

29   *A History of Jubilees* <https://www.royal.uk/history-jubilees>
30   *The Scotsman*, 4 July 1887, p.4.
31   'The Volunteer Review', *The Times*, 4 July 1887, p.10.
32   'The Volunteer Review', *Morning Post*, 4 July 1887, p.3.
33   'The Jubilee Review at Aldershot', *The Times*, 9 July 1887, p.7.

After the Queen's reply came a single bugle note that signalled three cheers and then the march past began. It would take nearly three hours. All regular army regiments were allowed to be played past Her Majesty by their own bands, who were massed by brigade. All volunteer corps, however, were played past by the massed bands of the Foot Guards, except for the London Scottish:

> Under Major Nicoll, in four double companies, who strode by with great precision and suitable Highland swagger, to the sound of the pipes …. They were loudly applauded. The Earl of Wemyss, as honorary colonel, rode past at its head, as usual.[34]

The entire Pipes and Drums led the way on this historic occasion, with Drum Major Goodman at their head and with Pipe Major Halley playing the silver-mounted pipes that had been presented to the regiment back in 1861.[35]

Halley took the opportunity to retire on a high, leaving the London Scottish in November of 1888, and allowing the ten-year veteran piper Alexander 'Sandie' Reith to take the reins. Pipe Major Reith would lead the band for the next 14 years, transforming it in the process into a pipe band with few equals and cementing his place as the most influential pipe major in London Scottish history. In 1888 there were still only eight pipers; not a small number for that period, but Reith began vigorously recruiting to increase the numbers to above 20. Similar enlargement of the drum corps also took place, along with closer liaison and extension of the bugle corps and with more emphasis placed on musical excellence to bring increased quality alongside increased quantity.

This last objective was aided greatly by structural changes to the Volunteer Army that came about in 1889, when the War Office finally 'recognised the fact that the Volunteer Army of some 225,000 men ought to be assigned a distinct place in the Army of home defense [sic].'[36] Under this scheme, volunteer corps would, for the first time, 'act on their own resources and initiative and be wholly commanded by their own officers, whereby their efficiency and discipline as soldiers will be thoroughly tested.'[37] This involved brigade drills at Easter and brigade camps for at least a week every summer. With the London Scottish also running their own camps[38] and weekend marches, this provided extended opportunities for the Pipes and Drums to practise and play together and to perform more frequently alongside the military bands of the 'Grey Brigade' and those of other associated regiments.

Many other opportunities to display their musical prowess were provided to the Pipes and Drums in addition to their routine regimental engagements, and their services were very much in demand. One of the most high-profile events during this period was the Royal Military Exhibition that took place at Chelsea Barracks during the first week of July 1890. The exhibition was open from 1000 hours until 2200 hours each day. Between 1500 hours and 1800 hours, a 'Grand Descriptive Piece' representing the Battle of Waterloo was performed. Providing the musical accompaniment for this large-scale re-enactment were the bands of the Royal Military School of Music, the 14th (King's) Hussars, the 1st Battalion, Liverpool Regiment, the Drums and Fifes of the 2nd Battalion, Grenadier Guards and the Pipes and Drums of the London Scottish.[39] The band found itself, again, in first class company and playing at a continuingly improving level.

---

34 'The Jubilee Review at Aldershot', *The Times*, 9 July 1887, p.7.
35 They would be played again by Pipe Major Reith at the 1897 Jubilee parade.
36 'The Easter Volunteer Operations', *The Times*, 19 April 1889, p.8.
37 'The Easter Volunteer Operations', *The Times*, 19 April 1889, p.8.
38 Taking place at Bisley after the NRA moved there following the last Wimbledon meeting in 1889.
39 See *Pall Mall Gazette*, London, 1 July and 3 July 1890, issues 7888 and 7890.

The pipe band's reputation for excellence went hand in hand with that of the London Scottish Regiment as a whole. More and more often it was the London Scottish that the crowds looked out for on parades and who the newspapers singled out for comment. Take, for example, the following report from *The Times* of the volunteer Easter manoeuvres at Dover in 1891:

> Next came quite the sensation of the proceedings – the approach of the London Scottish, commanded by Lieutenant-Colonel Nicoll, their pipers playing, and playing admirable at their head 'Highland Laddie.' The physique of the men on this occasion, at all events, was not heightened by the garb, for the London Scottish are composed of lads who would make a colonel of one of the old kilted corps weep with envy.[40]

'The garb' refers specifically to the tall feather bonnets worn by other kilted troops, that made shorter men seem taller, in contrast to the flat Glengarry bonnets worn by all ranks of the London Scottish at this time. Despite their impressive appearance, however, it is hard to imagine that London Scottish soldiers marching past without the Pipes and Drums would have been the 'sensation of the proceedings.' Likewise, without the bearing and precision of the marching companies, the Pipes and Drums would have had no specific purpose to serve and, thus, both units heightened the appeal, dignity and bearing of the other. As C.A. Malcolm states in *The Piper in Peace and War*, 'no good piper ever belonged to a bad regiment'[41] and this has always been very much the case with the London Scottish.

This self-perpetuating pursuit of excellence also had a positive effect on recruiting. As the reputation of both the regiment and the Pipes and Drums grew, so did applications to enlist. The 1870s had been the doldrums of the London Scottish, with significant recruitment difficulties, and while the 1880s saw some slight increase, it was through the 1890s that numbers began to surge. By the end of the decade permission had been granted for the formation of two more companies, taking the total to ten. Recruitment then had to be capped and a waiting list begun, as numbers were already well over the one thousand mark established.

Pipe Major Reith's attempts to enlarge the Pipes and Drums were also bearing fruit, and the size of the band was beginning to steadily grow. In 1893, the *Chambers Journal* reported on a volunteer review at Aldershot:

> What more popular, after a heavy field day … than the 'Elcho Tartan' and swinging stride of the London Scottish; while their dozen or sixteen pipers, stationed opposite the saluting base, played them by.[42]

The number of pipers had, thus, already doubled in the five years since 1888 and would continue to steadily increase over the proceeding five.

In their bid to match quantity with quality, the Pipes and Drums were provided further competitive musical incentive in 1893, with the reintroduction of a professional regimental military band. The volunteer band, that had never quite reached the mark, was wound up and replaced by 32 professional musicians under the direction of Scotsman Ronald MacDonald. The military band performed admirably for a number of years but would, again, prove to be a short-lived innovation and would ultimately suffer an ignominious demise. They would certainly never rise to the heights of accomplishment and regimental affection achieved by the Pipes and Drums but did, in addition

---

40 'East Manoeuvres Dover', *The Times*, 31 March 1891, p.4.
41 C.A. Malcolm, *The Piper in Peace and War* (London: John Murray, 1927), p.vii.
42 'Volunteer Review at Aldershot', *Chambers Journal*, 70 (1893), p.828.

COMING OF AGE 1881-1913   83

to the bugle corps, provide enhanced musical opportunities and a friendly competitive challenge to Pipe Major Reith and his men.

On 16 January 1896, for instance, all the bands of the London Scottish played at a New Year's Gathering, organised by the regiment. The entertainment over the evening went as follows:

> At 9 o'clock the Buglers and Drummers preceded a performance of the Battalion Band, under Bandmaster Ronald MacDonald … and then … a brave show of Pipers, under Pipe-Major Reith, led by Sergeant-Drummer Goodman, had a grand reception, appearing again at a later hour.[43]

As is so often the case, the drummers are not mentioned with the pipers but would have performed with them after playing with the buglers. A month later, at the distribution of prizes parade on 17 February, the 'Volunteer Pipers, under Sergeant-Piper Reith, and the Professional Band, under Bandmaster Ronald Macdonald, were in great form during the evening.'[44] The recruitment drive and musical competition had ensured that 'this season they are in a higher position than ever, for efficiency and numbers.'[45]

Such efforts were, whether intentional or not, extremely well-timed, with 1897 incorporating both Queen Victoria's Diamond Jubilee festivities and celebrations to commemorate Her Majesty becoming the longest reigning monarch in British history, which had been held over from the previous year. It would be at the main Jubilee celebration that the London Scottish Pipes and Drums would receive their very highest accolades.

Earlier in the year, the London Scottish took part in the Volunteer Easter manoeuvres at Shorncliffe camp, Dover; marching through Maidstone en route. Colonel Termoloff, the Russian Tzar's military attaché, had been specifically assigned to the London Scottish in order to observe the efficiency and effectiveness of the British volunteer army and he was on hand to watch, as:

> With a dozen of their pipers skirling out a pibroch, they marched as heroically into their camp on the grassy parade of Shorncliffe as if it had been another Lucknow they had relieved, or another Alma they had won.[46]

Colonel Termoloff was also in attendance the following day, as the Pipes and Drums played the regiment through at the march past, where:

> When the last company had swaggered past the saluting point, the reviewing officer, Major General E.A. Wood, CB, commanding at Shorncliffe, sang out after them with much sincerity in his voice, 'Well marched past, London Scottish!' And the compliment was unique.[47]

The regiment was, then, excellently prepared for Queen Victoria's Diamond Jubilee procession on Tuesday 22 June for what was, by far, the biggest event of the year. In fact, this may well have been the largest ceremonial event ever staged in Great Britain, with over three million people taking to the streets to watch a parade that represented the supremacy and global reach of the British Empire. The Golden Jubilee of 1887 had been big, but this was pomp and circumstance on the

---

43   'New Year's Gathering', *London Scottish Regimental Gazette* (1896), p.16.
44   *London Scottish Regimental Gazette* (1896), p.29.
45   *London Scottish Regimental Gazette* (1896), p.3.
46   *Maidstone and Kentish Journal*, 15 April 1897, p.7.
47   *Maidstone and Kentish Journal*, 15 April 1897, p.7.

Earliest known photograph of the London Scottish Pipes and Drums as a full band, 1891, with Drum Major Goodman centre rear, Bass Drummer and later Drum Major Hodgson right rear, Drum Instructor Morrison, front second left and Pipe Major Reith front third from right. (LSMA, used with permission)

William Lockhart Bogle, 'The Hallowe'en Dinner of the London Scottish Volunteers – Bringing in the Haggis', *The Graphic*, 1 November 1891, with Piping Instructor John MacKenzie leading the way. (LSMA, used with permission)

The London Scottish Pipes and Drums on the march, cross country, c. 1891. (LSMA, used with permission)

The only known photograph showing both the London Scottish Pipes and Drums and the professional brass band on parade together, Hythe Camp, Easter 1896. (LSMA, used with permission)

most lavish scale. *The Graphic* reported that 'the pageant witnessed in London on Tuesday has never been equalled. Never in the history of the world has such an imposing picture of world-wide Empire been displayed.'[48]

While the rank and file of the London Scottish took their place as a ceremonial guard along the route,[49] the Pipes and Drums were given the signal honour of marching in the procession itself. The significance of this accolade was heightened further by the fact that they were one of only three volunteer bands on parade and the only regular or volunteer army pipe band marching. They accompanied the colonial procession, comprising troops and dignitaries from around the empire, which led the way for the royal progress. To the fore and rear of the London Scottish were colonial infantry troops from Canada, India, Africa, Australia, New Zealand, and the West Indies; all marching to the sound of the Pipes and Drums.

Pipe Major Reith mustered 24 pipers on parade, along with one bass drummer, three tenors, five side drummers and 14 buglers. It was the biggest band the London Scottish had ever put together; most fitting for the biggest occasion at which they had ever performed. In addition, Drum Major Goodman strolled proudly at their head, winning plaudits for his bearing and marching as if the parade had been arranged specifically for his benefit. *The Globe* stated that 'yesterday was a proud day for two men. One was Captain Ames of the 2nd Life Guards,[50] the other was the Drum Major of the London Scottish.'[51] It was even reported, jokingly, at the time that Queen Victoria was jealous of Goodman for receiving more attention from the press than she did.

Regimental pride was at an all-time high, with the *London Scottish Regimental Gazette* reporting:

> It is with unmixed pride that we record the reception given to our Pipers in the Jubilee Procession. From beginning to end of the long route a wave of applause accompanied them, rising in places to deafening heights.[52]
>
> We are accustomed to see our Pipers look well; but they have never looked so well, they have never played more magnificently, they have never earned the thanks of the Corps more gallantly than in Her Majesty's Jubilee Procession.[53]

As usual, the drummers were not mentioned in the report, although the *Regimental Gazette* did recognise this omission and made a point of honouring them by name the following month.[54] The poor buglers received no mention at all.

The accuracy of the *Gazette's* claims was borne out by the photographic and cinematic recordings of the event. The Diamond Jubilee was the first great state occasion captured on cinematic film; a process that had only been invented a few years previously. Over 40 cameras, representing 20 fledgling film companies, were set up along the route, and the London Scottish Pipes and Drums appeared in much of this ground breaking coverage.[55] A report on the debut screening of one of these films at the Empire Music Hall, just days after the event, states of the film that 'the burly drum major of the London Scottish band came in for special recognition, for he is a notable

---

48 'The Diamond Jubilee', *The Graphic*, 26 June 1897, Issue 1439.
49 A wonderful personal account is given by a London Scottish solder in *The Aberdeen Journal*, 2 July 1887, p.6.
50 Captain Ames, the tallest man in the British Army, had the honour of leading the parade.
51 *The Globe*, London, 23 June 1897, p.3.
52 'Editorial Notes', *London Scottish Regimental Gazette* (1897), p.113.
53 'The Jubilee', *London Scottish Regimental Gazette* (1897), p.110.
54 *London Scottish Regimental Gazette* (1897), p.128.
55 see, S. Herbert and L. McKernan, *Who's Who of Victorian Cinema* (London: British Film Institute, 1996) for further details. Some of the film, including the seven titles made by R.W. Paul, are still held by the BFI. Unfortunately, the surviving R.W. Paul material does not include film of the Pipes and Drums.

and conspicuous figure in the procession.'[56] Impressive, considering that the procession included 46,881 troops of all ranks, 6,803 horses and 116 gun carriages.[57] These films were shown around the world and did much to heighten the reputation and influence of the London Scottish. The Pipes and Drums were certainly serving one of their most important purposes.[58]

The London Scottish Regiment was now instantly recognised wherever it went, with the Pipes and Drums often coming in for special attention. The march from the station after arriving in Cambridge for camp later that year, 'and indeed every occasion when the Scottish appeared in the streets ... with their Pipers, partook largely the character of a triumphal procession.'[59] Large crowds joined the march and 'did not disperse until the pipers had given an impromptu entertainment, in which *Cock o' the North* formed the *piece de resistance*.[60] A similar reception greeted them when they played in London at the Lord Mayor's Show in November 1897.

Such widespread fame brought additional opportunities that the Pipes and Drums were quick to grasp. In 1898, Pipe Major Reith marked his 20 years long service in the regiment with another historical first for the Pipes and Drums, when, alongside his brother, Corporal Piper Robert Reith, they were selected to perform the first ever recorded bagpipe music. Emile Berliner, who had invented the seven-inch gramophone disc[61] in 1894 in the USA, opened the Gramophone Company in the UK in late 1897, and produced his first discs the next year. The brothers Reith recorded the following 12 tracks over the course of three months in 1898:

Recorded London, 28 September 1898:

The Barren Rocks of Aden	Berliner 7700
(Solo recording by Corporal Piper Robert Reith)	

Recorded London, 6 October 1898:
Atholl Highlanders/The Lass	Berliner 7701
Lord Lovat's March	Berliner 7702
Cock o' the North	Berliner 7705
March, Strathspey and Reel	Berliner 7706
Tullochgorum/Reel of Tulloch	Berliner 7707
Johnnie Cope/Brose and Butter	Berliner 7708
Marquis of Huntley/Donal' Duncan	Berliner 7709

Recorded London, 24 December 1898:

---

56 'The London Music Halls', *The Era*, 24 July 1897, Issue 3070.
57 'The Diamond Jubilee', *The Graphic*, 26 June 1897, Issue 1439.
58 Unfortunately, no film of the London Scottish taken at the Jubilee survives today. While around 100 short, one minute sequences were taken of the procession, no more than 25 now survive. In private correspondence, Luke MacKernan, Lead Curator of Moving Images at the British Library and expert on Victorian Cinema, stated: 'One of the sets of films that does survive is that taken at the corner of Piccadilly and St James Street, which is described in the *The Era*, 24 July 1897. We know the name of the company... Professor Jolly's Cinematographe (an Anglicisation of the Joly-Normandin company). However, although some five minutes survive of the films taken by Professor Jolly, none shows the London Scottish band. Clearly Jolly did originally film the band but that portion of the film no longer exists. I have looked through all of the other films of the Jubilee procession, and I have not seen the London Scottish ... There is no one processing on foot.... So, unfortunately, I am fairly confident that no film exists'
59 *London Scottish Regimental Gazette* (1897), p.195.
60 *London Scottish Regimental Gazette* (1897), p.196.
61 As distinct from and with better audio quality than Eddison's wax cylinders.

March, Strathspey and Reel	Berliner 8807x
Highland Laddie March	Berliner 7713
Back o' Benachie/The Campbells Are Coming	Berliner 7714

Recorded London, date unknown
The Barren Rocks of Aden	HMV 12' Special

The quality of surviving discs has, obviously, deteriorated to a large degree over time, but they are clear enough to make out the contemporary fingering and arrangements. *Cock o' the North*, for example, is instantly recognisable, yet noticeably different from the standard composition generally used today.[62]

Not to be outdone, Drum Major Goodman was painted by Sir William Nicholson, as one of 13 images for his famous *London Types*,[63] which proved to be so popular that it was printed in three separate English language editions and two French. Nicholson's iconic woodcut block prints, hand-coloured, each with a quatorzain verse by W.E. Henley,[64] were amongst the most revolutionary British print images of the era, and their stylised simplification of shape and handling of perspective are said to have had no precedent in British art.[65] Goodman's inclusion here as a London 'landmark' provides further evidence that he had very much become the instantly recognisable public face of the London Scottish Regiment.

Looking inward, the less glamorous aspects of regimental life continued during these heady times and the regular duties and responsibilities of the Pipes and Drums still needed to be fulfilled. At Easter camp, from 5 to 11 April 1898, Captain Buckingham took 60 members of the regiment on extended marches in preparation for the latest London Scottish innovation, the 'March Through Scotland' to be inaugurated that summer. The easter marches saw the men marching to the alternate sound of drums and song. 'The drummers (four in number) deserve and received the greatest praise for the masterly and efficient manner in which they "played" their musical "monotony."'[66]

In the summer, it was the turn of the pipers and buglers. 13 pipers and six buglers accompanied the entire regiment as it took part in its first march through Scotland. This was an activity very much frowned upon by the military authorities during this period, who saw it as a waste of training time, but which would prove an innovation of extreme importance in the coming years. The rationale for the march was of dual purpose; to increase the fitness level of the rank and file, and to reengage the regiment with Scotland and her people. It was the first time in almost 40 years of existence that the London Scottish had organised a camp in Scotland and it would prove to be extremely popular both with the soldiers and with Scots themselves. This, and subsequent marches, also brought the London Scottish into contact with many Scottish and particularly, Highland regiments, helping to build strong and enduring ties that would last well into the future.

This first march took place over two weeks, with a route winding from Glasgow via Glen Ogle, Killin, Taymouth, and Aberfeldy to Perth. Captain Lyall Grant, who led the march, placed the pipers and buglers in the centre of the battalion, enabling them to be heard by companies at the

---

62 Further early recordings were made by the Reith brothers in 1908, when they recorded *Cock o' the North* and a set of Medley Marches for Zonophone Twin, No. 444.
63 W. Nicholson, *London Types* (London: Heineman, 1898).
64 Rudyard Kipling had originally been assigned to write the verse but was unable to fulfil this obligation.
65 The original, Japanese-influenced, woodblocks are now in the Victoria and Albert Museum and original prints sell for thousands of pounds.
66 'Easter 1898', *London Scottish Regimental Gazette* (1898), p.75.

front and rear of the column.[67] The importance of music on these long marches became apparent from the outset and is best summed up by the following comments:

> We cannot refrain from expressing at once our gratitude to both Pipers and Buglers for their efforts. However long the road, however steep the hill, however heavy the rain, when the singing flagged, or the men showed signs of weariness, one or the other struck up a lively tune, and restored the step to its original briskness.[68]

Thus, in addition to the ceremonial purpose it had always performed so well, the practical role of the Pipes and Drums, in camp and particularly on the march, became of increased importance. Similar comments relating to the contribution of the pipe band on the march for morale and *esprit de corps,* at a time before mechanised troop transportation, would be written time and time again by London Scottish soldiers throughout the First World War.

Ceremonial commitments also continued, however, and the next large-scale event was a Volunteer Review on Horse Guards Parade in July 1899. The salute was taken by the Prince of Wales, who was joined by, amongst others, the Dukes of Connaught, Cambridge and York, the Prince of Denmark, the Grand Duke of Russia and military attachés from Germany, France, America, Russian, Belgium and Japan. Over 26,000 men paraded and were played past the saluting dais by a massed band. This meant that the Pipes and Drums did not get the opportunity to play the regiment past, but they were on parade and played to and from the march past. 'Although their pipes were dumb, the London Scottish swung by with that magnificent presence which their dress and *esprit de corps* assures them.'[69] The impression on the watching foreign dignitaries was the best imaginable.

A second march through Scotland took place in the summer of 1899, this time with drummers joining the pipers. Piper Mackinnon, who took charge on the band, and Pipers Wills, Mackenzie, Keith and Legge were joined by Drummer Stoddart on side drum and Drummer Simmonds on 'the Old Presbyterian' tenor drum. The bass drum was deemed too heavy to endure 15-plus miles of marching each day for two weeks and so Simmonds resurrected an old tenor drum that he found hidden in the drum store and which had not been used for 16 years. Having shown it to the bandmaster, who said it was a fine quality instrument, Simmonds, with financial assistance from some of the pipers and other members of the corps, had it renovated.[70] The drum would become an institution over the next ten years and synonymous with the man who beat it.

While in Scotland, it seems Simmonds had a close encounter while trying to teach a herd of cows to march. Having been surrounded by enraged Highland cattle and having sounded a hasty distress call:

> Help was sent to rescue the 'Old Presbytarian.' For we could not have afforded to lose Simmonds at any cost. The pipers indeed would have broken into open revolt if anything had happened to him; and the whole detachment would have suffered by his loss. Drums being important articles on the march.[71]

---

67 In later years, companies would rotate to the front to be closer to the Pipes and Drums. Companies could also win the privilege as a prize for good performance.
68 *London Scottish Regimental Gazette* (1898), p.134.
69 'The Volunteer Review', *The Times*, 14 July 1899, p.14.
70 See letter from Corporal Drummer H. Simmonds, *London Scottish Regimental Gazette* (1897), p.104.
71 *London Scottish Regimental Gazette* (1899), p.152.

The London Scottish Pipes and Drums passing the grandstands at the National Gallery, Queen Victoria's Diamond Jubilee, 1897. (LSMA, used with permission)

London Scottish Bass Drummer, with pipers, drummers, officer and onlookers, c. 1899. (LSMA, used with permission)

London Scottish pipers and drummers and a Gordon Highlanders drummers relaxing in the Drum Store at 59 Buckingham Gate, c. 1898. (LSMA, used with permission)

London Scottish drummers parading with the newly designed 'Prussian model' rod-tensioned brass side drums and the traditional tenor drum nick-named 'The Old Presbyterian' with Scots Fusilier Guards instructor, c. 1898. (LSMA, used with permission)

The affection in which Drummer Simmonds was held within the regiment is strikingly obvious from this and other contemporary accounts.

Volunteer life would take on a more serious demeanour when, on 11 October 1899, war was declared between Great Britain and the two Boer republics of the Transvaal and the Orange Free State, beginning what would become the Second Anglo-Boer War. Initially, the expectation was that this conflict would be small in scale and short lived. After all, how could a mob of unruly farmers stand up to the might of the British Empire? This was certainly the feeling on 21 October, when the London Scottish Pipes and Drums marched a detachment of Scots Guards from Chelsea Barracks to Nine Elms station on the first leg of their mobilisation to South Africa.[72] The soon-to-be familiar cry of 'It will all be over by Christmas' made its ignominious début.

However, from 10 to 17 December 1899, afterwards known as 'Black Week' the British Army suffered three successive and devastating defeats at Stormberg, Magorsfontein and Colenso. This provided something of a wake-up call to the British government, who began to understand the huge effort that would be required to end a war that would eventually prove to be the longest, bloodiest and most expensive involving British troops since the Battle of Waterloo. By the time hostilities ended on 31 May 1902, nearly 450,000 men had been deployed, over £200 million spent and, for the first time, over 45,000 militia, yeomanry and volunteers had been sent overseas to fight alongside the regular army on the frontline.

The British government realised early in the conflict that large numbers of troops would be needed in South Africa and began a huge recruitment drive. As part of this campaign, a decision was made on 13 December 1899 to allow volunteers to serve overseas. Colonel Balfour immediately offered the entire London Scottish Regiment to the War Office for service, but his offer was rejected. The government preferred to control the influx of volunteers via existing yeomanry units, new volunteer corps specifically organised for the purpose and through incorporating volunteer companies into regular regiments. The London Scottish, and members of the Pipes and Drums, would volunteer for service within all three of these variants.

During this period, there was a large national debate about volunteers serving overseas, with the British press very much against the idea of citizens 'playing at soldiers.' Most Britons believed that the regular army should be expanded to meet the need, but troops had to be mobilised quickly and volunteers willing to serve overseas, and who agreed to sign up for one year or the duration of the war (whichever was shortest), were the most efficient, short-term solution. 216 men of the London Scottish answered the government's call and served in South Africa between 1900 and 1902, earning the regiment its first battle honours. Two drummers and a piper would be amongst that number.

Drummer J.W.A. Stoddart, with a small number of other London Scots, signed up with the newly created Imperial Yeomanry which had been formed by amalgamating existing yeomanry corps and enlisting additional volunteers. The Imperial Yeomanry received their Royal Warrant on 24 December 1899 and personified the War Office's designs for a nimble, mobile, mounted light infantry who could travel quickly and respond swiftly to the guerrilla attacks of the Boers. Over the next two years, 10,000 men, over half of whom were from the middle classes, served with the Imperial Yeomanry, who were among the first volunteer units to depart for South Africa. They arrived in February 1900 and initially saw action on 5 April with a victory at the battle of Boshof. Although a certain amount of disorganisation dogged the following six months, leading to a number of defeats, their war record was much improved in 1901. The original members of the

---

72   Pipe Major Reith had less than 12 hours' notice of the request but still managed to put together a band of 16 pipers and drummers. Links between the two regiments had always been close and the Scots Guards had been using the London Scottish drill hall for their mobilisation preparations.

Imperial Yeomanry stayed in South Africa the longest of any of the volunteer groups involving the London Scottish, returning home in June and July 1901.

A larger number of London Scottish volunteers,[73] including Drummer C.A. Shaw, enlisted in the City Imperial Volunteers (CIV) which was formed on 20 December 1899 after a conversation between the Lord Mayor of London and Field Marshal Wolseley, Commander-in-Chief of British Forces. The City livery companies initially agreed to finance 1,000 volunteers for South Africa but, with patriotic fervour running high, over 1,600 eventually served. The first detachments left for South Africa on 13 January 1900 and remained on active service until October. The London Scottish Pipes and Drums played the CIV from Wellington Barracks to Vauxhall on their departure. They had also played the evening before at a service for the CIV at St Paul's Cathedral. The CIV's baptism of fire arrived at Jacobsdal on 15 February, and their finest hour, came on 29 May at the Battle of Doornkop, outside Krugerdord. Here they were given the place of honour in the front line supporting the Gordon Highlanders and took the entrenched Boer positions after the Gordons had suffered heavy casualties. They would go on to fight in over 30 engagements and to march over 1,000 miles on foot during their service in South Africa.

Drummer Shaw and the City Imperial Volunteers returned to London on 29 October 1900 where their triumphal march through the City proved to be of epic proportions. A thanksgiving service at St Paul's Cathedral, a reception at the Guildhall, and a banquet in the grounds of the Honourable Artillery Company had been arranged for the occasion, but all planning went to pieces because of the sheer numbers of Londoners who came out to cheer the troops home. The Pipes and Drums of the London Scottish marched in the welcoming parade; one of 14 bands involved in the procession, which also included the Grenadier Guards.

Having arrived at Paddington station, the CIV marched down London's decorated streets through ever increasing crowds. A correspondent from *The Times* reported that the crowds were immense and 'much the most dense I have ever seen.'[74] By the time the procession reached Marble Arch, the situation had begun to get unruly and at Pall-Mall it 'all went wrong.'[75] The crowds burst through the barrier of troops and police lining the route and, by the time they reached The Strand, all order had been lost and the procession had to proceed in single file. The parade reordered into columns after fixing bayonets to enter the City of London but, at Ludgate Circus, the crowd grew uncontrollable and 'by sheer weight, swept away Life Guards, Foot Guards and police.'[76] There were many injuries, some very serious. The CIV finally entered St Paul's, with the London Scottish Pipes and Drums playing them in, one and a half hours late, and amidst scenes of total chaos.

The third and most numerous contingent of London Scots to serve in South Africa were given the honour of forming a complete London Scottish company of the 2nd Battalion, Gordon Highlanders. The strong links between the two regiments that had originally been forged in 1881 were taken to new heights by this arrangement, which saw London Scottish volunteers retain their identity as a company whilst wearing the uniform of the Gordon Highlanders. They would gain inimitable battle experience for the regiment from the regular soldiers alongside whom they fought. Piper A.R. 'Baby' Keith volunteered and was selected to join the first draft for this company, gaining the distinction of being the only volunteer piper serving with the entire South African Field Force.[77]

---

73   Approximately 40.
74   'Return of the C.I.V.', *The Times*, 30 October 1900, p.8.
75   'Return of the C.I.V.', *The Times*, 30 October 1900, p.8.
76   'Return of the C.I.V.', *The Times*, 30 October 1900, p.8.
77   Volunteer companies served with the Black Watch, Highland Light Infantry, Seaforth Highlanders and the Argyle and Sutherland Highlanders but none had volunteer pipers.

The company's departure from London Scottish headquarters en route to Aberdeen on Friday 19 January 1900 is immortalised in Louis Weirter's grand painting which hangs in the London Scottish drill hall. Standing on the right end of the rear rank is Piper Keith and visible in the background are the Pipes and Drums who, with the assistance of the band of the Royal Artillery, played the company through huge crowds to King's Cross station. After arriving in South Africa, the company went straight into action, joining the 2nd Gordons at Ladysmith on 24 March.

Piper Keith would lead the Gordons over hundreds of miles of veldt, as he had led the London Scottish on marches through Scotland and helped alleviate the boredom by performing for the troops during long periods of inactivity between encounters. The sound of the Pipes and Drums was, evidently, also enjoyed by the Zulu population:

> When they heard the banging of the drum and the skirl of the pipes, they (men, women and children) ran out from their different kraals and danced, shouted, laughed, and screamed alongside of us, and didn't leave off until the band had stopped.[78]

Piper Keith's war record shows that he was wounded at some point and spent time in the convalescent depot at Howick, KwazuluNatal.[79] His injuries are likely to have come at Lydenburg on 8 October 1900 when a Boer shell exploded directly over the London Scottish company as they marched to the front, killing three and injuring 22, and with two other regular Gordon's pipers among the seriously wounded.

The London Scottish volunteers acquitted themselves well and earned the following praise from Lieutenant Colonel W.A. Scott, Commanding Officer of the 2nd Battalion, Gordon Highlanders, and himself an ex-London Scot:

> During their time they have shown themselves worthy of their connection with their brothers of the Line Battalion of the Regiment. They have fully shared all the hardships of the campaign and they have fought with us side by side on many occasions in all of which they shared in the distinction earned by the Battalion.[80]

A relief London Scottish company left London on 15 March 1901, played away by the Pipes and Drums, and joined the Gordons at Pietersburg on 26 April.[81] The main body of the original company, including Piper Keith, arrived back in Great Britain aboard the SS *Tagus* on 29 April 1901 and were given a rapturous welcome by Londoners when they arrived at Victoria station. They were met by the Pipes and Drums and, joined by Piper Keith, still attired in the uniform of the Gordon Highlanders, complete with pith helmet, proudly marched back to 59 Buckingham Gate.

Whilst Stoddart, Shaw and Keith were serving in South Africa, the other members of the London Scottish Pipes and Drums continued their duties at home. 1900 saw the final demise of the regiment's professional military band after a number of years of unsatisfactory service, culminating in the bandmaster being found drunk on parade at Buckingham Palace. Charles Shaw, writing in 1951, and a bugler at the time, wrote of the incident:

---

78 Letter from J.D.A. Mitchell, *London Scottish Regimental Gazette* (1900), p.100.
79 Letter from Herbert G. Hoey, *London Scottish Regimental Gazette* (1900), p.113.
80 'Special Morning Orders' issued by Lieutenant Colonel W.A. Scott, reprinted in *London Scottish Regimental Gazette* (1961), p.121.
81 A third company, similarly, sent off by the Pipes and Drums, would later relieve the second at Pretoria on 27 April 1902.

As a matter of fact, I was there and can remember the Bandmaster going up Constitution Hill 'stottin' aboot like a gutta percha ba.' What a disgrace! But it finished the brass band. Colonel Balfour sacked it as soon as we returned to Headquarters.[82]

The Pipes and Drums would now only share their duties with the buglers, and there would never again be a London Scottish military band. However, in 1901 a proposition was put forward to start up a fife and drum band to assist the Pipes and Drums on the march, but this idea was quickly shot down, with members of the pipe band particularly vocal on the issue.[83] It is no surprise then that, with a need to assert their position, the turnout of pipers and drummers for the march through Scotland that year was particularly high.

Major changes took place within the band in 1902 with the double resignations of the long-serving pipe and drum majors. After the death of Queen Victoria the previous year, it seems fitting that these two men, who so personified the late Victorian era, should step down. Pipe Major 'Sandie' Reith resigned in February after 14 years as pipe major and 25 years of service with the pipe band, whilst Drum Major Alfred Goodman lay down his mace after 15 years of service in December. Plaudits for both men poured in from all directions and can be summed up by the following quote from Major James Alexander:

> You have for so long and efficiently guided the affairs of what I may say is the most important department of a Highland Regiment, for how could such a battalion exist without its Pipers?[84]

Reith and Goodman led the Pipes and Drums through the most important period of its development. They turned what was a small band of seven or eight pipers and four or five drummers into a proud corps of 30 to 40 members, able to turn the heads of queens and kings. In terms of quality, Goodman and Reith were able to secure the services of highly proficient instructors who ensured that the pipers and drummers sounded as good as they looked. Their dedication turned the Pipes and Drums, and to some degree the London Scottish Regiment as a whole, into household names. Reith secured his place in history by performing the first bagpipe recordings and Goodman was so famous during his lifetime that a popular music hall number written about him, composed by Corporal Duncan Tovey, was still being sung in London after the Second World War.[85] Their vision ensured that the Pipes and Drums kept pace with, and contributed to, the magnificence of High Victorian culture and London's position as 'Capital of the World' during this period.

'Sandie' Reith's younger brother, Robert, took over as pipe major and 'muckle drummer' Tommy Hodgson stepped into Goodman's shoes as drum major. Both were long time members of the Pipes and Drums, with Hodgson having joined the regiment in 1878. They were quick to stamp their mark on the band by announcing early in 1903 that the pipes, drums and bugles would in future be regarded as one band. This was a sensible advancement, as the drummers were playing for both bands anyway. The change ensured that all three sections practised together on the same evenings and could, therefore, better organise and raise their level of drill. Reith and Hodgson also worked at supporting as many regimental events as possible, including weekend company marches, to help cement the bands reputation as the hardest working unit of the regiment. The fact that a 'D' Company march in 1903, for example, was attended by 24 pipers, drummers and buglers highlights the success of this planning. The continuation of this policy over the next ten

---

82 Letter from Charles Shaw, *London Scottish Regimental Gazette* (1951), p.124.
83 Letter from H. Simmonds, *London Scottish Regimental Gazette* (1901), p.218.
84 Letter from Major James Alexander, *London Scottish Regimental Gazette* (1903), p.64.
85 Duncan Tovey, *The Big Drum Major* (London: Asherberg, Hopwood and Crew), 1901.

Painting by Scottish artist Louis Weirter, depicting the London Scottish, Gordon Highlanders contingent parading at Regimental Headquarters, 59 Buckingham Gate, before leaving for South Africa, 19 January 1900, with Piper Keith rear rank, far left and the Pipes and Drums behind, 1900. (LSMA, used with permission)

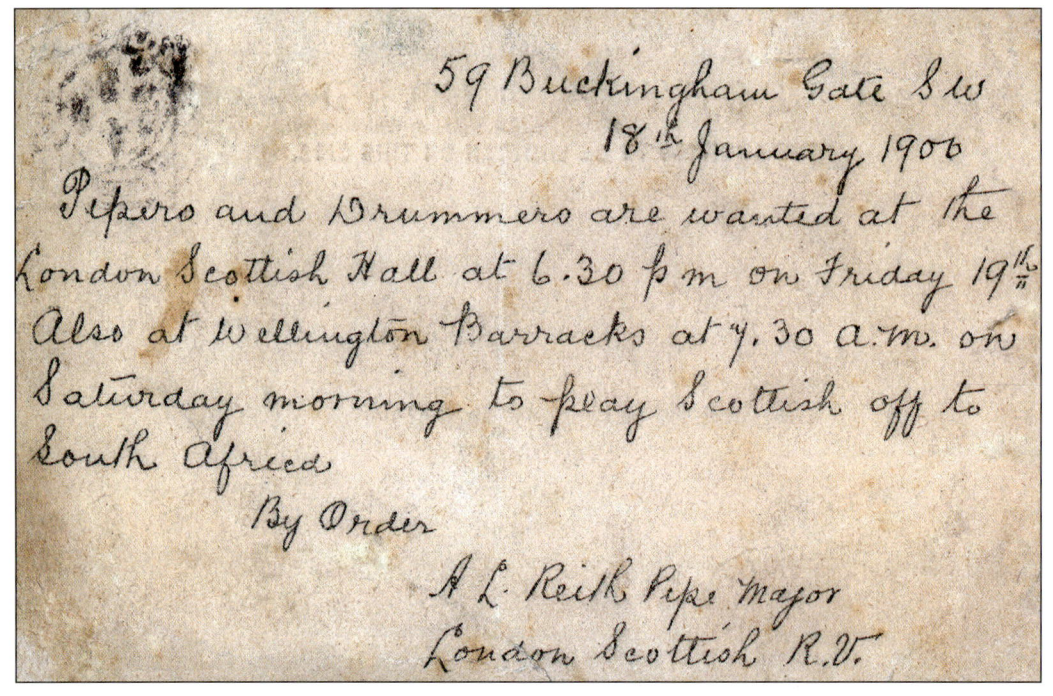

Postcard from Pipe Major Reith sent to all members of the Pipes and Drums relating to the above, 18 January 1900. (LSMA, used with permission)

COMING OF AGE 1881-1913 97

Postcard of the arrival of the London Scottish Regiment in Aberdeen during the 1901 March Through Scotland, 5 August 1901. The London Scottish are led by the Piper and Drums of the 1st Volunteer Battalion, Gordon Highlanders. (LSMA, used with permission)

Band practise at Easter Camp, with pipers playing practise chanters and drummers drumming on up-turned buckets, c. 1908. (LSMA, used with permission)

years also ensured that the Pipes and Drums were well prepared for the coming marching endurance tests of the First World War.

Reith and Hodgson also reintroduced an annual piping competition that first took place on 14 March 1904 during the annual school of arms meeting. The contestants in the competition performed a March, Strathspey and Reel and, although only four pipers took part, it was the beginnings of bigger things to come. Piper Kenneth Greig was adjudged to have won the competition after the top three had been asked to play a second time before the judges were able to reach a consensus. It was an impressive result for Greig who had only been in the band for six months and knew little of piping a year prior to that. He would go on to become Pipe Major of the 1st Battalion during the First World War.

1904 also saw the retirement of John Mackenzie from his role as piping instructor. He was now nearly 70 years old and had become unwell. Pipe Major Reith was instrumental in setting up a fund to help him financially and to repay some of the debt owed to Mackenzie for his role in the success of the band over the last 40 years. Pipe Major Henry Forsyth and Piper (later Pipe Major) William Ross, both of the 2nd Battalion, Scots Guards and both heavyweights of the pipping world, provided instructional assistance to the pipers over the next few years, continuing the 45-year association between the pipes and drums of the two regiments.

Comment was made by the press about the lack of a military brass band at the London Scottish annual inspection that year in Hyde Park. However, the following humorous exchange between a signaller and a member of of the crowd sums up the general feeling of those watching:

> Londoner (to one of the Signallers): 'Where's your brass band?'
> Signaller replies: 'We have no brass band.'
> Londoner: 'What! no brass band. Well (pointing his thumb over his shoulder at the pipers) that ain't so bad.'[86]

On 8 September 1905, King Edward VII took his first Royal Review of Scottish volunteers since his coronation in 1901. This was the first great review in Edinburgh since the 'Wet Review' of 1881, and this time 40,000 volunteers marched before their King. The London Scottish were represented by over 300 men, who again stayed at Younger's Holyrood Maltings. The Pipes and Drums were in attendance and it is recorded that, 'the faithful London Scottish … arrived at a local goods station at four o'clock in the morning and marched to the Holyrood maltings with their pipes playing *The Marchioness of Tullibardine*.'[87] The review fortunately took place in much more agreeable conditions than that of 1881.

The following year, the regiment was asked to perform for one night only at the Naval and Military Tournament[88] and on 19 May 1906 they performed a torchlight display of music and Highland dancing. This performance was so well received that they were asked to come back on 26 May to perform a second time and were then subsequently invited back repeatedly over the coming decades. A review of the performance stated that:

---

86 *London Scottish Regimental Gazette* (1904), p.128.
87 David Keir, *The Younger Centuries* (Edinburgh: William Younger, 1951), p.79.
88 Known more widely as the Royal Tournament and resurrected in 2010, after an 11-year, absence as the British Military Tournament; at which the London Scottish Pipes and Drums were again invited to performed.

Not only was the pipe band more than usually good and the bugles so excellent as to call forth loud applause by a crowded house, but the drums seemed to have made huge strides in their arts and left nothing to be desired.[89]

Later that year, the pipers received further incentive to excel when Colonel Greig, the Commanding Officer of the London Scottish, presented the 'Victoria Challenge Cup' as the trophy for the piping competition. The winner gained the title of 'Champion Piper' of the regiment for the forthcoming year, and it was Piper Greig that came away with the prize again. The competition was judged by London Scottish piping instructors Pipe Major Forsyth, now piper to the Prince of Wales (and later Sovereign's Piper), and his successor at the 2nd Battalion, Scots Guards, Pipe Major Ross.

Further assistance from the Scots Guards came in 1907, when drumming instructor John Morrison retired from the London Scottish to move back to Scotland.[90] He had spent the last 23 years as instructor with the Pipes and Drums and, along with piping instructor John Mackenzie, deserves a great deal of the credit for the tremendous success of the pipe band during that period. His position was taken by Drum Major J. Everett of the 1st Battalion, Scots Guards, who was joined at the London Scottish by his compatriot, Pipe Major John Ghillies, also 1st Battalion, Scots Guards, who took on the role of piping instructor. Both would still be instructing the Pipes and Drums in 1911, when Pipe Major Ghillies left for Canada to take up the position of Pipe Major to the newly-formed 72nd Highlanders, later known as the Seaforth Highlanders of Canada.[91] The coordination of this strong succession of instructors helped ensure that the London Scottish Pipes and Drums were in a healthy position to enter the new era of volunteer military service brought about by the Haldane Reforms and the creation of the Territorial Army in 1908.

The volunteer movement had been through an extremely difficult period following the end of the Second Boer War in 1902. The Conservative government of 1901-1905, under the direction of Secretary of State for War, William St John Brodrick, 1st Earl of Middleton and his successor Hugh Arnold-Forster, had made several disastrous attempts to reform the British Army which had left it demoralised and disorganised. The effects had been particularly acute on the volunteer movement which, despite its important role in South Africa, was close to collapse, with many corps short on recruits and funds. In the London Scottish Regiment, numbers had fallen dramatically[92] and there was concern about covering the mortgage for the headquarters building at 59 Buckingham Gate.[93] Even so, the regiment was much better placed than most. A Liberal election victory in 1905 saw Richard Haldane become Secretary of State for War, and he immediately set about constructing a programme of reform. By 1908, a British Expeditionary Force (BEF) had been formed, along with an Officer Training Corps, a new Imperial Staff, and a new operational and training doctrine as laid out in Major General Douglas Haig's *Field Service Pocket Book*.

On 1 April 1908, the Haldane Reforms also saw the passing into law of the Territorial and Reserve Forces Act[94] which completely reorganised the yeomanry, militia and volunteer corps. The London Scottish Regiment was now classified as the 14th (County of London) Battalion, The

---

89 *London Scottish Regimental Gazette* (1906), p.130.
90 Unfortunately, his retirement would only last three years and he passed away on 30 December 1910.
91 Pipe Major Ghillies would remain as a pipe major with the Seaforths of Canada until 1937. He was sent overseas as Pipe Major of the 72nd Overseas Battalion in 1916 and would serve with the C.E.F. in France and Belgium during the remainder of the First World War.
92 Nearly 400 below the 1,009 establishment.
93 A successful fundraising campaign was begun in 1907.
94 7 Edw. 7, c.9.

Pipe Major Robert 'Bob' Robertson, c. 1909. (LSMA, used with permission)

London Scottish pipers photographed during the March Through Scotland, 1911. Piper Chapman, seven from right, and Piper Latham, second from right, would be killed in 1914. Eleven others would serve overseas with either the London Scottish and/or as commissioned officers in other regiments during the war. Piper Oram, fourth from left, would serve from 1914-1919 in all three battalions of the London Scottish, on three fronts and, despite being injured multiple times, survived. (LSMA, used with permission)

Reaching Oban, during the March Through Scotland, 1911. (LSMA, used with permission)

London Scottish Pipers Sutherland-Graeme and Oram leading the funeral of the Earl of Wemyss at Gosford House, Aberlady, East Lothian, July 4 1914. Both pipers would serve with distinction during the First World War. (LSMA, used with permission)

London Regiment (London Scottish) of this new Territorial force. This army had been created specifically for home defence but soldiers could, in the event of the outbreak of war and after six months training, volunteer for service overseas. Men were asked to enlist in the Territorial force for a minimum of four years, and there were new regulations governing discipline and pay. The volunteer movement was officially dead, and those men who re-enlisted became part of a new Territorial Army (TA) that was now integral to the role of the British Army both at home and abroad.

Some 20 percent of London Scots did not re-enlist; many were put off by the four years minimum service, whilst others were debarred by new age restrictions. However, their places were soon taken by others who were attracted by the more 'official' structure of the Territorial Army, and numbers quickly recovered.[95] These men now wore a new London Scottish cap badge, specially designed to mark the occasion, and heavily influenced by the Commanding Officer, Colonel Greig of Eccles. It used the cap badge of the King's Own Scottish Borderers, with whom Colonel Greig had served in the Boer War, for inspiration, and included the regiment's new battle honours, 'South Africa 1900-1902.' The badge also incorporated into the design 'Strike Sure', the family motto of the Greig's of Eccles. This same cap badge was worn by the London Scottish until 2022 and is still worn by the Pipes and Drums today and is among the oldest cap badges still to be seen on parade in the British Army.

The structural changes brought about by the creation of the Territorial Army had a limited impact on the Pipes and Drums, which continued to play their usual part in regimental life. At the regiment's first camp as part of the Territorial force in the summer of 1908, the 'pipers, drummers and buglers were in the forefront of everything, be it work or play',[96] leading the nine-mile march past Stonehenge and with the pipers taking over the duty calls from the buglers. They also had to learn to slow march; a drill new to the Pipes and Drums, which was, apparently, the source of much amusement to those watching.

Non-military duties that year included accompanying the great music hall entertainer Harry Lauder (then the highest paid entertainer in the world) through the streets of London prior to his first visit to the United States of America.

> The pipers of the London Scottish paraded Lauder's car, over the bonnet of which the Saltire had been draped, from his house to Euston Station where he caught the New York boat train.[97]

This, apparently, was quite a march, from Lauder's home in Tooting, through throngs of enthusiastic admirers, who mobbed the band and the car and caused traffic in London to come to a complete standstill.

The year 1909 saw the resignation of Pipe Major Robert Reith and the appointment as pipe major of Robert 'Bob' Robertson. It was a very difficult decision and, if not for the effects of consumption (tuberculosis), Lance-Sergeant Piper Kenneth McNiven may well have been chosen for the position, for 'no one has ever served as a piper in the London Scottish who was so universally beloved as Kenneth …. What a splendid Pipe Major he would have made.'[98] Unfortunately, McNiven was

---

95 By early 1909 numbers had topped 800 and by the end of the year would reach 1,025 with a long waiting list.
96 *London Scottish Regimental Gazette* (1908), p.182.
97 Andrew Hurrall, *Popular Culture in London 1890-1918* (Manchester: Manchester University Press, 2001), p.69.
98 *London Scottish Regimental Gazette* (1910), p.76.

to finally succumb to his affliction on 9 March the following year. The band escorted his body to St Pancras Station, whence it was 'sent to his native land for burial.'[99]

> The band paraded under Pipe-Major Robertson, with the drums muffled and the pipes hung with black streamers in place of their usual gay ribbons, and several laments were played. A large crowd witnessed the incident and were very much impressed by it.[100]

The decision to appoint Robertson turned out to be an excellent one, however, and:

> It is no exaggeration when we say that he was probably the most successful and popular Pipe-Major the Regiment ever had; he ruled them, not by discipline, but by his wonderful personality.[101]

Pipe Major Robertson would prove to be the lynchpin that held the Pipes and Drums together from the lead up to the First World War through to the reconstruction of the regiment in the years after victory. His involvement in the wider regimental family would also prove to be of great influence and remarkable benefit. Robertson was an architect by trade and would go on to design many things for the London Scottish, from memorials to entire buildings. His first assignment came late in 1910 when the senior medical officer, Surgeon Captain Pirie generously offered to provide new pipe banners. One was made for each company, with an additional red pipe major's banner, and all were designed by Robertson himself.

The roll of the Pipes and Drums took on even greater importance in 1910, when the bugle band was finally disbanded. Private Douglas Kennedy recalled that the regiment had two bands, 'who took it in turns to play for the marching. Our Bugle Band was only fair, but our Bagpipe Band was rated very highly.'[102] The bugle band's demise came in a rather undignified fashion, at a review in Hyde Park. On a counter march, the bass drummer slipped:

> And he fell flat on his back, as helpless as an overturned tortoise, his kilt neatly covering his drum, leaving his most cherished possessions utterly exposed to the fascinated eyes of the huge gathering. The magnitude of the disaster had been quickly borne in on the buglers, for their brassy music faded into a dying fall, as the other drummers made a ring round their fallen companion and bore him to the rear.[103]

1911 was another important year for the Pipes and Drums and began in the soberest of tones with the news of ex-drumming instructor John Morrison's death on 30 December 1910. Two months later, on 14 February, came the news that Colonel J.A. Balfour, who had been the Commanding Officer from 1894 to 1902, had also passed away. The Pipes and Drums played at his remembrance service at St Columba's Church and Lance Corporal Piper R.G.P. Hare played at his funeral in Scotland.

---

99   *Evening Telegraph and Post*, Dundee, 16 March 2019, p.1.
100 *Evening Telegraph and Post*, Dundee, 16 March 2019, p.1.
101 'Obituary, Pipe Major Bob Robertson', *London Scottish Regimental Gazette* (1939), p.313.
102 Transcript of 'Douglas Kennedy 1893 – 1988', tape cassette, recorded by his son, Peter Kennedy, London Scottish Museum Archives, 1975, p.85.
103 Transcript of 'Douglas Kennedy 1893-1988', tape cassette, recorded by his son, Peter Kennedy, London Scottish Museum Archives, 1975, p.86.

Pipe Major Ghillies left for Canada in the spring of 1911, and, at the London Scottish pipers and drummers dinner, was presented with a 'token of esteem' for his work as piping instructor and instructor for the reel club. His position as piping instructor was taken up again by Pipe Major William Ross of the 2nd Battalion, Scots Guards. Pipe Major Ross, who joined the Scots Guards in 1896, served in South Africa during the Boer War, became pipe major in 1905 and went on to become the most influential piper of the twentieth century.[104] His appointment as instructor not only advanced the band's 50-year association with the Scots Guards, but continued the alliance of the London Scottish Pipes and Drums with the very best pipers of the era.

At the same dinner, mention was made of Piper Douglas Lyall Grant (the son of Major W. Lyall Grant, a senior officer in the London Scottish), who had accompanied the Scottish international rugby team to Paris for their match against France. Major Malcolm, who was taking over as Commanding Officer of the London Scottish and as band president, stated that, 'This son of a worthy sire, was shortly leaving the pipe band to take up a commission, as they wanted officers, and the pipe band was the place to find them.'[105] Piper Lyall Grant would go on to become the first of three consecutive London Scottish commanding officers during the inter-war years who had started their military career in the Pipes and Drums. He was also the first in the growing trend for recruitment of officers from the pipe band that would go on to reach epidemic proportions during the First World War.

The biggest ceremonial occasion of 1911 was the coronation of King George V and Queen Mary at Westminster Abbey on 22 June, followed by the Festival of Empire held in London to commemorate the event. The Pipes and Drums were involved in the royal procession, leading the veteran reserves to their places on Constitution Hill and then playing there throughout the day for the enormous crowds that came to watch the royal progress. Pipe Major Robertson was a proud man on the day, wearing for the first time his new red pipe major's banner, displaying the coat of arms of the new Commanding Officer, Colonel Malcolm.[106]

Later that evening, the London Scottish organised a dinner and concert at 59 Buckingham Gate to mark the coronation celebrations and the Pipes and Drums went down to the Scottish camp (which had been set up in Kensington Gardens for the Scottish regiments that had been assigned to the coronation) to gather in their fellow countrymen. Having rounded up a goodly number, 'the contingents were fallen in and swinging down the road behind our pipers marched into Headquarters about 400-500 strong.'[107] The band then played at the concert, marking the end of a long, but glorious, day.

---

104 He won the Gold Medal at Oban in 1907, the Gold Medal at Inverness in 1904, followed by clasps in 1905, '06, '07, '10, '12, '13, '19 and '28 – a feat that would remain unequalled for decades. He served in France from 1916 through 1918, when he was invalided home with rheumatism. He was appointed Principal of the new Army School of Piping in 1919, and appointed tutor to the Pirbaireachd Society in 1921. He compiled five seminal books on pipe music and was renowned for being a first-class instructor, with the great John D. Burgess amongst those he taught, as well as almost every Pipe Major in the British Army.
105 'Piper's and Drummer's Dinner', *London Scottish Regimental Gazette* (1911), p.28.
106 London Scottish pipe banners had always been blue but military protocol stated that a pipe major could carry a red banner, to differentiate it from the others, if it was commissioned by either the Commanding Officer or the Regimental Honorary Colonel. In a military setting, these individuals take the place of the Clan Chief who, under the Clan system, would have the honour of displaying a unique pipe banner to the Clan piper (represented by the pipe major in a military setting).
107 *London Scottish Regimental Gazette* (1911), p.136.

It was not always so glorious and there was one amusing occasion during this period which deserves to be highlighted. In 1947, an anonymous contributor to the *London Scottish Regimental Gazette* submitted the following:

> Shall I write of what I saw and heard in the pre-1914 band? Of the occasion when Drum Major Tommy Hodgson led the band, as he thought, across Hyde Park Corner, but the Pipe Major knew that was not the way the Colonel wanted to go, and took the Pipers and Regiment round a corner, while Tommy strode on in review order dignity of long plaid, white spats, black cock feathers and swinging mace all by himself across to the Park. Of his academic language afterwards when he pointed out to Rob Robertson that he had not got a lovely eye in the middle of his beautiful back – or words to that effect.[108]

Camp that summer consisted of a week at Dover followed by a week marching through Scotland. The regiment arrived at Dover Castle late at night, with one of the advanced party reporting:

> Sunday morning shortly before 3 a.m., the sound of bugles broke the stillness, then the pipes afar off pierced the air playing 'Queen Victoria's Welcome to Fiddoch' and 'The 75th Farewell to Edinburgh' alternately as they climbed the hill. Then we knew the regiment was approaching. Beds were forsaken in order to see the boys come swinging into camp, stepping proudly to our homing tune 'Highland Laddie.'[109]

The Pipes and Drums certainly knew how to make an entrance. They did more than just grandstand, however, playing their usual active part in camp life. For example, much use was made of Sandy Gow, the giant bass drummer who was 'simply invaluable when there was any strong man job on'[110] whether it be single-handedly stacking 450 lbs beer casks or helping to coal a steamer for the return journey from Scotland when the Glasgow dockworkers went on strike. Like many in the pipe band over the years, his great strength was only equalled by his immense thirst and Colonel 'Jock' Henderson, who was a piper at the time, later recalled the following tale of a back-firing practical joke played on Drummer Gow by a number of young pipers during the march that year:

> Seeing Sandy wending his way from the canteen they asked him if he would like a pick-me-up. Nothing loth, Sandy took the full glass of 'Kummel' proffered him in devilment, tossed it down his throat, made a grimace, exclaimed 'Ach-pepmint!' and strode off in disgust.[111]

The main item of note in 1912 was the retirement, after nearly 33 of service, of tenor Drummer Simmonds, who, during his first 25 years had only missed five uniform parades. His popularity within the regiment was so large that the Regimental Second in Command sanctioned the raising of a subscription throughout the battalion for a leaving present, something usually reserved only for a retiring commanding officer. A moving testimonial was given at the band dinner that year, to which Drummer Simmonds responded. 'He spak lang, an' the room rocked wi' roars o' lauchter, fur Simmonds' speech wi's brimfu' o' humour, wi' juist a tich o' pathos in it.'[112]

---

108 *London Scottish Regimental Gazette* (1947), p.116.
109 '1911 Training Camp – Dover', *London Scottish Regimental Gazette* (1911), p.167.
110 '1911 Training Camp – Dover', *London Scottish Regimental Gazette* (1911), p.168.
111 *London Scottish Regimental Gazette* (1951), p.75.
112 *London Scottish Regimental Gazette* (1912), p.69.

A year later, at the band dinner on 1 March 1913, Drum Major Hodgson announced his retirement, having himself, served for 35 years. Hodgson had been with the band through their glory years and had led them from the front for the last ten, when their fame had never been higher. He understood, however, that change was coming and that world events would demand that younger men take the helm. Piper Shand, in a toast given at the band dinner summed up, however, the importance to the regiment of Drum Major Hodgson and Pipe Major Robertson by remarking that:

> The band possessed the two most popular members of staff in the Drum and Pipe Majors. The crowds, he said, did not congregate to see the Colonel, or the Majors, or the Adjutant, however much they might fancy themselves; they gathered to hear the pipes, and to gaze on the Drum-Major.[113]

Drummer Percy A.E. Cunningham took over from Drum Major Hodgson and would hold the position for only a few short months until war broke out and the 1st Battalion was sent overseas. He would, however, go on to become Drum Major of the 2nd and then the 3rd Battalion until 1916.

On 10 October 1913, three pipers and a drummer joined the 15-man London Scottish team that demonstrated the fitness of these younger men who were taking the helm, by setting a new record marching from London to Brighton. They covered the 52.5 miles in 16 hours and 40 minutes with the pipers taking it in turns to play over much of the route. Drummer Gow, Piper Harry Latham, and the piping brothers Robert and William Porteous all played their part, the high point of which was the piping of the team over the South Downs. All four would go on to serve gallantly during the First World War.

Piper Latham was additionally a member of the London Scottish military marathon team that won the national competition in Edinburgh in 1913 and 1914. He was also a crack shot, ranking in the top 20 at the King's Prize at Bisley, further proving that members of the Pipes and Drums were valuable to the regiment for much more than just their musical skills. Unlike military bandsmen, pipers and drummers were riflemen first and musicians second, and were expected to take part in every aspect of regimental life, performing their musical duties as additional commitments. They were without doubt, some of the hardest working members of the regiment and would more than prove their worth in the coming war years.

Regimental life continued despite the increasing tensions around the world in 1914, but it became more and more obvious that the grand Victorian era of volunteer soldiering was now definitely dead and gone. The traditions of those times, including church parades, camps and annual reviews continued, but preparations for a very modern war, which now seemed almost inevitable, progressed at a pace. The London Scottish Regiment was already hugely oversubscribed by the early part of 1914, with a waiting list that would be of great benefit when permission was granted to form a second battalion some few months later.

As if to highlight the breaks with the past, the Regimental Honorary Colonel, the Duke of Argyll,[114] passed away in May 1914. The funeral took place at Westminster Abbey and the Pipes and Drums attended in full force, accompanying a Guard of Honour, with the 'music selected by the Pipe-Major ... very appropriate and splendidly rendered.'[115] In fact:

---

113 *London Scottish Regimental Gazette* (1912), pp.70-71.
114 Who had served as an officer in the London Scottish in the 1860s.
115 *London Scottish Regimental Gazette* (1914), p.108.

The pipes never sounded better; everyone seemed anxious to honour with his best efforts their beloved Honorary Colonel, who has on so many occasions shown how dearly he loved the old Highland music, and who took a keen interest in the Pipers.[116]

Then, as if to sever the oldest links completely, the Earl of Wemyss, revered founder, former Commanding Officer and past Honorary Colonel of the London Scottish, passed away on 4 August 1914; the very day that Great Britain declared war on Germany and war began. His funeral took place at his principal seat, Gosford House in East Lothian, with the funeral procession led by Pipers Sutherland-Graeme and Oram of the London Scottish, who would both go on to serve with distinction during the war. As the graveside service ended and the Countess and Lord Elcho turned to leave, the pipers struck up a last lament for the man who, 55 years earlier, had founded the London Scottish as a defence against foreign aggression.

The Earl of Wemyss never lived to see his regiment go into battle, but it would be only a matter of weeks before the London Scottish would begin four years of extreme, gruelling warfare that would test the modern methods and intense training that he, and his successors, had always insisted his regiment undertake. The Pipes and Drums would lead the way on every field of battle and in every engagement, playing their part as the London Scottish Regiment proudly continued to make history in wartime, as they had always done in times of peace. An immensely heavy toll would be paid for in so doing.

---

116 *London Scottish Regimental Gazette* (1914), p.108.

4

The Pipes and Drums at War 1914-1919

Forming a hollow square round the rows of open graves, we stood with heads bared, bowed over reversed rifles. The Padre read the Burial Service, and the pipers wailed a coronoch. Never did music sound so sweet in our ears, nor yet so plaintive. The last notes of the bagpipes died away, and all was still; not a murmur as, for a few seconds, we paid silent homage to our dead comrades.

Bernard Blaser, 1917[1]

Beat on drums; let the pipes play and the banners be unfurled for every triumphal march that shall be. But when the marches are played let us never forget that every march has grown more glorious by the war and the blood of the men who fell; that every march has woven around it a thousand memories of life and death, of hardship, of danger, and of victory.

Arthur Fetterless, 1920[2]

On 2 August 1914, the bulk of the London Scottish Regiment was en route to Ludgershall Camp on Salisbury Plain for their annual two-week camp. It was obvious to every man that a major war was imminent and rumours abounded regarding the role that Territorial Army troops might be asked to undertake. Service in South Africa one and a half decades prior had proved their mettle overseas and the relatively small size of the British Army meant any prolonged fighting might make their deployment necessary. However, Territorial soldiers had not signed up to fight beyond Great Britain's shores and, anyway, many believed that the fighting could not last for more than a matter of months. Most, then, prepared for and arrived at camp expecting it to be little different from previous years. For the Pipes and Drums, it was business as usual as they headed the battalion on the march from the train. An NCO in the advanced party wrote:

> All ready for the Battalion, but wars and rumours of war continue. News comes that the Battalion has arrived at Ludgershall …. Hear the pipes along the road, and break out the flag, 'the ruddy lion rampant in gold', as the head of the column comes into sight.[3]

---

1   Bernard Blaser, *Kilts Across the Jordan: Being Experiences and Impressions with the Second Battalion 'London Scottish' in Palestine* (London: H.F. and G. Witherby, 1926), pp.241-242.
2   Arthur Fetterless, 'The Piper in the Everyday Life of the War' in Bruce Seton and John Grant (eds.), *Pipes of War: A Record of the Achievements of Pipers of Scottish and Overseas Regiments During the War 1914-1918* (Wakefield: E.P. Publishing, 1920), p.244.
3   As quoted in Mark Lloyd, *The London Scottish in the Great War* (London: Pen and Sword, 2001), p.25.

Despite rumours all day about being sent back to London, Lights Out was sounded and the battalion settled down for the night. However, 15 minutes later, after receipt of a telegram from the War Office, bugle calls roused the camp and the men formed up to march back to the station, amid continual rumours of possible mobilisation.

On arrival back in London, the men returned to their homes and waited anxiously over the next two days for further news. When Germany invaded Belgium on 3 August, the Belgian Government invoked the 1839 Treaty of London which obliged Great Britain to come to its aid. The following day, Britain duly declared war on Germany and the task of mobilising the London Scottish began in earnest on 5 August. Men, including all members of the Pipes and Drums, reported to regimental headquarters at 59 Buckingham Gate where they were given medicals and issued arms and ammunition. They were joined by battalion reserves and flocks of other men hoping to join up in the 'elite' London Scottish. Those that lived nearby were sent home for a few days before War Office fears of possible German invasions recalled all men to billets in, or close to, headquarters:

> Cooped up as they were in overcrowded quarters the men began to suffer a good deal. But by the end of the week the bulk of the mobilisation work was done, and officers could be spared to take the men for short route marches in London. These marches, performed with gradual increase in weight carried and at last with full packs and ammunition pouches, proved a useful preparation for the more serious marches that were to follow.[4]

The Pipes and Drums would play an important role in this regard on all fronts throughout the war, through the mud of Flanders, the dust of Salonika and the desert of Palestine.

On 15 August the 1st Battalion, along with the rest of the 4th London Brigade, marched through Hyde Park to be inspected by Major General Thomas L.N. Morland, the recently appointed GOC 2nd (London) Division, and the following day orders came that the battalion was to march to Watford to begin training. The *Aberdeen Press and Journal* reported:

> An army has moved out of London not secretly by night but in full glare of this summer afternoon. The London Scottish swung past Buckingham Palace smartly, with the pipes and drums making a merry din.[5]

The London Scottish marched from Buckingham Gate, through the huge crowds in central London that had formed to see them off, to rendezvous with the rest of the brigade at Marble Arch. From there, the brigade marched up the Edgware Road, with the Pipes and Drums at their head, to camp under the stars on a warm summer's evening at Canons Park. The following day the march was continued to Watford and billets, mostly in farm buildings around Abbots Langley. Pipers and drummers billeted with the company to which they were assigned rather than as a unit in themselves, a practice which would continue for the first two years of the war.

Within a few days of arriving at camp, the London Scottish were formally asked to volunteer for overseas service. None could be forced to go, and it was a huge decision for all, especially for pipers and drummers who were often considerably older than those with whom they served, in some cases by a matter of decades. Like many of the men in the regiment, they came in the majority from white-collar, middle-class backgrounds and had well-paying civilian jobs on which they and their families depended. Many were also ex-public school and 'Oxbridge' educated and, thus, prime candidates for war-time officers. There was influence for agreeing to overseas service

---

4   J.H. Lindsay (ed.), *The London Scottish in the Great War* (London: London Scottish Press, 1926), pp.17-18.
5   *Aberdeen Press and Journal*, 17 August 1914, p.4.

from the War Office in the form of a guarantee that any battalion which secured over 75 percent volunteering rate would stay together and deploy overseas as a unit but:

> In the London Scottish care was taken to avoid any undue pressure upon the men. Each was asked for his decision, individually and in private. He was given time to consider the matter, and his decision, when given, was accepted without comment by his officers. Not all volunteered. It was a very serious thing to ask of the men, especially in the circumstances of the time.[6]

An unnamed private was to later write: 'We appreciated this as being the way a gentleman should handle this delicate question, and as being so much better than in some Battalions we heard.'[7]

In the end, more than four out of five men chose to volunteer for service overseas, including most of the Pipes and Drums. Others chose to volunteer for service but as commissioned officers either within the London Scottish or in other units. Piper Douglas Lyall-Grant had already commissioned as a London Scottish officer before war was declared and Piper Alexander Seaton Robertson took a commission that would later see him fighting with the Australian Army at Gallipoli. Piper Alan Vincent Sutherland-Graeme and Piper Lionel Durham Henderson were two others from the band who decided straight away to take up commissions and transferred together to the 4th Seaforth Highlanders which were billeted a short distance away in Bedford. Others who took a similar route also found their way into the homely atmosphere of Highland regiments.

On 26 August, the War Office decreed that all Territorial regiments which had volunteered for overseas service would be authorised to raise a second battalion. In typical London Scottish fashion, the regiment were the first in the country to do so and had secured enough recruits within just seven days. So popular was serving in this 'elite' regiment that a further 1200 men – more than another battalion strength – were passed on to other Highland regiments, with the 4th Seaforth Highlanders taking the largest number. The 2nd Battalion, London Scottish was initially designated a 'reserve' battalion to supplement the 1st Battalion as it transferred overseas and to perform its duties back in the UK. However, it would not be long until a 3rd Battalion was raised, and the 2nd Battalion began training for its own combat role fighting on foreign shores.

A 2nd Battalion also meant a second Pipes and Drums. Likewise, a 3rd Battalion meant a third, and men with experience with pipes or drum were eagerly sort after. Former band members re-enlisted while others were vetted for their musical prowess on recruitment. Piper Alfred Cairns-Wilson and Piper Walter MacKinnon along with bass Drummer Sandy Gow had all completed their service in the Territorial Army but re-joined and would go on to make their mark during the war. Older members of the 1st Battalion Pipes and Drums moved from the 1st to the 2nd Battalion and then, sometimes again to the 3rd. Pipe Major Robert Robertson, aged 47, transferred from the 1st Battalion to become Pipe Major of the 2nd Battalion in early October, and would later transfer again to become Pipe Major of the 3rd Battalion. The newly reacquired MacKinnon swapped pipes for a mace and became Drum Major of the 2nd Battalion a few days earlier but would remain in post for only a couple of months before taking a commission. The work of older members and in training, would-be pipers and drummers was to be of great importance once war began and casualties were taken overseas. The pipers and drummers of the reserve battalions would also become one of the regiment's most powerful recruiting tools at home.

Recruiting pipers and drummers, however, was not always plain sailing, as this report from the *Chelsea News and General Advertiser* makes apparent:

---

6 Lindsay (ed.), *The London Scottish in the Great War*, p.20.
7 Fleur de Lys, 'A Dream of 1914', *London Scottish Regiment Gazette* (1933), p.72.

A recruit for the London Scottish. Angus MacKenzie, 28, a hairdresser, of 66 Wood Street, Walthamstow, appeared to answer a charge of being drunk and disorderly at Buckingham Gate. The prisoner pleaded guilty. PC McKenna 469A, said he created a disturbance at the headquarters of the London Scottish. He had gone there for the purpose of enlisting. The Magistrate: That is an operation you had better carry out when you are sober. You really want to enlist? The prisoner: Yes, I am a piper and I could get into the London Scottish at once. The Magistrate: You will pipe much better when sober than when drunk. The prisoner: Yes, l am very sorry. I met a few Canadian soldiers and I took one drink too many. I am going to enlist to-day. The Magistrate: Very well then, I will give you an opportunity of going to the headquarters with the officer. You are discharged.[8]

Quite what happened to Angus MacKenzie after he was returned to London Scottish headquarters at 59 Buckingham Gate is unknown but, as far as the records show, he never became a regimental piper.

Around the Commonwealth and beyond, from India to Australia and Canada to South America, mobilisations were also taking place and former members of the Pipes and Drums were heeding the call to defend the 'mother country'. Most notably Piper Alexander Keith, who had been the first London Scottish piper to serve overseas when he joined the Gordon Highlanders contingent during the Boer War, returned south from his gold mining adventures in Northern Ontario. On first arriving in Canada, he had originally joined the 97th Algonquin Rifles as a pipe sergeant but at the outbreak of war he signed up with the 48th Highlanders, whose headquarters were in Toronto, and was appointed Pipe Major of the 15th Battalion Canadian Expeditionary Force (The 48th Highlanders).. He would go on to serve for the duration of the war without injury.[9] Amongst other new recruits to the London Scottish would come men such as Piper Oscar Machell-Varese, a bank clerk who was born and raised in Gibraltar; Piper Archibald Angus, who had spent most of his young life in Chile and Piper Donald Pinnington who drew lots with his brother in Buenos Aires, Argentina to see which of them should have the 'honour' of travelling half-way around the world to join the Pipes and Drums of the famous London Scottish. Piper James Young also travelled from Argentina specifically to join the band.

Such circumstances were echoed throughout the regiment and by the end of the first week in September 1914 the 1st Battalion was fully composed of men willing to serve overseas; with a full pipe band amongst them. On 12 September, a matter of days after this feat had been achieved, orders were received for the 1st Battalion to entrain for Southampton and so it stood that barely a month after arriving in Hertfordshire for what was meant to be a minimum of six months training, the London Scottish were selected to be the first of the Territorial force to be deployed overseas. Another historic 'first' for the regiment, and one that in time, would have devastating consequences for both the regiment and the Pipes and Drums.

---

8 *Chelsea News and General Advertiser*, 13 November 1914, p.7.
9 He held the rank of Pipe Major until the end of the war and was discharge 10 May 1919 in Toronto, Ontario. A remarkable period film clip <http://www.youtube.com/watch?v=lFeCyssGK_Q> briefly depicts the band in France, followed by the 15th Battalion marching through Toronto upon its return with Pipe Major Keith leading the band on its final parades.

1st Battalion

At 0800 hours on 15 September, the first four companies set off on 'almost a triumphal march through Watford to the Station through cheering crowds'[10] followed, a few hours later, by the second half of the battalion. Pipers and drummers, as always, leading the way, '… pipers playing and battalion in big heart.'[11] Upon arrival at Southampton, troops immediately embarked on the SS *Winifredian* and just had time to write a last letter home before sailing in the early hours of 16 September. Bugler Francis Brockett Coward wrote:

> Well dears I must close as the boat will soon be leaving and I want someone to post this for me. No danger attached to the job we are going to do so don't worry.

However, just two months later, in a letter dated 25 November 1914 he would write:

> This is mechanical butchery, that is all you can call it.[12]

The SS *Winifredian* was the first boat to dock at Le Havre after the reopening of the port and she tied up with a London Scottish piper playing at the prow. On disembarking, the battalion 'marched through the town with the pipers playing the Marseillaise, and received a hearty welcome from the people, who saw in their arrival a sign that things were going well.'[13] Such was the warmth of the welcome, that:

> Our pipers were giving us a tune when the mayor of Havre came in this afternoon and tied the tricolour on all the pipes and all the chaps got a bit of ribbon stuck in their hats.[14]

Private Arthur G. Davidson recalled in his diary:

> In the afternoon give impromptu concert in shed attended by crowds of French. Give them much pipe music, and scotch songs. Pipers give French National Anthem on pipes, great enthusiasm.[15]

---

10 Sergeant Lancelot Edey Hall, 'F' Company (unpublished diary, London Scottish Museum Archives, 13 September 1914 to 9 April 1915), p.1.
11 Lance Corporal J.B.F. Cowper, 'F' Company unpublished diary, London Scottish Museum Archives, entry for 15 September 1914.
12 Bugler Francis Charles Brockett Coward unpublished letters, London Scottish Museum Archives, 15 September and 25 November 1914. Brockett Coward was a Bugler and part of No. 2 Platoon, Lewis Gun Section, 'A' Company. Buglers, like Pipers and Drummers played a regular part in the Battalion, in addition to their musical roles. Coward was wounded on Christmas Eve 1914 but, defying the connotations of his surname, continued to fight with the Battalion through four more years of war until he was tragically killed by a shell concussion at Bullecourt on 29 August 1918, a matter of weeks before the end of hostilities.
13 *The London Scottish in the Great War*, ed. Lindsay, p.24.
14 W.H. Petty, 'B' Company, 'The Lighter Side – 'Til We Went into Action', (unpublished diary, London Scottish Museum Archive), entry for 15 September 1914.
15 Private Arthur G. Davidson, unpublished diary, London Scottish Museum Archives, August 1914 – September 1915.

From this 'shed' in Le Havre, the 1st Battalion would soon spread out across Northern France, as individual companies were assigned to a huge variety of different tasks. Pipers and drummers were, for the most part, detailed along with their requisite companies and found themselves undertaking numerous roles which freed regular army units for fighting at the front. These duties included guarding German prisoners, assisting with injured troops returning from the frontlines, setting up camp for the arrival of troops from India, loading and unloading munitions, food and other supplies at railway depots, sentry duties at various headquarters, setting up temporary hospitals, as well as guarding British regular army troops who had been imprisoned for desertion, drunkenness and other transgressions of military law. Private Alex Moffat, a London Scottish soldier, wrote 'It is reputed that the Scottish were sent here in order to set an example, as there is very little discipline left amongst the Tommies.'[16]

Troops were also required to provide guards of honour and grave diggers for burial parties and the regiment's pipers and drummers were very much in demand on such occasions. At this early time in the war there was still the opportunity for individual funerals for those whose bodies were not sent back to Britain, and the 1st Battalion made every attempt to ensure such burials were as dignified as possible. Between 18-27 October, 'F' Company, who were stationed in Boulogne, played a large part in such activity:

> We march a tremendous way with arms reversed and the sight of 3 hearses with bearers and our party must have been fine. We had some magnificent men with us the first 8 being about 6'2" a piece. The corpses are of 3 English privates and they are buried in the special part of the cemetery. Corp Piper Carey plays laments. We come back to a merrier tune.[17]

Private George Wilson of 'F' Company stated:

> We bury twelve a day. When we can spare them there is a party formed which marches behind the coffin with arms reversed, a piper leads playing a lament and two buglers play the Last Post when the coffins are all in the graves.[18]

German war dead were given an equally honourable send-off:

> We have also to supply Bearer Guards for the Dead; the first of these was a German Prisoner who had only a slight wound, but on being operated upon by the Doctor his stomach was found to be full of raw potatoes.[19]

A few days later, Lance Corporal J.B.F. Cowper wrote:

> In charge of bearer party to cemetery in afternoon. 3 officers and 4 men. We marched 2 miles through town in slow time with pipers playing laments. Firing party march behind with arms reversed.[20]

---

16 Private Alex Moffat, 'F' Company, (unpublished diary, London Scottish Museum Archives, 1914 to 1915), p.2.
17 Hall unpublished diary, p.2.
18 George Wilson, *Mobilised: Being the Record of Private George Wilson of F Company London Scottish. From the Call to Arms to his Return Wounded* (The Complete Press, undated), p.21.
19 Moffat unpublished diary, p.2.
20 Cowper unpublished diary, entry for 24 August 1914.

Lance Corporal C. Black's experience with a burial party saw him participate in 'the most impressive funeral I have ever been at. I never thought I would ever march through a French town to the wailing of the pipes. It was a strange experience.'[21]

Piper Harry Latham recorded that 'Stuart, Aires, Canny and myself catch the stunt of a lifetime'[22] as part of a funeral party for Major General Hubert Hamilton, who was the first British divisional commander to be killed in France on 14 October 1914. After a funeral parade on the dockside, the four men were assigned to accompanying his coffin aboard ship back to England. This duty gave those involved a rare few days with very little to do, although pay back came on their return to France which saw them unloading telegraph poles. Piper Latham was also involved in setting up a canteen for 'comfort items' that were being sent over from regimental headquarters back at 59 Buckingham Gate. Drum Sergeant Harold Simmonds, who had retired from the Territorial Army in 1912, returned to the reserve battalion and was responsible for the packing and distribution of these items. This new canteen is 'to be a miniature Selfridge's. Anything from a tooth-brush to a tin of dubbin, so to speak.'[23]

Pipers found the chance, and were indeed very much encouraged, to pick up their pipes and play for every possible reason. Unlike drums, pipes could be carried easily and be on hand at short notice. The significance of the piper in the everyday life of the regiment had been ingrained over the last 50 years and their importance for morale and *esprit de corps* was more important than ever, even at this early stage of the war. The plethora of diary entries from this period which mention the pipes serves to highlight their standing and the importance of Scottish martial music to the men. Sergeant Duncan Tovey's diary entry for 23 September states: 'Shifted out of our guard room. Found new one in truck of oats. Slept well. Got Parkyn to bring his pipes.' For 8 October, 'Got Parkyn to play in evening.' Even the lack of music is mentioned for its rarity, such as this entry from 5 October: 'Left Triage at 6. Marched across Paris. Pipers didn't play.'[24] Other diarists talk of impromptu performances during transportation breaks: 'At one station, where we stopped some time, our pipers gave a performance which the French got tremendously excited over.'[25] At other times, pipers played for sister Highland regiments that were passing through, 'Gordons leave with a Captain in command and very young Lieuts in command of Coys. Our 2 pipers play them down the road.'[26]

Drummers often played when companies or groups of companies marched together; and more formal concerts were given from time to time during this period although, with the battalion so spread out, it is unlikely that the entire band played together on many occasions after their initial arrival. As is usual, we must search harder for mention of drummers, but we do know that they had their instruments to hand and that some may have been lost or broken for which there were spares available as replacements. The quartermaster's field service records state that, on 21 October, 'Drum (side) handed over to Drummer Tovey of 'D' Coy.'[27]

---

21 Lance Corporal C. Black, 'F' Company unpublished diary, London Scottish Museum Archives, entry for 24 October 1914.
22 'A Private's Diary', *London Scottish Regiment Gazette*, 1914, p.238.
23 Private Bert France, 'F' Company unpublished diary, London Scottish Museum Archive, entry for 25 August 1914.
24 Sergeant Duncan Tovey, 'A' Company unpublished diary, London Scottish Museum Archives, entries for 23 September, 5 October and 8 October 1914.
25 Davidson unpublished diary entry for 19 September 1914.
26 Davidson unpublished diary entry for 20 September 1914.
27 QMS John Gibson, 'Army Book 152, Correspondence Book (Field Service) Sept 1914-Feb 1915', London Scottish Museum Archives, entry for 21 October 1914, p.15.

It may have been the case that the British Army saw the London Scottish and the wider Territorial Army continuing with the sort of rear echelon duties initially undertaken by the 1st Battalion for the remainder of the war. However, this notion was to be re-evaluated in very short order. Early October 1914 saw stalemate between opposing armies at the front on the Aisne after the German retreat from the Marne in September. Lack of troops, supplies and ammunition caused a lull with both sides entrenching, literally and figuratively. By the middle of the month, however, both the Germans and the French began outflanking manoeuvres that pushed the battle lines further and further north. The 'race to the sea' had begun. The British Expeditionary Force (BEF) were positioned on the northern end of this front and so came under increasing pressure from German assaults, resulting on 20 October with the beginning of the First Battle of Ypres. As Field Marshal Sir John French's troops came under increased attack, it soon became obvious that the thin British line could not hold without the assistance of every trained soldier who could hold a rifle. This would need to include not only Indian troops in the area but, in what was perceived as the bigger gamble, the untried and as yet untested representatives of the Territorial Army. Despite their lack of battlefield experience, their lack of pre-deployment training, their scattered status throughout Northern France which meant they had not even been able to practise firing the short magazine Lee Enfield rifles they had been issued on deployment, or their lack of opportunity to train as a battalion since arrival in France, Field Marshal French turned in his moment of need to what he saw as the elite of the Territorial Army. On 25 October, Lieutenant Colonel George A. Malcolm, Commanding Officer, the London Scottish Regiment, received the order they had all been waiting for with word that the 1st Battalion were being called to the front.

For the most part, London Scottish soldiers were very keen to see action and had, in fact, raised concerns that the fighting would be over before they had a chance to take part. They reacted enthusiastically when their companies were ordered to collect at St Omer and within three days almost the entire battalion had reformed. On 29 October, they were ordered forward. A fleet of London buses, complete with their Cockney drivers, drove the battalion for nine hours through horrendous rain, to Ypres, arriving at 0300 hours on 30 October. Such was the rush that the battalion's much prized Vickers machineguns were left behind as they were deemed too heavy to transport. Men took what rest they could for a few hours in and around the famous Cloth Hall before marching out of town before being ordered, a few hours later, to march back in again. They re-boarded the London buses to be transported to St Elois, where they disembarked and billeted for the night. The following morning, they marched to the front under orders to take the place of the Coldstream Guards – who had suffered appalling loses – and counter-attack in support of dismounted cavalry units who were holding a ridge between the West Flanders towns of Wytschaete and Messines:

> This indeed must have been a glorious chapter in the military history of the London Scottish Regiment to have the honour to take the place of the 1st Battalion Coldstream Guards in battle, 1914. I well remember the London Scottish Band playing 'Scotland the Brave' when they arrived.[28]

The 1st Battalion, London Scottish were about to make history again, as the first Territorial Army infantry regiment ever to go into battle.

In *The Salient: Ypres, 1914-18*, Alan Palmer states that:

---

28 *London Scottish Regiment Gazette* (1969), p.78.

New recruits to the Pipes and Drums, August 1914, with Piper Archibald Angus to the right of Piper Major Robertson. Piper Angus would be killed in action just months later at Messines. (LSMA, used with permission)

Drummer Cairns, left with snowball, November 1914. (LSMA, used with permission)

London Scottish piper leading a burial party for the funeral of a British serviceman, France, September 1914. (LSMA, used with permission)

Corporal Piper (later Pipe Major) Greig and a platoon of 'F' Company at Villeneuve St. Georges Station, France, September 1914. (LSMA, used with permission)

> The London Scottish … were roused from billets in the town and set out before dawn, 750 grey kilted 'exiles' following their pipers up the 4-mile road to Wytschaete.[29]

However, no first-hand evidence for this statement is provided and we cannot know for sure whether the battalion did indeed march this final distance to the sound of the pipes. The London Scottish regimental war diary states that this movement was carried out under heavy shellfire, which would not have necessitated a stealthy approach but may also not have been conducive to companies marching behind their pipers. Drummers would almost certainly have been without instruments and would have prepared for battle in their primary role as infantrymen. We do know that the men were in high spirits and sang songs including the popular music hall tune *The Big Drum Major* written by Sergeant Duncan Tovey in honour of Drum Major Goodman.

As will be described later, there is one first-hand account of pipes being present at the subsequent Battle of Messines and pipers almost certainly had their instruments with them even if they were not played. Lindsay states that the battalion paraded before the Cloth Hall: 'each man carrying full kit and two blankets.'[30] Full kit would have included pipes for each company piper but not a single first-hand account of the battle mentions the sound of bagpipes; before, during or after engagement. Considering the attention that the pipes and drums receive in diary entries on other less memorable occasions at this time, it might be thought a strange omission. It is worth noting though, that the heroic image of lone pipers leading their men in full charge 'over the top' would not come until later in the war and the more straightforward, if less glamourous, explanation for the omission of the sound of the pipes is that all members of the band were far too busy concentrating on fulfilling their primary roles as infantrymen to be sounding the charge.

The Germans, however, did bring their own musicians to the battle and their officers were well aware of the importance of military music for martial spirit. Many first-hand accounts mention the sound of German brass band music wafting between explosions and special orders would be given during this period stating that 'Regimental musicians who play during assaults will be awarded Iron Crosses.'[31] With crack German Grenadiers lined up against dismounted cavalry units, Indian Punjabi troops and the untested Territorials of the London Scottish, German generals were so confident that their forces would easily break through these makeshift lines that Kaiser Wilhelm II himself had travelled to join Crown Prince Rupprecht behind the forward lines in anticipation of opening an unassailable pathway that would eventually lead straight to Paris. 'It was evidently intended to be a very grand affair for they had a band playing somewhere behind the scenes.'[32] An unfinished letter from an unknown London Scot states, 'and I heard the bands playing in the German lines, an eerie, rotten sound.'[33] The German bands played light music during the day and more stirring airs later in the evening when a breakthrough seemed most imminent. Private Alex Moffat wrote: 'An awful din going on and can hear the German Imperial Band playing the Austrian National Anthem.'[34] Private George Wilson stated: 'We hear a German brass band playing the Austrian National Anthem and hear the order by the German Officer. Enemy about

---

29   Alan Palmer, *The Salient: Ypres, 1914-18* (London: Constable Press, 2007), p.23.
30   Lindsay (ed.), *The London Scottish in the Great War*, p.29.
31   Daily Orders, General der Infanterie von Deimling, Commander XV Corps, 3 November 1914.
32   E.M. Wilkins, 'A Brief Account of the Experiences of Private Eric Millward Wilkins on the 1st Battalion London Scottish During the Action of October 31st and November 1st, 1914 Near Messines Belgium', (unpublished manuscript, London Scottish Museum Archives).
33   Unfinished letter from unknown London Scot, who fought at Messines, (London Scottish Museum Archives).
34   Moffat unpublished diary, p.5.

fifty paces off before our charge.'[35] It was at this point that the London Scottish Regiment was thrown into action.

The events of the battle at Messines and all subsequent engagements of the war are described comprehensively in J.H. Lindsay's superb *The London Scottish in the Great War* and it is not the intention for this chapter to replicate that work. A general outline of events will instead be attempted, with specific focus on the function, purpose, activities and outcomes of pipers and drummers during the four years the regiment was deployed. Both Lindsay's work and the official London Scottish war diaries, held in the National Archives, are recommended reading for those wishing to join the dots and fill any gaps regarding the wider war history of the London Scottish Regiment.

As their comrades back home at headquarters in London were listening to the Pipes and Drums of the 2nd Battalion playing after the conclusion of the regiment's traditional Hallowe'en dinner, the 1st Battalion received their baptism of fire. Far from counter-attacking as initially ordered, the London Scottish had been pinned down under heavy bombardment in positions they had taken up on the Messines ridge earlier that afternoon. At 2100 hours, in the post-dusk darkness, the first of four German assaults on the line began. Pipers and drummers fought in their individual companies, with rifle and bayonet. The fighting was extremely fierce and four bayonet charges by the Germans over the next four hours meant close combat of the most bloody and ferocious kind. The older, Mark IV Lee-Enfield service rifles which the London Scottish had been issued would not accept the Mark VII magazines that had been issued along with them for rapid fire, and so each bullet had to be loaded one at a time. In addition, intense hand-to-hand bayonet combat with the cream of Germany's infantry pushed the London Scottish to their very limits. Men who, only two months earlier, had been sat at their desks in banks and insurance offices, fought for their lives, their friends and the honour of their regiment, to hold the line against overwhelming odds. A German breakthrough came at 0200 hours and was repulsed but another attack came an hour later with more success. However:

> The Companies in the trenches … hung on gallantly until daylight when finding themselves surrounded, they fought their way out and fell back on WULVERGHEM and KEMMEL.[36]

The importance of preventing a German breakthrough cannot be over emphasised and the exploits of the London Scottish on this night would be lauded at the very highest levels throughout the war and long after. But it came at a high price. A price that would be paid repeatedly over the next four years of war. From a total strength of 812 officers and men in action that evening, 395 were either killed, wounded, or posted as missing. The numbers of pipers and drummers included in these returns prove that they were at the very heart of the action. From a band of 14 pipers and ten drummers,[37] four pipers were killed, with six other pipers and six drummers wounded severely enough to require hospitalisation. This represented a 67 percent attrition rate from this one battle alone and was 18 percent higher than the losses realised by the battalion as a whole. Pipers Charles Oram, Bertram Gordon-Forbes, Charles William Donaldson Mackay, Bertram Nicol, Robert

---

35 Wilson, *Mobilised*, p.26.
36 '1st Battalion, 14th London Regiment (London Scottish), War Diary', The National Archives (TNA) WO 95/1266) entry for 1 November 1914.
37 Extensive efforts have been made by myself and Corporal Piper Andrew Parsons, Curator of the London Scottish Museum and Archives, to track down all pipers and drummers who fought with the London Scottish during the First World War but incomplete records, particularly regarding drummers, dictates that the list may not be fully accurate.

Porteous and William Porteous together with Drummers Horace Keeler, John Mann, Kenneth Sexton, Cecil William Piper-Smith, Percival 'Peter' Tovey and Walter Wallace were all hospitalised.

Of the four pipers that died that night, it is Piper Douglas Robert Parkyn about whom we know the least. On 2 November, Sergeant Tovey wrote in his diary: 'No news of Flockhart or Parkyn'[38] but there are no further details mentioned in any other source. Like so many, Piper Parkyn had been lost in the chaos. Along with the other three missing pipers, Piper Parkyn was still listed as missing in various newspapers on 31 January 1915 and a notice in *The People* on Sunday 28 February stated:

> PARKYN 1341 Pte (Piper) D. R. 1st London Scottish A coy – reported missing, Nov 1 at Messines. Any information from a comrade will be gratefully received by his parents.[39]

It would not be until early 1916 that Piper Parkyn would finally be listed as 'Presumed Killed.'

James Carey had joined the London Scottish back in 1904 and became 'H' Company Lance Corporal Piper in 1913. According to Seton, he was killed while acting as a forward observer[40] but was reported missing directly after the battle and was not listed as Presumed Killed in Action until mid-1915. Lance Corporal Piper Carey was subsequently found to have been wounded and taken prisoner, and it only came to light much later that he had died in enemy hands. The *Dundee People's Journal* reported at the time:

> AFTER MESSINES. DUNDEE LONDON SCOT MISSING
> Mr James Carey, cabinetmaker, 65 Nethergate, Dundee, has been notified by the authorities that his son, Lance-Corporal Piper James Carey, the London Scottish, has been missing since the Battle of Messines, in which, it will be remembered, the crack Territorial unit gained rich laurels. Lance-Corporal Carey, who was 32 years of age, was an architect in the employment of the London County Council, and had attained considerable eminence in his profession, when he was mobilised with his battalion in August.[41]

The third piper to make the ultimate sacrifice was Piper Archibald Angus, who left school in Edinburgh and travelled south to join the Scottish on 3 September, soon after war broke out. He was initially assigned to the 2nd Battalion but lied about his age and volunteered for service overseas. He was only 17 years old and the youngest London Scot to be killed at Messines. 'Archie' had been an officer cadet and pipe major of the pipes and drums at Edinburgh Academy and was keen to fight against the Germans who he felt were responsible for his family having to return to Scotland from their home in Chile. When his father complained about his son's deployment overseas, Archie wrote back to him, saying 'What would you expect me to do?'[42]

Craig Mair states, in his book about Archibald's father David Angus, that 'Archie was killed piping the charge of the London Scottish at Messines Ridge on 31 October 1914.'[43] Unfortunately there is no first-hand evidence to support this statement. However, Piper Angus' friend, Private

---

38 Tovey unpublished diary entry for 2 November 1914.
39 *The People*, 28 February 1915, p.8.
40 Brian Seton and John Grant (eds.), *Pipes of War: A Record of the Achievements of Pipers of Scottish and Overseas Regiments During the War 1914-1918*, p.143.
41 *Dundee People's Journal*, 6 February 1915, p.9.
42 Letter from Archibald Angus to his father David Angus, October 1914, Angus Family Letters, Inventory Acc. 7658, Manuscript Division, National Museum of Scotland.
43 C. Mair, *David Angus, The Life and Adventures of a Victorian Railway Engineer* (Stevenage: Strong Oak Press, 1989), p.205.

C. Brown, in a letter dated 26 November 1915, wrote to Piper Angus' parents detailing the events surrounding his death. According to Private Brown, he had seen Archie wounded when returning into no man's land to retrieve his pipes.[44] The pipes he was recovering actually belonged to Piper Gordon Forbes, who stated at the time that 'I was sent back with some prisoners and gave him my pipes. When I got back to the regiment, I heard he was missing and that he had my pipes on his back at the time.'[45] Piper Angus had played G Company to the train station at Rouen only a few days earlier, and it is unknown why he was not carrying his own pipes. According to Private Thomas, who was visited in Craigleith Military Hospital, Edinburgh by Archie's mother, Mary Angus, in a desperate search for news of her missing son, Piper Angus had been slightly wounded between 1800 hours and 2000 hours on 31 October and then seriously wounded in the thigh after creeping out of the trench sheltering what remained of G Company shortly after 2200 hours to retrieve the bagpipes.[46]

Corporal Cameron, in two letters to Archie's parents, wrote:

> I was in the same trench as your son on November 1st and as I left the trench I saw him lying at the bottom of it still alive. He turned his eyes in my direction, but did not move or speak, so I called to him that I would go get some help. I could do nothing myself as I had been shot and bayoneted through both shoulders. I wish I could hold out to you some hope of his recovery, but unfortunately the British line was retiring as we got back to them; and as far as I can gather, the ground has never been regained.[47]

In the second letter, he added more bad news:

> I know of the fact that all our wounded were bayoneted by the Bavarians several times whilst lying on the ground. I do not think there is any hope of his safety.[48]

These first-hand accounts regarding Piper Angus prove that London Scottish pipers had their pipes with them at the Battle of Messines. It seems very unlikely that these pipes were played during the fierce and unrelenting fighting, but it portrays vividly the importance of the bagpipes to both individual pipers and the battalion. To borrow Piper Gordon Forbes' pipes and then surrender his own life in a brave attempt, under heavy artillery and machine gun fire, to retrieve them is certainly proof positive of the value Piper Angus placed on these 'instruments of war.'

The fourth piper to be killed that evening was Lance Corporal Piper Eric Glenn Chapman of 'A' Company, a 22-year-old bank clerk who had signed up with the London Scottish in 1909 aged 17. Chapman was initially reported as 'Wounded and Missing' after the battle and finally 'Killed in Action (Presumed)' in March 1916. It would not be until 1921 that his body was discovered, identified, and reburied at Wytschaete Military Cemetery near Messines. Lance Corporal Piper Chapman was found buried in L'Enfer Wood, near the site of the London Scottish Regimental

---

44   Letter from Private C. Brown to Mr and Mrs David Angus, 26 November 1915, Angus Family Letters, Inventory Acc. 7658, Manuscript Division, National Museum of Scotland.
45   Letter from Bertram Gordon Forbes to Major W. Lyall-Grant, dated 2 February 1915, Angus Family Letters, Inventory Acc. 7658, Manuscript Division, National Museum of Scotland.
46   Letter from Mary Angus to David Angus, dated 7 November 1914, Angus Family Letters, Inventory Acc. 7658, Manuscript Division, National Museum of Scotland.
47   Letter from Corporal Cameron to Mrs Angus, dated 13 February 1915, Angus Family Letters, Inventory Acc. 7658, Manuscript Division, National Museum of Scotland.
48   Letter from Corporal Cameron to Mrs Angus, undated, Angus Family Letters, Inventory Acc. 7658, Manuscript Division, National Museum of Scotland.

Aid Post (RAP), which had been abandoned after the fighting on 1 November 1914. It seems likely that Chapman was wounded and taken to the RAP, where he either died of his wounds or was killed by advancing German soldiers, who later buried him. A letter, dated 15 September 1921, from the Infantry Record Office to Chapman's father confirming that his body had been found, and states that, with regret, 'it must now be definitely accepted that the late soldier was Killed in Action or Died of Wounds.' The letter goes on to state that 'the removal was undertaken with every measure of care and reverence, and … the reburial was conducted by a Military Chaplain.'[49] Lance Corporal Piper Chapman is the only member of the Pipes and Drums killed at Messines with a known resting place and one of only three men from the 85 London Scots who died that day with an official grave and headstone.

After the frenetic combat of the night before, just eight members of the band reported for roll call on the morning of 1 November 1914. French Impressionist painter Paul Maze, who was acting as an interpreter for the Royal Scots Greys, took photographs after the Battle of Messines, including one of London Scottish survivors at Wulverghem, near Kemmel. This image would become famous in the following months, as reports of the battle were taken up by newspapers and magazines around the world. In the centre of the photograph, amongst the other dishevelled soldiers, can be seen Sergeant Piper Kenneth Greig, still clutching his rifle and looking very much in a state of shock.

Of the others that survived uninjured, we know that Lance Corporal Piper Harry Latham, a crack shot in competitions before the war, used his rifle at close quarters, killing at least four Germans with his bayonet, for which he would be Mentioned in Dispatches. Lance Corporal J.B.F. Cowper recorded in his diary that German troops 'stopped at a hedge and Harry Latham jumping up said, "Let's charge the beggars." He was off first an easy winner and had got four before the line caught up.'[50] In a letter home to his parents after the battle, Sergeant Lance Hall stated:

> Part of No. 4 Section away to the left was nearly overwhelmed. They shot Germans down by the hundreds, Latham, Purvis and Allsop being in the trenches there. They did not miss many. They fired over 200 rounds each, not one being fired without a distinct aim at a man who could be seen within 100 yards. Many were shot at two yards. Poor Purvis was killed and then as they ran out of ammunition Latham organised a Bayonet Charge. He ran four men through himself and did not get a scratch.
>
> I never imagined it possible that everyone could be so cool. They advanced across that field as if they were attacking the Red House at Wimbledon and lines were kept much better.[51]

Latham was also widely reported in the British press for saving the life of Private H. Phelps who had been surrounded by German soldiers. In a letter home to his family, Private N. L. McLellan wrote:

> Then suddenly bullets began to arrive from behind us as well as in front! Cheerful, wasn't it? We could hear the little beggars going 'Thew-u-! phew-w-u!' as Piper Latham put it, exactly as if they were whispering ' 'Cheerio! Cheerio!' in our ears. All this time the Germans were blowing the 'cease fire' whistles in the hope of deluding us into stopping and calling out: 'Here you are, Scottish – over here. Back to your trenches, Scottish' and 'Scotland for ever' in a highly entertaining manner. I don't think they caught many people with their tricks

---

49 Letter from Infantry Records Office to J. Chapman, 15 September 2021, TNA WO 364/661/35055.
50 Cowper unpublished diary entry entitled 'Messines' 1914.
51 *London Scottish Regimental Gazette*, (2004), p.127.

though, except in one case. Piper Latham heard a plaintive voice from the middle of a group of Germans saying, 'No, I want the Scottish, I want the proper Scottish' and a small youth named Phelps suddenly burst forth with two of the Germans after him trying to bayonet him. Latham stood and shouted, 'Here we are, Latham, F Company!' and shot the leading Germans. Little Phelps rushed in, wounded in the arms, and gasped, 'Good God, Latham, I am glad to see you!'' and collapsed fainting in Latham's arms. Poor little chap.[52]

Respite from the battle at Messines was short-lived. The remnants of the battalion bivouacked at La Clytte on the night of November 1st and then marched to billets east of Ballieul on 3 November. They were inspected by GOC II Corps Lieutenant General Sir Horace Smith-Dorrien the following day and then had two days in camp to regroup and reorganise before marching to Ypres with 1st Division headquarters on 7 November. They were then back in the trenches near Zillebeke the following day and would remain there under heavy shelling and regular attack until the night of 13 November. The following day, the battalion were finally placed in brigade reserve and moved away from the front line. However, casualties from shelling were still taken over the next few days. During this period, two more pipers would be killed and two drummers and a piper wounded. Thus, over a short but bloody two-week period, virtually the entire London Scottish Pipes and Drums had been wiped out.

On Monday 9 November, Piper John Forbes Bennie was killed whilst under heavy attack in trenches along Brown Road, in woods southeast of Zillebeke. A report of the horrific conditions surrounding his death and burial were given in an anonymous soldier's diary entry:

> This morning (Tuesday) we had the sad duty of burying a certain piper of 'Ours', who had been killed the day before. We buried him in a big shell-hole, and I made a cross out of a box. We had scarcely finished this when the shelling started. We had to get into our dug-outs and listen to the storms of the cannonade and try to look happy at every earth-shattering explosion. The storm increased in violence and the earth rocked and sprang under the tremendous blows.[53]

A letter written to a friend by another unidentified London Scottish solder stated:

> I heard that a young piper was lying in a farmhouse, so bolted for it, as I had a presentimeant [sic] it might be. Met two Guards stretcher-bearers carrying a chap – had a look, and sure enough it was our Bennie. The bullet had either richochetted [sic] or was a dum-dum, and it caught him in the left eye. He must have been killed at once ... Two odd chaps and I buried Bennie in a Jack Johnson hole as we were being shelled. We three, the adjutant and I and a handy officer just gathered round and offered a prayer of one sentence – 'O Lord, we commend the body of this soldier to Thy care: and may every member of the London Scottish do his duty as nobly as this young piper.' And we covered him up. The Scouts made a little wooden cross, and I wrote his name on the back.[54]

Piper Bennie was 20 years of age and a graduate of the prestigious George Heriot's School in Edinburgh, where he had been pipe major in the OTC band, and sadly became 'the first Herioter

---

52 *Croydon Advertiser*, 21 November 1914, p.6.
53 '"Twelve Days" – Saturday November 7th to Wednesday November 18th, 1914', *London Scottish Regiment Gazette* (1918), p.59.
54 *The Glasgow Herald*, 2 December 1914, p.3.

of the new army to give his life for his country.'[55] He had worked in London in the Paymaster-General's Office in Whitehall.

Seven days later, Lance Corporal Piper Harry Gould Latham was 'blown to pieces by a shell.'[56] A specialist sniper section had been formed within the battalion after Messines, to which both Latham and Sergeant Piper Greig belonged, and it was whilst sniping on the front line that Latham was killed.

> Piper Latham, who volunteered for active service with the London Scottish Regiment on the outbreak war, was a splendid specimen of manhood, standing over 6ft …. He took part in the historic charges of the London Scottish at Ypres, where it has been stated there were only 2,000 British against 35,000 Germans. Striking testimony of the gallantry displayed by Piper Latham has been received from independent sources …. Another Briton has made the supreme sacrifice …. Lance-Corpl Latham joined the London Scottish 15 years ago, and soon came to the front as a marksman. On half a dozen occasions he was in the King's Hundred at Bisley, and one year secured third place for the King's prize. He was also a member of the London Scottish team which secured the 'Daily Telegraph' Cup and was also in the Marathon winning teams. He was about 34 years of age, and unmarried. When the news of Piper Latham's death was received, his brother, Mr Albert Latham, gave up his business at Croydon and joined the London Scottish for active service.[57]

Five of the six pipers killed during this period are commemorated on the Menin Gate in Ypres, Belgium, along with the names of over 54,000 other servicemen who were killed in action on the Ypres salient and have no known grave. Piper Bennie we know at least had a burial, but four further brutal years of fighting destroyed almost any possibility of identifying graves or bodies buried in these early days of the war. The recovery and reburial of Lance Corporal Chapman's body in 1921 would have provided some comfort to his family and provided them, seven years later, with a sense of closure unattainable to so many others whose loved ones were never found or identified.

For the survivors there now came a period of rest and recuperation, along with the opportunity to begin to process the horrors and intensity of the past few weeks. The *esprit de corps* of the London Scottish, built before the war, played a large part in holding the battalion together when in the line, but now that the men were away from imminent danger, 'the health of some broke down.'[58] Piper William Porteous was diagnosed with one of the first recorded cases of shellshock, having been buried alive by an explosion during the battle at Messines. Drummer James Smail, who had contracted pneumonia, was returned home after a period of hospitalisation, and many others began to assess the situation in which they now found themselves.

Piper Oram would remain in hospital for many months before returning home to join the newly formed 3rd (Reserve) Battalion, then later joining the 2nd Battalion and again embarking overseas. For many other pipers and drummers, a future as an officer beckoned. Casualties amongst officers throughout the war were generally high but were particularly so in the earliest days. London Scots were seen as prime officer material and 'it is a proud boast that through the course of the war more than 2,750 other ranks were commissioned to be officers in the Army, the Royal Navy and in the

---

55   George Heriot's School, *Roll of Honour 1914-1919* (War Memorial Committee: Edinburgh, 1921), p.20.
56   *The Cornishman*, 3 December 1914, p.8.
57   *The Cornishman*, 3 December 1914, p.8.
58   Lindsay (ed.), *The London Scottish in the Great War*, p.49.

Royal Flying Corps.'⁵⁹ More than from any other regiment. For pipers and drummers, a commission was insurance of much better pay and conditions which, after the rigours of Messines and the realisation that the war would certainly not be over by Christmas, must have been especially tempting, particularly for those who had been injured and were about to be released from hospital.

Piper Mackay took a commission in the 8th Battalion, Cameron Highlanders, while Piper Robert Porteous and his brother Piper William Porteous joined the Royal Garrison Artillery and the Royal Army Service Corps respectively. Piper Nicol became an officer in the Labour Corps and Piper Forbes also took a commission, whilst Drummer Sexton joined the West Riding Regiment and then the Royal Flying Corps. Drummer C.W. Piper-Smith joined the 20th London's and Drummer John Arthur Cairns was commissioned into the 8th Argyll and Sutherland Highlanders, Highland Cyclist Battalion, before also transferring to the Royal Flying Corps where he had the dubious 'honour' of being shot down by the German fighter ace the 'Red Baron' Manfred Von Richthofen. Cairns lasted just eight days as a pilot before being shot down. He crashed behind enemy lines whilst von Richthofen flew above him waiving his gauntlet. He was taken prisoner and travelled to a POW camp with Captain Michael Bowes-Lyon, brother of Elizabeth, the future Queen, Queen Mother and Honorary Colonel of the London Scottish Regiment. He was sentenced to 9 years in prison and finally released in 1919. Private Robin Bailes went overseas as a bugler whilst learning the pipes but never got to play with the 1st Battalion band. Injured at Messines, he returned home and joined the 2nd Battalion Pipes and Drums before taking a commission in the 14th Argyll and Sutherland Highlanders and then the Royal Flying Corps. He too was shot down and spent the remainder of the war in hospital, needing 28 operations and losing his right eye and left leg. Drummer Frank Wilkins transferred to the 2nd Battalion, Highland Light Infantry, while Drummer Wallace was commissioned to the 12th Middlesex Regiment and Drummer Sexton to The Duke of Wellingtons Regiment. In fact, of all the pipers and drummers wounded at Messines, only Piper Mackay, who returned briefly to the band before being hospitalised again and taking a commission with the 8th Cameron Highlanders, and Drummer Tovey would return to the ranks to play with the 1st Battalion Pipes and Drums. After being wounded for a third time in 1915, Drummer Tovey would also take up a commission later in the war.

The heroics performed by the 1st Battalion, London Scottish at Messines earned them the signal honour of being attached to the prestigious 1st Guards Brigade, who had themselves been mauled in the early months of the war. Of over 4,000 men from the 1st Coldstream Guards, 1st Scots Guards, 1st Black Watch and 1st Cameron Highlanders, fewer than 500 remained, of whom only five were officers. From nearly 1,000 men who were sent overseas in September, the London Scottish had just 280 to add to that number. A draft of five officers and 187 men arrived from the 2nd Battalion on 28 November, including Piper Machell-Varese, but the battalion remained seriously under strength. Piper Machell-Varese himself lasted only 12 days before receiving a wound that would return him to London.⁶⁰ Sergeant Piper Greig, Pipers Alexander Joss, Mackay and Machell-Varese plus the remaining few drummers, including Drummer Alexander Cleland Cunnison who had arrived with the November draft, paraded with the battalion on 3 December for review by His Majesty, The King, and looked forward to Christmas away from the front line. Unfortunately, on 19 December 1st Brigade was ordered back into the fighting and the following day the London Scottish began a long march that would return them to the front line, where they would stay throughout Christmas and New Year. The battalion had no transportation and so were

---

59 Andrew D. Parsons, 'The Men in Hodden Grey: The London Scottish Regiment' in Paul MacFarland (ed.), *Scots in Great War London: A Community at Home and on the Front Line 1914–1919* (Warwick: Helion and Co. Ltd., 2018), p.52.
60 TNA WO 323: 'Machell-Varese' Soldier's Service Records.

required to march over 30 miles in 24 hours. Sergeant Tovey wrote in his diary on 20 December, 'One sings occasionally [on the march] and our three pipers play us along.'[61] There may only have been half a dozen of the original Pipes and Drums left, but they continued to play an important part in assisting the battalion through difficult circumstances.

A letter from an unidentified London Scottish soldier published in the *Daily Record* on 22 January 1915 states:

> We had the bagpipes going nearly all the way back on our march from the trenches. The French in their trenches could hear them and were tremendously bucked. As the Germans were only 70 yards further on, I expect they heard them also. The pipes are a wonderful help on the march.[62]

Christmas and New Year were spent in wet, cold, and collapsing forward trenches. 'We moved off about 5.30 on the 11th and did about four miles to ____, where we spent the night … On the way it rained and hailed, but we were cheered up by the pipes.'[63] On 14 January, 'our Company went for a short route march, which took the form of a triumphal procession, as we had two pipers.'[64] It would not be until 17 January that the battalion returned to Bethune for a few days of rest but, just three days later they were back in action before finally earning extended relief on 28 January, taken in billets near Lillers. While in the trenches, the 1st Division managed to organise a concert to celebrate Burns Night on 25 January. Men of the Scots Guards, Black Watch, Cameron Highlanders and London Scottish were able to honour this national tradition and, at the end of the evening, 'headed by pipers of the various units went merrily to their billets, ready for the morrow, and all it might bring forth.'[65]

This period of rest and reorganisation presented the first real opportunity to review how best to assign the strength of the battalion in times of war. A headquarters company was formed, along with bombing parties and increased specialisation in other areas. With only three pipers and a similar number of drummers remaining, it became obvious that, for the overall morale of the battalion, the Pipes and Drums needed to be assigned duties that, although not necessarily keeping them out of harm's way, at least kept them slightly removed from the worst of the fighting in the front-line trenches. The unique value of the Pipes and Drums to the regiment in terms of *esprit de corps*, regimental and national identity, and troop efficiency on the march was ingrained into both officers and men. Replacing trained pipers and drummers would not prove to be an easy enterprise, and the attrition rate so far attained could not be sustained. To be blunt, they could no longer be 'wasted' as 'cannon fodder.'

In their new more protected roles, pipers and drummers would lead companies on the march and to and from front line trenches before taking on other responsibilities. They would begin to assume more specialist roles, in addition to their musical duties, mostly as runners and guards for the new headquarters company. Pipe Major Greig also took on an unofficial role to 'act as a kind of bodyguard to Colonel Newington when, as a junior officer, he commanded the Company.'[66] Interestingly, it may have been the case that the Pipes and Drums were intended to work as specialist

---

61 Lieutenant Duncan Tovey unpublished diary, London Scottish Museum Archives entry for 20 December 1914.
62 *Daily Record*, 22 January 1915, p.4.
63 *London Scottish Regiment Gazette*, (1915), p.40.
64 *London Scottish Regiment Gazette*, (1915), p.40.
65 *Newcastle Journal*, 28 January 1915, p.3.
66 *London Scottish Regiment Gazette*, (1948), p.84.

runners/guides, armed with pistols, rather than riflemen, from the beginning. An amendment to Battalion Orders signed by Captain and Adjutant C.H. Campbell, on the eve of sailing for France on 14 September 1914, read:

> No. 12 Pipers, Drummers and Buglers. The Pipers and Drummers mentioned in Battalion Orders of the 10th August, Part II No. 2, will return their rifles to the Q.M.
> All Buglers will carry rifles.[67]

However, haste in deployment to the front line and the necessity for all available officers and men to assist in the fighting at Messines may have rendered this directive impractical. It would not be until 14 December that the Quartermaster's records show that, finally, 'Pistols and holsters issued to Corpl. Piper Greig, Piper Mackay, Piper A. S. Joss'[68] the only three remaining pipers.

These changes of role did not always make the men who managed to avoid the worst of the fighting popular with their peers:

> Specialists did not appear to be very popular ... I don't know why. We had all been in the ranks at Messines – [they] ought to have been sorry for us! Having to undertake a role with which we were unfamiliar ... Anyway, the first day's guard was made up of Specialists from different Sections .... I believe there was one Piper and the rest Signallers.[69]

It is not particularly surprising, however, that those infantrymen left in the trenches, with no option to apply for a commission or perform specialist roles, might have shown resentment towards those spared at least some of the horrors of war.

Drummer Tovey, Sergeant Piper Greig and Piper Mackay were all back in hospital by February 1915 and, shortly after, Mackay left for a commission with the 8th Cameron Highlanders. He would be killed in action on 17 August 1916 leading his men over the top during the Somme offensive. Drummer William Hamilton was hospitalised in March during shelling of the battalion headquarters at Richebourg St Vaast. Hamilton would be evacuated to Great Britain where he saw out the rest of the war in the Pipes and Drums of the 3rd Battalion. Drummer Cunnison was also injured and never returned to the regiment, passing through the Middlesex Regiment and the Labour Corps before becoming a flying officer in the RFC in 1917. This left Piper Joss and Drummer Tovey, who had returned from hospital, as the only remaining members of the Pipes and Drums, before the newly appointed Pipe Major Greig returned some days later. An anonymous letter to the *London Scottish Regimental Gazette* detailed a battalion concert on 28 March in 'the cleanest midden in France', where two officers 'danced an impromptu one-step to the pipes.'[70] Burial of the dead, when possible, continued and a more sober report of the funeral of Corporal J. Kinross, killed by a sniper's bullet on 21 March, is given in *The Advertiser*:

> I arranged for the burial in the little soldiers' cemetery, which one of the regiments out here bought, and all soldiers who have fallen in the fighting round here are buried. The Chaplain

---

67 '1st Battalion Orders: August-September 1914', (London Scottish Museum Archives), p.52.
68 QMS John Gibson, 'Army Book 152, Correspondence Book (Field Service) Sept 1914-Feb 2nd, 1915', London Scottish Museum Archives entry for 14 December 1914, p.29.
69 *London Scottish Regiment Gazette*, (1934), p.244.
70 *London Scottish Regiment Gazette*, (1915), p.108.

From Left: Lance Corporal Piper Latham, Piper Carey and Pipe Major Greig, France, October 1914. Carey and Latham would both be killed in action the following month. (LSMA, used with permission)

J.W. Hepburn, The Band's dug-out in trenches at the Citadel Camp, Bayencourt, The Somme, 4 September 1916. (LSMA, used with permission)

THE PIPES AND DRUMS AT WAR 1914-1919   129

Pipe Major Greig and Piper Joss, the two remaining 1st Battalion pipers, entertaining the crowd at a battalion sports day, 29 April 1915. (LSMA, used with permission)

1st Battalion Pipes and Drums under Pipe Major Edgar in France, April 1916. (LSMA, used with permission)

read the service and Segt-Piper Grey [*sic*], the doctor and myself ... attended as mourners. The whole regiment would have liked to have come ... but we were in the trenches.[71]

A battalion sports day took place on 29 April, with a report stating that 'our two pipers Sgt. Greig and L/Cpl Joss also lent their aid',[72] while a draft of reserves on 23 April brought assistance in the form of Piper Donald S. Pinnington. Unfortunately, he was almost immediately wounded in the leg by a stray round which had been accidentally thrown into an incinerator.[73] This draft also saw the return of ex-piper, now Second Lieutenant, Alfred Cairns-Wilson as acting Officer Commanding, B Company.

2 May saw the few remaining pipers and drummers march the battalion back to the front line for a disastrous assault on Aubers Ridge that was finally launched on 9 May. Further marches took place in successive days to Hingette and then Givenchy, and then on to Bethune. On 14 May, after being relieved from front line trenches at Bethune, an officer wrote, 'Dawn duly broke and shortly after we met Greig and Joss who were waiting to pipe us in. We arrived about 4.30am, dead to the world ....'[74] Lieutenant Higgins, who had arrived in a draft that day and was waiting behind the lines for the London Scottish to come out, wrote:

> Some men moved off – they were pipers setting off to play the Companies out …. Other Companies, surprisingly small in number, went by, and from one of them a voice called out that the 'Scottish' were behind. A quarter of an hour passed, and then the Scottish pipes were heard, faintly at first, then louder as they approached. We stood up in this moment of meeting the 'First' and lined the road. 'A' Company, reduced to the size of a Platoon, came up. We realised the tragedy of numbers.[75]

The next few months of summer saw relative quiet along this stretch of the front and the London Scottish were in and out of trenches but with little action other than regular enemy shelling. During one such episode on 2 July, Lieutenant Cairns-Wilson was seriously injured by shrapnel when he refused to leave his post during an attack. The 24 July saw the loss of Pipe Major Greig when his commission to the Royal Army Ordnance Corps finally came through.

> I have almost forgotten to mention that Ken Greig left us the day we came up here. He piped us part of the way, and when he broke off each platoon cheered him heartily. It was the removal of another landmark.[76]

This 'landmark' meant the pipers were back down to two in number and the death knell for the original pre-war band came ever closer. The regimental history records that 'On August 5th the London Scottish Pipers celebrated the opening of the second year of the war by playing *God Save the King*. The Germans replied with *Wacht am Rhein* and then came a brief exchange of shells and bombs.'[77] Acting Pipe Major Joss and Piper Pinnington, newly released from hospital, would

---

71 'Letter from 2nd Lt. F.A.J. MacFarlane', *The Advertiser,* 9 April 1915, p.3.
72 *London Scottish Regiment Gazette*, (1915), p.133.
73 *London Scottish Regiment Gazette*, (1915), p.263.
74 *London Scottish Regiment Gazette*, (1915), p.148.
75 *London Scottish Regiment Gazette*, (1924), p.22.
76 *London Scottish Regiment Gazette*, (1915), p.213.
77 Lindsay (ed.), *The London Scottish in the Great War*, p.67.

soldier on with Drummer Tovey until the Pipes and Drums finally succumbed to the two-pronged assault of casualties and commissions during the Battle of Loos, which began the following month.

The Battle of Loos represented the British Army's 'big push' of 1915, as it attempted to overcome the stalemate of the trenches and get the war moving again. It was the first time divisions of the 'New Army' were sent into the fighting, amongst which was the 47th (London) Territorials, that included the London Irish Regiment. It was also the first time that the British used poison gas and the battle itself took place over two cold, wet, wintery weeks beginning on 25 September and ending in stalemate on 8 October. British casualties would amount to approximately 50,000 men. The London Scottish, who entered the battle 600 strong, lost five officers and 260 other ranks killed or wounded, including one piper and the last remaining drummer.

The London Scottish were a component of the initial assault as part of 1st Division and one of 12 battalions that, from a strength of over 10,000 men, would take 8,000 casualties in the first four hours alone. An unnamed officer, writing in the *Regimental Gazette*, reported that, after going over the top, two companies:

> 'D' and 'A' (who lost a lot), reformed and we marched on with a piper prepared to play, but he got a bullet through the arm and retired from the battle delighted, saying 'Ma word, ma lad, bit I've got a beauty.'[78]

This was Piper Pinnington who, having been returned to the fighting after his initial wound earlier in 1915, now had a 'Blighty' wound which would see him evacuated home and a period in hospital in Chichester.[79] His delight at being away from the horrors of the frontline is obvious, and he ensured that he would never have to return by taking up a commission in the Royal Navy on his eventual release from hospital.

Drummer Tovey, who had already been wounded and hospitalised twice, was also wounded on the first day of fighting and returned to Britain. He would eventually take up a commission with the 6th Duke of Cambridge's Own, Middlesex Regiment, in February 1917. Rising to the rank of Captain, he would go on to be awarded the Military Cross for conspicuous bravery.

On the evening of this same opening day of battle, the lone remaining piper, Sergeant Piper Joss, was earning his laurels performing his duties as a runner during the chaos of battle. In the early hours of 26 September, the London Scottish had been relieved from their position in the German trenches which they had successfully captured and returned to the original British firing trenches. They had to march back past their dead comrades, whose bodies still lay in no man's land. Rations had been ordered up to them by 2nd Brigade headquarters, but the ration party had been unable to find them in the darkness and had returned to headquarters at Vermelles.

> At Vermelles they found Piper Joss of the Scottish, who had been sent back with a message. Thereupon Captain Webb insisted on breaking away with his party ... and, with Piper Joss as guide, found the Battalion in the old British front line. It is believed that few, if any, of the other troops engaged got their rations before the night of the 26th.[80]

After sustaining heavy losses of 265 officers and men, the London Scottish were finally pulled out of the fighting on 1 October and a thankful soldier wrote:

---

78 *London Scottish Regiment Gazette*, (1915), p.271.
79 *The Motherwell Times*, 8 October 1915, p.5.
80 Lindsay (ed.), *The London Scottish in the Great War*, p.80.

Got out of it at 1 a.m. and struggled to a village not far back. J ___ played the pipes and we were all cheered up considerable-like. Beards were removed and we were quite cheerful by mid-day when we moved further back to where we are now.[81]

In his book, *Cannonfodder: An Infantryman's Life on the Western Front*, Stuart Dolden wrote of the same event:

> The piper met us on the way down and though we were weary and spent, it was marvellous how the skirl of the pipes put new strength into us and gave us just that little extra strength to get to our destination.[82]

It is undeniable, then, that even one solitary piper was able to make a considerably positive impression in such desperate times.

Relief would again be temporary, and the battalion moved up to the front line again on 7 October for one last, short-lived, attack on 13 October, before being withdrawn at dawn the following day. In other sectors of the same battlefield, the 2nd Battalion, Highland Light Infantry and 12th Middlesex Regiment found themselves at the heart of the action, and two young officers laid down their lives. Ex-drummer Frank Wilkins was killed in action on 9 October whilst serving with the Highland Light Infantry; he was 20 years old. Two weeks later, on 21 October, Second Lieutenant and ex-drummer Walter Wallace of the Duke of Cambridge's Own, Middlesex Regiment also made the ultimate sacrifice.

In early October, Pipe Major Joss was to return to Britain on leave and, whilst home, followed the path of Pipe Major Greig in securing a commission in the Army Ordnance Department. He would be returned to France almost immediately, and a letter home from a London Scottish officer states that, on 14 October, 'At lunch we were joined by J ___, ex-piper and now a man of note in the Ordnance Dept.'[83]

And, with that, the 1st Battalion London Scottish Pipes and Drums were no more. The battalion would now be without pipers and drummers for the first time in their existence. Thankfully, this situation was not to last long, and plans were already in place to begin reforming the band and ensuring that the casualty levels would never again reach the heights of the first full year of war. The colonel and senior officers of the London Scottish were acutely aware of the importance of the Pipes and Drums and set about sending over pipers and drummers from the 2nd Battalion with the next draft, which arrived at the end of October. The diary of Private Donald Bliss records details of how two pipers in this draft passed the time while travelling by train to France: 'Later the pipers putting away their set of chess, produced their reeds for a spot of Scottish music.'[84]

At the same time, in France, Captains Patterson and Worlock were already taking a keen interest in rebuilding the Pipes and Drums and called for willing volunteers from within the ranks. 'Freddie' Worlock who, as band president, 'had the honour of being nursemaid to the First Battalion Band during the war …'[85] and 'Pattie' Paterson, who would go on to be Commanding

---

81 *London Scottish Regiment Gazette*, (1915), p.271.
82 Stuart A. Dolden, *Cannonfodder: An Infantryman's Life on the Western Front, 1914-18* (Poole, Dorset: Blandford Press, 1980), p.35.
83 *London Scottish Regiment Gazette*, (1915), p.270.
84 Private Donald Bliss, (unpublished diary, London Scottish Regimental Archives, September 1914 to July 1916), p.71.
85 *London Scottish Regiment Gazette*, (1937), p.154.

Officer of the 1st Battalion later in the war, both saw the importance of the Pipes and Drums to the regiment. In fact, as Pipe Major Robertson, writing in April 1916 states:

> The London Scottish have been most fortunate in this, that the Officers who have held highest rank in the Battalion have always considered the Pipe Band to be a most important part of the Regiment and have taken the keenest interest in its duties and equipment.[86]

Patterson asked his wife to send out nine practise chanters 'with reeds and some music of simple tunes from McDougal of Aberfeldy' and the volunteers 'practised dolefully, some distance from our billets and discreetly downwind, until, at last, promoted to the fellowship of the re-formed Band.'[87] Piper Robert Marshal would be the first of them.

> I remember L/Cpl. Piper Edgar and two others arriving with a draft to the 1st Battalion at Lilliers about the beginning of November 1915. …. On the day Edgar came I was transferred from the ranks to Piper, so when the Battalion marched to Loos four pipers played them up.
> Edgar soon gathered more pipers and drummers and a pipe band worthy of the Scottish gradually came into being, he being promoted Pipe-Major.[88]

In fact, Lance Corporal Piper Harry Ferguson Edgar had arrived some weeks prior and 'joined in time to play the Battalion from the trenches after the attack of October 13th.'[89]

Private Morgan of 'D' Company wrote, in a letter home dated 27 October 1915:

> We … must have been a curious sight. Different sorts of headgear (some German helmets), scraps of equipment welded to torn uniforms with thick mud, unshaven and very dirty, we marched along singing to the tune of the bagpipes.[90]

Edgar (listed as Piper Eggar) is also included on the programme as playing a set to open the battalion Hallowe'en dinner which took place in Lilliers on 31 October. Thus, the battalion was technically only without any pipers and drummers for a matter of a few weeks, but the ability to hold a chanter or a pair of drumsticks does not immediately a musician make, and this period was not to be without its difficulties. The new band played the battalion back up to the front on Sunday 14 November and a report 'From the Ranks' ironically remarked 'We now have four young pipers and I am afraid it is true that it takes years to learn the pipes.'[91]

The march back from the trenches on Sunday 21 November and the effect on the men was reported in even more brutal fashion:

> In fact, we have a young piper who has not yet learned to play, and when we met him and he started 'making noises' he was actually 'yelled at' from the Company. Generally, we are glad to meet a piper when we come out of the trenches, to help us on the way a bit, but we were all so tired out that we would have yelled at anything. In fact, before we got here, there were calls of 'What about a halt?' etc., from the Company, and cries of 'Shut up' each time the piper

---

86 *London Scottish Regiment Gazette* (1916), p.112.
87 *London Scottish Regiment Gazette* (1954), p.121.
88 *London Scottish Regiment Gazette* (1951), p.74.
89 *London Scottish Regiment Gazette* (1916), p.123.
90 *London Scottish Regiment Gazette* (1996), p.50.
91 *London Scottish Regiment Gazette* (1915), p.296.

started. I have never seen the Company show their feelings so much before, and the end of the Company trailed out to a few men to each ten or twenty yards of road.[92]

Such reports portray the importance to the regiment, and its serving soldiers, of maintaining a first-class pipe band, and the newly installed Pipe Major Edgar made it his duty to bring one about as quickly as possible.

The 1st Battalion would remain at the front from November 1915 until January 1916, with tours in the trenches followed by 'maximum' periods of rest. Piper William Keith was one of the two other pipers who arrived with Edgar in October (the other being Piper William Warren Zambra) and, whilst acting as a runner during this period, he was buried in a collapsed shelter in forward trenches by a shell explosion and had to be dug out.[93] The weather was horrendous and the stalemate of trench warfare depressing, despite low casualties, but a much more positive description of the importance of the pipers from this time states:

> To struggle out of the muddy trenches in the autumn of 1915 in France, and across the dreary land to flop down on a waterlogged road and go to sleep until all had assembled. Then to form up, heavy with mud and fatigue, behind the Coy Piper who had come to lead us out. At the first skirl of the pipes some of the tiredness fell from the weary bodies and legs took up the old swing. Like a mother hen gathering her brood, the song of the pipes took us to our rest.[94]

A second report during this difficult period declares:

> After a turn in the trenches, unwashed or shaved, covered with mud, tired and hungry, thirsty in spite of all the water about, the men were on the verge of exhaustion when they were relieved. It was then that the big effort was necessary.
> The move was by Company and tired as they were, when the Company Piper filled his pipe bag and the lilting skirl of the pipes filled the air, the spirit of the men rose and the heavy feet took on a full swing as they got into step.[95]

However, as is the norm with soldiers, battlefield humour was still to be found even in these trying conditions. Piper Marshall would recollect:

> On the afternoon of Christmas Day, 1915, three pipers, of whom I was one, went into the trenches at Loos, and after playing at our Battalion H.Q., proceeded to the front line, where we played some selections for the benefit of the Germans, whose trenches were very close at this point.
> Having finished our performance, my friends and I proceeded on our way back, and presently, passing some men of another regiment, were asked by one of them: 'Was that you playin them bloomin toobs?' We admitted it. 'Ear that, Joe?' he remarked to his pal, 'These blokes ave bin givin the Uns a toon.'
> 'Serve em right' said Joe, 'they started the blinkin war.'[96]

---

92 *London Scottish Regiment Gazette*, (1916), p.20.
93 *London Scottish Regiment Gazette*, (1963), p.74.
94 *London Scottish Regiment Gazette*, (1978), p.61.
95 Bliss unpublished diary, p.104.
96 'The Best 500 Cockney War Stories', *The Evening Standard News*, (London: 1921).

It was imperative that the Pipes and Drums stepped up to expectations. Extensive practise and the ability to have the band together as a unit during this period and in the months to follow soon brought about noticeable improvement and, under Pipe Major Edgar's leadership, 'The Band was then formed and drummers instituted, and the Battalion is now justly proud of it.'[97]

The New Year was to bring big changes to the battalion. 15 January 1916 saw the entire 1st Division moved away from the front for an extended period of rest and training. The current battalion strength was fewer than 250 men, with more being lost to casualties and commissions than were being renewed in drafts. Only 56 men remained of the original 800 that had left on the SS *Winifredian* less than one and a half a years earlier, with Piper Marshall being one of them. With this in mind, it was decided that the battalion needed time to return to full strength and that their experience as veterans of the front was better served in supporting the formation of a new division, the 56th (London), consisting of mostly un-blooded Territorial soldiers from London. Both officers and men were disappointed at having to leave the prestigious 1st Division, but this was tempered by the knowledge that they would gain an extended period of respite from the trenches.

On 6 February, Brigadier-General Reddie, GOC 1st Brigade, 1st Division and General Rawlinson, GOC of the newly-formed Fourth Army, both addressed the men of 1st Battalion. Reddie 'made a short speech of farewell, and the pipers played The General Salute.'[98] Two days later, 'headed by the pipers of the Camerons and Black Watch, the London Scottish marched to the railway to entrain for Pont Remy.'[99]

Over the next three and a half months, the battalion would be brought up to strength amid intensive training for the coming summer's campaigning in what would in due course be remembered as the Battle of the Somme. More drummers and pipers were trained from the ranks and others arrived with drafts, while further changes were made to their specialist duties. Captain Patterson wrote a letter to Captain Whyte, his counterpart in the 2nd Battalion back in the UK, who was looking for advice on how to make best use of their own Pipes and Drums when they came to be deployed overseas. The letter provides an invaluable first-hand account of the situation in May 1916:

> Bugles we don't use, but in their place we are trying to raise a strong band!
> Our pipers play Reveille and Lights out and the full band on marches and at Retreat. Skinny Anderson, Worlock are here and they say, 'it is the best Tonic in the world.' They wear diced hose and glengarry bonnets with cock feathers.
> We support 3 side drum
>   1 big drum
>   And all the pipers you can muster
> We keep our band out of the Trenches and use them as extra stretcher bearers if required in action.
> When nothing much on they help sort the mail etc.[100]

---

97 *London Scottish Regiment Gazette*, (1916), p.123.
98 Dolden, *Cannonfodder*, p.58.
99 *The London Scottish in the Great War*, ed. Lindsay, p.94.
100 'Correspondence between R. Whyte and Captain J. Peterson [sic] regarding Bugles, Pipes and Drums, 24 May 1916', F.5, Transfer Procedures, Box 9, WWI 1914-18 Official Documents, 2/14Bn London Scottish, University Library Archives and Research Collection, McMaster University, Canada.

This role as stretcher bearers, with additional roles as runners when needed during action, would continue throughout the remaining years of the war. The band was assigned to HQ Company and spent much more time together as a unit. In effect, their specialist role resorted to being primarily pipers and drummers when out of action, with guard duties and other rear-echelon commitments as required. The positive impact for the men themselves was a reduction in their chances of becoming casualties and an increase in time to practise and train to become a band of high quality, with the increased numbers to be effective. The impact on the battalion was of increased cohesion and *esprit de corps*, as well as musical assistance to and from the trenches and on long marches, in addition to the pride in Scottish and regimental identity which came with adherence to national tradition. On a purely practical level, it also provided an additional number of stretcher bearers who were invaluable during action. As spring came to an end that action was approaching fast.

Preparation and training for the Somme offensive continued at pace through the early days of summer 1916, and the 1st Battalion was brought back up to strength with over 850 officers and men. Pipe Major Edgar transferred from the band at the end of May to take up a commission within the 1st Battalion and his place was taken by Corporal Piper Keith, who would remain in this role until the summer of 1918. Known, as 'Baby', Keith was only 20 when he was appointed Pipe Major 'and looked about 17 years old.'[101] More drummers and pipers arrived with further drafts, in addition to volunteers trained up through the ranks, and 'Keith was the main force in the welding of a somewhat motley mob into the semblance of a proper band.'[102] Pipe Major Keith was instrumental in building on the strong foundations that Pipe Major Edgar had left him and:

> Under Keith the band grew in size and in efficiency, and from that time onwards, despite casualties and departures for commissions, the Battalion always had a corps of pipers and drummers of which it could be proud.[103]

Some pipers and drummers continued in their battlefield role as runners, with the rest now trained as stretcher bearers when in action and wore armbands to denote this. The battalion had a total of 21 stretcher-bearers at the Somme and around half of these were from the Pipes and Drums.

During this period, ex-piper, now Captain, 'Duggie' Lyall-Grant became a POW in the most bizarre of fashions:

> Stationed away from the Front as an embarkation officer at Boulogne, he had been home briefly on leave in Wimbledon, and set out after breakfast to return by aeroplane from Farnborough. His pilot, on his first trip to France, got lost, inadvertently crossed over into German-occupied territory and they were duly shot at. Believing they were on course for St Omer, and this must have been 'friendly fire' from their own side, they decided the safest thing was to land in the nearest field. 'Little did I think', wrote Lyall Grant ruefully, in a diary from which the Regimental Gazette published extracts in the 1920s, 'on leaving home yesterday morning that by seven I should be in German hands.' The illicit diary – an extraordinary 50,000 words … was eventually sewn into his kilt waistband and inside his bagpipes so he could smuggle it out when he was freed in April 1918.[104]

---

101 *London Scottish Regiment Gazette*, (1950), p.43.
102 *London Scottish Regiment Gazette*, (1963), p.74.
103 *London Scottish Regiment Gazette*, (1963), p.74.
104 Parsons, 'The Men in Hodden Grey', p.60.

The Somme offensive was a series of engagments that took place over 141 days from 1 July through 18 November 1916 involving over three million men, from both sides, of whom over one million would be killed or injured. It remains one of the largest and bloodiest campaigns in human history. The objective was to take the German salient around Gommecourt and thus open up the Western Front to a moving war once again. The first day of battle remains the costliest single day of warfare in British history with over 57,000 casualties, and 19,240 men killed in action. The casualties of the 1st Battalion, London Scottish would be disproportionately large, even by these horrendous standards. Of the 854 officers and men who went into battle that first day, only nine officers, 236 other ranks and all 21 stretcher-bearers would remain that evening.

Final training for the 1st Battalion took place at Pas-en-Artois, finishing up on 26 June, with the expected attack date set for the 28 June, although bad weather set the date back to 1 July. The battalion, led by the Pipes and Drums, were famously photographed and captured on cine camera at this time by photographer Ernest Brooks and British film director Geoffrey Malins, who had both been assigned roles by the War Office to capture the action at the Somme. By October 1916 it is estimated that over 20 million British people had seen Malins' film *The Battle of the Somme* and witnessed the Pipes and Drums lead the 1st Battalion, London Scottish into action. Brookes' photographs clearly display the Pipes and Drums, senior officers and A Company marching through the north-west outskirts of Pas-en-Artois. Pipe Major Keith, Pipers John Foulis, Zambra, Marshall, Alexander Cornell and Ralston Gordon, along with bass Drummer Charles Hull and side Drummers John H. Risdale, David S. Middleton and Robert Wallace Somerville are all clearly identifiable. The reclassification of roles meant that all these men would survive the terrible first day of battle, although as runners and stretcher-bearers, the horrors they witnessed and would have to live with are beyond imagining.

> For while the great value of its pipe-band to a regiment on active service is taken as a truism, few, other than the pipers (and drummers), themselves, appreciate what it takes to measure up to what is expected of them.[105]

The work of the stretcher-bearers was particularly commendable as they waited on the battlefield on the evening of the battle to carry off any wounded men who managed to crawl back towards British positions. Through their efforts, many lives were saved.

Despite their terrible loses, the battalion were back in the trenches the following evening and would stay there for the next four days. Rest was short as they were again brought forward on 10 July and were not finally relieved until the 17 July, going into divisional reserve at Bayencourt, where a large draft of men, including drummers and pipers, brought the strength of the battalion back up to about 500. Whilst deployed in the trenches at this time, Piper Alexander Alan Connell was severely wounded by shellfire.

During this period, word came through that the London Scottish Regiment was, finally, to be affiliated with the Highland regiment with whom they had maintained strong ties since the 1880s. The *Daily Graphic* reported that:

> A landmark in the history of the London Scottish is the announcement that by Royal Warrant, dated July 12th, the regiment is affiliated to the Gordon Highlanders … Now they are affiliated to a regiment with which they have complete affinity.[106]

---

105 *London Scottish Regiment Gazette* (1963), p.74.
106 *Daily Graphic*, 7 August 1916, p.4.

On the evening of Saturday 21 July whilst in reserve and recovering from the fighting, the band held a dinner and the following first-hand account by one of the attendees provides an excellent insight into the mindset of the members of the Pipes and Drums three years into the war:

> Since the advent of the Battalion in this sanguine country (now ancient history), many momentous events have been placed on record, but surely none more worthily than the Band Dinner … The mirthful musicians assembled in one of the village estaminets and sat down 16 strong (and willing). Zero was at 8.15pm, and every objective accomplished with astounding vigour [sic] ('What a hungry crowd!').
>
> A great reception was accorded to the late Pipe-Major Edgar, who had rejoined the Battalion (not specially) the same day, as an officer, upon his taking the chair. Likewise, there were roars of clap after his able speech, in which he rather lamented his elevated status, and hoped he would still be privileged to meet us sometimes as a comrade (privilege granted). An even great ovation was given to Piper Copeland upon his resuming his seat (he is our prime orator), after his unrivalled eloquence over no one knows what.
>
> Pipe-Major Keith proposed 'The King', after which no excuses were required. Piper Willie Cowie treated the company to a little inspiring music on the pipes, and Bob Marshall an action song, 'Willie brewed a peck o' maut', the troops supplying the actions (there was Scotch wine by Messrs. Dewar and Walker, and the wine of France).
>
> The party dispersed after singing the 'Evening Hymn' – and we'd a long march next morning![107]

Over the next month, the battalion would be in and out of trenches at Hébuterne before entraining for St Riquier on 22 August and marching to Drucat for extensive training for the next big push. There was even time for the Pipes and Drums to play at church parade on Monday 4 September, although this was cut short when orders came for the battalion to move up to the front. During this time, news came through that on 17 August in fierce fighting further along the line, ex-piper, now Second Lieutenant C.W.D. MacKay of the 8th Cameron Highlanders had been killed in action.

A sketch by J.W. Hepburn shows the band dug out, used during the fighting, located in the transport lines at 'The Citadel' near Frégicourt and the front at Morval. An unknown officer wrote that 'It was while confined at the transport lines by the aggravation of a long-standing complaint that I was relieved at 'solo', of several weeks army pay by these expert makers of music.'[108]

Fighting commenced on 3 September and by the evening of the 5 September, in torrential rain, the 1st Battalion had made their way to the front. Not to trenches for once, as the British push had advanced into open land, but to a small wood and then in support of the London Irish Rifles who had sustained heavy casualties holding off a German counter-attack. Here they would stay until relieved on 8 September but immediately went back into heavy fighting the following day in an attempt to take and hold a German strong point known as the Quadrilateral. Over 100 men of the London Scottish would become casualties, including Piper Henry Woodcock, who was killed in action, aged 21. He had only joined the battalion overseas on 19 July, less than two months prior to his death. Piper William Pratt was also seriously wounded in the same fighting, being hit by shrapnel from a shell. He suffered extensive damage to his face and right arm and was permanently blinded. He arrived at the 1st Battalion position in France five days after Piper Woodcock and was wounded just 51 days later. Their adjoining Regimental Numbers were 6951 and 6952 and

---

107 *London Scottish Regiment Gazette*, (1917), p.123.
108 *London Scottish Regiment Gazette*, (1920), p.163.

they went through training together in the 3rd Battalion before being posted to the 1st Battalion in France.

The 1st Battalion were relieved the following day and were out of the fighting until the 15 September when they were brought up to Angle Wood where they remained, mostly in reserve, until 25 September for the assault on Combles and Morval. The advance was most successful but came at the cost of 4 officers and 50 other ranks. One of these officers was ex-piper, Second Lieutenant Alfred Cairns-Wilson, who was 40 years old and was posthumously awarded the Military Cross for his bravery.

The 1st Battalion were withdrawn from the fighting on 26 September and marched back to Ville-sur-Corbie, where they had been promised an extended period or rest and recuperation after months at the front. They reached Corbie on 29 September:

> But scarcely were our packs shed before an orderly Sergeant arrived with the news that the Battalion was to return up the line the next day. At first the intimation was hailed as a joke in very poor taste, but it soon became evident that this time rumours were right. Next morning we retraced our steps 'fucked off, fed up and far from home.' After a while the route led downhill, where the Regimental Headquarters were, to halt and the band formed up on the right. From my vantage point in the rear I saw the Battalion below. As the first notes of *Heilan Laddie* struck up, a sort of shiver seemed to pass through the marching lines and in an instant the rather reluctant trudge had become smart and purposeful. I can still feel a thrill of pride at the thought.[109]

Written 50 years after the event, this anonymous soldier's account poignantly brings home, once again, the huge impact the Pipes and Drums had on the moral and *esprit de corps* of the London Scottish.

The weather continued to be horrendous and the shelling constant as the men dug trenches in preparation for another assault on 6 October, by which point they had not slept under shelter for more than a month and had 'began to approach the limit of human endurance.'[110] The attack was made but with the battalions on both flanks being decimated by machine-gun fire, the London Scottish took heavy casualties and returned to their trenches. Thankfully, this engagement marked the last action of the 1st Battalion at the Somme and the men were relieved from the trenches on 8 October and given two weeks rest at Frémont.

Over 531 men were killed and injured in these four weeks of fighting, including Pipers Ian Grieve and Alec Patterson who were both wounded. Grieve returned to Britain where he was eventually discharged in May 1918, having never fully recovered from his wounds, while Patterson recovered and took a commission in the Scottish Rifles. Piper Connell, who had been wounded back in July, died in hospital of his wounds on 29 September. Further casualties were taken amongst the drummers and once again the Pipes and Drums paid a heavy price, although less brutally then in previous years of the war. The 1st Battalion, in total, took over 1,000 casualties during the Somme offensive, more than an entire battalion strength. The *Regimental History* states that:

> Despite this tremendous strain the Battalion had done very well indeed. It won honour in every operation and stood out pre-eminently as a Battalion that never lost its spirit and was always ready to perform whatever task was assigned to it.[111]

---

109 *London Scottish Regiment Gazette*, (1966), p.137.
110 *The London Scottish in the Great War*, ed. Lindsay, p.132.
111 Lindsay (ed.), *The London Scottish in the Great War*, p.133.

1st Battalion entertained by the Pipes and Drums whilst trench digging at Mont St. Eloi, 2 April 1918. (LSMA, used with permission)

1st Battalion Pipes and Drums under Pipe Major Gordon, in front of the ruins of Arras Cathedral, shortly before marching to their final battle of the First World War, 1 November 1918. (LSMA, used with permission)

1st Battalion Pipes and Drums under Pipe Major MacHattie, Hilden, Germany, March 1919. (LSMA, used with permission)

The 1st Battalion's final homecoming, marching from Charing Cross Station to Regimental Headquarters, 59 Buckingham Gate through huge crowds, 16 May 1919. (LSMA, used with permission)

With the battalion once again decimated, an extended period of rest and reorganisation was required. It got just ten days, before moving north to take over a section of the line near the border with Belgium. After an initial warm welcome by German artillery, the front here remained relatively peaceful through a very wet and miserable winter in trenches that needed considerable work to repair. However, 'compared with the weeks on the Somme battle-ground this time in the Laventie sector was a holiday from the enemy's shot and shell.'[112]

While out of the line, extensive training took place including lengthy route marches with pipers and drummers fully utilised. With the band starting the day with reveille undertaking full training with the rest of the battalion and other regular duties during the day, performing at battalion and company 'Smokers', officers' and sergeants' mess dinners and other entertainments in the evenings and then playing *Lights Out*, it was a long and arduous day. But any day in reserve was better than a day in the trenches. The band, as it would have done at home, took a central part in the Hallowe'en dinner and concert and an even bigger role in the Hogmanay concert, held in 'Bow Bells Hall' on 30 December. The band played together three times during the evening, whilst Piper Harold Davidson danced a highland fling, Piper Marshall sang *I'm Courtin' Bonnie Leezie Lindsay* and various mini-band groupings accompanied the dancing of foursome reels and the singing of traditional songs.

Shortly after New Year 1917, Piper Zambra would return to Great Britain and in June was commissioned into the Suffolk Regiment, before transferring to the Yorkshire Hussars in early 1918. Zambra was the grandson of Joseph Warren Zambra of Negretti and Zambra Optics and Instruments and worked for the family firm before signing up with the Scottish. Many of the field binoculars, telescopes and gun sights used by the British Army were made in their factories after they were engaged by the Ministry of Munitions. Attesting, again, to the quality and breadth of skills and knowledge within the Pipes and Drums, is the following remembrance from Major (later Lieutenant Colonel) Patterson. A senior officer from 1st Corps had sent out an enquiry asking if any battalions happened to have an officer with expertise in telescopes:

> The message asked for a skilled officer – we replied that we had a skilled piper! We were recipients of a furious message – they thought we were pulling their legs! So I sent Zambra (of Negretti and Zambra) escorted by an officer; and received apologies and thanks.[113]

Piper Zambra carved onto his practise chanter the name of every town and village the battalion stopped at during his time with the London Scottish, creating a wonderful physical documentation of the activities of the Pipes and Drums at this point in the war.

Further recruitment from the ranks, in addition to pipers and drummers arriving with drafts from the 3rd Battalion, meant that the band was now larger and more competent that at any point since Messines. One of the pipers that arrived in January 1917 was Piper Gordon Allan, who would stay with the battalion through to war's end. Piper Morrie Mills would later say of him:

> His initiation to the line was as a battle-runner, and, despite the wounding of one of the four pipers on their way to their assignment, the unperturbability, which was one of his marked assets, was quite unruffled, and he proved to be a very dependable and capable soldier.[114]

---

112 Lindsay (ed.), *The London Scottish in the Great War*, p.137.
113 *London Scottish Regiment Gazette*, (1951), p.109.
114 *London Scottish Regiment Gazette*, (1961), p.31.

The action that this account describes took place during the Battle of Arras, which would again see heavy casualties for both the battalion and the Pipes and Drums.

The new year brought new optimism on the Western Front and a series of advances along the line. A major offensive was planned for the spring in an attempt to break through the German Hindenburg Line, with British forces concentrated in the region around Arras. After a series of marches beginning on 9 March 1917 the 1st Battalion, London Scottish arrived behind their pipers and drummers at Ivergny for two weeks of intensive training. 27 March saw them continue on to Agny, where they spent five days digging assembly trenches during the night to avoid detection, before moving up to Achicourt on 1 April and more assembly trench digging. On the morning of 3 April, the British began a six-day constant bombardment of German positions in preparation for the attack which would begin on Easter Monday, 9 April.

The 1st Battalion proved their worth once again as a first-class fighting force, advancing over 1,400 metres of no man's land, through the mud and detritus of more than two years of warfare and a fierce barrage of enemy machine-gun and artillery fire. They took their primary objectives with relatively light casualties, capturing nearly 300 German soldiers and large quantities of weapons, ammunition and stores. One of those injured on that first day of battle was Piper Morrie Mills, who had recently been sent out to France and who would go on to play an important role in the Pipes and Drums over the next three decades.

Piper Mills had begun his service with the London Scottish as Drummer Mills, joining the 2nd Battalion, very much underage, on 5 November 1914 during the excitement after Messines. He was only 16 years old, yet still made full corporal by early 1915. Having lied about his age, he volunteered for service overseas and was sent to France, as a fledgling piper, with the 2nd Battalion in June 1916. The 2nd Battalion wished to send the largest contingent of Pipes and Drums as possible, and senior officers understood their importance on and off the battlefield. Corporal Piper Mills 'dropped a rank to become Piper in 1916 at the CO's request in order that the 2nd Battalion might go abroad in June 1916 with a full complement of six pipers.'[115] When Piper Mills' father heard of his deployment, he wrote a stern letter to the regimental colonel, requesting that Morrie be sent home:

> Dear Sir
> I am writing to ask that you will give orders for my son 3466 Piper M E Mills to come back to England until he attains the age of 19 years (27th June 1917). He should not have been sent up to the front until then according to army regulations, most especially as he is short-sighted.
> Trusting … that you will attend to this matter.
> Yours obediently
> A J Mills
> PS. He was in trenches in France the last letter he sent his mother.[116]

Piper Mills was duly sent back to Britain before the forthcoming battle of Vimy Ridge and remained in reserve with the 3rd Battalion until volunteering at the earliest opportunity to be sent back to France with a draft to join the 1st Battalion Pipes and Drums in early 1917. His injury at Arras was not severe enough for a return to England, and he would remain overseas with the Pipes and Drums through to 1919.

---

115 *London Scottish Regiment Gazette*, (1997), p.29.
116 TNA WO 364: 'Letter dated August 3rd, 1916, from A. J. Mills to Colonel, Headquarters, 14th London Scottish Regt', Mills, Maurice, E., record 11442. War Office: Soldiers' Documents, First World War 'Burnt Documents', Microfilm Copies.

Piper Mills would have been evacuated back to Arras with the other casualties. The rest of the battalion did not get relieved until the afternoon of 11 April and, even then, had to march through a driving snowstorm to open trenches with no cover, before heading back into the fighting the following day and staying in trenches in Cojeul in horrendous weather until relieved on 19 April:

> The march down to Arras was a very trying one, owing to everyone being so thoroughly tired out, but when we found the Company piper waiting at Beaurains to 'pipe' us the remainder of our way, it was remarkable to see the effort everyone made to 'buck up', and 'D' Company arrived at our billets in good spirits.[117]

They were back on the march on 24 April and continued moving until the 28 April in a complete circle which took them back to divisional reserve in Arras. Action would soon find them again, however, and the 1st Battalion would move back into front line trenches on the evening of 3 May, near Guémappe, immediately coming under heavy and deadly accurate enemy artillery fire that would continue for two weeks duration.

> The pipe band, who were acting as stretcher-bearers, suffered severe losses during this period, the relay aid post which they manned receiving a direct hit from a high explosive shell.[118]

Om 13 May, several unnamed drummers and Piper Davidson were injured in this attack, which also saw Pipers Campbell and Paton both killed. Piper Simon 'Sam' Campbell was 19 years old from Lochboisdale on the Isle of South Uist in the Outer Hebrides and had been working as a footman in Chelsea before enlisting in February 1916. He was sent overseas to join the 1st Battalion Pipes and Drums on 10 December 1916. Piper Andrew Buchanan Paton was a civil servant before the war, having moved from Glasgow to join the London Telephone Department. He enlisted in the London Scottish in October 1914 and became B Company piper on joining the 1st Battalion in France. He was 26 years old when he was killed.

It is worth noting that the only known reference to a London Scottish piper playing troops 'over the top' during the First World War comes during this period. Colonel Duncan Bennett, who had been a drummer in the Pipes and Drums when first joining the London Scottish in 1914 wrote, in an obituary for Pipe Major Keith in 1963, 'He played HQ Coy over the top in 1917 at Arras.'

The obituary goes on to say:

> He would surely have thought that this was the highest valedictory tribute that the Regiment could pay him, that we recall, and honour him for all that is implicit in that simple statement of fact – he played his Coy over the top.[119]

From 17 May to 10 June, the 1st Battalion had three weeks of extended rest and training prior to moving back into divisional reserve at Archicourt, where they stayed until 20 June before heading back into the line east of Arras. They would remain here in the monotony of trench-life on a relatively quiet front until 22 July when training began for the Third Battle of Ypres. Twelfth August found the London Scottish in reserve at Dickebusch, only a few kilometres from where the war

---

117 *London Scottish Regiment Gazette*, (1918), p.78.
118 Lindsay (ed.), *The London Scottish in the Great*, p.146.
119 Obituary for P.M. William Patterson Keith, M.V.O, *London Scottish Regiment Gazette*, (1963), p.74.

had begun for them back in October 1914 at Messines. The battalion was at full strength with over 1,000 officers and men:

> The band, too, had increased in proportion. It had always been the ambition of successive Commanding Officers to have one piper per platoon, and this was almost realised on leaving Dickebusch, when thirteen out of sixteen platoons marched out each with a piper at its head.[120]

With a similarly sized contingent of side, tenor and bass drummers, this was the largest the Pipes and Drums had been since arriving overseas three years earlier and it would stay at such size for the remainder of the war. A growth in personnel allowed the band to play an increasingly active role within the battalion both in and out of action.

This began with movement up to the front line on 16 August but, after severe loses in other units of 56th Division, the 1st Battalion was held back from participation in the Battle of Langemarck, a sub-battle of the Third Ypres campaign, and returned to Dickebusch camp. They then marched to Moulle before being informed that they would entrain for Bapaume and the Somme on 30 August. Here they would stay in a relatively quiet stretch of the front at Lagnicourt for another three weeks before the Battle of Cambrai began on 20 November. The London Scottish involvement was heavy and lasted from 22 November to 30 November, with many casualties resulting from fending off the furious German counter-attack that came after the initial British tank-led assault faltered. Ex-Pipe Major, now Second Lieutenant Edgar was injured on 24 November with the *Dumfries and Galloway Standard* reporting that Edgar 'had passed through the dressing station that day suffering from wounds to the head and arms, but that he appeared to be bright and cheerful.'[121] He was, however, seriously wounded and was evacuated back to the UK. His substantial contribution to the Pipes and Drums, the regiment and his country, finally at an end.

HQ Company, including all members of the Pipes and Drums, were heavily involved in the fighting when infiltrating German infantry stormed British trenches containing the 1st Battalion's headquarters. The battalion lost 363 killed, injured or missing and 'had had a trying task, but they had held their own, and they had done not a little to avert the disaster which threatened the whole British front before Cambrai.'[122] The winter of 1917-18 would see a further sustained German counter-offensive and the 1st Battalion would be in the midst of this defensive action.

On 3 December, the Pipes and Drums began marching the battalion from Cambrai to the Vimy area of the front. Three initial days on the road before entraining and then further days of marching saw the London Scottish arrive, on 7 December, in brigade reserve at Écurie. The battalion would spend most of the next three months here, in a sector of the front line that remained relatively quiet. German trenches were less than 200 yards away and, on Christmas Day, London Scottish pipers gave their now traditional greeting to the enemy with a selection of tunes, bringing about a short exchange of mortars and shelling. Hogmanay was spent out of the line celebrated with the usual 'London Jock' passion before it was back to business as usual, repairing trenches and support areas in preparation for the expected attack in spring. Hundreds of men joined tunnelling parties while others repaired secondary trenches known as the Red Line, placed wires and set up communications.

Private Stuart Dolden documents one such activity on 17 February 1918 where he and Piper Gordon pushed a railway truck full of cook's dixies from the railhead:

---

120 Lindsay (ed.), *The London Scottish in the Great War*, pp.151-152.
121 *Dumfries and Galloway Standard*, 5 December 1917, p.5.
122 Lindsay (ed.), *The London Scottish in the Great War*, p.164.

Piper Gordon and I had to push one of these trucks and, by Jove, it was stiff work. After half an hour's solid pushing we reached the 'Red Line', and there waited for a light engine. During this time we sat on one of the trucks. The Germans suddenly put up shrapnel, and as one large piece hit the truck on which we were sitting we decided to quit. Shortly after, an electric engine arrived and as soon as the trucks had been coupled on to it we set off in the darkness. It was a very exhilarating ride, for two or three times we were very nearly shot clean off the truck and had to hang on for dear life. At one point a shell landed and only missed hitting the rails by a yard. This happened in front of us, but luckily we passed the spot before the second shell arrived.[123]

Despite such activity, this was still the calm before the storm. The Russian Revolution in 1917 had brought about a conclusion of hostilities on the Eastern Front and a signed armistice between the new Bolshevik regime and the Central Powers that permitted more than a million German troops to begin moving to the Western Front. Germany knew that, with the USA entering the war and a significant volume of newly trained British forces embarking for mainland Europe, they had a short window of opportunity to push for victory before large numbers of Allied troops arrived in theatre to help tip the balance against them. The westward movement of German troops took place throughout late 1917 and early 1918, with seasoned soldiers and new tactics for their use on the battlefield in place by the middle of March. On 21 March the anticipated enemy offensive finally opened, although not initially in the area around Vimy Ridge where the 1st Battalion were entrenched. It would not be until 28 March that a massive German assault began, with the 1st Battalion in the 'Red Line' support trenches watching massed German troops pour across no man's land, capturing the British front line. The London Scottish found themselves engaged in furious fighting in the Red Line, followed by three hours of heavy shelling that obliterated their positions.

During this fighting, the last member of the Pipes and Drums to be killed in action during the First World War lost his life. Drummer Alexander Macpherson, aged 19, was killed fighting off this German assault on the Red Line. Macpherson had enlisted in the London Scottish in October 1916 just before his 18th birthday and had been posted with the Provisional Training Battalion throughout 1917 as a drummer in the Pipes and Drums. He was sent out to France in a draft to the 1st Battalion on 12 January 1918 and was killed less than three months into active service. Piper Macpherson and his good friend Private B.P. Lindsay were directly hit by a mortar shell, which so intermingled their remains that it was impossible to separately identify them. They would later be buried together at Canadian Cemetery No. 2, Neuville St. Vaast, in one shared grave, with two separate headstones.

The British line had held and with the initial German offensive beaten back the 1st Battalion moved into reserve near Mont St Eloi. An iconic photograph of Piper Stewart leading the column during this march was published in many newspapers at the time. The enemy would have greater success in the coming months, reaching to within 40 miles of Paris. After minor but important action holding the line in April, the 1st Battalion moved to Arras and stayed there until August. May and June saw them move in and out of the line and, although German attacks raged around them, the London Scottish remained clear of any major action. However, during shelling on 2 June, Pipe Major Keith was seriously wounded and sent back to Britain. He was listed as still being in a convalescent home in Plymouth on 4 November. With the German offensive finally halted later that month, the British High Command planned a counter offensive that would begin in early August and eventually lead to the conclusion of four years of bloodshed and misery on a

---

123 Dolden, *Cannonfodder*, p.142.

scale the world had never encountered before. The London Scottish, as always, would be in the thick of the action.

On 17 August the 1st Battalion were taken out of the line and, after three days of marching and train travel, billeted at Lignereiul. 20 August saw them trek 10 miles behind the band to La Cauchée where details were received of an attack planned for the coming days. The battalion were to attack from positions more than 16 miles from their current location, and a hasty march was necessary to arrive in time to receive orders and battle stores. Years of route marches behind the Pipes and Drums made this a less arduous task than it would have been for many regiments. The attack itself came on the morning of 23 August and, despite stubborn resistance, all objectives were taken without major loss. This advance at Arras was the beginning of a major push which saw German forces forced further and further back over the next three months until the armistice was signed at 1100 hours on the 11th day of the 11th month in 1918. The 1st Battalion fought at Bullecourt (twice) in the final days of August, and it was during this action that Piper Alexander Wood Urquhart, who had only days earlier been transferred to the Scottish from the 5th Battalion Gordon Highlanders, became the last member of the Pipes and Drums to be wounded in action during the war. He was hit during a minor attack at Bullecourt on the Hindenburg Line and was assisted back to the Regimental Aid Post by Drummer Charles 'Chappie' Chapman and Piper Mills who later reported that Piper Urquhart was 'whisked smartly away by the Aid Post people and, as was usual, disappeared into a limbo, and so far as we knew never returned to the Battalion.'[124]

The 1st Battalion undertook other minor assaults in the following months before moving up to the line on 31 October to take their part in the last great battle of the war, which began on 1 November, exactly four long years since their baptism of fire at Messines in 1914.

The main action for the 1st Battalion took place on 5–6 November around Sebourg at Audregnies and was the last battle for the London Scottish in the First World War. After fierce fighting and enemy bombardment, the battalion was relieved in the early hours of 7 November and returned to Sebourg. The 8 and 9 November saw the men marching behind the Pipes and Drums in terrible weather on muddy roads to Erquennes, then on to Blairegnies near Mons on 10 November. It would be at 0700 hours the next day, in billets in the village of La Dessous, that the battalion would be told of a cessation of the fighting:

> It was announced to the Battalion, which was on parade preparing to leave for a road-repairing fatigue. The news was received quietly. There was, of course, deep heartfelt satisfaction at the successful ending of the tremendous struggle, and the personal sense of good fortune in having fought through more or less of these years of war, done well the duty of the time, and survived its dangers. But among the Scottish there was no inclination for noisy 'mafficking', the day's work was carried on. The news of the last hours of war were discussed, and there was interested conjecture aroused by rumours that the next move of the Battalion would be to join the Army of Occupation that was to go forward to the Rhine.[125]

The war was finally over, but it would be many months before some of the men, including a large contingent of the Pipes and Drums, would get to head home.

Pipe Major Keith, who had returned to Britain seriously injured in June would eventually be replaced as Pipe Major by Corporal Piper Ralston Gordon, who is pictured in a famous band photo taken in Arras on the morning of November 1st before the battalion marched on towards

---

124 *London Scottish Regiment Gazette*, (1995), p.20.
125 Lindsay (ed.), *The London Scottish in the Great War*, p.214.

its final battle. Pipe Major Gordon would stay in post for only a matter of months before he was demobbed and his position taken up by Corporal Piper John MacHattie who would continue to lead the Pipes and Drums through their remaining time overseas in Germany at Hilden, southeast of Düsseldorf.

After the Armistice, the 1st Battalion moved to Givry on the Belgian border, where they were to stay through Christmas and New Year. Assigned activities took place each morning with the afternoons free for recreation. Pipers and drummers were in great demand for battalion, brigade and division activities. On 13 January, the battalion found out they were to leave the 56th Division, with whom they had spent most of the war and join the 9th (Scottish) Division in Germany. On 16 January they marched the eight miles to Mons, receiving the finest of send offs from the other battalions in the 56th:

> We just got outside Givry when we ran across the Kensingtons lining the route with their band … about a quarter mile past them the Fuzzies *(4th London Rifle Fusiliers)* with more music. At the next village all the London Rifle Brigade turned out with a brass band … and so the good work went on till we got to Mons, where three bands of the 167th Brigade met us and played us to the station. We had dinner there while the Divisional Band played selections. At 4:30 the Battalion fell in and marched into the station past the massed bands, playing *Hielan' Laddie*. It was decidedly impressive and forms a last very impressive memory of the good old 56th.[126]

Two days of slow travel by troop train finally saw the battalion arrive at Hilden and the men marched to billets in schools and public buildings, including a concert hall. The situation was very calm and the troops generally well received. Mornings were again taken up with classes and drills, including route marches every Tuesday and Thursday. The streets of Hilden grew accustomed to the sound of pipes and drums, with Beating Retreat and church parades a regular occurrence.

Demobilisation began on 13 March and, on 29 March, the battalion was officially ordered to reduce to cadre strength, numbering just over 50 officers and men. Men slowly began to be sent home or to the 2nd Battalion, which would remain overseas for another seven months. The Pipes and Drums for the main, would remain with the cadre, although a number had begun to be demobbed, including Piper Mills who had returned to Great Britain in January.

On 3 May news came that the cadre was finally to return home. After three days in Dunkirk, the remains of the 1st Battalion sailed for Southampton before spending a few days winding up in camp at Sandling and then entraining for London. At 1530 hours on 16 May, they arrived at Charing Cross for their final march back to headquarters and found an enormous crowd ready to provide them with a hero's welcome. The *Leeds Mercury* reported:

> Amid the hissing of escaping steam, the whistles of impatient engines, and the fevered rush and scurry at Charing Cross station, the skirl of the pipes and the beat of the drums were heard this afternoon.
>
> There was an exuberance and jollity about the proceedings that I have rarely seen on similar occasions. Everybody was in the highest spirits.[127]

Lindsay sums up the scene as follows:

---

126 *London Scottish Regiment Gazette* (1919), p.31.
127 *Leeds Mercury*, 17 May 1919, p.8.

Great crowds had gathered in and around the station, hundreds of them being old comrades, who had worn and fought in the Hodden Grey. A pipe band (which included five Pipe Majors) was waiting on the platform and falling in behind it the Scottish marched out amid ringing cheers. The old comrades fell in behind them, forming in fours to lengthen out the little column of kilted veterans which passed along between cheering crowds across Trafalgar Square, and then by Pall Mall, Waterloo Place, Piccadilly, Grosvenor Place and Victoria Street to Buckingham Gate .... With the pipes playing *Heilan Laddie* they marched into the drill hall.[128]

The Pipes and Drums played the Royal Salute for Her Royal Highness, Princess Louise, The Duchess of Argyll, who gave a short speech before tea and cakes were served and the 1st Battalion, London Scottish officially ended their military campaign.

1st Battalion Piper Robert 'Bob' Marshall was one of only a handful of London Jocks who had seen the war from start to finish, having boarded the SS *Winifredian* in September 1914 and been demobbed in Germany on 18 January 1919. The battalion had played an enormously important role in the four and a half years they had served overseas, and the Pipes and Drums had been an integral component from beginning to end. Apart from a few short weeks in 1915, pipers and drummers had always been present to fulfil their roles as infantrymen, snipers, forward observers, runners, guides, stretcher-bearers, medics, trench diggers, funeral attendants, guards, specialist musicians, harbingers of regimental and national tradition and most importantly, morale-lifters, strength-givers and the embodiment of battalion *esprit de corps*. 'Twice the soldier' indeed. The men of the Pipes and Drums, like the regiment they represented, had served well, with courage and distinction, despite the heavy price asked of them.

2nd and 3rd Battalions

As described previously, the 2nd/14th (County of London) Battalion, The London Regiment (London Scottish), came into existence on 31 August 1914. Initially raised as a reserve battalion to supplement and supply drafts to the 1st Battalion, it would soon turn these duties over to a 3rd Battalion before being sent to Ireland, Flanders, around the Mediterranean and back again. The battalion distinguished itself in three theatres of war, building a reputation to match that of the 1st. The influence and importance of their Pipes and Drums was arguably even more substantive, as the 2nd Battalion was required to cover vast distances on the march in a variety of trying conditions. Regimental *esprit de corps* and the London Scottish tradition and experience of extensive route marches were to stand the 2nd Battalion in good stead for what was to come.

The earliest of these marches took place while the battalion was still stationed in London and were often high profile and ceremonial in nature. On 29 October 1914, the Pipes and Drums headed a guard of honour at the funeral of the Chief of the Imperial General Staff, General Sir Charles W. Douglas, who, whilst a captain and then major in the Gordon Highlanders, had been Adjutant to the London Scottish from 1886-1893. As news of the heroics performed by the 1st Battalion on Hallowe'en filtered back to Britain, the London Scottish at home basked in the glory created by the men at Messines, with stories of heroic charges, hand-to-hand combat and stoic defence of the British front-line filling local and national newspapers. Pride and patriotism were high, and the 2nd Battalion was given a prominent position at several important national events during this period.

---

128 Lindsay (ed.), *The London Scottish in the Great War*, pp.221-222.

In the first few days of November, the battalion undertook a 20-mile route march through central London in a show of regimental pride that saw thousands line their route. The *Western Mail* reported that, 'The London Scottish were headed by their pipers and, 1,200 strong, they made a brave show as they passed Buckingham Palace.'[129] A number of such route marches took place in the city, carrying full pack, rifle and five rounds of ammunition.

> The route was always lined with admirers or perhaps sympathisers? Our uniforms of Hodden Grey had been designed … to 'escape observation' but, as we marched up Constitution Hill towards Piccadilly, I always felt that we were the most conspicuous Regiment in the British Army.[130]

On 8 November the battalion was given the honour of leading the Lord Mayor's Show through the streets of the City of London and the famous front cover of *The Graphic* shows nine pipers and eight drummers led by Drum Major MacKinnon marching 600 men of the battalion past St Paul's Cathedral, surrounded by an enormous crowd. 'The 2nd Battalion of the London Scottish, with the pipers at their head, were clearly the heroes of the day.'[131]

Two days later, the London Scottish lined the route for the State Opening of Parliament by King George V. Once again, the battalion was given pride of place, with particular prominence for the Pipes and Drums:

> Great scenes of enthusiasm marked the passage along the Whitehall, which was lined by the London Scottish, one of the finest and certainly the most popular of the Territorial forces in the Metropolis. Immediately opposite Horse Guards the pipers of the London Scottish were drawn up, and as the Royal coach was seen they broke into a wild skirl. Their majesties graciously acknowledged the warm-hearted reception.[132]

The *Northern Whig* reported that 'a detachment of Indian troops took a prominent position, and, like the London Scottish reserve battalion, its pipers opposite the Horse Guards, came in for tribute to the fame of their comrades in the firing line.'[133]

On 19 November, the battalion were in the spotlight again, heading the funeral procession of Field Marshal Frederick Roberts VC, 1st Earl Roberts, from Westminster Abbey to St Paul's Cathedral. The importance of this event is emphasised by the fact that Lord 'Bobs' Roberts and Sir Winston Churchill half a century later, were the only two people outside of the Royal Family to be given a state funeral during the twentieth century. It was, therefore, an enormous honour for the Pipes and Drums of a 2nd battalion Territorial regiment to be chosen to lead the procession. A lament was played up Ludgate Hill to the cathedral, where: 'Shortly after eleven o'clock the troops heading the procession arrived in the churchyard, headed by the pipers of the London Scottish.'[134]

The impact of Messines so early in the war, stimulated by these high-profile public appearances around London and their subsequent reporting in the press, attracted hundreds of men to enlist with the 2nd Battalion, which was soon hugely oversubscribed. By the end of November, permission had been granted for a 3rd Battalion to be formed with the express purpose of receiving

---

129 *Western Mail*, 9 November 1914, p.4.
130 Major John L. Hyslop, 'A Terrier in Flanders' unpublished diary written from notes by his son Sam, London Scottish Archives, p.47.
131 *Aberdeen Press and Journal*, 10 November 1914, p.3.
132 *Western Mail*, 12 November 1914, p.11.
133 *Northern Whig*, 12 November 1914, p.2.
134 *The Scotsman*, 20 November 1914, p.4.

this over-spill and retaining all members, old and new, who signed up only for home service or were deemed too old or unfit for service overseas. Drafts to the 1st Battalion at this time came exclusively from the 2nd Battalion and continued in this vein until July 1915. Hence Pipe Major Robertson, who was 47 years of age and not eligible for overseas service, quickly moved from the 1st Battalion to the 2nd on 2 October 1914 and then to the 3rd in late November. Pipe Major David Wills took over from Robertson, officially being appointed Pipe Major of the 2nd Battalion on 1 February 1915. Drum Major MacKinnon, who had also been a regimental piper, took a commission within the 2nd Battalion on 1 December and his position was taken over by Drum Major Percy Cunningham, who had been heading up the 3rd Battalion drummers and who had led the Pipes and Drums before war broke out. As if things were not confusing enough, his position as Drum Major was taken over by Corporal Piper George Shand.

The final ceremonial task undertaken by the 2nd Battalion Pipes and Drums in London took place on 17 December at Horse Guards Parade when the battalion took part in the last inspection of the old 'Grey Brigade', by General Sir Reginald Pole-Carew. Then, after Christmas and New Year at home with their families, the battalion marked the beginning of 1915 by moving to billets in Dorking on 4 January. Here intensive training would begin, despite steady redeployment of soldiers from the ranks to the 1st Battalion overseas.

While the 1st Battalion had to deal with the continual loss of good men through commissions and heavy casualties, the 2nd Battalion had to manage the continuing depletion of men, especially NCOs, brought about by both commissions and drafts to the 1st Battalion to replace their combat losses. This was echoed in the Pipes and Drums, with replacements for men leaving to become officers or for service overseas coming either from the 3rd Battalion, direct recruitment of those who could already play or by training up soldiers from the ranks. Trained pipers and drummers were extremely sought after and several men who could play but were found to have enlisted underage were retained within the 2nd and 3rd Battalions purely to serve as drummers or pipers. Included in this number was Ian Hutcheson, who later volunteered to be drafted overseas as soon as he was old enough and would serve as bass drummer with the 1st Battalion from August 1917 until April 1919. He was only 16 years and five months when he enlisted with the London Scottish in December 1914 and was assigned to the 3rd Battalion. Pencilled across the top of his attestation paper is 'Drummer', whilst his medical inspection report sheet includes the note 'Band Only.'[135]

An integral part of the intensive training undertaken at Dorking was route marching over increasing distances and with progressively heavier loads. Having trained pipers and drummers on the march was a considerable aid to these gruelling assignments. The 2nd Battalion war diary detailing the first few weeks at Dorking offers an instructive insight. On 6 January, two days after arriving, the battalion marched for ten miles. On the 9th, another eight miles, followed by 14 miles on the 14th and 16 miles on the 18th. The 22nd saw them march from the Epsom Downs back to Dorking and on the 25th they marched 13 miles via Leatherhead with full kit before a simulated attack exercise. The regularity of such route marches would continue as a staple of training throughout the war, and the capacity to march long distances and be 'fighting fit' upon reaching their destination would become a source of pride for the battalion during their time on active service overseas.

Back in London, the 3rd Battalion were gearing up for a move to Richmond Park, where they would be stationed until 1916. Recruits were marched from headquarters in Westminster to Richmond, as detailed in the diary of Private James Graham, who had joined the London Scottish straight from school:

---

135 TNA WO 363: Hutcheson, Jan [sic], records 0622 and 0623, War Office, Soldiers' Documents, First World War 'Burnt Documents' Microfilm Copies..

Then came the big day, we had to march in public with a Pipe Band, leading all the way to Richmond Park to join the rest of the Battalion and other Territorial Regiments who were training there.[136]

He goes on to state, 'a Piper sounded the réveillé at 6:30am' and that, as in the 2nd Battalion, training included regular 'long route marches, sometimes lasting three days.'[137] These route marches would also be increasingly used throughout the war for recruitment purposes. The *Surrey Advertiser* reported an early recruiting march through Guildford 'Headed by the pipes of the 4th [sic] London Scottish.'[138] Pipe Major Robertson detailed the role of the 3rd Battalion Pipes and Drums, including heading up these roughly twice-weekly route marches, playing daily battalion duty calls, Beating Retreat, Sunday church parades, parades to see off drafts, as well as regular band practises,[139] in addition to their regular training as stretcher-bearers, runners and first-aiders. The Pipes and Drums of both the 2nd and 3rd Battalions were also much in demand for soldier's funerals, fund-raising concerts, officer's dinners, static recruiting events and other brigade and divisional activities, such as assault-at-arms and sporting events. Such activities would be staples of the 3rd Battalion Pipes and Drums for the remainder of the war.

Examples of such 'extra-regimental' activities taking place during this period give a flavour of the variety of work undertaken. The *Dorking and Leatherhead Advertiser* for 30 January 1915 reports on a soldiers' concert at the local YMCA attended by 'two London Scottish Pipers'[140] and reports again the following month about a similar concert at St Martin's Church Room and Men's Club, which was open to troops, stating that, 'The performance of Piper McGilvray … deserved special mention.'[141] On 29 March, the *Aberdeen Press and Journal* reported on a recruiting rally that took place on a 'gigantic scale' in Highbury Fields, London, attended by over 100,000 people, in which the 3rd Battalion London Scottish participated:

> The detachment of the London Scottish attracted a good deal of attention as, headed by their pipers, they marched in the procession, which consisted mostly of men in the Kitchener armies.[142]

In April, the *Pall Mall Gazette* reported on another high-profile event in which the 3rd Battalion Pipes and Drums performed. The British Red Cross held a fund-raising concert at the Royal Albert Hall in the presence of Queen Alexandra. The Pipes and Drums played a selection of tunes and accompanied a performance by highland dancers from the battalion.[143]

A 3rd Battalion church parade took place on Sunday 24 January 1915 that was reported in various newspapers. The battalion marched from 59 Buckingham Gate to the regimental church and, depending on which report you read, was either 900 or 600 strong. The *Aberdeen Press and Journal* stated that so many people wished to attend the service that they could not all get in the church: 'There were six hundred of the men of the 2nd Reserve Battalion under Colonel Greig, and they marched through the streets behind their pipers.'[144] *The Scotsman* had the total at 900 who

---

136 James Graham unpublished diary, 1915-1918, London Scottish Regimental Archives.
137 Graham unpublished diary.
138 *Surrey Advertiser*, 20 January 1915, p.1.
139 *London Scottish Regiment Gazette*, (1916), p.102.
140 *Dorking and Leatherhead Advertiser*, 30 January 1915, p.5.
141 *Dorking and Leatherhead Advertiser*, 13 February 1915, p.5.
142 *Aberdeen Press and Journal*, 29 March 1915, p.7.
143 *Pall Mall Gazette*, 15 April 1915, p.6.
144 *Aberdeen Press and Journal*, 25 January 1915, p.4.

'headed by their pipe band and buglers, marched four abreast to St Columba's Church of Scotland in Pont Street, Belgravia, where the service was held.'[145]

Meanwhile, the 2nd Battalion was preparing the largest draft it would send out to the 1st Battalion. It would consist of over 380 officers and men, constituting the cream of the 2nd Battalion, along with men from the 1st Battalion who had returned to Great Britain as casualties but were now classified as recovered and fit again for active service. Lindsay calls this draft 'as fine a body of men as had ever been got together', of whom nearly all 'were subsequently granted commissions.'[146] The draft left to embark at Southampton from Westminster on March 7th and the diary of Private Herbert C. Maben states:

> We were then marched to headquarters where we were inspected by the Adjutant who made a good speech. Headed by band (pipers and buglers) we set out for Waterloo, big crowds following. Great cheering and band playing as we steamed out.[147]

Piper Oliver Machell-Varese was the only piper or drummer who left with this famous 'March Draft' but a number of others would subsequently go on to join the band, including Private John Henry Ridsdale, who became a drummer in January 1916 and Private David Middleton who would later serve as both drummer and piper. Total drafts to the 1st Battalion numbered nearly a full battalion strength and would continue until the middle of July when the 2nd Battalion began to be prepared for service overseas. All unfit and home service men were transferred to provisional battalions (notably the 104th) or the 3rd London Scottish Battalion which took over the role of providing drafts for both the 1st and 2nd Battalions.

The 2nd Battalion had moved to Watford on 29 March, then to Saffron Walden in the middle of May and on to Bishop Stortford on 26 October. It was here in Bishop Stortford that the battalion would be informed that it was to undertake the necessary six months pre-deployment training that the 1st Battalion never had, before being sent to join the British Army overseas. Training would take place on Salisbury Plain, and the battalion marked the beginning of 1916 by moving to No. 9 Camp at Sutton Veney on 21 January. Here the Pipes and Drums would concentrate on their fighting roles but as well as passing through musketry, bombing and other courses directly related to combat, they were also taught about roles as runners, guides and stretcher-bearers. In some of the only entries that explicitly mention members of the band, the 2nd Battalion war diary for February 1916 also records that, over a number of days, the Medical Officer gave first aid 'lectures to … Stretcher Bearers, Buglers and drummers [sic] in his hut.'[148]

A large contingent of the battalion was sent to various counties in Ireland on 28 April, following the Easter Rising, to patrol and search for weapons. However, they returned to Salisbury Plain two weeks later after word was received that overseas deployment of the 60th (London) Division, to which the battalion belonged, was imminent. A review inspection of the entire division by King George V was planned for 31 May and the battalion war diary for 30 May states: 'Rehearsal for Review by King on 31st night. Five pipers and three drummers lent by 3rd Battalion arrived from London.'[149] The Pipes and Drums were to play a central role in the review and planned to field the largest band possible to generate the most favourable impression. Directly after the inspection, all

---

145 *The Scotsman*, 25 January 1915, p.10.
146 Lindsay (ed.), *The London Scottish in the Great War*, p.229.
147 Herbert C. Maben unpublished diary March to September 1915, London Scottish Regimental Archives.
148 TNA WO 95 3030/4: 60th Division, 179th Infantry Brigade, 2nd/14th Battalion London Regiment War Diaries, January 1915 to November 1916 entry for 28 February 1916.
149 TNA WO 95 3030/4 entry for 30 May 1916.

154   STRIKE UP, STRIKE SURE

2nd Battalion March, St. James's Park, London, November 1914. (LSMA, used with permission)

2nd Battalion Pipes and Drums performing at Dudular Camp, Salonika, November 1916. (LSMA, used with permission)

2nd Battalion Drummers Ferguson and Turner photographed at camp on the Mount of Olives, Jerusalem, with Turkish ceremonial drums captured at Nebi Musa, February 1918. (LSMA, used with permission)

2nd Battalion Pipes and Drums practising at bivouacs near Es Salt, Palestine, March 1918. Note the Turkish ceremonial drum. (LSMA, used with permission)

men were given four days leave, staggered over eight days, before final arrangements were made for embarkation. As part of these preparations, pipers were issued revolvers and taught to shoot them. On 19 June, 48 hours before departing overseas: 'All officers, Pipers and those who carry revolvers fired 50 rounds this day.'[150] Unlike the departure of the 1st Battalion, which took place in a blaze of glory in front of cheering crowds but after very little training and preparation, the 2nd Battalion left Southampton in a dirty, rundown paddle steamer named SS *La Marguerite*, with no rapturous send off, but 'well equipped, well trained, in fine physical condition, and as eager as the many thousands who preceded them to measure themselves against the foe.'[151] So began a three year odyssey that would see them travel through France, Egypt, Greece, the Balkans, Palestine, Italy and back again to France and Belgium. They would travel by boat and train but more frequently by foot on the march behind the Pipes and Drums; over 1,000 miles of foot slog through some of the most trying conditions imaginable.

After arriving in France, the 2nd Battalion travelled slowly by train to Petit Houvin, marched through the rain to Averdoingt and then, on 25 June, to Marœuil, near Vimy Ridge, where they took over fatigue duties for the Royal Engineers. Sixth July saw the battalion move to the front line for the first time and take over a section held by the 51st (Highland) Division. They would remain in this section for the next four months, in a revolving system either in front line trenches, in support or in reserve. This section of the front was relatively quiet during this period and whilst casualties were light, they were constant. Lindsay states that, while the 1st Battalion were in the thick of the action at the Somme, in this sector 'one tour of duty much resembled another [as] there was no intention on the part of the High Command to take the offensive in this area.'[152] The 2nd Battalion war diary records casualties being taken almost every day, mainly from German trench mortars, during these periods at the front. Not all deaths during the war, however, were a direct result of enemy action. Soldiers were susceptible to the same diseases as civilians, and the conditions in which they lived greatly enhanced their vulnerability. One such case was that of 2nd Battalion Drummer Frank Albert Gosling, who was taken to hospital on 18 August with spinal fever and would succumb to the illness ten days later. Drummer Gosling had enlisted in Glasgow in October 1914 with the express intention of joining the London Scottish. He was initially a bugler, but it seems he already had existing medical issues that meant playing the bugle: 'proved a little too much for him'[153] and he instead took on the role of drummer. He was first assistant for Hobbies model-makers at their Glasgow branch and their weekly magazine provided a report of his death in December 1916, including a photograph of Gosling and two other drummers. Gosling was the only member of the 2nd Battalion Pipes and Drums to lose his life during the First World War.

It is a matter of both design and good fortune that this was the case. The horrific experiences of the 1st Battalion Pipes and Drums had taught senior officers the importance of restricting risk to members of the band but their roles as runners for company commanders and stretcher-bearers during action still brought them into considerable danger, as German shelling and mortar bombs killed and wounded men whether in front line, support or reserve positions. As such, the Pipes and Drums were extremely fortunate not to lose any other men to either illness or action while overseas.

On 22 September, the battalion was in front line trenches when confirmation was received that the new commanding officer had arrived in reserve positions. Drummer Hector 'Curly' Turner,

---

150 TNA WO 95 3030/4 entry for 19 June 1916.
151 Lindsay (ed.), *The London Scottish in the Great War*, p.233.
152 *The London Scottish in the Great War*, ed. Lindsay, p. 36.
153 *Hobbies*, 23 December 1916, p.3.

in his role as runner 'had the unique distinction of being the first person to meet Colonel Ogilby when he took command of the 2nd Battalion from Colonel Dunsmore.'[154] Lieutenant Colonel Robert James Leslie Ogilby of Ardnargle and Pellipar was owner of a large estate in Londonderry and had spent his military career as a cavalry officer in the (Royal Irish) Dragoon Guards and the 2nd Life Guards. He had fought dismounted at Messines and had, in fact, handed over part of the line to the 1st Battalion, London Scottish on Hallowe'en 1914. He was a traditional calvary officer with traditional views of how a battalion should be run which included extremely strict rules regarding discipline. Upon taking over the 2nd Battalion:

> The initial impact of both on each other … became historic! However, they came to understand one another and he personally never regretted the meeting, which for him commenced a love of all things Scottish.[155]

This would very much include the Pipes and Drums who, in traditional pipe band fashion, often had a healthy disregard for matters disciplinary. Colonel Ogilby, however, came to see the importance of the band to the battalion and over time a grudging respect was returned to him; a sentiment that seemed to be echoed by the entire battalion. Drummer Turner and his right-hand man, Drummer Alfred 'Fergie' Ferguson were notable characters within the band whose exploits during the war were particularly memorable. Whilst close friends, they did not always see eye to eye. Soon after Colonel Ogilby's arrival, German action began to increase, making use of new trench mortars and howitzers in an attempt to destroy British front-line positions. On returning to the line on 7 October, it soon became obvious that all forward trenches were beyond repair and that bomb craters matching the forward positions should be manned whilst new trenches were dug further to the rear. German bombing continued over four more days and nights and Piper Davie Pullar, who was acting as a company runner, 'jumping from sump hole to sump hole', recalled that, 'the funniest thing I ever saw was our two Drummers having a stand-up fight during a bombardment, as to who was going to get into "that sump-hole first."'[156]

The battalion were in and out of the line until 22 October and on 25 October started a four-day march that would see them arrive at Montigny-les-Jongleurs on 29 October, where they were able to celebrate Hallowe'en. 'Resources and accommodation being both very limited, the festivities could not be termed elaborate, but all that was lacking in that respect was more than made up for by gaiety and good spirits.'[157] The Pipes and Drums were able to assist most handsomely in this regard. Exactly one year later, the 2nd Battalion would add their own incredible story to the London Scottish regimental Hallowe'en tradition.

Back in Richmond Park, the 3rd Battalion were celebrating their own Hallowe'en dinner. Over 800 strong, the men of the battalion paid their respects not just to those lost during the Battle of Messines two years earlier but to the hundreds that had been killed since. *The Scotsman* reported that 'The toast of "Fallen Comrades"' given by Colonel Greig 'was responded to in silence, the pipers afterwards played a dirge.'[158]

Life for the battalion in 1916 continued much as it had done in 1915, training men for drafts, recuperating the wounded from both 1st and 2nd Battalions for return to action and supporting the war effort in as many ways as possible. The biggest change came about in May when Pipe

---

154 *London Scottish Regiment Gazette*, (1965), p.95.
155 *London Scottish Regiment Gazette*, (1956), p.72.
156 *London Scottish Regiment Gazette*, (1941), p.16.
157 Lindsay (ed.), *The London Scottish in the Great War*, p.240.
158 *The Scotsman*, 2 November 1916, p.10.

Major Robertson retired after nearly 25 years with the band. Various celebratory events took place in his honour, including a sergeants' mess dinner, a band farewell dinner, an officers' mess dinner and a final farewell dinner on 30 May. It would be fair to say that he was a much-loved pillar of the regiment. In a letter to the *Regimental Gazette* on 16 April Pipe Major Robertson observed:

> The London Scottish have been most fortunate in this, that the Officers who have held highest rank in the Battalion have always considered the Pipe Band to be a most important part of the Regiment and have taken the keenest interest in its duties and equipment. No one who served in the Regiment can imagine a London Scot …, no matter how tired or weary, failing to square his shoulders and proudly step out with head erect when the pipes and drums break into *Highland Laddie*.[159]

His appointment as pipe major was taken by Drum Major Shand, and Shand's appointment as drum major was taken by bass Drummer 'Teddy' Hall. Shand and Hall would remain in charge of the 3rd Battalion Pipes and Drums until it was disbanded in 1918.

The Pipes and Drums would continue to play a particularly significant role in public-faced recruiting and fund-raising events throughout the next two years. In April 1916, the *Surrey Mirror* reported on a large recruiting parade in Caterham that included a march past by troops from the Grenadier, Coldstream, Scots and Irish Guards: 'A contingent of the London Scottish Territorials, with their fine band of pipers, arrived, and acted as the guard of honour at the saluting base.'[160]

In September, the Dutch Red Cross held a fund-raising garden party at the Bishop of London's residence, Fulham Palace, which was being used by the British Red Cross as an auxiliary hospital for wounded servicemen. The Pipes and Drums provided quite the spectacle:

> About 3 o'clock there was a diversion, for weird noises were to be heard in the field. The responsible individuals were pipers of the London Scottish, who were getting their lungs in working order for the big blow that was to follow. This parade was an attractive spectacle, and when the men halted in a circle and played faster and faster, and even faster than that the crowd that gathered round was an admiring one.[161]

The band were involved in a more sombre occasion in October when they participated in a military funeral at St Dunstan's Church, Cranford, for Private Reginald A. Roots of the 1st Battalion, London Scottish, who had been wounded at the Somme and died in hospital back in Britain. 'A small detachment of the London Scottish, headed by pipers, the men with rifles at the reverse, came next' and as three rifle volleys were shot over the coffin 'the pipers played *MacIntosh's Lament* between each volley.'[162] The band contained pipers and drummers who had themselves been wounded overseas, including tenor Drummer Percy Lingwood and Piper R.A. Porteous, both of whom would have found such occasions particularly poignant. Other recovered 1st Battalion band members were now back in France serving with the 2nd Battalion, for whom the war was about to take a considerable change of course.

After celebrating Hallowe'en in 1916, the 2nd Battalion, London Scottish began training intensively for what they thought was going to be their involvement in the continued fighting at the

---

159 *London Scottish Regiment Gazette*, (1916), p.112.
160 *Surrey Mirror*, 16 April 1916, p.7.
161 *Fulham Chronicle*, 22 September 1916, p.8.
162 *West Middlesex Gazette*, 19 October 1916, p.6.

Somme. However, on 3 November the battalion were astounded to receive orders to prepare for a move to Salonika, a theatre of war that many had not previously known existed.

While the killing of an Austrian Crown Prince by a Bosnian Serb played a crucial role in beginning the 'Great War', little thought was given by most British people to the situation in the Balkans once war in France and Belgium had been declared. By September 1915, attacks by Austro-Hungarian and German forces had pushed the Serbian Army back into southern Serbia. Bulgaria, who had been at war with Serbia on two previous occasions, joined the Central Powers and commenced a two-fronted attack in early October, pushing the Serbian army out of their own country and creating a front line through Albania and along the border with Greece. This threatened the vital port of Salonika, which the Germans wanted as a submarine base from which to attack Allied convoys in the Mediterranean. The Allies sent a token force to support Serbia but, with manpower issues on the Western Front and a decision to throw weight into the Gallipoli campaign taking precedence, it was not until the spring of 1917 that any serious action was taken by British and French troops. It was in preparation for this spring campaign that the 60th Division, containing the 2nd Battalion, London Scottish, were being mobilised.

One person who would not be going to the Balkans, however, was Piper Charles Warren Cummins. Cummins joined the 2nd Battalion Pipes and Drums soon after the battalion formed and became a piper in February 1915. He volunteered for overseas service despite being 46 years old, although the 'apparent age' he declared on his medical report in February 1915 states 39 years and 11 months.[163] He was deemed fit enough and 'acted as runner to 'C' Company in the trenches in France, and the work he performed compared favourably with that of many a younger man.'[164] However, the climate on the British held section of the Balkan front line near Dorian was particularly harsh, with freezing winters and boiling summer heat. When the battalion left for Salonika, Piper Cummins was invalided home, where he joined the 3rd Battalion until his discharge in late 1917. The other member of the band who returned to Great Britain at this point was Pipe Major David Wills. Wills had joined the London Scottish on 2 September 1914 aged 30 and had been with the 2nd Battalion since its inception, taking over as pipe major from Bob Robertson. He was designated as unfit with pleurisy on 18 December and it was decided he should be sent home on 29 December, where he joined the 3rd Battalion despite continued bad health which led to his discharge on 9 March 1918. His position as pipe major would be taken by John Armour McGilvray, who had joined the London Scottish in 1908 and was a corporal piper when war broke out. He had been immediately transferred to the 2nd Battalion to help form the nucleus of the new Pipes and Drums and would go on to lead the pipe band until his demobilisation after the armistice in late 1918.

Pipe Major Wills did, however, parade with the rest of the Pipes and Drums as the battalion marched to Longpré on 15 November to entrain for Marseilles. They would arrive on 17 November and, at dawn on 22 November, embarked on the White Ocean Liner HMT *Megantic* for the voyage to Salonika. Conditions onboard this luxury liner were rather better than their previous troopship experience, and the crossing of the Mediterranean took place in smooth waters and warm weather. Intensive training continued while onboard and, in addition, the Pipes and Drums played at many evening concerts for both officers and men. This life of relative comfort would end abruptly on 29 November when the *Megantic* docked in Salonika harbour.

---

163 TNA WO 364: 'Charles Warren Cummins', record 887, War Office: Soldiers' Documents, First World War 'Burnt Documents', Microfilm Copies.
164 *London Scottish Regiment Gazette* (1940), p.22.

Upon disembarking, the battalion marched six miles to Dudular Camp 'over atrocious roads, deep in mud and filth' to a camp which was 'a stretch of bare, muddy, uncultivated land.'[165] With the roads in terrible condition, and a lack of railways and motorised transport, the bulk of all movement in this theatre of war would be on foot. Transportation of battalion equipment would be accomplished entirely using 143 mules that had been shipped from South America, 'all unbroken, and all imbued with the spirit of Satan.'[166] The first week in camp was spent learning to feed, harness and load these brutes, a situation made particularly difficult by the actions of the Pipes and Drums. An extended quote from Private Robert Murray's war diary paints a vivid picture of the first time the battalion attempted a route march with their mule transport section, held under the watchful eye of their ex-cavalry commanding officer. Getting the mules lined up on the road had itself been a major exercise, however:

> This beginning was quite trivial compared with what was to follow. Our bagpipers began to play a Scottish tune, and that was the end. At this time, the mules' ears went up, their eyes almost fell out of their heads, their front feet went up in the air, and after a while the valley was full of mules rushing away from the terrifying sounds, as if the Devil himself was chasing them.
>
> The musicians saw the effect of their music and so many laughed that the music came to an inglorious end. Less than a quarter of the mules remained on the road. The others were far away on the plain. … Oh, what a day!
>
> Because of this fiasco, the colonel decided that they should teach the mules to appreciate and love the music of the bagpipes. So, every morning the regimental bandsmen came to the transport section of camp and marched between the mule lines and for half an hour played the tunes they usually played on the march, as we laughed and applauded them mockingly, while the poor mules were completely terrified. We had our revenge for the previous laughter of the bandsmen.[167]

By 10 December, the animals were deemed suitably under control and a proportion of the battalion marched off through the night to Topsin. Two more days of marching would see them arrive at Guida and then another three days took them to their objective, the town of Katerini and the outpost at Kolokuri, just north of Mount Olympus. An advanced guard consisting of 'C' Company, London Scottish, including Drummer Turner, left the same day by sea to prepare the landing of other elements of the brigade. They embarked on a paddle-steamer, then boarded a lighter and were told to wade ashore. Drummer 'Curly' Turner disembarked and promptly went under in full kit before being hauled back to the surface by an unknown comrade. 'Curly maintained that I saved his life, but no one gave me a life-saving certificate. We had the satisfaction of not losing that cheery little bloke.'[168] The battalion would remain around Katerini, guarding the mountain pass and helping to repair roads and bridges, until 5 January 1917. Christmas and Hogmanay were celebrated with as much Scottish tradition as the circumstances allowed and the Pipes and Drums were greatly in demand.

13 January 1917 saw the arrival in Salonika of a draft from the 3rd Battalion, which included Pipers Charles Oram, Donald Hay, John MacMillan and Charles 'Bob' Stewart, although

---

165 Lindsay (ed.), *The London Scottish in the Great War*, p.243.
166 Lindsay (ed.), *The London Scottish in the Great War*, p.244.
167 Robert Murray, 'My Adventures in the Great War: War Diary 1915-1919' unpublished manuscript, London Scottish Museum Archives, 1933, p.24.
168 *London Scottish Regiment Gazette*, (1973), p.14.

transportation difficulties meant they would not join up with the battalion until weeks later. Piper Oram was a pre-war London Scottish piper who had been wounded at Messines and discharged from the army in October 1915. He decided to re-join in January 1916 and became a member of the 3rd Battalion Pipes and Drums shortly after, before deciding to volunteer again for service overseas. Piper Hay had seen pre-war service from 1902 to 1910 with the 4th Black Watch and 6th Seaforth Highlanders and was called up in December 1915. He was living in Clapham Junction with his wife and three-year-old son at this point and so asked to join the 3rd Battalion, London Scottish, as a piper, in May 1916. When informed that he was to be sent overseas with the draft to Salonika, Piper Hay went absent without leave from the 9-15 December. For this offence he was deducted seven day's pay and jailed for 14 days. Both pipers served with the 2nd Battalion for the remainder of the war.[169]

Meanwhile, the rest of the battalion moved again on 5 January 1917 to Hani Miljas, where training took place and then moved again on 13 February, to Petra, where the weather deteriorated considerably. Rain often turned into snow and the entire area was a sea of mud, but despite suffering harsh conditions in the trenches, at least there was little enemy action. On 1 March, the battalion returned to Katerini behind the Pipes and Drums and 'the fine physical condition of the men was reflected in the march, the 18 miles being covered in 6¾ hours marching time, and for the greater distance in pouring rain, without one man falling out.'[170] The rigours of this march, however, would pail into insignificance compared with what was yet to come. On 10 March, the 2nd Battalion 'commenced a march which surely must be set down among the most notable marching feats of the British Army.' In seven days, the battalion covered nearly 100 miles over muddy cart tracks 'at best.' The men experienced 'dust, intense heat, intense cold, torrential rain, snow, sleet, and that piercing of all winds, "the Vardar."'[171] Sections consisted of eight miles, then 13, 14, 19, 13 and 10, with a final 15-mile trek into Kalinova on 16 March. Due to the weather and with proximity to enemy positions requiring secrecy, most of these marches was made without the benefit of the Pipes and Drums. However, only 15 men dropped out, including one 'D' Company private who died of fatigue.

After just one recovery day, the 2nd Battalion were sent into the line at Dâche where trenches had to be blasted from solid rock. A small enemy attack took place on 4 April, but otherwise this section of the line remained quiet until the London Scottish successfully attacked into no man's land on the evening of 8 May. During this fighting, Piper Alec Paterson would be seriously wounded. The 2nd Battalion was relieved on 10 May after 38 days in the line and by early June it was common knowledge that the London Scottish would be leaving the sector. From 8-12 June the battalion, this time following the Pipes and Drums, marched back to Dudular Camp in Salonika from where they had started out seven months earlier. Here they 'stayed a week at the Barracks, where we held sports etc. The band gave a great display daily, which most of the inhabitants turned out for, as the big drummer was quite a juggler with his sticks.'[172] The 'big drummer' was Alexander 'Sandy' Gow, another legendary pre-war band member who was known for his size and

---

169 Piper Hay was demobbed in January 1919 and then promptly disappeared. A letter sent from his son in Winnipeg, Canada in 1934 to the London Scottish asking for any information about his whereabouts mentions that he may have been suffering from shellshock and so hospitalised but the family had had no contact since a letter he sent home to his wife in September 1918. An obituary appears in the *London Scottish Regiment Gazette* in 1943, and his wife presented his wartime pipes to the Regiment, so it seems probable that his whereabouts were eventually discovered.
170 Lindsay (ed.), *The London Scottish in the Great War*, p.250.
171 *London Scottish Regiment Gazette*, (1935), p.91.
172 Private Neil Hendry, 'My Experiences with the London Scottish 1914-18' unpublished manuscript, London Scottish Museum Archives.

2nd Battalion Sergeant Piper Oram in Pith Helmet (note London Scottish cap badge) and shirt-sleeve order, Palestine 1918. (LSMA, used with permission)

2nd Battalion London Scottish, led by the Pipes and Drums under Pipe Major McGilvary, marching out after capturing Es Salt, 27 March 1918. (LSMA, used with permission)

2nd Battalion Pipes and Drums at Aire, near St. Omer, France, 1918. (LSMA, used with permission)

2nd Battalion Pipes and Drums at a French farm near Étaples, January 1919. (LSMA, used with permission)

strength. However, due to his age, he did not leave with the battalion but was evacuated to Malta where he would remain running canteens for Allied troops until discharged in 1918.

On 30 June the London Scottish boarded HMT *Aragon* to join General Allenby's army in Egypt and prepared to enter their third theatre of war. Conditions during their time in the Balkans had been horrendous and, while very few men were casualties of combat, hundreds fell ill and spent time in hospital. This harsh environment made it extremely hard for pipers and drummers to keep their instruments in a playable condition. Drumheads and wooden shells cracked with the extreme temperature variation and 'owing to the submarine campaign and to the distance from home, supplies ran short, and the pipers were compelled to make pipe bags from goat skins soaked in whale oil.'[173] Whale oil had been issued to all troops as a protection against trench foot and was available, therefore, in plentiful supply. Marching in such circumstances was effort enough but playing and keeping their instruments going at the same time was a feat of real endurance. At no point did any piper or drummer fall out, and the positive effect on the men (if not mules) of the 2nd Battalion had been enormous. Conditions in their next theatre of war would be equally demanding, although this time they would also find themselves very much in the thick of the fighting.

On 22 February 1917, the 3rd Battalion back in London were involved in the funeral procession of 1st Battalion CSM Jock Forbes, who had died from illness while on leave in Great Britain. A guard of honour from the London Scottish marched the coffin to the train station for the return of his body to his family home in Perthshire. 'Then, in an impressive silence, the cortège moved off at Slow March, the Pipers playing *The Flowers of the Forest*. First came the firing party with arms reversed; next the Pipers, Drummers and Buglers.'[174] On arrival at the station, the guard of honour presented arms and the Pipes and Drums played a second lament as the coffin was loaded onto the train.

The battalion moved to Hazeley Down Camp near Winchester in October 1916, along with the 3rd Battalions of several other London regiments. The drum major reported that:

> Every Friday the Band, Pipes, Bugles and Drums play 'Retreat' in front of the Orderly Room much to the delight of the local inhabitants, who turn out in large numbers … to admire the 'Braw, braw lads' and especially, especially, especially the Big Drum Major.[175]

The Sportsman of 5 June reported on a piping competition in the 3rd Battalion camp at Hazeley Down, with Lance Corporal Piper James Stewart taking all the prizes.[176] He is mentioned again in a report in the *Hampshire Advertiser* in July 1917, playing along with Piper Ian Mackenzie and a London Scottish concert party at a fund-raising concert in Chine, Southampton.[177] Stewart would later join his brother Piper Charles Stewart, who was already serving with the 2nd Battalion overseas, but not until the battalion returned from their current theatre of operations. For while Piper Stewart played in Southampton, his brother and the men of the 2nd Battalion were about to go into the line in Palestine for the first time against yet another enemy, the Turks.

In February 1915, German-led Ottoman forces had attacked British troops in Egypt with the intent of taking control of the strategically important Suez Canal. This offensive had been beaten off, aided by the Arab Revolt, and by early winter of 1916, British and ANZAC forces had instead

---

173 *London Scottish Regiment Gazette*, (1919), p.32.
174 *London Scottish Regiment Gazette* (1917), p.55.
175 *London Scottish Regiment Gazette* (1917), p.70.
176 *The Sportsman*, 5 June 1917, p.3.
177 *Hampshire Advertiser*, 28 July 1917, p.3.

3rd Battalion Pipes and Drums at camp in Richmond Park, June 1915. (LSMA, used with permission)

gone on the attack. Ottoman troops were pushed out of Sinai by January 1917 but after initial gains into Palestine a stalemate ensued throughout the spring. In June, General Sir Edmund Allenby, who had been commanding the Third Army in Flanders, was ordered to take command of the Egyptian Expeditionary Force and take up the offensive with the aim of capturing Jerusalem and tying up as many Ottoman forces as possible to relieve pressure in other areas. A large strength of Allied forces, including the 2nd Battalion, London Scottish, arrived in theatre for a big autumn push that hoped to reach Beersheba, Gaza and ultimately Jerusalem. The 'Holy City' had been under Muslim control for the last 400 years and its fall would be a huge propaganda blow for the Turks. General Allenby had written a letter of congratulation to the Commanding Officer of the 1st Battalion, London Scottish after Messines and was well-acquainted with the regiment and its abilities. He was also very well disposed towards Colonel Ogilby. As such, Allenby would make hard use of the 2nd Battalion over the next year but would also honour them with particular respect.[178]

The 2nd Battalion disembarked at Alexandria, Egypt on 3 July after four glorious days relaxing at sea. The luxury continued upon arrival, as they travelled by passenger train to Moascar Camp in Ismailia on the west bank of the Suez Canal, only 70 miles from Cairo. The camp was a haven after Salonika, and men were given only light duties, leaving time to swim in the canal and take leave to visit the 'delights' of Cairo, climb the pyramids and take photos on the Sphinx. Officers and men made good use of their free time but were ready when, in late afternoon on 17 July, they marched out through Ismailia towards the desert.

---

178 A public indication of this respect was shown when General Sir Edmund Allenby (GOC Egyptian Expeditionary Force) gave permission for the London Scottish to become the only battalion in the entire EEF entitled to wear their regimental cap badge on their pith helmets.

As we passed along smooth, tarred macadam roads shaded by large overhanging trees, numbers of the population, both European and native, stood by the wayside watching us, actuated by that curiosity always excited by troops marching to the skirl of pipes and the beat of drums.[179]

They bivouacked that evening in the desert near El Ferdan next to the Suez Canal and the following morning 'Soon after daybreak … the sound of bagpipes woke us and we got up from our desert beds and prepared to do physical exercises.'[180] After breakfast, they were able to swim in the sea before setting off again to Balah. The London Scottish were given the honour of leading the brigade on this march through the desert, which had the added benefit that the Pipes and Drums were able to play without being covered in the horrendous dust that was kicked up by the trail of marching troops. On these and subsequent marches, the band would play for the first ten minutes of each hour, then the column would march for the next 40 minutes before having ten minutes rest. In this manner large distances were efficiently covered. The first ten minutes marching after each rest period were deemed the hardest, and the music of the Pipes and Drums was both an incentive to march and something for which the men could look forward.

After two further days marching through the desert, they reached Kantara and, following a day's rest 'headed by the pipes and drums, the Battalion moved to the military station and entrained for the railhead' at Deir el Belad.[181] A further march took them to camp at Shabasi on the Mediterranean coast where they spent the next week and got acquainted with another species of transport animal. Despite being as wilful as any mule, camels took to the sound of the Pipes and Drums with much less terror.

On 29 July, the brigade marched to the front line for the first time. It was a horrendous 17-mile slog through sandstorms and dust. The marching was hard, but the strong tradition of route marches in the regiment meant that the London Scottish were 'the only Battalion not to have a man fall out.'[182] No man's land was an odd sea of sand hills, with the enemy out of sight and the heat and monotony of sitting in trenches hard to bear. Discipline became harder to maintain and several men allowed their feelings to boil over during this difficult time and were duly made examples of.

One of those was Drummer 'Fergie' Ferguson, whose disciplinary record states that: 'Whilst on active service, Conduct [sic] to the prejudice of good order and military discipline, in that he at Retreat on 6 August 1917 was insolent to a superior officer.'[183] The witnesses to the incident were Regimental Sergeant Major Duncan and Pipe Major McGilvray. The charges were heard by Major Young, and Drummer Ferguson was sentenced to seven days Field Punishment No. 1. This meant being strapped to a post or wheel and left in the sun for two hours each day. It must have been an excruciating punishment in the desert heat.

A month later, on 15 August, the battalion were moved to El Shauth, another waterless and featureless area known colloquially as the 'cactus garden.' Here intensive training for desert warfare took place, including instructing the men to limit the amount of water they needed to sustain themselves on the march and practising marching through the night to avoid the intensity of the desert heat. The hardships of desert life were interspersed with battalion and brigade concerts and sporting competitions, all of which required involvement from the Pipes and Drums. Retreats were performed, as well as nightly playing at both officers' and sergeants' mess dinners,

---

179 Blaser, *Kilts Across the Jordan*, p.32.
180 Murray, 'My Adventures in the Great War', p.47.
181 Lindsay (ed.), *The London Scottish in the Great War*, p.262.
182 Murray, 'My Adventures in the Great War', p.47.
183 TNA WO 363: 'Alfred Ferguson', record 3360, War Office: Soldiers' Documents, First World War 'Burnt Documents', Microfilm Copies.

along with half-time performances at football matches and other sporting and social events. Pipers and drummers also performed Highland and sword dances, with Pipers Stewart and Hay both particularly gifted in this regard. The Pipes and Drums performed at a large brigade concert held on 19 October, with Pipers Stewart and Hay dancing a reel with two NCOs.

The battalion would remain at El Shauth through most of October, as plans were finalised for the coming Battle of Beersheba. On 5 October, the entire battalion spent three hours in the blazing sun rehearsing for a ceremonial inspection parade planned for the following day by General Allenby. The rehearsal and the preparations for the inspection were 'not enjoyed by regular soldiers'[184] as along with many hours of drill practise, all items of kit had to be cleaned and polished. The Pipes and Drums, as expected, would have a major role in the parade. The next morning, pipers sounded reveille at 0300 hours and the men were on parade an hour later. 'A sergeant, then lieutenant, then captain, then Colonel inspected them – then they marched away to division HQ to be inspected by General Allenby.'[185] The whole show was over by 0900 hours. To balance against these 'annoyances', all men were given extended leave and many made the trip back to Egypt again to further explore Cairo and the Nile.

Preparations for battle were completed by 21 October and the battalion moved out in secrecy to Esani where they stayed in camouflaged bivouacs for the next week, in the hopes of avoiding detection and springing a surprise attack. On 28 October they moved again to Abu Ghalyun and remained there for two days, where engagement with the enemy was planned for 31 October. 'There was a lively satisfaction in the Battalion when it became known that a chance would be presented to them of making memorable yet another Hallowe'en.'[186] Battle commenced at dawn with an artillery barrage, and the London Scottish went over the top at 1215 hours to cross the 1,200 yards to the Turkish positions. The 2nd Battalion swept through the Turkish front line and onwards to their reserve and communication trenches. Fighting would continue until dark when Beersheba itself was finally taken and the vital water supplies it guarded were secured. The London Scottish had fought bravely at the centre of the attacking line 'and it was no small compliment to them that the divisional password for the night was "Strike Sure."'[187]

The battalion moved forward again on 3 November and were back in action on 6 November at Kauwukah, despite having received precious little water in the preceding days. On 7 November they were ordered to take the wells at Sheria, where they suffered heavy casualties but accomplished their mission. Here, news came through that Gaza City had fallen with the Turks in full retreat and the London Scottish were ordered to continue the advance the next day. As the battalion marched forward, they passed through the former headquarters of the Turkish corps commander, where 'every step displayed fresh evidence of the hurried flight of their former occupants. Equipment, stores, personal belongings lay everywhere.'[188] Drummers Turner and Ferguson took this opportunity to 'liberate' a brass Turkish side drum and a bugle to replace issue regimental drums that had lost their own private battle with the desert climate. The battalion's replacement drums were in stores back at Kantara in Egypt and unlikely to be accessible during the campaign. This side drum and bugle would be supplemented by other instruments acquired in even more bizarre circumstances in the coming weeks.

The pipers were also having trouble keeping their instruments in playable condition, finding their sheepskin pipe bags extremely difficult to keep from drying out and splitting. Pipers would

---

184 Murray, 'My Adventures in the Great War', p.64.
185 Murray, 'My Adventures in the Great War', p.64.
186 Lindsay (ed.), *The London Scottish in the Great War*, p.271.
187 Lindsay (ed.), *The London Scottish in the Great War*, p.275.
188 Lindsay (ed.), *The London Scottish in the Great War*, p.282.

often use whale oil, treacle or honey to help keep their bags supple and airtight but 'in the operations subsequent to the fall of Beersheba, no treacle or honey being obtainable, water, often from the pipers own scanty store, had to be used in order to keep the pipes going.'[189] Both drummers and pipers were doing everything possible to continue to play their part.

The battalion pushed on through the intense heat, suffering light casualties as they took Muntaret el Baghl, and ending the day on the heights of Tor Dimre having covered 17 miles under constant fire. They were now 50 miles further forward than the front line at Beersheba which they had attacked only ten days earlier. Jerusalem was now firmly in sight.

The next few weeks consisted of constant long marches, through desolate country with large swarms of flies and minimal water. After two days rest at Tor Dimre, the 2nd Battalion marched eight miles to Nelilieh and then on 16 November, the 17 miles back towards Sheria, to camp at Jindy, where they would stay until 18 November. At Jindy, the pipers had the pleasing task of sorting and handing out a large mail drop of rare post and parcels from home, which did a great deal to enhance morale. Further marches took place each day until reaching Junction Station on 22 November, then on to Bab el Wad on 23 November and Beit Nakuba the following day. Here the Turkish line was again engaged, just six miles from Jerusalem, with the battle for the Holy City planned for 8 December. It would be here that London Scottish Corporal Charles Train would win his Victoria Cross and bring further glory to his battalion and the regiment.

This and other acts of bravery secured the objective of storming Tumulus Hill and a secondary objective by 0900 hours on 24 November and by 1700 hours, news came through that the Turks were pulling out of Jerusalem. The following morning, the London Scottish were given the honour of leading the brigade into the city, on the exact date that Judas Maccabeus had conquered the city and returned it to Jewish control over 2,000 years earlier in 164 BC. It also marked the end of precisely 400 years of Ottoman Turk control after Suleiman the Magnificent seized Jerusalem in 1516. It was, then, a seminal moment of the war and a seminal moment in the history of the Middle East. The Pipes and Drums, as always, led the way and ensured that the men of the battalion were able to enter the city and commemorate this landmark event in a manner that they would remember forever:

> After some difficulty our pipers managed to tune up their instruments (which had suffered considerably from the recent damaging conditions), and they played us along the white road towards the western suburbs. The skirl of the pipes, accompanied by the drums, created a great sensation amongst the few Arab and Jewish pedestrians whom we passed, and, as we marched between the houses, the excitement rapidly rose to such a pitch that it was difficult to maintain a clear passage for the column.[190]

Private Neil Hendry recorded in his diary:

> Early the next morning we marched into Jerusalem with the Pipers in full skirl. The crowds soon turned out and we got a rousing reception. We were just getting to the outskirts of the town and the head of the battalion had turned a corner, when machine gun bullets started to whistle down the street, being fired from a house on the hill in front. We sent out two parties on either flank and they were soon silenced.[191]

---

189 *London Scottish Regiment Gazette* (1919), p.32.
190 Blaser, *Kilts Across the Jordan*, pp.119-120.
191 Hendry, 'My Experiences with the London Scottish'.

A third report from an unknown soldier's diary observed:

> Our pipe band, as you may guess, did justice to us as we marched in on this occasion, and though it was a cold and wet morning, yet our reception from the inhabitants was a warm one and spoke for itself.[192]

The battalion were billeted in an old Syrian orphanage and, in the first rainfall for many months, the London Scottish were able to enjoy a well-earned rest: 'the first night we have been under a roof since we left Katerina in March.'[193] Fighting continued, however, around the Mount of Olives and the 2nd Battalion would remain in the advance until 15 December when they returned to billets in various Jewish schools in Jerusalem. With the battalion remaining in the city until Christmas Eve, there was ample opportunity to explore all the Holy City had to offer. Many were disappointed not to have the opportunity to celebrate Christmas in Jerusalem but on 24 December the London Scottish went into brigade reserve at Shafat amidst fears of a Christmas Day counter-attack by the Turks. The attack never materialised, and the men ate a gloomy Christmas dinner in a rainstorm. However, the Turks did attack on Boxing Day, but the battalion were not seriously engaged in the action and, despite heavy action on other sections of the front, they were not involved in further fighting. The counter-attack had been a disaster for the Turks and they were forced back a further 10 miles from Jerusalem, allowing the London Scottish to return to their billets where they had the opportunity to celebrate Hogmanay in a manner that made up for the disappointment of Christmas Day. 'The haggis was brought in with the state befitting a chieftain, the pipes screaming a heroic chant.'[194] Even a 'certain amount of liquid refreshment was procured',[195] but not enough to result in sore heads for the march out of Jerusalem the next morning to take over the line at Es Suffa.

The Scottish were relieved from the line on 9 January 1918 and billeted on the Mount of Olives, where they would stay until mid-February. During this time, the commanding officer organised for the battalion to undertake a route march led by the pipe band to Bethlehem where they visited and stood guard at the Church of the Nativity. Burns Night was also celebrated in style on 21 January where 'the pipers played at intervals songs of the motherland, and Burns was duly honoured within hearing of the guns of the enemy.'[196]

Movement came again on 18 February, with further fighting on 20 February to take Jebel Ektief and then Neby Musa the following day. Here the battalion raced a mounted ANZAC squadron to take the large mosque and monastery which stood on the hill that marked the burial-place of the Prophet Moses. The 2nd Battalion arrived first and were able to secure both buildings. Whilst searching the monastery, the inimitable Drummers Ferguson and Turner again 'liberated' two drums that 'were not Turkish but ceremonial ones which we understand were used by the monks at the monastery in connection with the visit of pilgrims to the tomb of Moses.'[197] Drummer Ferguson states in regard to the same incident that 'permission was granted to both 'Curly' Turner and myself for their "safe" keeping.'[198] Drumsticks were whittled from tent-pegs and these drums, along with the Turkish brass side drum, would be played by the drum corps for the remainder of

---

192 *London Scottish Regiment Gazette* (1918), p.44.
193 *London Scottish Regiment Gazette* (1921), p.180.
194 *London Scottish Regiment Gazette* (1921), p.142.
195 Lindsay (ed.), *The London Scottish in the Great War*, p.306.
196 *London Scottish Regiment Gazette* (1921), p.142.
197 Letter from Hector Turner to Bernard Blaser, London Scottish Regimental Archives, 12 November 1961.
198 Letter from Alfred Ferguson to Bernard Blaser, London Scottish Regimental Archives, 14 November 1961.

the campaign in Palestine. They would eventually be brought back to regimental headquarters in London where they remain on display in the museum.

The 2nd Battalion would retire back to their billets on the Mount of Olives in preparation for their next major engagement which would take place at Es Salt, a town on a strategically placed hill near Amman in what is now Jordan, overlooking the Jordan valley. The march took them across the Jordan river, which General Allenby aimed to free to allow transport along its length. Fighting began around the hill at El Haud on 24 March and Es Salt was taken the following day. On 27 March, the 2nd Battalion was ordered to march back from Es Salt and formed up for another moment of history that would be captured in text, photographs and cinematic film. The famous photo and film of the London Scottish marching out of Es Salt is brought to life by Private Bernard Blaser's wonderful description:

> Away up on the hillside the roofs of houses were packed with people and the road itself was lined on either side … all gathered to witness the wonderful sight of a kilted regiment on the march …. The order was given to 'Quick-march!' The drums gave a warning roll, captured Turkish drums to boot, the pipers commenced to skirl and the delight of the natives soared to the highest pitch … As we marched, a multitude of men and boys pushed and scrambled for places alongside the pipers, succumbing to the charms of the music like iron filings to the attraction of a magnet. The bagpipes made an irresistible appeal to the Arabs … For two or three miles they kept up with us … until eventually we were unaccompanied except for the echoes that danced around the rocks on the hillside.[199]

The battalion would be back in Es Salt briefly two days later, however, to repel a joint Turkish and German counter-attack before a long march in the desert sun through Jericho to Talaat ed Dumm. 'It was a most trying march, all uphill. The pipers and drummers played magnificently.'[200] Further gruelling marches over the next four days brought them back through Jerusalem, up the Mount of Olives to bivouacs near Shafat, which they reached on 6 April. 'Through the village of Et Tor we passed, and round the sleeping curves through Bethany, the sound of the bagpipes bringing crowds of villagers hurrying to the roadside to see us pass.'[201] After two day's rest, they were back on the march again, travelling along desolate, mountainous, roads and arriving at Wadi El Jib on 10 April. They would go straight into the line the following day.

The front-line here was noticeably quiet and proved something of a rest after the weeks of constant marching. However, it was not to last and only eight days later the battalion was informed that it would be returning once again to Jerusalem to prepare for a second attack on El Haud which had recently been retaken. On Sunday 7 April, a church parade to St George's Cathedral was organised. 'The pipers played us there and back again.'[202] A five-day trek back to Shafat was followed again by the difficult march down the Jordan valley, finally reaching Wadi Nimrin in the early morning of 29 April. During all this time, not a single man fell out and Bernard Blaser gives the following praise to the Pipes and Drums for their contribution during this incredibly difficult time:

> Thanks be to our pipers and drummers we derived considerable stimulation from their music during these long marches. The third and fourth hours of a march are by far the worst, and

---

199 Blaser, *Kilts Across the Jordan*, pp.211-212.
200 Lindsay (ed.), *The London Scottish in the Great War*, p.326.
201 Blaser, *Kilts Across the Jordan*, pp.235-236.
202 *London Scottish Regiment Gazette* (1918), p.119.

you feel as though you can hardly drag one weary leg after the other. Your back begins to bend beneath the weight of your pack, and the step changes every other minute. The periodical halts seem a terribly long time coming, and you are convinced that the Colonel's watch has stopped, and you have already marched half an hour overtime. Then a preliminary roll of drums travels down the column, and the pipers burst forth once again to help you on your weary way. The effect is wonderful. Your back, and the back of your neighbour, in fact everyone's back, immediately straightens; shoulders are squared, and the step again goes with a swing as though each man is anxious to convey to his fellow sufferers that he is not at all tired, but, on the contrary, quite fresh. In ten minutes the unwelcome double beat of the drums is heard, one more round, and the music stops. The rhythm of the step again falls to pieces, backs begin to droop, heads drop lower, and chins rest on chests in the struggle with the strain on endurance.[203]

The attack on El Haud began on 30 April and the fighting would be extremely fierce. Enemy numbers had been grossly underestimated and the attack up-hill over rocky, open ground under intense Turkish shelling and machine gun fire caused substantial casualties. A Victoria Cross for Private Robert Cruickshank along with one Distinguished Conduct Medal and two Military Medals would be awarded to men of the London Scottish for the day's action and reflects the heroics performed by the 2nd Battalion in capturing their objectives, despite the failure of the overall assault. More than 170 men became casualties, including 33 killed in action. On 1 May the London Scottish were relieved and held a service at Wadi Nimrin to bury their dead: 'the transport men had already dug graves. We had a very impressive service here where our poor chaps were laid to rest to the wail of *The Flowers of the Forest*.'[204] The ceremony took place at twilight and the battalion was marched forward, company by company to form a square:

> The centre of the square are mounds of earth, each surmounted by its little cross, carefully and neatly finished, those that are closed, but twelve or more are still open. Then, on the still night air the pipes give forth *The Flowers of the Forest*, that beautiful plaintive cry of grief for the fallen. It finishes and one can hear men catching their breath. Three rounds of blanks fired by the firing party, each followed by the salute of the pipers.[205]

The band then played the companies back to camp and the final major battle for the 2nd Battalion in Palestine was over. Their time in the Middle East was coming to an end.

After months of gruelling marching and hard campaigning, the London Scottish were promised a significant period of rest but as was so often the case, it was not to be. Following just two weeks recuperation at Ain Arik, the battalion were ordered out to dig roads near Ram Allah for a week, before a march to the coast saw them entrain out of Palestine and back to Kantara. Here it became obvious that the 2nd Battalion would be moving again to another theatre of war and on 15 June they entrained for the port of Alexandria and directly on to the *SS Canberra*. The major German offensives that took place on the Western Front in the spring of 1918 had been checked but the outlook was still ominous and a major effort was underway to muster as many troops as possible, including the newly arrived Americans, to break the German line and finally win the war once and for all. The experience and efficiency of the 2nd Battalion, London Scottish as a fighting unit meant they, and battalions like them, were highly craved by British military commanders in

---

203 Blaser, *Kilts Across the Jordan*, p.236.
204 Hendry, 'My Experiences with the London Scottish'.
205 *London Scottish Regiment Gazette* (1918), p.110.

France and Flanders and it was decided that they would leave the 60th Division and return to the Western Front.

The *Canberra* made port safely at Taranto, Italy on 18 June 1918, after a journey fraught with German U-boat attacks. Here the men climbed aboard troop trains for the long, slow journey back to France. They would arrive in Marseilles on 1 July to join the 90th Brigade of the 30th Division, which had been destroyed by the German counter-attack in March 1918 and was now being rebuilt. The 2nd Battalion arrived back in Europe to be greeted by the 1918 influenza epidemic, which particularly affected men used to the dry heat of the desert. Despite this, movement was made back to France and 8 July saw 2nd Battalion in corps reserve at Cassel and soon on the front at Eecke. Here they would stay, rotating in and out of the line, until their first major assault on 20 August at the Dranoutre Ridge. Over the next few months, the courage of the 2nd Battalion would continually be relied upon to push the Germans backwards and, of the 28 times the 30th Division attacked, the London Scottish led the way on no less than 26 occasions. This fighting took them close to Messines Ridge, where the 1st Battalion had made such a reputation, seemingly so long ago, and forward over ground devastated by four years of constant warfare.

On 19 September, the 2nd Battalion took over the front line at Hill 63 where they would stay until 24 September, in the vain hope that they could take back the village that had been the scene of so much London Scottish glory in 1914. This wish would partially come true on 27 September as Allied forces pushed successfully forward on a front 24 miles wide, which would see the 2nd Battalion pass through Messines. They would be relieved on 3 October and withdraw to the Messines Ridge, with many men taking the opportunity to visit the exact location of the famous 1914 Hallowe'en battle. On 10 October they were back in the line again and fighting forward, with another major assault taking place on 14 October at the Menin-Wervicq road. This action was a great success and proved to be the last major attack by the 2nd Battalion during the First World War, although further fighting would take place on 18 and 20 October before relief came, followed instantly by another major outbreak of Spanish Flu. The Pipes and Drums were able to supply some good cheer on 31 October when a sports day was followed by the traditional meal, allowing the 2nd Battalion to properly celebrate their own Hallowe'en exploits in Palestine for the first time. A return to the line in early November saw the Germans in full retreat and the 2nd Battalion were near Moen when news came through of the signing of the Armistice. It would, however, be a long time yet before the men were to finally see home.

Nineteen-eighteen passed very much like the previous year for the Pipes and Drums of the 3rd Battalion back home in England. Pipers and drummers were trained and were sent out to both the 1st and 2nd Battalions over the course of the year, whilst wounded men returned and re-joined, including Piper James Wood Young who would rise to the rank of pipe sergeant under Pipe Major Shand. The band continued to play at regimental and mess dinners as well as at funerals and fund and morale raising events but, by the latter half of the year, 'the ranks of the band have been sadly thinned.'[206] Finding trained pipers and drummers at this point in the war was almost impossible, and the talent and temperament of those willing to learn was not always of the highest calibre. The *Chelsea News and General Advertiser* reported on the court case of Piper Bernard Gilbert Rodgers, aged 17: 'a piper in the London Scottish Regiment, who was charged on remand … with stealing a quantity of silver goods, six boxes of cigars, articles of apparel, etc.'[207] worth about £50. Rodgers admitted to the offenses and stated that the men he found around him had money and he 'wanted

---

206 *London Scottish Regiment Gazette* (1918), p.175.
207 *Chelsea News and General Advertiser*, 2 August 1918, p.2.

to keep up a position.'[208] The generally middle-class stature of many of the men in the Pipes and Drums may well have played a part in the young Rodgers' decision to break the law.

This was a late and rather unwelcome event in the history of the 3rd Battalion Pipes and Drums but it would not be long before both band and battalion were demobilised and their sterling work training men for overseas service and providing a range of musical services on the Home Front came to an end. The Pipes and Drums had offered a home for those who could not fight overseas as well as those that did but returned injured. Many pipers and drummers would re-join the regiment after the war and were instrumental in rebuilding the post-war band and taking it forward to new heights.

Unlike the 1st Battalion, the 2nd Battalion would not go on to play a part in the army of occupation in Germany but, despite this, they would not be demobilised until months after the final 1st Battalion cadre returned to headquarters in May 1919. The Pipes and Drums headed a divisional ceremonial victory parade near Marcke on 26 November. Four days later, they were leading the battalion through a series of long marches from 30 November to 4 December that saw them arrive at Les Ciseaux. From there they went on to La Lacque, where Colonel Ogilby arranged for the battalion to take over a newly built POW camp, where they would stay until mid-January 1919. Here, the battalion were able to relax for the first time and recover from the brutalities of the last few years, and they went about it with great gusto; the Pipes and Drums leading the way as always.

A large Christmas dinner was organised, along with other sporting and social events to mark the season, before Hogmanay was celebrated in true London Scottish spirit. Matters within the pipe band hut, in particular, were close to getting out of hand, as this excerpt from a speech given some years later by Captain J. Stuart Monro ascertains:

> On New Year's Eve … according to RSM Danson, I saved Piper Pullar's life. The first New Year's Eve after Armistice had been decidedly hectic. At 3am Hell's Delight was going on, and *Réveillé* was at 5.30. As most of the officers and NCO's, including both Orderly Officer and Orderly Sergeant, were otherwise engaged in assessing the value of the liquid assets in the Sergeant's Mess, I set out alone to endeavour to quell the riot. By sheer bad luck I first entered the Band hut. You yourself (talking to the CO) have been a distinguished member of the Band and can realise the position. I walked in one door, and decided it was politic to walk out the other and go back to bed. Later on, Danson told me that Piper Matheson, who was chasing Pullar with a spade, saw me (in duplicate as it were), and decided it was wiser to go to bed![209]

All members of the Pipes and Drums managed to attend full reveille next morning, dressed and able to function, and thus no more was said about the incident until years later.

The battalion moved a short distance on 3 January and again on 16 January nearer to Étaples, where the demobilisation process would begin for many but for only a handful in the Pipes and Drums. The band was considered essential for morale and *esprit de corps* and, therefore, would be amongst the last to be finally demobbed. Pipe Major McGilvray was one of the lucky ones and, due to his age and service, was demobbed on 21 December 1918. He was presented with the Belgian Croix de Guerre by a thankful nation, despite most of his service having taken place in the Middle East. He would also be further rewarded for his outstanding military service by being made a Commander of the British Empire. His position was taken by Sergeant Piper Charles Oram, whose own war experience was an extraordinary one, having fought and been wounded at

---

208 *Chelsea News and General Advertiser*, 2 August 1918, p.2.
209 *London Scottish Regiment Gazette* (1935), p.12.

Messines, only to continue his service on recovery with the 3rd then 2nd Battalions. He was one of only a handful of men from the London Scottish who fought and survived the entire length of the war, serving as he did with all three battalions and fighting in three different theatres of war. Pipe Major Oram returned to Britain on 25 February 1919 and Piper Davie Pullar took over, officially appointed pipe major on 20 June. Pipe Major Pullar would see out the final duties of the 2nd Battalion Pipes and Drums during the war, finally earning his own demobilisation on 29 September 1919.

When the 1st Battalion went down to cadre strength in March, some members of the 1st Battalion Pipes and Drums were sent to the 2nd Battalion, along with 100 other ranks of the 1st Battalion and 700 men from the Gordon Highlanders. This could not have come at a better time as, by this point, Pipe Major Pullar and Piper Gillies were the only two pipers left with the band. The battalion stayed near Abbieville from 25 May onwards, guarding prisoners of war during the spring and summer of 1919, where the Pipes and Drums were given friendly competition by a newly created battalion jazz band. They would finally move back to England on 17 September to Cherry Hinton camp, via Folkestone before moving on to Clipstone camp, near Mansfield in October. By the first week of November 1919 the last man from the 2nd Battalion was finally a civilian again.

The 2nd Battalion had proudly lived up to the reputation of its more glamorous sister battalion and had played an equally important role during the war. As with the 1st Battalion, a huge amount of their success was due to the regimental spirit and prestige that both battalions fostered and emphasised. It was a characteristic of the regiment much commented on by numerous generals and other senior ranking officers, 'and so Lord Haig is right when he says that it is to their 'esprit de corps' that the London Scottish owe their success.'[210] In facilitating this, the 2nd Battalion Pipes and Drums had done their duty, and so much more.

Whilst fewer members of the 2nd Battalion band paid the ultimate sacrifice in comparison to their counterparts in the 1st Battalion, many were wounded as they played their part in action as runners and stretcher-bearers, whilst others succumbed to diseases and the debilitations of desert warfare. It is worth noting that, of the 33 stretcher-bearers who served with the 2nd Battalion during the war, four were killed and 19 wounded. As with all of the men in the battalion, they suffered the hardships, horrors and brutality of modern conflict. Ultimately, however, their place in history is assured as the only regimental Pipes and Drums to see active service in Ireland and three separate theatres of war during the First World War. As is recorded so eloquently in the *Regimental Gazette*:

> They played in the lowlands of Flanders and France, under the shadow of Mount Olympus and among the Macedonian hills, in the plains and hills of Palestine, across the desert and on the high seas, and their value to the Battalion in its long marches, as well as in its leisure moments, cannot be estimated too highly. They wailed a coronach over the dead on the banks of the Jordan and for the first time in history the bagpipes were heard on the road to Bethlehem. Their music has lightened the step of many a weary mile and helped to brighten the soldier's life in camp and billets in days of rest.[211]

---

210 Lindsay (ed.), *The London Scottish in the Great War*, p.306.
211 *London Scottish Regiment Gazette*, (1919), p.32.

5

The Inter-War Years 1919-1939

It will, I think, be generally admitted by men of wide experience, whatever may be their private opinion of bagpipes, that for marching to, there is nothing to compare with a pipe band.

The pipe band strikes up and your feet suddenly forget their weariness; that extra demon of weight, which threatened to overcome you, silently slips from your shoulders; and the telegraph poles by the roadside evince a new and friendly nearness to each other. There is a magic in the pipes, with their old familiar marching tunes and the undercurrent of the drums with their enlivening beat.

In many regiments, the drum-beats are not written down at all; they are simply handed down from one generation of drummers to another, in at least one case, as many of you know, actually from father to son. The pipe tune itself is an affair of notes, carefully recorded in black and white that all may read it; but the drum-beats, the undercurrent of the music, are not in the realm of written things at all: they are in the province of Tradition reverently guarded by a long line of devoted drummers.

Reverend Dr Archibald Fleming
Chaplain, The London Scottish Regiment (1903-1922)
Sermon, St Columba's Church, London Scottish church parade in the early 1920s[1]

The men of the 1st and 2nd Battalions, London Scottish, returned to a vastly different world when they were demobilised and sailed back to Great Britain at the end of the 'Great War'. While the country had not suffered the physical devastation by aerial bombardment that would take place during the Second World War, the social, political and economic impact created by four years of total war was on a scale never previously witnessed. The *Representation of the People Act* of 1918 meant that some returning soldiers would obtain the vote for the first time, while for others that vote was extended to their wives and daughters. With a crippling national war debt, equivalent to 136 percent of gross domestic product, it soon became obvious that the radical reconstruction and social reform programme promised at war's end, including large scale building of social housing and the creation of a national health and welfare system, would be replaced by swingeing cuts to service the national debt and ward off rampant inflation.

Nearly one million British men had been killed, and a further 1.7 million seriously wounded during the war. This represented approximately two percent of the British population. The human cost had been enormous and the ongoing physical and mental issues for the wounded would impact the nation for decades to come. What is striking, however, when reading diaries of London Scottish and other soldiers who served during the war, is the numerous comments on how much they 'enjoyed' their war experiences. Diary keeping became an offense punishable by death in July 1915, but many men decided to carry on writing. Men like Private Sandy Innes, who wrote, 'I hope to smuggle this

---

[1] The 'drum-beats' in question are the 'Big Drum' beatings of Sergeant Drummer 'Sandy' Gow and his son, Drummer Tom Gow, who took over from his father as bass drummer in the London Scottish Pipes and Drums.

one home.'[2] Soldiers wanted to continue keeping diaries to commemorate their experiences which, despite the horrors they witnessed, would for many, be remembered fondly. Sergeant Henry T. Smith, who fought with the 1st Battalion from July 1915, wrote on the day he was demobbed in 1919, 'now I have actually finished my Army career. Looking back, I know that I have had the time of my life.'[3] Many men enjoyed the adventure, camaraderie, organisation and excitement that military life during wartime created, and returning to the normality of civilian life in a debt-ridden country that would gradually descend into the 'Great Depression,' left a hole some were eager to fill.

While countless others were understandably glad to be rid of military life, some wished to extend it. Thus, when the London Scottish were re-established in 1919, many who had served during the war looked to re-enlist. This was particularly prevalent in the Pipes and Drums, where pre-war members, such as Pipe Major Rob Robertson, who had remained the heart and soul of the regiment back in Great Britain during the war, were joined by others that had volunteered or been conscripted to serve in the two battalions overseas. They would, in turn, be joined by pipers and drummers who had served in other Scottish regiments and now found themselves in post-war London, in addition to younger men who had not been old enough to serve and felt they had missed out on the Great War experience. In this way, men who had fought on every battlefield of the war or none, came together to form the post war Pipes and Drums of the London Scottish Regiment. Between them, they would take the pipe band to musical heights never previously envisaged. With three former band members also taking the helm as commanding officer of the regiment throughout the inter-war period, these were to be glorious days indeed for the London Scottish Pipes and Drums.

22 May 1919 saw a total of 46 pipers and drummers, including seven previous pipe majors, sit down for the restoration of the annual band dinner with Pipe Major Robertson presiding. Showing typical humility, 'Pipe-Major Robertson thought, that with such a noble army of Pipe-Majors who had done their bit in the war, that he had no business to occupy the Chair.'[4] Pipers and Drummers who had served through the war were honoured, while those who had died while overseas were remembered, as indeed, they are to this day. Captain 'Dougie' Lyall-Grant gave his remembrances of piping whilst a Prisoner of War in Germany, and it was noted that band practise had begun again on the traditional Thursday evenings. Rebuilding the regiment was of the greatest importance to all present, and Pipe Major Robertson stated that he 'had no doubt but that the Pipes and Drums would be in the forefront of the rejuvenated London Scottish.'[5] They would most certainly play a major role in this regard.

On Saturday 5 July 1919, before the 2nd Battalion had even returned to Great Britain, a victory parade was organised in London for Territorial troops that had served overseas. 'London's Day: The March of the London Territorials' started on the Chelsea Embankment and ended in the City of London at Somerset House. A contingent of ex-London Scottish soldiers marched in the parade behind the Pipes and Drums. A concert was held in the evening back at 59 Buckingham Gate, which doubled as a celebration of the appointment, two days earlier, of Field Marshal Sir Douglas Haig as Honorary Colonel of the London Scottish Regiment. This was an honour of huge significance, deemed a massive coup for a Territorial regiment and an indication of the prestige accorded the London Scottish for their war-time exploits. The Pipes and Drums took centre stage at this concert, with Pipe Major Robertson in charge. Considering that there were several ex-pipe majors available to lead the pipe band, it is a sign of the respect and regard in which he was held that Robertson was chosen to take authority over

---

2   A.G.S. Innes, Unpublished diary, London Scottish Museum Archives, July 1915.
3   Henry T. Smith, 'Diary of the Great War 1914-19', Unpublished diary, London Scottish Museum Archives, entry for 19 February 1919.
4   *London Scottish Regiment Gazette* (1919), p.98.
5   *London Scottish Regiment Gazette* (1919), p.78.

the post-war Pipes and Drums. It may also have been a politic way of ensuring none of the war-time battalion pipe majors felt slighted. Pipe Major Robertson would go on to add extensively to his already considerable contribution, not only to the band but to the regiment, and his successful leadership built strong foundations for the success of the Pipes and Drums over the next 20 years.

The most important event in the regimental calendar for 1919 came on 29 October when a massive Hallowe'en dinner was organised at the Olympia Exhibition Centre. 31 October had always marked the end of the Volunteer year and had been celebrated in the London Scottish with a regimental dinner since at least 1866, but the heroics of the 1st Battalion in 1914 and the 2nd Battalion in 1917 were to add great significance from this point onwards. Only 19 men had taken part in both Messines and Beersheba, the two great Hallowe'en battles of the war, including Piper Charles Oram who performed with the band that evening. The 'London Scottish: Great After-War Reunion' was attended by over 1,500 officers and men who had passed through the regiment during the war and the newly created Earl Haig gave a rousing speech before a performance by the Pipes and Drums brought the men to their feet.

While the Hallowe'en dinner was a celebration of all the regiment had achieved during the First World War the memorial service held a few days later, on Sunday 2 November, was very much an occasion for commemoration and reflection. It is a tribute to the band, and to the music of pipes and drums in general, that such opposing emotions could both be so eloquently expressed. 'At the conclusion of the service the pipe band of the regiment with muffled drums played the 'Lament' and the buglers sounded last post.'[6] Regimental Chaplain, Dr Archibald Fleming, wrote to Pipe Major Robertson about the pipe band's contribution to the service, remarking:

Many, including Lord Haig, said to me that it was the most impressive service of the kind that they had ever attended. … this was in no small measure due to the wonderful playing by you and your pipers of the most moving music in the world. Perhaps you will have the opportunity of telling them of my deep gratitude and appreciation.[7]

The commitment by the Pipes and Drums to remember the fallen was further highlighted in February 1920, when they organised a 'Grand Concert' at regimental headquarters that raised a significant amount of money towards a proposed London Scottish war memorial, commemorating the names of all those who had fallen in action while wearing the Hodden Grey. The concert was a great success and 'The Band (we call them that collectively – they are a band of brothers) put their hearts and, what is more moment, their money and their work in the promotion of this … event.'[8]

Later that year, the band were involved in a recruiting concert on June 10th and joined the rest of the regiment in August for the re-inauguration of the traditional march through Scotland. The regiment travelled to Scotland by boat and were hosted by the Royal Navy at the headquarters of the Torpedo Boat Flotilla at Port Edgar, Edinburgh where the Pipes and Drums made quite an impression. They set off the first morning to rousing cheers from sailors on the base, 'but they did not let us go unattended, for a select party of Naval Petty Officers accompanied the detachment all the eight miles to Linlithgow, two of them carrying the big drum when it wasn't being beaten.'[9] They were also astounded when ex-piper, Captain Lyall-Grant:

True to his old love, took his place in the pipe-band for a time and felt and looked, as all true pipers do, like ten. This tickled our Naval friends immensely and one was heard to remark 'Just imagine our 'Number One' playing in the band.'[10]

---

6   *Dundee Evening Telegraph*, 3 November 1919, p.4.
7   *London Scottish Regiment Gazette* (1919), p.182.
8   *London Scottish Regiment Gazette* (1920), p.32.
9   *London Scottish Regiment Gazette* (1920), p.117.
10 *London Scottish Regiment Gazette* (1920), p.117.

Piper Oram stood in as acting pipe major, and ten other pipers and drummers who marched that week had served overseas with either the 1st or 2nd Battalions.

July 1921 saw the first annual camp since the reformation of the regiment, which travelled to their old pre-war stomping ground at Shorncliffe. The Pipes and Drums led the regiment through Victoria and Pimlico to the train and then performed their normal camp duties over the next week, including a Scottish night in Folkestone on the last evening where 'Our pipe band played to the natives and visitors for the good of their souls.'[11]

An interesting event took place on October 6th when the band played alongside the Pipes and Drums of the 1st Battalion, Scots Guards at a concert organised by current and past members of 'A' Company. 'Perhaps the most outstanding features were the pipe-bands.'[12] The London Scottish band opened the concert, followed by the Scots Guards and then, most interestingly, 'the pipers of the 1st Scots Guards and drummers of the London Scottish showed us what first-class pipers and drummers of two crack units could do together; a fine combination.'[13]

Company dinners were major affairs during this period, with hundreds of serving soldiers and veterans, attending. Over ten thousand men had passed through the three battalions of the London Scottish during the war, and company dinners were a way of staying in touch with former comrades and remaining part of the regimental family. They were generally relaxed affairs, with officers, the majority of whom had come through the ranks, mixing freely with the men. As all pipers and drummers were assigned to a specific company, and with the Pipes and Drums constantly in demand for regimental dinners, members of the band were always in attendance at such events. At the 'A' Company dinner in 1922, Captain Lyall-Grant, who had been an 'A' Company piper, piped in the haggis and at the 'C' Company dinner, no less than four pipe majors from that company played the guests to the table.

It was not, however, all jollity and light-heartedness. The harsh realities of the post-war economy were making life exceedingly challenging for many and some members of the Pipes and Drums were having difficulty finding work. In 1922, the *Regimental Gazette* published an appeal from Piper Bertram Nicol who 'would be glad if any member of the Battalion would help him to obtain employment. Preferably as draughtsman but failing that anything and anywhere – home or abroad.'[14] Fortunately, Nicol found work in London, became an architect, and was able to continue as a member of the Pipes and Drums for the next decade. He had been wounded at Messines in 1914 and spent the remainder of the war using his draughtsman's experience as an officer in the Labour Corps but, like several other ex-officers, happily re-joined the London Scottish as a private to play once again in the band.

A highlight of 1922 was an attempt by the regiment to win back the world record for the 'longest route march in the quickest time,' which the London Scottish had inaugurated in 1890. The original time for a platoon of men, marching 52 and a half miles from London to Brighton, carrying full kit and rifle weighing over 50lbs, was just over 19 hours. Competition between the Scottish and, in particular, the London Rifle Brigade had seen the Rifles bring the record down to 14 hours and 23 minutes in 1914. Pipers and drummers had taken part in this event on several previous occasions and on 8 April 1922 five pipers and four drummers would accompany two officers and 27 other ranks as they attempted to win the record back. Despite torrential rain, the team set off 'as Pipers Allan, Cross and Allan commenced the first of an endless repertoire of pipe tunes.'[15] As

---

11 *London Scottish Regiment Gazette* (1921), p.116.
12 *London Scottish Regiment Gazette* (1921), p.150.
13 *London Scottish Regiment Gazette* (1921), p.150.
14 *London Scottish Regiment Gazette* (1922), p.40.
15 *London Scottish Regiment Gazette* (1922), p.72.

is so often the case, the drummers receive no mention, but the representatives of both sides of the band played through every hour of the march. Despite the hardships of not only marching for over 50 miles but also carrying and playing instruments:

> Again and again our pipers, like true sportsmen, came to the rescue, piping as though they had first started, so that one and all, had they ever doubted their capabilities, redoubled their efforts and strode out afresh for the goal.[16]

That goal was achieved when the team arrived in Brighton in 13 hours and 59 minutes, smashing the record by 24 minutes; a truly remarkable feat of endurance.

On 23 July, the regiment took part in the Royal Review of the 1st and 2nd London Divisions by King George V and Queen Mary. This parade of over 10,000 Territorial troops took place in Hyde Park in terrible weather. As had happened on some many occasions during the Victorian era, the London Scottish were given a distinguished individual honour. As each regiment paraded in front of the Royal saluting dais during the march-past, the massed bands of the Guards division played them through, while their own bands remained mute. 'The London Scottish, however, marched past to the accompaniment of their pipes.'[17]

This honour was not awarded just because of regimental prestige. While the London Scottish name carried a huge degree of honour, the musical abilities of the Pipes and Drums were beginning to make a name for themselves too. Their performances at annual camp in Aldershot in September, for instance, met with rave reviews. *The Scotsman* observed:

> The pride of the London Scottish Territorials just now is their pipe band. They have become more fully conscious of its superiority by the tributes paid to it by officers and bandmasters of other regiments during the recent period of encampment at Aldershot.[18]

The Pipes and Drums at this point comprised 18 pipers and 12 drummers, including four ex-pipe majors who had given up their appointments to play in the band. As well as representation from pre-war and war-time battalion drummers and pipers, a contingent of excellent younger musicians was coming through the ranks, six of whom had learnt their instrument at the Royal Caledonian School. The band also attracted interest from the regular army and contained five ex-Scots Guards pipers. This group joined under the auspices of Piper David 'Dusty' Smith, who had enlisted as a piper in the 1st Battalion, Scots Guards in 1907 and served with them until his promotion to Pipe Major of the 3rd Battalion in 1916. When his battalion were disbanded after the war, Pipe Major Smith was discharged and, in 1921, joined the London Scottish bringing four other pipers with him. This combination of older, younger, Territorial, regular, pre-war, wartime and post-war musicians proved to be the perfect blend. Indeed, the *Aberdeen Press and Journal* commented:

> The London Scottish pipe band is credited with being the finest musical combination of any regiment stationed at Aldershot within recent years. Its admirers suggest that it should be able to challenge any pipe band in Scotland, and claim that no Territorial, maybe no Regular, Scottish battalion has more musical vitality or ability than the London Scottish.[19]

---

16 *London Scottish Regiment Gazette* (1922), p.73.
17 *Aberdeen Press and Journal*, 24 July 1922, p.5.
18 *The Scotsman*, 18 September 1922, p.5.
19 *Aberdeen Press and Journal*, 18 September 1922, p.4.

Talk began to grow of possibly competing in the World Championships at the Cowal Games in Dunoon as early as the following year, but Pipe Major Robertson understood that a great deal more practise and preparation would be needed to make such a dream reality. It would not, unfortunately, arrive under his tenure, but it would come soon after.

More important regimental duties took place on 5 November 1922 when the regimental church parade was given added significance by Earl Haig unveiling a memorial at St Columba's Church to commemorate the officers and men of the London Scottish who laid down their lives in the Great War. The quality of the band's performance that day is portrayed vividly in the following account:

> Again, the throbbing of drums and the skirl of pipes raised in the soul-stirring lament, dying into silence as the pipers circled the church and gradually passed out, and then a silence which seemed an eternity, until broken by the ringing notes of the Last Post. Again silence, and then the call of Reveille, and it seemed to bring to the listeners a message of a new life opened, a great and glorious life, free from petty cares and strife.[20]

Sunday 21 January 1923 saw an equally impressive ceremony at the unveiling of the First World War memorial at regimental headquarters, 59 Buckingham Gate. Once again, it was Regimental Honorary Colonel, Earl Haig, who led the unveiling, with the Pipes and Drums, as always, playing a significant role.

August saw six pipers and five drummers under Sergeant Piper Smith accompany a London Scottish detachment of 50 officers and men who travelled to Canada at the invitation of the Toronto Scottish Regiment. Formed originally as the 75th Battalion CEF during the First World War, they had been re-designated 'The Mississauga Regiment' in 1919 post-war reforms. However, with many NCOs and men of Scottish decent, they petitioned to be reclassified as a Highland regiment and renamed the Toronto Scottish, for which permission was approved in September 1921. As a Canadian militia unit, the Toronto Scottish wished to model themselves on the Territorial London Scottish and advances were made for an affiliation, which was endorsed initially by Colonel Green and other London Scottish officers, and then given official approval by the War Office on 22 March 1922. As a mark of respect, the Toronto Scottish asked for permission to assimilate the Hodden Grey as their regimental tartan and to use the basic design of the London Scottish cap badge for their own. Permission was again granted and they became, and remain, the only other regiment in the world with consent to wear Hodden Grey.[21] The London Scottish were invited to Toronto for a series of events to honour this new affiliation and the contingent departed on August 17th.

> They marched from their headquarters in Buckingham Gate to Euston headed by the Scots Guards pipe band (who played alternately with the London Scottish Pipes and Drums) and were given a send-off at the station which had all the gusto of the war-time departures, with none of the sadness.[22]

The London Scottish detachment was treated royally while in Canada, performing at events in Toronto, Montreal and Quebec. The London Scottish Regiment was given the Freedom of the City of Toronto and, most poignantly, the Pipes and Drums played at the Christie Military Hospital for men disabled by the war, 'which seemed to greatly interest the patients.'[23]

---

20 *London Scottish Regiment Gazette* (1922), p.177.
21 For further particulars, see Timothy J. Stewart, *Toronto's Fighting 75th in the Great War 1915-1919: A Pre-History of the Toronto Scottish Regiment* (Waterloo, Ontario: Wilfrid Laurier Univ. Press, 2017).
22 *Western Mail*, Cardiff, 18 August 1923, p.7.
23 *London Scottish Regiment Gazette* (1923), p.149.

THE INTER-WAR YEARS 1919-1939   181

This period in charge for Pipe Sergeant Smith would prove to be a good rehearsal as, in June 1924, Pipe Major Robertson retired for the second and last time and Smith was appointment pipe major. Robertson had already resigned in 1916, only to come out of retirement when asked to help reform the Pipes and Drums after the war. Now, at the age of 57, he decided to pass the baton on to a younger man. 'The excellence of our Pipe Band bears eloquent testimony to his enthusiasm and tact.'[24] Pipe Major Smith already had experience gleaned while a pipe major in the Scots Guards, and he also managed his own civilian pipe band which played regularly as part of a cabaret act at the London Palladium. It is to his credit that he was accepted to lead the band having only joined three years earlier.

Piper Charles Oram, who was another of the war-time London Scottish pipe majors in the band, would also retire during this period due to ill health, exacerbated by his wartime service, which left Piper Davie Pullar as the only remaining war-time pipe major still serving. Pullar would miss out on the top job this time round, but his patience would prove to be worthwhile. Pipe Major Smith continued to build on the musical legacy left by Pipe Major Robertson, and the Pipes and Drums continued in their quest for musical excellence which would eventually take them onto the world championship stage; 'He handed over to his successor, Sergeant-Piper Smith, probably the finest Pipe Band the Battalion has ever had.'[25]

Pipe Major Robertson was, however, still in charge for the most significant regimental event of 1924, which took place on 5 May with the unveiling by Albert I, King of the Belgians, of the London Scottish war memorial on Messines Ridge at the site of the 1914 Battle of Messines. The London Scottish took a large contingent to the unveiling and this initial undertaking would evolve into a five-yearly regimental pilgrimage that continues to this day. The officers stayed at the Hotel Sultan in Ypres where, 'with our fellow guests, the senior members of the pipe band, we soon settled down. The pipers became prime favourites with Madame, Mademoiselle and the 'jeune filles' of the establishment, as they always do wherever they go!'[26] The ceremony was an impressive affair, beginning in Ypres' heavily battle-scared and ruined centre, before moving on to Messines and then to the new memorial on the ridge. 'The Guard of Honour mustered in the railway station square, where the pipers treated the populace to a selection of the music of the hills.'[27] That guard of honour included Major Lyall-Grant and Piper Nicol who had both fought at Messines. The drums were muffled in black crepe and the pipes played a lament before the bugles sounded Last Post and reveille in front of an audience of current and ex-London Scottish soldiers and a plethora of dignitaries, including King Albert who had flown himself to the memorial service by plane.

From 24 August to 26 September the Pipes and Drums participated in the Torchlight Tattoo, which exhibited the varying capacities of the British armed forces as part of the British Empire Exhibition at the newly built Wembley Stadium. For once, it was the drummers who would come in for special praise: 'I wonder who trained those London Scottish drummers, they are the best in the massed pipe band!'[28] Presciently, within the next three years they would come to eclipse even the pipers.

After the traditional Hallowe'en dinner, 1924 would conclude with a retirement dinner for Pipe Major Robertson. With Major Lyall-Grant in the Chair, 'all ranks were forgotten'[29] and, after the current band played, an ensemble of former members took to the floor:

---

24   *London Scottish Regiment Gazette* (1924), p.101.
25   *London Scottish Regiment Gazette* (1924), p.112.
26   *London Scottish Regiment Gazette* (1924), p.86.
27   *London Scottish Regiment Gazette* (1924), p.92.
28   *London Scottish Regiment Gazette* (1924), p.151.
29   *London Scottish Regiment Gazette* (1925), p.6.

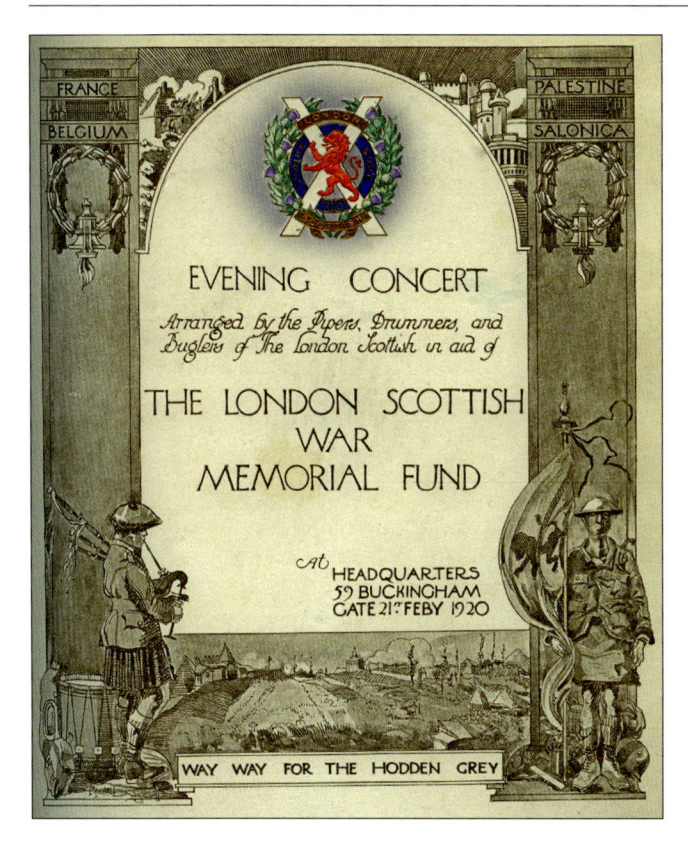

Poster for the concert organised by the Pipes and Drums to help fund the London Scottish First World War memorial, February 1920. (LSMA, used with permission)

The Pipes and Drums, led by Pipe Majors Wills and Oram, leading the London Scottish Victory Parade through Admiralty Arch and on to The Mall, July 1919. (LSMA, used with permission)

Setting a new record of 13 hours 59 minutes for the 52.5-mile London to Brighton March, with five pipers and four drummers playing the entire route, 8 April 1922. (LSMA, used with permission)

The London Scottish detachment en route to Canada on the S.S. *Montrose* to visit the Toronto Scottish, August 1923. (LSMA, used with permission)

Among the eleven ex-pipers who formed this band were six commissioned officers – five majors and a captain – and the big drums were beaten by the ever-young septuagenarian Tommy Hodgson, and his very much junior, Old Sandy Gow.[30]

The 'Ancients and Moderns' then played together, starting a tradition that was taken up at the 1925 band supper and which continues to take place today. This dinner was a fitting end to his time as pipe major but Robertson's commitment to the Pipes and Drums and to the regiment was far from over.

The Burns Night season of 1925 was given special importance by the fledgling British Broadcasting Corporation. On the evening of Saturday 4 January, 'a concert at the Albert Hall will be relayed, including selections on the pipes. Items by the band of the Scots Guards and the drums and pipes of the London Scottish.'[31] This marked the first occasion that a pipe band had played live on national radio.

Later in the year, another march through Scotland saw the London Scottish in Aberdeenshire with the Pipes and Drums again at their head. The march to Crathes Castle found the regiment 'Stepping out in good style, the men singing and whistling during the intervals when the pipe band was not playing.'[32] The approach towards the Castle 'heralded by the strains of the pipes and the beating of the drums brought large crowds to the main thoroughfare.'[33] The week concluded with the London Scottish parading at Balmoral Castle, where the band played a set before marching the regiment from the grounds.

1926 saw the inauguration of the now famous Macleod Medal, which was first reported in the commanding officer's notes in the *Regimental Gazette*:

> I have to thank the following for their kindness in presenting prizes for battalion competitions:
> Lieutenant T MacLeod, for a medal to be held for the year by the best piper in the band, below the rank of lance-corporal.[34]

It was won, in its inaugural year, by Piper L.G. Booth and has been hotly competed for by pipers of the regiment ever since. Interestingly, 1926 was also the year that a certain Private Hugh Attwooll first joined the London Scottish and was assigned to HQ Company. Having climbed through the ranks, he would go on in later years to inaugurate a similar prize for drumming.

In October, ex-piper and band president Major Lyall-Grant became Lieutenant Colonel Lyall-Grant and took his place as Commanding Officer of the London Scottish. By special order, he received permission to stay on as band president, a position normally held by the second in command or another major or captain within the regiment. Re-joining the regiment from the reserve of officers to take his place as Second in Command was Major Lionel D. Henderson who:

> Will be better known to many old members by the sobriquet 'Jock,' borne by him for ten years from 1904 till the outbreak of the War, while serving with that enthusiastic band of brothers – the pipers. Soon after mobilization he was one of the first two (both pipers) members of the 'Scottish' to be commissioned.[35]

---

30 *London Scottish Regiment Gazette* (1925), p.6.
31 *Tamworth Herald*, 17 January 1925, p.7.
32 *Aberdeen Press and Journal*, 6 August 1925, p.6.
33 *Aberdeen Press and Journal*, 6 August 1925, p.6.
34 *London Scottish Regiment Gazette* (1926), p.42.
35 *London Scottish Regiment Gazette* (1926), p.165.

It was perfect timing for the Pipes and Drums to have both senior positions in the command structure taken by ex-band members, both of whom retained a love for the music and who understood the importance to the regiment of a strong, competent band. As the commanding officer pointed out, 'I wonder if any other Regiment has a CO and Second-in-Command who were Pipers. I ha'e ma doots!'[36] Both men would be extremely influential in providing every opportunity for the Pipes and Drums to fulfil their full potential. This encouragement began with the band entering, and winning, pipe band competitions in London and the South-East, which lead to a growing belief that they were good enough to compete at the very highest level.

In January 1927, a letter arrived at Buckingham Gate from Mr J. Quigley of the Cowal Games Organising Committee. Winners of the pipe band competition that took place as part of the Cowal Highland Gathering had been crowned 'world champions' since 1906, and only the very best bands were invited or considered entering. Alongside the world championships ran a competition especially for Territorial Army bands that had never seen a band enter from outside Scotland. Mr Quigley's letter stated:

> As a member of the Cowal Games Committee, I am interested in the rumour that we are to have the London Scottish at Dunoon this year; if such an event comes to pass we shall all be delighted, and the band will be assured of a most hearty welcome, and the place of honour in the march past of the thousand pipers.[37]

To receive such a sincere invitation was too good to ignore, and the officers of the London Scottish promptly raised the money needed to send the Pipes and Drums to the championships in August.

Practise began in earnest. The band at this point consisted of over 30 members, but only 20 would be selected to compete. There were places for 12 pipers and eight drummers and competition for places was friendly but fierce. The band had so far only competed in 12 local competitions during the preceding few years and very little was expected of their visit to Cowal, but the opportunity and experience gained from participating would prove to be invaluable.

On 26 August, Drum Major Mills, Pipe Major Smith and the pipers and drummers of the London Scottish travelled to Gourock by train and then caught the boat to Dunoon:

> On nearing Dunoon Pier, we were delighted to see the magnificent Pipe Band of the 8th Argyll and Sutherland Highlanders paraded on the pier to meet us. As the steamer drew alongside, the Pipe Band greeted us with 'The Road to the Isles', and after many handshakes, our band fell in behind the 8th Argylls and we were marched through the town to the Headquarters.[38]

Here, the band was greeted by the Games Reception Committee, as well as many old friends of the London Scottish, including Pipe Majors Ross and Forsyth of the Scots Guards who had both been piping instructors to the London Scottish before the war. The band would stay as guests of the 8th Argyll's at their headquarters on Queen Street.

The Scotsman reported on Saturday 27 August that 'The Cowal Highland Gathering opens at Dunoon today, and a special interest is being taken in the appearance of the London Scottish Pipe Band, which will compete for the world's championship.'[39] The London Scottish fared much better in this competition than anyone anticipated. They received full marks (as perhaps would be

---

36 *London Scottish Regiment Gazette* (1926), p.172.
37 *London Scottish Regiment Gazette* (1927), p.39.
38 *London Scottish Regiment Gazette* (1927), p.162.
39 *The Scotsman*, 27 August 1927, p.11.

expected) for both turn-out and march discipline, but they also managed a more than respectable ninth place in the World Championships out of the 32 bands that competed. In addition, they managed fourth place overall in the Territorial competition, whilst the drummers achieved an excellent seventh place in the World's and second in the Territorial competition. These were significantly better results than had been expected, with most observers believing that the band would not measure up to Scottish standards. The London Scottish Pipes and Drums were justly proud to take the place of honour at the march-past, of which a cinefilm recording was made:

> A fitting climax to a most successful gathering was the march past of 'The Thousand Pipers' to the tune of 'Heilan' Laddie', played by the London Scottish Band. As they passed the grand stand the long stretch of bands nearly encircled the field. When all had passed they formed into line, the hodden grey of the Scottish in the position of honour.[40]

Their success was fittingly celebrated and, the next day, the Games organisers took them, perhaps ill-advisedly, on a celebratory and rather raucous sea trip around the isles. The Pipes and Drums then proudly, if with rather sore heads, returned to London the following day.

After a pat on the back for their successful weekend, it was straight back to regimental life as usual, epitomised by this report of their attendance a few weeks later for a B Company weekend camp, which not a single member of B Company actually attended. 'The officer in charge of 'B' Company finally arrived and apologised for the non-appearance of his Company, but the Band magnanimously overlooked the omission and played themselves to Waterloo and eventually to Box Hill.'[41] During the next few months, amongst their many other regular regimental duties, the band entered a team for an inter-platoon rugby competition, played for General Allenby at the annual Hallowe'en dinner, put out a band of 36 pipers and drummers for the annual church parade and performed at the second annual Armistice Day Service on 11 November. Their excellent playing on Armistice Day was mirrored by their drill and deportment, with one report stating, 'it is well to put on record that a spectator was overheard to remark how smart the Band looked compared with the other half of the Battalion!'[42]

This good work paid off, and an appeal was put around by the commanding officer to raise money for the Pipes and Drums to enter the World Championships at Cowal once more in 1928. The band were now practising twice a week, on Tuesdays and Thursdays, but this concentration on musical prowess didn't always sit well with the rest of the battalion, who were sometimes deprived of their services. A practise march took place on 4 March for the regimental Daily Telegraph Cup team, led by CSM Murray who personally provided the musical accompaniment. 'His singing made up for the lack of pipers, who had let us down again.'[43] However, it was not only concentration on the World's that was taking up the band's time. As usual, they remained 'the hardest working unit' in the regiment and continued to perform on the national stage.

On 29 January 1928, Earl Haig died unexpectedly at the relatively young age of 56. While his exploits as Commander-in-Chief of British Forces during the First World War and his role as Honorary Colonel of the London Scottish are well documented, it is sometimes forgotten that Earl Haig was also the founder of both the Royal British Legion and their Poppy Appeal, and the instigator of the tremendous work done by that organisation over the years for British servicemen and women. The London Scottish played a major role in the funeral arrangements for Earl Haig,

---

40   *The Scotsman*, 30 August 1927, p.12.
41   *London Scottish Regiment Gazette* (1927), p.187.
42   *London Scottish Regiment Gazette* (1927), p.207.
43   *London Scottish Regiment Gazette* (1928), p.92.

providing guards of honour during the two days of laying in state at St Columba's Church, an escort for the coffin from London to Edinburgh for interment at his country home at Bemersyde and a 420-strong contingent at the national ceremony that took place at Westminster Abbey. During the ceremony at the Abbey, the Pipes and Drums of the London Scottish played what many commentators described as the most moving laments which had a strong emotional effect on the congregation:

> This appeal was too poignant in its simplicity, too direct in its message to the hearts for the composure of the great majority. Women broke down and were heard sobbing unashamedly in the intervals between music. Men struggled to keep back a rising mist of tears, and the most hardened of warriors were touched as never before.[44]

With the funeral transmitted live on BBC Radio, the impact of this poignant performance would have been felt by millions listening around the country and throughout the British Empire.

Pipe Major Smith had been told in rehearsal that, for the sake of timings, the lament would have to be cut short. Smith went to Colonel Henderson who agreed that the lament should be played in full and damn the consequences.[45] The emotive influence on the congregation saved the band from any reprimand.

The London Scottish contingent later led an enormous parade of troops from Great Britain, France and Belgium through the streets of London from St Columba's Church to Waterloo, with the Pipes and Drums at their head.

> Slowly to the muffled music of the band he loved, Earl Haig passed on his last journey through the saddened streets of London. Soldiers of three nations in a procession more than a mile long came to bear him company.[46]

The Pipes and Drums proved, once again, that they had the skill and capacity to perform both musical and ceremonial roles at the very highest level.

The support of the Commanding Officer during these busy times also helped the men of the battalion understand the level of commitment provided by the pipers and drummers. Stating his thanks for their attendance at a concert at Bisley, Colonel Lyall-Grant wrote:

> Some people seem to think that because a Band is a Band it should appear anywhere at any time. Having been a member of it myself, I know the difficulties that face members when there are a large number of calls on their time.[47]

'Revenge' on those that questioned their commitment came in several guises, such as that described in the following review of the 1928 annual camp:

> Comparatively few of us had the unbounded delight of seeing a certain orderly officer arriving at the Guard Tent at 6 a.m. and enquiring where the dickens the Guard was, and why the Band wasn't playing the Reveille. His discomfiture on being informed that Reveille was at

---

44 *Dundee Courier*, 4 February 1928, p.5.
45 *London Scottish Regiment Gazette* (1964), p.72.
46 *Hull Daily Mail*, 3 February 1928, p.14.
47 *London Scottish Regiment Gazette* (1928), p.152.

5:30, and that the Band had played and the Guard dismissed while he was still asleep, was highly diverting but, unfortunately, only enjoyed by a few.[48]

After a busy summer of activity including annual camp, an inspection parade in Hyde Park, a Scottish gathering at the Duke of York's Headquarters and, for Pipers Booth and Bruce, the honour of leading out the British team at the Olympic Games opening ceremony in Amsterdam, it was time once again to journey north to Cowal. During the first half of the year, Pipe Major Smith had left the London Scottish and Pipe Sergeant 'Davie' Pullar finally got his chance to become pipe major, almost ten years after he had last done so at the close of the First World War. He was still accompanied in the competition band by five others who had fought during the Great War and were still giving their service to the regiment. In total, Drum Major Mills and six drummers joined Pipe Major Pullar and his 11 pipers on the boat to Dunoon, along with a group of supporters which included both Colonel Lyall-Grant and Major Henderson.

They would, once again, stay as guests and competitors of the 8th Argyll and Sutherland Highlanders, but this time it would be the guests who would emerge victorious. The London Scottish performed a March, Strathspey and Reel consisting of the tunes *Highland Wedding*, *Arniston Castle* and *Lord MacDonald* and their months of hard work was over in around three minutes. The performance was good enough to win both the Territorial band and drumming competitions and placed them sixth out of 50 in the Worlds for the full band and fifth for the drummers. An incredible performance of which the regiment was justifiably proud. The London Scottish were given the honour of playing all 50 bands into position for the march-past and presentation of prizes, as the rain began to pour down. 'Down it came for a good half hour, and all that time the 'Scottish' Band stood steadfastly at their post, not a move, not a shake of the head or a movement of a foot; there they stood, a splendid example of training and discipline.'[49] It did, however, completely ruin the drum heads but, as one band member stated, 'What if it has commenced to rain, I don't give a hoot!!! We've got it!!!'[50] Drum Major Mills took command of the march-past and, after it was over:

> Out of the grounds we march, playing a tune of Victory … bearing the Trophies triumphantly aloft, and as we pass through the gates Clan MacLean, the Open Champions, form an impromptu guard of honour, and give us three rousing cheers. That, indeed, was a proud moment.[51]

The importance of this victory to the regiment, at this time, is hard to overestimate. The 1920s had been a difficult period for the country, for the Army and especially for the Territorials. War-weariness, alongside economic and social hardship, meant that not only was funding for the Territorial Army at an all-time low but that most regiments had great difficulty in recruiting and were significantly below their established numbers. The London Scottish had managed to reach their establishment for the first time since the war in 1928 and the publicity and pride associated with the band's victory would do wonders for future recruitment and retention. Of equal importance, the success at Cowal also enhanced the authenticity of the London Scottish in regard to their Scottish roots and traditions. Neither factor was lost on senior officers in the regiment, as the Commanding Officer pointed out:

---

48   *London Scottish Regiment Gazette* (1928), p.177.
49   *London Scottish Regiment Gazette* (1928), p.198.
50   *London Scottish Regiment Gazette* (1928), p.196.
51   *London Scottish Regiment Gazette* (1928), p.196.

> One is apt to forget that the winning of both the Band and the Drumming Competitions was a result of months of hard work, and the whole Battalion should thank those members of the Pipes and Drums who have brought such honour to us …. Drum-Major Mills and Pipe-Major Pullar are proud men to-day, but I doubt if they are much more proud than those who had the privilege of accompanying the Band and of hearing, and seeing, its performance.[52]

A report in the *Regimental Gazette*, written by another senior officer asserted:

> What we are bucked about most is that we have proved, beyond all possibility of error, to our countrymen North of the Border that the London Scottish are not people who merely have skirts in the Perth Dye Works, but are fully capable of upholding Scottish traditions in London, and that the London Scottish has been, is, and always will be a fine Corps, to which any man will feel proud to belong, and, finally, that any young fellow who has made up his mind to come South to prise the Sassenach loose from his filthy lucre, will always find a home from home at 59 Buckingham Gate.[53]

1928, then, was a seminal year that retains particular resonance amid the illustrious history of the London Scottish Pipes and Drums.

The London Scottish annual children's party would begin again in January 1929 and would run until relatively recent times, when changes to safeguarding legislation made it impossible to continue. The Pipes and Drums had always played a significant role in the event, not just performing but in organising and managing. Ex-Pipe Major Robertson was responsible for bringing the party back to life after it had originally begun in 1914, before the war brought it to a premature end. The parties were attended by hundreds of young people each year, both children of members of the regiment as well as orphans and disadvantaged youngsters from homes in the surrounding area. Many of the original themes, including magicians, the circus ringmaster and 'Spider' the pantomime horse, continued throughout its existence. Drummer J.M. Campbell was the first ringmaster and produced the routine for 'Spider' that would continue down the years. The full band always performed, with the children allowed to march alongside them, and there are several Pathé films from the 1930s showing the band in action, trying hard not to trample children under foot.

The band dinner in February was a particularly triumphant affair, with the two Cowal trophies on prominent display and another letter from the Cowal Games Committee stating that 'your success in the Territorial Contest was the most pleasing result of the Gathering,[54] and going on to mention that they hoped the London Scottish would return to defend their trophies. The issue, however, was one of cost, and the band did not want to ask the regimental family to pay for a third year when the economic situation in the country was so dire. Thankfully, help was at hand as, in late spring, the Honorary Colonel of the Toronto Scottish Regiment, Colonel F.B. Robins, visited 59 Buckingham Gate and offered to defray the costs of sending the Pipes and Drums back to Dunoon. Colonel Lyall-Grant wrote, 'It was an offer that, needless to say, we accepted, and I feel that there can be no better way of thanking him than by the Band retaining both the trophies that they won last year.'[55]

---

52 *London Scottish Regiment Gazette* (1928), p.174.
53 *London Scottish Regiment Gazette* (1928), p.197.
54 *London Scottish Regiment Gazette* (1929), p.93.
55 *London Scottish Regiment Gazette* (1929), p.93.

The Pipes and Drums at the ruins of the Cloth Hall, Ypres during the regimental visit to commemorate the opening of the London Scottish memorial cross on Messines Ridge, May 1924. (LSMA, used with permission)

Of the six men at annual camp in 1930 who had fought during the First World War, three had been pipers. Piper Nicol, standing far left and Colonels Lyall-Grant and Henderson, seated, who were both awarded the Military Cross during the First World War. (LSMA, used with permission)

THE INTER-WAR YEARS 1919-1939 191

Drum Major Mills and Pipe Major Pullar leading the band that won both the Campbell Challenge Trophy and the Walter Scott Challenge Trophy, and placed sixth in the world at the Cowal Highland Gathering, August 1928. (LSMA, used with permission)

Drum Major Mills leading a leashed Pipe Major Pullar and band at annual camp, 1928. (LSMA, used with permission)

Before Dunoon in August came another march through Scotland in July. During the march, the London Scottish camped at Craigievar Castle as the guests of Lady Semphill, where the band had the privilege of playing in the famous pipers' gallery. The *Aberdeen Press and Journal* reported closely on the march and published an illustrated account which captured wonderfully the characteristics of the regiment during this period. Reporting on a 17-mile march on day three, the author, 'A Civilian on Trek', observed:

> The pipe band did especially well, and Pipe-Major Pullar really deserved that kindly word of praise the Colonel gave him at the end of the march. The intervals when the band were resting were filled vocally. The entire repertoire of war-time songs, even 'Fred Karno's Army', were sung – with discreet modulations, of course – but somehow the pipe band did not appreciate these vocal efforts, and, at the end of each, struck up a terribly mournful dirge of their own. 'Oh, my, what a rotten song!'[56]
>
> The pipers play ten minutes and then 'rest' ten minutes. I don't know how they manage it in this heat, though, after all, this is what one would expect from the champion pipe band of the Territorial Army.[57]

One ten-minute period in particular was something special:

> Perhaps, being Sunday, the battalion was affected by the holiday spirit. In all events, the Colonel departed from convention by joining his 'old love' the pipe band. An old Glenalmond boy, the Colonel – perhaps I might as well call him 'Dougie', as everybody else in the regiment does – advanced to the pipe band, and for ten minutes on the route between Lumsden and Gartly he relieved Pipe-Major Pullar, a typical Dundonion by the way. 'It was a long ten minutes', said the Colonel to me afterwards.[58]

At Carrbridge, the regiment was joined by the Pipes and Drums of the 6th Seaforth Highlanders and then, on the last day, by pipe bands from the Black Watch and the Cameron Highlanders. 'The sight and sound of the three bands … massed and playing our Regimental March as we approached the Cameron's Parade Ground, will be a memory not soon forgotten.'[59] Furthermore:

> Those last few miles of marching were as nothing, even to men with tired and blistered feet and shoulders aching with the weight of full equipment. The spectacle as the battalion marched in to barracks, to the music of the massed pipes and drums, was stirring and inspiring. It was an unforgettable sight, one that quickened the pulse and caused the heart to beat faster.[60]

The Cowal Highland Gathering came around quickly just weeks after and, for a third time, the London Scottish put on a magnificent show. The band had been practising at the Royal Hospital, Chelsea, for the previous few months to allow them to perform outside and away from the echoes of the regimental drill hall, which was a definite advantage. The drummers again took first place

---

56 A Civilian on Trek, *On Trek with the Hodden Grey: Being an Illustrated Account of the Route March of the London Scottish from Aberdeen to Inverness, July 15th-26th, 1929* (Aberdeen: The Aberdeen Press and Journal, 1929), p.14.
57 A Civilian on Trek, *On Trek with the Hodden Grey*, p.30.
58 A Civilian on Trek, *On Trek with the Hodden Grey*, p.20.
59 *London Scottish Regiment Gazette* (1929), p.169.
60 A Civilian on Trek, *On Trek with the Hodden Grey*, pp.36-37.

in the Territorial competition and managed an incredible third place in the World's, whilst the full band placed second in the Territorial band competition and sixth overall in the World's. Captain Scott Freeman of 'A' Company wrote. 'We have always been very proud of our Band, and I know the whole Company will join with me in congratulating them on the magnificent show they put up.'[61]

This would be the pipe band's final visit to Cowal and their last competition for many years. The Great Depression was about to hit the western world and economic woes, coupled with the rise of fascism, brought a new emphasis to Territorial life in the 1930s. The money to support the Pipes and Drums in their 'non-military' activities was in short supply, whilst the martial build-up around Europe placed a more intense emphasis on new and diverse infantry training and skills. Camps and training weekends took place more often by company, with pipers and drummers requested on each occasion, in addition to performing their infantry roles. This meant that band members had to spread themselves around and so had less time to spend as a unit.

1930 saw more emphasis placed on the 'in-house' piping competition, with the Macleod Medal given increased publicity. Previously, the medal had been competed for on a normal Thursday practise night, with only band members and friends in attendance. Now it was given greater prominence and opened to a much bigger audience. It was won, appropriately, that year by Piper MacLeod.

Hallowe'en 1930 was also of great importance to the Pipes and Drums, as it was Colonel Lyall-Grant's final evening in command of the regiment. As Band President and Commanding Officer, he had been an incredible supporter of the Pipes and Drums. Thankfully, his position was taken by Major Henderson, who had also been a London Scottish piper before the war. Major Henderson's position as Second in Command was taken up by Major L. Duncan Bennett, who had joined the London Scottish as a 3rd Battalion drummer in 1915 before taking a commission in 1916. Major Bennett would take over as band president, ensuring that the influence of the Pipes and Drums upon the two top command positions was retained.

5 March 1931 saw the first involvement of Her Royal Highness, The Duchess of York with the London Scottish, when she consented to present the regimental prizes at the annual award ceremony. Her future involvement and influence on the London Scottish, and particularly on the Pipes and Drums, would be enormous.

Two months later, from 28 May to 6 June, the band and a team of highland dancers from the regiment performed at the Royal Tournament. *The Scotsman* reported:

> An innovation at the Royal Tournament to be opened May 28 at Olympia will be a display by the London Scottish (14th London Regiment) who will present a piece of high pageantry in the form of piping, drumming and dancing. The full strength of the regimental bandsmen and dancers, about 80 strong, will take part, and famous marching airs will be played.[62]

It was also recounted that, 'When the time came the Regiment acquitted itself splendidly and the Pipe Band and Highland Dancers received unstinted praise from "experts" and general public alike.'[63]

Colonel Henderson reiterated the importance of involving the Pipes and Drums in such high-profile events when he wrote:

---

61 *London Scottish Regiment Gazette* (1929), p.188.
62 *The Scotsman*, 20 May 1931, p.8.
63 C.N. Barclay (ed.), *The London Scottish in the Second World War 1939-1945* (London: William Clowes, 1952), p.29.

To appear at Olympia in the Royal Tournament, where only the pick of His Majesty's Services are performing, is a very great honour in itself, but to have performed with credit is something to be really proud of. The 'Scottish' did this, which should do good in many ways, both to us and to the Territorial Army which we represented.[64]

It was also further proof that Scottish traditions were alive and well in the regiment and being preserved and well-exemplified in the capital of the British Empire.

As a direct consequence of the Great Depression, 1932 brought with it major concerns for the Territorial Army in the form of deep cuts to the budget which would have a major impact on functionality. The London Scottish annual camp only took place because money was found from regimental funds and by individual members contributing to their own expenses; much as had been the case 70 years previously when the regiment was first formed. The Pipes and Drums, however, did as they had always done and contributed even further towards basic costs by using monies from the band fund and contributions from individual pipers and drummers to assist other soldiers who had financial struggles. Despite the hardships, the pipe band would continue to ensure that the regiment had their support, no matter what difficult circumstances arose.

At the Distribution of Prizes parade in 1933, Colonel Henderson stated in his speech; 'The Pipers and Drummers are as keen as ever and turn up in a splendid manner for every Company or Battalion Parade or other function,'[65] and it is obvious from reading through the *Regimental Gazette* that their participation in platoon, company, regimental and external events continued with the same steadfast commitment as always.

On 17 April, Colonel G.A. Malcolm, who had commanded the pre-war London Scottish and led the 1st Battalion charge at Messines, died. At his funeral, 'Six pipers, under Pipe-Major D Pullar, played the lament as the coffin was lowered into the earth.'[66] From 16 to 30 July, the Pipes and Drums led the regiment on their latest march through Scotland, starting in Stirling and marching 160 miles to Edinburgh. The regiment were taken to and from Scotland on the new London, Midland and Scottish Railway locomotive No.6124, named 'London Scottish' in their honour, and the pipe band played the new steam engine into the station to take them north. The band, as always, turned out in force and 12 pipers and nine drummers marched the men past Taymouth, Blair and Drummond Castles, joined at various times by the Pipes and Drums of the Royal Engineers and the boys of the Queen Victoria Military School in Dunblane. In a show of extra commitment, after every day's march, Drummer Shelley who was a trained butcher, went to the cook house to do the butchering. 'This generous offer is one that stands out as an example of "war-days" comradeship.'[67]

And 'war-days' were fast approaching. Adolf Hitler's Nazi Party had taken control of Germany in the spring of 1933, and the march toward another world war had begun. 'Every Territorial Army soldier was now required to train and fit himself for war on an almost professional basis.'[68] This would, naturally, hold true for the hard-working Pipes and Drums. In addition to their regular infantry training, pipers and drummers still attended practise nights and performed as and when required by the regiment. At the annual assault-at-arms competition in March 1934, for example:

---

64 *London Scottish Regiment Gazette* (1931), p.135.
65 *London Scottish Regiment Gazette* (1933), p.92.
66 *London Scottish Regiment Gazette* (1933), p.101.
67 *London Scottish Regiment Gazette* (1933), p.202.
68 Barclay, *The London Scottish in the Second World War 1939-1945*, p.31.

Of the pipes and drums one can have no criticism, and the audience is always ready with a special cheer for Davy Pullar and his plaided pipers. They put on two shows during the evening, apart from their support of the Maze run, the Reel Club, and the final Parade – a full night's work.[69]

With the threat of war came greater numbers of recruits, who quickly learnt the joys and quirks associated with membership of a Scottish regiment. The *Regimental Gazette* published a letter from one new recruit that he sent home from the 1934 annual camp to his mother:

When we march out of camp in the morning, after a few hundred yards the pipes and drums stand at the side of the road and play very fast while we march past. The fellows say that they go back to camp and practise playing their pipes, also tent-pitching.[70] Other chaps say, 'Do they, hell', and lick their lips.[71]

It is important that all Scottish traditions are kept alive, after all.

In the same year, and despite no longer being a serving soldier in the regiment, ex-Pipe Major Robertson gave substance to the saying 'Once a London Jock, Always a London Jock' with two important contributions. The first was the design of a memorial to the 2nd Battalion to be invested in the Scots Church in Jerusalem, commemorating the officers and men that gave their lives to free Palestine, Jordan and the Holy City during the Palestine Campaign. It was unveiled on St Andrew's Day 1934 by ex-2nd Battalion Commanding Officer Colonel Robert J.L. Ogilby and Lieutenant General Sir Arthur Wauchope, after having been initially dedicated at St Columba's on 4 November. The 1st Battalion, Gordon Highlanders sent a detachment from Haifa, 150 miles away, which included six pipers, and the Seaforth Highlanders also sent 12 pipers as part of their detachment.

Robertson's second major contribution was to design and build a shooting lodge for the London Scottish at Bisley, where the regiment had been shooting since the move of the National Rifle Association from Wimbledon in 1890. This was a major development for the London Scottish and meant that they now had first class accommodation whenever they required use of the ranges. The building, complete with Robertson-designed piper weathervane, was opened on 15 June 1935. The Pipes and Drums had their first shooting weekend there in October.

The regimental prize distribution parade in 1935 was again attended by The Duchess of York and soon after (and after much delay and lobbying) she consented to become Honorary Colonel of the London Scottish Regiment. It had been seven years since Earl Haig died, and many wondered why the regiment had gone so long without a replacement honorary colonel. In fact, the regiment had made multiple requests to His Majesty, King George V, for the Duchess of York to be allowed to become the honorary colonel-in-chief but, as she would state to Regimental Colonel John Clemence many years later:

'The old king did not altogether approve of women in these appointments and said so.' 'But' she said, 'your predecessor just went on badgering the King until he became tired and, in 1935, gave in on the grounds that if that was what they wanted, then so be it.'[72]

---

69 *London Scottish Regiment Gazette* (1934), pp.78-79.
70 For some reason, the band always won the tent pitching competition at annual camp, although it was apparently lost after an 8-year run in 1934 through 'trying to be too brainy.'
71 *London Scottish Regiment Gazette* (1934), p.224.
72 *London Scottish Regiment Gazette* (2002), p.51.

Maxwell Scott, Poster for the regimental Hallowe'en Dinner, October 1933. (LSMA, used with permission)

The London Scottish Rifle Lodge at Bisley, designed by Pipe Major Robertson, 1936. Note the London Scottish piper on the weathervane. (LSMA, used with permission)

THE INTER-WAR YEARS 1919-1939   197

Reveille at Burley Camp, 1938. The dark days of war would not be far away. (LSMA, used with permission)

It would prove to be a stroke of genius, and the dedication shown by the regiment in securing her as honorary colonel would be paid back ten-fold over the next 65 years. Her love of the regiment, and of the Pipes and Drums, would become legendary and would prove to be instrumental in safeguarding the regiment's very existence in the latter half of the twentieth century.

On 20 January 1936, King George V died. His state funeral took place on 28 January and, while 350 London Scottish troops had the honour of lining the route from the Duke and Duchess of York's residence in Piccadilly to Hyde Park Corner, 'It was a great disappointment to the Pipers and Drummers that the band was not allowed on parade.'[73] Despite the quality of the band in both musicality and deportment, they would be usurped by their brethren in the regular army.

The Pipes and Drums made up for this disappointment at the Hyde Park Review on 16 May when they turned out an impressive number of pipers and drummers. The band had been recruiting vigorously after a slight drop in members in previous years and managed to bring in a handful of experienced pipers, including ex-Pipe Major 'Tommy' Marshall from the Cameron Highlanders and Sergeant Piper Alec 'Dusty' Millar from the Seaforth Highlanders. Marshall took over as Pipe Major of the London Scottish in August 1936 when the long-serving Davy Pullar retired. Miller would go on to lead the 2nd Battalion band as pipe major throughout the vast majority of the Second World War.

Pipe Major Marshall had joined the Scots Guards in 1916, serving throughout the Great War and in the army of occupation in Germany afterwards. He became a pipe sergeant in 1920 and then transferred to the 2nd Battalion, Queens Own Cameron Highlanders in 1924 as a pipe major. He received the Medal of the Royal Victorian Order from King George V at Holyrood in 1927 and left the regular army in 1935, before joining the London Scottish a few months later. He took over as pipe major almost instantly.

At camp in August 1936, Pipe Major Marshall was thrown straight into the deep end as acting CSM for HQ Company, whilst Drum Sergeant List took the role of acting CQMS. The London Scottish were at camp with a new brigade after the merging of the 47th and 56th Divisions, whose other composite battalions were not used to hearing *revéillé* quite as early as were the London Scottish:

> Prompted by their antipathy to early rising, the Pipe-Major arranged a pot-pouri of Heilan' music to woo them gently from the Land of Nod, ending up with 'Johnnie Cope.' The length of this selection took the Band to all the nearer training areas[74]

In addition to the divisional changes that took place in 1936, the London Scottish became officially associated with the Gordon Highlanders; 55 years after it had first been suggested during the Childers Reforms. The War Department directed that all Territorial regiments should be a subsidiary of a regular army regiment, and the Gordon Highlanders made representation to claim the London Scottish. From 1937, the regiment would be officially designated 'The London Scottish, The Gordon Highlanders.' The close association between these two regiments, which had started back in the 1880s and which had been given some associated status during the First World War, was now official and to commemorate the event, the pipers of the London Scottish changed their pipe bag covers to Gordon Highlander tartan. This tradition, along with the later incorporation of black spat buttons in 1953, remains to this day.

---

73 *London Scottish Regiment Gazette* (1936), p.62.
74 *London Scottish Regiment Gazette* (1936), p.227.

On 1 November, the Pipes and Drums 'had the honour of playing the Lament at the Ypres Day Memorial Parade held under the auspices of the Ypres League, on the Horse Guards Parade,'[75] and, the following week, led a detachment of London Scottish at the Lord Mayor's Show for the first time in many years. Another first for the band came on St Andrew's Day when Pipe Major Marshall and pipers and dancers from the regiment became the first ever to perform on the ground-breaking new BBC television service.

The momentous events of 1936 took on even greater import for the London Scottish in December, when King Edward VIII abdicated and his brother, Prince Albert (assuming a regnal name) became George VI. The Duchess of York, Honorary Colonel of the London Scottish, was now Queen Elizabeth. Her new royal position and dedication to the regiment that had fought so hard for her patronage ensured a level of pride and prestige in the London Scottish to match any in its illustrious history. Her Majesty was a particular admirer of the Pipes and Drums and her support would bring much honour through the coming war years and into the decades that followed.

Annual camp and the march through Scotland were amalgamated in 1937, with the London Scottish combining tactical training with their traditional route marching over a two-week period from 11 to 25 July. The regiment arrived at Inverness by train with 24 officers and 577 men, who then 'marched from the station to the Cameron barracks, piped in turn by the Band of the Cameron Highlanders and our own.'[76] Training took place there for a week before the long marches began. After complaints in previous years from C and D Companies, who were always at the back of the marching column, companies were rotated to be closer to the Pipes and Drums while on the march. The effect on morale is made obvious from the following D Company notes:

> It was always the best part of the day when we were up in front of the Battalion and we had the Pipe-Admiral to say good-morning to. One can really enjoy the pipes when one is just behind them, and the cheer which greeted the end of a tune showed how we appreciated the efforts of the Band.[77]

Ex-Sergeant Alex Fraser reported on a 'Grand Tattoo' given by the Pipes and Drums during the march in the main square at Invergordon:

> They started most effectively, with the drums and slow march; they marched and counter-marched slowly and in quick time, all the time playing stirring tunes; everything seemed to me done so perfectly and in unison. It was wonderful to me, too, how the Pipe-Major controlled and intimated the changing of the tunes and pace. It must have been, surely, by raising his eyebrows or a glance or a nod! Anyhow, I could see no sign nor hear a jarring note.
>
> The 'Scottish' should be, and no doubt is, proud of its Band. They certainly performed their part most efficiently and acceptably to all who heard and saw them. After twenty-four years' service in the 'Scottish', I know what a valuable asset such a Pipe Band is to a Regiment.[78]

The fortnight in Scotland ended at Dingwall, allowing the regiment to hold a ceremony at the war memorial of the Seaforth Highlanders, with whom Colonel Henderson had commanded a battalion, and won his Military Cross and Bar, during the First World War. In front of thousands

---

75 *London Scottish Regiment Gazette* (1936), p.268.
76 *London Scottish Regiment Gazette* (1937), p.225.
77 *London Scottish Regiment Gazette* (1937), p.217.
78 *London Scottish Regiment Gazette* (1937), p.225.

of spectators from the surrounding towns and villages, 'The London Scottish provided the guard of honour, as they marched to the memorial headed by their pipe band.'[79] Colonel Henderson laid a wreath while the pipers played a lament, which was followed by a march-past, with the London Scottish band joined by the Pipes and Drums of the 4/5th Seaforth Highlanders. This was a fitting conclusion to Colonel Henderson's tenure as Commanding Officer of the London Scottish, which would formally come to an end on Hallowe'en.

12 May 1937 had seen the coronation of King George VI at Westminster Abbey. The London Scottish provided a small detachment which joined the procession, and had men lining the route, but there was no part, again, for the Pipes and Drums here or later in the year when 430 men of the London Scottish lined Fleet Street for a visit by Their Majesties to the City of London. However, on 16 October, Queen Elizabeth, as Honorary Colonel of the London Scottish, invited the regiment to be inspected in a Royal Review at Buckingham Palace. This was a signal honour for the London Scottish as up to that point, only the Scots Guards had ever before been inspected as a regiment at Buckingham Palace. It was also a mark of unique respect to Colonel Henderson. 27 officers, over 500 other ranks and 50 'old and bold' from the newly raised Defence Company 'paraded, and headed by their pipes and drums marched into the grounds of the Palace, where Her Majesty stood on a scarlet covered dais to take the salute.'[80] Queen Elizabeth then inspected the troops while 'the band played Scottish airs,' and the 'inspection concluded with a march past headed by the band.'[81] A film of the review was made by Pathé News, which The Queen reportedly enjoyed watching at Buckingham Palace and which was widely distributed to cinemas around the country.

Colonel Henderson's last official engagement as Commanding Officer was at the regimental Hallowe'en dinner, which was attended by over 500 people. He handed over to his Second in Command, Major, soon to be Colonel, L. Duncan Bennett who made it three in a row for the Pipes and Drums. This time, however, an ex-drummer rather than an ex-piper was in command. Pipe Major Marshall wrote a march entitled *Colonel L D Henderson MC, TD* to mark the occasion. Colonel Henderson had stayed in post as Commanding Officer of the London Scottish for three years longer than was usual and his steady hand during this critical pre-war period ensured the regiment was at peak strength. Colonel Bennett took over command of a battalion that was 20 percent above its established numbers, at a time when many other Territorial units were seriously below strength and virtually every observer could see a major conflict with Germany was now almost inevitable.

With war looming, life as a Territorial soldier took on even greater intensity in 1938 with increased training and more large-scale exercises, in addition to which, the London Division finally became mechanised. HQ Company, to whom the Pipes and Drums belonged, was expanded to over 300 men and provided with armoured Bren gun carriers. The Pipes and Drums were to make up the battalion anti-aircraft platoon and now numbered 20 pipers and 18 drummers. Learning new tactics, new vehicles and new weaponry in readiness for the possibility of war obviously took precedence, but the Pipes and Drums still managed to perform their musical duties, as the regiment had come to expect. They were joined at the annual Presentation of Prizes parade in 1938 by the Drums and Pipes of the 1st Battalion, Gordon Highlanders to mark the name change of the regiment to 'The London Scottish, The Gordon Highlanders.' The band also performed at the Territorial Army sports day at the Duke of York's Headquarters. However, despite the many

---

79   *Aberdeen Press and Journal*, 26 July 1937, p.9.
80   *Aberdeen Press and Journal*, 18 October 1937, p.6.
81   *Aberdeen Press and Journal*, 18 October 1937, p.6.

changes taking place around them, the big event of the year for the Pipes and Drums was their annual band dinner.

This took place on 12 May and over 100 men attended. The evening began with the youngest member of the band, Drummer Riddell, being called upon to lay a wreath on the First World War memorial, while a piper played a lament. The new Commanding Officer and the two previous Commanding Officers were all in attendance, as was the new Band President, Captain Hugh Wilson, while ex-Pipe Major Davy Pullar was in the Chair. Drum Major Morrie Mills retired after 24-years' service with the Pipes and Drums and was presented by Colonel Lyall-Grant with the Claymore sword that he had worn on so many memorable occasions. His service to band and regiment had been immense. This left Piper Gordon Allan as the only London Scottish First World War veteran still serving with the Pipes and Drums. Pipe Major Marshall gave a review of the year and the speeches were then concluded by Captain James Peddie of B Company, who would go on to have a greater association with the band during and after the Second World War. He stated:

> We all have our own ideas as to who is the backbone of the Regiment, but there is no doubt that the Pipe Band is the heart of a Scottish Regiment. We march along in the dust blown up by your hoofs, but I can assure you that the cheer which goes up when you cease playing is not of relief but of gratitude.[82]

Seven days later, the MacLeod Medal and various dancing competitions took place, with the medal being won for the third time by Piper Ken Wright. Piper Wright was one of four brothers who had been pipers in the London Scottish since 1922, with all four playing together from 1927 to 1931. Colin, Gordon, Donald and Kenneth were all in the band on the three occasions it played at the Cowal Games and Ken was the last still to be serving. His marriage ceremony took place at 59 Buckingham Gate on June 4th and he left for a new life in New Zealand on 1 July. A few months later, his brother, Donald, who had won the MacLeod Medal in 1934 before moving to Jamaica, sadly died of blackwater fever aged just 30 years.

Brigade camp took place in July at Burley in the New Forest, where the Pipes and Drums trained in their roles as company runners, anti-aircraft gunners, stretcher-bearers and ammunition carriers; all functions they would shortly undertake in combat during the Second World War. This increase in intensive training was not always appreciated by the previously 'semi-autonomous' Pipes and Drums, as was made apparent when the new HQ Company Commander ordered a snap rifle inspection before camp pay parade:

> Whence came the rifles, I know not …. But such was the reproachful expression on the Wing's collective face during the inspection that I doubt whether the Company Commander will have the nerve ever to drop such a frightful brick again.[83]

Burley camp also saw the beginning of the exploits of 'Drumfamily' as they were to be colloquially known over the next few years in highly entertaining reports from Drum Sergeant Archie MacLeod in the *Regimental Gazette*, which usually concentrated on more 'traditional' pipe band behaviour. For example, night operations were the highlights of the second week of camp that year. While mock battles ensued, the drum corps spent the evening whizzing around the designated war-zone in a commandeered vehicle until, 'enough of this, they changed cars and headed

---

82 *London Scottish Regiment Gazette* (1938), p.151.
83 *London Scottish Regiment Gazette* (1938), p.223.

straight for the "local", as it was a very warm evening.'[84] The next day was casualty drills with the Medical Officer. 'The MO reads casualty label: "Bullet wound in the chest. What do we do now?" "Don't know" said Drumcow, bursting with knowledge.'[85]

All self-deprecation aside, the Pipes and Drums, along with the rest of the regiment, prepared themselves for war. The war scare that came in September 1938 during Prime Minister Chamberlain's series of meetings with Adolf Hitler demonstrated that at least one member of the band was rather too keen to see battle commence:

> Take the embarrassment of that Piper, a keen soldier of H.Q. Wing, who, seeing a news placard, 'Territorials Mobilized', and, quite rightly, not wishing to waste a penny, just rushed home, packed his kit-bag and, with a haversack full of hard-boiled egg sandwiches, presented himself at H.Q. in full marching order, to an astonished and scandalised P.S.[86]

Unfortunately, he would not have too much longer to wait. In early 1939, training for the London Scottish would be stepped up to three times a week as the regiment was put on a war footing. The drummers now made up the majority of the anti-aircraft platoon, with most of the pipers employed in a variety of other roles. War was now almost inevitably on the horizon.

The Pipes and Drums, however, still had a part to play in state ceremonial activities and were involved in the parade for the royal visit of President Lebrun of France on 22 March. A Sovereign's Escort of Life Guards and the combined Guards' band marched from Buckingham Palace, down The Mall and on to St Paul's Cathedral. The route was lined by men from the Brigade of Guards, amongst other units and 'Emphasising the "Auld Alliance" was the presence of the London Scottish with pipes and drums.'[87]

In April, the War Department announced that the Territorial Army would be doubled in size and the London Scottish were given permission to implement a second battalion. This meant the transfer of many officers and NCOs to assist with the 'immediate rush of old members of the Regiment, and new men, to join up.'[88] As had been the case prior to the First World War, the London Scottish were the first regiment in the country to raise a second battalion, taking just a couple of weeks. A 2nd Battalion Pipes and Drums were raised as a matter of priority, with newly appointed Pipe Major A.C. 'Dusty' Millar tasked with the job.[89] When war was finally declared on 1 September 1939, the next generation of London Scots were ready to take up arms and march once more into battle behind their Pipes and Drums.

The 1920s and 1930s had, then, been a time of immense highs and some lows for the London Scottish which, as always, was reflected in the history of the Pipes and Drums. The regiment entered into the 1920s on the crest of a wave of glory, sustained by its exploits during the First World War. The Pipes and Drums helped to maintain and elevate regimental pride during the lean years of cuts and recruitment difficulties that followed, as the nation felt the effects of post-war upheaval and the Great Depression. Both regiment and band weathered these storms and, buoyed by royal patronage from the latter half of the 1930s, prepared for the bigger storms to come.

Once again, the London Scottish were headed to war.

---

84   *London Scottish Regiment Gazette* (1938), p.225.
85   *London Scottish Regiment Gazette* (1938), p.225.
86   *London Scottish Regiment Gazette* (1938), p.259.
87   *Aberdeen Press and Journal*, 23 March 1939, p.7.
88   Barclay (ed.), *The London Scottish in the Second World War 1939-1945*, p.34.
89   Further details of this and other preparations for the declaration of war on 1 September 1939 are taken up in detail in the following chapter.

6

The Second World War 1939-1946

By this time there were only three ways out of Anzio for the Infantryman: Stalag, the grave, or a hospital ship.

Focke-Wolfes strafed the harbour and the coast road beside our camp. We listened to the Pipe Band playing retreat and remembered that we had watched this same band marching and counter-marching during a golden summer sunset on the greenswards of Broome Park. The Pipe Band, in my memories, played a sort of Intermission at every stage of our war journey, providing a connecting theme as it were - and many were the men who had listened to the band in towns, villages, camps and lanes in England, on troopships, in the barren Iraqi desert, in Palestine and Egypt, on gay piazzas in Sicily and in war-torn Italian towns; men who would never hear the wailing, lamenting pipes again.

Keith Spooner[1]

By January 1939, and despite Chamberlain's September 1938 decree of 'Peace in Our Time', the military build up to a possible war with Germany had begun in earnest. In March, Chamberlain finally realised that negotiation with Hitler was impossible and, on 31 March, Britain and France announced their support for Polish independence. On 12 April, as German pressure along the East Prussian border grew stronger and with Italian forces invading Albania, Leslie Hore-Belisha, the Secretary of State for War, granting permission for Territorial Army regiments to begin raising second battalions. The London Scottish, as they had done before the First World War, became the first regiment to achieve this honour, taking just 19 days and leaving a long waiting list. Many of those enlisting came to London from Scotland specifically for the purpose of joining the London Scottish, which helped ensure the 2nd Battalion retained its proud heritage. The thoughts of one of these recruits, J.M. Lee Harvey, seemed to have been shared by many: 'Opting for the army, I tried to enlist in the London Scottish, the regiment my elder brother had joined … Why not, I thought, enlist in a glamour regiment?'[2] However, like many others, he found both battalions already full.

Thankfully, a third, slightly left field, option was to become available when retired artillery officer Major K.S. Thorburn and three ex-Colonels of the London Scottish were approached by Major-General Sir F. Pile, G.O.C., of the 1st Anti-Aircraft Division, regarding the possible formation of a Scottish-linked Territorial anti-aircraft regiment for the protection of London. Support for this idea was afforded, as long as the new unit would be officially part of the London Scottish Regiment and 'conform in every way to the rules and regulations governing recruitment'[3] with

---

1 Keith Spooner, 'Personal Memories of 1st Bn in Action', London Scottish Regimental Gazette (1948), p.137.
2 J.M. Lee Harvey, *D-Day Dodgers* (London: William Kimber, 1979), p.11.
3 C.N. Barclay (ed.), *The London Scottish in the Second World War – 1939 to 1945* (London: William Clowes and Sons, 1952), p.248.

Major Thorburn as Commanding Officer. Despite huge initial resistance from the War Office, the 97th Heavy Anti-Aircraft Regiment, Royal Artillery, TA (The London Scottish), became the 3rd Battalion of the London Scottish and would remain so throughout the course of the war. Recruiting for this anomalous and uniquely kilted Royal Artillery battalion began in late April 1939. While 'Ack-Ack' was not seen as a glamour role, the 'London Scottish name brought in the men who would have hesitated to join another regiment, and the quality of recruits was very high.'[4] Men like Lee Harvey, who would serve with the 3rd Battalion for the next five years.

The fledgling 2nd and 3rd Battalions required a great deal of assistance from the 'old-timers' in the 1st Battalion, some of whom had served in the last Great War. Experienced officers, NCOs and specialists volunteered to join these new ventures and ensured London Scottish traditions were incorporated from the very outset. As such, the formation of 2nd and 3rd Battalion pipe bands was deemed a matter of urgency and 1st Battalion pipers and drummers would play an important role in assisting the emergence of both the pipe bands and the battalions they represented. At the same time, appeals for pipes, drums and specific items of band uniform to equip the new bandsmen went out to old comrades, resulting in pipes, sporrans, leopard skins and other much needed equipment arriving from far-flung corners of the British Empire.[5]

Initially, the 2nd Battalion drilled at Wellington Barracks, with the 3rd at the Royal Hospital, Chelsea and, before they had working bands of their own, the 1st Battalion Pipes and Drums would often attend drill nights to play the battalions from their parades. Piper A.C. 'Dusty' Millar was soon transferred to become Pipe Major of the 2nd Battalion, taking other long-serving members, such as Pipe Sergeant William D. Paterson, with him.[6] The 3rd Battalion Pipes and Drums would be slightly slower in taking shape but, thanks largely to the commitment of Battalion Second in Command Major H.V. Kerr, their incorporation was always given top priority.

On 2 July 1939, King George VI and Queen Elizabeth attended a Royal Review of National Service units in Hyde Park. The 1st Battalion were invited to provide the Sovereign's Guard, in recognition of the London Scottish becoming the first regiment to raise a 2nd Battalion. This event was the first official function to which the 2nd Battalion contributed, with their pipers and drummers massing with those of the 1st Battalion to march the Sovereign's Guard into position, before taking 'the position of honour, opposite the Royal dais.'[7] The massed band was led by 2nd Battalion Pipe Major Millar[8] and Drum Major Morrie Mills, who was asked to come out of retirement to perform. The event was broadcast live on the radio and a picture of the band appeared the following day in *The Times*.[9] Despite the inexperience of the 2nd Battalion Pipes and Drums, it was reported that the massed bands 'made a fine show and their marching and countermarching was very effective. We have seldom heard them play better.'[10]

Many changes were taking place within the band as the country geared up for war, as this example from a single month's report from the drum corps of the 1st Battalion portrays:

---

4   Barclay (ed.), *The London Scottish in the Second World War*, p.248.
5   For example, two sets of pipes, one silver-mounted and another having been used during WW1 by the Seaforth Highlands, were sent over from Canada by D.B. McMonnies. See *London Scottish Regimental Gazette* (1939), p.131.
6   Paterson would soon transfer to the 3rd Battalion to provide similar assistance.
7   *The Scotsman*, 3 July 1939, p.11.
8   1st Battalion Pipe Major T.K. Marshall was quite ill at this time with a stomach complaint that would force him to retire from active service.
9   'Citizen Army of Defence', *The Times*, 3 July 1939, p.5.
10 *London Scottish Regimental Gazette* (1939), p.201.

Drumcorp Archie MacLeod has left us for the 2nd Battalion. Drumcow (Dougie Cowie) has left us for the RAF, Tendrums Fearnside and Dodd have gone to Trinidad and 2nd Battalion respectively. Drumsarge is taking a commission in an Anti-Tank Regiment …[11]

As was the case in the Great War, many members of the band, would leave to take up a commission. In the regiment as a whole, nearly 1,300 men, well over an entire battalion strength, became officers during the war: the highest of any British army regiment. Whilst this was a huge drain on the regiment's resources, it was also a profound indication of the qualities and training of the London Scottish soldier.

Recruitment from Scotland, however, continued to be strong, ensuring the unique heritage of the regiment and providing would-be soldiers who had Highland piping and drumming backgrounds. Drafts of new recruits leaving Scotland for London were often piped from railway stations by Highland regimental pipers and, on at least one occasion, by a piper from the Toronto Scottish Regiment who was attending the School of Piping at Edinburgh Castle.[12]

While these recruits were mainly Scottish, it was often the case that they 'had very little in common with the original pre-war members of the Battalion',[13] which would bring its own challenges. English recruits had even less in common and, according to Private Ron Pottinger, who would quickly leave the 3rd Battalion to fly Typhoons in the RAF, 'were not wanted in the Scottish.'[14] Pottinger states that the Scottish were a 'pretty snooty territorial unit … not pleased at having Sassenach conscripts drafted into them.'[15] He found it strange that duty calls 'cookhouse, lights out, fatigues, last post, and the rest, were all played on the pipes',[16] moaned about the sound of reveille on his first day being played on the pipes and was very concerned about having to wear a kilt, 'which seemed ridiculous to me.'[17] However, even this dissenting voice was not immune to the power of the pipes and drums when, later at camp in Broome Park:

> There was an Armistice Day service with two minutes silence, and then a file of half a dozen pipers wended their way through the wooded slopes above the house playing the last post. In that setting and atmosphere, the sight was most impressive and brought a lump even to my throat.[18]

By Easter 1939, drummers of both the 1st and 2nd Battalions were formed into the nucleus of Number 2 (Anti-Aircraft) Platoon in their respective headquarters companies; a role they would continue undertaking for much of the war. The effectiveness of such anti-aircraft measures however, given the gunnery available, was questioned by many:

> Twin Vickers and twin Brens, mounted on 15-cwt trucks joining in a barrage against hostile aircraft, always reminds me of a very small boy singing in a very large choir – it couldn't really make any difference if it were not there. However, Bn AA Platoon appeared to be a formation

---

11 *London Scottish Regimental Gazette* (1939), p.185.
12 *London Scottish Regimental Gazette* (1940), p.109.
13 John Ferguson, 'Pioneer Commando – A Memoir of Special Service in Norway, The Mediterranean and North-West Europe, 1940-1945' unpublished manuscript, London Scottish Museum Archives, p.3.
14 Ron Pottinger, *A Soldier in the Cockpit: From Rifles to Typhoons in WWII* (Mechanicsburg, Pennsylvania: Stackpole Books, 2007), p.5.
15 Pottinger, *A Soldier in the Cockpit*, p.3.
16 Pottinger, *A Soldier in the Cockpit*, p.3.
17 Pottinger, *A Soldier in the Cockpit*, p.2.
18 Pottinger, *A Soldier in the Cockpit*, p.5.

on establishment, and so there it was, consisting chiefly of drummers, an odd bugler or two, and various other people such as mess cooks, whose normal employment ceased when the Bn was in action.[19]

General guard duties would also accompany this more specialised role. As a formal platoon, the self-styled 'Drumfamily' were now under the auspices, for the first time, of an officer.

> We believe this month History has been made – correct us if we are wrong – in the posting of a serving officer to Drumfamily, and we are happy to welcome 2/Lieut. Jim Hollebone (Drumloot to us) to our midst.[20]

In summer, the 1st and 2nd Battalions were at annual camp together in Burley, which provided a chance for the 2nd Battalion band to be brought up to scratch, with 2nd Battalion Pipe Major Millar stating:

> Even allowing for the customary modesty of this part of our Regiment, it is felt that the 2nd's Band is shaping up well and is capable of upholding the tradition particular to the Pipes and Drums.[21]

Meanwhile, the pipers were beginning their training in the role of stretcher bearers and first aid medics. Their first call to action, dealing with 'casualty' Drummer Clark, during a mock-battle along Holmsley Ridge at Burley camp, accurately describes how seriously they were taking their responsibilities:

> We whistled up Pipecorp Alec Murray, who unceremoniously tips Gordon Allan off the only available stretcher, where he was having a well-earned nap, and dashed to Clark's assistance. Clark, proving more obstinate than usual and not helping in the least to get his 14 1/2 stone on to the stretcher.[22]

The rest of Burley camp was spent in 'an orgy of Ack-Ack Bren Guns, drum practise and hours of tuning of pipes.'[23]

The 3rd Battalion Pipes and Drums was still very much in its infancy at this point and so the 1st Battalion provided the band for the regimental inspection at the Royal Hospital, Chelsea on 15 August, whilst the 2nd Battalion band played them off to camp later the same month.

It is worth making note here of the contribution of the Royal Caledonian School to the success of the London Scottish bands during the Second World War. A contribution that cannot be overstated. In late 1939, nearly 20 former pupils could be found in the combined Pipes and Drums of the regiment.

Military life for members of the London Scottish bands began to be taken more seriously after Hitler's invasion of Poland and Great Britain's subsequent Declaration of War, on 1 September 1939. The 2nd Battalion were, at this time, stationed in London's Docklands and members of the band continued the London Scottish tradition of historical 'firsts' by taking the very first German

---

19 'Bn AA – By 6666317', *London Scottish Regimental Gazette* (1954), p.39.
20 *London Scottish Regimental Gazette* (1939), p.185.
21 *London Scottish Regimental Gazette* (1939), p.219.
22 *London Scottish Regimental Gazette* (1939), p.241.
23 *London Scottish Regimental Gazette* (1939), p.244.

prisoners of the Second World War. Half an hour after war was declared, the 2nd Battalion were ordered to remove the crew of the German steamer, the *Royal Eagle*, under armed guard. While the 'Band's request for the vessel as a Band Room was promptly ruled out',[24] the steamer was requisitioned by the 2nd Battalion and the drummers did practise there before the battalion moved to Kent on 21 October. The 1st Battalion also moved to Kent that month, being stationed at Broome Park. Meanwhile, the anti-aircraft batteries of the 3rd Battalion took up station in various high-profile spots in central London.

As the 'phoney war' dragged on, discipline, drill and training took on new seriousness and a good number of pre-war members of the regiment, who were older or less fit, were de-mobbed. Many would join the Middlesex National Defence Company,[25] to which the London Scottish contributed a distinct platoon. This included members of the regimental Pipes and Drums, some of whom had fought in the Great War. Pipe Major Davy Pullar and three other ex-pipers ensured the London Scottish Platoon had suitable musical accompaniment.

Pipe Major Marshall of the 1st Battalion was another casualty of 'anno domini.' His position was taken over in February 1940 by Pipe Major Charles Turnbull, who came with 21 years' service from the 2nd Battalion, Gordon Highlanders and who was the Senior Pipe Major in the British Army. Although in his 40s, he was incredibly fit and represented the regiment at cross country running. He was an excellent piper and, 'due to his skill and untiring enthusiasm in the face of many difficulties, the Pipes and Drums of the Battalion were brought to a very high standard and played no small part in the life of the Battalion in the war years.'[26]

In the early days of the war, much of the support provided by the Pipes and Drums revolved around the basics of battalion life at camp. Bugles had been issued to the drummers and, for a short while, took over the daily duty calls, as the drummers became proficient. Drummers also assisted with drilling new recruits by providing a steady beat on the drill square. For many recruits, however, the most popular part of training was the route marches. 'Perhaps the skirl of the pipes has something to do with that.'[27] Companies were taken out one at a time and the presence of the band made a huge impression on the green recruits:

> The pipe band arrived in a lorry from Battalion and I shall never forget that blood-quickening cacophony as pipers tuned drones in Earls Avenue, drummers tightening pipe-clay thongs – those drums scrolled with Battle Honours, South Africa and my father's war. R Company formed up and stepped off to an 8-point roll reverberating against the houses, the great rising cry of the pipes … and every apprehension about the army and what was to come flew away as we swung into a proud pace behind that glorious rant.[28]

Regular Retreats were beaten at battalion headquarters at Chiddingstone Castle, with the Pipes and Drums 'marching out over the drawbridge as though to ancient war',[29] and providing the essential *esprit de corps* that allowed those serving to feel heartily that, 'By God we belonged.'[30]

---

24 *London Scottish Regimental Gazette* (1939), p.268.
25 National Defence Companies were the precursors of the Home Service Battalions, often known as the 'Home Guard'.
26 Barclay (ed.), *The London Scottish in the Second World War*, p.42.
27 'The First Months – Impressions of a Recruit of the 1st Battalion', *London Scottish Regimental Gazette*, (1940), p. 3.
28 Keith Spooner, *The Battalion* (London: LSR Trust, 1979), p.11.
29 Spooner, *The Battalion*, p.32.
30 Spooner, *The Battalion*, p.24.

A perplexed Luftwaffe pilot is taken prisoner at Broome Park after his ME109 was shot down during the first days of the Battle of Britain. He is led away by 1st Battalion Piper McDougall, 8 July 1940. (LSMA, used with permission)

1st Battalion Pipes and Drums at Broome Park, Kent, Summer 1940. After five long and bloody years of war, two of these pipers and two drummers would be dead, two pipers and a drummer would be prisoners of war, one drummer would be awarded the Distinguished Conduct Medal for bravery and three pipers would have served as Pipe Major. (LSMA, used with permission)

THE SECOND WORLD WAR 1939-1946   209

1st Battalion Pipes and Drums marching out from a memorial service at St. Andrew's Church, Jerusalem, June 1943. (LSMA, used with permission)

J. Ford, 'Into Battle', 1st Battalion London Scottish piper leading his company at the Battle of Primosole Bridge, 7 July 1943. (LSMA, used with permission)

Her Majesty, The Queen, as Honorary Colonel, paid a visit to the 1st Battalion on 10 April at Broome Park on a very cold day. Her Majesty was greeted by the Royal Salute and the pipe band playing *The Point of War* before she inspected the troops to the accompaniment of *The Skye Boat Song*. What 'perhaps the Queen heard that afternoon most faithfully expressed the feelings of every London Scottish heart – the strains of *Will ye no come back again?*'[31] played on the pipes as the royal car drove slowly away.

Meanwhile, the 2nd Battalion band were performing two shows that would exemplify the public face of their contribution to the war effort over the next five years. On 28 March, they performed at a 'Scottish Night' at the Royal Opera House, Covent Garden, as a morale boosting concert, and in April they performed at the Queen's Theatre in the West End as part of a fundraising concert in aid of the All-Services Canteen.

On 10 May 1940, Hitler invaded France and the Low Countries. Chamberlain chose to resign and was replaced by Churchill, and the 'phoney war' was officially at an end. Just over two weeks later the British Expeditionary Force was being evacuated in the 'miracle of deliverance'[32] that was Dunkirk, with France then quickly surrendering on 22 June. By 16 July, Hitler had approved plans for the invasion of Britain and the London Scottish found themselves confronting the same invasion scare scenarios that had brought about the regiment's birth in 1859 and indeed that of their original predecessors in 1798 and 1803 respectively. Before such an invasion could take place, however, Germany needed air superiority, and so the 'Battle of Britain' began in the skies over Southeast England.

The London Scottish Regiment, as always, played its part, but from the ground. The 1st Battalion achieved the first capture of a Messerschmitt ME109 fighter pilot and his intact plane, after a crash landing near Broome Park on 8 July 1940. Piper Willie McDougall was one of three guards that led the bemused pilot away to captivity. What this six-foot two-inch, blonde haired, blued eyed member of the 'Master Race' thought of being captured by a short, hairy, stocky Scottish piper is anyone's guess. Meanwhile, the 2nd Battalion were guarding Duxford Fighter Airfield,[33] where the Station Commander was very fond of the pipes.

Retreat was played many times at the airfield and was the first in a string of associations between the 2nd Battalion and the RAF during the war. The post-war rise of RAF pipe bands may very well be attributed to this period.

The 3rd Battalion were also scoring a 'first' when, on 1 September, 319 Battery, based at Shirley and including members of the Pipes and Drums, became the first Anti-Aircraft battery to shoot down a German bomber over London.[34] They would continue to play an important role in the defence of the capital at a time when Hitler, with the Battle of Britain lost and an invasion now impossible, took his revenge on the people of London through heavy bombardment of non-military targets. What followed was 76 consecutive nights of mass bombing of civilian areas that would come to be known as 'The Blitz.' War had come to the British people and casualties were high.

59 Buckingham Gate, Headquarters of the London Scottish Regiment, and St. Columba's Kirk, Regimental Church of the London Scottish, would both succumb to aerial attack on the same night. Three were killed at Buckingham Gate on the night of 10-11 May 1941 with the building significantly but only partially damaged. Unfortunately, St. Columba's was completely destroyed.

---

31 *London Scottish Regimental Gazette* (1940), p.105.
32 Winston Churchill, 'We Shall Fight on the Beaches' speech, House of Commons, 4 June 1940, *Hansards*, 1940, vol. 361 cc.787-78.
33 Now home to the Imperial War Museum's Aviation Museum.
34 The scared tailplane of this Junkers Ju88 bomber is on display in the London Scottish Regimental Museum.

59 Buckingham Gate, however, continued to be the rallying point for the regiment during the war, with the basement turned into a centre of operations and, most importantly, home to the ever-open war time bar.

The pipe band's own first casualty of war came on 15 August 1940 with the death of ex-Drummer Douglas Cowie who was known as 'The Babe' and 'Drumcow'. He had enlisted as a drummer in the 1st Battalion's pre-war band, having joined as a boy piper at the age of just 16. Eager to take the fight to the Germans, he transferred to Bomber Command, where he trained as a sergeant wireless operator and air gunner. He was tragically killed, aged 19, during a training accident when the Handley Page Hudson bomber T9320, in which he was a crew member, collided with a barrage balloon cable shortly after take-off. The *Regimental Gazette* reported: 'The passing of ex-Drummer D B Cowie illustrates once more that in the midst of life we are in death.'[35]

Three weeks later, news also came through of the death from the skies of 1914-18 war veteran Drummer Joss (John Arthur) Cairns. On 1 September, Joss was caught in an air raid on his way home from working at The Admiralty. His leg and body were badly burned by an incendiary shell and he died the next day after amputation. Cairns' exploits in the Great War are described in Chapter 4 of this volume and it seems perverse that, having been shot down by celebrated 'Red Baron' Manfred von Richthofen and survived, it should be a bomb from an anonymous German aircraft 26 years later that would take his life.

Band members continued to leave the regiment searching, as Douglas Cowie had, for quicker ways to join the fighting against these German air raids or through advancement by the taking of commissions. In peacetime as part-time soldiers with his own paid job, a piper or drummer had no reason to strive to be anything else within the Territorial Army. In wartime, however, as a regular soldier, 'he has to think of pay and allowances in relation to his family.'[36] Commissioning as an officer was, therefore, a very attractive proposition. However, not all those who became officers left the regiment, with the *London Scottish Regimental Gazette* in late 1940 reporting 'it should be known that the serving Officers of the 1st Battalion can produce a Band of four Pipers and one Big Drummer.'[37] By early 1941, the pre-war drum section alone had provided five Captains, one 2nd Lieutenant and the RQMS. The influence of the band throughout the regiment continued, as always, to be extraordinarily strong.

Such drains on the regiment's pipe bands did, however, mean that more aggressive policies for training new pipers and drummers had to be found. When the 2nd Battalion moved to divisional reserve at Llanwit Major, Monmouthshire, the band president, Major Henderson, and Pipe Major Millar set in place an intensive training course for volunteer pipers and drummers. This paid healthy dividends as, within three months, five of the six pipers and five learner drummers 'were good enough to play on ceremonial parades.'[38] Additional band members also meant the need for additional kit, and the call went out again to old comrades to part with their treasured sporrans, belts and slings to help dress the three battalion bands.[39]

The move to Wales in October 1940 involved the 2nd Battalion band in a slightly sensitive diplomatic incident. The battalion had stopped in Cardiff en route to Llanwit and, with enthusiastic support from a huge local crowd, decided to march through the city with bayonets fixed,

---

35 *London Scottish Regimental Gazette*, (1940), p.230.
36 Barclay (ed.), *The London Scottish in the Second World War*, p.189.
37 *London Scottish Regimental Gazette* (1940), p.241.
38 Barclay, *The London Scottish in the Second World War*, p.189.
39 The *London Scottish Regimental Gazette* tragically reported that ex-London Scot Angus Munro sent in his belt with a note stating that, while he had always intended to pass it on, his son 'and his wife have just been killed by one of Hitler's bombs and, being childless, his race is finished.' p.251.

behind the Pipes and Drums. Unfortunately, the bestowed honour of the 'Freedom of the City' of Cardiff was the sole preserve of the Royal Welsh Fusiliers, who were reportedly less than happy about having their rights usurped. This may be one of the reasons why the 2nd Battalion's stay in Wales was a short one. By April 1941, they had moved again, this time back to the South Coast, to be stationed close to Brighton. This was only the beginning of the 2nd Battalion's extensive wartime journeys around Great Britain, which would see them continually move, at short intervals, and to their great annoyance, around England, Scotland and Wales but, much to their intense chagrin, never overseas.

In the meantime, the 3rd Battalion had acquired a fourth battery with the application by 376 Battery RA, which included a large number of Scots, to join the London Scottish. On 11 January 1941, this request was approved by the War Office and the new battery 'marched in, headed by the embryonic Pipe Band and already wearing Tam O'Shanter bonnets.'[40] This was one of the very first official jobs for the 3rd Battalion's fledgling pipe band, which had only really begun to take shape in December 1940 and which was led by Pipe Major WD Fielding, who would soon leave for a commission with the Royal Warwickshire Regiment. His position would be taken by Pipe Major WD Paterson, who, like Fielding, served in all three battalions of the London Scottish.

While the 3rd Battalion's band took its first tentative steps, the 1st Battalion's nearly took its last when, in January 1941, 2nd A.A. Platoon, including all drummers and a number of pipers, was heavily bombed while on 'Ack-Ack' duty. Thankfully, however,

> Out of the ten bombs which surrounded us, only one went off, and that very considerately waited two days before doing so, thus enabling us to make a strategic withdrawal in fairly good order.[41]

Meanwhile, the 2nd Battalion Pipes and Drums, stationed on the 'Front Line' against bomber raids, in Sussex, 'now have Ack-Ack added to their multifarious duties'[42] and can 'promise Jerry a warm reception if he comes, unless it happens to be a Thursday, when our Ack-Ack Gunners will be out playing drums!'[43]

The relatively close proximity of the three battalions along the South Coast would remain throughout most of 1941 and allowed for an unprecedented level of regimental interaction. Contemporary issues of the *Regimental Gazette* mention numerous inter-battalion visits which invariably included members of the three pipe bands. One of the most important came on 13 July which witnessed a 'unique occasion in the Regimental history.'[44] At a cricket match against the 1st Battalion, hosted by the 3rd Battalion at Chislehurst, the massed bands of all three battalions performed together for the very first time. 'Under the Pipe-Major of the 1st Battalion, 26 pipers and 14 drummers took the field, and who could not have been stirred by the tunes they played and the picture they made?'[45] Officers and men from the entire regimental family were in attendance and 'a more enjoyable party could not have been had, even in the piping times of peace.'[46]

August 1941 saw the 2nd and 3rd Battalion bands playing for the first time with the Pipes and Drums of their sister regiment, the Toronto Scottish, while the 1st Battalion band had the

---

40 Barclay (ed.), *The London Scottish in the Second World War*, p.258.
41 *London Scottish Regimental Gazette* (1941), p.2.
42 *London Scottish Regimental Gazette* (1941), p.52.
43 *London Scottish Regimental Gazette* (1941), p.77.
44 *London Scottish Regimental Gazette* (1941), p.187.
45 *London Scottish Regimental Gazette* (1941), p.195.
46 Barclay (ed.), *The London Scottish in the Second World War*, p.262.

solemn duty of playing at the funeral of Colonel G Clowes, Honorary Regimental Colonel of the London Scottish Regiment. On 6 September, the 1st Battalion organised a Scottish Gathering near Ashford in Kent, to which all three battalions were invited. Many sporting events were held, but particular interest was paid to the piping and dancing competitions. Piping began at 0900 hours and continued through to 1715 hours, with nine piping and four dancing competitions in total. The 1st Battalion won the lion's share of the prizes, with Corporal Piper John Cheffins winning the open and Piper George 'Spud' Donaldson the junior competitions. The 2nd Battalion did win the novice marches but the young, and inexperienced, pipers of the 3rd Battalion went away empty-handed.

The standard of playing, particularly in the 1st Battalion, was now at such a high level that Pipe Major Turnbull, with the full support of his commanding officer, re-introduced the teaching and playing of *Piobairechd* for the first time in decades. This was no mean achievement and meant many additional hours of practise, culminating in nine different pieces added to the band's repertoire. In a letter to the *Regimental Gazette*, dated 19 November 1941, pipers of the 1st Battalion stated that:

> The rebirth of piobairechd in the Battalion has been a laborious and difficult task but emerges now in a standard of piping higher and stronger than it has ever been in the history of the Regiment.[47]

The drummers of the 1st Battalion, however, had not fared so well. The drive to play a more direct part in the war effort influenced many to transfer to the RAF. This was not helped by a belief that they were undervalued, both within the band and within the battalion. On moving to new barracks, the anti-aircraft platoon (made up almost exclusively of pipers and drummers) found themselves, with all their stores, quartered in three ancient bell tents, which, 'upon erection and inspection, proved to have rather more ventilation than was originally allowed for in their construction.'[48] While the pipe major used his position to requisition a marquee to move the pipers into, the drummers had to stay put. The December 2nd A.A. Platoon notes, written by a drummer and published in the *Regimental Gazette*, stated candidly that this was:

> A period which will be remembered with sorrow and bitterness and we hope that the Powers-that-be will prevent a recurrence of the state of affairs we experienced there. Now is the time to put our band among the foremost in the country. Despite insults and ridicule suffered in the past, we still retain our enthusiasm. We have the material and the ability; all we need is co-operation and we'll do the rest.[49]

The 'powers-that-be' were quick to take note and the asked for co-operation would soon be forthcoming. In fact, by the end of 1941, the standard of the band was so good that Private Keith Spooner would later write in his excellent war memoir, *The Battalion*:

> Pipey, who was, I believe, senior pipe-major in the British Army at the time, a twinkle-toed little man with head tilted like a bird ... had shaped a collection of war-joined Jocks and a

---

47 *London Scottish Regimental Gazette* (1941), p.299.
48 *London Scottish Regimental Gazette* (1941), p.175.
49 *London Scottish Regimental Gazette* (1941), p.275.

Territorial nucleus … into as good a band as any in the pukka highland regiments … who heartened and kept us going on all the roads of war.[50]

Meanwhile, the Pipes and Drums of the 2nd Battalion were showing their own prowess on the radio. The BBC decided to broadcast a new series entitled *Off Parade* and chose the London Scottish to provide the inaugural performance, which was recorded live on 19 December 1941. The Pipes and Drums opened and closed the half-hour show, which also included a solo performance by Pipe Major Millar, as well as a variety of musical turns by other members of the battalion.

Such activity at the end of 1941 and during the first six months of 1942 helped to lighten what were probably the darkest days of the Second World War. While Germany's invasion of the Soviet Union in June 1941 had provided some respite to the bombing of Britain, the Axis war machine continued to appear invincible as it swept through the Russian plains to the gates of Leningrad and Moscow. An Allied counter-offensive in North Africa had been rebuffed by January 1942 and further defeats throughout the next four months saw Axis forces close to Alexandria in Egypt, with the strategically important Suez Canal in sight. In the East, Japan's declaration of war on 7 December 1941 heralded the loss of British colonies, including Hong Kong, Burma, Singapore, Malaya, Borneo and Brunei, as one disastrous defeat after another seemed to befall the Allies. Even Australia was under threat of invasion. The arrival of the United States into the war brought some hope for the future but, with crippling US shipping loses off the American Atlantic coast causing an even harder squeeze on rationing, hopes of a brighter future seemed a long way off to the beleaguered British people. Efforts to boast morale and bolster a sense of cohesion, for both British soldiers and civilians, was of particular importance during this dark time.

Despite this sense of desperation, plans were already being made to turn the tide. While Britain's civilians rolled up their sleeves, kept calm and carried on, Britain's military took training to a new level of commitment as the country gritted its teeth and prepared for what was to come. This dedication to training and the advance to a more intense war footing was obvious in the London Scottish Regiment. While the three bands of the regiment continued to practise hard and increase and retain their numbers, the vast majority of their time was now spent training for their specific fighting roles. Band notes in the *Regimental Gazette* talk more often of lessons in un-armed combat and the joys of river crossings than they do of practise and performances, while the *Gazette* itself, following increased security measures, no longer provided battalion, platoon or battery identification and ceased to mention their locations. In addition, training with live ammunition increased, sometimes, tragically, with fatal consequences.

On 13 April 1942, the Army and RAF organised a joint demonstration at Imber Downs near Warminster. A delegation from the 2nd Battalion London Scottish, which included Pipe Major Millar, was involved, along with many other military officials who were stationed 800 yards from a large target of dummy human figures. As Spitfires and Hurricanes swept in low to strafe the targets with machine-gun fire, an inexperienced pilot mistook the military enclosure for the dummy figures and poured thousands of rounds onto those below. One young lieutenant from the London Scottish was amongst three men who died that afternoon, while Pipe Major Millar was lucky to survive. He was hit four times, being shot three times through the legs and arms, whilst one bullet miraculously ricocheted off his belt buckle. He would subsequently make a full recovery from his injuries and re-joined the battalion two months later.

Two days after this incident, to vividly juxtapose the very differing responsibilities of the Pipes and Drums, the 3rd Battalion band provided entertainment at Craven Cottage, home of Fulham Football Club, for the military divisional football final which saw the London Scottish take on a

---

50   Spooner, *The Battalion*, pp.44-45.

team from the Honourable Artillery Company. The band, which was slowly beginning to come into its own, was able to turn out eight pipers, a bass, tenor and two side drums despite the rigors of training and continued anti-aircraft duty protecting London and the South Coast. Their impressive performance did not, unfortunately, positively influence the result of the game.

The following month, in May, the 3rd Battalion headquarters moved from Dibden Manor to Beaulieu Palace in Hampshire with the Pipes and Drums brought together here from their various batteries for an extended period of practise. They were then 'loaned to Batteries from time to time to keep up morale during long periods of work.'[51] One of these, 298 Battery, was responsible for guarding the Fleet Air Arm aerodrome at Worthy Down and the Pipes and Drums made a number of appearances there in the coming months. The commanding officer of the aerodrome was a Scotsman and on the first night the band performed decided to join them as a drummer. He hitched a drum to the buttons of his braces and off they went:

> They set off through the camp with the Commander in his gold-braided cap, drumming as if inspired and hoping that the buttons would stand the strain, while crowds lined the way cheering and marvelling. The whole thing was such a success that we were implored to repeat the Saga, which we did three days later.[52]

Performances by the band became a regular fixture at Beaulieu, with local people and soldiers and airmen billeted nearby attending Beating Retreat every Saturday evening. In addition, with all the battalion's officers now stationed together at the Beaulieu headquarters, the first opportunity arose to inaugurate an officer's mess:

> It did much for morale and officers of different batteries got to know each other. Sergeant-Piper Paterson here came into his own, and on many occasions he entertained the Mess with his playing, as did Bdr D Fielding and Pipers C Wicks and H F Richardson.[53]

The 3rd Battalion of the London Scottish Regiment, although still part of the Royal Artillery, was now beginning to function much more along the traditional lines of her two sister London Scottish battalions.

Despite being physically confined to Great Britain, the influence of the London Scottish Pipes and Drums could still be felt overseas. Colonel 'Duggie' Lyall-Grant was continuing his illustrious military service, which stretched back to his time as a London Scottish piper prior to the Great War, as the Officer Commanding on various troop ships moving Allied soldiers around the world. Mid-1942 saw him taking command of 2,000 Australian troops heading across the Pacific. Colonel Lyall-Grants uniform and accent stood out and on his first parade there came from the ranks of 'Diggers' a shout of 'Give us a tune on the pipes, Scottie.' Duggie, being Duggie, replied that he would willingly do so, if a set could be found. Miraculously, and in short order, a set of pipes were duly delivered and 'Duggie did give them a tune, after which the Aussies ate out of his hand.'[54]

With major turns in the tides of war, it would not be long until two battalions of the London Scottish would, themselves, soon be on troopships heading for war service overseas. After the US victory at the Battle of Midway and with British and Commonwealth troops again halting

---

51 Barclay (ed.), *The London Scottish in the Second World War*, p.269.
52 *London Scottish Regimental Gazette*, (1942), p.132.
53 Barclay (ed.), *The London Scottish in the Second World War*, p.278.
54 *London Scottish Regimental Gazette*, (1942), p.82.

1st Battalion marching through a Sicilian village, July 1943. (LSMA, used with permission)

The Boys in the 1st Battalion Band, Iraq, 1943. (LSMA, used with permission)

Massed Pipes and Drums of the 1st Battalion London Scottish and 6th Battalion, Gordon Highlanders, under shellfire at Anzio Field Hospital, 11 February 1944. (LSMA, used with permission)

'C' Company, 1st Battalion, headed by Pipers Fraser and Munro, marching from Morciano to a farm 3 miles southeast for two days rest after fighting at Croce and Palazzo Ridge, September 1944. (LSMA, used with permission)

Rommel's advance at El Alamein, there were signs that the Axis war machine might be beginning to stall. In the summer months of 1942, discussions began in earnest amongst the Allied military about how best to advance the war in Europe. Whilst most US Generals advocated strategic landings in France as soon as possible, Churchill convinced President Roosevelt that no such offensive could realistically take place until mid-1944 at the earliest. With Soviet Premier Stalin pressing strongly for a second front in Western Europe to relieve pressure on his troops in the East, it was agreed that an invasion of Sicily would take place in 1943 which, if successful, could lead to a full invasion of Italy. Churchill claimed this would allow for swift advances through 'the soft underbelly of Europe', opening up the Mediterranean to Allied shipping and tying up much needed German troops.

By May 1943, North Africa was fully reconquered by Allies forces and, whilst major Soviet offensives were steadily pushing back German troops on the Eastern Front, preparations for 'Operation Husky' – the invasion of Sicily – were being finalised. This operation, and the subsequent invasion of Italy, would involve both the 1st and 3rd Battalions of the London Scottish, who would remain at the heart of this conflict for the next three years. This supposed 'soft underbelly' would prove, in the words of American General Mark Clark, to be one 'tough old gut.'[55] The Pipes and Drums of both battalions would feature in the thick of this heavy fighting from the very beginning. Contrary to popular belief, 'No Campaign in Western Europe cost more that the Italian Campaign in terms of lives lost and wounds suffered by infantry forces',[56] and London Scottish losses would prove to be substantial in a campaign that would very much come to take second place in the eyes of the world after the Normandy landings in France on D-Day.

7 August 1942 saw the 1st Battalion training hard at Highham in Suffolk. Here they would receive a visit from King George VI who 'after listening to the Pipes and Drums, inspected training by all companies and departed to the echoes of tumultuous applause from all ranks.'[57] 20 days later, all those applauding would be at sea. The last published Band Notes in the *Regimental Gazette* for August included the following passage:

> As this will probably be our last communication to the outside world before our complete confirmation of Darwin's theory, we trust that our readers (if any) will not forget us and will regret our passing, even if only for the reason that we looked such pretty little boys when we were all dressed up. Cheerio![58]

On 27 August, the 1st Battalion embarking aboard HMT *California* with other units of the 168th Brigade, totalling around 4,000 men and women. 24 hours later the ship left Gourock on the Clyde, to begin the first leg of their journey to join the war. The Pipes and Drums played the ship away from port, making quite an impact:

> How many readers have heard a pipe band play at sea? To see 'Pipey' and his stalwarts perform within the limited space of the promenade deck brought a lump to your throat. At the Captain's request they played and have given of their best daily since then. Maybe the

---

55 Richard Holmes, *The World at War: The Landmark Oral History from the Classic TV Series* (London: Random House, 2011), p.442.
56 J. Keegan, *The Second World War* (London: Penguin, 1990), p.368.
57 Barclay (ed.), *The London Scottish in the Second World War*, p.58.
58 *London Scottish Regimental Gazette* (1942), p.105.

wind caught up the silver skirl and deep throb and carried them back to the native heath. We like to think so, anyway.[59]

The only other entertainment on board was the Fife and Drums of the Royal Berkshire Regiment, with whom the Pipes and Drums would regularly Beat Retreat, ensuring that the London Scottish band remained in much demand. Performing at sea did, however, occasionally come at a price:

> Pipey and his boys have been giving us a tune twice daily. One day he was playing with three others while the deck heaved and rolled rather more than comfortable. When given leave to fall out Pipey remarked to nobody in particular, 'Thank you, now I can carry on being sick!' Pipe music sounds lovely at sea.[60]

The first stop in the voyage came in West Africa on 9 September when the convoy reached Freetown in Sierra Leone, although no shore leave was granted. It would not be until 25 September that the *California* would reach Cape Town, South Africa. A short stay ensued and with all re-embarked, they set sail again on 29 September. Joining them on board were the 1st Battalion, London Irish Rifles and 90 female sister nurses of the 93rd General Hospital. The London Scottish were quick to seize on this boon. Pipe Major Turnbull and Pipe Sergeant Cheffins began conducting Highland dancing classes, which automatically drew the interest of the female nurses on board and ensured that the band and the London Scottish officers were the envy of all.

Another short stop came at Bombay on 22 October, where the battalion left the *California* and boarded HMT *Neuralia*, which set sail on 25 October. Hallowe'en was spent at sea, with the captain and crew invited to join the traditional London Scottish celebrations. Pipe Sergeant Cheffins piped throughout the evening, which was heartened greatly by the ship's captain who broke out the rum. After much merriment, members of the band carried the chief engineer to bed having, once again, cemented their special status and added a great deal to the ship's general morale.

The *Neuralia* finally ended her journey on Guy Fawkes Night, 1942, greeted by a band from the Gurkha Rifles when tying up just outside Basrah in Iraq. After disembarking, the 1st Battalion were driven 15 miles into the desert to spend the next eight days at Zubair transit camp. Here 'to regain land-legs we marched over miles and miles of fuck all … The pipes played us on as always.'[61] 13 November saw the battalion entrain for a two-day journey to Kirkuk, where they would stay for the next four months as part of Persia and Iraq Command, PAIFORCE, protecting oilfields and undergoing vigorous pre-deployment training.

On arrival in Kirkuk:

> 'Pipey' and his stalwarts were soon making the evenings sweet with their lilt, and their shadowy figures silhouetted against the twilight of a desert sky added to the wistfulness and grandeur of their tunes.[62]

---

59 *London Scottish Regimental Gazette* (1942), p.190.
60 Letter dated 1st-8th September 1942, 'Overseas and All That – By 5451', *London Scottish Regimental Gazette*, (1948), p.30.
61 Spooner, *The Battalion*, p.55.
62 *London Scottish Regimental Gazette* (1943), p.69.

Camp calls would continue to be performed by the orderly piper, with a full band reveille performed once a week by the Pipes and Drums in 'shit order' of denims and PT shoes.[63] The other two infantry battalions of the 168th Brigade were the aforementioned London Irish Rifles and the Royal Berkshire Regiment, both of whom were camped within hailing distance. At *Lights Out*, the brigade's soldiers settled down and:

> Listened to the orderly piper up at Battalion HQ's ridge playing *Donald Blue*, followed by the distant London Irish piper who played *Oft In The Stilly Night*. Finally, a bugler from The Royal Berkshires sounded *The Last Post*, and hundreds of young Britons so far from home composed themselves for slumber beneath 'strange-eyed constellations.'[64]

Captain C.A. McIntyre of the London Scottish wrote in his journal entry for Monday 9 December; 'Amazing how sweet the pipes sound here and what a grand sight they look in the desert dusk.'[65]

Maintenance of bagpipes and drums would be a continuing issue while the band were overseas. While those back home did their best to send out any spare parts they could lay their hands on, Pipe Major Turnbull and his men had to improvise with anything that would come to hand. Reeds were a particular issue, although 'The Iraqis have a kind of reed bagpipe affair, and we could get reeds from them.'[66] The accompanying change in pitch very much lent the bagpipes to their new surroundings. Keeping pipe bags and chanters from drying out involved the concoction of a preservative made from sugar and water. Drumheads also needed protecting, as did thongs and ropes that would split and crack in the heat. Despite this, and the more direct rigours of war, the 1st Battalion bass drum, complete with a drumhead signed by band personnel and listing all their places of deployment, made it through the entire war and is still today, proudly on display in the regimental museum.

Christmas 1942 was celebrated with a brigade drumhead service followed by much drinking, which would pale into insignificance in comparison with the forthcoming London Scottish celebrations at Hogmanay. Heavy drinking continued throughout the day and late into the evening and, as is want to happen, the singing of opposing sectarian football songs in support of Glasgow Rangers and Glasgow Celtic descended into a mass brawl that left many injured. A huge bonfire was started in the camp and the situation threatened to get out of hand. However, instead of sending for the Military Police, the quick-witted commanding officer[67] sent in the Pipes and Drums, who:

> Formed a wide circle round the conflagration and a great drunken dance stamped itself out into eventual exhaustion. What in Allah's name did those neighbouring Kurds make of it all?[68]

Training continued apace including more frequent and longer route marches. On 9 January, a 20-mile march took place, leading back through Kirkuk, 'which turns out en masse and marvels

---

63 See Spooner, *The Battalion*, p.57.
64 Spooner, *The Battalion*, p.60.
65 C.A. McIntyre, Unpublished Diary, London Scottish Museum Archives, 28 August 1942 to 28 April 1943.
66 Pipe Major Turnbull, as quoted in *Eighth Army News*, August 1943.
67 Lieutenant-Colonel H.J. Wilson, O.B.E., T.D. who was affectionately known by the men as 'Harry the Horse.'
68 Spooner, *The Battalion*, p.62.

at the pipes.'[69] Two weeks later, at the end of another all-day march, the pipe band strikes up 'and tired troop's spirits lift again as they near home.'[70] Meanwhile, duties continue in the Officer's Mess. MacIntyre's entry for Friday, 5 February states that 'Pipey entertains, with a grand selection, Alec Murray plays, also 'Pipe Captain' Aitchison and 'Pipe Lieutenant' Glover.'[71]

Flying Officer Ian Smith, who would many years later become Prime Minister of Rhodesia, recalled the advantages the Pipes and Drums gave the 1st Battalion, London Scottish rugby team when he played against them as part of No. 237 (Rhodesian) Squadron, RAF in Kirkuk. The squadron had a crack rugby team and their only defeat came at the hands of the London Scottish:

> When they came to play us on the first day, foolishly we agreed that their pipe band could play up and down the field before the game, and that was the first time we were beaten. We never forgave the pipers for that – we played them a second time, and when we didn't let the pipers on the field, we won the second game.[72]

A more sombre duty came for the band in early March 1943, when Private Jenkins of D (Don) Company was accidently shot and killed during intensive live-fire exercises. On a fittingly overcast and rainy day, the band slow marched the battalion to the burial site and played *The Flowers of the Forest* before his coffin. With the spectre of combat now only months away and very much on the horizon, Private Jenkins would prove to be 'the only man of the Battalion's accumulated dead for whom there was time and circumstance for such full military honours.'[73] His death was a subtle but sharp reminder of what lay ahead.

During this period, the 3rd Battalion would themselves head overseas, leaving behind Pipe Major Paterson who was deemed too old for active service. The 15 December 1942 saw them arrive, like the 1st Battalion before them, at Gourock on the Clyde where they embarked on HMT *Britannic*, along with over 4,000 other troops. As with the 1st Battalion, the Commanding Officer of the London Scottish was asked to perform the duties of OC Army Troops while onboard, which would provide benefits for the Pipes and Drums. The convoy set sail on 17 December into stormy weather that would last until their next sighting of land at Freetown, Sierra Leone, on New Year's Eve.

Despite the conditions, the London Scottish were quick to set up an officer's reel club, run under the direction of newly promoted ex-Bombardier, now Pipe Sergeant J Speirs, who was even quicker in inviting to the classes all 20 of the RAF nurses who just happened to be the only females on board.

Christmas had been celebrated at sea:

> The Pipe Band of ten pipers and five drums have got into their stride and have been greatly appreciated by all on board. Christmas Day was a field day for them, as they gave continuous performances on deck and below. Furthermore, Bdr. Speirs piped the CO on his round of the troops at dinner, and later piped while the Officers had their dinner (both sittings) and later still piped for the WO's in their Mess.

---

69   McIntyre, Unpublished Diary entry for 9 January 1943.
70   McIntyre, Unpublished Diary entry for 22 January 1943.
71   McIntyre, Unpublished Diary entry for 5 February 1943.
72   Philippa Berlyn, *The Quiet Man* (Salisbury, Rhodesia: Collins, 1978), p.52.
73   Spooner, *The Battalion*, p.64.

> In fact he was still piping when we turned in, so that in congratulating him on behalf of his very able band we must add a personal bouquet for his individual and prodigious performance throughout the day and night.[74]

Hogmanay celebrations on arrival at Freetown were especially vigorous, no doubt heightened by the rough voyage. For the first time since leaving Scotland, portholes could be opened and light and fresh air allowed into the ship.

> Being New Year's Eve, it was a great occasion for all Scots on board and from every quarter of the boat could be heard the Scottish reels and dances accompanied by the twirling of the bagpipes.[75]

Needless to say, celebrations continued long into the night:

> At midnight, the band assembled on the fore decks and, with the ship's searchlight from the bridge focused upon them, piped in the New Year.[76]

No shore leave was permitted and on 3 January 1943 the convoy set off again on a much smoother second leg. The Pipes and Drums would flourish in these conditions and:

> Under its new leader, Sergeant Piper Speirs, gave two performances each week on the main deck and was a constant delight not only to the Regiment but to all other personnel on board. On one occasion their programme was broadcast to the whole convoy.[77]

19 January saw the convoy arrive for a brief rest at Durban, South Africa, with the decks manned and the London Scottish Pipes and Drums playing the *Britannic* alongside the quay. 'It was early in the morning and a lump came into all throats.'[78] The men disembarked the following day and marched behind the band to a bivouac transit camp some four miles inland. 'We were given a rapturous welcome from residents who entertained us in their homes and we put on a fine parade or two for them with the pipe band.'[79]

The battalion embarked again on HMT *Dilwara* on 27 February but engine problems saw her return to Durban where the London Scottish transferred to HMT *Cap Tourane*. Mombasa was reached on 31 March for a refuelling stop where:

> In accordance with the now established custom the Pipe Band played the ship into port, and in return many shouts and cheers were received from personnel lining the sides of other ships already in harbour, and also the running up of the St Andrew's Cross by HMS *Revenge*, which was not slow to recognise the arrival of Scottish troops.[80]

---

74 *London Scottish Regimental Gazette*, (1943), p.75.
75 Harvey, *D-Day Dodgers*, p.36.
76 '3rd Battalion at Sea', *London Scottish Regimental Gazette* (1943), p.84.
77 Barclay (ed.), *The London Scottish in the Second World War*, p.282
78 Harvey, *D-Day Dodgers*, p.37.
79 *Memoirs of the 'A' Troop Commander, 298 Battery, 3rd Battalion 1939-1946*, (Unpublished Manuscript, London Scottish Museum Archives), p.3. This personal account was penned by one of the four 'A' Troop Lieutenants: J. B. Bewsick, I. H. Miller, G. L. O. Bell or J. B. Watson.
80 Barclay (ed.), *The London Scottish in the Second World War*, p.288.

The 8 April saw the *Cap Tourane* arrive at Aden for another refuelling stop, with the Pipes and Drums playing the ship in to harbour with, of course, *The Barren Rocks of Aden*. Seven days later, on 15 April, the demanding voyage finally came to its conclusion, some four months after leaving Britain, on arrival at Port Tewfik, near Suez. The 3rd Battalion immediately entrained for Qassasin, 60 miles northeast of Cairo and just 15 miles from Ismailia, where the 2nd Battalion, London Scottish had been stationed during the First World War. During this period, the 1st Battalion were also stationed on the Suez Canal and Commanding Officer Lieutenant Colonel Harry Wilson, accompanied by Major Torrance Law, made the journey to visit the 3rd Battalion camp and offered an invitation for a return visit. It was the first occasion that the two battalions had been able to arrange a meeting in over two years, and a party consisting of officers, NCO's and the Pipes and Drums made the return trip the following Sunday. 'This reunion was a somewhat unique and memorable occasion and cemented the friendship which already existed between the two Battalions.'[81]

> The Pipe Band was able to put in a good amount of practise at Qassasin and used to play 'Retreat' on two evenings a week. They also played and achieved an enthusiastic reception at a military demonstration organised by Area Command. This was the last occasion on which the Band was to perform as a unit for many months. Its members were scattered amongst the batteries, where each man had his operational job and from which, in the field, he could not be spared.[82]

As with the 1st Battalion, it would not be long before the 3rd Battalion entered the war proper.

Back in Britain, the 2nd Battalion, much to their frustration, remained firmly tied to the homeland. Whilst her sister battalions headed overseas, the 2nd Battalion was deployed to New Milton and the Hampshire coast. In early November 1942, the Pipes and Drums joined with the other bands of the now fully 'Celtic' 141st Brigade to Beat Retreat in Bournemouth. A Massed Pipes and Drums of the London Scottish, the 8th Battalion Black Watch and the Royal Irish Fusiliers performed before a large crowd, including the brigade and divisional commanders. The 'playing and marching were excellent, including a complicated manoeuvre of getting from eights to threes evolved by Pipe-Major Millar.'[83]

By February 1943, however, the battalion had moved again[84] and the pace of training had reached such a level that the band had very much taken a back seat. So much so, in fact, that 'it is not uncommon to be asked by new members of the battalion if the London Scottish possesses a band.'[85] The hope very much remained that the 2nd Battalion would follow the 1st and 3rd overseas and that being so well trained would guarantee their ticket. Unfortunately, the opposite would prove to be the case. The well-trained men of the battalion were siphoned off for officer training, as training instructors or for drafts to the London Scottish overseas battalions and those of other regiments. Turnover of personnel, including those from within the Pipes and Drums, would

---

81 *London Scottish Regimental Gazette* (1943), p.141.
82 Barclay (ed.), *The London Scottish in the Second World War*, p.292.
83 'C.O.'s Notes', *London Scottish Regimental Gazette*, (1942), p.202.
84 To Boscombe, Hampshire followed by another move in March to Southampton.
85 '2nd Battalion, 2nd Platoon Notes, February', *London Scottish Regimental Gazette*, (1943), p.20.

1st Battalion Pipes and Drums Beating Retreat at Regimental Headquarters, Pula, Italy, July 1945. (LSMA, used with permission)

1st Battalion Pipes and Drums under acting Pipe Major McLeod, inspected by the Corps Commander after the Colours Parade, Trieste, 26 March 1946. (LSMA, used with permission)

THE SECOND WORLD WAR 1939-1946   225

Robert Souter, watercolour from a photograph of the 1st Battalion Pipes and Drums Beating Retreat in the Piazza San Marco, Venice, May 1945. (LSMA, used with permission)

remain high throughout the war years,[86] while the battalion would continue to move around the country;[87] its frustration almost personified by its restlessness.

In March 1943, as the 2nd Battalion moved once again to Southampton, the 1st Battalion received orders to move forward. The preceding month had been one of continual rain and intense training and the move could not come soon enough for most. As always, the pipe band were able to use their influential position to artfully express the opinions of the common soldier. On 26 March, the brigade commander spent the evening at the London Scottish Officer's Mess. MacIntyre's diary entry for the day reads; 'Brig. comes to dinner in evening and 'Pipey' plays, including a subtle pibroch *Too Long in This Condition*.'[88]

It did the job, and on 31 March, the battalion entrained for an over-night journey to Baghdad; a journey that would have 'exciting' consequences for Drum Sergeant 'Bertie' Brand:

> During the 'wee sma" hours', Bertie, our leading 'tipper' or side-drummer, woke for a leak, thought he was in a tent or hut, unbuttoned his flies and stepped out of the moving wagon. He rejoined us after several weeks having crawled along the tracks with a broken ankle until he was discovered by some goat-herds.[89]

From Baghdad, a long journey by road took the battalion through western Iraq, Jordan, Palestine and the Sinai Desert, crossing the Suez Canal near Ishmalia, before arriving at the Combined Operations Centre in Kabrit, Egypt for the rigours of final combat assault training.

On 8 May, with the course successfully completed, the 1st Battalion departed back over the Sinai to Gaza, following in the footsteps of the London Scottish's First World War 2nd Battalion. This interlude would only last six days but allowed enough time for a side visit to Jerusalem and a memorial service at St Andrew's Church, where Pipe Major Turnbull and Pipe Sergeant Cheffins played a lament. Directly after the service concluded, 'the Band played selections in front of the Church, to the delight of the Scots residents of Jerusalem',[90] including a number of members of the regiment's Old Comrades Association.

It was here in Gaza that Pipe Major Turnbull would later reminisce about 'The Remarkable Story of a Latrine.' Pipe Sergeant Cheffins was the camp Orderly Officer and gave orders to a London Scottish private to clean out the latrines. The private dumped an entire barrel of petrol into the latrine and then sat down on one of the 12 seats to have a smoke. Having lit his cigarette, he rather absent-mindedly decided to drop the match down the hole. 'I heard the explosion some fifty yards away, and I saw the Orderly Officer who reached my office in record time to make his report.'[91] Mercifully, despite the collapse of ten tons of concrete, no one was hurt, although the battalion was sent a bill for £250 which reached them months later on the beachhead at Anzio and which was, justifiably given the circumstances, summarily ignored.

On 15 May, the battalion embarked again for a return to Egypt, this time to the southern end of the Suez Canal at Ataka, where their time was mostly occupied with route marches. They embarked again on 1 July, only to disembark on the 4th, before finally departing on 8 July to play their part in 'Operation Husky' the long-anticipated invasion of Sicily.

---

86 The battalion sent over 100 soldiers for officer training between March 1942 and March 1943.
87 Moves came on average every four months from 1939 until after the D-Day landings in 1944. The battalion was stationed in over 20 different locations during the course of the war.
88 McIntyre, Unpublished Diary entry for 26 March 1943.
89 Spooner, *The Battalion*, p.64.
90 Barclay (ed.), *The London Scottish in the Second World War*, p.78.
91 *London Scottish Regimental Gazette* (1958), p.180.

No attempt will be made in this chapter to give a detailed chronological or tactical account of the many and varied combat operations undertaken by the 1st and 3rd London Scottish battalions during their war service in Italy. All major actions will be mentioned, but if the reader requires further detail, it can be found in Brigadier C.N. Barclay's edited volume *The London Scottish in the Second World War*, which is both comprehensive and exceedingly well written.

The invasion of Sicily began on 10 July 1943, with amphibious and airborne landings by the US 7th Army under General Patton at the Gulf of Gela and the British 8th Army, under General Montgomery, north of Syracuse. The 1st Battalion, London Scottish landed at Syracuse three days later. Here they:

> Disembarked on to a wharf which was literally alight with burning petrol fumes – several officers had their kit burned. We marched through the recently captured town to the tune of the pipes and camped for the night outside Florida.[92]

All five drummers, in their role as Ack-Ack Platoon, five pipers and the Pipe Major made the landing, while the rest of the band were strung out in various locations from Tel Aviv to Cairo working as rear parties. These remaining members, under Pipe Sergeant Cheffins, would take until 21 September to re-join the main party in Sicily. Meanwhile, the Pipe Major and a second piper were assigned to Headquarters Company, while the four remaining pipers were each assigned directly to a rifle company.

On 14 July, the battalion marched to a forward holding area with each company headed by their newly assigned piper. The march was in excess of 15 miles across rough country, in stifling heat and with little water. Sergeant Souter depicts it as the hardest route march the battalion had endured thus far. A diary entry of Corporal George Smith explains that it began at 0800 hours and the final destination was not reached by most until after 1930. Smith goes on to state that 'At two villages the people turned out and 'gave us a hand' – or was it the pipers?'[93] Marching in itself was a feat in such conditions, with many men needing medical attention en route. Marching whilst piping was, then, an exploit of true dedication and endurance:

> By afternoon there was a whole rabble of stragglers, staggering along behind what looked like the original Drunken piper. This was a good chum of mine, Bill[94] ... and his dogged performance that day should have been worth a medal.[95]

There would be no time to recover, however, as the battalion moved up again the following day, under heavy shell fire and with pipes playing, to the front line near Primosole Bridge. A sketch by Sergeant J. Ford, entitled *Into Battle* and drawn on the day itself, depicts this march into action with troops following their company piper. This battle, for most in the battalion,[96] would begin at 2200 hours on 17 July, with orders to take the bridge, utilising intense artillery support:

> In view of the projected artillery support, each company had permission to take one piper to play them into their first action, but as they reached the start line, orders were received that

---

92 Lt. Col H.J. Wilson OBE TD Unpublished Diary, London Scottish Museum Archives, n.d.
93 Cpl. George Douglas Smith Unpublished Diary, London Scottish Museum Archives, 25 August 1942-25 May 1945, entry for 14 July 1943.
94 Piper William Cowie.
95 Spooner, *The Battalion*, p.72.
96 'A' Company had actually seen their first action of the war the previous evening.

the earlier support had been cancelled and that the initial attack, to the disgust of the pipers, would be silent.[97]

Private Spooner describes the moment in detail:

> 'Hallo Toc Four, hello Toc Four. Report my signals, over.' There followed a message that the advance would, despite previous information, be silent. I told Jim, who told The Duke, who told the CSM, who told Spud. Pipers had been ordered to play their companies through the presumed barrage: the film of 'Desert Victory', shown to us as a preview, must have gone to Harry the Horse's head![98]

Don (D) Company's piper, George 'Spud' Donaldson quite prosaically summed up his annoyance at not being able to play by stating: 'Ah feel like a spare prick at a weddin', so ah do.'[99]

The proceeding action was chaotic and violent with intense German resistance from machine guns and mortars. The drummers were heavily involved in the fighting: 'those members of the platoon still on their feet were hurled into battle, while the remainder hurled themselves on the ground in varying stages of unconsciousness.'[100] Primosole Bridge was taken and the operation deemed a success, but not without casualties. Over 30 soldiers were injured and 12 had been killed, mostly by German mortar fire. One of these was Corporal John Bryden, who had been hit while attempting to dig in.

> We became aware of a terrible catarrhal snoring from the half-dug slit below, about which stretcher-bearers knelt. It was Johnny, the Coy HQ corporal, a dark, dapper Londoner who had once been a drummer in the pipe band and was older than most present; he whom death had given a preliminary prod on the road to Primosole Bridge.[101]

Johnny Bryden was 35 years old and had been a tenor drummer with the band from at least as far back as 1940, before initially transferring to D Company on promotion to corporal.

Private 'Trigger' Holohan would also die on that first night of fighting. He had been stretchered back to the Regimental Aid Post, having been hit by shrapnel. 'Seriously wounded in several places, he refused morphia and told the stretcher-bearers to leave him and attend to the other wounded. His only request was for 'Spud' Donaldson to play *Heilan' Laddie* to him.'[102] While Piper Donaldson solemnly played the regimental march, 'Trigger died – just like someone in a war film. Battle, it seemed, would touch the innermost, immense hidden things in our fellows.'[103]

Primosole Bridge was, however, no war film, and the 1st Battalion's inaugural battle of the Second World War was certainly no repeat of the 'glories' that made headlines around the world when the London Scottish went into action for the first time at Messines during the Great War. Glories that had come at enormous human cost and decimated the Pipes and Drums. Despite later portrayals in print and film of the 'heroic lone piper' leaving the trenches and bravely

---

97   Barclay (ed.), *The London Scottish in the Second World War*, p.85.
98   Spooner, *The Battalion*, p.86.
99   Spooner, *The Battalion*, p.87.
100 *London Scottish Regimental Gazette* (1944), p.31.
101 Spooner, *The Battalion*, p.83.
102 *London Scottish Regimental Gazette* (1943), p.70.
103 Spooner, *The Battalion*, p.89.

leading troops over the top into no-man's land (a heroic perception shared by soldiers and senior officers alike) the pipers and drummers of the London Scottish went into battle both at Messines and at Primosole Bridge as infantrymen, fighting alongside the rest of the men in their respective companies. Despite Piper Donaldson's obvious annoyance at not being able to repeat the perceived heroics that myth and war films had assigned to British Army pipers (and which he and his commanding officer may have felt was expected of them), cancellation of the preliminary artillery barrage probably saved the lives of many London Scottish pipers at Primosole Bridge. Instead, Piper Donaldson was in a position to employ his talents consoling a dying comrade as he passed from this life.

Pipe Major Turnbull wrote a tune to commemorate the event, entitled *The London Scottish at Primosole Bridge*, and Volume One of the *Gordon Highlanders Pipe Music Collection* gives an insight into its composition and naming. A few days after the battle:

> Pipe Major Turnbull was playing a tune he had composed when one of the Cockney Jocks asked what it was. On being told it had no name, he shouted 'Call it Primosole Bridge.' Sadly the Jock was killed in action a few days later.[104]

The 1st Battalion would spend the next 12 days dug in on the front line, until finally moving out on 5 August to the recently captured town of Catania. B Company notes from the period mention 'congratulations and thanks … to Piper Horne, first man to pipe through Catania, whose music lent wings to our feet.'[105]

The battalion would lead the advance out of Catania the following day and continue fighting in difficult conditions, harassing the German rear guard through hilly country around Mount Etna, before being ordered to stand fast at Machia on 13 August. Four days later, the campaign in Sicily was over and the 1st Battalion were finally able to rest. Over 100 men had given their lives and the pipers and drummers had more than played their part, both on the battlefield and, as was so reminiscent of the Great War, on the long marches in between.

Keeping the pipes going was particularly difficult in the harsh conditions found in Sicily. All the band's spares were lost when the band stores disappeared in transit, and new reeds and pipe bag liners had to be fashioned from whatever was available. Pipe Major Turnbull stated that:

> Even when the sun goes down and stops cracking the reeds and chanters, you've got to watch the ants don't eat the bags. We use sugar and water as a preservative, and these big Sicilian ants seem to go for them in a big way.[106]

Two sets of pipes were also lost in direct action, with one set being blown apart while strapped to the back of Piper Donaldson. He was firing a Bren gun at the time, when a German mortar round exploded behind him. The wooden drones and chanter almost certainly saved his life.

Ingenuity was employed and repairs somehow made; indeed, it was imperative to the battalion that they were. As Pipe Major Turnbull asserted, 'We've got to keep the pipes going, for the lads wouldn't go on without them.'[107]

---

104 P. Graham and B. MacRae (eds.), *The Gordon Highlanders Pipe Music Collection, Volume 1* (London: Hal Leonard, 2004), p.50.
105 *London Scottish Regimental Gazette* (1943), p.53.
106 Interview with Pipe Major Charles Turnbull, 'Sicily Ants are Piper's Headache', *Eighth Army News*, August 1943.
107 'Sicily Ants are Piper's Headache', *Eighth Army News*, August 1943.

At the end of August, the battalion moved to Zafferana Etnea, on the slopes of Mount Etna, for intense training and, with the injured recuperated and the arrival of the remainder of the band from Egypt, along with the band supplies that had been lost en route to Sicily, the Pipes and Drums were able to turn out a band of ten pipers, five side drummers, two tenors and a bass. They were put to good effect:

> Each morning the pipe band paraded on the piazza and presented the brave, ceremonial side of army life, which lifted all hearts after recent weeks, and not only those of the soldiery. The bambini strutted up and down besides the pipers and drummers as children the world over. Lovely girls gathered in blooming clusters as to any social event. The old men sat out at tables on the pavement with their little flasks of vino, memories perhaps stirring of that older war. Young men, of course, other than those adolescent students, were conspicuously absent.[108]

Here, at Zafferana Etnea, contact was also made with both the 1st and 5/7th Battalions, Gordon Highlanders, and the massed pipes and drums Beat Retreat on more than one occasion.

Whilst the Sicily campaign was over, and the pipe band could enjoy playing together once again for a short while, the war itself merely moved on, and it would not be long before the battalion had to move with it. On 10 October, the 1st Battalion, London Scottish moved to the destroyed port of Messina. From here they would embark for mainland southern Italy, landing at Salerno on 14 October, to begin their involvement in the next phase of the war.

The 3rd Battalion had a slightly more convoluted journey to join their sister battalion in the Sicily campaign, beginning with a gruelling over-land journey from the Suez Canal to Sousse in Tunisia. This expedition across North Africa began on 14 June 1943 (taking a route via Tobruk, Alexandria and El Alamein) and did not end until 3 July. The troops withstood terrible thirst and hunger in the blazing desert sun. On arrival, the battalion was sent to a holding area with the 51st (Highland) Division, where they were greeted royally. There were over 100 officers serving with battalions within 51st Division who had transferred from the London Scottish, and the 3rd Battalion was welcomed with open arms. From Sousse they sailed directly for Sicily and, only two days after the 1st Battalion had landed at Syracuse, the 3rd Battalion arrived at Augusta harbour: 'the ship glided into the harbour, a piper standing in the bows playing them in to the strains of *Highland Laddie*.'[109]

Their anti-aircraft guns were set up immediately to defend the newly captured port from Luftwaffe raids, and it would not be until 24 July that the harbour had a raid-free night. Enemy snipers were also a problem in the early days until the area had been properly secured. Air raids continued, all be it more sporadically, for another month and it was during one such assault that the 3rd Battalion suffered their first casualties from enemy action. On the evening of 9 August, D Troop took a direct hit during bombing by German Junkers Ju.88s and Focke-Wulf FW 190s and four men were killed while in action at their guns. One of their number was Gunner Piper William Turnbull. 'He was a piper of merit, extremely popular and known affectionately as 'Tumshie' and he died, as he would have wished, doing his job.'[110] Little else is known regarding the aftermath of Turnbull's death, but it is a comforting thought to know that other pipers were close by to play a lament over his body.

With air raids finally ending on 25 August, the battalion began preparations for the next phase of the war; 'Operation Baytown', the first Allied invasion of mainland Europe. The 299 and 319

---

108 Spooner, *The Battalion*, pp.97-98.
109 Barclay (ed.), *The London Scottish in the Second World War*, p.303.
110 *London Scottish Regimental Gazette* (1943), p.216.

Batteries were selected to accompany the first assault, while 298 Battery was to remain behind in Sicily, close to Messina, and assist with the great artillery barrage which would accompany the landings. Preparations were in place by the end of the month and the Eighth Army duly landed, north of Reggio, on 3 September.

Some 299 and 319 Batteries came ashore on the first LSTs (Landing Ship, Tanks) that hit the beach and were soon set up at the mouth of a dried-up river bed. They were the 'very first heavy ack-ack guns to fire on the mainland of Europe'[111] and were soon involved in very heavy action. The beachhead was packed with men and machinery and made a concentrated target for enemy fighter bombers who soon began descending in swarms, despite fierce anti-aircraft fire that seemed to have little effect against the fast-moving Focke-Wulf fighters. Both batteries held their own but, on 4 September, the command post of F Troop, 319 Battery suffered a direct hit, resulting in nine killed and another eight badly wounded:

> The killed were buried that evening in a mass grave near the gun position; a chaplain of the Canadian Forces officiated at the ceremony and at its conclusion a lament was played by Sergt-Piper Speirs.[112]

Thankfully, German forces soon began to pull out northward and, with the capitulation of Italian armed forces on 8 September, hostilities in the area were soon at an end. The forward advance, however, was swift and the 3rd Battalion (including the newly arrived 298 Battery) were soon on the move again, arriving two weeks later at Bari (via Pizzo, Cotrone and Scanzano), over 300 miles north from their landing point. The battalion set up around Bari and Barletta and were involved in sporadic fighting against enemy bombing raids over the next few months to protect both port towns. While the Allied advance moved forward, all three batteries stayed put, which 'meant that their hitherto interesting life with the forward formations, full of excitement and movement, would come to an end',[113] at least in the short term.

There was plenty of action to keep them busy, however, and on the morning of 2 December, the Germans mounted one of their most successful air raids of the Italian campaign, causing major damage to the town of Bari and setting the packed harbour ablaze, including direct hits to an ammunition ship and 12 other boats. Drummer Gunner W Pert performed acts of bravery during this attack that led to him being mentioned in dispatches by Lieutenant General Sir Oliver Leese:

> The G.O.C. desires to place on record the act of gallantry described below, performed by the undermentioned O.R.
> 1473376 Gunner Pert, W., R.A.
>
> On the evening of 2nd December 1943 when Bari harbour was heavily attacked by enemy aircraft Gnr. Pert was on leave in the Dock Area when he heard a Naval Officer call for volunteers in rescuing personnel from the burning ships.
>   Without hesitation, Gnr. Pert volunteered despite the grave risk of further explosions. He saw in the water between the blazing ships a considerable number of men. He rescued one by means of a rope and carried him to a waiting ambulance. By this time he had contacted two sailor companions of his and with their help rescued three or four men from the water. With complete disregard for his own safety, he remained in the Dock Area until 02.00hrs. to

---

111 Harvey, *D-Day Dodgers*, p.63.
112 Barclay (ed.), *The London Scottish in the Second World War*, p.313.
113 Barclay (ed.), *The London Scottish in the Second World War*, p.317.

2nd Battalion Drummer Connelly seeing in the New Year in style, Royal Wanstead Orphanage, Essex, Hogmanay, 1939. (LSMA, used with permission)

2nd Battalion Pipes and Drums marching a company through the ruins of East London, August 1940. (LSMA, used with permission)

2nd Battalion marching through Cardiff, with fixed bayonets, October 1940. (LSMA, used with permission)

see whether he could give any further assistance. The G.O.C. directs that an entry be made on the conduct Sheet of the above-named O.R. in accordance with paras. 1713 and 1718(b) (XVII) K.Rs. 1940.[114]

Despite such intermittent excitement, this period granted the 3rd Battalion relative quiet and a chance to regroup and reorganise. It also meant that all members of the Pipes and Drums were in the same place for an extended duration, allowing the band to practise and perform together for the first time since leaving Egypt. Their first performance was at a brigade sports meeting, where, despite casualties, they were able to muster nine pipers, a bass drummer, three sides and a tenor. Band performances on Sundays in the square at Barletta became a regular occasion and 'fetched them out in their thousands. Pity we couldn't have taken a photo of the occasion!'[115] This was further enhanced, on two occasions in December, by performances with both the Scots and Irish Guards who had arrived with the 1st Division, and who were stationed at Cerignola: 'and a grand sight it made with the Royal Stuart, the Saffron and the Hodden Grey.'[116]

Christmas was a busy time, with the band in great demand. A performance by Pipe Sergeant Speirs was broadcast on the Allied Forces radio and pipers were required at battalion headquarters, at A Battery, and for a 'series of visitations from Brigade.'[117] Pipe Sergeant Speirs followed up his Christmas Day performance with a second broadcast on Hogmanay, this time accompanied by Bombardier Piper T Millen. The year 1944 would begin as 1943 ended, with training and a lull from front-line fighting, but it would not be long before the 3rd Battalion were pushing forward into the action once again.

Back on the home front, the 2nd Battalion were continuing their listless journey around Great Britain. On 29 May 1943 they left Southampton to take up a counter-offensive role on the Isle of Wight, to repel any possible invasion threat. 'The Band had a busy time playing at local 'Wings for Victory' parades.'[118] A battalion games took place on 1 July and training continued unabated. On 3 August, the battalion were on the move again, back to the mainland at Portsmouth to begin assisting in the initial preparations for the planned invasion of Northwestern Europe. The role here for the 2nd Battalion was mainly administrative, and it became increasingly obvious to the men that the unit would not be used as a frontline fighting force. However, their responsibilities in setting up camps and assisting with the preparations for D-Day should not be underestimated. Nor can the importance of training and conditioning men who passed through the battalion and went on to see active service in other units.

One such man was Lance Corporal Peter Quilliams, who had been the bass drummer with the 2nd Battalion Pipes and Drums before volunteering for reassignment to the 1st Battalion, The Parachute Regiment. He had taken part in the assault on Primisole Bridge, having been dropped in with the rest of the 1st Battalion, Parachute Regiment on 17 July 1943 to hold the bridge before the London Scottish and other units arrived. His bravery in more secretive actions on 2 October earned him the Military Medal. His citation, signed off by General Alexander and which includes the hand-written note *No publicity to be given to this citation* states:

---

114 Eighth Army Routine Order No.1, Lieut-General Sir Oliver Leese, Bt., K.C.B., C.B.E., D.S.O., 5 January 1944.
115 Capt. L.E. Proctor, Letter dated 29th December 1943, *London Scottish Regimental Gazette* (1944), p.29.
116 Barclay (ed.), *The London Scottish in the Second World War*, p.321.
117 '3rd Battalion Notes', *London Scottish Regimental Gazette* (1944), p.71.
118 Barclay, *The London Scottish in the Second World War*, p.228.

> On 2 Oct 43 L/Cpl. Qulliams was one of ten men of the 1st Bn. Parachute Regiment dropped by parachute behind the enemy's lines in the area of ANCONA, N.E. Italy. His task was to collect escaped Allied prisoners of war and assist them to rejoin our own forces. Until the middle of December, L/Cpl. Quilliams carried out this difficult and dangerous task. He was responsible for the safe return of many ex-P.O.Ws. His bravery and great devotion to duty is an inspiration to all.[119]

Quilliams was the first of three London Scottish bass drummers to be awarded medals for outstanding bravery during the Second World War.

The nomadic lifestyle of the 2nd Battalion continued in September when they moved again to the Dorchester area for yet more training and then again in November to Chichester. Hallowe'en was celebrated there and Colonel Ogilby, who had led the 2nd Battalion through Palestine in the First World War, attended. His address was aimed particularly at the younger members of the battalion as he:

> Referred to the memories stirred by the anniversary, which was being celebrated, memories of pride and sadness. He emphasised the honour and privilege which rested on every man posted to the Regiment, who became thereby, for all times, a London Scot.[120]

This was an important message at a time when morale in the 2nd Battalion was relatively low and the turnover of officers and men increasingly high. Morale, as always, was a major component of the *reason d'être* of the Pipes and Drums, and their role in ensuring it remained as high as possible was an important one. Equally important was their less glamorous responsibilities of duty calls, weekly performances and attendance on route marches, all of which helped to keep the distinct London Scottish spirit alive.

On 2 December 1943, a 2nd Battalion reunion took place at regimental headquarters in London, which included the handing over for safe keeping of the Roll of Honour of members of the battalion who perished in the Great War. This roll had previously been held in the regimental chapel at St Columba's Kirk but the church had taken a direct hit from German bombing on 10 May 1941 and was now totally destroyed. Fortunately, however, the Roll of Honour, along with a number of other regimental items, had survived. A contingent of the serving battalion attended, and Pipe Sergeant J Bruce played at a special ceremony held in the ruined Church House Chapel at St Columba's as the roll was entrusted to the regiment.

Christmas and Hogmanay passed with much celebration and the band's involvement was as high profile as always. New Year's Eve celebrations involved guests from the United States Army, who seemed to particularly enjoy the piping. 'An impromptu tune on the way back to company HQ billets earned Piper Cameron two glasses of pre-war whisky and a couple of mince pies. He gave the mince pies away!'[121] On 21 January, the battalion moved again, this time to Whitby for more anti-invasion exercises. The 17 March saw the next move, back to the Southampton Staging Area and more preparations for D-Day. There was much contact with Canadian and American troops during this period and a great deal of work went into keeping the troops entertained in the slightly dismal conditions of the camps. American resources were optimised to obtain films and gramophone records and the Scottish and American forces worked together to put on shows and

---

119 The National Archives, UK, Ref: WO 373/5/477.
120 Barclay, *The London Scottish in the Second World War*, p.234.
121 '2nd Battalion Notes', *London Scottish Regimental Gazette*, (1944), p.24.

concert parties. 'The pipes and highland dancing were much appreciated, while the Jocks took a liking to 'Hill Billy' music and the mandolin.'[122]

March 1944 also saw the drafting away from the battalion of all fit and able men under the age of 30, in readiness for D-Day. Most went to other Scottish units, primarily the 1st and 5/7th Gordon Highlanders, the 1st Tyneside Scottish and the 7th King's Own Scottish Borderers. Drummer Bill Connoly was one of those men who went to the Borderers. He would go on to fight in the fateful attack on Arnhem, where the 7th KOSB were deployed as glider-borne troops. After having a finger shot away during the fighting, he was eventually captured and saw out the rest of the war in a POW camp in Germany. Along with the redeployment of men such as Drummer Connoly went the very last hope of the 2nd Battalion, London Scottish Regiment ever becoming an overseas fighting force.[123]

Another of the men who transferred at this time was Drummer James Hutchison who had been the 2nd Battalion bass drummer prior to his reassignment to the 5/7th Gordon Highlanders, with whom he landed on the Normandy beaches in June 1944 and fought through North-Western Europe for the remainder of the war. Drummer Hutchison was a stretcher bearer with C Company and his heroic actions on 9 August, during the fighting at Conteville along the Seine in Normandy, resulted in him being awarded the Military Medal. His citation, which was signed off by Field Marshal Montgomery and which originally recommended a Distinguished Conduct Medal, stated that:

> There was a wounded man out in the open and whenever anyone went to get him in, the enemy opened fire at them.
>
> Pte. Hutchison with complete disregard for his own personal safety and scorning the enemy ran over 200 yds of bullet swept ground. He then carried the wounded man on his back to the road which was also covered by enemy fire. Being unable to get down the road he crawled about 100 yds along the ditch, at the side still carrying the wounded man, until he reached comparative safety.
>
> Shortly after this the enemy M.G. and rifle fire became so intense that it was impossible to evacuate the wounded to the R.A.P. which owing to the nature of the action had to be some way back.
>
> Pte. Hutchison realising the situation took command of all the Stretcher Bearers and set up his own R.A.P. Here he personally attended to all the casualties of his own company and also men of other companies and the Derbyshire Yeomanry who were in the area. This he did under Mortar and M.G. fire until the enemy were driven off and the wounded could be properly evacuated.
>
> As a Private soldier Pte Hutchison took upon his shoulders the duties of the M.O. and there is no doubt that he saved the lives of many of his comrades.
>
> His superb personal courage and devotion to duty as well as the very great responsibility he took upon himself were an inspiration to all with whom he came in contact and his wonderful example was responsible for the very high state of morale of the other stretcher bearers who instinctively turned to him for orders through all stages of the battle.[124]

Another transferee was Captain Donald Ross Spence, who was sent to join the 2nd Battalion, Gordon Highlanders. 'The piping of Donald Spence will be greatly missed by all ranks, and I know

---

122 Barclay (ed.), *The London Scottish in the Second World War*, p.241.
123 It also saw the promotion of L/Sgt Bruce to 2nd Battalion Pipe Major.
124 The National Archives, UK, Ref: WO 373/50/353.

the Pipe Band will miss his services sorely.'[125] Captain Spence landed on the beaches of Normandy on D-Day and would be killed in action two short months later, bravely leading the men of D Company in a frontal boat attack, attempting to cross the River Seine, on 27 August 1944.[126]

The 2nd Battalion became an administrative unit in the preparation and execution of the D-Day landings and then, once completed, transferred to the 48th (Reserve) Infantry Division to work at training centres in Scotland, preparing other units for fighting overseas. The battalion moved to Carronbridge in September 1944 and, just before they left:

> The Battalion bade farewell to their American friends of the 1st Bn., 29th Infantry Regt., U.S. Army ... who were ordered to North-West Europe. The Scottish presented them with a plaque of English Oak in which was fixed a silver Regimental Badge ... The Pipe Major also composed a march in their honour, which he played when marching at the head of the Battalion – playing them from the camp to the boat.[127]

The 2nd Battalion remained at Carronbridge until after the Victory in Europe armistice of 8 May 1945 and formally ceased to exist on 1 March 1946. Whilst, as a battalion, it was never to achieve its objective of taking the fight overseas, hundreds of individuals who passed through the ranks, including members of the Pipes and Drums, went on to serve in combat units on all fronts during the war. The battalion may not have played the role it had desired, but its influence and contribution was nothing short of exemplary.

Back in Sicily, the men of the 1st Battalion were ready to join the 3rd Battalion on the Italian mainland. They landed at Salerno on 14 October 1943 and on 28 October they went into action outside of Teano, which the London Scottish captured on Hallowe'en; adding another important victory to that illustrious date in the regiment's history. 7 November saw the battalion move up to the Cassino Line and, on 2 December, the second battle for Mount Camino began in earnest. Fierce fighting followed and by 6 December the London Scottish had taken control of the monastery on top of the mountain. Whilst A, C and D Companies occupied the mountain top, B Company, along with all other available troops, including any available men from the Pipes and Drums, worked as load carriers, moving supplies and ammunition from the Jeep-head to the three companies at the top, while under continual shell and mortar fire. Pipers and drummers led mules and carried loads on their backs through freezing storms of rain and hail to make certain the position was fortified and ensure that their fellow soldiers remained well-supplied:

> During their stay at the top of the mountain the Battalion never went without rations, water or ammunition – the porter parties performed prodigious acts of physical labour and endurance, scrambling over boulders and ploughing ankle deep through mud.[128]

13 December, relief arrived and the battalion were moved back from the frontline to Vezzaro and, from there, to the divisional rest area at Falciano, where they spent Christmas.

---

125 '2nd Battalion Notes', *London Scottish Regimental Gazette*, (1944), p.154.
126 My grateful thanks to Bert Innes at The Gordon Highlanders Museum for his assistance and comprehensive research into the service and fate of Captain Spence.
127 Barclay (ed.), *The London Scottish in the Second World War*, p.242.
128 Barclay (ed.), *The London Scottish in the Second World War*, p.101.

There was a Christmas morning church parade, marching behind the heart-lifting rant of the pipes and drums, who were together again after being used in carrying parties, or manning Brens for the air defences of Battalion HQ.[129]

Hogmanay was spent close by in Carinola and it would have been a heavy-headed battalion that made its way back up to the frontline on 1 January 1944.

The next major obstacle in the advance northwards was the Garigliano river. Dual assaults undertaken here and amphibiously at Anzio would be the key to a successful strike on Rome. The riverbank was heavily fortified and, on 11 January, as part of a major assault, the London Scottish were ordered to attack two heavily defended enemy positions. The attack was successful, but there were substantial casualties. Amongst those who gave their lives that day was Lance Sergeant William Ian Hamilton, who had served much of the earlier part of the war behind the bass drum, before being promoted and transferred to D Company. 'Tall, genial, an imposing figure with the big drum in far away England was killed'[130] attacking a fortified position codenamed 'Haybag' during the action to capture the riverbank. He was 23 years of age. William, known to all by his middle name Ian, had joined the pre-war 2nd Battalion and went overseas with the 1st Battalion in the summer of 1942. 'Thus another London Scot has joined that glorious Company of wearers of Hodden Grey who have laid down their lives for King and Country.'[131]

Control of the south side of the river was consolidated over the next few days in horrendous weather conditions. During this brief 'lull', a young Spike Milligan, serving as a Royal Artillery gunner stationed in support of the attacks, observed in his diary:

> To add to the depressed atmosphere a lone piper wails in the rain-filled dark 'The Skye Boat-song.'
> 'It's the London Scottish, they're burying their dead' said Fuller, who had come in to replace the Batteries telephone. 'Poor bastards, buryin' 'em in the bloody rain, their graves are 'alf full of bloody water.'[132]

The attack on the Gagliano river itself took place on 17 January, to coincide with the landings at Anzio, and on 20 January the London Scottish, along with the rest of 168th Brigade, were over the river and consolidating positions in the foothills nearby around Damiano. There they encountered bitter fighting and constant counter-offensives by the enemy. During one such attack, on 21 January, Piper William Kilgour McDougall was shot and killed.

Piper McDougall was another pre-war London Scot and an excellent piper who had won the regiment's prestigious McLeod Medal for piping. An obituary, written in April 1944 by former Drum Sergeant, Captain Ian Thompson related the following:

> He was a great support to me when, on the outbreak of war, we were without a Pipe-Major, and that august body of men, the Pipers, were in the hands of a drummer; and when Pipe-Major Turnbull joined the Regiment, Wullie was one of the first to rally round, and we soon had the Pipers and Drummers going out together in the evenings and lying down to sleep together in the same rooms.

---

129 Spooner, *The Battalion*, p.118.
130 *London Scottish Regimental Gazette* (1948), p.105.
131 *London Scottish Regimental Gazette* (1944), p.58.
132 Spike Milligan, *Mussolini: His Part in My Downfall* (London: Penguin, 1980), pp.260-261.

We were touched to hear that after he was buried, the Regimental Pipers and Drummers held a special service of remembrance over the grave and Pipe-Major Turnbull played the Piobaireachd 'I got a Kiss of the King's Hand.' I feel sure Wullie McDougall has not died in vain, and I know that wherever London Scottish Pipers and Drummers meet hereafter, he will be remembered.[133]

We know, from another contemporary letter, that 'All the remainder of the Pipers are OK'[134] as the fierce fighting continued. It was during one such action, just two days after Piper McDougall's death, that Private George Allan Mitchell would earn his Victoria Cross and immortal honour for himself and the regiment.[135]

After almost four months of continual fighting, the 1st Battalion were eventually pulled out of the line on 30 January and took immediate transport to Giuliano, near Naples, where they had scant time to attempt to reorganise before re-embarking to be transported to the Anzio beachhead. It was here that the London Scottish faced their sternest test of the war, and where the battalion and their Pipes and Drums paid a heavy price.

The initial landings at Anzio had been a great success for the Allies, as German forces consolidated further inland and allowed the beachhead to develop virtually unmolested. However, as Allied troops attempted to push away from the coast, their hastily prepared numbers came up against extremely strong and, more importantly, well-rested and well-prepared opposition. The London Scottish, as part of 168th Brigade, had been sent to Anzio to reinforce this initial thrust to break out of the beachhead, which was in grave danger of grinding to a halt and being thrown back into the sea.

Landing on 3 February, the London Scottish moved directly to the frontline to assist the 6th Gordon Highlanders, who were under fierce assault and had lost three of their four rifle companies. 'It was a memorable reunion with Lieut.-Colonel James Peddie, one-time Second-in-Command of the Scottish'[136] and Headquarters Company Officer Commanding, responsible for the Pipes and Drums back in 1939.

The role at Anzio of the battalion anti-aircraft platoon, which consisted mostly of drummers, was summed up by the platoon sergeant as follows:

> Aircraft recognition was not important, we shot at whatever bigger guns in the distance shot at. We manned our little guns, and like excited puppies chasing and snapping at a fast car, without the slightest hope of catching it and small hope, if they did, of being able to inflict any real injury, we frolicked into action, the excitement for several minutes being so intense that only the burning hot cartridge cases ejecting from the guns and finding their way down the back of the neck, brought us literally back to earth.[137]

In the extremely heavy fighting during their first three days on the frontline, the 1st Battalion, London Scottish lost 120 men killed, wounded or missing, feared taken prisoner. The objective,

---

133 Ian Thompson, Obituary for Piper William K. McDougall, *London Scottish Regimental Gazette* (1944), pp.92-93.
134 Piper Jimmy Lord, letter to G.N. Smith dated 12 April 1944, *London Scottish Regimental Gazette* (1944), p.88.
135 See Barclay (ed.), *The London Scottish in the Second World War*, pp.104-106 for citation and further information.
136 Barclay (ed.), *The London Scottish in the Second World War*, p.111.
137 'Bn AA – by 6666317', *London Scottish Regimental Gazette* (1954), p.39.

however, was achieved and the battalion were able to rest briefly and to reorganise, before fighting began again in earnest on 7 February.

For the next three days, the 1st Battalion were involved in the heaviest fighting they had so far encountered during the war and, tasked with holding the line at any cost against vigorous attack, would suffer severe losses. By 10 February, the fighting strength of the battalion was down to 500, with D Company in particular, suffering the heaviest casualties. D Company's position had been overrun in the early hours of 9 February and over 30 men were missing. A number of these, including Lance Sergeant Drummer Geoffrey Davies, were taken prisoner and would spend the rest of the campaign as Prisoners of War in Germany.[138] He would be joined there by Piper Andy Kidd and Piper T.C. 'Tam' Weir who were also taken prisoner during the Anzio campaign.

A few days of rest saw the battalion sleeping under canvas a short distance from the frontline at No. 2 Casualty Clearing Station (CCS) camp, where the Pipes and Drums paraded through the tented encampment in a massed band with the 6th Battalion, Gordon Highlanders.

> There was strafing by day, shelling and swarms of anti-personnel bombs by night, the latter rattling and rumbling about the woods like jumping crackers. The Pipe Band played, prudently wearing their steel helmets.[139]

15 February saw renewed contact, and Axis forces continued to attack the Allied lines fiercely for the next three weeks. Then, on 4 March, relief troops arrived and the 1st Battalion were finally able to withdraw from the front. During this period of fighting, on the afternoon of 27 February, tenor drummer Corporal Tommy Robson was killed when the battalion came under intense shell fire. Very little is known about his death, as it came in the middle of such sustained combat, but he was buried later in the Anzio Beachhead war cemetery, along with so many other London Scots. Corporal Robson was part of A and B Echelons, who were generally stationed away from the frontline but, because of the intensity of the fighting, would join the rifle companies at short notice to help plug gaps and take the places of those killed and injured. As such, the battalion found itself during this action:

> Losing many men who, by virtue of the useful jobs they were performing for the fighting troops, had been considered inviolate; the water-truck driver, Hugh Hubble, Robson the Tenor Drummer, and many more.[140]

In addition to the death of Corporal Drummer Robson, every other London Scottish drummer as well as a number of pipers received battlefield injuries of various degrees of severity during this period. These casualties, in addition to the capture of Lance Sergeant Drummer Davies and Piper Kidd and Piper Weir, torn apart the Pipes and Drums at Anzio. As ever, the condition of the pipe band proved a microcosm of the situation within the wider battalion. In total, the 1st Battalion suffered 483 killed, wounded or missing. 'But the line was always held, although the price was a high one.'[141]

Whilst January 1944 saw the 1st Battalion heading for Anzio, the 3rd Battalion begin a move to positions around Foggia airfield that concluded with the arrival of 299 Battery on St Valentine's

---

138 L-Sgt. Davies eventually ended up in Stalag VIIA, Germany's biggest prisoner of war camp, situated near Moosburg in Bavaria. The camp was liberated by American forces on 29 April 1945.
139 *London Scottish Regimental Gazette* (1948), p.136.
140 *London Scottish Regimental Gazette* (1947), p.137.
141 *London Scottish Regimental Gazette* (1947), p.127.

Day. Later that month the battalion were temporarily assigned to the 12th AA Brigade of the United States Fifth Army and in early March begun the journey to the front at the Gustav Line around Monte Camino and Monte Cassino. At this point, their role began to switch from anti-aircraft to general artillery, and the battalion played their part on 15 March in supporting the advance of New Zealand troops on the town of Cassino and its famous mountain monastery. Fighting continued throughout March and April with limited forward movement on the German fortifications, until a third and decisive push began with a massive artillery bombardment all along the Gustav Line on 11 May. The battalion made an important contribution to what would 'prove to be the biggest and fiercest artillery barrage in the history of warfare.'[142] Within a few hours, they had fired over 4,000 shells as part of an 800-gun bombardment. 'Oil in the gun buffers reached boiling point and paint peeled off the gun barrels'[143] and by 18 May the Gustav Line had been overrun along its entire length. The Hitler Line was next, and with that overrun on 23 May and a breakout from the Anzio beachhead finally successful days later, the road to Rome lay open. The 3rd Battalion took a few days to recover from the 12 days of continuous fighting that had taken toll on both men and machinery, but they would march into Rome on 5 June, just hours behind the first units of the American Fifth Army who had entered the day before.

Celebrations, however, would be short-lived:

> The limelight and the glory of this theatre of war lasted for only twenty-four hours, for on 6th June the Allies invaded Europe and from then on, the glorious achievements and the men who had made them possible were forgotten.[144]

After D-Day, the Italian campaign, like the war in the Far East, was very much seen by the British public, unfairly, as a sideshow. However, fierce fighting continued and the war was still a very long way from being over.

The 3rd Battalion continued its dual role of anti-aircraft and medium field artillery, deployed both defending airfields and supporting troops in the drive north. The pace, however, was slightly less frenetic and some official rest was possible. 'Rest' for the members of the Pipes and Drums meant an opportunity to practise for performances, for which there had been little opportunity over the proceeding months. This practise would be put to good use on 27 July when His Majesty, The King landed at Castiglione airfield, where he was cheered by off-duty personnel from 319 Battery and 'most members of the Pipe Band who, as the King's car slowly approached, broke into the Regimental March.'[145] His Majesty was

> ... intrigued when he heard the strains of the pipe band, and asked his driver to stop, and requested to speak to our Colonel. He promised to convey to Her Majesty the Queen (our Regimental Colonel) the Colonel's loyal greetings from all ranks.[146]

On another occasion, 'we joined forces with Bands of the Scots and Irish Guards, and a grand sight it made with the Stuart, the Saffron and the Hodden Grey' although 'the Italians thought it all a bit weird.'[147] Further opportunity to play came on 13 August, in a medieval castle near Casciano,

---

142 Harvey, *D-Day Dodgers*, p.111.
143 Harvey, *D-Day Dodgers*, p.113.
144 Harvey, *D-Day Dodgers*, p.137.
145 Barclay, *The London Scottish in the Second World War*, p.342.
146 Harvey, *D-Day Dodgers*, p.149.
147 *London Scottish Regimental Gazette*, (1944), p.190.

The formative days of the 3rd Battalion Pipes and Drums, Dartford, Kent 1939. (LSMA, used with permission)

3rd Battalion Pipes and Drums with Colonel Courtney at the final of the 1st A.A. Division Football Trophy Final, Craven Cottage, Fulham, 15 April 1941. (LSMA, used with permission)

3rd Battalion Pipes and Drums in the desert of North Africa near Tobruk, Libya, during their journey to Souse, Tunisia, June 1943. (LSMA, used with permission)

3rd Battalion Gunner Drummer Pert in the ruins of Bari Harbour, where he was 'Mentioned in Dispatches' for an act of gallantry, rescuing military personnel from burning ships during a German air raid, 2 December 1943. (LSMA, used with permission)

into which had moved the battalion headquarters. The 6th Gordon Highlanders, commanded by ex-London Scot, Lieutenant Colonel Peddie, were also stationed in the area and a Beating Retreat was hastily organised, utilising the combined Pipes and Drums of these 'sister' regiments.

The period that followed would see the last major action of the 3rd Battalion's war, as they supported the advance on the Gothic Line. The fighting was some of the fiercest in the history of the British Army, as the battalion fought its way ever north, reaching Rimini and setting up to defend the airfield before pushing on again to Santarcangelo di Romagna, where for a short time they were to come into contact with the 1st Battalion. Senior officers visited each other, with members of the two pipe bands in tow, but while the 1st Battalion were to continue fighting, the 3rd Battalion received news on 11 October that they were to leave the 8th Army and reorganise as a brigade school for teaching the use of the 3.7-inch anti-aircraft gun for ground support; a role they had perfected in the previous months in close support of the infantry:

> On October 18th the old Regiment held its last parade, on Rimini airfield. In spite of weather and living conditions and the fact that the Regiment had been in the line for many months, the turn-out was up to a remarkably high standard. The Regiment was inspected by the MGRA, Major-General A H Hornby, who had flown over from Army Group especially for the purpose. After inspection the General gathered the Regiment round him, addressed them and complimented them on the part they had played in the campaign that was now nearing an end. The Regiment reformed and led by the Pipe Band marched round the airfield, and passed the saluting base, from which the Regimental Flag was flying.[148]

The Major General's affection for the battalion and for the Pipes and Drums was evident in his desire to say farewell by having them play at 8th Army headquarters on the anniversary of El Alamein, before the official 'ceasefire' for each battery was received on 24, 25 and 26 October. The battalion moved away from the frontline, down the Adriatic coast to Bari where, on 6 November, the 3rd Battalion was placed in suspended animation, to be immediately reborn as 97th Garrison Regiment, Royal Artillery, (The London Scottish). Large numbers of men were transferred (usually against their will) to other regiments, but senior officers fought hard to, and were ultimately successful in, keeping all members of the Pipes and Drums together. Their importance to *esprit de corps* during this difficult time was fully understood and, indeed, could not be overestimated. In point of fact:

> The Band, with its keen and enthusiastic Pipe-Major, J Speirs, still in command, now came fully into its own for the first time since the beginning of the war. It was now possible to relieve them of all but a minimum of extra duties, and their time was practically fully given over to practise and playing. New equipment was ordered from England, and their brave show and magnificent playing soon became a part of the life of Bari and the surrounding district.[149]

Duties, however, were not all ceremonial. Soon after arriving in Bari to take over garrison duties from the Green Howards, a riot by local communists overwhelmed the resident police force, who were subsequently locked in their own cells, and the London Scottish were called out to quell the rioting. On the second day, 'the Band was also despatched … and marched at the head of a column of troops through the streets.'[150] Whether it was down to the wild sound of the Pipes and Drums,

---

148   Barclay (ed.), *The London Scottish in the Second World War*, p.351.
149   Barclay (ed.), *The London Scottish in the Second World War*, p.354.
150   Barclay (ed.), *The London Scottish in the Second World War*, p.354.

or the sight of experienced armed troops, is not known, but there were to be no further violent outbreaks in the area under London Scottish control during their occupation.

With peace came a more regular garrison lifestyle. The Pipes and Drums had their own band hut for practise and 'They have been playing Retreat three times a week, and there is a full Pipe Band Reveille each Saturday morning',[151] with a church parade one Sunday each month. The band also played regularly at local military hospitals, and it was at one such hospital that they played a remarkable role in the recovery of Captain, later Lieutenant Colonel, George Bailey. Bailey had enlisted in the London Scottish in 1939, before transferring to the Royal Signals and later training as a pilot in the Army Air Corps:

> A week before Christmas 1944 I was rather badly 'smashed-up' in Italy. Wound up in RAMC 98 General Hospital Bari. It seems I was not expected to survive but came to on Christmas morning to the sounds of the pipes and drums. This has always remained in my mind as a miracle. The Pipes and Drums of my own Regiment calling me back to life. Bless them all, they brought me back to the land of the living at Christmas.[152]

Christmas Eve 1944 saw the band playing for church parade at St Augustine Church, which was soon to become the garrison church. Here, the battalion was inspected by the area commander before marching back to camp through the town with the Pipes and Drums at their head in what would become a regular event over the next nine months. The band's public displays brought out a large proportion of the population, including a sizable number of local children who came to be known by the battalion as the 'Dead-End Kids', who would loyally follow the Pipes and Drums and seemed to know all the tunes:

> During the playing of the Retreat the actions of the drummers are simultaneously carried out by the children on imaginary drums, and imaginary sticks, and we are certain that any one of them could carry out the entire ceremony with perfect precision and without hesitation.[153]

January 1945 began an extremely active period for the Pipes and Drums. The band 'seem to have become the most popular British Band serving in Italy'[154] and were in constant demand for sporting events, concerts, ceremonial duties and radio performances. On 25 January, they were broadcast to Allied troops all over the world via British Forces Radio and were such a hit that they were asked back again to perform a longer set on 24 February. That same afternoon they played in front of 10,000 spectators during the interval of a United Services versus New Zealand rugby match. Captain MacLeod, ex-drummer and now an officer in the 3rd Battalion, stated: 'I don't think it is really necessary for me to say that they played perfectly, and from the studio end it sounded absolutely beautiful.'[155] The previous day, saw the band Beat Retreat at the Area Rest Camp with the Pipes and Drums of the Seaforth Highlanders and two days later they commenced a series of Retreats at outlying Royal Artillery batteries by playing at Bitonto, 'where it appeared as if the whole population had turned out to watch the "Scotsesi Soldati" who were duly applauded by much hand-clapping and shouts of "Benissimo! Benissimo!"'[156] The month was rounded off

---

151 *London Scottish Regimental Gazette* (1945), p.41.
152 *London Scottish Regimental Gazette* (2001), p.102.
153 *London Scottish Regimental Gazette* (1945), p.257.
154 *London Scottish Regimental Gazette* (1945), p.125.
155 *London Scottish Regimental Gazette* (1945), p.92.
156 Barclay (ed.), *The London Scottish in the Second World War*, p.358.

with a full Beating Retreat on 27 February alongside the band of the Royal Scots Fusiliers. These highlights were capped off at the end of February when Pipe Sergeant Jock Speirs finally received his appointment as Pipe Major. 'It is mainly due to his hard and untiring efforts that the Band has reached its present high standard and is so much in demand, not only by the Regiment, but also by other Units in the area.'[157]

March was just as busy, with a report in the *Regimental Gazette* detailing a whole list of events, including battery visits, football matches, a Retreat at the Repatriated POW Camp, concerts in town squares and various events for the American Red Cross, American military hospital, the RAF headquarters and the RAF hospital. The Americans in particular 'went wild about the Band!'[158] and repeatedly requested performances. March also saw the first member of the band to gain home leave. By this point, the 3rd Battalion had been overseas for nearly two and a half years and, luckily, Headquarters Company, which included the Pipes and Drums, came out of the draw 'and the lucky fellow who started his journey home on 19 March was Gnr. Pert, of the Drum Section of the Band.'[159]

April continued this busy trend but included a more sombre note. On 9 April, an ammunition ship exploded in Bari harbour causing extensive damage and loss of life. Fortuitously, no London Scots were killed, despite the fact many were working in the docks at the time. Two days later:

> A collective funeral of British Service victims took place in the military cemetery and the Pipe Band played for over an hour, as coffin after coffin was carried slowly through the cemetery.[160]

A solemn reminder that the war in Italy had not yet ended.

That end would come less than a month later when, at 1400 hours on 2 May 1945, Axis forces in Italy surrendered unconditionally. Führer Adolf Hitler had committed suicide on 30 April and Berlin was close to falling. Victory in Europe was finally declared on 8 May 1945 and a victory thanksgiving service was held at battalion headquarters on Sunday 13 May:

> This was a most impressive ceremony and included reading out the names of those members of the Regiment who had been killed or who had died during the war. The service concluded with the Buglers playing the 'Last Post', followed by 'The Flowers of the Forest' by the Pipes and Drums, and finally 'Reveille' by the Buglers.[161]

Over the next few months, the 3rd Battalion would be slowly stripped of men destined for other duties; most specifically for regiments still fighting in the Far East. None of the battalion wanted to be reassigned at this point, especially because it meant leaving their comrades of four or five years to join other units on the other side of the world as strangers. Knowing that the Pipes and Drums embodied regimental togetherness and tradition, senior officers fought hard to keep the band together. They would be successful in ensuring pipers and drummers were not transferred and the band continued to play an important role within the battalion until the very end.

Their last big parade came on 15 July at the opening of a new British church within the castle at Bari:

---

157 *London Scottish Regimental Gazette* (1945), p.86.
158 *London Scottish Regimental Gazette* (1945), p.103.
159 *London Scottish Regimental Gazette* (1945), p.112.
160 Barclay (ed.), *The London Scottish in the Second World War*, p.359.
161 Barclay (ed.), *The London Scottish in the Second World War*, p.405.

> Another bit of history was made on this occasion, for the Church is in the Castello which was built in the eleventh century, and Ours is the first Scottish band ever to have played in the inner courtyard – or for that matter, anywhere in the Castle.[162]

After the ceremony and the playing of a selection of music in the courtyard:

> The whole parade, headed by the Band, then marched out of the castle, across the bridge spanning the moat and back to camp through the town. This impressive ceremony was a fitting finale to all those parades which had been held, in so many places, during the years of the Regiment's service in the Second World War.[163]

A wonderful photograph commemorates this event complete with the 'Dead-End Kids' performing in the moat below as the band passes above.

By the time the Second World War officially came to an end with victory over Japan on 2 September, only 165 men remained in the 3rd Battalion, including all 18 members of the Pipes and Drums. These men, who had now been on active duty overseas for nearly three years, were finally given the chance to return home on leave for 28 days. 'The silence of Headquarters, due to the absence of the Band ... is having such an uncanny effect on us that we are all creeping about on tip-toe, almost afraid to make a noise.'[164] They returned to play their first Retreat in five weeks on 25 October, which required both pipers and drummers to 'practise furiously .... This cancels our remarks of last month about the silence of these head-quarters.'[165]

Final disbandment of this unique battalion would take place on 9 December 1945 and a last Retreat was played at regimental headquarters at 1600 hours on Sunday 2 December. As a mark of respect to the invaluable service to the battalion performed by the Pipes and Drums during the war: 'After the ceremony the Colonel presented to Pipe-Major Speirs the Regimental Flag which had flown from the flag-pole outside the Regimental Headquarters at Bari.' This symbolic relic of a disbanded battalion would accompany the Pipes and Drums on their final journey as they became the last members of the 3rd Battalion to be reassigned to the 1st Battalion, London Scottish, who had just concluded their own war in Pola, Northern Italy.[166]

There would remain many miles, much combat and mass casualties for the 1st Battalion after Anzio and before they finally reached the relative peace of Pola. Those who had survived the horrors of Anzio entrained for southern Italy and, on 29 March 1944, embarked for Egypt to rest, recover, re-equip and reinforce:

> A memorial service for the fallen was held in the first-class lounge .... The pipe-major played the Lament, slow-marching out to the open deck until his plaintive grace-notes mingled with the cry of the gulls.[167]

On arrival at Port Said, 'Our pipes massed with those of the London Irish on the boat deck in a brave jigging skirl and the pastel patchwork of saffron and Hodden Grey kilts.'[168]

---

162 *London Scottish Regimental Gazette* (1945), p.210.
163 Barclay (ed.), *The London Scottish in the Second World War*, p.405.
164 *London Scottish Regimental Gazette* (1945), p.258.
165 *London Scottish Regimental Gazette* (1946), p.18.
166 Now in modern day Croatia.
167 Spooner, *The Battalion*, p.147.
168 Spooner, *The Battalion*, p.147.

3rd Battalion Pipes and Drums leading the battalion on a victory parade through Bari, Italy, to celebrate victory over Japan, September 1945. (LSMA, used with permission)

The 1st Battalion had been decimated at Anzio and would need a prolonged period out of the fighting to train and assimilate the hundreds of new recruits who had joined from a wide variety of English, Scottish and Irish regiments. They would stay in Egypt for the next three months and for most of that time the battalion was stationed in Sidi Bishr Camp, on the Nile Delta, just outside of Alexandra and not far from Cairo. This extended period out of action also gave the Pipes and Drums a chance to reorganise, recruit and train new members to replace those killed, captured and wounded in the previous year's fighting. The drummers had been hit particularly hard, but a number of those injured at Anzio recovered from their wounds and helped bring on the new members of the corps. The pipe band were a very popular addition to military and civilian life in Alexandra and Cairo and played at numerous events, including a garden party given by the British Military Mission to the Egyptian Army, which came with a specific request to play the Egyptian

3rd Battalion Pipes and Drums, Rimini, Italy, October 1944. (LSMA, used with permission)

3rd Battalion Pipes and Drums leaving Regimental Headquarters at Bari Castle for Church Parade. Note the local 'Dead-End Kids' watching from the moat below, 15 July 1945. (LSMA, used with permission)

National Anthem. Pipe Major Turnbull 'and his merry men rose to the occasion as usual, and after some excruciating rehearsals produced a completely recognisable version.'[169] Unfortunately, it was wasted on the Egyptian Army representatives who didn't even notice it was playing until the British officers stood to attention.

13 July 1944 saw the battalion reembark for Italy. Morale was particularly high due to their extended break away from the frontlines and because of the success of the D-Day landings that signalled the opening of a second front in Western Europe. With Axis forces retreating around the world, the war finally appeared to have an end in sight.

The battalion landed in Taranto, precisely where they had when first invading Italy back in 1943. On marching to camp, 'There was a cacophonic clash of pipe music as our band passed that of the 8th Argylls, coming the other way.'[170] The battalion then began the long journey north, until reaching camp at Tivoli, just ten miles outside Rome. All troops had leave to visit the 'Eternal City', and the Pipes and Drums had the opportunity to play a number of times in Rome which 'attracted great attention.'[171] On one occasion they performed in the Piazza Venezza, from where Mussolini had given many of his most infamous speeches.

> On another memorable occasion in this camp the Pipes and Drums of the 6th Gordons, in the presence of their late and present Commanding Officers, Lieut.-Colonels J Peddie and J B Clapham, both of the Scottish, played massed with the Scottish Band.[172]

16 August saw the battalion move back up to the front at Tolentino for the big push against the Gothic Line; a series of large-scale strategic defensive positions that followed a natural ridge running across the country from east to west. The major fighting for the 1st Battalion began on 7 September at Morciano on the Palazzo-Croce Ridge, but on 5 September the convoy taking the battalion forward was sighted and shelled by enemy gunners. During this attack, Captain James Charles Hollebone and one other soldier were killed. Captain Hollebone had been the original 'Drum-Loot', who had commanded the Anti-Aircraft Platoon and it's contingent of drummers back in early 1939. During this period, he joined the Pipes and Drums on various occasions as a tenor drummer and deserves to be remembered here for his service and ultimate sacrifice.

The battalion engaged in heavy, often hand-to-hand fighting and battalion headquarters, stationed in a local farm, came in for sustained bombardment from enemy 88mm artillery.

> The battle really raged, shells smashing continually about the farm. Two ack-ack wallahs, both drummers in the pipe band, were relieved from slits outside where they have been posted as sentries.
> 'If you can stand an hour of that – you're a man!' said one, angry pride covering his fear.[173]

Private L.W.G. Brown would later state that, during this fighting, 'Piper Bill Cowie and I walked 'neath shell bursts together on the last time that a piper 'went in' with the lads – very inspiring too.'[174] It seems then that, despite their disappointment at Primosole Bridge, the pipers managed

---

169 *London Scottish Regimental Gazette*, (1947), p.164.
170 Spooner, *The Battalion*, p.154.
171 Barclay (ed.), *The London Scottish in the Second World War*, p.130.
172 Barclay (ed.), *The London Scottish in the Second World War*, pp.130-131.
173 Spooner, *The Battalion*, p.161.
174 *London Scottish Regimental Gazette* (1991), p.11.

to find ways to play the men into battle on this and various other undocumented occasions during the war.

Sustained combat continued until the evening of 20 September when the battalion were able to pull back a short distance from the frontline. 'Next morning Charlie Company filed out of Marciano, two young pipers in battle bowlers at the head, blowing brawly and managing a kiltless swagger.'[175] The battalion had lost 335 men of all ranks killed or wounded. The three rifle platoons were down to only 80 men at one point and the battalion had to be reinforced again by men from other decimated regiments.

Their time away from the fighting was to be short, but during this lull:

> There was … a memorable visit from the Commanding Officer, Second-in Command and Adjutant of the 3rd Battalion of the Scottish (who were participating in the battle on an adjoining sector), who listened to the Pipes and Drums playing 'Retreat' in the ruined farmstead of Bn H.Q. with the line of battle only a few miles away.[176]

Sergeant Spooner wrote of the occasion: 'The Pipes and Drums … playing the brave affirmative tunes, and we all gathered to watch and listen with lifted hearts.'[177]

Fighting began again on 27 September:

> 'We're moving at last light' said the Company Commander, an officer with whom I had not been in the line before. And who was he? None other than Alec, a Major now but once Recruit Company's piper, who had played 'Donald Blue' in two feet of snow at Folkestone, January 1940 – a khaki lifetime ago.[178]

It was heavy fighting once again until 5 October, and the battalion were finally pulled out of the battle on 13 October and sent to camp at Puerto St Giorgio on the coast near Ancona. The men were able to enjoy two months of rest, recuperation, training and reorganisation in a well-equipped camp and in good weather. In a letter home, Pipe Sergeant Cheffins wrote:

> As you know, we have had a damned sticky time, and now we are enjoying a period of rest in a pleasant coastal town. Band parades are in full swing, and tho' we are working dashed hard, I would rather be doing this than dodging shells.[179]

As always, the Pipes and Drums were much in demand and 'collected the usual curious and sometimes elated crowds.'[180] They were also able to sit down together as a battalion at Hallowe'en for the first time since leaving Great Britain. The Pipes and Drums performed for guest of honour, ex-Commanding Officer Colonel Duncan Bennett, who had been a drummer in the London Scottish in the early years of the First World War.

---

175 Spooner, *The Battalion*, p.165.
176 Barclay (ed.), *The London Scottish in the Second World War*, p.143.
177 Spooner, *The Battalion*, p.177.
178 Spooner, *The Battalion*, p.166. The Major in question was Alec Murray who had started the war as a piper and had been a member of the pre-war band for many years.
179 Pipe Sergeant Cheffins, letter dated 5 November 1944.
180 Spooner, *The Battalion*, p.178.

Another two months of fierce fighting began on 17 December which saw Christmas and Hogmanay come and go with little respite, before the battalion was pulled out of the line on 11 January 1945 and relieved to billets in Forli, where they would stay for three weeks.

> On occasion at this period the Pipes and Drums of the Scottish combined with those of the 6th Argyll and Sutherland Highlanders in St Andrew's Square, Forli, and as usual attracted huge crowds.[181]

German forces were steadily being pushed further and further north across the plains and towards the River Po which was the last natural defensive feature before Venice. While the end now seemed inevitable, it would still be another three months before surrender would come, and the fighting continued unrelentingly. The 1st Battalion found themselves returned to the front on 2 February 1945 until relieved on 11 March. They were then able to regroup and to train the recently arrived, and much needed, new recruits. These included many men from the now disbanded 3rd Battalion and brought each company back up to four rifle platoon strength. March 1945 also saw a new commanding officer and the first to be appointed who had not been a member of the pre-war regiment.

5 April saw the battalion begin their last campaign of the war as they assaulted the River Reno en route to the River Po and after fierce fighting at the Argento Gap. Crossing the Reno in boats and barges under heavy fire proved to be a challenging task, and it was here that CSM J.K. Duncan was awarded a Distinguished Conduct Medal.

> Our Able Company ferried the attackers over the Reno, its CSM subsequently awarded the DCM for swimming about under fire and rescuing riflemen from capsized canvas assault craft. A remarkable man … erstwhile bass drummer in the pipe band … and as diffident a fellow as you would ever meet. Heroes don't often come in the swaggering mould the movies would have you believe.[182]

Duncan's citation, signed off by Field Marshal Alexander, concludes with the following paragraph:

> The behaviour of CSM DUNCAN, who was not a member of the assaulting Bn. and in no way responsible for the tasks he undertook, deserves the highest praise. His duties were limited to organising boats and to ferrying across the river. These tasks he performed successfully but his high sense of duty and esprit-de-corps prompted him to do things entirely out of his own sphere of duty. His complete disregard for personal safety, his super-human effort of swimming three times the R. RENO and his regard for the needs of the wounded inspired all who worked with him. The fact that the river and the area beyond were continually under mortar, shell and small arms fire did not deter him in any way. His services were invaluable and most courageous.[183]

The main objective of crossing the River Po was finally accomplished on 27 April 1945 and, two days later, Field Marshal Alexander accepted the unconditional surrender of all German forces south of the Alps. By 2 May, all hostilities had ceased and, after 22 months of fighting, the 1st

---

181 Barclay (ed.), *The London Scottish in the Second World War*, p.150.
182 Spooner, *The Battalion*, p.198.
183 TNA WO 373/13/366.

Battalion's war was finally over. However, it would be another 19 months before the last members of the battalion returned home.

The 1st Battalion were moved directly to very comfortable billets in the border town of Gorizia in an attempt to keep the local Yugoslavs in check and restrain them from starting a civil war that might spill over on to Italian soil. 'The pipes and drums proclaimed our presence by beating Retreat in the town centre.'[184] Unfortunately, the US Army's 91st Division arrived a few days later and the London Scottish were removed to less salubrious accommodation. The Pipes and Drums played at a service of thanksgiving on 13 May, and then joined other ranks on short term leave in Venice, where the band famously had the honour of performing in the Piazza San Marco (St Mark's Square), surrounded by a crowd of thousands.

5 June saw the battalion's last move of the war, to the Pola enclave on the Adriatic coast, in what is now Croatia, where regimental life was able to return to 'normal.' Field Marshal Alexander inspected the battalion for the last time on 4 August and the Pipes and Drums proudly played as one of their own, CSM Duncan, was presented with his Distinguished Conduct Medal. Men were demobilised and sent home in small groups over the coming months, although there were some small drafts arriving, concluding with the entire Pipes and Drums from the 3rd Battalion after the battalion's own disbandment in December 1945. One of the first to be demobbed, on 2 July, was Pipe Major Turnbull, who had spent five and a half years with the band and who was now in his late forties. His position as pipe major was appointed to his trusted right-hand man, Pipe Sergeant Cheffins who, contrarily, became one of the London Scottish Regiment's youngest ever Pipe Majors.

Over four nights in September 1945, the Pipes and Drums performed with the Pipes and Drums of the 1st Battalion, Scots Guards and the London Irish Rifles at XIII Corps Searchlight Tattoo in Trieste. This event was of epic proportions and was shown in newsreel back in Great Britain. It included detachments from every Allied unit fighting in the Italian campaign, from the US Army's 34th Division, on one side of the globe, to the 10th Indian Division on the other. 'The sight of the Royal Stuart kilt flanked by the Hodden Grey and the Saffron – picked out by searchlight – was magnificent.'[185]

By early 1946, other members of the pipe band were also being sent home, including the newly promoted Pipe Major Cheffins, who was suffering with heart problems. Cheffins' position was taken over by Pipe Major Speirs, who thus attained the unique honour of having been appointed pipe major of two battalions of the London Scottish during the Second World War. It would not be long before he himself would also be demobbed with Lance-Corporal Piper Alec McLeod taking over as acting Pipe Major, while Corporal Piper 'Wullie' Smith was back in Edinburgh taking the pipe major's course. By this point, acting Pipe Major McLeod was one of only two remaining pipers who had originally gone overseas with the battalion back in 1943. The other was Piper John Young, who achieved the honour of being the longest serving London Scottish piper during the Second World War. As a mark of respect, ex-piper Major Alec Murray was also given the honour of acting as pipe major on his last Sunday reveille with the battalion before returning home in January.

In February, the remainder of the 1st Battalion, London Scottish were moved to Trieste and, on 26 March, the Pipes and Drums played the battalion through as they undertook their last 'first' of the war. The Commanding Officer had the regimental colours flown out from Great Britain and the 1st Battalion London Scottish became the first unit to hold a full Colours Parade on Italian soil after the end of hostilities. Sergeant Keith Spooner, such a strong advocate of the band, 'took

---

184 Spooner, *The Battalion*, p.213.
185 *London Scottish Regimental Gazette* (1945), p.233.

a far more conspicuous part than even his wildest dreams would have predicted and was seen bespatted and clad in the National Dress thumping a tenor drum with a good deal of zeal, if limited technique.'[186]

By late April, a large majority of those men still remaining, including Sergeant Spooner, were demobbed and sent home.

> The band formed up and Pipey (merely a corporal piper now, his seniors already demobbed) waited for the driver to climb into his cab, whereupon drums rolled and the truck moved off to the strains of 'Happy We've Been A'Taegaither.' The truck turned through the barrack gates. Prisoners gestured from the guardroom, the sentry and a regimental policeman saluted.[187]

By the first anniversary of the secession of hostilities on 2 May 1946, only two skeletal companies and the Pipes and Drums remained. However, the Pipes and Drums, made up of 12 London Scottish pipers, nine drummers plus two pipers and four drummers from the 2nd Battalion, Cameron Highlanders who could not themselves field a full band, headed up the anniversary victory parade and marched the entire brigade past Lieutenant General Sir John Harding to the strains of *Hielan' Laddie*. July saw the band travel to Vienna for three weeks to take part in the Vienna Tattoo. They formed a massed band with the Scots Guards, Royal Inniskilling Fusiliers, Royal Irish Fusiliers, Cameron Highlanders, Argyll and Sutherland Highlanders, and the London Irish Rifles, which encompassed over 70 pipers. It also saw a new Pipe Major with the return of Corporal Piper Smith from his pipe major's course, during which he had also found time to get married.

In September, the 56th (London) Division, to which the 1st Battalion belonged, was dissembled and moved to Bassano near Venice, and it quickly became evident that the battalion itself would shortly be disbanded.

> The news that the Battalion is to be broken up was received with alarm, despair and regret by the Band. Things were just beginning to get more and more like the standard of the old Band when release and Python shook our foundations[188]

'Python leave' meant that any man sent home on leave with over four years' service could not be posted back overseas and should remain on home service when his leave came to an end until his eventual demobilisation.

In November, Pipe Major Smith was demobbed and his responsibilities taken over by Pipe Sergeant George Lord. One of his first jobs was to organise the band to play at a farewell ball in Trieste to mark the eventual break-up of the 1st Battalions of both the London Scottish and the London Irish Rifles.

On 5 December 1946, the 1st Battalion was placed into suspended animation and the London Scottish Regiment's commitment to armed service overseas during the Second World War was officially at an end. On 12 January 1947, with Pipe Major Lord at the head, the regiment's colours were laid up at the bomb-destroyed St Columba's Church back in Knightsbridge, with a memorial service held at Jehangier Hall and, with that, the 1st Battalion, London Scottish Regiment ceased, temporarily, to exist.

---

186 *London Scottish Regimental Gazette* (1946), p.88.
187 Spooner, *The Battalion*, p.215.
188 *London Scottish Regimental Gazette* (1946), p.191.

However, the London Scottish presence in Italy, and that of the Pipes and Drums, would continue past that date. Allied Forces Head Quarters Defence Company included Lance Corporal Piper Duncan and Piper McAffer who were much in demand for both social and military occasions. After Duncan's demob, it would be Piper McAffer, as a guard at the British Embassy in Rome, who would be the last member of the Pipes and Drums to remain on active service overseas and whose eventual return to the UK would close out the Pipes and Drums involvement in the Second World War.

During the war the London Scottish lost 382 men killed in action, with over 3,000 more wounded or taken prisoner. This number includes eight confirmed killed and an unknown number of others killed and wounded with direct links to the Pipes and Drums. Nearly 1,300 other ranks were commissioned. As had been the case in the First World War, this was the most of any single regiment in the British Army, and the Pipes and Drums provided more than their fair share. Over 9,000 men passed through the three battalions and the Pipes and Drums played a part in the military experience of each and every one of them. Some, like Privates John Ferguson and Ron Pottinger, initially loathed the sound of pipes and drums and could not understand their importance within a Scottish regiment. For others, like Sergeant Keith Spooner, they represented a constant, connecting presence. A link to home and an ever-present force that personified the values, traditions and *esprit de corps* of the regiment and the loyalty of the men who belonged to it.

The Pipes and Drums suffered the same hardships, defended the same ground, attacked the same objectives and suffered the same mortal consequences as all the other officers and soldiers of the regiment within the three battalions they embodied. They brought honour in life and comfort in death, a lifting of hearts in the hardest times, strength and courage before battle and the wild skirls of pride when victory came after. They marked the London Scottish out as being different. Unique, even. The Pipes and Drums, to all intents and purposes, were the personification of the regiment. Most importantly, however, they brought about a sense of normality, comfort and order in the most trying of times. If the band were still playing, then the war was not lost and the men listening had lived to fight another day. Their importance to each battalion cannot be overestimated and their dedicated service to battalion, regiment and country is deserving of the very highest regard.

7

The Post-War Years at 59 Buckingham Gate, 1946-1985

You do remember the Pipes and Drums, don't you? They are the body of men who march in front of the Battalion in war and peace time and through some unaccountable magic of music make the miles seem less long. Individually their members turn up at your reunions and foregatherings and play their pipes for your pleasure, and move you to tears, and comparison, and nostalgia, and wipe away the years, straightening your back, recalling the laddie who marched alongside you, flashing the whole history of Scotland through your mind's eye, and causing you to nod knowingly to your contemporaries – that little secret nod that puzzles the outsider but speaks volumes to those within.

Editorial, *The London Scottish Regiment Gazette*, 1957[1]

Despite all three battalions of the London Scottish being stationed overseas or away from London during the course of the war, regimental headquarters at 59 Buckingham Gate remained the spiritual home of the regiment, as it had done since the building was first constructed in 1886. The regimental offices remained at the drill hall and it became a centre for old comrades, families and friends of the London Scottish to gather. Despite suffering severe bomb damage on 11 May 1941 that killed three people, peppered the hall with shrapnel and partially destroyed the First World War memorial, the building was a hub of activity, with parcels full of food, clothes and cleaning products, as well as other essentials like haggis, whisky, replacement uniforms and parts for drums and bagpipes, packaged up and sent out to the two overseas battalions and to London Scottish prisoners of war. These activities were undertaken, in the main, by the 'Old and Bold' which included many ex-pipers and drummers. 59 Buckingham Gate served as a home from home for all London Scots but also for officers and men of other Scottish regiments who found themselves in London, whether on leave or after demobilisation, and the canteen and bars stayed open throughout the war years.

By late 1946, then, unsure of its future, severely battered from bomb damage and misuse but still standing proud amidst London's rubble-filled streets, 59 Buckingham Gate characterised the condition and fortitude of the regiment and the pipes and drums that called it home.

In late November 1946, ex-Drum Sergeant Archie MacLeod, with assistance from former Commanding Officers 'Dougie' Lyall-Grant and 'Jock' Henderson and ex-Drum Major Morrie Mills, organised the inaugural post-war band supper. It was the first major attempt within the regiment to ensure that pre-war traditions were kept alive and a grand total of 52 London Scottish pipers and drummers of all ages, plus friends of the pipe band, attended the dinner held at regimental headquarters. The state of the building presented issues, particularly the low gas pressure, which made cooking and staying warm difficult on the coldest night of the year, but those who attended foresaw the importance of such events for the future of the Pipes and Drums and, indeed, for the regiment.

---

1   *London Scottish Regimental Gazette*, (1957), p.102.

A selection of music was played on the pipes by ex-2nd Battalion Pipe Major 'Dusty' Millar, ex-1st Battalion Pipe Major 'Jimmie' Lord, along with ex-1st Battalion Piper Bill Cowie and pre-war and 2nd Battalion Piper Alan Raich. In his reply to the formal toast, Colonel Lyall-Grant emphasised the importance of rebuilding the band and ensuring that younger pipers and drummers who had been demobilised from the three wartime battalions be approached and encouraged to remain active. 'The intention throughout was to revive something on as nearly pre-war lines as possible.'[2] This would prove to be extremely difficult but was, in true London Scottish fashion, ultimately successful.

5 December 1946 saw the 1st Battalion placed into suspended animation and, on 12 January 1947, the battalion colours were placed into the care of the demolished regimental kirk, St Columba's Church on Pont Street, Knightsbridge. With this ceremony, the war service of the London Scottish finally came to an end. Within weeks, news arrived regarding funds to begin the rebuilding of 59 Buckingham Gate and days later, on 1 March, the 1st Battalion, The London Scottish, The Gordon Highlanders, was reformed, ready for their own rebuilding. Their Commanding Officer would be Colonel F. Gordon Maxwell, who had been in command of the 2nd Battalion in the early years of the war. He observed that 'The first sub-unit to be formed will be Battalion Headquarters Company,'[3] which included the Pipes and Drums, and assigned Captain Derek Hollebone as Company Commander. Captain Hollebone made his own request and hoped 'that many ex-members of the Regiment with experience of … piping will return and re-join in order that the Battalion may be assisted in obtaining that standard for which the Regiment is renowned.'[4] A recruiting pamphlet was duly produced with the first heading asking for experienced pipers and drummers.

Recruitment after the horrors of the First World War had been difficult but now, at the end of a devastating Second World War and after the enormity of the loss of life and the atrocities committed by the Nazis, Japanese and Soviets came to light, national war-weariness and anti-military feeling was at a high. The Labour Party had won a landslide victory in 1945 and changes that had been promised but then reneged upon in 1918 finally began to come to fruition. A National Health Service and associated welfare system, along with policies of nationalisation and reconstruction of social housing, gave working men and women a glimpse of a progressive world away from war and imperial aspirations. Many of the men who fought overseas with the London Scottish had been away from home for over three years and felt they had seen and done more than enough in service to their country and had no wish to return to a military role. In addition, the introduction of compulsory National Service for all men turning 18 years old would make it more difficult for individuals to volunteer specifically with the London Scottish.

However, as had been the case after the First World War, there were a core of men from the three wartime battalions for whom the London Scottish represented a spiritual home from home, which brought with it a sense of camaraderie and belonging found nowhere else and an opportunity to continue serving their country in an uncertain world. Along with a core of 'Old and Bold' pipers and drummers who were 'London Jocks' through and through, and a new group of younger bandsmen who had been too young to see action in the war, these men would build foundations which would ensure that the London Scottish Pipes and Drums advanced steadily into the new 'Atomic' age. They would be joined by Second World War veterans from other Scottish regiments, who found themselves residing in London, such as Piper John Williams, who had served through the war with the 10th Battalion, The Black Watch, and who was amongst the very first to join the post-war London Scottish Regiment.

---

2   *London Scottish Regimental Gazette* (1946), p.42.
3   *London Scottish Regimental Gazette* (1947), p.71.
4   *London Scottish Regimental Gazette* (1947), p.72.

Erstwhile Drum Sergeant, Archie MacLeod, would continue to take a central role, helping to recruit and organise the drummers, while another pre-war piper, William Paterson would do the same with the pipers. 'Stiffie' MacLeod had begun the Second World War as a drum sergeant, helping to build the 2nd Battalion band, before being posted to the Gordons Depot in Aberdeen in 1941. He was commissioned into the ROAC in June 1942, spending the rest of the war in Italy. He was demobbed as a captain in April 1946 and immediately returned to London and to his first love, the London Scottish. William 'Pat' Paterson passed through the 1st and 2nd Battalions before becoming Pipe Major of the 3rd Battalion from its formation in 1940 until 1943 when, due to his age, he was forced to remain in Great Britain as the battalion left for service overseas. He spent the rest of the war serving in the London Scottish National Defence Company, helping to protect important buildings around London. These men were helped considerably by CQMS Roland 'Gibbo' Gibbons, who had joined the Scottish as a piper in 1928, aged 16, and entered the Second World War as a pipe sergeant with the 1st Battalion, before taking a commission with the Indian Army. He gave up his rank of major to re-join the London Scottish in 1946 and, although he did not re-join the band, was a huge supporter of the Pipes and Drums.

Their first job was to pull together a small band of pipers and drummers to play on 12 April 1947 at the opening of a Second World War memorial for men from the Richmond and London Scottish Rugby Football Clubs who had given their lives for their country. Piper Jimmy Lord was one of those few who attended and he had previously 'officiated at practically every function requiring pipers during the gap before the present Battalion was formed.'[5] Soon after, notice was given via the *Regimental Gazette* that 'Band Practise is starting right away, and, of course, in accordance with tradition, on Thursday evenings'[6] and on 29 May the Pipes and Drums paraded officially for the first time as part of the new 1st Battalion. Corporal Piper Bruce Ledgett was leading the band at this point. Ledgett had served throughout the Second World War with the 2nd Battalion Pipes and Drums and was an expert Weapons Training Instructor. When the 2nd Battalion was disbanded, he became Pipe Major of the training battalion of the Black Watch for a short time before his own demobilisation. He would go on to play an especially important role with the Pipes and Drums over the next eight years.

The call was put out to other ex-members of the pipe band to think about re-joining, including those that had taken war-time commissions:

> A Piper or Drummer remains a Piper or Drummer at heart, and no matter if, in the course of war, he collects a few pips or crowns or flying O's, he cannot resist, eventually, having another smack at it with the Band. It has always been the happy custom on Thursday evenings to welcome any ex-members and invite him to join in.[7]

However, in these early days, it was new recruits to the Pipes and Drums that outweighed old members and new members required specific training in all aspects of soldiering and musicianship, in addition to attending general band practise. Ex-Piper and Drum Major, Morrie Mills, who had written all the beatings for the drummers during the glory days of the late 1920s and 30s, was drafted in to assist and immediately contributed by facilitating expert external tuition for the pipers.

As had, serendipitously, been the case from the very birth of the London Scottish Pipes and Drums in 1860, when a piping instructor was required, a Pipe Major from the Scots Guards

---

5   *London Scottish Regimental Gazette* (1947), p.127.
6   *London Scottish Regimental Gazette* (1947), p.93.
7   *London Scottish Regimental Gazette* (1947), p.111.

answered the call. On this occasion it was Pipe Major James Blair Robertson who had been Pipe Major of the 2nd Battalion Scots Guards from 1932 to 1941, having initially joined their 1st Battalion as a 17-year-old piper. He was a piper of the highest regard, having won the Gold Medal at Oban in 1932 and at Inverness the following year; indeed, his record of winning the former winners 'March, Strathspey and Reel' at Inverness nine times, still stands. On becoming a Scots Guards pipe major in 1932, he joined London Scottish Pipe Major Davy Pullar, along with Lewis Beaton, David Ross and Dr W.H. MacPhail to form the Scottish Piping Society of London. The SPSL inaugurated and still hosts the famous Bratach Gorm solo piping competition. Robertson had been a regular visitor at Buckingham Gate in the 1930s, officiating at the annual MacLeod Medal piping competition and attending band suppers and Thursday evening practises. From 1948 to 1949, he would add Pipe Major of the London Scottish Pipes and Drums to his distinguished list of achievements, although effectively as a stop-gap until his replacement attained the necessary qualifications and experience.

For the remainder of 1947 however, Pipe Sergeant Ledgett remained in charge when the Pipes and Drums were on parade. Archie MacLeod and Pipe Sergeant Ledgett had been vigorously recruiting and were able to turn out a band of decent size for their first regimental church parade on Sunday 2 November. 'A detachment, under Lieutenant F A Henderson, with a band 21 strong, marched from Head-quarters'[8] to the Great Hall at the Imperial Institute in South Kensington.[9] The *Aberdeen Press and Journal* reported slightly higher numbers: 'Although recruiting has disappointed during the last few months, there was nevertheless a brave show at the first post-war church parade … with twenty-five pipers and drummers in the band … the smart parade impressed Londoners who stood and watched.'[10]

The annual church parade has always played a significant role in London Scottish tradition, being as it is, an opportunity for the entire regimental family to assemble and parade through the streets of London. Prior to the First World War, the annual church parade took place on Easter Sunday but was moved after the war to coincide with Remembrance Sunday in November. A parade of serving London Scottish soldiers, veterans, cadets and associated military personnel march behind the Pipes and Drums from regimental headquarters to the regimental kirk, St. Columba's Church, where a service of thanksgiving and remembrance is held. Regimental tradition, begun in distant times unknown, dictates that the Pipes and Drums, minus one selfless piper who is tasked with playing during the church service, retire to a nearby public house to refresh and recover in preparation for the rigours of the return march back to regimental headquarters when the service ends. Family and friends meet the returning parade for tea and cakes, speeches and the opportunity to explore headquarters and the regimental museum. Tradition dictates that the Pipes and Drums play a range of tunes through the hour march in each direction, with *Lord Lovat's Lament* played on approaching St Columba's and *The Black Bear* played on returning to headquarters. The band break into the regimental march, *Heilan' Laddie*, shortly after leaving the kirk as the parade marches past the Regimental Colonel and takes the salute, before returning to the Pipe Major's selected tunes.

The Pipes and Drums had played a selection of tunes at the 1947 regimental Hallowe'en dinner a few weeks prior to church parade and, although the quantity of pipers and drummers was high, the quality of the playing at this early point in their reformation was better suited to route marching. Numbers, however, were crucial and with all sections of the regiment attempting to expand rapidly, the success of the band's recruitment campaign was often remarked upon, as

---

8   *London Scottish Regimental Gazette* (1947), p.195.
9   St Columba's was still in ruins in November 1947 and would not be rebuilt until 1955.
10 *Aberdeen Press and Journal*, 3 November 1947, p.4.

1st Battalion Pipes and Drums on the Lord Mayor's Show, 9 November 1948. (LSMA, used with permission)

Her Majesty, The Queen, Honorary Colonel of the London Scottish Regiment speaking with newly appointed Pipe Major Ledgett, 19 December 1949. (LSMA, used with permission)

The London Scottish on the march through Scotland, Aberdeen 1954. (LSMA, used with permission)

Band practise at Dibgate Camp, 1956. (LSMA, used with permission)

demonstrated by this report from the 'C' Company Commander: 'Eight newcomers have been posted to the Company. We have not had the chance of meeting them all yet, and by the time we do shall probably find they have been annexed by the Band!'[11]

The Pipes and Drums were so successful at recruiting, in fact, that in January 1948, the battalion Commanding Officer, Colonel Maxwell observed:

> I want to congratulate the Band, under Sergeant Ledgett, with the untiring support of ex-Sergeant Archie McLeod; this is due not only for the standard of both Band and individual playing which they have worked up, but for the tremendous esprit de corps which they have shown in getting such a strong sub-unit of the Battalion (nearly 50 per cent of total strength!) together by this excellent example of 'roping in old friends.'[12]

As had been the case from the very earliest days of the London Scottish, the Pipes and Drums also took advantage of welcoming non-serving volunteers and old comrades into the band to supplement numbers, particularly for high profile occasions.

The first annual band supper for the new London Scottish Regiment Pipes and Drums took place on 5 February 1948, amidst scaffolding and builder's rubble in the Drill Hall at 59 Buckingham Gate. Despite the inconveniences, and with many ex 1st and 3rd Battalion pipers and drummers now finally returned from overseas, there were 63 present to celebrate the rebirth of the building, of the regiment and of the Pipes and Drums. Many of these returnees were commissioned officers and 'It was rather striking to see among the Old and Bold two ex-Commanding Officers of the Regiment piping, a Lieutenant Colonel beating the drum, and Majors and Captains galore either piping or drumming.'[13]

It was noted at the supper that the drum section was now being led by acting Drum Sergeant Walter 'Jimmy' Riddell, who had first joined the London Scottish as a drummer in 1937, aged 15, and who had attended every parade and practise since the reforming of the regiment. Riddell was called up to the 1st Battalion in 1939, then reassigned to the 2nd Battalion via a short stint with the 77th Regiment, Royal Engineers, before being moved on again to the 3rd Battalion. Here, he passed through the hands of all three gun batteries and had made the rank of bombardier by the time the 3rd Battalion went overseas. In Egypt he was told he would need to revert to the rank of gunner or be reassigned to another unit. He took the latter option, fighting throughout the rest of the war with the 2nd Regiment, Royal Artillery as a sergeant in charge of his own gun. He re-joined the London Scottish in 1947 as a private, along with his younger brother John, the first London Scottish cadet to sign up after the war, who also joined him in the drum section. 'For a man who was 'pushed around,' he has managed two remarkable feats. He has retained his grand sense of humour and his loyalty to the Scottish.'[14] His loyalty and commitment would be indispensable to the post-war success of the Pipes and Drums.

The London Scottish Regiment's first military exercise took place at Bisley in April alongside the 21st SAS (Artists). The exercise consisted of a night attack by the SAS on the London Scottish, which was extended slightly by the over-exuberance of a gung-ho London Scottish piper:

> The battle over, Piper Williams was told to sound 'the Close.' Some little time had elapsed since he had tied his pipes in a tree and gallantly joined in the war. Like cats, all trees look alike at night, but the pipes were eventually found and the war was officially over. By 11

---

11 *London Scottish Regimental Gazette* (1947), p.196.
12 *London Scottish Regimental Gazette* (1948), p.6.
13 *London Scottish Regimental Gazette* (1948), p.42.
14 *London Scottish Regimental Gazette* (1953), p.73.

o'clock everyone was washed and changed, and headed by Piper Williams, marched over to the SAS hut, where they were royally entertained until well into Sunday morning.[15]

Annual camp in August was at Dover, where recruiting issues for both regiment and band were becoming more noticeable. While the process of recruiting 'old friends' and volunteers to supplement numbers in the Pipes and Drums was useful for big parades, only six enlisted pipers and three enlisted drummers were able to attend camp. It did, however, afford them 'the first real opportunity since re-forming to practise drill, marching, and the many details that go to the making of a good team.'[16] The remainder of the regiment were themselves only able to put out two composite companies, each around platoon strength, and it was apparent that recruiting was going to remain a major issue for some time to come. The pipe band did, however, make a good first impression on the other regiments in camp. 'Comments on the pipers and drummers were complimentary in the extreme, studded with superlatives, with but one reproach: "but is that all you've got?"'[17]

The Pipes and Drums took part in various recruiting drives for the regiment during this period, playing outside Westminster Abbey and at Lloyd's in the City of London during lunchtimes throughout October 1948. They were assisted by an article in the *London Evening News* of Wednesday, 29 September which gave details of the history of some of the more famous Territorial Army regiments. Regarding the London Scottish it concluded: 'Men with experience in piping and drumming, anti-tank guns, mortars and mines are wanted by them.'[18] The pipe band also marched with the Pipes and Drums of the London Irish Rifles in the London Mayor's Show, although the band was not large in number and were not all able to parade in No. 1 dress due to limited available uniforms. 'We could not help feeling that if the London Irish could turn out a Pipe Band all in full dress so could the Scottish.'[19] The Pipes and Drums managed to put together a larger band for the regimental church parade on Sunday 14 November, but the rest of the battalion was not so imposing; 'although the turn-out and the standard of marching were what is expected of the Regiment, the numbers – other than the Band – left a good deal to be desired.'[20] Recruitment would continue to be a concern over the next 20 years and was a critical factor in the major structural changes that appeared to be on the horizon for the London Scottish Regiment.

1949 began with another 'first' for the Pipes and Drums when they performed the first ever live televised pipe band performance, shown on the BBC on 7 February, alongside the Pipes and Drums of the London Irish Rifles. Although, *The Scotsman* noted:

> It is surprising to learn that most of these pipers will be wearing the kilt of the London Irish. Their pipe band is now 26 strong, compared with the 12 pipers and six drummers of the London Scottish.[21]

This band of 18 included non-serving members, and reports from the band supper of 17 March highlighted the continued issue with recruiting enlisted pipers and drummers: 'After supper the serving band played downstairs under Sergeant E Bruce Ledgett. Six pipers (one borrowed) and four drummers (one borrowed).' Conversely, the 'Old and Bold played in two relays, and …

---

15 *London Scottish Regimental Gazette* (1948), p.68.
16 *London Scottish Regimental Gazette* (1948), p.162.
17 *London Scottish Regimental Gazette* (1948), p.139.
18 *Evening News*, London, 29 September 1948, p.7.
19 *London Scottish Regimental Gazette* (1948), p.189.
20 *London Scottish Regimental Gazette* (1948), p.193.
21 *The Scotsman*, 18 January 1949, p.4.

must have represented about 50 years of ex-members.'[22] Two days later, these eight serving pipers and drummers played at Twickenham Rugby Stadium before the England versus Scotland Five Nations international rugby match and can be seen in the crowd on a contemporary Pathé News film of the game.[23] Their musical encouragement was, however, unable to affect the final score in favour of Scotland.

On 22 May, Pipe Sergeant Ledgett accompanied Regimental Colonel Ogilby and a party of officers and NCOs to Rome for a dedication of the first memorial to London Scottish soldiers who gave their lives during the Second World War. A plaque, designed by Sergeant Ford, was unveiled by the British Ambassador at St. Andrew's Scottish Church. 'Regimental Piper Bruce Ledgett played the Lament after the dedication, and the whole party in their kilts of hodden grey and their fine military bearing made a deep impression on all who saw them.'[24] The group went on to visit Anzio for a further memorial service at the British and Commonwealth cemetery.

On his return, Pipe Sergeant Ledgett welcomed several new recruits to the band over the summer, ensuring that, in preparation for annual camp at Shorncliffe, 'We paraded at HQ … 14 strong, eight collodion players and six tub thumpers.'[25] Much of the fortnight at camp was spent specifically on band practise with a Beating Retreat performed on the promenade in Folkstone at the end of each week.

A London Scottish detachment travelled to Aberdeen on 20 August to participate in the annual Freedom of the City parade with the Gordon Highlanders. While the London Scottish Pipes and Drums were not officially on parade, Headquarters Company representation came from RQMS (and ex-Piper) Gibbons, Drummers Riddle, Paterson, Thompson and Wales, along with Pipers Scott and Dunnett. Piper Dunnett managed to pipe on the parade and, a couple of years later, the entire pipe band would be invited back to Aberdeen, playing alongside the massed bands of the entire Gordon Highlanders regimental family. On 22 August, the band were on parade for another associated regiment when Major Moffat, Second-in-Command of the Toronto Scottish Regiment, visited 59 Buckingham Gate. The Major, accompanied by the Toronto's Regimental Sergeant Major, presented 'on behalf of their Regiment, a handsome Skean Dhu to be competed for annually and awarded to the Best Novice Piper.'[26] This sgian dubh remains on display in the Regimental Museum.

September saw the re-dedication at regimental headquarters of the London Scottish 1914-18 War Memorial which had been heavily damaged by bombing during The Blitz. Over 1,200 individual replacement oak pieces were hand-carved and reinserted as part of the restoration process and the renovation of the memorial in the drill hall at 59 Buckingham Gate was a fitting representation of the continued restoration of the building itself. RQMS Gibbons played *Flowers of the Forest* at the ceremony, 'fading away down the stairs through the labyrinth under the hall until we could but faintly hear the pipes and then retracing his steps to give the swelling impression of vigorous life with our reveille "Hey, Johnnie Cope."'[27]

The most important regimental event of 1949 came on 19 December when Her Majesty, Queen Elizabeth attended headquarters to preside over the annual prize giving parade in her role as Honorary Colonel. Her Majesty 'received a real Scottish welcome. To greet her as she entered the

---

22   *London Scottish Regimental Gazette* (1949), p.59.
23   *England vs Scotland – Rugby (1949)* <https://www.youtube.com/watch?v=EgRAJicrEcI>
24   *Brechin Advertiser*, 7 June 1949, p.7.
25   *London Scottish Regimental Gazette* (1949), p.135.
26   *London Scottish Regimental Gazette* (1949), p.145.
27   *London Scottish Regimental Gazette* (1949), p.180.

drill hall were the skirl of the pipes and the roll of the drums.'[28] The Pipes and Drums were led by newly appointed Pipe Major Ledgett, who had been promoted in the weeks prior to the event, having completed the Army pipe major's course. It was fitting reward for his commitment and dedication to the band. Pipe Major Ledgett led the Pipes and Drums in a set before receiving the award for best highland dancer from The Queen, after which Piper Dunnett was presented with the MacLeod Medal. At the end of the parade the Pipes and Drums played Her Majesty from the hall. The band were pleased to be mentioned in a letter from The Queen's private secretary to the Commanding Officer, dated 20 December, which stated: 'It gave Her Majesty much pleasure to note the high standard of turnout and playing shown by the Pipes and Drums.'[29]

Pipe Major Ledgett's experience and confidence leading the band grew to such a degree that he formally took over the organisation of the Pipes and Drums from Archie MacLeod early in 1950 and, from this point, it became very much Ledgett's band. With no drum major appointed at this time, he was assisted by Corporal Drummer Riddell, who would become Drum Sergeant the following year. Ex-Pipe Major, J.B. Robertson, started his own civilian competition pipe band in 1949 and his position as piping instructor at the London Scottish was taken by James Clark 'Jim' Caution, who was himself a distinguished piper and very involved with the Scottish Piping Society of London. He entered his first competition in 1947, before famously beating Pipe Major Robertson in a piobaireachd competition and would go on to become a renown piping competition judge. Caution would help the London Scottish Pipes and Drums achieve a close second-place finish behind the J.B. Robertson Pipe Band at the London Caledonian Games at White City on 13 May, winning the princely sum of £20.00. Robertson's band contained four ex-London Scottish pipers who accompanied him when he left the regiment in order to spend more time on the burgeoning post-war competition scene.

Military pipe band life, however, had perks of which competition bands could only dream. The biggest of these were the major state ceremonial occasions. Battalion camp in 1950 had seen the Pipes and Drums spending more time than usual building their infantry skills, driving trucks, instructing on mortars and PIATs, and rifle shooting, with Piper Dunnett coming fourth in the regimental shooting competition. However, there had still been time to practise, and the hard work paid off when, in the middle of August and with only two weeks' notice, the Pipes and Drums were called up to participate in Beating Retreat on Horse Guards Parade, alongside the massed bands of the Household Division. They played on both nights (30 August and again on 6 September), joining with the Pipes and Drums of the 1st Battalion, Scots Guards, 1st Battalion, Irish Guards and the London Irish Rifles. Several pipers and drummers were on holiday when the news came through and rehearsal opportunities were difficult, but the band acquitted themselves well, despite the horrendous weather conditions on both evenings.

With the Territorial Army year ending, as always, on Hallowe'en, details of the number of training periods completed by each serving member were released. These figures highlighted the huge commitment that the Pipe Major and Drum Sergeant were making to ensure the London Scottish were represented by a Pipes and Drums of the very highest quality. A report in the *Regimental Gazette* states:

> We notice that ... Sgt. Drummer W G Riddell heads the list with 217 periods and Sgt. Piper Bruce Ledgett comes next with 211. As an old member of the band we are proud to see that

---

28 *Aberdeen Press and Journal*, 20 December 1949, p.1.
29 *London Scottish Regimental Gazette* (1950), p.10.

the present members of that august body are maintaining our old boast 'the hardest worked men in the Regiment.'[30]

As had so often been the case throughout their history, the Pipes and Drums during this period were completely self-supporting with no money coming from regimental funds. Specialist kit that was not available from stores, as well as musical instruments and associated items, had to be purchased from band funds raised from non-military paying jobs and from donations. These private jobs, overseen by the band president, took place on evenings and weekends outside of the battalion training schedule. In addition, the band was working hard to compete in pipe band competitions in and around London, with practise taking place twice a week (on Mondays and Thursdays) prior to competition season, in addition to their duties supporting all regimental and other military functions. It is not surprising then, that the Pipes and Drums were, and have always been, some of the 'hardest worked' members of the regimental family.

The year 1951 was a particularly busy year for the Pipes and Drums but one in which their skill and hard work would be recognised and well-rewarded. On 15 May, the Mayor of Westminster hosted a ceremony conferring the Freedom of the City of Westminster on the London Scottish Regiment. This was the first time that Westminster had afforded this honour to any military unit, and gave the London Scottish the unique, historical right to march through Westminster with drums beating, colours flying, and bayonets fixed. The regiment, led by the Pipes and Drums, marched from 59 Buckingham Gate to Wellington Barracks and then on to Horse Guards Parade for the actual ceremony. As the parade ended 'The Pipe Major "slung up" almost before he had stepped off the square and played us all the way back. Thank you, Band, you looked and played as well as we always expect you to.'[31]

Two weeks later, on 26 May, the Pipes and Drums competed in the London Caledonian Games at White City in front of 25,000 spectators. Their main competition was, again, the J.B. Robertson Band and the Old Caledonians Pipes and Drums, which also contained ex-members of the London Scottish, including drummer Archie MacLeod and piper Ian MacDougall, the younger brother of Piper Willie MacDougall who had been killed during the Second World War. Both would also play as non-serving members of the London Scottish Pipes and Drums in later years. The Scottish were the last to compete and had as delay of two hours due to heavy rain. In the end, they had to play in the rain regardless but 'the ovation from the spectators as we entered the stadium lifted our spirits and the whole band rose to the occasion. Another big ovation as we left.'[32] The judges of the competition, including the Sovereign's Piper, Pipe Major Alex MacDonald, and Drum Major W.G. Graham of the 1st Battalion, Scots Guards, awarded the London Scottish first place, and their first major competition win since Cowal in 1928. Fittingly, a 3rd Battalion reunion was taking place back at headquarters when the 13 pipers and five drummers returned with the Forth Bridge Trophy. Three of the winning band members had fought with the 3rd Battalion during the Second World War and the attendees helped ensure that the trophy 'had the usual christening, and the band members were invited to stay and enjoy the evening, a gesture which was greatly appreciated.'[33]

Hot on the heels of this success came the major event of the year for the Pipes and Drums when, on 3 July, Her Majesty, The Queen visited headquarters to present new pipe-banners to the regiment. The previous pipe banners, including those originally presented to the regiment in 1861,

---

30   *London Scottish Regimental Gazette* (1951), p.8.
31   *London Scottish Regimental Gazette* (1951), p.101.
32   *London Scottish Regimental Gazette* (1951), p.120.
33   *London Scottish Regimental Gazette* (1951), p.120.

had been damaged or destroyed during 'The Blitz' and in 1950 the major cities of Scotland had been approached with the suggestion of funding new banners portraying each city's coat of arms. Her Majesty, as Honorary Colonel of the London Scottish, had also graciously offered to provide a Royal pipe banner for her pipe major, which provided an additional incentive for the Scottish cities to agree to fund their own banners. Aberdeen, Dundee, Edinburgh, Glasgow and Perth all consented, along with banners funded by Regimental Colonel Ogilby, out-going Commanding Officer Colonel Borthwick and his replacement Colonel Maxwell. The event itself was a major occasion for the entire regiment and widely reported in the national press. The Lord Provost of each Scottish city attended in their formal robes, along with the Lord Mayor of Westminster and many prestigious military guests, including Colonels Bennett and Lyall-Grant, both ex-pipe band members. Her Majesty arrived and inspected the guard and band before Colonel Ogilby inquired if the Queen would graciously present her banner.

> Pipe Major Ledgett marched forward and had the signal honour of receiving the Banner from Her Majesty's hands, who then, as Honorary Colonel of the London Scottish, graciously consented to receive the Pipe Banners presented to the Regiment by the Cities of Edinburgh, Perth, Glasgow, Dundee and Aberdeen.[34]

After the Pipe Major, eight pipers individually marched forward to collect a banner, before tying them to their pipes. 'The pipers, proudly bearing their new banners, then gave a short programme of Highland music,'[35] before playing the Royal Salute and piping The Queen from the building to the regimental march. In the words of ex-Drum Major Morrie Mills, who had led the band through the glory days of the late 1920s:

> The Pipes were magnificent and the drums their worthy counterparts. If you who were not there have any doubts, let me still hear them forever. The music could not have been bettered. It has been ringing in my ears ever since.[36]

At the end of July, the Pipes and Drums spent their second week of annual camp in Scotland visiting the five cities that had presented them with pipe banners. It was a hectic tour with two or three parades and performances each day, and the band were relieved at the end of the week to be played onto the train in Edinburgh by pipers from the Royal Scots. As Pipe Major Ledgett stated, 'it is our hope that what we did in our small way will be of material benefit to the Regiment from a recruiting angle.'[37]

Recruiting was still a major issue at this point and would cause growing concern for the regiment over the next decade. The first National Service men had begun to arrive in 1951 but, with the London Scottish requirement of Scottish ancestry, aligned with the hopes of attracting more men who chose to join the regiment rather than those obliged because of National Service, new recruits were limited. The Pipes and Drums, however, were continuing to thrive and at one point in the mid-1950s accounted for over one tenth of the entire regiment's manpower. On occasions, recruiting new members required regimental pressure for rules to be bent, as was the case with Piper Alan Withey, who would go on to be a stalwart of the band for over 30 years, serving under six pipe majors. Piper Withey had been in the RAF during the Second World War and

---

34 *London Scottish Regimental Gazette* (1951), p.146.
35 *Dundee Courier*, 4 July 1951, p.3.
36 *London Scottish Regimental Gazette* (1951), p.151.
37 *London Scottish Regimental Gazette* (1951), p.169.

came to the London Scottish to learn the pipes under Jimmy Caution in 1950. He could not join the Territorial Army because he worked at The Admiralty but, in 1952, the regiment lobbied Opposition Whip MP Ted Heath, who spoke to the Minister of Defence, who arranged for an exception to be made. Others, however, like Drummer Dougie Chowns who was serving in the RAF, played with the band in the time-honoured position of volunteer. The role of the non-serving, volunteer piper or drummer would also become increasingly important over the coming decades and into the next century.

The band's role as a recruiting tool had never been more vital, and the prestige and public image they provided for the regiment became progressively more essential in this regard. That level of prestige was soon to rise markedly, but not without some small degree of controversy.

The following report of an officer's dinner on 23 June 1952 states:

> Bruce Ledgett was accompanied at this dinner by Piper Leslie de Laspée, late Pipe Major of the 1st and 2nd KOSB (King's Own Scottish Borderers), who after 24 years as a regular was invalided out of that grand regiment after having a motor cycle accident which lessened the use of an arm. He could not keep away from things military and recently joined us. Refreshing is the news that he hopes to bring along half-a-dozen ex-KOSB comrades to join our ranks![38]

Piper de Laspée soon became a corporal piper and very soon after that, a pipe sergeant. He was a natural showman of strong military bearing and brought with him a wealth of experience and contacts. Along with a clutch of pipers, he also brought with him Drummer Mike Crowley, another ex-KOSB who had served in the later stages of the Second World War and in Korea where he had been badly injured. Drummer Crowley would go on to become a major force in the drum corps over the next 30 years.

Pipe Major Ledgett and Pipe Sergeant de Laspée became the most public-facing members of the regiment and performed together on numerous occasions, the most high-profile of which was on 1 December 1952, when Her Majesty, Queen Elizabeth, who had recently become the Queen Mother on the death of her husband, dedicated the new London Scottish Second World War Memorial at 59 Buckingham Gate. The two men piped in the Royal party and Pipe Major Ledgett joined Her Majesty in laying a wreath at the memorial. The ceremony was shown on BBC news bulletins, with a British Movietone film unit in attendance for future showings in cinemas around the country. A Pathé news film also clearly depicts de Laspée as the Union Flag covering the memorial is pulled away.

With no drum major to lead the Pipes and Drums at this point, Sergeant Piper de Laspée's military experience was of great benefit to Pipe Major Ledgett on big parades like the Royal Review of ex-service men and women at Hyde Park on 5 July 1953. Here, a column of 122 London Scots, 51 of whom had served during the First World War, marched behind the band.

> And what a thrill it was to march again behind the pipes! As we went down Buckingham Gate, past the Palace, and up Constitution Hill, each man's mind was filled with memories, memories of other marches, behind other pipers. Marches in South Africa, perhaps, more than 50 years ago; in France and Flanders; in Palestine, in Sicily, Egypt and Italy, or in Scotland. We had to leave the Band at the Albert Gate; we did so with real regret. As we passed into the park and the strains of the pipes grew softer, we knew it had been worth turning out, whatever the rest of the day might be like.[39]

---

38 *London Scottish Regimental Gazette*, (1952), pp.123-124.
39 *London Scottish Regimental Gazette* (1953), p.199.

This working arrangement, of a less experienced pipe major and a more experienced and militarily senior pipe sergeant, was a difficult one to manage. It would become even harder in December 1953 after the Queen Mother decided she would like to appoint her own personal piper.

The appointment had first been raised, quite informally, as a secondary point in a letter sent from Her Majesty's private secretary to Colonel Ogilby on 3 November 1953, responding to a request to sign a portrait to be sent out to the Bulawayo Branch of the London Scottish Old Comrades Association. The letter stated:

> Queen Elizabeth raised one other matter, about which she thought you might be able to give her some advice. Her Majesty wondered if you know of any retired Pipers who might be able to come and play at Clarence House sometimes. By long-standing tradition, the Piper plays at Buckingham Palace at 9 o'clock every morning, waking around the Palace, in the garden, and I think something on this line was in Her Majesty's mind. I do not know if there are any ex-members of the Regiment who might be able to fill this role from time to time, or if the appropriate dress would be available for them?[40]

Her Majesty very much enjoyed the sound of the pipes and the role that the Sovereign's Piper had played for the late King and herself. With the coronation of her daughter, Queen Elizabeth II, in June 1953, The Queen Mother lost the services of the Sovereign's Piper and this letter made preliminary inquiry about creating her own unofficial appointment. Colonel Ogilby saw the opportunity to make this position more official and binding to the regiment and so recommended a London Scottish piper as being most appropriate for the task.

The question then became, who should be put forward? In normal circumstances, a position of such honour and prestige would have gone without question to the Pipe Major, who had already received a Royal pipe banner from The Queen Mother herself when she was still The Queen, only two years previously. However, the required duties not only meant playing at Clarence House three times a week in the early morning but playing, when requested, at state functions and other events outside of the capital. There was also no financial reward for these duties. This would have been no issue for a piper serving in the regular army but Territorial soldiers needed their civilian jobs to support themselves and their families and such a large commitment would have been difficult for most to fulfil.

Pipe Major Ledgett was offered the position but could not guarantee that he would be able to commit the necessary time, on top of his already considerable duties as pipe major. Instead, he put forward the name of his pipe sergeant, Leslie de Laspée, who expressed a definite interest in the post. His long experience of regular army service, added to the fact that he worked as a clerical officer at London Scottish regimental headquarters which was within walking distance of Clarence House, made Pipe Sergeant de Laspée an ideal second choice. The suggestion was put to Her Majesty, who replied through her private secretary: 'Her Majesty felt it would be very nice if we could arrange to try out his services here and suggested asking him to come and play the pipes on Tuesdays, Wednesdays and Thursdays at 9 o'clock in the morning.'[41]

It must have been a bitter pill for Pipe Major Ledgett to swallow for 'despite the brave face he put on it, it grieved him deeply.'[42] Having put so much time and effort into re-building the Pipes

---

40 Letter from Captain Oliver Dawnay, Private Secretary to H.M. The Queen Mother, to Colonel R.J.L. Ogilby, 3 November 1953, London Scottish Museum Archives.
41 Letter from Captain Oliver Dawnay, Private Secretary to H.M. The Queen Mother, to Colonel R.J.L. Ogilby, 12 November 1953, London Scottish Museum Archives.
42 *London Scottish Regimental Gazette* (1985), p.18.

and Drums after the war and turning them into such an excellent band, it was as if he was now missing out on the grand prize. It also led to a strange situation within the Pipes and Drums, as the seniority of de Laspées experience and position as the Queen Mother's personal piper, was seen by some to supersede that of his own pipe major.

It was, however, a huge distinction for the London Scottish and the December *Regimental Gazette* broke the news as follows:

> As we go to Press, news has reached us of a great honour befallen the Regiment through one of its serving members.
>
> Sgt L.V. de Laspée of the Pipe Band has been appointed Piper to Her Majesty Queen Elizabeth, the Queen Mother, our Honorary Colonel, with effect from December 2, 1953. Three times a week in the mornings he will parade in full dress at Clarence House, where he was summoned to learn of the honour, to play his pipes.
>
> As far as can be discovered, this is the first time on record that a member of the Territorial Army has received such a distinction.[43]

To his credit, de Laspée attempted to mollify the situation by stating 'The honour of being made Piper to the Queen Mother is one of which I am very proud, but it is an "award" to the Regiment and I just happen to be the person representing the Scottish – it could well have been someone else.'[44]

There does not seem to have been any animosity between the two men, but pressure was subsequently applied to Pipe Major Ledgett from certain quarters within the regiment who felt in 'right and proper' that the Queen Mother's personal piper should also be the pipe major:

> Since the Battalion was only allowed one such appointment, it looked like an impasse. Bruce, however, resolved the problem in a manner which truly reflected his gentlemanly qualities and his love of the Scottish by changing places in the band with de Laspée.[45]

During spring 1954, Pipe Major Ledgett announced that he was retiring as Pipe Major and that he had taken a job in Brighton. On this news, de Laspée was, possibly, rather too hastily appointed as his successor. There is little reporting of the situation in the *Regimental Gazette* and no cover article on the retiring Pipe Major Ledgett as is usually the case for an outgoing pipe or drum major, which hints at a degree of institutional unease around the situation.

Ledgett continued in the role of pipe sergeant for another 18 months and then, in late 1955, he and his family emigrated to Australia. He was given a last regimental goodbye in a packed Sergeant's Mess after band practise on Thursday, 15 December. It was a fitting send off for the man who RQMS Gibbons held 'solely responsible for the post-war Band.'[46] In a show of camaraderie, Pipe Major de Laspée appeared in full review order on the platform at St. Pancras railway station and piped Ledgett and his family onto the train taking them to Southampton to catch the boat that would carry them to their new life. When the Ledgetts arrived in Sydney some weeks later, there were two London Scottish old comrades there to meet them, proving once again that, no matter the circumstances, once a London Jock, always a London Jock.

---

43 *London Scottish Regimental Gazette* (1953), p.281.
44 *London Scottish Regimental Gazette* (1954), p.13.
45 *London Scottish Regimental Gazette* (1984), p.18.
46 *London Scottish Regimental Gazette* (1956), p.2.

Pipe Major Ledgett's contribution to the Pipes and Drums and to the London Scottish Regiment cannot be over-estimated. His hard work safeguarded the survival of the pipe band in the post-war era and his personal commitment as Pipe Major guaranteed it was a Pipes and Drums of exceptional quality and one of which the regiment could be justifiably proud. No greater compliment to Pipe Major Ledgett could be made than this 1954 report of the band at Hallowe'en:

> The Band performed with even more than its usual skill, and Old Comrades were glowing in their praise of its rendering and of the numbers mustered for the occasion. A veritable forest of drones, pennants and drumsticks marked its progress up and down the hall.[47]

The summer of 1954 saw de Laspée installed as Pipe Major and his first significant undertaking came in June when the London Scottish travelled to Scotland for annual camp for the first time in 17 years. The first week was spent at Buddon Camp in Barry, Angus with the Gordon Highlanders, who had recently returned from a three-year tour of Malaya. The next four days were then spent on the road marching to Aberdeen via Dundee and Carnoustie. In the evenings after each march, the Pipes and Drums Beat Retreat and also played at Crathes Castle as well as Aboyne Castle, ancestral home of the Marquess of Huntly, the original 'Cock O' The North', whose forefather, the 4th Duke of Gordon, had raised the Gordon Highlanders.

The regiment's arrival in Aberdeen was timed to coincide with a parade to commemorate the award to the Gordon Highlanders of the Freedom of the City. In the morning, the London Scottish marched into the city to take the salute from their own commanding officer:

> The men made a brave show as they marched past the saluting base headed by their pipes and drums. Hundreds of people – including several former members of the London Scottish who were in a special enclosure at the base – took pictures of the parade.[48]

That afternoon, a detachment of Gordon Highlanders returning from Malaya was led on parade to a civic reception by the Massed Bands and Drums and Pipes of the Gordon Highlanders Regiment, comprising the 1st, 4/7th and 5/6th Battalions, the London Scottish Regiment and the Aberdeen Depot, Gordon Highlanders. This was 'the first time in history all the pipe bands of the regiment will have played together'[49] and was, thus, a moment of great significance.

The London Scottish returned home the following morning:

> We had a pleasant surprise when the Band of the 4/7th Gordons swung out of a side street in front of the Battalion as we neared the station and played us in, and also played sets on the platform while the train was waiting to move out.[50]

It was noted that, while on the march in Scotland, '*The Black Bear*' became so popular with the Battalion that on our return home, when the Band was playing on King's Cross Underground Station, the whole battalion shouted for "Black Bear."' [51] This customary 'return to barracks' tune remained popular with the regiment and has, by tradition, become the last tune played on the return march to headquarters during the annual church parade each year.

---

47 *London Scottish Regimental Gazette* (1954), p.298.
48 *Aberdeen Evening Express*, 18 June 1954, p.9.
49 *Dundee Courier*, 24 May 1954, p.4.
50 *London Scottish Regimental Gazette* (1954), p.192.
51 *London Scottish Regimental Gazette* (1954), p.155.

Pipe Major Leslie de Laspee with a chimpanzee 'piper' in a promotional shot for the Searchlight Tattoo at White City Stadium, June 1959. (LSMA, used with permission)

Pipe Sergeant Ferguson giving actress Anne Taylor a blow on his pipes at the London Scottish Centenary Press Evening, 12 March 1959. (LSMA, used with permission)

Actor Anthony Newly (far left) joins the Pipes and Drums on the set of the film *Idle On Parade*, 1959. (LSMA, used with permission)

The Pipes and Drums on the set of This Is Your Life, with John Mills and Eamon Andrews, 19 December 1960. (LSMA, used with permission)

1954 had been a momentous year for the London Scottish Pipes and Drums. 1955 would prove to be much more settled. The highlights of the year began with a trip to Twickenham Rugby Stadium on 19 March to perform, alternately, with the Scots Guards for the England versus Scotland international rugby match, followed by band supper a few days later which saw Captain Alan Niekirk take his seat for the first time as band president. Pipe Major de Laspée, Pipe Sergeant Pearson, Piper Milner, along with Drummers Riddell (Jnr) and Wardley assisted the London Scottish Cadet Pipes and Drums at the Royal Tournament in June, where they were performing as part of a County of London ACF massed band. The Cadet Pipes and Drums had initially been set up during the First World War and had been revived in the 1950s, with pipers and drummers from the regimental band assisting with organisation and instruction. They would become an excellent source of new recruits, including Piper Robert Hay and Drummer James Taylor, who was given special permission to join the Regimental Pipes and Drums in 1955 despite being only 16 years old. The pipers were instructed by ex-Metropolitan Police Sergeant Findlater, son of Pipe Sergeant George Findlater of the Gordon Highlanders who won a Victoria Cross at the Battle of Dargai Heights in 1897. The drummers were assisted by the Drum Major of the Metropolitan Police Brass Band, Ted Owens, whose association with the London Scottish Pipes and Drums would grow considerably over the next few years.

The two biggest news items for the regiment as a whole in 1955 came in October with the announcement that Major Hugh Attwooll would be taking command of the regiment and that ex-Commanding Officer (and ex-Drummer) Colonel Duncan Bennett would be taking over from Colonel Ogilby as Honorary Colonel. Having an ex-member and such a firm friend of the Pipes and Drums as Honorary Colonel was, naturally, a source of enormous pride for the band.

With the Pipes and Drums at full strength and the rest of the serving battalion at close to established numbers, the condition of the regiment appeared to be extremely positive at the start of 1956. However, around 75 percent of the men serving with the London Scottish were on National Service and Prime Minister Anthony Eden announced plans that year to drastically cut the National Service programme and to undertake a major review regarding the purpose and composition of the Territorial Army.[52] Nineteen fifty-four would mark the beginning of decades of change and uncertainty for the London Scottish Regiment which would prove to have a particularly marked effect on the Pipes and Drums.

The band had the highest number of serving soldiers who had chosen to join the regiment, in proportion to National Service men who had been assigned to it, of any unit in the battalion. It also contained, as has always been the case since its founding, various 'volunteer' members who were not serving in the battalion but practised and turned out with the band, particularly for big occasions. This included several pipers and drummers from the Metropolitan Police who, due to police regulations, were not permitted (or did not wish) to join the Territorial Army. None of these non-serving members received any financial reward for playing with the Pipes and Drums and did so, as had always been the case, for the honour and pride of the regiment whose uniform they wore. Circumstances dictated that the services of these ancillary members would begin to increase markedly from this point onwards.

25 March 1956 saw the dedication of the London Scottish Regimental Chapel at the newly rebuilt Church of St Columba's in Pont Street, Knightsbridge. Her Majesty, Queen Elizabeth, The Queen Mother was in attendance, as were the Pipes and Drums and the occasion was recorded for a half-hour television programme on BBC Scotland. That April, the band also made recordings for

---

52   As it turned out, the brunt of initial changes to the Armed Forces brought about by the Government's programme of reorganisation was born by the Regular Army, which was to see dramatic cuts. The Government initially attempted to push the Territorial Army with trade unions and employers as a cheaper option.

a BBC radio programme on the history of the London Scottish Regiment and in September the entire pipe band appeared on the popular radio programme, the *Billy Cotton Band Show*. This was the first job for a young tenor drummer named Bryan Alderson, who would still be parading with the Pipes and Drums 50 years later. These performances marked the beginning of a ten-year period where the Pipes and Drums were very visible on television and in film, which helped considerably in keeping the London Scottish Regiment in the public eye.

The band also now had a Drum Major to lead them on these high exposure events. Drum Sergeant Walter 'Jimmy' Riddell was appointed in June, having recently returned to the Pipes and Drums after a long illness. This was the first time since Morrie Mills had fronted the pipe band in the 1930s that the regiment had boasted a drum major. It was just reward for Sergeant Riddell who had worked tirelessly with Pipe Major Ledgett to ensure the rebirth of the Pipes and Drums after the war.

A smaller but noteworthy event came in the summer of 1956, when Pipe Major de Laspée performed for a dedication of remembrance at the rose garden in front of the London Scottish shooting lodge at Bisley. The London Scottish had been shooting at Bisley Camp since the National Rifle Association (which they helped form) moved there from Wimbledon in 1890. The London Scottish lodge was designed by Pipe Major Robertson in 1935, complete with a cast iron piper on the weathervane. A rose garden was planted at the lodge and a tradition began for the ashes of deceased members of the regiment to be scattered there. In future years, the remains of many pipers and drummers, including Drum Sergeant Bryce List and Pipe Major William Ferguson would rest there.

A second important dedication service came on 21 October at St Columba's Church where the Pipes and Drums played for the rededication of the First World War memorial. The original bronze plaque had been repaired and replaced after receiving severe bomb damage during the destruction of St Columba's during the Second World War.

In early 1957, the band president, Major Niekirk, began campaigning for funds to send the Pipes and Drums back to compete at the Cowal Highland Gathering for the first time since their successes in the late 1920s. After an appeal in the *Regimental Gazette*, pledges were received from 'North and South America, Australia, New Zealand, Pakistan, the West Indies, Hong Kong, Singapore, Malaya, South Africa, East Africa, West Africa, the Channel Islands and all over Scotland,'[53] in a show of support for the band that was representative of their affection within the regiment, especially with old comrades. The Cowal Games took place on 31 August and the band stayed, as they had in the 1920s, at the 8th Argyll and Sutherland Highlanders headquarters in Dunoon. One piper nearly ended up in the Firth of Clyde when, having left something on the coach, he had to make a running jump to catch the ferry. 'Along galloped our hero, took one flying leap, touched the gang-way once, and landed on deck, kilt under his armpits, a bit shaken but pleased with himself.'[54] The competition at Cowal was tough and, in the words of Drummer Alderson, 'needless to say we were outclassed'[55] but they were given the honour, as of old, to lead the final parade of over 80 bands into the arena. With Colonel Attwooll and a host of old comrades in attendance, it was another excellent opportunity for the London Scottish to fly the regimental flag north of the border and provided great experience for the Pipes and Drums.

Joining them on the bus to Dunoon was Drum Major Ted Owens of the Metropolitan Police Brass Band. A reoccurring illness meant that Drum Major Riddell had been unable to perform

---

53 *London Scottish Regimental Gazette* (1957), p.155.
54 *London Scottish Regimental Gazette* (1957), p.160.
55 Bryan Alderson, *MacNamara's Band to Drum Major: A Drummers Anecdotes and Pictures* (London: self-published, 2009), p.4.

with the Pipes and Drums on many occasions since his appointment and it would ultimately compel him to retire. Drum Sergeant Jeff Wardley, who played the bass drum with the band, was hopeful that the position would go to him, but the regiment again decided to appoint a newcomer, with Ted Owens approached and selected for the role, despite never having been a member of the Pipes and Drums or having led a pipe band. This caused a degree of discomfort, particularly with Drum Sergeant Wardley, but one which was ultimately overcome. Drum Major Owens was a mounted Metropolitan Police officer, based in Hammersmith, and had previously served in India and Shanghai with the Mountain Battery, Royal Artillery, having joined them in 1923 as a boy trumpeter, at the age of 14. He was most well-known for leading the Metropolitan Police Brass Band during half-time performances at Arsenal Football Club during every home game. He was required to leave the Metropolitan Police in order to become Drum Major of the London Scottish, but the regiment pulled some strings and organised a civilian administrator post for him with the City of London Police. A moustachioed native-speaking Welshman, Owens cut a dashing figure to match the showmanship of Pipe Major de Laspée. They would lead the Pipes and Drums together for the next ten years.

Summer 1958 was exceptionally busy for the band. It started with the Royal Review of the Territorial Army in Hyde Park on 22 June, followed closely by the City and County of London Tattoo at White City Stadium where they played alongside the Pipes and Drums of the London Irish Rifles. Annual camp followed in July with two weeks spent again in Scotland, including one week on the march from Elgin to Aberdeen, where:

> They played more on the line of march than we can ever remember, they gave us an excellent Retreat (in full dress) each night after marching all day, they went over Bennachie and, we understand, they did quite a bit of walking after duties. Iron men, indeed.[56]

In addition, whilst in camp, 'Each day there would be a duty piper and a duty drummer, playing the calls of the day. A couple of times during camp there would be a full band reveille and of course many "Beating Retreats."'[57]

During their time at annual camp, the Pipes and Drums were afforded the unique honour, although at short notice, to Beat Retreat at Edinburgh Castle, which they duly performed on 26 July. Upon their return to London the band was also invited, again with little prior warning, to perform Beating Retreat on Horse Guards Parade with a massed pipe band comprising of Scots Guards, London Scottish, 2nd Canadian Guards and the 57th (City of London General Hospital) RAMC. The London Scottish also provided the Guard of Honour while the military band of the Highland Light Infantry played for the last time wearing kilts. After participating in the two rehearsals, it was decided at the last minute that there were too many drummers and the London Scottish, as the last unit to be invited, were asked to leave their drummers behind. The regiment was represented by 11 pipers and the drum major and it 'seemed to be the general opinion that the Scottish Drum Major was the smartest on parade,'[58] but it was a huge disappointment to the drummers.

Next came a performance at Twickenham Rugby Stadium for a rugby tournament organised by Colonel Lyall-Grant, followed by another performance at White City Stadium for the SSAFA Searchlight Tattoo. A second trip to Dunoon for the Cowal Gathering came in August, before another tattoo, this time in Sevenoaks at the RAF Association Battle of Britain Tattoo. The annual

---

56 *London Scottish Regimental Gazette* (1958), p.129.
57 Alderson, *MacNamara's Band to Drum Major*, p.9.
58 *London Scottish Regimental Gazette* (1958), p.135.

Hallowe'en dinner and regimental church parade rounded off an extremely busy and high-profile year. It would prove to be sterling preparation for the event-filled regimental centenary year that was to follow in 1959.

Keeping the regiment in the public eye was of increasing importance. The enormous reduction in National Service enlistments pledged by the government had begun to kick in at the end of 1958 and the battalion was now down to just 140 men. Senior officers knew that they had to recruit, and recruit vigorously, or else a battalion strength regiment would no longer be viable. The Pipes and Drums had always been a key asset in this regard, and they would increasingly be put to work advertising the regiment over the coming years.

On 12 March 1959, the London Scottish organised a press night party at headquarters to mark the centenary of the regiment and to garner some much-needed publicity. 59 specially invited Scottish guests attended 59 Buckingham Gate, where 'The Pipes and Drums performed and won attention from all sides.'[59] The band played with pop singer Nancy Whisky and the Pipe Major danced with actress Anne Taylor who was also famously photographed blowing Pipe Sergeant Ferguson's pipes. Subsequent articles such as 'Londoners in Kilts' that appeared in the London *Evening News* provided exactly the publicity hoped for. A few weeks later, Pipe Sergeant Ferguson, in full uniform and accompanied by his wife, made two appearances on the Sunday night ITV show *Beat the Clock* hosted by Bruce Forsyth. With two dozen uniformed members of the London Scottish in the audience, this was precisely the type of advertising the regiment required. A high-profile performance with the London Irish at Mansion House for the Lord Mayor's Easter Banquet was followed by a television appearance on the *Easter Parade*, a television interview by the Pipe Major before their performance at the England versus Scotland rugby match and, biggest of all, an acting role for the entire band in the new Anthony Newley film, *Idle on Parade*. The film, starring Newley, Sid James, Lionel Jeffries and Bernie Winters amongst a plethora of other household names, was the story of a young rock and roll star joining a regiment for National Service. It came out at the same time Elvis Presley was being drafted into military service in the United States and did very well at the box office.

Regimental commitments to commemorate the centenary year were multifarious, but the celebrations also brought several additional benefits for the Pipes and Drums. The first came in April with the annual competition for the MacLeod Medal. Colonel Attwooll, the out-going Commanding Officer, presented a prize for drumming to match that given for piping, and the Attwooll Trophy, won in its inaugural year by Drummer Mike Crowley, is still competed for today.

The regiment were invited to mount a ceremonial guard at the Palace of Holyroodhouse, in Edinburgh on 23-24 May. This historic occasion marked the first time an English Territorial Army regiment had mounted a guard at the monarch's official residence in Scotland. One piper and one drummer accompanied each guard, with Lance Corporal Piper Milner and Lance Corporal Drummer Crowley playing on the first day and Piper Oswald and Drummer Sweetman on the second. Pipe Sergeant Ferguson paraded in the guard, as a private and not a piper, and had to remove his sergeant's stripes for the occasion. Lance Corporal Drummer Crowley, who had been working to reintroduce the instrument to London Scottish drummers, also played the bugle at the guard mount.

On 4 June, the Pipes and Drums attended a ceremony at regimental headquarters where Drum Major Owen, on behalf of the band, was presented with an elegant silver-mounted mace by Honorary Colonel Bennett, which had been graciously proffered by the Caledonian Society.[60] In

---

59 *London Scottish Regimental Gazette* (1959), p.58.
60 This unique mace was used on all parades until very recently, when the item was appraised and found to be far too valuable for everyday use.

addition, the Earl of Dundee, President of the Highland Society of London, presented the first of four modern pipe band rod-tensioned drums to replace the traditional rope tensioned drums still being used up until this point. In addition to funding the mace, Colonel Jamie Thomson, President of the Caledonian Society presented three more drums on behalf of the Royal Caledonian Schools Directors, Masters of the Regimental Lodge and the banking firm Glynn, Mills & Co. The drummers were now equipped with four of the very latest, pipe band specific side drums that would prove to be hugely advantageous when competing.

New regimental colours were presented by Queen Elizabeth, The Queen Mother, on 11 July at the Duke of York's Headquarters, where Her Majesty was joined by the Earl of Caithness, the Honorary Colonel of the Gordon Highlanders. The London Scottish Pipes and Drums were accompanied by the Military Band of the Gordon Highlanders for the inspection, which ran well over time as Her Majesty stopped to talk to many of the men on parade. The old colours, which had been presented by King Edward VII in 1909, were marched off as the new colours were dedicated on a drumhead altar built of side drums and a bass. The Pipes and Drums played the battalion on to the parade with the tune *Hot Punch* and off again at the conclusion to *Hielan' Laddie*:

> As the Pipes and Drums took the high road back to H.Q., a carefully timed drill operated in that the Gordon's Band skilfully picked up the strains of the Regimental March, blended in and took over, thus obviating echo and the faltering of the step from those out of earshot. It worked perfectly.[61]

The event featured on television and radio and was widely reported in the national press.

The following day was the centenary regimental church parade and a day later, The Queen Mother was back at Buckingham Gate specifically to make a presentation to the Pipes and Drums. Her Majesty had graciously given permission for the Pipe Major and Drum Major to wear her personal monogram on their plaid brooches and commissioned two solid silver brooches to be made for the occasion. It was Her Majesty's wish to pin them on to each man herself, however:

> As they stepped back, saluted and turned smartly to withdraw, Drum Major Ted Owen's brooch supplied an unrehearsed incident. It gently detached itself from his plaid and rolled across the floor. The Queen Mother clasped her hands in apprehension and laughed once it was found and returned by a senior officer.[62]

Her Majesty then gave a speech and sat and listened intently as the Pipes and Drums played a set in her honour. Highland dancing followed before a rendition of the famous *Hodden Grey* song. When singing the refrain of 'Three for the Colonel' during every verse, the entire audience rose and toasted Her Majesty, who was visibly moved by the occasion.

Three days later, the Pipes and Drums held their own centenary event, which proved to be the biggest of the year. Some 700 people had attended the regimental centenary dinner the previous day, where Colonel Morgan of the Toronto Scottish presented the regiment with a pipe banner, but over one thousand enjoyed the Thursday evening event hosted by the band and the regimental reel club. Thursdays were the only evenings that ladies were allowed into the canteen bar at 59 Buckingham Gate, which was permitted because the reel club met that evening before band practise, with regimental pipers and drummers played each week for the dancers. As such, Thursday evenings were often the most convivial of the week and the 'Bar was always crowded with old

---

61   *London Scottish Regimental Gazette* (1959), p.145.
62   *London Scottish Regimental Gazette* (1959), p.154.

comrades, the band, the dancers and lots of girls.'[63] So many wished to attend the band's centenary event that the Queen's Westminster Regiment Drill Hall next door had to be seconded in order to seat everyone for dinner. After the meal, the serving band played and:

> Then came the highlight of the evening when former Pipers and Drummers were invited to join the Band in a set. When they 'fell in' there were some 40 pipers and 20 drummers. How the spectators loved that Band and would have liked them to have gone on much longer.[64]

Bleary-eyed bandsmen and many of the guests then made their way the following evening to the regimental centenary ball held at the Grosvenor House Hotel in Mayfair. A contingent of the Pipes and Drums performed throughout the evening for the reels.

The band played for the third year in a row at the Cowal Gathering in August, which also included a military tattoo on the Friday evening with five other Territorial Army bands, which was performed completely unrehearsed. The Pipes and Drums did not achieve a place in the main competition but once again won the Milton Trophy for best drill and deportment.

The centenary year celebrations concluded with the regular dinner at Hallowe'en and regimental church parade on 8 November, where the old 1st Battalion colours were laid-up in the London Scottish Chapel at St Columba's. 'Preceded by the Pipe-Major and five pipers playing *My Home*, the Colour Party marched in slow time up the main aisle to the altar steps where they were awaited by Dr Scott (the Regimental Padre) and the Commanding Officer.'[65] The 100th anniversary of the regiment had been celebrated with huge pride and enormous gusto but, with enlisted numbers still less than 200, the future existence of the regiment looked extremely uncertain.

By mid-1960, numbers had improved to over 250, but this was still only a fraction of the 750 men required to realise the minimum numbers for full battalion establishment. Every other TA unit in the capital was also struggling to recruit as the country entered the 'Swinging Sixties,' where social and political attitudes shifted significantly. Britain's empire was slowly evolving into a commonwealth and public opinions concerning the military during the height of the Cold War, adjoined to the fears of this 'nuclear age' were turning many young men away from thoughts of joining the Territorial Army. Further concerns were raised when news came through that the TA was to be reduced in the summer from 266 to 195 major units as National Service came to an end. The London Scottish needed to bring in a significant number of recruits to substantiate their viability and effectiveness and avoid the threat of being disbanded or amalgamated with another regiment. Senior officers even set up a competition for each sub-unit of the regiment with the prize of an 18-gallon barrel of beer for whichever of them brought in the highest number of new recruits.

An announcement regarding proposed TA disbandments and amalgamations was reported in *The Times* newspaper on 16 August. The London Scottish had been lucky. The Commanding Officer, Lieutenant Colonel John McGregor, later wrote in the *Regimental Gazette*, 'By now all members of the Regiment will know that in the reorganisation of the Territorial Army, we are the only infantry regiment in London to escape amalgamation.'[66] Royal connections, regimental history and a huge publicity campaign, in which the Pipes and Drums had played a major role, helped to stave off the restructuring that had affected every other famous London Territorial unit, from the Honourable Artillery Company and the London Scottish's neighbours, the Queen's Westminsters, through to their close friends, the London Irish Rifles. The challenge now was to

---

63 Alderson, *MacNamara's Band to Drum Major*, p.3.
64 *London Scottish Regimental Gazette* (1959), p.180.
65 *London Scottish Regimental Gazette* (1959), p.217.
66 *London Scottish Regimental Gazette* (1960), p.141.

prove that the London Scottish Regiment was worthy of the confidence that had been conferred upon it.

The band travelled to Dunoon once again in August, where they won the Milton Challenge Trophy for the third year in a row, but their most memorable contribution was hosting a ceilidh for all the other army bands at the 8th Argyll and Sutherland Highlanders drill hall that was, by all reports, extremely well received. 'At Reveille, it was quite a feat to sort out our own band amongst all the various pipers and drummers,'[67] whose 'condition' had made it inadvisable for them to leave the premises the previous evening.

The 1960 regimental Hallowe'en dinner was provided with an extra twist from the Pipes and Drums, when, under the guidance of Drum Corporals Riddell (Jnr) and Crowley, the drummers presented not only a drummer's call but also a bugle fanfare as an additional set to the regular band performance. This was the first time the London Scottish had mustered a 'Bugle Corps' since the end of the Second World War and, by November church parade the following year, there were six drummer buglers who were able to perform regularly and to a high standard, under the direction of Drum Major Owens, who had himself been a fanfare trumpeter.

The year was rounded off with a visit to 59 Buckingham Gate on 10 November by Her Majesty, The Queen Mother to celebrate her 25th anniversary as Honorary Colonel, where she was presented with a silver statue of a London Scottish piper. In a letter thanking the regiment for their hospitality, Her Majesty wrote 'I was particularly pleased with the standard of the Guard of Honour, and the playing of the Pipes and Drums.'[68]

20 December 1960 saw the release of a major Oscar-nominated motion picture, regarded by Alfred Hitchcock as one of the greatest films ever made. *Tunes of Glory* is a dark psychological drama that tells the story of the change of command in a fictitious Highland regiment soon after the end of the Second World War. Alec Guinness and John Mills, both subsequently knighted, star respectively as Major Jock Sinclair and Lieutenant Colonel Basil Barrow in the film, which is based on James Kennaway's 1956 novel of the same name, which drew loosely on his own experiences in the Gordon Highlanders. The film highlights the importance of the Pipes and Drums and Highland dancing within Highland regiments, and the London Scottish were called upon to provide assistance, with the pipe band and members of the regimental reel club taking prominent roles. Regimental Colonel Hugh Attwooll was a successful movie producer who worked on many Disney films and other classics of the era (including *Reach for the Sky* and *Greyfriar's Bobby*) and he recommended the band for the role. Piper Hay mentioned that the filming was particularly 'memorable for dear old P/M de Laspée setting fire to the polystyrene snow on a hot summer's day by trying to put his fag out in it, it was that realistic!'[69] The Pipes and Drums would also be involved in several promotional events for the film in the first part of 1961, with Pipe Major de Laspée travelling as far afield as Canada, where he was graciously hosted by the Toronto Scottish Regiment.

The band was also invited to perform on the hit BBC show *This is Your Life* on 19 December to celebrate the lifetime achievements of one of the stars of *Tunes of Glory*, John Mills. To close the show, the host, Eamon Andrews, announced 'From your latest film, *Tunes of Glory*, the Pipes and Drums of the London Scottish. John Mills, this is your life' as the band marched on playing *Black Bear*. This should have been the end of the evening for the Pipes and Drums but, whilst the rest of the band got changed and went to the pub to celebrate their newfound fame, bass Drummer Bryan Anderson and Piper Alan Withey decided to head to the BBC canteen for something to eat.

---

67 *London Scottish Regimental Gazette* (1960), p.156.
68 *London Scottish Regimental Gazette* (1960), p.189.
69 *London Scottish Regimental Gazette* (1985), p.57.

On arrival they were informed that a meal was being laid on and were directed to the executive banqueting suite where they found John Mills surrounded by family and famous friends, along with Eamon Andrews and various high-level BBC executives, about to sit down to a sumptuous post-production dinner. Seeing two empty seats, the uninvited pair sat down and 'managed to enjoy an "Executive Supper" free, which is upholding the highest traditions of the Pipes and Drums.'[70]

Some 20 years later, now Drum Major Alderson bumped into John Mills and his wife at a function at Hampton Court Palace, where he reminded them of the incident. Mrs Mills replied 'Oh don't worry about it. I thought you were a couple of old 'winos' who had wandered in from the street!'[71]

Camp in 1961 was at the Army Civil Defence School at Millom, in what is now Cumbria. It was a busy camp for the Pipes and Drums with engagements on every evening along with their regular infantry activities, including daily show parades, drill sessions and fitness tests. Even Pipe Major de Laspée 'hammered the tarmac every day and proved himself fitter than men more than half his age who had only a fraction of his drinking potential.'[72]

The band went from annual camp straight to Scotland for another appearance at the Cowal Gathering, from where Piper Martin was rushed back to play at the funeral of one of the London Scottish Regiment's most notable soldiers, Robert Cruickshank, who was awarded the Victoria Cross for conspicuous bravery while serving with the 2nd Battalion during the First World War. His wife had initially planned a quiet funeral, but word got around about the death of this regimental and national hero and Piper Martin ensured Cruickshank was given a fitting farewell.

For unknown reasons, only three pipers played at the annual Hallowe'en dinner in 1961, but the dinner did see the promotion of another former piper (although not with the London Scottish Pipes and Drums) to the position of Commanding Officer. The outgoing Commanding Officer, Colonel McGregor, was replaced by Second in Command and band president Major Ronald T.S. 'Tommy' Macpherson. Macpherson was the most decorated officer in the British Army, having been awarded the Military Cross three times, the French Croix de Guerre three times, the Legion d'Honneur and a Papal Knighthood for his service behind enemy lines during the Second World War.[73] He had served with the Queen's Own Cameron Highlanders TA, No. 11 (Scottish) Commando and the 21st SAS TA before transferring to the Gordon Highlanders and on to the London Scottish. He would prove to be a great support to the Pipes and Drums during his tenure in command.

Nineteen sixty-two saw the release of the blockbuster epic film *The Longest Day*, with an all-star cast including the Hollywood stars John Wayne, Robert Mitchum, Richard Burton, Sean Connery, Henry Fonda, George Segal, Robert Wagner, alongside London Scottish Pipe Major Leslie de Laspée. De Laspée played the part of Pipe Major Bill Millen, who had been personal piper to Lord Lovat and who had piped the 1st Special Service Brigade ashore to *Heilan' Laddie* on D-Day, continuing to play throughout the ensuing battle. During filming for the landing scene in Normandy, de Laspée was washed overboard when the landing craft ramp opened too early and he had to be rescued. However, his final performance, although uncredited, is a scene-stealer.

The highlight of 1962 for both band and regiment came in July with a combined annual camp and march through Scotland, the latter of which experienced the extremes of Scottish

---

70 *London Scottish Regimental Gazette* (1961), p.27.
71 *London Scottish Regimental Gazette* (2005), p.192.
72 *London Scottish Regimental Gazette* (1961), p.134.
73 Details of his incredible exploits can be found in his excellent autobiography *Behind Enemy Lines: The Autobiography of Britain's Most Decorated Living War Hero* (London: Mainstream Publishing, 2010).

summer weather. The march began in Inverness at the Cameron Highlanders barracks and ended at Victoria Barracks in Ballater, home of the royal guard when the monarch is in residence at Balmoral Castle. The London Scottish were inspected by Queen Elizabeth, The Queen Mother at Ballater in extremely cold and windy conditions that resulted in the headdress of a number of officers and men flying loose. The Pipes and Drums took pride in not losing any.

The previous day, Commanding Officer Colonel Macpherson, had been spotted by London Scottish troops talking to a well-dressed woman by the roadside:

> There we were, hoofing it along the road, marching at ease, rifles slung and Davie Duncan now piping *Sarie Marais* … On the other side of the road we spotted the boss man, the MacPherson himself, standing bareheaded and in shirtsleeve order, talking to somebody who was seated on a crumbling old castle wall. That someone looked decidedly feminine but well concealed in an anorak and holding a fishing rod.
>
> Just to give our chief a bit of support we offered a few wolf whistles and coo-ees, when Paul Hammond exclaimed, 'Cheese and rice! It's the Queen Mum.' Bubbles called us to attention. No time to shoulder arms, so we pulled down on our webbing straps and tried to stop laughing at our act of lese majesty. Came the order 'Eyes Left!' The Queen Mother, already knew that we loved her, without all this fuss. She was a good Jock.[74]

On another occasion, while the battalion continued to march through driving snow over the forbidding Corrieyairack Pass, the band were, fortunately, diverted to Kingussie to Beat Retreat. However:

> The moment we marched off, down came the snow. We played in a combined dust and snow storm to an audience of nil, unless you count the people who looked out of their warm rooms and wondered who we were.[75]

Drummer Alderson recalled that the freezing rain and snow was so bad that, when they reached Braemar, 'Piper Alan Withey, another piper and I instead of returning to camp booked into a B&B'[76] before a thankful return to London. Camp in 1963 would take place very sensibly in Norfolk, and the following year moved even further south to Plymouth.

Nineteen sixty-four saw The Queen Mother attend Hallowe'en dinner at regimental headquarters to commemorate the 50th anniversary of the Battle of Messines, where she took wine with all surviving members. The Pipes and Drums played for Her Majesty on her arrival outside 59 Buckingham Gate, where:

> The skirl of the pipes announced that our Honorary Colonel had arrived. Handclapping preceded her entry and then, as she stepped through the door, ebullience sent protocol gasping through the rafters on a wave of full-throated, full-blooded cheering.[77]

In June of the following year, Pipe Major de Laspée, Pipe Corporal Davie Duncan and Drummer James Connor would perform again for The Queen Mother on a much bigger, but equally as welcoming stage, 3,500 miles away in Canada at the Toronto Scottish Regiment's golden jubilee

---

74 *London Scottish Regimental Gazette* (2002), p.51.
75 *London Scottish Regimental Gazette* (1962), p.92.
76 Alderson, *MacNamara's Band to Drum Major*, p.10.
77 *London Scottish Regimental Gazette* (1964), p.215.

celebrations. The Queen Mother had become the Colonel-in-Chief of the Toronto Scottish in 1938, and the main event of the jubilee was a colours parade at the university stadium on Friday 24 June in front of a crowd of over 20,000 guests. The London Scottish pipers and drummer massed with the Pipes and Drums of the Toronto Scottish Regiment on the parade 'which was carried out with precision and was generally very impressive.'[78] 900 sat down for dinner that evening at the Royal York Hotel, and Her Majesty was piped to and from the dinner by Pipe Major Wakefield of the Toronto Scottish and Pipe Major de Laspée. Both pipe majors also played together for The Queen Mother outside her hotel at 0845 hours every morning throughout her stay.

A regimental reunion took place at Toronto Scottish headquarters at Fort York Armoury on the Saturday evening, at which the London Scottish contingent attended and presented a pipe banner with the London Scottish cap badge on one side and the Toronto Scottish badge on the reverse. The London Scottish contingent were, as always, entertained most hospitably by their hosts and, as they began their journey home from Toronto International Airport, were piped into the departure lounge and down the tunnel to the plane by the Toronto Scottish Pipes and Drums.

They arrived back in Great Britain and headed straight to annual camp at Devizes, where rumours were beginning to circulate concerning plans for further reorganisation of the Territorial Army that would see personnel slashed from 120,000 to just 50,000. In July, the Labour Government announced that, as part of a wider plan to demilitarise Britain's political role at home and abroad, it intended to disband 73 Territorial infantry battalions, 42 artillery regiments and 19 armoured regiments. This would leave just 13 Territorial infantry battalions, and serious concerns began to mount regarding the future of the London Scottish. It soon became obvious that, even if the London Scottish managed to survive, it would not be at full battalion strength and the fight began to ensure that the regimental name remained alive, even if it was to be at a much-reduced establishment. This situation was particularly acute for the Pipes and Drums, as amalgamation into another battalion or the extinction of the regimental name would mean that the band in its current form would cease to exist.

In the meantime, the Pipes and Drums carried on as usual and continued to work on the quality and variety of their performances. With six drummers now trained as buglers, but only four modern side drums for them to play, Drum Sergeant Crowley approached the Sergeants' Mess president CSM Rylands about raising funds to provide the drum section with two additional side drums and a modern replacement for the bass drum. Funds were raised, the drums were duly purchased, and then formally presented to the band on 22 August. Crowley later wrote in the *Regimental Gazette*:

> The cost of these drums was made by personal contributions from past and present members of the Sergeants Mess. This was made possible by two very generous past members who wish to remain anonymous, to you two gentlemen please accept our most sincere thanks ... Since receiving these drums we have won two drumming awards and this is just the start of what's to come, somewhere in the near future we hope two tenor drums will make the Pipe Band the most up to date in the British Army.[79]

The drummers were able to make good use of their new drums when they performed for the first time since the 1930s at the televised National Festival of Remembrance at the Royal Albert Hall on Sunday 13 November.

---

78 *London Scottish Regimental Gazette* (1965), p.160.
79 *London Scottish Regimental Gazette* (1965), p.194.

Frank Scott watercolour of Pipe Sergeant Ferguson holding the pipe banner presented by Lieutenant Colonel Jackson, 1962. (LSMA, used with permission)

Her Majesty, Queen Elizabeth, The Queen Mother inspecting the Pipes and Drums, Royal Review, Ballater, July 1962. (LSMA, used with permission)

THE POST-WAR YEARS AT 59 BUCKINGHAM GATE, 1946-1985   285

Drum Major Ted Owens leading the Pipes and Drums on parade, c. 1965. (LSMA, used with permission)

Pipe Major Duncan playing on the top deck of London Bus 'Old Bill' as it enters the Imperial War Museum, London, 30 April 1970. (LSMA, used with permission)

The Government's proposed defence review announcement final came in February 1966, with the aim of passing legislation through Parliament in time for changes to be implemented by 1967. The Territory Army would in future be called the Territorial and Army Volunteer Reserve, consisting of T&AVR categories 'I' through to IV. T&AVR I constituted an 'ever-ready' force known as the Special Army Volunteer Reserve, consisting of six battalions ready for United Nations duties as and when required. T&AVR II necessitated soldiers to sign up for service if required overseas without the previous necessity of a Royal Proclamation and constituted the main body of the new force. T&AVR III constituted 87 lightly equipped infantry units, funded directly by the Home Office rather than the Ministry of Defence, for home defence purposes, while T&AVR IV constituted miscellaneous units such as university officer training corps:

> Reductions on such a scale effectively destroyed the regimental structure upon which the Territorial Army had been built since its foundation in 1908, and inevitably they provoked a good deal of vociferous opposition from the spokesmen of the force.[80]

Despite this 'vociferous opposition,' the changes went ahead and it was announced that the new structure would take effect by April 1967, although the London Scottish were informed that, from 4 January 1967, 59 Buckingham Gate would now house three different units of the new T&AVR force. The T&AVR II unit was named 'G' (The London Scottish Company), 51st Highland Volunteers, consisting of an establishment of five officers and 110 other ranks. Headquarters for this unit was located in Perth, Scotland and the other constituent companies came from the Black Watch, Seaforth Highlanders, Queen's Own Cameron Highlanders, Gordon Highlanders, Argyll and Sutherland Highlanders and the Liverpool Scottish. The two T&AVR III contingents constituted the Battalion Headquarters Company for the newly formed London Yeomanry and Territorials, with headquarters at 59 Buckingham Gate which, at battalion strength, also included 'C' (London Scottish) Company with an establishment of 100 men, alongside companies from the Inns of Court and the City Yeomanry. It was a complicated, ugly, mess, but at least the regimental name lived on.

Unlike many other Territorial regiments, the London Scottish had managed to survive the cull, but was now constituent, company strength units within two very different battalions. One a Highland battalion in the London Scottish tradition and the other reflecting the regiment's geographical location in London. The aim of the regiment from the initial implementation of these changes was to ensure that the T&AVR II Highland company was kept at full strength by transfers as required from the T&AVR III home defence company. While both companies would wear the kilt and retain their Scottish heritage, the London Scottish cap badge would no longer be worn and the regimental colours were no longer eligible to be carried. In fact, the 'regiment,' in the traditional sense within the British army, was no longer a regiment at all.[81]

In addition, neither company had the establishment for a pipe band, and so the London Scottish Pipes and Drums were now, technically, surplus to requirements. The 51st Highland Volunteers did have provision for a pipe band but, with seven composite companies, there were limited spaces available for the approximately 20 pipers and ten drummers in the London Scottish. The London Yeomanry and Territorials had no provision at all. However, the concept of the London Scottish existing without a full Pipes and Drums was not one that many were willing to consider. The pipe

---

80 David French, *Army, Empire, and Cold War: The British Army and Military Policy, 1945-1971* (Oxford: Oxford University Press, 2012), p.293.

81 However, reforms to the traditional regimental system that had begun in the 1950s and that are still taking place within the Army today have radically changed our concept of what constitutes a 'regiment'.

band had always been a fundamental part of London Scottish regimental integrity, and innovative ways of retaining such integrity, a golden thread during this period of immense change, would need to be devised. It was soon realised that, with the regimental colours now gone, the Drum Major's baldric, pipe banners and, most importantly, the side, bass and tenor drums now carried the only representation of regimental heraldry and history, including the London Scottish battle honours earned at such high cost. It was imperative that they be preserved.

The guest of honour at the Hallowe'en dinner in 1966 was Major General D'Avigdor Goldsmid, who was in over-all command of the new Territorial and Army Volunteer Reserve. After listening to the Pipes and Drums perform he stated the following:

> Tonight we have heard your splendid Pipe Band. Are you going to be without your Band? Of course not. You have simply got to support the new organisation so that your Regiment can survive in time of normal situation which is not really so bad as people make out.[82]

It was up to the regiment, then, to find the positives from this new 'normal' and to make the absolute best of the situation. As Commanding Officer Colonel Torrance Law stated in his response to the general's speech, 'We of the Scottish are accustomed to being regarded – even by our friends! – as being, shall I say, "peculiar" and so we are used to doing things a little differently.'[83] The regiment had always had its head and its heart in two places; London and the Highlands. Now this had become a 'peculiar' but geographical and political reality. Thankfully, the regiment's 107 years' experience of doing things differently would ensure that both band and regimental integrity would remain intact.

It was decided early on that the regimental Pipes and Drums had to be preserved, but it was an extremely complicated situation. Limited serving positions were available to London Scottish pipers and drummers in the 51st Highland Volunteer T&AVR II Pipes and Drums and decisions had to be made about who would take up these places. The training commitment to T&AVR II was greater than previously in the TA, and practise with the amalgamated Pipes and Drums meant travelling twice a month to the Black Watch drill hall, Tay Street, Perth. For any remaining pipers and drummers who signed up to the T&AVR III London and Yeomanry Territorials company, all pipe band practise and performances would be outside the remit of the battalion, and so would need to be taken on in a purely voluntary and auxiliary capacity.

As has been described throughout this volume, such 'supernumerary' service had been performed by pipers and drummers in the London Scottish to varying degrees throughout a large proportion of its history and represented a return, in some respects, to the original ethos of the unpaid volunteer who was 'twice the soldier.' The training commitment of T&AVR III was quite low, and the bounty rather small, and it was soon recognised that it would be unattractive for many who may prefer not to re-enlist. It was acknowledged that keeping the door open to those individuals who retained their commitment to the regiment would be advantageous, as would allowing further access to past members, other ex-servicemen and ancillary civilians willing to play on a completely voluntary basis. While this had been the case in small numbers throughout the history of the regiment it would now take on a much more pronounced role.

Added to the complications was the role of Pipe Major de Laspée as Personal Piper to Her Majesty, The Queen Mother. This was an honorary position given personally by Her Majesty to the London Scottish regiment and, while it was a role associated with the Pipe Major of the regiment, it had been given to de Laspée while he was still a pipe sergeant. Pipe Major de Laspée

---

82 *London Scottish Regimental Gazette* (1966), p.227.
83 *London Scottish Regimental Gazette* (1966), p.227.

remained a member of the London Scottish regiment permanent staff but, with the changes in structure and due to his age, he did not reenlist in either of the T&AVR II or III companies. This issue was solved, in the short term at least, with true London Scottish innovation, by making arrangement for two pipe majors:

> Yes – we have the advantage of two Pipe Majors, a perhaps unforeseen advantage of the reorganisation resulting in two companies. Whether or not we also get two Drum Majors we wouldn't know, but no doubt Ted Owens will double around until the situation resolves.[84]

Pipe Sergeant William Ferguson was appointed Pipe Major and joined Drum Major Owens in the 'voluntary' role of leading the regimental Pipes and Drums, while Pipe Major de Laspée took on the honorary title of Regimental Pipe Major and retained his appointment as Personal Piper to The Queen Mother. He would not, generally, turn out with the Pipes and Drums but would perform individually as required at regimental and other events, in addition to his duties at Clarence House.

As for the rest of the band, 'As soon as they were informed that the Pipe Band was to continue, they elected almost to a man to volunteer for AVR II where there is a small establishment for pipers and drummers, and AVR III in order that the military preservation should be maintained.'[85] With a small number of pipers and drummers vying for those few T&AVRII places, another 18 members of the Pipes and Drums joined the T&AVRIII company:

> Led by that old warhorse Sgt Ferguson as Pipe-Major, they will be a great source of entertainment, both on and off duty. Not many readers appreciate that behind those pipes and drums lies a multitude of soldierly qualities, they love their music, but they also like soldiering.[86]

Pipe Major Ferguson was certainly a 'soldier's soldier.' He enlisted in the 2nd Battalion Gordon Highlanders in 1932 before transferring to the 1st Battalion whilst in Singapore, where he first joined the regimental drums and pipes.[87] He had made corporal by the outbreak of war in 1939 and went to France with the 1st Battalion who had been sent to help bolster the 51st (Highland Territorial) Division that was fighting as part of the British Expeditionary Force. He was captured, along with 10,000 other men of 51st Division, on 12 June 1939 at St Valery, France, where the division had been ordered to stay behind and aid the French Army in slowing the German advance to enable major troop evacuations at Le Havre, Dieppe and, most famously, Dunkirk. He was sent to a prisoner of war camp in Poland, where he ran highland dancing classes after a British Sunday newspaper sent him out a set of bagpipes. He planned and executed an escape along with another soldier and was hidden for several weeks on a Polish farm until the two men were able to make their way to Russian lines, where they were mistaken for Germans and nearly killed. Having received a pass from a Russian general, they made their way back to Great Britain via Odessa and the Dardanelles before sailing into Gourock, Glasgow. Ferguson then spent the rest of the war at the Gordon's Depot in Aberdeen. He continued in the Drums and Pipes after the war for three years before being posted to Warminster, then returning to Aberdeen in 1950. He then joined the Highland Light Infantry for a short time before becoming pay sergeant back at the Depot at Brig

---

84 *London Scottish Regimental Gazette* (1967), p.54.
85 *London Scottish Regimental Gazette* (1967), p.189.
86 *London Scottish Regimental Gazette* (1967), p.88.
87 The Gordon Highlanders are almost unique in the Pipe Band world in correctly using the term 'Drums and Pipes' rather than 'Pipes and Drums'. As Drummers were on establishment centuries before Pipers they should, in military parlance, take precedence.

o' Don. Having accepted a job in London, he began playing with the London Scottish Pipes and Drums as a 'guest' before finally being discharged from the regular army and taking over as a pipe sergeant from ex-Pipe Major Bruce Ledgett in 1956 when Ledgett and his family emigrated to Australia. 'Fergie' as he was affectionately known by all ranks, was a popular choice as pipe major and was seen as a steadying hand during this time of sweeping change.

The regiment officially announced that 'While applicants for membership of the Band are encouraged to join AVR, we are prepared to accept, under certain circumstances, members in a civilian capacity'[88] and so it was when the Pipes and Drums appeared at St Columba's Church on 19 March 1967, to lay up the regimental colours:

> The Band was indeed a brave sight, with one Drum Major and probably for the first and last time, two Pipe Majors on a Battalion march. They were made up in strength by at least one Old Comrade and another Old Caley lad, Charles Redmond. Both have helped out in the past. The Old Comrade was the irrepressible Archie McLeod, erstwhile Drum-Sgt, and drumming fit to bust.[89]

Drummer Charles Redman, who worked for Post Office Telecommunications, was one of the most reliable members of the band during this period, and a great supporter long after he retired from playing, but he never served with the London Scottish Regiment. As the band president Roger Linford, himself now a civilian, stated at the time, 'It is through the Pipes and Drums that our Regiment as we know it, soldiers on', and further asked the regimental family to 'Be proud then of your Pipes and Drums – of your typical Scottish Private Army.'[90] Thankfully, such innovative thinking and strong support from the regimental family ensured the future existence and success of the London Scottish Pipes and Drums through into the next millennium.

Difficulties did occur during this early period of complex change but, in true London Scottish fashion, there was always help available to overcome any obstacle. With Drummer Bryan Alderson away at camp with the 51st Highlanders, a stand-in bass drummer was required on 15 July for a Royal British Legion event. The Commanding Officer and ex-band president, Colonel Niekirk stepped in and 'played like a champion!'[91] becoming at least the fourth Commanding Officer to perform with the band. A bass drummer was needed again on 13 August and Sergeant Bob Harman, who would later become the Regimental Secretary, came forward. Harman was a tenor drummer with the London Scottish before he joined the Gordon Highlanders as a regular soldier and 'when he heard we were short …, he stepped in and did a grand job playing the Bass Drum.'[92] Thankfully, Drummer Alderson was available when the Pipes and Drums again went to Dunoon to compete at the Cowal Gathering, later that month.

In September 1967, the French Department of War requested that the London Scottish Pipes and Drums lay a wreath at the Tomb of the Unknown Soldier at L'Arc de Triomphe, in Paris. Such a privilege is usually reserved for visiting Heads of State and as such, this was a major honour and a massive psychological boost to the band and the regiment at this difficult time.

> Piper Murphy carried the wreath; Piper Sutherland was escort and the Scottish were flanked by English 'Bobbies' who volunteered their services. Sgt Smith marched the party forward

---

88 *London Scottish Regimental Gazette* (1967), p.189.
89 *London Scottish Regimental Gazette* (1967), p.75.
90 *London Scottish Regimental Gazette* (1967), p.189.
91 *London Scottish Regimental Gazette* (1967), p.188.
92 *London Scottish Regimental Gazette* (1967), p.188.

to our Regimental march-past; the wreath was laid and one minute's silence observed. The Pipers sounded *The Flowers of the Forest* and salutes were exchanged …. It was a sight and occasion never to be forgotten.[93]

Eleven pipers and nine drummers turned out for annual Hallowe'en dinner that year and 'played superbly and were in great strength, despite being the most voluntary of Scottish volunteers.'[94] They earned the respect of the regiment that evening for fulfilling their role in 'raising morale as intended when things aren't going well, when they could all have stayed away.'[95] In the words of the band president:

> It is traditionally accepted and often a fact that the personnel of a Band of any Regiment give themselves airs and graces, and tend to be spoilt compared with other ranks and appointments … Our lads are no better or worse in this respect. They would not be pipers and drummers if they had not a guid conceit, but if ever they earned the right to swagger that much more, to look at themselves somewhat as a breed apart, they did so at Hallowe'en, 1967.[96]

He would go on to state the following year that 'one thing is for sure, whatever the outcome, good or bad, the pipes and drums of the London Scottish will wear the hodden grey and carry on as though nothing had happened.'[97]

That spirit was required in droves throughout 1968, when further major changes came to the band. In the early part of the year, Drum Major Ted Owens 'retired,' bequeathing his drum major's baldric to the regimental museum. He was coaxed back to play at Hallowe'en and church parade that year but 'We did not see the going of Ted, he seemed to disappear with no farewell. Maybe he had a grievance, we never saw him again.'[98] Drum Major Owens had a sometimes-testing relationship with Pipe Major de Laspée which, to a certain degree, related to pay and military respect. De Laspée's official rank whilst serving was as warrant officer second-class, while Drum Major Owens rank was as a sergeant. When on parade, the drum major is in overall charge of the band, and Owens felt this disparity in rank made it difficult for him to retain his authority. The Commanding Officer arranged for Owens to receive the 'unofficial' rank of WOII but without the pay, which may have helped to some degree but still did not level the playing field. Then, when the T&AVR changes came into effect, Owens completely lost his rank and pay while de Laspée continued to be supported by the regiment. Whatever the reason for his departure, it deprived the regiment of a loyal servant and left the Pipes and Drums without a figurehead.

By April, the band was also without a pipe major. At the band supper on 28 April, Piper Withey was in the chair after 15 years with the band, and 'backed up, of course, by his better half L/Cpl Bryan Alderson.'[99] It was reported here that:

> During the evening, when the speeches were being made, the Band President informed us that Pipe Major W. Ferguson had resigned from the London Scottish Pipe Band, for domestic and health reasons. It came right out of the blue and was quite a shock for most people.

---

93 *London Scottish Regimental Gazette* (1968), p.21.
94 *London Scottish Regimental Gazette* (1967), p.235.
95 *London Scottish Regimental Gazette* (1967), p.237.
96 *London Scottish Regimental Gazette* (1967), p.237.
97 *London Scottish Regimental Gazette* (1968), p.46.
98 Alderson, *MacNamara's Band to Drum Major*, p.11.
99 *London Scottish Regimental Gazette* (1968), p.105.

> Who is going to sing 'My Big Kilmarnock Bonnet' and the 'Miles to Dundee' is anybody's guess.
>
> 'Fergie' will be greatly missed and it will be a long, long time before someone with his personality and powers of persuasion joins the ranks of the Band.

Sergeant Ferguson continued serving for a short time in the T&AVR III company, occasionally playing with the band when they were short on numbers, before his health deteriorated further.

The Pipes and Drums were left rudderless at this important period but Pipe Sergeant Davie Duncan stepped up to take charge of the pipers, with Drum Sergeant Crowley taking control of the drummers, ably assisted by Corporal Drummer Alderson. Their commitment was of great importance as high profile military engagements and, of most benefit to the band fund, fee-earning civilian jobs that continued to come in. For example, on 15 September the Pipes and Drums went to Heathrow Airport to send of the British Olympic team for the games in Mexico. Their performance in the pouring rain was aired on BBC and ITV news broadcasts.

Hallowe'en saw the drum section bring more innovation to the proceedings by deconstructing their drums and installing different coloured lights inside to illuminate their performance, which received 'tumultuous acclaim.'[100] In his speech, Colonel Niekirk commented that 'In talking about the Regiment there is one other part of it that deserves special mention and that is our own very private army, the Pipes and Drums.' He went on to thank Pipe Sergeant Duncan for holding things together when 'Fergie' left, and finished up by saying:

> I think the best tribute I can pay to the success of Pipe-Sergeant Duncan's work is to ask him now to come forward and allow me to give him the insignia of Pipe Major.[101]

Pipe Major Duncan had been a radar mechanic in the RAF, before moving to London and joining the London Scottish in 1959. He worked for aircraft company Handley Page and then for British European Airways. With no pipe band on establishment, he served as an infantry NCO in 'G' Company in addition to his duties as Pipe Major, for which he received no pay or 'official' recognition.

The year was rounded off by another performance at the Royal Albert Hall for the National Festival of Remembrance, where the Pipes and Drums played in the presence of their Honorary Colonel, Her Majesty, The Queen Mother. The BBC commentator, Raymond Baxter, paid tribute to the London Scottish Pipes and Drums and their continued loyalty to their regiment despite their unestablished existence, and was quoted in the *Regimental Gazette* stating that they had been:

> Left with virtually nothing but their own determination … to carry them through and adding words to the effect that if he knew the London Scottish and its determination, this would be by no means the last occasion our Pipes and Drums would perform in the Festival.[102]

Indeed, throughout this difficult time, the London Scottish Pipes and Drums not only managed to survive but, as regimental family and friends rallied round, performances at 'Hallowe'en and the Festival of Remembrance and Church Parade saw the biggest Band since the war.'[103] Despite this,

---

100 *London Scottish Regimental Gazette* (1968), p.229.
101 *London Scottish Regimental Gazette* (1968), p.229.
102 *London Scottish Regimental Gazette* (1968), p.219.
103 *London Scottish Regimental Gazette* (1968), p.220.

however, their incredible hard work, and that of the London Scottish Regiment in general during this period, was about to be undermined once again.

In January 1969, the new Commanding Officer, Colonel Alan Bovington, reported that 'for the second time in as many years the Territorial Army and with it the London Scottish has again been cut.'[104] The Home Office had decided that, after two short years, it was no longer prepared to fund T&AVR III and so, just two months later on 31 March, the London Scottish Company of the London and Yeomanry Territorials, containing the vast majority of the members of the Pipes and Drums, would be completely disbanded. This meant that there was now no provision and pay of any kind for any members of the band except those few who made it into the 51st Highland Pipes and Drums. The entire T&AVR III battalion was to be replaced by a cadre of three officers, two NCOs and two other ranks, who were at least all London Scots, wearing the London Scottish uniform and cap badge, but it was another huge blow for both regiment and band.

Colonel Torrance Law, who was shortly to hand over his position as Regimental Colonel to Colonel G.F. Maxwell stated:

> Our Pipes and Drums certainly merit our pride and gratitude and will undoubtedly play an ever-increasing part in keeping the name of the London Scottish to the fore, nor will we allow their continued existence to be jeopardised for lack of funds.[105]

However, despite the reassurances of senior officers within the regiment to ensure the survival of the band, fears continued that the London Scottish company of the 51st Highland Volunteers might themselves also face the axe. In 1969, 'G' Company was the lowest strength of all the 51st Highland companies and the future looked increasingly bleak.

These further disincentives had a marked effect on membership of the Pipes and Drums, which quickly went from being the largest band since the war to 'a serious state, being composed of private volunteers who received nothing in the way of pay other than from some engagements.'[106] As a way of killing two birds with one stone, work began in an attempt to get the band re-established onto the army list as a military band, for which there was provision, and which would bring the additional benefit of increasing numbers in 'G' Company. However, the War Office concluded, in their infinite wisdom, that Pipes and Drums do not constitute a military band and so were not eligible.

The London Scottish contribution to the 51st Highland Volunteers Pipes and Drums at this time consisted of Pipers Walker, Rennie, Todd and Knox, along with Bass Drummer Alderson, who continued to wear London Scottish uniform, despite a change of cap badge, along with a change of headgear for Alderson who was presented with a feather bonnet. They joined the remainder of the 51st band and battalion to travel to St Valery for a parade on 6 June 1969 to commemorate 25 years since the 1944 incarnation of the 51st (Highland) Division liberated the town after D-Day and avenged the surrender of their 1940 forebearers four years earlier. The Pipes and Drums Beat Retreat at Bayeux Cathedral and an additional ceremony took place at the Highland Division Memorial on the cliff tops overlooking the town. It was an enormous shame that ex-Pipe Major Ferguson was no longer with the band and thus unable to perform in the town where he had been captured in 1940.

---

104 *London Scottish Regimental Gazette* (1969), p.3.
105 *London Scottish Regimental Gazette* (1969), p.27.
106 *London Scottish Regimental Gazette* (1969), p.120.

Hallowe'en saw the announcement of a new band president, Lieutenant Rutherford-Young, who was unofficially assisted by Archie 'Stiffie' MacLeod, and with a new Drum Major after the appointment of Corporal Drummer Bryan Alderson:

> The Drums from their ranks have produced the new Drum Major, Bryan Alderson, a step in the right direction, for although his skill and dexterity with the Bass Drum have been admired by many, he is but the second Drum Major to come from our drum section since the 1914-18 War. It is not any old bod that can handle the Mace with efficiency and head the parade with dignity and calm authority.[107]

His first major parade was 'the TA massed band retreat at Stirling Castle. It was the first time for me as senior Drum Major. I hadn't a clue what I was doing but managed to bluff my way through it.'[108]

Drum Major Alderson began his military musical journey as a bugler, then side drummer, in the Twickenham Sea Cadets. He was called up for National Service in 1951 and became a drummer with the Royal Army Service Corps Staff Band, with whom he toured around Britain and appeared on the BBC show *Music While You Work*. On completing his two year's National Service he spent a further two years with 901 Company, Royal Army Service Corps (TA). In 1956, he wrote to the London Scottish and was invited to join the Pipes and Drums by Captain Niekirk. He worked as a mounted police officer with the Metropolitan Police and was given special permission to join 'G' Company, 51st Highland.

On 30 April 1970, Pipe Major Duncan played on the top deck of B43 'Old Bill', an open-topped London bus of the type that had been used to ferry London Scottish troops to Messines in 1914, as it was laid up at the Imperial War Museum. In August, he also took the Pipes and Drums on another visit to Dunoon for the Cowal Gathering, where the band led the parade of bands into the arena for the march past and prize giving. Finances were tight and so the band stayed again at the old Argyll's drill hall, which was now an American Post Exchange (PX), where, to save money, Piper John Spoore and Drummer Charles Redman cooked all the meals. In November that year, Piper Spoore and Piper Baigrie spent five days in Austria at events run by the British Board of Trade, before joining the band for the traditional end of year events at church parade and the Lord Major's Show.

By this time, 'G' Company, London Scottish was up to strength and was given permission to recruit a further 20 percent over its establishment to make up for lower numbers in other companies within the 51st Highland Volunteers. This increase in numbers provided spaces for five pipers and three drummers from the London Scottish, up from four and one respectively. In fact, the London Scottish commitment to the 51st Pipes and Drums, along with that from the Liverpool Scottish, increasingly provided the backbone to the band and the provision for London Scottish pipers and drummers in 'G' Company would continue to steadily increase. Despite the change of cap badge, London Scottish pipers and drummers continued to wear the Hodden Grey, much as each battalion Pipes and Drums of the Royal Regiment of Scotland continue to wear their antecedent regimental uniforms when performing today. This not only helped to keep the regimental spirit alive, but also acted as a walking recruitment poster for the London Scottish.

1971 was a busy year for the Pipes and Drums, including a T&AVR parade in Hyde Park, a Royal British Legion parade along Whitehall to Horse Guards, the Festival of London, a televised appearance at the centenary re-enactment of Queen Victoria's opening of the NRA ranges at

---

107 *London Scottish Regimental Gazette* (1969), p.257.
108 Alderson, *MacNamara's Band to Drum Major*, p.14.

Wimbledon Common and a performance at the national remembrance parade at the Cenotaph on Remembrance Sunday with the Scots and Irish Guards. The main event of the year, however, was the 'Big Blaw' on 7 June on Horse Guards Parade, involving a massed pipes and drums consisting of the majority of the remaining British army pipe bands. The rows of pipes and drums made quite an impression as they marched from Wellington Barracks to the parade square:

> The sight of that massed Band moving down Birdcage Walk on its way to Horseguards, shaking the summer air with a mellow throb, kissing the sky with silver shrill and lazy goldenskirl, the swinging patchwork of many tartans, punctuated with the hodden grey into which they all resolve to you as a London Scot – the actual ceremony of Beating Retreat on the most famous military parade ground of pageantry and military pride in the world – is all too overwhelming for the senses.[109]

A week after this event, the band played at the Royal Albert Hall for the Hundred Pipers Pageant in aid of the Gurkhas Appeal. Unfortunately, Drum Major Alderson's wife mistakenly took the family car with the regimental mace still in the boot and so the regimental museum had to be raided to give one last outing for Drum Major Goodman's Victorian mace. Towards the end of the year, Drum Sergeant Crowley was seen off at Waterloo Station by nine members of the band as he left to travel to New Zealand for a few months. As an ex-King's Own Scottish Borderer, they played the train away to *All the Blue Bonnets are Over the Border* before finishing with *Heilan' Laddie*. The band had originally been told they would not be allowed to play in the station, but luckily one of the British Transport policemen on duty that day happened to be Piper Baigrie, who arranged for the rules to be bent.

The overall professionalism, quality and enhanced numbers of the London Scottish Pipes and Drums was to pay off in 1972, when both Pipe Major Duncan and Drum Major Alderson were asked to become Pipe and Drum Majors respectively of the 51st Highland Volunteers. While Pipe Major Duncan was able to continue to wear Hodden Grey, Drum Major Alderson was approached by the band president of the 51st, Major Halford MacLeod, about whether he would be willing to wear the feather bonnet and uniform of the Black Watch. Drum Major Alderson was happy to acquiesce and so the London Scottish took the two senior roles within the 51st Highland Pipes and Drums for the first time. They also contributed more pipers and drummers, with 11 men, three higher than the official establishment, performing with the band. It was a hectic schedule for these men who took on the infantry responsibilities of 'G' Company in addition to piping, drumming, tuition and administration for both the 51st and London Scottish pipe bands. Thankfully, there were more than 20 additional 'volunteers' in the London Scottish Pipes and Drums to help carry the burden.

Later during 1972, 'one of the most hilarious jobs the Band has ever known'[110] took place when, at very short notice, ten London Scottish pipers and drummers flew to Scotland for the filming of an advert for Seagram 100 Pipers whisky. The film company had originally employed the services of pipers from three, Grade One Scottish civilian competition bands, but one pulled out at the last minute and 'in desperation the film company asked if we could make up enough to fulfil the contract even if they were drummers as the film would be dubbed anyway.'[111] Filming took place over four days at the picturesque thirteenth century Eilean Donan Castle, north of Fort William and in the mountains on and around Ben Nevis. The film company had everyone

---

109 *London Scottish Regimental Gazette* (1971), p.108.
110 *London Scottish Regimental Gazette* (1972), p.89.
111 Personal correspondence with Piper John Haynes, 27 March 2020.

up at 0400 hours, dressed all the men as pipers, and then took shots of them marching through fields, across bridges, on the mountain, and even in small boats on the loch, while they pretended to play.[112] They were given feather bonnets that 'on inspection were found to be motorcycle crash helmets covered in feathers – last used in the film *The Battle of Waterloo*! [sic] You can imagine the hilarity!'[113] Filming was a litany of disasters and was not, by all accounts, taken very seriously by the attending cast, who were not even able to drown their sorrows in the whisky being advertised because the film crew hid the several crates that had arrived on set for their own indulgence.

On 18 May 1973, the London Scottish Regiment were invited for an official visit to Dainville, near Arras, France, to receive the Freedom of the Town and to officially rename the main thoroughfare 'Rue du London Scottish Regiment' in honour of the 1st Battalion's role in the area during the First World War. The Pipes and Drums were billeted in the local school for the weekend and Beat Retreat in the town centre on Saturday evening, before marching in the main parade which took place on the Sunday. They played at the French war memorial before the official renaming ceremony, where Regimental Colonel Maxwell unveiled a commemorative plaque. Later they moved on to the local cemetery which contains the graves of 13 London Scottish soldiers.

27 October saw Drummers Eric Newton and Tom Muir join four other London Scots for a week-long guard mount by the 51st Highlander Volunteers at Edinburgh Castle. While they were away, the rest of the Pipes and Drums performed as usual at the annual Hallowe'en dinner. Despite being two drummers down, the Officer Commanding stated that 'For a unit that does not have a band on establishment, the strength of the Pipes and Drums on this parade was remarkable.'[114]

In June the following year, Pipe Sergeant John Spoore led the 51st Highlander Volunteers Pipes and Drums, including four other pipers and five drummers from the London Scottish, to Beat Retreat on the Edinburgh Castle esplanade. Pipe Major Duncan was in Canada with Pipe Major de Laspée, where they played with the Toronto Scottish Pipes and Drums in front of 23,000 people as Her Majesty, The Queen Mother presented new colours to the regiment.

In October 1974, the band took a slight change in musical direction when they were approached by the Glasgow glam rock outfit, The Sensational Alex Harvey Band to perform on their third album, titled *The Impossible Dream*, which was to be recorded at the Apple Studios in London, made famous by The Beatles. The Pipes and Drums were specifically involved with the last track on the album, *Anthem*, which was released as a single and would become the signature track which The Sensational Alex Harvey Band used as a finale in their live performances. Pipers John Gilligan and Alexander 'Sandy' Baigrie feature on the album cover, sitting in a cinema, and the band and both pipers would later accompany the group on a tour of Germany. The Pipes and Drums also joined the group for three appearances at the London Palladium and played with them two years in a row at the Reading Festival. After living a wild rock and roll lifestyle, Alex Harvey died in 1982 at just 42 years of age. Piper Baigrie would play at his funeral.

Back on more common ground, the Pipes and Drums performed for Her Majesty, The Queen Mother the following year at the T&AVR Review of all London units, which took place in Hyde Park on 6 April 1975. The London Scottish Pipes and Drums, 30 strong, including Pipe Major de Laspée, led the parade, with 50 London Scottish soldiers forming the Guard of Honour. Both Guard and Pipes and Drums were inspected by the Queen Mother.

This event would prove to be Pipe Major de Laspée's last major parade with the London Scottish and as Her Majesty's Personal Piper, as he shortly announced his retirement after 22 years' service in that role. He was awarded the Royal Victorian Medal by Her Majesty in recognition of his

---

112 *Seagram's 100 Pipers Scotch – 1970s* <https://www.youtube.com/watch?v=BM3NJ22iL_g>
113 Personal Correspondence with Piper John Haynes, 27 March 2020
114 *London Scottish Regimental Gazette*, (1973), p.195.

Her Majesty, The Queen Mother speaking with her Personal Piper, Honorary Regimental Pipe Major de Laspee on his last parade, T&AVR Review, Hyde Park, London, 6 April 1975. (LSMA, used with permission)

The Pipes and Drums of the 1st Battalion, 51st Highland Volunteers, Thetford Camp, 1980. (LSMA, used with permission)

Drummers before the Regimental Church Parade, November 1978. (LSMA, used with permission)

Presentation of new side drums and pipe banners by Her Majesty, The Queen Mother, at Regimental Headquarters, 4 April 1979. (LSMA, used with permission)

outstanding service, before moving to Devon to enjoy his retirement. Pipe Major Duncan was duly appointed in his place and, with this hand-over, the tradition of the Personal Piper to The Queen Mother being Pipe Major of the London Scottish was finally and firmly established. The Pipes and Drums performed again for Her Majesty when she visited 59 Buckingham Gate on December 4th to celebrate her 40-year connection with the regiment. A letter from her equerry the following day stated that, 'The Pipes and Drums, who played most beautifully, illustrated so well by their bearing and turnout the 'esprit de corps' which was so evident throughout the evening.'[115]

Yet another first for the Pipes and Drums came in 1975, when Drum Sergeant Crowley and Drummer Michael 'Mickey' Powell were chosen as the first two Territorial Army soldiers to attend the six-week Army School of Bagpipe Music and Highland Drumming drummers course at Edinburgh Castle. The proficiency of their drumming skills earned glowing reviews and opened the doors for future attendees from the Territorial Army.

Further compliments for the Pipes and Drums came after the regimental visit to Messines and Ypres over the weekend of 24-26 September 1976. On the first day, the regiment formed-up in the main square in Ypres to be inspected by the British Ambassador to Belgium, after which 'the incomparable Pipes and Drums added lustre to this memorable occasion with a magnificent performance of Beating Retreat.'[116] The pipe band then led the regiment to the Menin Gate for the famous Last Post Ceremony, where they played under the arch. Sunday saw a parade to the London Scottish war memorial outside Messines but, in the words of the Officer Commanding, 'I think we will remember, in particular, the Pipes and Drums as they came through the Menin Gate arch.'[117]

The Queen's Silver Jubilee celebrations in 1977 saw the 51st Highlander Volunteers Pipes and Drums perform at another 'Big Blaw,' this time at the Palace of Holyroodhouse with the massed bands of the Scottish Division. They also performed at a Royal Review of Reserve forces at Wembley Stadium and again at a Beating Retreat at Edinburgh Castle. Camp that year for the 51st Highlander Volunteers was at Devizes, where their Commanding Officer, Colonel Graham Murray, who was an avid piper, filled in the blank space in the second row of pipers and played with the band at reveille almost every morning.

> This was a great boost to our morale but it posed some interesting problems for 'Drummie' on how to dismiss his Pipes and Drums when it included the CO. A drill was evolved which might or might not have satisfied the Guards, but which certainly proved to us that Drum-Major Bryan Alderson richly deserves his Silver Jubilee Medal; our congratulations to him.[118]

Long-serving Piper Allan Raich, three-time winner of the MacLeod Medal, accompanied a 168 Brigade, Second World War veterans' trip to the battlefields of Italy, where he played during commemorative events at Anzio, Minturno and Monte Cassino.

On 4 April 1979, Her Majesty, The Queen Mother visited 59 Buckingham Gate to present new drums and replacement pipe banners to the London Scottish Pipes and Drums in commemoration of her 80th Birthday. The drums were gifted by Mrs Marian Miles whose husband Peter had served during the Second World War, and by the Officers' Mess, Sergeants' Mess and the Regimental Masonic Lodge, who also gifted three silver bugles representing the three London Scottish recipients of the Victoria Cross. The pipe banners came again from the cities of Edinburgh, Perth,

---

115 *London Scottish Regimental Gazette* (1976), p.16.
116 *London Scottish Regimental Gazette* (1976), p.103.
117 *London Scottish Regimental Gazette* (1976), p.92.
118 *London Scottish Regimental Gazette* (1977), p.59.

Glasgow, Dundee and Aberdeen and helped to renew the regiment's links with those cities. After presenting the drums and banners, Her Majesty gave a speech which included the following:

> Bands, whether Military or Pipes and Drums, are such an important part of any Regiment, and for the London Scottish to be able to carry the banners of Cities and Districts of Scotland, is a constant reminder of the links the Regiment has always strived to keep with its heritage.
>
> You may be smaller in establishment today than you were in the past, but I have no doubt at all that if called upon you would acquit yourself with just as much distinction as your predecessors.[119]

Camp that year for the 51st Highland Pipes and Drums took place in Germany, as they had been invited to participate in the Berlin Military Tattoo. The band was flown out by the RAF to Hanover, then entrained for travel through East Germany to Berlin, where they stayed at Smut Barracks next to Spandau Prison which, at the time, held Rudolf Hess. The tattoo, which, according to Drum Major Alderson, was 'far and away the best tattoo I have ever been involved in or seen,'[120] took place at the 12,000-seater Deutschlandhalle and included 36 different military, pipe, bugle and corps of drum bands during 12 sold out performances spaced over two weeks. The London Scottish pipers and drummers were given the opportunity to spend a day in East Berlin, passing through Checkpoint Charlie, and Drum Major Alderson, Corporal Drummer Powell and Drummer Tam Muir wangled a ride in an Army Air Corps helicopter which took them along the Berlin Wall. During the final performance, when the RAF Regiment Queen's Colour Squadron Drill Team fired their last volley on their way out of the arena, members of the Pipes and Drums threw up feathers from an old pillow, much to the amusement of the crowd.

The London Scottish Pipes and Drums were also invited to perform at the Royal Tournament that year, with The Queen Mother attending as Guest of Honour on 24 July. At the finale, representation from all the military units of which Her Majesty was Colonel-in-Chief; The London Scottish, The Black Watch, the Toronto Scottish and the Black Watch of Canada, marched into the arena:

> Suddenly, from the Scottish ranks at the back, David Duncan moved forward to the Royal Box. The lights dimmed apart from a spotlight on him. He played a tune. *Castle of Mey*, specially composed by Major Duncan Beat, Director of Music, Scots Guards (and ex Band Master, Black Watch) for the occasion.[121]

At the reception afterwards, Pipe Major Duncan presented The Queen Mother with a framed score of the tune which had been beautifully hand-written by Pipe Sergeant Spoore. Two weeks later, Pipe Major Duncan was joined by ex-Regimental Pipe Major de Laspée to play for Her Majesty at Clarence House on her birthday.

Later that year, Colonel Murray decided that the Military Band and Pipes and Drums of the 51st Highlander Volunteers should record a long-playing album. While it may or may not have been, in the words of Drum Major Alderson, 'the worst Military LP ever produced,'[122] it was, nevertheless, an interesting and enjoyable experience for all involved.

---

119 *London Scottish Regimental Gazette* (1979), p.29.
120 Alderson, *MacNamara's Band to Drum Major*, p.18.
121 *London Scottish Regimental Gazette* (1980), p.55.
122 Alderson, *MacNamara's Band to Drum Major*, p.16.

1981 saw Pipe Major Duncan perform at the Royal Premiere of the film *Chariots of Fire*, while Lance Corporal Piper Ian King was appointed as the Honorary Piper of the Caledonian Society of London and Piper Christopher Macpherson performed on television at the centenary birthday celebrations for a London Scottish soldier. The Pipes and Drums Beat Retreat at Lancaster House for a Foreign and Commonwealth Office party, whilst The Queen Mother watched from across the road at Clarence House. 24 June, the Pipes and Drums of both the Toronto Scottish and the 48th Highlanders of Canada visited 59 Buckingham Gate prior to their performance at the Wembley Military Musical Pageant. A massed band of nearly 50 pipers and drummers performed in the London Scottish drill hall to a large and very appreciative crowd.

Stalwart ex-Drum Sergeant Archie MacLeod died on September 5th, with Piper Cowie and Drum Sergeant Crowley playing the lament and reveille at his funeral. 'Stiffie' MacLeod had first joined the London Scottish 67 years earlier in 1924 and his enormous contribution to the Pipes and Drums continued until the very last days of his life. It is true to say that his contributions through the six decades he was involved with the band were incomparable. A barstool to commemorate his dedicated service to the regiment was commissioned and, to this day, sits at his favourite spot at the end of the canteen bar.

The dramatic events of the Falklands War took most of the time and attention of the nation in 1982 but, due to legislation which meant units could not be called up individually, the Territorial Army had very little involvement in the conflict itself or in relieving pressure on the British Army on the Rhine (BAOR). Victory over Argentina did, however, have a markedly positive impact on national and regimental recruitment over the following years.

Another long-serving member of the Pipes and Drums, Drum Sergeant Crowley, celebrated 30 years with the Pipes and Drums in 1983 and, on February 5th, a secret party was organised for him by Drummer Redman at regimental headquarters. Some 170 guests watched as Drum Major Alderson made a presentation from all serving members of the Pipes and Drums. Ex-Regimental Pipe Major de Laspée, who had been his Pipe Major in both the King's Own Scottish Borders and in the London Scottish, did the same for former and non-serving members. Over 40 pipers and drummers then took to the floor to play in his honour. The drum section from the Pride of Murray pipe band, for whom Crowley also played, performed a drum salute, before the London Scottish drum section performed their own Salute *Men of Messines* which had been written by Crowley. It was a fitting tribute to another member of the Pipes and Drums who had made such a significant contribution.

In July 1983, the Pipes and Drums of the 51st Highland Volunteers joined the Royal Scots Dragoon Guards, Scots Guards, Gordon Highlanders, King's Own Scottish Borders, Royal Tank Regiment and five pipers from the Toronto Scottish in a massed pipes and drums at the Royal Tournament. This massed band paraded along The Mall on Sunday 10 July to publicise the event, with Her Majesty, The Queen attending on July 18th and The Queen Mother on the following evening.

Pipe Sergeant Spoore, Corporal Piper Baigrie and Pipers Macpherson and Rose bagged the trip of a lifetime in 1984 when the regiment was asked to provide pipers at a surprise birthday party in Saudi Arabia. The party was arranged for the British Ambassador, Sir James Craig, and was hosted by Crown Prince Zeid Sudairi, one of the richest men in the world. The four London Scottish pipers were flown out to Jeddah aboard the prince's private jet, where they were met by a cadillac limousine which drove them to the five-star Sands Hotel. No expense was spared during their trip, and they were taken on a guided tour of Jeddah, including lunch with the Sheikh where they received personal gifts, as well as on a boat trip on the Red Sea. The garden party for Sir James was given at the Crown Prince's 'beach hut,' where the London Scottish pipers were presented to the prince himself on arrival:

The four pipers were kept out of sight and well looked after by the son of Prince Sudairi, who had just passed out of Sandhurst, as of course did Prince Sudairi a few years ago. At the given signal, the pipes were inflated and we made our way through the jasmine and into the garden.[123]

The 70th anniversary of the Battle of Messines was commemorated on the weekend of 27-29 July with the first regimental pilgrimage to Belgium since 1976. Eleven pipers and nine drummers formed the band which played at memorial ceremonies in Ypres, Tyne Cot cemetery and Messines. The Pipes and Drums then Beat Retreat at the Menin Gate, where the drumming buglers played reveille after the Last Post, and played in Messines before, during and after the parade to the London Scottish memorial on Messines Ridge. Pipe Sergeant Spoore played his new composition *The Burning Mill at Messines*, which he had written especially for the memorial parade.

The Pipes and Drums entered 1985 on a high, after 16 years of stability and development under the dual control of Pipe Major Duncan and Drum Major Alderson. The band itself now consisted of 21 pipers, ten of whom were serving in the 51st Highland Volunteers, and 12 drummers, five of whom were also serving. Between them, the serving members made up nearly half of the entire 51st Highland Pipes and Drums. Many of the non-serving members had been with the Pipes and Drums in its former battalion strength days and some, including Pipers Cowie, Withey and Duff were veterans of the Second World War. Others, like Pipers Baigrie, Drum Sergeant Crowley and Drummer Redman had decades of service with the band, whilst Pipe Sergeant Spoore, Corporal Piper King and Piper Macpherson all went on to become Pipe Majors of the regiment, while Corporal Drummer Powell later became Drum Major. The drum section even included a serving officer, in Second Lieutenant Geoff MacAdam. Other characters like Corporal Piper Gordon Skilling and tenor Drummer Patrick King added weight to an incredibly experienced and professional Pipes and Drums, of whom the regiment could be justifiably proud. The commitment of these men, often over many decades, had ensured the survival of the Pipes and Drums during the most difficult of times. Many of these men received no pay and no plaudits or medals for their service and would often have to put their hands in their own pockets to cover expenses, replacement kit and practise equipment. The London Scottish Regiment was lucky indeed to warrant such dedication.

In addition to their robust composition, the quality of the pipe band's performances was also first class, as was evident when the Toronto Scottish visited on 30 April 1984:

> The highlight of the evening was the combined parade of the Pipes and Drums of both Regiments. … they gave a superb display of quick and slow marching, which drew tremendous applause from the appreciative onlookers massed on the balcony and on any available space on the Drill Hall floor. One could have wished for more, and more.[124]

It was fitting, then, that in Her Majesty, Queen Elizabeth, The Queen Mother's 50th anniversary year as Honorary Colonel of the London Scottish Regiment, the foundations of the Pipes and Drums were so strong. It also proved a particularly appropriate point for Pipe Major Duncan to retire and hand over to his successor, in good faith, a band that was in such excellent health.

The Queen Mother visited 59 Buckingham Gate for the last time on 4 June 1985, for an anniversary dinner. Here she presented Pipe Major Duncan with the Silver Medal of the Royal Victorian Order, Pipe Major Alderson with a second clasp to his Territorial Efficiency Medal and Drummer Muir with his own Territorial Efficiency Medal. Pipe Major de Laspée was in attendance as Pipe Major Duncan handed over the dual appointments of Pipe Major, the London Scottish Regiment

---

123 *London Scottish Regimental Gazette*, (1984), p.45.
124 *London Scottish Regimental Gazette* (1985), p.29.

and Personal Piper to Her Majesty, The Queen Mother, to Pipe Sergeant Spoore, who would officially begin both appointments the following day. Pipe Major Spoore's debut came a few weeks later, on Thursday 25 July at a royal dinner party, where he played for the first time in his official capacity alongside the Sovereign's Piper, Pipe Major Brian MacRae.

Pipe Major John Spoore had served with the 1st Battalion, Gordon Highlanders from 1957 to 1963 and had then spent nearly six years on 'A' Emergency Reserve after leaving the regular army. He joined the London Scottish and 'G' Company, 51st Highland Volunteers in February 1968, where he served in a variety of roles including recruit training platoon sergeant and battalion light machine gun instructor. His civilian role was as a Sergeant in the Metropolitan Police, which meant that both the Pipe Major and Drum Major of the London Scottish were now serving police officers. The Pipes and Drums had entered the post-war period within the Gordon Highlanders, and it was apt that this latest chapter of their history should come to a close with an ex-Gordon Highlander now in charge of the band.

The decades after the Second World War had been full of both extreme highs and lows for the London Scottish Regiment and for their Pipes and Drums. The initial rebuilding of the Pipes and Drums echoed the post-war rebuilding of the regiment and the band fulfilled an increasingly important part in regimental life during the enormous challenges brought about by the cessation of the battalion and the forming of the 51st Highland Volunteers and T&AVR III companies in the 1960s. With the loss of their regimental colours, the Pipes and Drums became the very heart, soul and repository of regimental history and tradition. They carried the battle honours, Hodden Grey uniform and London Scottish cap badge with them on each performance through these difficult times and preserved them for the future. Without the Pipes and Drums to keep them alive, these regimental assets may well have simply become museum pieces.

Moreover, without the willingness of many pipers and drummers to loyally remain with the band on a purely voluntary basis, the London Scottish Pipes and Drums could never have survived, while the serving members who played with the 51st Highland Volunteers band ensured that 'G' (The London Scottish) Company were a major force within their Pipes and Drums. Vain hopes of returning to battalion strength were firmly in the past by 1985, but the future of the regiment seemed well established in the 51st Highland Volunteers. With numbers well above establishment, and 'G' Company making up a large minority of the entire 51st Battalion, the foundations were in place for a settled future for the London Scottish Regiment. The loyalty and good will in such evidence from so many pipers and drummers also provided the foundations for a settled future for the regimental Pipes and Drums.

The foundations of the regimental headquarters building at 59 Buckingham Gate were, however, not so sturdy and, just one year prior to the 100th anniversary of its construction, the building was deemed unsafe and had to be closed at very short notice. While hard work, ingenuity and persistence through the most difficult of times had secured the future of the regiment and of the Pipes and Drums, the ground was, quite literally this time, pulled out from under their very feet.

8

95 Horseferry Road to the London Guards 1986-2022

The soldiering is rewarding and the stuff this pipe band does is unbelievable. The pipe band has been one of the defining features of the London Scottish since its foundation over 150 years ago. Long may that tradition continue.

Piper Andrew Parsons
The London Scottish Regiment Gazette 2011[1]

With their regimental headquarters at 59 Buckingham Gate condemned as unsafe, a temporary home had to be found for the London Scottish while final plans were prepared for a permanent replacement building. The old drill hall of the 4th London Regiment (Royal Fusiliers), on Wenlock Street in Hoxton, North London, was proposed and subsequently housed the London Scottish from 1986 to 1988. Interestingly, the 4th London's were the only English regiment with no Scottish or Irish connections to have had a pipe band during the First World War.[2] It was fitting that, after its sequestration, the London Scottish Pipes and Drums brought the music of the Highlands back to the building for the first time in many years.

Despite safety concerns, the Pipes and Drums were allowed back into 59 Buckingham Gate one last time on the evening of Saturday 23 January 1986 for a Ladies' Night dinner. 'Such an evening does not close; it gently merges into Sunday morning – very pleasant and very successful.'[3]

Recruitment during this period of temporary homelessness was extremely difficult for both 'G' (London Scottish) Company, 51st Highland Volunteers and for the band. Both sections assisted each other through this challenging time with the Pipes and Drums playing at a 'G' Company recruiting event in Hyde Park on 18 April and 'G' Company attending both the Richmond and the Harpenden Highland Games where the Pipes and Drums were competing. The most high-profile event of the year, however, came on 7 June with the pipe band once again performing with an all-army massed pipes and drums at Beating Retreat on Horse Guards Parade. 'The Pipes and Drums put on a splendid show, but then they always do, and we have run out of complimentary comments on their behalf.'[4] A month later, on 4 July, the serving pipers and drummers of the London Scottish paraded as a component of the Pipes and Drums of the 51st Highland Volunteers at North Inch Park, Perth, Scotland in the presence of Queen Elizabeth, The Queen Mother,

---

1 *The London Scottish Regiment Gazette* (2011), p.23.
2 See F. Clive Grimwade, *The War History of the 4th Battalion, the London Regiment (Royal Fusiliers) 1914-1919* (London: Good Press, 2019), p.237.
3 *London Scottish Regimental Gazette* (1986), p.46.
4 *London Scottish Regimental Gazette* (1986), p.107.

where Her Majesty presented new colours to the battalion. Drum Major Alderson and Pipe Major Spoore led the band.

The band president at this time was Captain David Rankin-Hunt, who would go on to become Regimental Colonel of the London Scottish Regiment. Drum Major Alderson recalls an incident during this period during company training in Thetford Forest when Captain Rankin-Hunt, Corporal Piper Macpherson and himself were digging a trench. 'At that moment the SPSI decided to liven things up a bit and decided that we should have some gas to test the Pipes and Drums.'[5] Unfortunately, only Captain Rankin-Hunt was carrying his gas mask and when he turned to ask the other two to buddy-check his mask, he realised they were not wearing them. Choking and with red eyes, the sprightly 53-year-old Drum Major Alderson made a run for it. When he came back with the masks, Corporal Macpherson was curled up close to unconsciousness in the bottom of the trench, from where he was swiftly removed by the Drum Major and band president. 'It was then that we decided that modern soldiering was not for the old or fainthearted and, in particular, not for Pipers and Drummers.'[6] The serious point to be taken from this amusing anecdote is that younger men and new recruits were very much needed to ensure the continued existence of the band.

Of the ten serving Territorial Army members of the Pipes and Drums in 1987, the average length of service was over 13 years. They were well educated men, with 30 percent having attended university. Their numbers included two policemen, four who worked in finance, two in telecommunications and one in public relations, but their average age was relatively high. Of the volunteers, Piper Bill Cowie and Piper Willie Duff were still playing, having both served in the Second World War with the London Scottish and Black Watch respectively, whilst Drum Sergeant Mike Crowley and Drummer Norman Lennie had enlisted in the early 1950s. Dedicated service from the likes of Pipe Sergeant Gordon Skilling and Piper Tommy Johnston, (who would still be regularly on parade with the band 30 years later) was invaluable, but new members were very much needed. A few younger men, including Piper Rob Blackledge and Drummer Gavin Macpherson, were joining the ranks but recruitment continued to be a problem.

On 16 May, the Pipes and Drums perform at Grosvenor House for the American Eagle Ball which included actress Joan Collins amongst the guests:

> It was one and a half hours after we should have played that the Band eventually went on. The reason for this being that our illustrious leader, Captain Rankin-Hunt, had staged a mutiny on our behalf – refusing to let us go on until we were fed and watered, according to his agreement with the organisers of the event.[7]

In June, the military band of the 52nd Lowland Volunteers spent a week at the London Scottish Regiment's temporary headquarters in Wenlock Street while they performed each day for the public in Regent's Park. The regular Thursday evening band practise that week turned into a lively ceilidh with the Pipes and Drums hosting the military bandsmen, who were deemed to be 'an excellent Band and a smashing bunch.'[8]

The 51st Highland Volunteers Pipes and Drums played at a Black Watch reunion at Balhousie Castle in Perth on 27 June and Beat Retreat at North Inch Park for their Commanding Officer

---

5   Bryan Alderson, *MacNamara's Band to Drum Major: A Drummers Anecdotes and Pictures* (London: Self-published, 2009), p.20.
6   Alderson, *MacNamara's Band to Drum Major*, p.21.
7   *London Scottish Regimental Gazette* (1987), p.37.
8   *London Scottish Regimental Gazette* (1987), p.37.

and guests on 11 July. Back in London, Drum Major Alderson was presented with his BEM by the General Officer Commanding, London District. In between these dates, Pipe Major Spoore played at two interrelated 'topping out' ceremonies. The first on 7 July was for the prestigious new Swire Group office building on the site of the old regimental headquarters at 59 Buckingham Gate, which was followed on 10 July by a second ceremony at the new regimental headquarters building at 95 Horseferry Road.

Hallowe'en was celebrated, for what was hoped to be the last time in temporary accommodation, at the drill hall in Wenlock Street and the highlights of the year concluded on 14 November, with six members of the Pipes and Drums joining the rest of the 51st Highland Volunteers Pipes and Drums leading a detachment of the Black Watch to Aberfeldy. Here a ceremony took place to commemorate the centenary of the construction of a memorial at Wade's Bridge on the River Tay, directly facing the spot where the original six independent companies of the *Am Freiceadan Dubh*, 'The Black Watch' first mustered as the 43rd Highland Regiment in 1739.

1988 opened with Piper Les Smith-Bowers flying to Marbella to play at a New Year's Eve party and, later that month, Pipe Major Spoore flew to Belgrade for a Burn's Night dinner at the British Embassy. The main event of the year, however, came on 26 April when Queen Elizabeth, The Queen Mother opened the new London Scottish Regiment headquarters building at 95 Horseferry Road.

Her Majesty arrived at 1900 hours to a Royal Salute from the Pipes and Drums and, after a short speech, declared the new building officially open. The Queen Mother then toured headquarters while the Pipes and Drums played a selection of tunes, as they had similarly done over 100 years previously at the opening of 59 Buckingham Gate in 1886. During the visit, Corporal Piper Macpherson and Corporal Drummer Powell both received their efficiency medals from The Queen Mother, in her role as Honorary Colonel of the regiment. Prior to Her Majesty's arrival, the Pipes and Drums made an additional, but unexpected, contribution to proceedings. 'We were all on parade silently awaiting Her Majesty to arrive. Suddenly from the rear of the Pipes and Drums came a clashing and banging.'[9] One of the drummers had fainted, and was shortly followed by another, with drums and sticks flying in every direction. Thankfully, the wife of Regimental Colonel Anderson, who was a trained nurse, came down from the balcony to administer First Aid. 'I have always maintained there should be a small plaque on the Drill Hall Floor, to the two fallen drummers!'[10]

1988 also saw a number of pipers and drummers leave the serving company for various reasons, including Drummer Geoff MacAdam, who was, interestingly, also a serving lieutenant in the regiment. He was forced to leave the London Scottish as he was joining the Metropolitan Police. 'Lieutenant Drummer' MacAdam had joined the London Scottish in 1981 and played an active role as both an infantryman and a drummer. He had initially won the prize as 'Best Recruit' on his training course, before having the honour removed for over-zealous celebrations. He would later come top of his Territorial Army commission course at Sandhurst, having uniquely been promoted to sergeant and appointed officer cadet at the same time, thus 'gaining the somewhat exclusive – if dubious – distinction of … dual membership of both the Officers' and Sergeants' Mess.'[11] His passion for pipe band drumming saw him continue to perform with the Pipes and Drums after receiving his commission, and he would remain with the band for many years as a volunteer member.

---

9 Alderson, *MacNamara's Band to Drum Major*, p.21.
10 Alderson, *MacNamara's Band to Drum Major*, p.21.
11 *London Scottish Regimental Gazette* (1988), p.104.

Joan Wanklyn, Painting of the opening ceremony for the new London Scottish Headquarters at 95 Horseferry Road, April 1988. (LSMA, used with permission)

Visit of Her Majesty, The Queen Mother to Regimental Headquarters, 26 February 1992, photographed with her three surviving personal pipers, Pipe Majors Duncan, Spoore and King. (LSMA, used with permission)

The Pipes and Drums of the London Regiment at the inauguration parade, Duke of York's Headquarters, 1 August 1993, led by Drum Major Powell of the London Scottish and his father, Drum Major Powell of the London Irish. (LSMA, used with permission)

Drum Major Powell leading the Pipes and Drums passed Her Majesty, The Queen Mother, at Clarence House to celebrate Her 60th Anniversary as Honorary Colonel of the regiment, 15 June 1995. (LSMA, used with permission)

However, overall losses to the Pipes and Drums were highlighted at Hallowe'en with a band of only seven performing and the Officer Commanding commenting in his speech that 'We need more serving Pipers and Drummers.'[12] Non-serving volunteers were now making up the majority of the Pipes and Drums, and a band of 16 led the regiment on the annual church parade in November. Now that the regiment had a permanent home with new, modern, facilities, it was fervently hoped that recruitment for both 'G' Company and the Pipes and Drums would begin to steadily increase.

Drum Sergeant Powell successfully completed the British Army Drum Major's course at the beginning of 1989, under the watchful instruction of Drum Sergeant Coventry, Scots Guards, and Drum Sergeant Boyd, Irish Guards. Powell reported that 'As I was the only Drum Major in kilt order it gave the instructors rise for sarcasm such as "You in the pink skirt!"'[13] He passed out second in his class. The five-yearly regimental pilgrimage to Messines took place over the weekend of 19-21 May with the Pipes and Drums again playing under the Menin Gate at Ypres and at the London Scottish memorial on Messines Ridge. On their return, they played at the Marriott Hotel in London for the Prime Minister, Margaret Thatcher, on the 10th anniversary of the 1979 Conservative general election victory.

The main event of the year for serving pipers and drummers, however, came on Saturday 23 September when the London Scottish Band President, Major Rankin-Hunt, arranged for the Pipes and Drums of the 51st Highland Volunteers to Beat Retreat in the grounds of Windsor Castle. Here, 'a little bit of history was written' as, prior to this point, 'this had been an honour accorded only to the Foot Guards.'[14] The band had the opportunity for two quick rehearsals before marching on parade in front of a large crowd of tourists as well as honoured guests including Admiral Sir David Hallifax, Constable and Governor of Windsor Castle, and Lieutenant Colonel Norman West, Staff Officer of the Military Knights of Windsor. The Pipes and Drums performed extremely well and 'should give the Guards reason to pause and reconsider any prejudices they might have had about TA Pipe Bands generally.'[15]

The four years since the closure of 59 Buckingham Gate and settling into new headquarters at 95 Horseferry Road had been disruptive and difficult both for the regiment and for the Pipes and Drums. Under the steadying hands of Drum Major Alderson and Pipe Major Spoore, this potentially stormy period was successfully weathered and the pipe band, while still relatively small in size, had been kept alive by a core of long-serving and dedicated members while new, younger, pipers and drummers were slowly recruited to ensure the band's continuity. Having seen out these difficult times, 1990 brought a number of high-profile, prestigious, parades and further momentous changes.

The year began with a performance in January at the London Scottish Golf Club on Wimbledon Common, to celebrate the 125th anniversary of the third oldest golf club in the world, which had been set up by the regiment in 1865. The following month, in a display of their soldiering prowess, members of the Pipes and Drums provided the GPMG (General Purpose Machine Gun) shooting team for 'G' Company at Garelochhead Camp in Argyll and Bute. Drum Sergeant Powell, Lance Corporal Piper Macpherson and Piper John Bracken took a creditable second place, before resuming their regular duties with the Pipes and Drums. Interestingly, Piper Bracken's bagpipes had been given to him by his first tutor, Wilfred Reid Morris, who had played them at the Somme, Arras, Ypres and the Marne during the First World War, while serving with the 6th Battalion,

---

12   *London Scottish Regimental Gazette* (1988), p.158.
13   *London Scottish Regimental Gazette*, (1989), p.4.
14   *London Scottish Regimental Gazette*, (1989), p.66.
15   *London Scottish Regimental Gazette*, (1989), p.66.

Cameron Highlanders. 21 May saw the 51st Highland Volunteers Pipes and Drums perform in London at the Caledonian Ball before preparations began in earnest for the two major events of the year that would take place that summer.

On 2 June, rehearsals began at the Guards' Depot, Pirbright for the latest 'Big Blaw' Beating Retreat which was to take place on Horse Guards Parade over three evenings from 12 June. It would be the first time since 1971 that the massed Pipes and Drums of the entire Scottish Division had Beat Retreat, with Her Majesty, Queen Elizabeth II attending as Guest of Honour on the final evening. This event would be closely followed by a special performance, again on Horse Guards Parade, on 27 June of a massed Pipes and Drums including the Irish Guards, Black Watch, Black Watch of Canada and the Toronto Scottish as part of Queen Elizabeth, The Queen Mother's 90th Birthday Tribute. With two such high-profile performances on the horizon, Pipe Major Spoore and Drum Major Alderson decided together that they would resign their positions after the events, allowing them to complete their long and dedicated service in the most memorable fashion. It would be the end of an era, as the two men had over 70 years of military service between them, with Drum Major Alderson having been at the helm as Drum Major of the London Scottish for over 20 years and Pipe Major Spoore having accumulated 33 years military piping experience.

The Gordon Highlanders and Black Watch used the new London Scottish headquarters as a base to prepare for the Big Blaw, which provided an excellent opportunity for the London Scottish to renew ties with two Highland regiments with whom they had strong historic connections. Tenor Drummer Patrick King, who worked in television and film production, arranged for Pipe Major Spoore and Drum Major Alderson to be interviewed on Sky News on the evening before the third and final performance. It would be at the conclusion of this final performance that Drum Major Alderson would be accorded a most signal honour.

The senior drum major on parade was Drum Major Bert Tomkins of the Gordon Highlanders who, having been informed of Drum Major Alderson's imminent retirement, graciously decided to allow him to lead the massed band off the parade square and back to barracks:

> Bryan had no knowledge of this, so as the Bands marched off House Guards up Horse Guards Approach, D/M Tomkins called over his shoulder to Drummy Alderson, 'Come hold, Bryan.' Bryan, bewildered, quickened his pace to the side of D/M Tomkins to be told 'Right, now stay out, Hold and take us back to Welly B.' D/M Tomkins dropped back into Bryan's vacant position – and Bryan led the whole Scottish and affiliated Divisions back down Birdcage Walk to Wellington Barracks and into Retirement. Well done Bryan – the end of an era.[16]

For Drum Major Alderson this was 'the most gracious thing' and 'a gesture I will never forget.'[17]

On the morning of the Queen Mother's Birthday Tribute, Pipe Sergeant Ian King had travelled to Heathrow Airport to pipe in members of the Toronto Scottish Pipes and Drums on their arrival in London to perform in the parade. The day after playing at the Birthday Tribute, he was officially appointed as Pipe Major of the London Scottish Regiment. He then accompanied Pipe Major Spoore to Clarence House on 4 August, to make his first appearance as Personal Piper to Her Majesty, The Queen Mother on her actual birthday. Pipe Major Spoore composed the tune *Queen Elizabeth's Birthday March* in honour of the occasion and, on his retirement, was awarded the Royal Victorian Medal by Her Majesty in the Birthday Honours List.

Pipe Major King was born in Argentina and moved to the United Kingdom at the age of 12. He initially studied physics, then astronomy, at St Andrew's University and joined the Officer

---

16 *London Scottish Regimental Gazette* (1990), p.59.
17 Alderson, *MacNamara's Band to Drum Major*, p.23.

Training Corps there. He soon joined the St Andrew's UOTC Pipes and Drums, where he learned to play the pipes under Pipe Major Bert Barron. After graduating in 1973, and wishing to keep up his piping, he joined the Black Watch HQ Company of the 51st Highland Volunteers in 1974. On moving to Reading a few years later to take up a trainee position with Metal Box Ltd, he transferred within the 51st Highland's to the London Scottish.

Pipe Major King was joined shortly after by newly appointed Drum Major Michael 'Mickey' Powell, who was also simultaneously appointed as Drum Major to the Pipes and Drums of the 51st Highland Volunteers.

Drum Major Powell began playing drums with the London Irish Association Pipes, Drums and Bugles, where his father was Bugle Major, before Drum Sergeant Crowley persuaded him to join the London Scottish as a volunteer civilian drummer in 1972. In 1974, he enlisted with the London Scottish, with the tantalising promise of a place at annual camp in Cyprus with the 51st Highland Volunteers. However, Turkey invaded the island just weeks earlier and camp was relocated to the slightly less glamourous surroundings of Salisbury Plain. He took a rest from the Pipes and Drums from 1984 to 1989, gaining the rank of corporal in 1986 and finally reached the rank of sergeant on his return to the band. As mentioned earlier, he completed the army drum major's course in 1989, in readiness to take over from Drum Major Alderson the following year.

It would be the job of Pipe Major King and Drum Major Powell to attempt to rebuild band numbers once again. They would receive invaluable assistance from Pipe Major Spoore who stayed on with the Pipes and Drums as band president and whose first important contribution in his new role was to persuade the Regimental Trust to commence a major programme to replace the Pipes and Drums' equipment and uniforms. Drum Major Alderson was also never far away and would provide assistance to the band as an occasional replacement bass drummer and stand-in drum major for many years to come.

At the end of summer 1990, on the August bank-holiday weekend, ten pipers and drummers from the London Scottish visited Belgium to celebrate the 150th Anniversary of the Messines civilian marching band, with whom they had paraded on many occasions during regimental pilgrimages. It was the perfect opportunity for pipers and drummers to let their hair down after a momentous summer and 'There followed a weekend of unbridled self-indulgence ….'[18]

The Pipes and Drums decided to perform from the balcony at headquarters for the first time at the annual Hallowe'en dinner in October, which turned out to be slightly more complicated than had been anticipated. However, after a restart of the first set, the rest of the evening went without issue. The year ended with the Pipes and Drums invited, once again, to participate in the Lord Mayor's Show, which had been a staple up until 1981 but, for some reason, had disappeared from the band's calendar. The London Scottish paraded with support from 51st Highland Volunteer pipers and drummers from the Black Watch and Liverpool Scottish contingents, as well as the 51st Highland's military band. The 1st Battalion, Gordon Highlanders also took part in the parade.

The announcement of the government's latest Armed Forces Review was expected at the beginning of 1991, however, Saddam Hussein's invasion of Kuwait created higher priorities for the Ministry of Defence. During the fast-paced reaction to this unexpected invasion, the 51st Highland Volunteers were mistakenly called-up for war service, leading to 75 eager London Scottish troops arriving at 95 Horseferry Road on 17 January, ready for action. Men had travelled from various places around the country to answer the call. Colour Sergeant Piper Skilling at the time was a senior reporter for *Soldier Magazine* and questioned the mobilisation with his superior who, as a brigadier in army media relations, quickly confirmed that it was a false alarm.

---

18 *London Scottish Regimental Gazette* (1990), p.83.

Political plans for large scale changes to both the Scottish Division and to the Territorial Army, anticipated in the delayed Armed Forces Review, created dual levels of apprehension for the London Scottish throughout 1991, but these concerns were held in abeyance at least for a little while longer. Regimental Colonel John Clemence reported that it was 'recognised that the future of the London Scottish lay in association with a TA unit in London'[19] which would necessitate the termination of the 25-year relationship with the 51st Highland Volunteers and the Scottish Division. An early recommendation by the MOD was for the 8th Queen's Fusiliers to be allowed an additional rifle company, which would be formed from the amalgamation of the London Scottish and the London Irish, with the loss of heritage identity for both Celtic regiments. Other related recommendations within the regular army included the merging of the Gordon Highlanders with the Queen's Own Highlanders, which would see the identity of the London Scottish's parent regiment also disappear. It was, then, another fight for survival for the London Scottish, and a huge amount of diplomacy and lobbying would take place behind the scenes, with unofficial support and concern from Her Majesty, The Queen Mother very much appreciated. In a break with protocol, Her Majesty directly penned a letter herself, rather than through her private secretary, to be read to the regiment at the 1991 annual Hallowe'en dinner:

> I send my greetings on the occasion of the Hallowe'en Reunion, with an assurance that my thoughts are very much with the Regiment at this anxious time in its loyal and distinguished history.[20]

Thankfully, there was vociferous support from the Fusiliers and the London Irish Rifles to create a more amenable solution, and a counter recommendation was put forward endorsing the reformation of the London Regiment for the first time since it had been disbanded in 1938, prior to the Second World War. It now became a waiting game for the final decision.

In the meantime, on 30 April 1991, Pipe Major King performed at the dedication of a memorial stone in the rose garden at the old London Scottish shooting hut at the Bisley Shooting Ground in Surrey, commemorating those London Scots whose ashes were scattered there. He then travelled to Valençay in France on 6 May, to accompany Her Majesty, The Queen Mother in unveiling a memorial to the 104 men and women of the Special Operations Executive who gave their lives working behind enemy lines to liberate France during the Second World War. Later in the year, he attended the two-week TA Advanced Pipers and Band Management course at Edinburgh Castle, whilst ensuring throughout the year that he tended to the beehives that he had set up on the roof of regimental headquarters, the produce of which was sold as regimental honey!

In January 1992, news came that a decision had finally been made by the MOD concerning the future of the London Scottish. Regimental Colonel Clemence reported that, through intense lobbying:

> We have gained a concession ... that the Battalion, of which we would form part, would be the only four Company Battalion in the Territorial Army made up of a Company from each of the Queen's, The Fusiliers, The London Irish Rifles and ourselves.[21]

The Ministry of Defence announced that a re-constituted London Regiment would be formed as a new unit within the Queen's Division and entitled to its own colours. Most importantly

---

19 *London Scottish Regimental Gazette* (1991), p.75.
20 *London Scottish Regimental Gazette* (1991), p.90.
21 *London Scottish Regimental Gazette* (1992), p.3.

and, again, as somewhat of an anomaly within the British army, it would be a multi-cap badged regiment safeguarding the continued identity of the constituent regiments from whence its four composite companies were derived.

This decision represented the best of all possible outcomes for the London Scottish as it not only ensured the survival of the regiment, its traditions and its Pipes and Drums, but it returned, after 25 years, the London Scottish cap badge and Hodden Grey uniform lost in the formation of 'G' Company that the London Scottish Pipes and Drums, alone, had kept alive during the intervening period. It is fair to say that, without this continued presence from the Pipes and Drums, the uniform and cap badge may well have gone forever, and it was, thus, wonderful news that 'A' (London Scottish) Company, The London Regiment would be wearing the cap badge which their predecessors had designed in 1907 and first worn back in 1908.

On 26 February, after news of the finalised arrangements had been revealed, Her Majesty, The Queen Mother attended a lunch at 95 Horseferry Road hosted by the serving officers of the regiment for a viewing of Joan Wanklyn's painting of the opening ceremony of the new regimental headquarters at 95 Horseferry Road, back in April 1988. All her surviving Personal Pipers past and present; Pipe Major Duncan, Pipe Major Spoore and Pipe Major King, joined together to play a set.

It was understood that the official formation of the new London Regiment would commence on 1 April 1992 and, therefore, a re-badging ceremony was arranged for 31 March. It proved to be an emotional occasion, particularly for the older members of the regiment who had witnessed the loss of the regimental cap badge 25 years earlier, and the performance of the Pipes and Drums, especially at the closing, added great poignantly to the proceedings. As it transpired, the London Regiment was not officially formed until April the following year, with an interim arrangement involving the 8th Queen's Fusiliers in place until that time, but the passion to reinstate the cap badge was so strong that it is impossible to imagine that the London Scottish were prepared to wait an additional 12 months to see it happen.

The band supper in 1992 saw the Pipe, Drum and Bugle Majors from the Queen's Fusiliers and London Irish bands invited as guests of honour, as discussions began about the musical formation of the new London Regiment. Meanwhile, on 23 May, the serving London Scottish pipers and drummers performed with the 1st Battalion, 51st Highland Volunteers to commemorate the 25th anniversary of their founding and to bid a fond farewell. At annual camp that summer the London Scottish no longer constituted a proportion of an amalgamated pipe band. They were now, once again, a full pipe band in their own right. However, the disruption of the preceding year and the uncertainty surrounding their continued existence meant that the only a handful of pipers attended camp, along with a drum major without any drummers. Thankfully, the Corps of Drums of the 8th Queen's Fusilier Regiment offered their services and were enlisted to lend a helping hand.

The newly formed London Regiment officially appeared on the Army List on 20 April 1993, and an inaugural formation parade was organised for Sunday 1 August at The Duke of York's Headquarters, Chelsea, in the presence of Field Marshal, The Lord Bramall, in his capacity as Lord Lieutenant of Greater London. The Pipes and Drums of 'A' (London Scottish) and 'D' (London Irish) Companies, while continuing as independent pipe bands, would play together for the first time as an amalgamated London Regiment Pipes and Drums. Pipe Major King was appointed Pipe Major of the London Regiment with Drum Major Powell as Drum Major. His father, Jim Powell, was Drum Major of the London Irish at the time but was no longer a serving soldier, so Drum Major Powell, the younger, took precedence.

Later that day, Pipe Major King flew out to the Ukraine to perform at the British Embassy for Her Majesty, The Queen's official birthday celebrations and in October, ex-Pipe Major Spoore joined the London Scottish Association battlefield tour in Italy which visited Anzio and Monte

Cassino. During this tour, Regimental Colonel Clemence presented a pipe banner, marking his tenure as Regimental Colonel of the regiment, which Pipe Major Spoore received on behalf of the Pipes and Drums.

The uncertainty and adjustments of the previous two years continued into 1994 as the London Scottish endeavoured to support a high-profile campaign to save the Gordon Highlanders from amalgamation with the Queen's Own Highlanders (Seaforth and Camerons). This had been proposed in the Ministry of Defence 'Options for Change' review which had been initiated by the collapse of the Soviet Union and the Warsaw Pact. Various support events were organised in London, with 95 Horseferry Road utilised as a base of operations for the Gordons in the capital. Ultimately, however, and incongruously in their 200th anniversary year, the battle was lost and on 17 September 1994 the Gordons became a composite unit of The Highlanders (Seaforth, Gordons and Camerons). It was a major blow, especially after the euphoric high of keeping the London Scottish alive.

Within the London Scottish Regiment, Pipe Major King and Drum Major Powell continued with their intense efforts to strengthen the Pipes and Drums, by recruiting more personnel and improving the quality of the sound and performance of the band. Numbers had become dangerously low, and unofficial assistance was requested from Pipe Major Brian MacRae (Gordon Highlanders), the Sovereign's Piper. Pipe Major MacRae's involvement helped to attract younger, talented pipers to join the Pipes and Drums including Pipers Nicholas Tuckey, Jim McLucas, Douglas Gardiner, Manoj Goonewardene and Andrew Parsons, along with Drummers George Wilson and Phillip Mason. The results were immediate, with the London Scottish winning both first and second places at the Cranford and Ashbourne mini-band competition that year.

Alan Morris, the retiring regimental secretary, was accorded the honour of chairing the annual band supper on 8 April 1994. He had 'accompanied the Pipes and Drums on many occasions as a dancer, and has long been secretary and quartermaster, and it was felt that it was about time we recognised this.'[22] His position as regimental secretary was taken by Robert 'Bob' Harman, who had started his military career with the London Scottish in 1956, where he often played tenor drum with the band, before joining the 1st Battalion, Gordon Highlanders, where he performed with the Drums and Pipes and became an excellent Highland dancer. Harman's association with the London Scottish had been strengthened in 1966 when he was posted from the Gordons as the Permanent Staff Instructor (PSI) Sergeant and he would continue as an 'emergency' member of the Pipes and Drums, both as a drummer and later as a piper, for many years.

The weekend of 5-7 August saw the London Scottish Regiment visit Belgium for the 80th anniversary of the Battle of Messines and the 70th anniversary of the unveiling of the regimental memorial on Messines Ridge. The ceremony was shown on Belgian television and further commemorations took place that weekend at Tyne Cot Cemetery, Hill 60 and Sanctuary Wood.

In December 1994, further reorganisation of the Territorial Army was undertaken with a categorical commitment that all infantry regiments would now, and in the future, follow a three company, single cap-badge, structure. The London Regiment, after more heavy lobbying, again received authorisation to be the only exception to this rule and were granted permission to retain their four, highly individual, companies. While not officially granted permission, they were also given a 'degree of flexibility' to preserve their four cap-badge status.[23] The unique position of the London Scottish, once again, managed to survive, and the regiment were able to march confidently into what would be another momentous year for the Pipes and Drums.

---

22 *London Scottish Regimental Gazette*, (1994), p.48.
23 *London Scottish Regimental Gazette* (1995), p.3.

The year 1995 marked the 50th anniversary of the liberation of Europe, victory over Japan and the end of the Second World War, which was commemorated by a series of high-profile celebrations attended by the Pipes and Drums. The first of these was a VE Day celebration in Perth on 13 May which saw the unveiling of a memorial to the 51st Highland Division, depicting a Second World War piper being handed a rose by a Dutch child, commemorating the liberation of Holland, in 1945. 13 members of the London Scottish Pipes and Drums 'some of whom were returning to old stomping grounds from the days with 1/51st Highland Volunteers'[24] joined 400 other pipers, drummers and musicians who performed in front of serving troops and over 2,000 veterans who lined the streets throughout the city. The procession was 'cheered along by the young and veterans alike, and by widows proudly wearing their husbands' medals'[25] and the parade concluded with a drum-head service at the unveiling of the memorial.

Another important anniversary came that year with the celebration of Her Majesty, The Queen Mother's 60th year as Honorary Colonel of the London Scottish Regiment. With typical humility and concern for the regiment, 'Her Majesty has particularly requested that we do not make any presentation to mark the occasion and prefers that we do so by raising money for a Regimental Purpose.'[26] Regimental Colonel Clemence deemed the most pressing need to be uniforms and accoutrements for officers and pipers and drummers and over £30,000 was subsequently raised for this purpose, which included a new set of side drums for the drum corps.

Due to ill-health, Her Majesty was not able to attend the celebration planned for her at regimental headquarters on 23 February, but more than made up for any disappointment in the summer. As Regimental Colonel Clemence observed:

> One of the most memorable events of my tenure took place on June 15th when the Pipe Band, Serving Company and Cadets marched past Her Majesty at Clarence House, and then had group photographs taken in the garden.[27]

The Pipes and Drums, at a strength of 13 pipers and five drummers, lead the march-past and the regiment exercised their Freedom of the City of Westminster by marching back to 95 Horseferry Road, along The Mall and past Buckingham Palace, with 'drums beating, banners flying, and bayonets fixed.' On return to headquarters, the parade joined a second large-scale regimental celebration to mark the 50th anniversary of VE Day, at which the Pipes and Drums also performed.

Around this time, Corporal Piper Macpherson piped for the Lord Mayor of Westminster at The Savoy Hotel, London, at a formal, white tie, dinner to which Regimental Colonel Clemence had been invited. Colonel Clemence, in full London Scottish mess dress, was approached after the dinner by a distinguished gentleman who had recognised the regimental uniform. Much to the Colonel's chagrin, he was asked by the older gentlemen if he was the piper, to which he was quick to respond, 'No, Sir, but I sometimes call the tune.'[28]

In June 1995, the pipe band attend the Chateau Balleroy Hot Air Balloon Festival in Normandy for further VE Day celebrations. While bad weather meant no balloons could fly, the Pipes and Drums did their bit to ensure the entertainment made up for the deficiency. In fact, the party they created went on all night 'with Colour Sergeant Piper Skilling at the Joanna, Piper McLucas on

---

24   *London Scottish Regimental Gazette* (1995), p.82.
25   *London Scottish Regimental Gazette* (1995), p.82.
26   *London Scottish Regimental Gazette* (1995), p.5.
27   *London Scottish Regimental Gazette* (1995), p.63.
28   *London Scottish Regimental Gazette* (1995), p.40.

the small pipes and a group of Frenchmen celebrating someone's birthday. Roll-call was a bit frail the next day.'[29]

On 30 July, the serving company and Pipes and Drums paraded with the rest of the London Regiment at an open day at The Duke of York's Headquarters, where a ceremony was held for the new drums which had been purchased with donations to mark the Queen Mother's 60th anniversary. Regimental drums, adorned with the insignia and battle honours of the regiment, are treated with similar reverence to the regimental colours themselves, and provide remembrance of the men who were killed, injured and served in the campaigns honoured on the drums. The 'newly emblazoned drums were blessed, presented and then played. The musical display which followed was excellent and the whole day was a resounding success.'[30]

London Regiment annual camp that summer saw members of the London Scottish heading in three separate directions, with a composite London Regiment platoon flying to Cyprus, a second contingent heading to the Falkland Islands and the remainder, including the Pipes and Drums, going to Sennybridge Camp in the Brecon Beacons. A few days after arriving, the pipers were leading a party of London Regiment soldiers as they marched to the day's exercise, when they came across a soft-topped Land Rover belonging to a unit of the Welsh Air Training Corps which had careered off the road, down a 15-foot bank and overturned into a stream. All seven occupants were injured, five of them seriously. The London Scottish contingent stopped to recover the occupants and provide first aid, whilst radioing for further assistance. Pipe Major King took the majority of the London Regiment soldiers on to exercise, while some remained with the injured. Corporal Piper Macpherson took the two lesser-injured air cadets to a junction with the main track to wait for and direct further assistance when it arrived, where he was joined by a second group of cadets who had also witnessed the incident:

> A number were in shock and upset. To distract the youngsters, he gave them a lesson on the pipes and then played for them. This helped greatly to reduce their fears and tension and stopped several of them becoming hysterical.[31]

Corporal Piper Macpherson would later receive official commendation for his actions.

The last major event of the year came on 20 October, when military units that had been granted 'City Privileged Regiment Status' by the Corporation of the City of London, marched past Mansion House, where His Royal Highness, The Duke of Edinburgh took the salute to mark the 50th anniversary of the end of the Second World War. The parade included contingents from the Royal Navy, Blues and Royals, Coldstream Guards, Royal Fusiliers, Princess of Wales Royal Regiment and the Royal Air Force. The London Regiment Pipes and Drums played alongside the Bands of the Royal Marines, Grenadier Guards, Queen's Division, Honourable Artillery Company and the Minden Band of the Rifles: 'with Bands playing, Bayonets fixed and Colours flying, they came down via the Bank of England, past the Mansion House and up Cheapside to the Guildhall – a wonderful sight to see.'[32]

It had, then, been another momentous year for the Pipes and Drums as they continued the band's tradition of taking their place at the most prestigious military and civilian events, which always requires a huge degree of commitment and dedication from pipers and drummers, both serving and volunteer. Colour Sergeant Piper Skilling, who would celebrate 30 years in the TA

---

29 *London Scottish Regimental Gazette* (1995), p.85.
30 *London Scottish Regimental Gazette* (1995), p.63.
31 *London Scottish Regimental Gazette* (1995), p.68.
32 *London Scottish Regimental Gazette* (1995), p.122.

in 1996, conveyed the following reflection regarding the participation of pipers and drummers at such events:

> Musicians hold a peculiarly privileged position, being at the heart of ceremonies, and sometimes the focal point. There is often, however, little chance to enjoy the spectacle; you have to concentrate on the music and drill; and in a massed band you can often only catch glimpses of any activity.[33]

It is, indeed, a universal truism that a piper or drummer's gratification from their involvement in high-profile events generally takes the form of retrospective satisfaction in a job well done, rather than pleasure derived from the event itself.

A quieter year came in 1996, which focused more on London Scottish regimental activities and, with it, a continued push to further the quality and performance of the band. In April, the Pipes and Drums played at the Cranford mini-band event and again won first and second places in the London and South-East quartet and mini-band competitions in Grade 4. They would also attend the Territorial Army Pipe Band Cadre in Edinburgh from 26-28 April, before performing at the Royal Caledonian Ball in London on 2 May in the presence of Her Royal Highness, Princess Margaret. There was a strong turnout for the internal MacLeod Medal competition, judged again by the Sovereign's Piper, Pipe Major Brian MacRae, and won by Piper Gardiner.

The Reserve Forces Act of 1996, which passed into law on 22 May that year allowed for reservists, including all members of the Territorial Army, to be called-up for peacekeeping and humanitarian operations overseas for up to nine months at a time. World-wide instability, highlighted by the dissolution of the USSR, widespread fighting in Yugoslavia and a genocidal civil war in Rwanda, together with troop reductions in the regular army, meant that greater reliance would be placed on Territorial forces, including the ability to deploy overseas should the need arise. It would prove to be an extremely intuitive move.

A sign of this greater reliance on, and further acceptance of, the abilities and dedication of Territorial Army soldiers came on 28 July when the Pipes and Drums of the London Scottish and the London Irish were given the honour of becoming the first TA bands to ever perform at the Changing of the Guard ceremony at St James's Palace and Buckingham Palace. This combined London Regiment Pipes and Drums, under Drum Major Powell and Pipe Major King, numbered 16 pipers and eight drummers, plus the London Irish Drum Major. They would lead a Royal Guard from the Grenadier Guards to their positions guarding both palaces. The importance of making a good show at this extremely public duty resulted in considerable pressure, as the combined band was effectively representing the entire Territorial Army and was very much under the scrutiny of senior army officers for the standard of their playing, drill, deportment and dress. However, the event was widely deemed a success and repeated the following weekend.

After the annual regimental events at Hallowe'en, Lord Mayor's Show and church parade in 1996, the year's events concluded on 23 November with the 100th anniversary dinner of the London Scottish Sergeants' Mess. The four sergeants in the Pipes and Drums were joined by Lance Corporal Piper Tuckey and Pipers Gardiner and Johnston who played two sets during the evening. They were also to witness an infamous address to the haggis by Colour Sergeant Piper Skilling who 'delivered a rendition fit for the Bard himself, and his dirk welding was such that the look of horror on the face of the chef was a joy to behold'[34]

---

33 *London Scottish Regimental Gazette* (1996), p.24.
34 *London Scottish Regimental Gazette* (1997), p.15.

On 11 June 1997, the Pipes and Drums of The Highlanders (Seaforth, Gordons and Camerons) Beat Retreat at 95 Horseferry Road with over 300 people in attendance. In honour of the occasion, the band played *The Heights of Cassino*, which commemorates the Second World War battle at Monte Cassino in which both the 1st and 3rd Battalions of the London Scottish had been involved. The following month, on 25 July, new colours were presented to the London Regiment at The Duke of York's Headquarters, Chelsea:

> It was a fine sight during the actual parade to see the four Companies marching past, led by the Drums and Pipes of The London Regiment.[35]

Former tenor Drummer Pat King produced a film of the colours parade entitled *A Capital Regiment*, through his Westminster-King production company. King had already produced and directed the multi-award-winning *Instrument of War* and *When the Pipers Play* trilogy, detailing the history of the Highland bagpipes in war and peace, which became a staple on the History Channel and a best seller in America. Regimental Colonel Clemence stated that this achievement was, 'Not bad for an ex-drummer, but then he is a London Scot.'[36]

Over the 1997 August Bank Holiday weekend, Pipe Major King travelled to Plymouth to participate in the Navy Day celebrations. Twenty-three Royal Navy ships were open to the public and a military tattoo took place on the Sunday evening. Pipe Major King performed on the Russian ship STV *Sedov*, the largest sailing ship in the world, and was also given special permission to pipe to the crowds from the bridge of HMS *Argyll*, the lead ship at Navy Day, which usually carried a piper from the Argyll and Sutherland Highlanders.

The Commanding Officer of the London Regiment organised an invitational piping competition on 16 October for pipers from the 1st Battalion, Scots Guards, the London Irish Rifles and the London Scottish Regiment. Each regiment was allowed to enter three pipers and the competition was judged by the Sovereign's Piper, Pipe Major Brian MacRae, alongside the famous piping composer Pipe Major Roddy S. MacDonald. The March, Strathspey and Reel (MSR) competition was won by London Scottish Piper Gardiner, with Piper Cowan of the 1st Battalion, Scots Guards taking second place. Piper Cowan would also take first place in the Piobaireachd competition, with Lance Corporal Piper Tuckey and Piper McLucas, both of the London Scottish, taking second and third places. It was an excellent example of the quality of piping amongst the London Scottish pipe corps.

A mark of respect for their achievements came two weeks later at the regimental Hallowe'en dinner when the Pipes and Drums, who normally ate in the canteen while preparing to play the various duties and sets performed throughout the evening, were invited by 'A' (London Scottish) Company Officer Commanding, Major Stuart Young, to join the guests to eat in the drill hall. In his report, Major Young stated of the Pipes and Drums:

> They are an extremely good advert for the Company and the Battalion and should be encouraged to excel to greater heights. To this end we are allowing them to eat with us tonight for the first time in over 100 years. They must be hungry by now.[37]

Three days later, three London Scottish pipers proved they were already excelling at great heights with success at the Scottish Piping Society of London Cup hosted by Harrow School. Here, Piper Andrew Parsons won two silver medals in B Grade March and B Grade Strathspey and Reel,

---

35   *London Scottish Regimental Gazette* (1997), p.73.
36   *London Scottish Regimental Gazette* (1997), p.118.
37   *London Scottish Regimental Gazette*, (1997), p105.

whilst Lance Corporal Piper Tuckey won the *Ceol Mor* (Piobaireachd) and silver and bronze in A Grade March and A Grade Strathspey and Reel. Piper Gardner won two gold medals in A Grade March and A Grade Strathspey and Reel and the overall first prize for the day was shared between Tuckey and Gardiner.

In 1998, after nearly 140 years of unofficial assistance and cooperation, it was announced that the London Scottish were to enter an official affiliation with the Scots Guards. The Scots Guards had played an important role in the history of the London Scottish since the founding of the latter in 1859. Links with the Pipes and Drums were particularly strong from the very earliest days, with piping instructors from the Scots Guards assisting and performing with the London Scottish throughout the Victorian era and into the twentieth century. The two regiments had fought together through the early years of the First World War and the geographic proximity of their headquarters, both in central London, and overlapping duties as the representatives of Scotland in London had forged close relationships at various points over the previous one and a half centuries. The London Scottish had no parent regiment following the amalgamation of the Gordon Highlanders, and formalised affiliation with a regular army battalion, especially with yet another Ministry of Defence strategic defence review on the horizon, made tactical sense. Pre-review rumours were again beginning to circulate concerning the possible final demise of the London Scottish regiment, with reports of major cuts again being potentially inflicted on the Territorial Army.

An inaugural association party was held at 95 Horseferry Road on 16 April attended by His Royal Highness, The Duke of Kent, Colonel of the Scots Guards, and Major General John Kiszely, Regimental Lieutenant Colonel, Scots Guards, who stated:

> This association has been universally acclaimed and welcomed by Scots Guards past and present. The London Scottish have at present five of their soldiers serving alongside Scots Guards in Northern Ireland. The London Scottish are reputed to have taken every position they were ordered to take and held every position they were ordered to defend.[38]

The London Scottish Pipes and Drums performed a set at the party and were followed by the Military Band of the Scots Guards, which had just returned from a tour of the USA. Drum Major Powell then led both bands in a combined performance, before requesting permission from His Royal Highness, The Duke of Kent to march off. The two bands then left the hall playing their shared regimental march, *Heilan' Laddie*.

The London Scottish Pipes and Drums were invited to join a massed band at the Royal Artillery Sunset Ceremony, on Horse Guards Parade, held over four nights in June that year. The event was televised, with Her Majesty, The Queen attending as Guest of Honour. The London Scottish invitation came because of the link with the Second World War 3rd Battalion, which had officially been a battalion of the Royal Artillery. Ten members of the Pipes and Drums attended ten days of rehearsals at Woolwich Barracks before the four evening performances, one of which coincided with Scotland's first match at the football World Cup. Unable to watch the game on television, the band came up with an ingenious way for the match result to be communicated to the men on parade. A lone piper played a lament at the end of each performance and because he was off parade for the majority of the evening, he had access to a radio. It was agreed that a different lament would be played to signal either a win, lose or draw. 'Never in the history of piping was a lament more keenly anticipated but the opening bars of *Sleep Dearie Sleep* made the outcome depressingly clear.'[39] Unsurprisingly, Scotland had lost 2-1 to Brazil.

---

38 *London Scottish Regimental Gazette* (1998), p.44.
39 *London Scottish Regimental Gazette* (1998), p.37.

Better news came the following month when the results of the government's latest Strategic Defence Review were announced. After a considerable amount of lobbying and hard work behind the scenes to ensure the survival of the London Scottish, a final decision had been made to increase the size of the already anomalous London Regiment from four companies to six, with the inclusion of two companies from the Royal Green Jackets. Most importantly, all composite companies would again retain their original, unique cap badge. The new London Scottish Regimental Colonel, Colonel Richard Halliday, had led the battle, lobbying MPs, generals and cabinet members after it had become clear that the Ministry of Defence would have preferred to see an amalgamated, three company, single cap-badge London Regiment. Miraculously, the London Scottish had been saved yet again. Unfortunately, others, like the Liverpool Scottish Regiment, which the London Scottish had helped raise in 1900 and had marched along side in the 51st Highland Volunteers, did not survive the cull.

The Strategic Defence Review White Paper was officially published on 15 October and feelings were running high at the annual Hallowe'en dinner. The guest of honour was General Sir Jeremy Mackenzie, First Colonel of The Highlanders and following his speech:

> The Pipes and Drums played their Second Set which stirred the blood and made one proud to be part of the London Scottish. When the Regimental March was played instead of remaining seated, as is customary during a dinner, everybody rose and stood to attention. This demonstrated the intense feeling for the future of the Scottish.[40]

With the prospects of the regiment intact, at least for a while longer, three London Scottish pipers closed 1998 by achieving yet another 'first' when they travelled to San Carlos de Bariloche, in the Andes, for the 2nd Festival of Military Bands and Scottish Bagpipes. This was the first official visit by British Army soldiers to Argentina since the end of the Falklands War in 1982. Pipe Major King, who was born in Argentina, along with Colour Sergeant Piper Skilling and Piper Stuart Walker were flown out at the request of the British Ambassador and played at a series of events. They marched through the streets of Bariloche, playing alternatively with the military band of the Argentinian 26th Mountain Infantry Regiment, and performed with members of the South American Piping Association. Pipe Major King would diplomatically state 'is it probably only fair to say that their style has developed separately from mainstream piping in Britain.'[41] The trio also undertook a photoshoot on the top of the 2,400m Mount Cerro Catedral, which they reached by cable car and then by chair lift. The main event, however, was a military tattoo in Bariloche in front of 1,500 people, where Pipe Major King performed a solo of *Amazing Grace*. The evening concluded with the Argentinian military bands playing *The Song of the Malvinas* and the pipers marching off to *The Black Bear*. 'It must be supposed that playing *The Crags of Tumbledown Mountain* would be a tad controversial.'[42]

After another unsettled period, but with their future now reassured, the London Scottish Regiment was well placed to see out the end of the twentieth century and move forward confidently into the new millennium. Their role, and the remit of the Territorial Army in general, would change drastically as demands on the British army in a variety of theatres overseas ramped up, beginning with the continued build-up of troops in Kosovo through the latter part of 1999. The situation within the Pipes and Drums, however, would remain uncertain and unsettled over

---

40 *London Scottish Regimental Gazette* (1998), p.117.
41 *London Scottish Regimental Gazette* (1999), p.12.
42 *London Scottish Regimental Gazette* (1999), p.16.

the next three years, seeing as it did several changes in key senior personnel, coupled with an element of controversy.

The first major change came in early 1999, when Pipe Major King announced that he would be relinquishing his appointment after the annual children's party that took place in early spring. The reasons behind Pipe Major King's decision to leave are unclear, but soon after he would join the Royal Signals Pipes and Drums as a pipe sergeant and later became involved with the Air Cadets. On relinquishing his role as Pipe Major of the London Scottish, he initially hoped to continue in his role as Personal Piper to the Queen Mother but was made aware that this appointment belonged to the London Scottish Regiment and would be inherited by his successor. That successor would be Pipe Sergeant Christopher Macpherson, who had been with the London Scottish Pipes and Drums since 1975 and who was now 60 years old.

Pipe Major Macpherson was a well-liked and affable member of the Pipes and Drums and had been good friends with Drum Major Powell over the previous 15 years. As such, he was a popular choice within the band and the wider regimental family. Pipe Major Macpherson was an excellent organiser who could get the best out of people but was open about his limitations as a piping instructor. He decided that the Pipes and Drums would benefit from expert tuition and so, with the assistance of Regimental Secretary Bob Harman, turned to Pipe Major Brian MacRae, the Sovereign's Piper, who already had a close relationship with the London Scottish, to take on a more formal role. Pipe Major MacRae accepted a paid position as Piping Instructor to the London Scottish Pipes and Drums which was particularly helpful for the talented younger pipers and for encouraging the recruitment of new members.

The initial success of this venture led Pipe Major McRae to recommend bringing in a drumming instructor in the form of Tony Burns, a Grade 1 drummer who had learned his trade as a pupil of the great Alex Duthart at the British Caledonian Airways Pipes and Drums. It was hoped that this would similarly attract new members to the drum corps, which had been very stretched for several years but, unfortunately, despite some initial success, it did not quite have the desired impact.

These changes took place during a very busy year for the band. On 7 February 1999, 12 members of the regiment visited Number 10 Downing Street at the invitation of Alastair Campbell, the Prime Minister's press secretary. Regimental Secretary Bob Harman had, on various occasions, lent bagpipes to Mr Campbell, a keen piper, and in way of repayment it was arranged that a party of London Scots would visit the Prime Minister's official residence. Tony Blair met the party on the staircase at Number 10 and took the time to shake hands and speak to everyone. Two months later, the Pipes and Drums played at a Scottish tattoo at the Royal Albert Hall on 18 April, where Corporal Piper Tuckey played a lament and Bob Harman performed with a Scottish country dancing team, and the band performed once again at the Caledonian Ball two weeks later, on 29 April. During April, the London Regiment Pipes and Drums also performed public duties by playing again at the Changing of the Guard ceremony at Buckingham Palace, with ex-Drum Major Alderson returning on tenor drum and ex-Pipe Major Spoore piping in the ranks to ensure that the largest band possible was on parade.

Both men would lend a hand again in May, when the Pipes and Drums were invited to Warsaw to take part in the unveiling of a memorial to the men of the Polish Division who had fought and died alongside the 1st and 3rd Battalions of the London Scottish in May 1944 at Monte Cassino. Drum Major Powell was unavailable for the weekend trip and so Bryan Alderson stepped back into his old shoes as drum major. Having flown to Lodz to play in support of a British Trade and Industry show, before flying back to Warsaw, Pipers McLucas and Parsons then played at a nightclub for the British Council Trade mission, in support of Ballatine's Whisky, before rehearsals began the next morning at 0800 hours. The London Scottish played with the orchestra of the Polish Army at the unveiling ceremony, where they were introduced to the President of Poland, Alexander Kwasniewski. The event itself took over five hours, after which the band went to the Presidential Palace to join a guard of honour alongside various units from the Polish army. As the guard fell-out and marched from the courtyard, Drum Major Alderson saluted and the parade commander ordered 'Eyes Right', whereupon 'the whole parade marched past the Pipes and Drums doing the "Goose Step" returning our salute with an eyes-right. That was a moment to remember.'[43] Most of the band returned home the following day, but Pipe Major Macpherson and Pipers Bracken, Parsons and McLucas stayed on to play at a reception at the British military attaché's residence for around 20 Polish veterans who were finally receiving British medals they had been awarded during the Second World War.

Two weeks later, the London Scottish Regiment was in Messines and Drum Major Alderson again headed the Pipes and Drums, due to Drum Major Powell's continued absence. A week later, on 18 June, the band was back in Normandy for the Balleroy Balloon Festival, where they Beat Retreat in the chateau forecourt in front of a celebrity crowd. Drummer Andrew Abbess, a keen parachutist, brought his parachute and persuaded a balloon owner to agree to take him up and allow him to jump out. Unfortunately, the winds were too strong to make the attempt and Drummer Abbess had to content himself with a Highland dancing display with Rose Murray, who had joined the band for the occasion.

Ms. Murray would again perform with Drummer Abbess at the Scots Guards summer ball, held at 95 Horseferry Road on 1 July, and Drummer Abbess would perform an impromptu sword dance a few weeks later at the Royal Hospital, Chelsea, after the London Scottish Pipes and Drums had played with the Military Band of the Highland Division. Both bands had been invited into the pensioner's bar after the event to a reception where the Highland Division's ceilidh band were performing. When the band had a break, Pipers Parsons and McLucas were asked to play some tunes and Drummer Abbess danced over band president Major Gareth Blyth's sword.

After a large number of other jobs both military and civilian, the Pipes and Drums concluded the year with performances at the St Andrew's Ball at Banqueting House in the City of London, the Ceremony of the Keys at the Tower of London, and a banquet for the Worshipful Company of Distillers; a natural connection for the Pipes and Drums. Drummers were then free to see in the new millennium with family and friends whilst pipers, as customary, earned a small fortune playing at private New Year's Eve parties; it was ever thus!

The year 2000 was another busy year for the band, beginning with four London Scottish pipers assisting at a concert by Isla St Clair at 95 Horseferry Road on 22 March. Later that month, the MacLeod Medal was won by Piper Chris MacTernan who, along with other high-quality pipers including Piper 'Sandy' Gibb (an ex-Scots Greys and Royal Scots Dragoon Guard) and two South Africans, Piper Russell King and Piper Andrew Morty, were recent recruits, attracted by the piping tuition, high standards and military aspect of the band. Piper Parsons was in the chair for the annual band supper on 7 April, at which bass and tenor Drummer Norman Lennie was presented with a silver quaich to celebrate his 50th year with the Pipes and Drums. The Territorial Army pipe band concentration took place at Cameron Barracks in Inverness over the weekend of 14-16 April, with Piper Parsons, Drummer John Conlon, (now ex-) Drummer Abbess and band president Major Blyth instructing the cadet cadre. As senior drum major on parade, Drum Major Powell would lead the massed band for the final Beating Retreat. The London Scottish came 2nd and 3rd in the Quartets.

6 June saw the regiment again invited to Clarence House, on this occasion to celebrate Her Majesty, The Queen Mother's 65th anniversary as Honorary Colonel of the London Scottish. Here, Drum Major Powell was presented with a bar to his TEM by Her Majesty. Regimental Colonel Holliday stated:

---

43 Alderson, *MacNamara's Band to Drum Major*, p.25.

A good turn up and turn out by the Pipes and Drums, which formed up right opposite, and only twenty or thirty yards from, Her Majesty, played with precision and vigour and were greatly appreciated.[44]

Alongside Her Majesty's position as Royal Honorary Colonel, there had always been a Regimental Colonel in the London Scottish to head up the regimental organisation. The Queen Mother's advancing age, combined with the pressures and changes of the previous 15 years, prompted the regiment to seek permission from the military secretary at the MOD to appoint an additional post of Honorary Regimental Colonel. 'This post will be offered to a person of high public profile who will, by his acceptance, become our "champion" and be able to put our case to the relevant authorities should the need arise.'[45] With the proposal having been approved, this position was offered to, and graciously accepted by, Lord George Robertson of Port Ellen, Secretary General of NATO, who was officially appointed later that year.

The Pipes and Drums performed at a concert at the Army School of Music, Kneller Hall, in Twickenham on 14 June and again supported the Royal Artillery at their Sunset Tattoo at Larkhill Garrison later that month. The two major events of the year, however, would come the following month in celebration of Her Majesty, The Queen Mother's 100th birthday. The first of these events occurred on 19 July with Beating Retreat on Horse Guards Parade. This event involved over 1,000 military personnel and 8,000 civilians and was broadcast globally. The London Scottish Pipes and Drums joined 12 other military pipe bands from around the world at the event, including the Toronto Scottish, Black Watch of Canada, Transvaal Scottish and Cape Town Highlanders, as well as several military bands. At the post-parade reception, Drum Major Powell and Drum Major Millar of the Toronto Scottish were presented to Her Majesty. When asked if she could tell which one was which, she light-heartedly replied:

He, (Drum Major Millar) is Canadian and he (Drum Major Powell), is mine.[46]

The canteen at regimental headquarters was open all week during rehearsals and became the home of the various pipe bands involved in the event, many of whom would soon be travelling up to Edinburgh with the London Scottish to begin a week of rehearsals for the 'Big Blow', which would take place on 27 July at Edinburgh Castle. Band members took the train to Edinburgh, but their kit was in a van which was involved in an accident on the A1 motorway and ended up scattered across the carriageway. Luckily, the driver, Corporal Anderson, was not badly hurt, but it meant that only enough undamaged kit could be found to dress five pipers for a reception at Gosford House, hosted by the Earl of Wemyss, grandson of the regiment's founder, Lord Elcho. Replacements and repairs ensured that the London Scottish Pipes and Drums took their place with ten other Scottish military pipe bands and eight others from the Commonwealth for the main event itself. Six-hundred musicians in total performed, of whom over 400 were pipers and drummers. Prior to the performance, the director of the newly amalgamated Army School of Bagpipe Music and Highland Drumming, Major Gavin Stoddart, addressed the London Scottish, professing his satisfaction with their performance during the week and further stated that he would have no hesitation in asking the band back again for other major performances in Scotland. Importantly, as Piper Parsons wrote in the *Regimental Gazette*:

---

44   *London Scottish Regimental Gazette* (2000), p.63.
45   *London Scottish Regimental Gazette* (2000), p.63.
46   *London Scottish Regimental Gazette* (2000), p.69.

95 HORSEFERRY ROAD TO THE LONDON GUARDS 1986-2022

Parade at 95 Horseferry Road to mark the first official association of the Scots Guards and the London Scottish, 15 January 1998. (LSMA, used with permission)

The Pipe and Drum Majors on parade for Her Majesty, The Queen Mother's funeral parade, 9 April 2002, including newly promoted Pipe Major McLucas and Personal Pipers to Her Majesty, Spoore and Macpherson. (LSMA, used with permission)

Pipe Major McLucas at NATO Headquarters to pipe out London Scottish Honorary Colonel George Robertson on leaving his post as Secretary General to NATO, December 2003. (LSMA, used with permission)

The Pipes and Drums leading the regiment through the streets of Messines on their five-yearly pilgrimage to honour the men of the regiment who fought during the First World War, August 2004. (LSMA, used with permission)

Credit here is due to the association members of the band who don't get thanked enough. Ten of our pipers and drummers took a whole week off work without recompense for a job that reflected well upon the London Scottish Regiment as a whole.[47]

Reliance on the 'Old and Bold' and younger volunteer members who wanted to play their part but could not, or did not, want to join the Territorial Army, would become even more pronounced in years to come, and their involvement would guarantee that the London Scottish Pipes and Drums remained a vibrant and viable band. These dedicated members would give up large amounts of their time and money for the privilege of representing the regiment and it would not have been possible for the Pipes and Drums to survive without their service.

In August, serving Pipers Parsons and McLucas attended the two-week army piping course at the Army School of Bagpipe Music and Highland Drumming at Inchdrewer House in Edinburgh. In September, the Pipe and Drum Majors would join the other serving pipers and drummers for the London Regiment annual camp in Romania. Here, Piper McLucas performed in Bucharest at the invitation of the British Ambassador to Romania. October saw the band join the rest of the London Regiment for a parade to celebrate National Territorial Army Day at The Duke of York's Headquarters, Chelsea, followed later in the month by the annual regimental Hallowe'en dinner. After performing their set, the outgoing Regimental Colonel, Colonel Halliday, proposed a toast to the Pipes and Drums, stating 'There is no other sound I would want to follow into battle.'[48]

The winds of change would, once again, begin to blow at the end of the year, when Pipe Major Macpherson announced that he planned to retire on 25 January 2001. At 62 years of age, Pipe Major Macpherson had been kept on as a serving soldier for as long as possible but decided that it was now time to step down. Pipe Sergeant John Bracken was appointed to take his place, both as Pipe Major of the London Scottish and as Personnel Piper to Her Majesty, The Queen Mother. This was a challenging appointment, as Pipe Major Bracken had relatively recently returned to the band, although he had previously served in 'G' Company 1st Battalion, 51st Highland Volunteers and in the London Regiment. His leadership style contrasted somewhat with that of Pipe Major Macpherson's and, on appointment, Pipe Major Bracken made clear his intention to steer the Pipes and Drums towards becoming a Grade Two standard competition band. These ambitions were not necessarily shared by all band members, especially those who felt they could not, or did not, want to perform at this competition standard or who saw the role of a regimental pipes and drums in a wider context; primarily supporting the military and ceremonial functions of the regiment and serving company. While competing was not such a high priority for Drum Major Powell, the Pipe and Drum Majors maintained a good working relationship that would have helped balance regimental commitments with competition aspirations. Unfortunately, Drum Major Powell would soon resign his appointment which, unwittingly, created an imbalance that would have significant consequences.

Disagreements with band president Major Blyth led to the conclusion of Drum Major Powell's tenure after 11 years leading the London Scottish Pipes and Drums. Having resigned from the band, Sergeant Powell remained in the London Scottish for two more years before moving to 'B' (Princess of Wales Royal Regiment) Company, The London Regiment, where he was soon promoted to Company Sergeant Major. He would later transfer to begin a successful and long-running appointment as Drum Major of RAF Halton Pipes and Drums. With a new pipe major still finding his feet, the regiment turned once again to an old hand to help steady the ship, asking veteran Drum Major Alderson to return to provide assistance and lead the Pipes and Drums

---

47   *London Scottish Regimental Gazette* (2000), p.69.
48   *London Scottish Regimental Gazette* (2000), p.106.

at high-profile performances. Drum Major Alderson graciously accepted. 'I was back with old friends; it seemed I had never been away.'[49]

The disruption caused by events during the previous six months, including the untimely death of the London Scottish piping instructor, Pipe Major MacRae, in September 2000, allied with the change in musical direction and style of leadership within the band, led to the departure of numerous pipers and drummers during 2001 and, subsequently, to a dearth of band performances. Pipe Majors Bracken and Macpherson performed together at Buckingham Palace on 11 July at a royal garden party and Pipe Major Macpherson played his composition *The London Scottish Regiment Salute to The Queen Mother* at a Second World War veterans' dinner. A framed copy of the piece was sent to Her Majesty, to which a reply was received stating that, 'Her Majesty much appreciated your kind thoughts in giving her this pipe music, which will be hung in a place of honour at Clarence House.'[50] Full band performances, however, were very rare and the Pipes and Drums were becoming unsustainable as a unit, with four more pipers and a side drummer leaving to join the developing RAF Halton Pipes and Drums.

In a more positive vein, the Cowal Games at Dunoon introduced a new award for juvenile drumming presented in memory of ex-London Scottish Drum Drummer Mike Crowley, who had been so influential in the pipe band world and who had died in 1999. The award was designed and presented by ex-London Scottish piper and band president, Roger Linford. An anonymous donor also arranged for a new London Scottish drum major's baldric to be presented to the regiment at church parade in November. At the donor's request, the presentation was made by Mrs Monica Gibson in memory of her brother Drum Sergeant Crowley. While wishing to remain anonymous at the time, Roger Linford, the generous donor, who had also previously presented a regimental bass drum, may now be rightfully identified and publicly thanked.

The al-Qaeda terrorist attacks on New York City and Washington DC on 11 September 2001, and the subsequent invasion of Afghanistan by the United States and United Kingdom the following month, brought about enormous adjustments in the responsibilities and recruitment of the Territorial Army. The 1996 Reserve Forces Act had permitted individuals, sub-units and units of the Territorial Army to be deployed for operational service both at home and overseas, alongside, and more often within, regular army units. Various TA personnel had been called-up during the Bosnian and Kosovan conflicts in the early 1990s (including Drummer Jamie Ryan who served in a London Scottish platoon embedded with The Highlanders) and intelligence units of the TA were now amongst the first to be called up after '9/11' as the occupation of Afghanistan began. With a country to run and al-Qaeda and Taliban forces to fight, the emphasis of the Territorial Army was now focused on operational readiness and overseas activity with the introduction of extended nine-month call ups for entire companies, rather than for individuals and smaller sub-units. The situation would become even more acute for the British Army 15 months later, after the invasion of Iraq doubled Britain's fighting commitments, with medical, logistical, signals, intelligence and engineering specialists in particular demand. London Scots, including members of the Pipes and Drums, began to prepare for potential operational service in warzones overseas.

During these hectic times, changes within the Pipes and Drums also continued at a pace and in January 2002, Pipe Major Bracken relinquished his appointment after only one year in post. Discussions regarding his replacement centred on two potential candidates, Piper Parsons and Piper McLucas and it would be McLucas who, much to his surprise, was announced as the new Pipe Major at band supper in early March.

---

49 Alderson, *MacNamara's Band to Drum Major*, p.25.
50 *London Scottish Regimental Gazette* (2001), p.81.

Pipe Major Philip 'Jim' McLucas began playing the pipes at the age of nine under the tuition of Pipe Major Jimmy McMinn of the Seaforth Highlander's Association Band in Pleasley. He would eventually join that band as a full member and played with them until he was 18. He performed as a guest piper for highland dancing groups on tours throughout Europe over the next few years and then began playing seriously again in the early 1990s under tutors Jimmy Banks and Pipe Major McRae. He was invited to join their fledgling City of London Pipes and Drums, based at Flemings Bank in The City, who were looking to form a Grade 2 competition band, however this project never quite got off the ground. Having seen the London Scottish Pipes and Drums at the Lord Mayor's Show in 1994, McLucas decided to attend practises with them and, soon after, committed to joining the Territorial Army, completing his combat infantry course at Catterick in 1996. Numbers in the London Scottish Pipes and Drums were very low at that point, and his loyalty through the hard times helped cement his position as the successful candidate when changes came in 2002.

As the paperwork was completed on McLucas's appointment as Pipe Major, but while he waited for final confirmation of is appointment as Personal Piper to The Queen Mother, the sad news arrived that, on 30 March 2002, Her Majesty, Queen Elizabeth, The Queen Mother had died in her sleep at the age of 101. As Regimental Colonel Stephen Henwood observed:

> With the end of the life of our Royal Honorary Colonel we have suffered a very great loss as have many other regiments at home and abroad – she will be irreplaceable and will leave a great void in our lives for many years to come.[51]

Her Majesty had been a staunch supporter and friend of the London Scottish for 67 years and had played no small part in the survival of the regiment on numerous occasions. Her death, both for the regiment and for the country as a whole, very much represented the end of an era.

As preparations began for a state funeral, planned for 9 April, assumptions were made that the London Scottish, Black Watch and Toronto Scottish, of whom The Queen Mother had been Honorary Colonel since 1935, 1937 and 1938 respectively, would each play a central role in the proceedings. However, it soon became obvious that the Household Division would exert their precedence and the three Scottish regiments would be relegated to play bit parts. The main involvement of the London Scottish would be in the massed pipes and drums which would lead the funeral procession but, even here, their responsibilities and participation would be limited. They were asked to form one rank within the massed band, along with the Pipes and Drums of the 51st Highland Regiment, which limited their contribution to just five pipers and three drummers. Newly appointed Pipe Major McLucas fronted the column, along with two ex-Personal Pipers to Her Majesty, Pipe Major Spoore and Pipe Major MacPherson, followed by Pipers Johnston and Parsons. The three drummers selected were Conlon, Foulis and Lloyd. There was no place for London Scottish Drum Major Alderson, despite his 50 years of service. It was the same situation for other regiments. In order to participate at all, the Drum Major of the Black Watch was relegated to playing a tenor drum.

Pipe Major McLucas, having been appointed just days earlier, was very much thrown in at the deep end but, despite having to sew on his new pipe major's chevrons during rehearsals, proved his qualities and justified his appointment by ensuring the London Scottish pipers and drummers who were chosen to participate did the regiment proud. Rehearsals began at RAF Uxbridge on 4 April, with two days perfecting drill and honing the tunes that had been selected for the occasion. This was followed by repeated night-time rehearsals on-site between 0400 hours and 0600

---

51 *London Scottish Regimental Gazette* (2002), p.35.

hours prior to the big day. On 9 April, the massed pipes and drums arrived at Wellington Barracks at 0700 hours and assembled on the parade square at 1000 hours, before marching in silence to Westminster Hall (where Her Majesty was laying in state), behind the empty gun carriage that would later carry Her Majesty's coffin to Westminster Abbey. Pipe Major McLucas, wearing The Queen Mother's pipe banner, and the rest of the massed band stepped off to Her Majesty's favourite tune, *My Home*, which was followed by *The Mist Covered Mountains*, said to be a favourite of her husband, King George VI. Upon reaching Westminster Abbey, the massed pipes and drums stood to attention in front of the grandstand erected for the world's media for the entire duration of the service, before moving into position in front of the abbey doors for the return march. Pipe Major McLucas would later observe:

> At the conclusion of the service, the bearer party carried the coffin through the Abbey and upon reaching the doors, the command was given to begin the lament. We struck up with *Oft in the Stilly Night* as the Irish Guards carried the coffin out of the Abbey and into the hearse. It was difficult not to be affected by the emotion of the moment.[52]

The massed pipes and drums then led the guard of honour and senior military personnel through Parliament Square, down Birdcage Walk and back to Wellington Barracks, playing the retreat marches *Green Hills of Tyrol* and *When the Battle's O'er*. It would be an unforgettable experience for the few London Scots that were lucky enough to be involved.

Two weeks later, at the request of the organising committee, Pipe Major Macpherson, wearing Her Majesty's pipe banner, played a lament at the opening of the Royal Caledonian Ball on honour of The Queen Mother. Viscount Dupplin, Chairman of the ball, wrote to thank Pipe Major Macpherson, stating: 'there was not a dry eye in the house … It will remain an indelible memory on all the many hundreds who were there. You played quite beautifully.'[53] Pipe Major Macpherson refused to take payment for this engagement, asking instead that a donation be made to his preferred charity.

Her Majesty's pipe banner would be worn on one last solemn occasion when Pipe Major McLucas played the lament at the London Scottish memorial service at St Columba's Church on 29 September. Regimental Colonel Henwood stated in his eulogy:

> We have always been proud to provide Her Majesty's personal piper and I know the significance of this to the individuals concerned. Today Pipe Major Jim McLucas carries the Queen Mother's pipe banner for the last time.[54]

It was fitting, then, that Pipe Major McLucas who, while waiting for confirmation of his appointment never got to perform for The Queen Mother as her Personal Piper, should be the last to wear her Royal banner. The banner itself now resides, on proud display, in the regimental museum.

On the last weekend of July 2002, the Pipes and Drums were invited to attend a ceremony to mark the unveiling of a memorial statue at Longueval in France commemorating all pipers who had died during the First World War. A band of 18 pipers and drummers joined seven from the London Irish Rifles to represent the London Regiment, which had contributed 88 battalions during the Great War. They were the biggest band on parade and the only Territorial Army band invited. The Somme Battlefield Pipes and Drums were also invited to perform, with their members

---

52 *London Scottish Regimental Gazette* (2002), p.57.
53 *London Scottish Regimental Gazette* (2002), p.61.
54 *London Scottish Regimental Gazette* (2002), p.123.

wearing the various uniforms of regiments who served in the First World War. 'One of them wears Hodden Grey and for the parade and ceremony, he marched in the ranks of the London Scottish.'[55] The parade marked the last time Pipe Major Macpherson would perform with the London Scottish in full regimental uniform. It was also the first time a female piper had played on parade with the band when Piper Abby MacDougall became the first woman to wear the Hodden Grey. Unfortunately, it was to be her one and only performance in uniform, and it would be another 15 years before the next female piper joined the band.

Drum Major Alderson's extended two-year temporary cameo came to an end in November 2002 when Colour Sergeant David 'Nobby' Foulis was appointed as Drum Major by Regimental Colonel Henwood. Drum Major Foulis had joined the Argyll and Sutherland Highlanders in January 1964 with the objective of becoming a piper but was immediately sent to the Borneo Confrontation on heavy weapons duty and lost the opportunity. He served in the Malayan Peninsular and later at Aden with Lieutenant Colonel Colin 'Mad Mitch' Mitchell, as the 15 pipers famously played *Scotland the Brave* on retaking The Crater. Drum Major Foulis would also see service in Northern Ireland and went on to serve with the Royal Scots, Gordon Highlanders and with the Small Arms School Corps, before leaving the regular army in April 1990. On moving to London, he joined the London Scottish, having been PSI there from 1984 to 1986 whilst with the Gordons, and he began playing tenor and bass drum with the Pipes and Drums in 1994. He took the army drum major's course in 2001 and his first time 'behind the mace' was at church parade in November that year, where he took over from Drum Major Alderson on the return march to regimental headquarters from St Columba's Church.

Drum Major Foulis and Pipe Major McLucas immediately struck up an effective and efficient working relationship, emphasising the military aspect of the Pipes and Drums whilst also actively working to recruit both serving and volunteer members; particularly to the drum corps which was still running at a bare minimum. They would also push others within the Pipes and Drums to take on specific responsibilities, which helped widen the structure and organisation of the band whilst building a core of dedicated pipers and drummers, both serving and non-serving, with vigorous loyalty to both band and regiment. The current success of the London Scottish Pipes and Drums is the ultimate testament to the accomplishment of this strategy, over 20 years into their joint tenure.

Several new pipers joined during this period, including Pipers Stuart McMillan, Haydn Cottam, David Stewart and Stuart Hume, with the latter three still core members in 2022. Piper McMillan would go on to become a Member of the Scottish Parliament, where he is also the Parliamentary Piper, playing the pipes at official functions while still proudly wearing a London Scottish cap badge on his glengarry. Drummers Gary Dillon, David Morris, Duncan de Silva and bass Drummer Bob Edwards, under lead tip Drummer Gordon Lloyd, bolstered the drum corps, helping to build firm foundations through 2003 before more recruits arrived early the following year. Drummers Chris Smith, a TA soldier in the serving company, and Joe MacMahon swelled the ranks of side drummers, whist tenor Drummer Jason Newman and bass Drummer Nicholas Gair arrived from successfully competing with the Pride of Murray Pipe Band. With a strong core, recruiting became easier and a strong, stable Pipes and Drums began to emerge once again.

The Pipes and Drums attended the Territorial Army Pipe Band Concentration at Redford Barracks on the weekend of 22-24 May 2003 which helped re-establish links within Scottish pipe band circles and particularly with the Army piping organisation. While Pipe Major Gordon Walker's Grade Two 52nd Lowland band scooped all the prizes, it was excellent experience for the newer members of the London Scottish. A series of concerts were held again with Isla St Clair in early June, including one at the Royal Hospital, Chelsea, and Pipe Major McLucas played for the

---

55 *London Scottish Regimental Gazette* (2002), p.75.

400th anniversary of the Royal Scottish Corporation, for whom he would be made honorary piper. The major focus of 2003, however, was a summer visit to Gibraltar and the first large scale overseas engagement undertaken for some years.

The London Scottish, along with the Corps of Drums of the 2nd Battalion, Royal Anglian Regiment, had been invited by the Royal Gibraltar Regiment to undertake a number of state ceremonial duties to assist the regiment's military band and pipers and to coincide with an inspection visit by the Inspectorate of the Corps of Army Music. It was an important commitment and a risk for the newly invigorated London Scottish Pipes and Drums, but one which garnered enthusiastic support and encouragement from the wider London Scottish family. In the end, a band of 21 flew to Gibraltar, including Pipe Major Spoore and Drum Major Alderson who would make their final appearances with the band. The musicians were accompanied by 33 officers, soldiers and Regimental Association members who paid their own way to support the band and help fly the flag for the London Scottish. Major Mark Ludlow stood in for Major Stuart Young as band president and provided first class support and assistance.

The Pipes and Drums were billeted in Devil's Tower Camp, next to the airport's military runway, and rehearsals took place at the Devil's Bellows Camp on the other side of the isthmus. A ceremonial guard mount, one of only four carried out each year, took place on the Saturday afternoon, where Pipers Newton and Morty played *Highland Cathedral* from a balcony overlooking The Convent, the Governor's residence. A charity concert took place that evening in St Michael's Cave, a natural amphitheatre within the Rock of Gibraltar, in aid of the Red Cross and War Child, which had sold out weeks in advance. The band came on in complete darkness, descending very steep, damp stone steps which nearly precipitated a disaster, but their performance, which included backing Isla St Clair on *When the Pipers Play* was very well received. The week was the perfect opportunity for the band to bond as a unit, enjoy their surroundings and enhance military aspects in terms of drill, deportment and life in barracks for the newer members.

Colonel Randall of the Royal Gibraltar Regiment wrote to his counterpart at the London Scottish stating that, 'I would like to pass on my sincere congratulations to the Pipes and Drums of the London Scottish Regiment for the most excellent of visits to Gibraltar and their outstanding performances throughout.' He went on to state that the Inspectorate of the Corps of Army Music had been 'very impressed with what they saw.'[56] The success of this tour not only led to six subsequent invitations to return to Gibraltar over the coming years but also began to raise awareness of the band within the Corps of Army Music and wider army circles who now had first-hand experience of the proficiency of the London Scottish Pipes and Drums.

The efficiency of the serving company was also becoming more apparent and their services were much in demand. The Company Commander, Major Marc Overton, stated at the regimental Hallowe'en dinner that, 'For the first time since the Second World War soldiers from this unit have been compulsory mobilised to go to war.'[57] The multinational invasion of Iraq had seen over 30 London Scottish soldiers volunteer to supplement the regular army in Operations TELIC 1 and 2, alongside the continuing operations in Afghanistan. Having been called-up, another 21 London Jocks deployed to theatre in January 2004 with the 100-strong London Regiment Cambrai Company for TELIC 3. Those serving overseas included Drummer Gary Dillon, a company medic attached to the RAF medical centre at Basra Airport, ex-piper Colour Sergeant Nick Tuckey as CQMS and ex-drummer Lance Corporal Jamie Ryan, now serving with The Highlanders. London Scottish soldiers would be involved in multiple further deployments to both

---

56 *London Scottish Regimental Gazette* (2003), p.98.
57 *London Scottish Regimental Gazette* (2003), p.117.

Iraq and Afghanistan over the coming years, beginning with Messines Company for TELIC 4 in May 2004.

Honorary Regimental Colonel Lord Robertson left his post as Secretary General to NATO in December 2003 and Pipe Major McLucas ensured that he 'was marched out from NATO Headquarters in Brussels to the sound of the London Scottish pipes.'[58] It was the end of a critical and historic year for the London Scottish and marked the beginning of an important period in the regiment's history.

January 2004 sadly witnessed the first London Scottish operational casualties since the Second World War. The most severe of those injured was Lance Corporal Ian Dawson, a strong supporter of the Pipes and Drums, who sustained a serious head injury and lost an eye in an IED explosion whist on convoy escort duties in Iraq. Lance Corporal Dawson had previously served overseas in Bosnia, attached to The Highlanders, and would later go on to become Company Sergeant Major.

Back at home, the Pipes and Drums recorded their first album, when ex-drummer Pat King took the band into the studio in March to record *Strike Sure*. The 17-track album contained medleys and sets of the full band, solos on Highland and small pipes and the first recording of the London Regiment's regimental march, *The London's Return*. Pipe Major McLucas composed the tune *Cambrai's Return* during this period, to commemorate the return of Cambrai Company, who would finish their deployment to Iraq in May. The tune was first aired in public on 30 May during a reception at London Scottish headquarters to welcome home Cambrai Company and bid farewell to Messines Company who would leave for deployment to Iraq in June. It was a poignant ceremony with Cambrai Company returning home after nine months overseas. 'The balconies were full of families and the reception as the Company marched in to the sounds of the Pipes and Drums was very emotional.'[59]

Ten days earlier, the pipe band had Beat Retreat at regimental headquarters for His Royal Highness, The Duke of Gloucester at the unveiling of the Royal Caledonian Schools Trust Scottish clan crests wall, which was followed later that evening by the entire band heading to East London to attend the opening of a gallery exhibition of landscape and portrait paintings by distinguished artist Piper Cottam. Later in the month the Pipes and Drums would Beat Retreat at the Royal Hospital, Chelsea with the Highland Band of the Scottish Division before leaving for a second trip to Gibraltar in early June.

Tercentenary celebrations throughout 2004 marked the capture of Gibraltar from Spain during the War of the Spanish Succession in 1704. The military importance of 'The Rock' for the British Navy, Army and RAF over the following 300 years cannot be overestimated, but Gibraltar's sovereignty has been continuously and fiercely disputed by Spain. Consequently, for diplomatic reasons, there was no royal involvement in the 300th anniversary celebrations, which was a major disappointment to the population of Gibraltar. A band of 19 London Scottish pipers and drummers took part in a guard mount at the Governor's residence and then at the Queen's Birthday Parade at the Victoria Stadium on 10 June. There, they joined a massed band of over 100 musicians including the Clive Band of the Prince of Wales's Division, the Royal Gibraltar Regiment Military Band and Corps of Drums, as well as the Corps of Drums of the 1st Battalion Royal Anglian Regiment. A guard from the Royal Artillery, Royal Engineers, Royal Marines and Royal Gibraltar Regiment escorted the colours of the Royal Gibraltar Regiment and there was a fly-past of Royal Navy and RAF aircraft. The following day was spent at the Royal Gibraltar Regiment Association building, with pipes being played and London Scottish CDs sold. It was here that Piper Hume 'solved a 60-year-old mystery by deciphering a WWII Japanese flag. I am no longer surprised by

---

58   *London Scottish Regimental Gazette* (2004), p.8.
59   *London Scottish Regimental Gazette* (2004), p.63.

anything this band does.'[60] Being a fluent Mandarin speaker, Piper Hume had been able to translate the adopted Chinese characters common between both written languages.

A second overseas visit came later in the summer, when the London Scottish regimental family made a 90th anniversary trip to Messines and Ypres. The Pipes and Drums performed at the Last Post ceremony at the Menin Gate before Beating Retreat on the exact spot in front of the Ypres Cloth Hall where the 1st Battalion had mustered before the Battle of Messines in 1914. A parade on the Sunday to the London Scottish Memorial on Messines Ridge was followed with a reception hosted by the town council of Messines, during which the Pipe Major was presented with two hand-made statues of pipers, cast from lead dug up by farmers ploughing the battlefield on which the London Scottish had first gone into battle.

December included celebrations to mark the return of Messines Company from Iraq, and Pipe Major McLucas played at the SSAFA Carol Concert on Christmas Eve at the Guards Chapel, Wellington Barracks, which was transmitted around the world on British Forces Broadcast Radio. Christmas saw London Scottish pipers and drummers celebrating in New Zealand, Newfoundland, South Africa, USA and Iraq:

> On a more sombre note, Piper Chris MacTernan, who is currently working in Northern Iraq, played his pipes at Christmas time at an American MASH unit (field hospital) for the survivors of the tragic bombing in Mosul.[61]

News began to filter through in early 2005 concerning details of plans for further amalgamation within the British army that had first been announced by the Secretary of State for Defence in December 2004. It had already been decided that Scottish infantry regiments would join together and, in some cases, amalgamate to form a new Royal Regiment of Scotland with effect from April, with the loss of all previous cap-badges but with a degree of regimental identity preserved. It was also announced that all regular army regiments would now integrate an associated Territorial Army battalion, which would also wear the same cap badge. These proposals presented, yet again, another problematic situation for the position of the London Scottish within the London Regiment. While the future was still not clear, it was heavily rumoured that the London Regiment would become the TA support battalion for the Guards Division, wearing a new London Regiment cap-badge and losing individual company identities. Thus, began yet another round of intense lobbying and campaigning to keep the London Scottish identity alive, although it would be another year before the outcome was finally known.

Within the Pipes and Drums, recruitment continued at a pace, including Drummer Stephen Hill, who would go on to become a cornerstone of the band, and Piper Bill Ferguson, son of former London Scottish Pipe Major 'Fergie' Ferguson. Increased numbers meant that 20 pipers and drummers competed for the in-house piping and drumming competitions, with the MacLeod Medal won by Piper Parsons and the Attwooll Trophy, reinstated for the first time in many years, won by Drummer Hill. The prizes were presented by Colonel Jackman of the Toronto Scottish Regiment who was visiting the London Scottish.

The London terrorist attacks of 7 July 2005 coincided with a dinner commemorating the end of the Second World War which was due to take place at 95 Horseferry Road that evening. In true 'Blitz Spirit' it was decided to go ahead, although transport disruption made it impossible for many of the band to make their way to regimental headquarters. Pipers Parsons, Skilling, Stewart and Blackledge, however, did find a way and 'the full programme was played by a pipe quartet rather

---

60 *London Scottish Regimental Gazette* (2004), p.66.
61 *London Scottish Regimental Gazette*, (2005), p.144.

than the full band. This was greatly appreciated by all present'[62] including Lord Robertson and the many veterans in attendance.

In August, the Pipes and Drums were invited for a third trip to Gibraltar and performed again at a Trooping of the Colour, this time in Casemates Square. They also played at an evening concert at the Governor's residence, The Convent, and at the departure of a cruise liner; slightly surreal, but possibly another 'first' for the band. For the third year, the band were accompanied by Ron Younger, the ex-Scots Guards, ex-London Scottish, regimental bar steward, who was of invaluable help and 'whose kazoo intro to Killaloe was the highlight of the trip for many.'[63] The band would show their appreciation by playing at Mr Younger's wedding a few weeks later at the regimental kirk, St Columba's.

Over the weekend of 23-25 September, the London Scottish joined 12 other regiments at the Loos British cemetery in France for a 90th Anniversary Service of Remembrance. 'With the Pipes and Drums prominently formed up in front of the Sword, the Hodden Grey could be proudly seen on all four sides of the parade.'[64] A massed pipes and drums comprising the Black Watch, King's Own Scottish Borderers, London Irish and the London Scottish also marched through the town before the London Regiment attended a parade at Auchy-Les-Mines. They also attended a wreath-laying ceremony with the Durham Light Infantry and the Royal Sussex Regiment at St Mary's military cemetery and a remembrance ceremony at the exact spot where Piper Laidlaw of the King's Own Scottish Borderers earned his Victoria Cross during the First World War.

The weekend of church parade in November also included the first recording sessions for a second album by the Pipes and Drums. *Tunes of Glory: Salute to the Scottish Regiments*, again produced and recorded by ex-drummer Pat King, was created to supplement the band's involvement with the forthcoming, award-winning, touring theatre production by Middle Ground of the original 1960 film *Tunes of Glory*, in which the London Scottish Pipes and Drums had also featured. The current Pipes and Drums were involved with the new play and had spent a day earlier in the year being filmed at the Royal Artillery Barracks, Woolwich Arsenal, wearing the costumes originally used in the film for a series of recorded clips that were to be projected on stage during the live performances. The album included 10 tracks of duty calls, military standards, sets and solos which were well received. Tracks from the album which have subsequently been uploaded online, including *Highland Laddie* and *Cock O' the North*, have received well over two and a half million views on YouTube.

The year 2006 would prove to be another momentous year for both the London Scottish Regiment and the Pipes and Drums. Confirmation came in late spring that the London Regiment would be operationally aligned with the Foot Guards and, in May, the regiment was formally transferred from the Queen's Division to the Household Division. 'A' (London Scottish) Company would be aligned and officially associated further with the Scots Guards but would retain the London Scottish cap badge and their unique Scottish regimental traditions. To commemorate this increased level of association, the Scots Guards and London Scottish Pipes and Drums gave a performance on 2 May at 95 Horseferry Road. The Regimental Lieutenant Colonel of the Scots Guards, Colonel Alastair Mathewson, stated:

> The Regimental Colonel and all ranks Scots Guards send the Regimental Colonel and all ranks of the London Scottish their warmest best wishes on the historic occasion of the formal

---

62 *London Scottish Regimental Gazette*, (2005), p.203.
63 *London Scottish Regimental Gazette*, (2005), p.211.
64 *London Scottish Regimental Gazette* (2005), p.247.

pairing of the two Scottish regiments with their headquarters in the British capital, in anticipation of a long and fruitful association.[65]

This formal pairing came after nearly 150 years of informal association and affiliation dating back to the very founding of the London Scottish Rifles Volunteers in 1859.

April saw the premier of the *Tunes of Glory* theatre production attended by the Pipes and Drums and a large number of London Scottish Association members. 'We knew the Pipes and Drums had been used to record the score for use on stage and would be piping on the night but until we saw them play we did not fully appreciate the extent of their influence.'[66] The pipe band scenes were projected onto a huge backdrop on stage, whilst reproductions of regimental paintings adorned the sets. The play won rave reviews, with the *Daily Telegraph* declaring it 'a triumph' and honouring it with their critics' choice award.

In May, the Pipes and Drums again returned to Gibraltar for another tour, accompanied by new band president Lieutenant Colonel Peter McLelland, who had previously been the Commanding Officer of the London Regiment. In June, with both the Scots Guards and Irish Guards serving in Iraq, the London Scottish and London Irish Pipes and Drums were invited to join the massed bands of the Household Division for Beating Retreat on Horse Guards Parade. The drum major of the London Irish was none other than ex-London Scot, Drum Major Alderson, brought out of retirement once again. July saw the London Scottish Regiment at Thiepval for the 90th anniversary of the Battle of the Somme, followed by a visit to the pipers' memorial at Longeuval. In August, the Pipes and Drums were invited to the 6th International Bagpipe Festival at Xixon, Spain, where they joined bands from all over the Celtic world for a long weekend of celebrations which included concerts, street parades and exchanges of musical traditions, and which also happily coincided with the local cider festival. 'The cider was working well and at 1:30 in the morning an improvised band of French, Spanish and Escocias marched through the Astorian countryside playing *Scotland the Brave* … a truly memorable day.'[67]

A further highlight of 2006 was the attendance of the Pipes and Drums of the Toronto Scottish Regiment at the Lord Major's Show and the London Scottish church parade in November. A combined band of 49 from the London Irish, Toronto Scottish and London Scottish paraded on Saturday for Lord Mayor's, and a band of 50 London and Toronto Scottish pipers and drummers led the regiment on church parade the following day. It proved to be an arduous weekend of marching for many of the 'Toronto Jocks' but was a wonderful opportunity to renew ties between the two sister regiments.

All in all, the Pipes and Drums performed at over 20 full band events during 2006, involving a series of high-profile and overseas performances totalling around 30 days. Additionally, solo pipers provided by the regiment undertook more than 30 other performances. This represented an enormous commitment, especially from volunteer members who received no pay, used their own annual leave entitlement and often paid their own expenses and costs for the honour of representing the regiment. Such dedication was proof that the Pipes and Drums were now in excellent shape, and this busy year would be a sign of what was to come.

March 2007 saw the latest London Regiment overseas operation with Somme Company, containing 28 London Scottish soldiers including Drummer Chris Smith, deploying to Afghanistan on Operation HERRICK 6. They operated as a company within the 1st Battalion, Worcester and Sherwood Foresters battle group, alongside their regular counterparts. Sadly, Grenadier

---

65 *London Scottish Regimental Gazette* (2006), p.4.
66 *London Scottish Regimental Gazette* (2006), p.11.
67 *London Scottish Regimental Gazette*, (2006), p.11.

Guardsman Daryl Hickey was killed while serving with Somme Company after an engagement with the Taliban and others in the company were seriously injured during the tour.

On 19 April, back at regimental headquarters, the Pipes and Drums supported a charity concert for the London Scottish Benevolent Fund and the Not Forgotten Association which provides support for injured servicemen and the families of soldiers killed in action. The band also performed, slightly surreally, that month at the opening of the new Church of Scientology Headquarters in the City of London, in front of 5,000 happy Scientologists before heading to Gibraltar for their fourth tour on 25 April. In May, the Pipes and Drums played for the London Scottish Rugby Club's final game of the season, where a win against Richmond RFC guaranteed the club's promotion. The band's performance appeared on Sky Sports and in *Rugby World Magazine* and was utilised to make a recruiting appeal at the game and highlight Somme Company's current service in Afghanistan.

Having acquitted themselves well at Beating Retreat the previous year, the London Scottish were invited back to perform again on 6-7 June and joined with the London Irish as the combined London Regiment Pipes and Drums. They were the only pipe band on parade and played a set on their own to an appreciative crowd of over 3,000 spectators each night. 28 June saw the London Scottish Pipes and Drums Beat Retreat with the Military Band of the Royal Signals at the Royal Hospital, Chelsea, for the centenary celebrations of the First Aid Nursing Yeomanry in the presence of Her Royal Highness, The Princess Royal, their Commandant-in-Chief. The band then travelled to Holland for the Voorhuitzon Military Tattoo, with the Pipes and Drums of RAF Waddington, the 1st Battalion, Royal Tank Regiment and the Royal Scots Dragoon Guards. In July, Piper Hume was interviewed on Chinese national television during a band performance at The London Gathering at the Inner Temple as part of a Scottish trade show. The Chinese reporter was somewhat shocked to find a Scottish piper in London wearing full military uniform who could speak fluent Mandarin.

The Pipes and Drums led a homecoming parade at the Guildhall on 14 October 2007 to welcome back Somme Company from Afghanistan. The joint London Scottish and London Irish Pipes and Drums were on hand to welcome home the troops including London Scottish Drummer Chris Smith and London Irish Piper Will Aspinall. The ceremony was shown on BBC News and made the front cover of the *Daily Telegraph*. The following week the Pipes and Drums departed for the Fulda Military Tattoo in Germany. October ended with the traditional regimental dinner on Hallowe'en where the new Regimental Colonel, Colonel David Rankin-Hunt, personally thanked Pipe Major McLucas and Drum Major Foulis for turning around the fortunes of the Pipes and Drums and for fostering such high standards and an even higher public profile:

> I claim no personal credit for their achievements but bask in their reflected glory. They do a tremendous amount to promote the London Scottish and the London Regiment and I was particularly proud to watch them take part in Beating Retreat on Horse Guards as part of the Household Division earlier this year.[68]

Piper Parsons won the Messines Trophy for best London Scottish soldier of 2007 and Drum Major Foulis made a presentation to the outgoing Regimental Colonel, Colonel Henwood.

The London Regiment provided the guard of honour at the Lord Mayor's Show in November, which included the London Scottish Pipes and Drums and, the following day, at church parade, Drum Major Foulis ensured his place in London Scottish history by making a wrong turn on the march from regimental headquarters to St Columba's Church. This resulted in the entire

---

68 *London Scottish Regimental Gazette* (2007), p.18.

column marching along Knightsbridge, causing somewhat of a traffic disaster and an enormous logistical headache for the accompanying police escort. His performance would instigate a new award, a set of tom-tom drums, inaugurated by the band president Lieutenant Colonel McLelland at the following band supper, to be presented to the bandsman that had made the most significant contribution to band morale (in other words, the biggest 'cock up') during the preceding 12 months. In his defence, Drum Major Foulis maintained that he was simply following the police horse in front of him. At the reception after church parade, Colonel Christopher Van de Noot, Gordon Highlanders (retired), presented the pipers with a new banner on behalf of the Gordon Highlanders Association. Pipe Major Spoore, in Gordon Highlanders uniform, piped the banner in and transferred it to Piper Bob Harman, in London Scottish uniform, who played it out. The two men having previously served together with both the London Scottish and the 1st Battalion, Gordon Highlanders.

On 18 November, the band paraded at the Cenotaph in Whitehall with the Devon and Dorset's Regimental Association, for whom they had played at this prestigious event over the last few years. Having initially been mistakenly missed out of the invitations to attend the inaugural Armistice Parade at the Cenotaph in 1920, amends had been made to the Devon and Dorset Regiments, along with the Royal Tank Regiment (which had also been omitted), by permitting them to parade at The Cenotaph in their own private ceremony, the following Sunday. This tradition has continued to modern times and is jealously guarded. Four days later, on 22 November, pipers and drummers from the London Scottish joined the Military Band of the Scots Guards to march 'F' Company, Scots Guards through the streets of Westminster and Chelsea from Chelsea Barracks to their new home at Wellington Barracks where they were inspected by His Royal Highness, the Duke of Kent, Colonel of the Scots Guards.

The year 2008 began with the annual regimental children's party that had been held since 1914. Piper Bill Ferguson, who had attended these parties as a child, brought his own adult son, Tom, who was also a piper and persuaded him to march with the band. The following year, Tom would join the Pipes and Drums, making it three generations of London Scottish pipers from the Ferguson family. A performance of a quite different kind came on February 28th, when the band were invited to appear on stage with the Welsh rock band, the Manic Street Preachers, at the O2 Arena in London for the New Musical Express Big Gig in front of a capacity crowd of 20,000 people. The Pipes and Drums were well looked after by the 'Preachers' who provided them with a crate of Welsh Penderyn whisky at the after party.

On 7 May, Piper Parsons played a solo performance at the top of the dome of St Paul's Cathedral during the City Salute event hosted by Their Royal Highnesses Prince William and Prince Harry to raise money for British service personnel wounded in Iraq and Afghanistan. Later that month, the London Scottish joined a massed pipes and drums at Windsor Castle for A Hero's Welcome; another largescale fund-raising event for British troops which would take place over four evenings, along the lines of the old Royal Tournament. On the last evening, the Pipes and Drums were reviewed by Her Majesty, The Queen and the participating pipe and drum majors, including Pipe Major McLucas, Drum Major Foulis and Drum Major Alderson, who was on parade with the London Irish Rifles Pipes and Drums for the final time after 57 years' service, were presented to Her Majesty. 'The setting was perfect, yet another memorable parade.'[69]

The highlight of 2008 for many in the pipe band came from 12-17 June with an invitation to participate in the 90th anniversary commemorations in northern Italy of the First World War battles of Piave, Asiago and Vittorio Veneto, which had taken place in May and June 1918 and brought about ultimate victory for the Allies on the Italian front. The 2nd Battalion, Gordon

---

69 Alderson, *MacNamara's Band to Drum Major*, p.29.

Pipe Major McLucas and Drum Major Foulis at Devil's Tower Barracks, Gibraltar, 2005. (LSMA, used with permission)

The Pipes and Drums of the London Scottish and Toronto Scottish, Church Parade 2006. (LSMA, used with permission)

Recreating the famous photograph of the 1st Battalion London Scottish at the Piazza San Marco, Venice in 1945 during the tour of Italy, June 2008. (LSMA, used with permission)

Members of the Pipes and Drums at the Peace Village, Messines recreating the inimitable style of their predecessors who fought at the Battle of Messines 100 years previously, June 2014. (LSMA, used with permission)

Highlanders had fought in these campaigns and their Drums and Pipes were well remembered in the local area. The London Scottish band travelled throughout the region, playing at many different cemeteries and local towns. At Piave, band president, Lieutenant Colonel McLelland, talked his way into the seat of a First World War Tiger Moth bi-plane for the fly past. On the last day, the Pipes and Drums went to Venice and recreated the famous 1945 photograph of the London Scottish Pipes and Drums parading in the Piazza San Marco (St Mark's Square), where they Beat Retreat in front of a large and appreciative crowd.

On 21 June, the Pipes and Drums performed at the Territorial Army's TA100 celebrations, marching the entire column from Horse Guards Parade, past Buckingham Palace to Wellington Barracks. Pipers Parsons and Bowler (who would later rise to the rank of Major in 1st Scots), attired as First World War pipers, led two files of similarly dressed actors and a period Rolls Royce armoured car. A week later, the band attended a military tattoo near Arnhem, Holland, filmed a television advertisement in Battersea Park for a Vietnamese scooter company and, in August, returned once again to Asturias for the Xixon International Bagpipe Festival. A band of more than 20 performed at the regimental Hallowe'en dinner, at which a delegation from the Toronto Scottish, including Drum Major Johnny Millar and Drummers Bill Bain and Joe Blake were guests. Drummer Blake joined the band for church parade two weeks later. The year ended with the sad news of the death of David Charteris, 12th Earl of Wemyss and March and grandson of Lord Elcho, founder of the regiment. At the funeral, two London Scottish pipers piped the coffin, draped in Hodden Grey, into the church.

The year 2009 marked the 150th Anniversary of the London Scottish Regiment, and a series of commemorative events were organised throughout the year. The annual band supper took place in April, where ex-Drum Major Alderson, ex-Pipe Majors Spoore and Macpherson and 'Old and Bold' drummer Pat King related some of their favourite memories from their time with the Pipes and Drums. 16 April saw the band play at a regimental cocktail party and, later in the month, perform at the Royal Caledonian Ball. A regimental garden party took place on 24 May at Loseley Park in Surrey, where 'The Band played to their inimitable high standard, which completed a memorable day.'[70] Regimental Colonel Rankin-Hunt also staged a ceremony at 95 Horseferry Road to present commemorative 150th Anniversary medallions to all serving soldiers and all members of the Pipes and Drums, both serving and volunteer.

13 June saw a regimental association ceilidh held at headquarters and, later in the month, the Pipes and Drums Beat Retreat at a charity event in Pimlico with the Corps of Drums of the Coldstream Guards, before heading off once again for a weeklong tour of Gibraltar during the first week of July. On their return, they played at the regimental 150th anniversary dinner, in the presence of His Royal Highness, Prince Edward, Earl of Wessex, whose association with the London Scottish and the London Regiment was to become much closer in the coming years. Pipers Parsons and Skilling represented the London Scottish in July at the Gordon Highlanders International Homecoming event, where regiments throughout the Commonwealth that could trace their lineage to the Gordon Highlanders were invited to parade in a massed band. Piper Parsons was also involved in piping in The King of Tonga when His Majesty visited regimental headquarters on 20 August.

The main regimental commemorative event of the year, however, was the pilgrimage to Messines where the London Scottish were invited to participate in the Last Post Ceremony at the Menin Gate. The Pipes and Drums would, unexpectedly, take centre stage:

---

70   *London Scottish Regimental Gazette* (2009), p.4.

At the very last moment (after we had marched into position at the ceremony) we were informed that we would be Beating Retreat within the 'parade square' of the Menin Gate itself. This was a great honour and it is certainly something none of us will ever forget. All of us in uniform were standing ten feet tall with pride.[71]

The visit to Messines and Ypres rounded off a hugely successful 150th anniversary year. The regiment was in excellent shape, with recruiting at a high and an additional platoon authorised. Amiens Company, which included ex-Corporal Drummer Ryan who had newly re-joined the London Scottish, had been mobilised and would deploy to Afghanistan for HERRICK 2 in January. Ex-piper and current CSM Tuckey would also deploy separately to provide security at the British Embassy in Kabul. Four further deployments to Operation HERRICK would take place over the following three years, taking the total London Scottish deployment to Iraq and Afghanistan over the eight years since 2001 to approximately 500 men.

On 15 December, Rifleman James Brown of the 3rd Battalion, The Rifles was killed whilst engaging a suicide bomber at a checkpoint in Sangin, Afghanistan. He had arrived in country less than two weeks earlier and had been on operations for only four days. Rifleman Brown was the partner of Hayley Morris, daughter of London Scottish Drummer David Morris. On 14 January 2010, members of the London Scottish Pipes and Drums had the honour of playing at his funeral in Bromley. 'This was the first full military funeral in London in the last 20 years. At the request of the family, three drummers and four pipers played at the cemetery as this 18-year-old soldier was laid to rest.'[72]

The 150th Anniversary of the London Scottish Pipes and Drums occurred in 2010, highlighting the band's standing as the fourth oldest pipe band in the world and the oldest outside of the regular British army. Under Drum Major Foulis and Pipe Major McLucas, the band was experiencing somewhat of a renaissance and was at its strongest point of any time since the Second World War. The piping contingent was particularly robust, and the drummers were finally catching up in both quality and quantity with well-respected Drummer Andy Withers arriving to take over as leading tip from Drummer John Morrison. Band membership was soaring with recent arrivals such as Pipers Robert Vowles, Malcolm Wright, Christopher Blenkinsop, Robert Green, Stephen Noble and Alexander Bourne-May joining a core of dedicated serving and non-serving pipers and drummers who went above and beyond in service to the regiment. In celebration of the 150th anniversary, the objective of the year was 'to make the year a memorable one for the band members and to raise the profile of the Regiment in ways that perhaps traditional military publicity channels could not.'[73]

This began on 20 January with the Pipes and Drums performing at a centenary dinner for the London Youth Trust (LYT) at St James's Palace, in the presence of Her Royal Highness, Princess Anne, The Princes Royal in her position as patron of the LYT. St James's Palace is the most senior royal palace in the United Kingdom and, as such, is the official residence of the monarchy. Here, the Pipes and Drums were provided the rare privilege of Beating Retreat in the Colour Court, where Her Royal Highness took the salute, accompanied by Major General Sir Evelyn Webb-Carter, President of the LYT, and London Scottish bass Drummer Nicholas Gair, Chairman of the LYT. Having had his uniform prepared specially for the occasion, Drum Major Foulis left the dry-cleaning ticket on his plaid, to the general amusement of all. Colonel Peter McLelland also attended the dinner, as did Major General, The Duke of Westminster, who was at the time the

---

71 *London Scottish Regimental Gazette*,(2009), p.12.
72 *London Scottish Regimental Gazette* (2010), p.13.
73 *London Scottish Regimental Gazette* (2010), p.15.

senior serving TA officer in the army. After the dinner, LYT presented the band with a case of champagne, which was used at the band ladies night supper a few weeks later.

Piper Rob Blackledge and family organised a Winter Warmer at 95 Horseferry Road on 3 February to raise funds for the Royal Hospital, Chelsea, Help for Heroes and the London Scottish Benevolent Fund, which was a great success. The internal band competitions took place on 4 March, with the MacLeod Medal won by Piper King, the Macpherson Quaich won by Piper Johnston and the Attwooll Trophy won by Drummer Andy Withers. 13 March saw a 150th anniversary solo piping competition at regimental headquarters, organised by ex-London Scottish piper, WO2 Tuckey, who was assisted by Adam Sanderson, President of the Scottish Piping Society of London. The event attracted top soloists from around the country, as well as Pipe Major Alan Clark of the Cameron Highlanders of Ottawa, who flew over to attend. It was judged by Pipe Major Lewis Barclay of The Highlanders and gold medallist Tom Speirs, son of the Second World War London Scottish Pipe Major Jock Speirs. The open competition was won by John Angus Smith and the amateur event by Alan Dunsmore.

The largest band supper since its inception in the 1860s took place later in March, with over 100 guests and Tom Speirs as guest of honour. Tom's son, Iain Speirs, one of the world's elite pipers, gave a recital, and Piper Blackledge and Drummer Hill spoke on behalf of the pipers and drummers. Drummer de Silva gave a concise history of the last 150 years, illustrated with images of the Pipes and Drums through the ages. Drummer de Silva also presented a new prize, the 150th Anniversary Claymore, awarded to the piper or drummer who had made the biggest contribution to the band over the preceding year. The inaugural award went to Piper Blackledge. A veritable army of pipers and drummers then took to the drill hall floor for the traditional march and counter-march to end the formal segment of the evening.

The ladies night, mentioned previously, was organised on 24 April to recognise and thank long-suffering wives, girlfriends and partners and the band played at the Royal Caledonian Ball on 39 April, where officers of the London Scottish Regiment had a table. A mini-band joined ex-Pipe Major King at the Caledonian Society summer ball on 4 June, with a performance the following day at the regimental ceilidh and another the day after with the Grade 1 Vale of Athol Pipe Band at the newly revived Richmond International Highland Games. Later that month, the Pipes and Drums were invited to shoot at Bisley by the Muzzle Loaders Association of Great Britain, organised by Piper Bill Ferguson. The band stayed at the old London Scottish shooting lodge, now owned by the Army Rifle Association, where Piper Ferguson played a lament at the rose garden, where the ashes of many London Scots, including his father Pipe Major William Ferguson, are scattered. The Muzzle Loaders taught the band how to shoot the Pattern 1853 Enfield rifle used by the London Scottish at Wimbledon in 1860 and the Short Lee Enfield .303 used by the regiment during the Battle of Messines in 1914. The band performed for Lieutenant Colonel Marc Overton at his garden party which was taking place nearby and then Beat Retreat outside the Exhibition Lodge at Bisley before a dinner hosted by the Muzzle Loaders. During the weekend, 'because of time constraints and for the hell of it'[74] the band participated in 100-yard target shooting in full dress uniforms and were, thus, attired very similarly to their predecessors from 1860 and 1914. The overall shooting competition was won by Pipe Major McLucas, with Lieutenant Colonel Ludlow second and Drummer de Silva third.

On 26 June, the Pipes and Drums played at five different venues throughout London in one day for National Armed Forces Day. In July, the band's seventh and final trip to Gibraltar took place, with ceremonial events including a guard mount at The Convent, the official residence of the Governor, where they performed with the Corps of Drums and Military Band of the Royal

---

74 *London Scottish Regimental Gazette*, (2009), p.45

Gibraltar Regiment. Despite the cessation of this annual trips, the association with the Royal Gibraltar Regiment would continue back in the United Kingdom with the band regularly assisting in Gibraltar Day celebrations at the Guildhall, which took place in 2010 on 18 October. The Pipes and Drums played again at the Guildhall on 24 October for the homecoming parade of Amiens Company and the newly mobilised Ypres Company who would join 5 SCOTS (Argyll and Sutherland Highlanders) on Operation HERRICK 13. 'The Homecoming Parade reinforces the idea that we are fully part of the London Regiment and that our primary job is to support the Battalion in whatever way possible.'[75]

In further celebration of the 150th anniversary, a request was made to Colonel Mark Cuthbert-Brown, Commandant at Kneller Hall, which resulted in an invitation for the London Scottish Pipes and Drums to participate at the Royal Military School of Music's summer concerts in July and August.

On 5 November, Lance Corporal Piper Parsons finally celebrated his promotion after 14 years as a private by piping in His Majesty, King Hussein of Jordan on a royal visit to regimental headquarters. Lance Corporal Piper Parsons now vacant position as the longest serving private in the regiment's serving company was kept within the traditional confines of the Pipes and Drums by Drummer Smith.

Following their performance at the LYT dinner at St James's Palace the band were invited by Major General Sir Evelyn Webb-Carter to perform at the newly instigated British Military Tournament, in aid of ABF – The Soldier's Charity (formerly the Army Benevolent Fund). Bass Drummer Gair remembers:

> Evelyn and I were having lunch in Belgravia and bumped into Christopher Joll – Event Director and Producer of the BMT. Evelyn asked Christopher, 'Do we have any Pipes & Drums in the Tournament?' and Christopher said 'No.' Tapping me on the arm, Evelyn said 'Well, we do now!!'[76]

After the success of the Windsor Tattoo in 2008 and 2009, it had been decided to bring a Royal Tournament-style event back to Earl's Court in London, which took place on 4-5 December with four performances in front of over 60,000 spectators. The Pipes and Drums helped re-enact the Victorian era story of the daily 1600 hour guard change at Horse Guards, with barman Ron Younger taking a cameo role as John Brown. The involvement of the Pipes and Drums enabled the London Regiment recruiting team to set up a promotional stand at the event and demonstrated once again the importance of the Pipes and Drums in keeping the London Scottish in the public eye. It was a wonderful way to bring the 150th anniversary of the band to a close.

The weekend of 4-6 March 2011 saw 'Exercise London's Return' take around 200 serving soldiers, association members and the Pipes and Drums to tour the First World War battlefields around Ypres, with the objective of bringing together the widest possible London Regiment family to learn more about the regiment's combined history. On the Friday evening, the Pipes and Drums marched the regiment to the Last Post Ceremony at the Menin Gate before an impromptu Beating Retreat outside the Ypres Cloth Hall. Most of Saturday was spent touring various battlefield sites relevant to the London Regiment before a second, official, Beating Retreat in Ypres. Sunday was spent at the Loos cemetery before the regiment moved to Vimy Ridge for a moving drumhead ceremony in freezing weather conditions.

---

75 *London Scottish Regimental Gazette* (2011), p.23.
76 Nicholas Gair, Personal correspondence with author (June 2021).

In May came the announcement that His Royal Highness, The Earl of Wessex would assume the appointment of Honorary Colonel of The London Regiment and would wear the uniform of the London Scottish in memory of his late grandmother, Her Majesty, Queen Elizabeth, The Queen Mother. It was also announced that Pipe Major McLucas would serve as the Earl's personal piper, and he was duly presented with a Royal pipe banner in October. Further honour came in June, when the London Scottish Pipes and Drums were invited to participate once again at Beating Retreat on Horse Guards Parade in a massed pipes and drums with the Scots Guards and the Irish Guards, with His Royal Highness, The Duke of Edinburgh as guest of honour. The massed band played the newly composed pipe tune *En Ferus Hostis* named after the motto of the 1st Battalion, Scots Guards, which translates as 'Behold a Fierce Enemy.' The composition, arranged with drum beatings representing battlefield noise, was dedicated to the fallen of the Scots Guards during their recent tour of Afghanistan and was played during the performances in memory of all those from the Guards Division who had made the ultimate sacrifice:

> It was extremely pleasing that our contribution to Beating Retreat was commented on most favourably by both the Major General Commanding the Household Division and the Senior Director of Music, Household Division. However, perhaps the greatest compliment came as we marched off after the final rehearsal, when WO1 (GSM HQ London District) 'Billy' Mott, HM Ceremonial Warrant Officer, expressed the opinion in a typically understated way, that the Massed Pipes and Drums had the makings of a reasonable performance![77]

In April, Piper Gary Anderson and Drummer Hill were selected to represent the Pipes and Drums on a tour of Uzbekistan, at the invitation of the British Ambassador, to celebrate Her Majesty, The Queen's official birthday and to coincide with the royal wedding of His Royal Highness, Prince William and Catherine Middleton. The duo played a series of engagements during their week-long trip, including events at the British Ambassador's residence, the Romanov Palace, the State Conservatory and, most importantly as it would transpire, the Ministry of the Interior. On arrival in country, the duo had been greeted by the British Defence Attaché, who had rather set views regarding the perceived irrelevance of military bands in the modern British armed forces. By the end of the trip, however, he stated, 'You have walked through doors it has taken me three months to knock at. I may change my view on musicians.'[78] The success of the trip would lead to a number of repeat invitations to Uzbekistan, fulfilled by other members of the Pipes and Drums over the coming years.

After the traditional Hallowe'en dinner, the Lord Mayor's Show and the annual regimental church parade, the year ended with another performance at the British Military Tournament at Earl's Court Arena, with the London Scottish Pipes and Drums accorded the honour of closing the show and being the last unit off parade on each of the five performances. The highlight of the tournament came on 2 December when Her Majesty, The Queen attended the first performance and took the Royal Salute.

The annual internal band competitions took place on 8 March 2012 with Piper Les Hain winning the MacLeod Medal and Drummer Iain Withers, son of leading tip Drummer Withers Snr, winning the Attwooll Trophy. Piper Hain went on to become a stalwart of the band, taking on compositional duties for new sets, as well as piping instruction. A new element was introduced that year by Drummer Hill who organised an internal mini-band competition to round off

---

77 *London Scottish Regimental Gazette* (2011), p.39.
78 *London Scottish Regimental Gazette* (2011), p.36.

proceedings, which was sponsored by the Worshipful Company of Distillers, and which would become a staple of the event over the next decade.

A mini-band performed at the Caledonian Club on 8 June at the request of ex-London Scottish Pipe Major Ian King to support their diamond jubilee ball, with a full band performance the following evening at the London Regiment ball, with Drummer Joe Blake of the Toronto Scottish Regiment guesting with the drummers. June saw the band invited to join the Pipes and Drums of the Irish Guards for Beating Retreat on Horse Guards Parade, with the first performance falling exactly 30 years to the day and hour since the 2nd Battalion, Scots Guards engaged in the Battle of Mount Tumbledown during the Falklands War. The morning after that battle, Pipe Major James Riddell of the 2nd Battalion, Scots Guards played a commemorative quick march on the top of the mountain in honour of the fallen, having purportedly written the tune on the back of a cigarette packet or ration pack only hours previously. While both the cigarette packet and ration pack stories are in circulation, it is also possible that the story is apocryphal, and that Pipe Major Riddell had drafted the tune previously and had it ready 'in his back pocket' for such an event. Either way, the tune conveys moving tribute and honour to the men who lost their lives that day:

> Imagine how incredibly poignant it was to be formed up in the middle of Horse Guards, precisely thirty years later, playing *The Crags of Tumbledown Mountain* with the massed bands of the Household Division.[79]

In July, as Piper Hain joined Piper Anderson and Drummer Hill for a second tour of Uzbekistan, Pipe Major McLucas and Lance Corporal Piper Parsons undertook tours of Jamaica and Trinidad and Tobago, to commemorate both Her Majesty, The Queen's Diamond Jubilee and Jamaica's half-century of independence. Thankfully, white No. 3 Tropical Dress tunics had been issued, which didn't stop four members of a composite Canadian Army Pipes and Drums passing out on parade due to the heat. On their return, Lance Corporal Piper Parsons assisted Drummer Hill in assembling care packages for London Scottish soldiers currently serving in Helmand Province, Afghanistan, purchased with funds raised by all members of the Pipes and Drums and including a substantial monetary contribution from the very same Defence Attaché in Uzbekistan who had been converted the previous year as to the importance of military musicians.

In late July, having performed four days earlier aboard carousel horses at a London Scottish Regiment garden party, celebrating Her Majesty, The Queen's Diamond Jubilee, the London Scottish Pipes and Drums left for the Loreley Military Tattoo in Germany. The band played a solo set on stage in the spectacular natural amphitheatre on the crest of the Loreley cliff-top, in addition to joining a massed band to close the show. The band opened the ITV *Alan Titchmarsh Show* on 19 September to promote the next British Military Tournament, which was to take place again in December. 4 November saw the Pipes and Drums perform with the Military Band of the Guards Division for the homecoming and medals parade at Guild Hall Yard for Vimy Company, returning from Afghanistan. A week later Drummers Smith and Withers (Snr) performed at the Royal Albert Hall for the Royal British Legion Festival of Remembrance, accompanying two pipers from the 2nd Battalion, Scots Guards who were both veterans of the Battle of Mount Tumbledown, playing *The Crags of Tumbledown*. Two days after this, the band began rehearsals at Wellington Barracks for the Household Division *Scarlet and Gold* concert held at Central Hall, Westminster. As well as performing with the Household Division Concert Band, the London Scottish Pipes and Drums also played a solo set, highlighting the recognition given to the ever-increasing quality of the band's musical abilities.

---

79 *London Scottish Regimental Gazette*, (2012), p.103.

Through his contacts with ABF – The Soldiers' Charity, bass Drummer Nick Gair had been asked by the event producer to put together a massed pipes and drums for the British Military Tournament, as they wished to feature the sound of the pipes as part of a celebration of Her Majesty, The Queen's Diamond Jubilee. The additional challenge set was for this to be the largest massed pipes and drums ever to appear at an Earl's Court event. In true London Scottish fashion, and with Pipe Major McLucas, Drum Major Foulis and others pulling in several favours, a massed band of 128 was eventually assembled, with the London Scottish joined by the Pipes and Drums of RAF Halton, RAF Leuchars, RAF Waddington, Nottinghamshire Police, Aberdeen Universities OTC, and Glasgow & Strathclyde Universities OTC; Drummer Joe Blake from the Toronto Scottish also put in a solo guest performance. Piper Les Hain adapted pipe scores and, together with Drum Major Alastair Pether from RAF Halton, who was senior Drum Major for the event, devised drill movements, whilst Drummer Withers (Snr) arranged the drum beatings. Piper Gardiner opened the massed band's performance playing solo whilst being raised into the arena through a trapdoor and subsequently closed the finale by being lifted up into the roof on a hoist as the massed pipes and drums joined in playing *Heilan' Laddie*, the London Scottish Regimental March.

By year's end, the Pipes and Drums had performed together on 38 separate occasions over the preceding 12 months, as well as providing individual pipers and drummers at approximately 50 other events. An undertaking which demanded huge commitment from serving and volunteer members alike. Many of these events were extremely high profile, playing in front of members of the Royal family, senior military officers and large audiences. The professionalism of the London Scottish Pipes and Drums would continue to develop at a pace over the coming years, providing increased opportunities for the Pipes and Drums to keep the London Scottish, the London Regiment and the Territorial Army firmly in the public eye.

As well as their regular military support duties, the Pipes and Drums undertook various corporate and hospitality functions in the first half of 2013, including performing once again at the 165th Royal Caledonian Ball. The backstage preparations appeared in a humorous article by Peter Ross in *The Scotsman* on 12 May, which included the following insightful observations regarding life in the band:

Upstairs, in a room off the balcony, the Pipes and Drums of the London Scottish Regiment are preparing to perform, some of them sipping bottled largers or whisky … Rob Green, a 29-year-old Londoner, is standing in T-shirt and underwear, ironing his plaid. He used to be a Highland dancer but found there was more beer to be had in a pipe band. Although he himself is English, his grandmother was from Glasgow and his great-grandfather came from Lewes. 'That's a beautiful story', jokes a passing drummer, 'It almost makes up for how shit you play your pipes.'[80]

Later in the article, Ross states:

Drum Major David Foulis, known as Nobby, is a 66-year-old Glaswegian, specifically a Partick man, and has been in the army since joining the Argyll and Sutherland Highlanders at 17 …. Nobby gives the strong impression of being considerably tougher than the toughest pair of old boots one might hope to find, mentioning in passing that just four weeks ago he suffered a 'wee haemorrhage' of the brain. I can't believe you're here tonight I tell him. 'Neither can my wife', he grins.[81]

The main overseas trip of the year would come in September when the band travelled to the German Military Tattoo in Schalke, where a world record attempt was made for the most pipers

---

80   Ross, Peter, 'The Royal Caledonian Ball', *The Scotsman*, 12 May 2013.
81   Ross, Peter, 'The Royal Caledonian Ball', *The Scotsman*, 12 May 2013.

and drummers playing the famous tune *Highland Cathedral*. On 21 October the London Scottish supported the Military Band of the Royal Gibraltar Regiment at the annual Royal Gibraltar Day parade at Guildhall in the City of London, with the bands marching off to *The London Scottish at Primosole Ridge*, played to commemorate the 70th anniversary of the 1st Battalion's opening action of the Second World War. Hallowe'en dinner followed at the end of the month and the London Scottish Pipes and Drums joined the London Irish to form the composite London Regiment Pipes and Drums to lead the guard of honour at Mansion House for the Lord Major's Show.

Participation for the fourth and final British Military Tournament saw the London Scottish Pipes and Drums lead a detachment of Chelsea Pensioners into the arena for the finale. London Regiment Honorary Colonel, His Royal Highness, The Earl of Wessex took the Royal Salute at the Saturday performance and very kindly sent his equerry to find the Pipes and Drums to deliver a crate of beer. An extremely kind and most welcome gesture. Following the final performance, Piper Blackledge and Drummer Gair were presented to His Royal Highness, The Duke of Cambridge who had been the guest of honour that evening.

The Pipes and Drums opened 2014 on 27 January at a dinner at 95 Horseferry Road to commemorate the 150th anniversary of the forming of the London Scottish Regimental Association. On 2 March, Pipe Major McLucas was joined by Lance Corporal Piper Parsons, Pipers Stewart, Stuart Nicholson, Iain Barratt, Calum Galleitch and Robert Green to participate in the South of England Quartets at Broxbourne. This was the first time the band had competed for some years and it was a healthy reintroduction to the competition scene. On 6 March, Piper Galleitch won the McLeod Medal for the second year running, mirrored by Drummer Withers (Jnr) in the Attwooll Trophy. The band played for the Queen's Body Guard of the Yeomen of the Guard on 7 April, then at the Royal Caledonian Ball at the Grosvenor House Hotel on 2 May and performed on 7 June at the annual charity garden party hosted by ex-Regimental Colonel Clemence in the grounds of his home in Kent.

The major regimental undertaking of the year came over the weekend of 20-22 June with a tour of Ypres and Messines to mark the 100th anniversary of the start of the First World War and the entry of the London Scottish into the fighting at the Battle of Messines. A century earlier, four pipers had been killed and 12 other pipers and drummers wounded in this initial engagement, which saw heavy casualties throughout the regiment. This event would mark the first of many commemorations over the next four years to honour the approximately 10,000 men of the London Scottish who fought, were injured, taken prisoner or gave the ultimate sacrifice during this so-called 'war to end all wars':

> As always, this was a stunningly memorable occasion on so many levels … all at once being entertaining, informative, solemn, moving, reflective and an opportunity for all sections of the Regiment … to bond closer over shared history, common experiences and the odd dram.[82]

The Pipes and Drums played at the Last Post Ceremony at the Menin Gate and Beat Retreat at Ypres Cloth Hall on the first evening. Battlefield tours took place on Saturday before a march from Messines to the London Scottish Memorial Cross on Messines Ridge on Sunday and a civic reception hosted by the citizens of Messines and the surrounding area, on whose land bones and bullets from four years of war 100 years previously are still regularly found.

The following weekend, on 28 June, the Pipes and Drums joined the London Irish Rifles to lead a guard of honour from the London Regiment at a drumhead service of remembrance at the Royal Hospital, Chelsea. Her Majesty, The Queen, His Royal Highness, The Duke of Edinburgh

---

82 *London Scottish Regimental Gazette* (2014), p.57.

and London Regiment Honorary Colonel, His Royal Highness, The Earl of Wessex attended the service to honour the men of the Territorial Army, now newly renamed the Army Reserve, and all other military volunteers who served during the First World War.

The band took their first trip to Switzerland on 9-13 July to participate in the St. Gallen Military Tattoo. A six-day trip for a two-day tattoo left much time for sight-seeing, swimming, and general merriment. The Pipes and Drums had a solo spot at the beginning of the second section of the show which took place atop a stage-set wooden castle, behind microphones hooked up to the stadium public address system. On the last performance Drum Major Foulis managed to nearly destroy these microphones while exuberantly flourishing his mace, prompting an accompanying high-pitched squeal from the amplified distortion that threatened to deafen the audience!

Pipe Major McLucas and Piper Nicholson played at, or more correctly, attended a reception at Number Ten, Downing Street on 17 July for the signing of the new Armed Forces Covenant. Having arrived to find they were not on the guest list, the duo were finally allowed entry and told they would be supporting a concert band of the Irish Guards every 20 minutes to allow them breaks. However, having started to play on the first occasion, the two pipers were hurriedly told to refrain as the Prime Minister was on the phone and couldn't hear himself think. On the second occasion they began to play, they were again soon stopped as an important NATO meeting was also taking place nearby. Apologies were made to the Irish Guards and the duo proceeded to enjoy the contents of the drinks table.

Pipe Major McLucas and Piper Nicholson were joined by Drummer Withers (Snr) to perform at Buckingham Palace on 13 October in support of The Duke of Edinburgh's Award. The trio played through the White Room, Music Room and Blue Room into the State Dining Room and, from there, through to the Throne Room; a truly unique experience. The full band performed five days later at the Guildhall to provide ceremonial and musical support to the inaugural Lord Mayor's Ball for the chosen charities of Dame Fiona Woolf, only the second female Lord Major of London in over 800 years. Dame Fiona was also on the council of the London Regiment.

The regimental Hallowe'en dinner was a particularly poignant affair in 2014, as would be expected on the one hundredth anniversary of the Battle of Messines. The Pipes and Drums, as tradition decreed, debuted, to thunderous applause, their new medley set that would be used for the following year. Following the formal reports, speeches and responses, the band then returned to play their second set, comprising of company marches, before Drum Major Foulis asked permission from the new Regimental Colonel, Brigadier Alastair Bruce of Crionaich, to march-off. One week later, a combined band of 30 saw the London Scottish, led by Drum Major Foulis, and the London Irish, led by Drum Major Smith, ex-drummer of the London Scottish, lead the London Regiment at the Lord Major's Show on November 8th, before a London Scottish band of 22 pipers and drummers led the regimental family through the streets of Westminster and Chelsea the following day to St Columba's on church parade. Commemorations continued at 1100 hours on 11 November when the Pipes and Drums once again led the Western Front Association parade to their service of remembrance at The Cenotaph in Whitehall:

> A detachment of Royal Marines formed a Guard of Honour at the four corners of the Cenotaph and, as Big Ben rang out the hour, a Bugler from the Grenadier Guards sounded 'Last Post', which signified the start of the traditional two-minutes silence, during which time London really did stand still. No traffic noise, no Police sirens, no talk. A very eerie but peaceful hush.[83]

---

83 *London Scottish Regimental Gazette*, (2014), p.111.

After the wreath laying, Welsh rock singer and radio presenter Cerys Matthews beautifully read the poem *In Flanders Field*, followed by Pipe Major McLucas slow marching around The Cenotaph playing *The Flowers of the Forest*. The exhortation from *For the Fallen* was given before the bugler played *Sunset* and the Pipes and Drums, playing the London Scottish regimental march and led the parade off for the return march along Whitehall. An unforgettable honour and an incredible way to conclude the most memorable of years.

Pipers Nicholson, Galleitch, Callum Young, Hamish Young, Hain and Johnston represented the London Scottish Regiment and the Pipes and Drums at the funeral of ex-regimental colonel Sir Ronald 'Tommy' Macpherson at St Columba's Church on 18 February 2015. Lance Corporal Piper Parsons was unable to take up his regular position as duty piper, being snow-bound in his native Canada, and his responsibilities on this prestigious occasion were taken up at short notice by Piper Nicholson. He accompanied the church organist and a solo singer in a rendition of *A Scottish Soldier*, set to the famous pipe tune *The Green Hills of Tyrol*, before joining the other five pipers to play from the balcony.

Piper Galleitch and Drummer Withers (Jnr) made it three in a row in the MacLeod Medal and Attwooll Trophy on 19 March. Pipers Nicholson, Galleitch and Stewart played on 12 April in Caterham to mark the 100th anniversary of the London Scottish marching through the town on a recruitment day in 1915. On 14 May, a film crew came to 95 Horseferry Road to film the Pipes and Drums for a new display at the National Army Museum, Chelsea, highlighting the reach and influence of the bagpipes in the British Army. The band were filmed marching and then playing a static set with Highland dancers to portray the importance of British army pipers and drummers in conserving bagpipe music and creating a legacy of bands and competitions on every continent.

Early June saw the Pipes and Drums invited to join the 1st Battalion, Scots Guards and their association band on Horse Guards Parade for Beating Retreat, the theme of which was the 200th anniversary of the Battle of Waterloo. The massed pipes and drums played a solo set in a thistle formation before later helping to recreate a scene from the Duchess of Richmond's Ball, famously held on the night before the battle, before joining the massed bands for the finale, which comprised of:

> A cleverly choreographed tableau of the battle of Waterloo itself, with each of the participating bands providing a representation of the various forces deployed during hostilities, moving in stops and starts across the parade ground as the battle unfurled.[84]

The Pipes and Drums joined members of the serving company, regimental lodge and association for the wedding of Corporal Daniel Holbrough on 9 May, at Albright Hussey Manor, Shrewsbury. Unbeknownst to the new Mrs Holbrough, Corporal Holbrough became a tenor drummer for the afternoon, joining the Pipes and Drums on the march, complete with leopard skin and much flourishing of beaters. Performing with the Pipes and Drums was obviously influential as, six years later, on 10 March 2021, Corporal Piper Holbrough, now serving with the Royal Scots Dragoon Guards, graduated from his Class 3 pipers' course at the Army School of Bagpipe Music and Highland Drumming.

The Pipes and Drums embarked on their longest tour in decades when they accepted an invitation to perform over 12 days in July at the Lorient Festival at Interceltique, in Brittany. The festival attracts tens of thousands of visitors, celebrating all things Celtic, and the Pipes and Drums played in a massed band with a combined Scottish Universities OTC Pipes and Drums and other special guests. The massed band played static performances, marching sets, parades through towns, a

---

84 *London Scottish Regimental Gazette* (2015), p.56.

pipe band competition, innumerable side shows and an unexpected 50-minute performance at a marina next to the ruins of a Second World War German U-boat pen. A highlight of the trip was a performance in Port Louis at a memorial held on the battlements of the coastal defences where members of the French Resistance had been executed by firing squad by occupying German forces:

> It meant so much to the locals to have a British Regimental Band commemorating the courage and sacrifice of these extremely brave individuals.[85]

At the regimental Hallowe'en dinner, Drummer Alex Cooper ceremoniously carried the haggis around the drill hall behind the duty pipers in his role as 'Chef of Honour' and provider of the evening's catering. It also saw Lance Corporal Piper Parsons receive his second chevron to finally become a full corporal. The band played at a regimental cocktail party on 5 November before being joined by the Tayforth and Aberdeen Universities OTC Pipes and Drums, with whom they had performed as a massed band at the Lorient Festival, and who were subsequently invited to attend the 800th Lord Major's Show and the regimental church parade on the following day. A band of nearly 50 pipers and drummers lent an additional degree of grandeur to each occasion. The Western Front Association armistice service at the Cenotaph on 11 November saw a guard of honour from the 2nd Battalion, Royal Gurkha Rifles join a Scots Guard bugler and the London Scottish Pipes and Drums leading the parade.

The year 2016 brought several changes to the Pipes and Drums, beginning on 16 January with the death of long-serving piper Gordon Skilling. Piper Skilling had joined the band back in the 1970s and, like Drum Major Foulis and Piper Tommy Johnston, had over 40 years' experience with the British Army and was a stalwart and much-loved member of the Pipes and Drums. A large band attended his funeral, along with many members of the regimental family, playing the hearse to St Andrew's Garrison Kirk at Aldershot. Pipe Major Macpherson piped the coffin into the packed church, where Isla St Clair sang a moving rendition of *The 51st's Farewell to Sicily* which was then taken up by Pipers Johnston and Nicholson on the pipes.

Lead tip, Drummer Andy Withers took early retirement in the spring of 2016 and relocated to the warmer climes of the south of France where he would join Pipers Hain and Anderson who had both independently preceded him there a few years earlier. The role of lead tip was taken up by Drummer Hill who currently retains the position. New members, including Pipers Euan McCorquodale, William Arndell, Ranald Gibson and Drummers Leo Both, Peter Ellis, Tafadzwa Garikayi and Peter McDonald bolstered numbers and helped bring down the average age of the band. Piper Gibson was following in the footsteps of his uncle, Tom Gibson who had been a private in the 2nd Battalion, London Scottish during the First World War. Active recruiting by Pipe Major McLucas and Drum Major Foulis built links with the various Scottish Universities Officer Training Corps bands and ensured that the next generation of military pipers and drummers would be attracted to the London Scottish, helping to safeguard the continued longevity of the band.

With this outcome in mind, the London Scottish accepted an invitation from the Aberdeen Universities OTC Pipes and Drums to attend Armed Forces Day on 25 June in Aberdeen. The London Scottish and Aberdeen UOTC bands were joined by the Gordon Highlanders Association, Ballater and District, Banchory, Kintore and Lonach pipe bands for the parade through Aberdeen city centre. The London Scottish were billeted in Dargai Block, Gordon Barracks, Bridge of Don where, 52 years prior, a young Private Foulis had passed-out into the Argyll and Sutherland Highlanders following basic training.

---

85 *London Scottish Regimental Gazette* (2015), p.102.

Two weeks earlier, the London Scottish had joined the Pipes and Drums of the Scots Guards and Irish Guards once again in Beating Retreat on Horse Guards Parade. Part of the parade performance that year was a commemoration of the 100th anniversary of the Battle of the Somme. The massed pipes and drums played *The Battle of the Somme* which had been written by Pipe Major William Lawrie of the Argyll and Sutherland Highlanders, who was killed in action in 1916. Pipe Major Lawrie's bagpipes were paraded in front of the massed bands, adding additional symbolism to the performance.

Piper Callum Young and Drummer Cooper headed off to Uzbekistan at the end of summer and, on 30 June, Piper Stuart McMillan, Member of the Scottish Parliament for Greenock and Inverclyde played as Her Majesty, The Queen opened the fifth session of the Scottish Parliament. Resplendent in his London Scottish glengarry, Piper MacMillan played *The Rowan Tree* as part of the official opening ceremony.

The Regimental Colonel hosted a dinner for the Worshipful Company of Distillers at regimental headquarters on 3 November. The London Scottish Regiment is the company's affiliated army unit, and the livery company has particularly close links with the Pipes and Drums, who provide pipers for their annual banquet at Mansion House, whilst the Distillers provide the annual mini-band competition prize to the band. Two days later the band travelled, in an unofficial capacity, to Sussex for the annual Lewes bonfire night celebrations at the invitation of Pipers Cottam and Barratt, both Lewes residents, and as guests of the Waterloo Bonfire Society Pipes and Drums. The event itself is somewhat anarchical, involving an interesting combination of alcohol, fireworks and flaming torches which resulted in 'another surreal band night where the Ps&Ds lit the blue touch paper, stood back, played up and Struck Sure!'[86]

A three day 'marchathon' followed the next weekend with the Pipes and Drums on the Friday supporting the Western Front Association at The Cenotaph, on Saturday leading the London Regiment on the Lord Mayor's Show (both of which were covered by national television), and on Sunday leading the regimental church parade. A large contingent from the Tayforth Universities OTC accompanied the London Scottish Pipes and Drums over the weekend, contributing to a massed band of 40 for church parade. The London Scottish Regimental Trust kindly provided the Pipes and Drums with a substantial grant to feed and water the visiting pipers and drummers over the course of the weekend. Church parade also saw another first for the Pipes and Drums when they were joined on the march by a uniformed serving officer of the Royal Navy. At the invitation of the Regimental Colonel, ex-London Scottish and ex-Tayforth UOTC Piper, now Sub-Lieutenant Hamish Young, joined both of his former military pipe bands and his brother Piper Callum Young for the return to headquarters from St Columba's Kirk.

On 17 November, 170 guests packed the drill hall at 95 Horseferry Road for a 'Winter Warmer' ceilidh organised by Drum Major Foulis and family and catered by Drummer Cooper, ably assisted by another pipe band chef, Drummer Jamie 'Paddy' Wilson. The Pipes and Drums played a set, as did Isla St Clair, before the George Buchannan Highland Ceilidh Band took over. This highly successful new 'tradition' would become an annual event added to the regimental calendar.

The year 2017 was a typically busy and important for the London Scottish Pipes and Drums. It opened with a personal highlight for bass Drummer Gair who was awarded an MBE in the New Year's Honours List for 'Services to Military Personnel and to young people in London', recognising his significant work with the Association of Trauma and Military Surgery, the Royal British Legion 'Battleback' Centre, the London Youth Trust and the Outward Bounds Trust.

After full band jobs at the Royal Caledonian Ball on 28 April (which saw the debut of Piper Alex Mackison), for the Worshipful Company of Butchers at Guildhall Yard on 17 May, and for the

---

86   *London Scottish Regimental Gazette* (2016), p.106.

Regimental Colonel's summer party on 8 June, the Pipes and Drums were again invited to participate with the Household Division at Beating Retreat on Horse Guards Parade from 12 to 15 June. While the full band were undertaking public duties at Horse Guards on 15 June, a series of other London Scottish piping engagements were taking place around the world on the same day. Piper Edward Robson and Drummer David Lowe were performing at the British Embassy in Ashgabat, Turkmenistan, having previously played that afternoon at the British Ambassador's Residence in Tashkent, Uzbekistan. Pipers Brenton Johnston, Green and Hume were playing at the annual Waterloo Dinner of the Naval and Military Club, in St James's Square, London and serving Piper Gibson was visiting the Toronto Scottish Regiment at their headquarters, the Captain Bellenden Seymour Hutcheson VC Armoury, Toronto, Canada.

The importance of the international reach and public face of the Pipes and Drums to the London Scottish Regiment cannot be overestimated. The fact that it is now provided predominantly by the good will of volunteer pipers and drummers who seek only to honour the regiment they 'serve', is particularly noteworthy. While they work alongside and subsidiary to, their serving colleagues, the band could not survive without them and their contribution to the regiment and to the preservation of military piping cannot be overlooked.

Ten days after Beating Retreat, the Pipes and Drums travelled to Aberdeen to join the Armed Forces Day Parade, once again at the invitation of the Aberdeen UOTC. Ten days after that, the band performed at 'Kilted in the Capital' a charity evening at regimental headquarters attended by over 200 guests and organised by Major Rob Pitt, Officer Commanding, 'A' (London Scottish) Company. As Major Pitt stated, whilst other bands and singers performed during the evening, including folk singer Ian Bruce, whose father had been Pipe Major of the 2nd Battalion during the Second World War, it was 'our own inimitable Pipes and Drums who, as always, steal any show.'[87]

On 29 July, Corporal Piper Parsons and Pipers Nicholson, Brenton Johnston and Nathan Kwan participated in the Gordon Highlanders Victoria Crosses commemoration parade held in Buckie, Banffshire. Two weeks later the Pipes and Drums travelled to Belgium to mark the 100th anniversary of the Battle of Passchendaele and to take part in a series of events commemorating the contribution of Scottish regiments in the campaign. On 17 August, the band performed at the Last Post Ceremony at the Menin Gate. The following day, the London Scottish lead a parade to the memorial to Scottish troops at Frezenberg near Zonnebeke for the opening of a new supplementary memorial to the original Scottish granite cross. Ten metal silhouette figures of Scottish troops had been designed and erected to surround the cross. That evening a concert was held in Zonnebeke where the London Scottish performed a solo set before joining a massed band for the finale. The return journey on the final day saw the band stop to pay their respects at the London Scottish Memorial on Messines Ridge.

On 8-10 September 2017, the band performing at the Goodwood Revival weekend, West Sussex, where they led out vintage racing cars on to the starting grid from Scottish racing team 'Ecurie Ecosse', which had won the Le Mans 24-hour race in both 1956 and 1957, 50 years previously. On 23 September, the Pipes and Drum supported The Princess of Wales's Royal Regiment in Canterbury at the presentation of their new colours. The band joined the military bands of the host regiment and the Queen's Division, along with the Drums and Fifes of the Danish Royal Life Guards. After the usual round of Hallowe'en dinner, Lewes bonfire night, armistice parade at The Cenotaph, regimental church parade, Caledonian Society dinner and Winter Warmer, the Pipes and Drums ended the year on a high with a performance at Buckingham Palace on 29 November. The band played for the Royal Household Reeling Club in the State Ballroom, which provided the first opportunity for many in the band to perform in this prestigious setting.

---

87 *London Scottish Regimental Gazette*, (2017), p.53.

Over remembrance weekend, Corporal Piper Parsons joined a small party of London Scots in Israel to commemorate the 100th anniversary of the 2nd Battalion, London Scottish Regiment's campaign through Palestine during the First World War and, specifically, the capture of Jerusalem on 9 December 1917. Having travelled to various battlefields and played at several British military cemeteries containing London Scottish graves, Corporal Piper Parsons played a lament at a remembrance service held at St Andrew's Scottish Memorial Church in Jerusalem next to the London Scottish memorial plaque originally unveiled in 1934. The 1st Battalion, London Scottish Pipes and Drums had also played there as they passed through Jerusalem in 1943.

The Pipes and Drums supported the serving company, the London Regiment, the London District and the wider Scottish military community in a host of events during an extremely active 2018 to commemorate the 100th anniversary of the final year of the First World War. Thankfully, consistent strong recruitment into the band meant it was now at such a size that this level of activity could be comfortably sustained.

Recruitment to the serving company was also high during this period, but enormous changes were about to take place within the regiment which were instigated by a Ministry of Defence decision to no longer rent the London Scottish headquarters at 95 Horseferry Road with effect from April 2018. This left the regiment with a headquarters building in the heart of London that would no longer contain serving soldiers and the headache of providing a sustainability plan for the future that would keep the building as the heart and soul of the regiment but which would also raise enough revenue to cover operational costs. A major part of the proposed scheme to safeguard the traditions of the regiment at 95 Horseferry Road included enhancing the regimental museum, ensuring serving company training and events regularly took place in the building and keeping the Pipes and Drums on site in their traditional regimental home. On 6 March, the Pipes and Drums undertook the sad duty of piping out 'A' (London Scottish) Company from regimental headquarters and around the corner to their new home at the Army Reserve Centre, Rochester Row. The front rank of pipers was made up of serving soldiers in the form of Pipe Major McLucas, Corporal Piper Parsons and Piper Gibson as they marched the half mile to their new base of operations.

Piper Barratt was in the chair for band supper on 9 March and Piper Cottam presented an oil painting, of the Pipes and Drums marching to St Columba's on church parade, to Piper Tommy Johnston who, having just turned 80, still turned out with the Pipes and Drums on static jobs and competed in the in-house piping competitions. On 17 May, Corporal Piper Parsons and Drummer Lowe flew out to Uzbekistan for the now annual tour, while back in London the band performed on 21 May at a regimental cocktail party hosted by the Regimental Colonel for the Honorary and Regimental Colonels of the Toronto Scottish who were in London to attend a garden party at Buckingham Palace, celebrating the 70th birthday of His Royal Highness, The Prince of Wales, the Royal Honorary Colonel of their regiment. Pipe Major Andrew Killick of the Toronto Scottish joined the Pipes and Drums to perform the two regimental marches.

The week 14-20 June saw the Pipes and Drums travel in their own footsteps on a second tour of northern Italy commemorating the decisive battles that ended the First World War in 1918 on the 'Forgotten Front.' They had previously attended the 90th anniversary commemorations in 2008 and were welcomed back again with open arms for the centenary. Piper Hain provided a last-minute pipe arrangement for the popular Italian patriotic song *La Leggenda del Piave*, which had previously been the Italian national anthem. This was hastily learnt by the band on the journey to Italy and played by the Pipes and Drums, along with *Scotland the Brave*, at the end of every performance on the tour, 'much to the obvious delight of the spectating crowds, many of whom cheered and sung along to the tune.'[88] The band performed at the Sacrario Militare del Monte Grappa

---

[88] *London Scottish Regimental Gazette* (2018), p.22.

Performing with the Scottish Universities OTC Pipes and Drums at the Lorient Festival, Brittany, July 2015. (LSMA, used with permission)

Parading at the Sacrario Militare del Monte Grappa memorial, Northern Italy, June 2018. (LSMA, used with permission)

The massed bands of the London Scottish and Aberdeen University OTC at The Sword and Crown, Horse Guards Parade, July 2020. (LSMA, used with permission)

Members of the mini band who competed at the Army Pipe Band Championships, and Band President, Colonel G. Strickland, with their trophies, Edinburgh, February 2022. (LSMA, used with permission)

memorial and at the Giavera Cemetery which contains the graves of many 2nd Battalion, Gordon Highlanders and Beat Retreat in numerous Italian towns over a long six-day trip in Full Dress uniform. Ex-band president Lieutenant Colonel McLelland joined the trip to provide battlefield tours, and current band president Lieutenant Colonel Geoffrey Strickland, latterly Commanding Officer of the London Regiment, ensured logistical support, as well as wholeheartedly personifying his role in verse three of *The Hodden Grey* song.

On 26 June, a celebrative book launch took place at regimental headquarters for the publication of *Scots in Great War London: The Scottish Community on the Home Front and in Battle, 1914-1919*, edited by Paul MacFarland and Hugh Pym, which included a chapter on the London Scottish Regiment, written by Corporal Piper Parsons, who is also the curator of the London Scottish Regimental Museum. A series of additional events were held at 95 Horseferry Road through October and November recognising the contribution of Scottish organisations, including the London Scottish Regiment, during the First World War.

The Army's London District organised a programme of events commemorating the last 100 days of the First World War, including a drumhead service of remembrance at the Royal Hospital, Chelsea, on 1 September. Representative units from the Royal Navy, the Army and Royal Air Force, including the London Regiment were in attendance and the Pipes and Drums were joined by the Royal Yeomanry Band and the North London Military Wives Choir. 4 October saw the Pipes and Drums, supported by various members of the regimental family, including the ubiquitous Ron Younger, travel to Dainville, France to provide ceremonial support for a rededication and slight renaming ceremony of the 'Rue du London Scottish' (previously misnamed the Rue du London Schottish!), titled in honour of the regiment, which runs through the heart of the town. The band also played at a special Last Post Ceremony at the Ploegsteert Wood Memorial to the Missing which contains the names of 11,447 allied soldiers who died in the area during the First World War, but whose remains were never identified.

Hallowe'en dinner in 2018 concluded with the Pipes and Drums marching out to *Caller Herrin'*, the exact same tune to which they had marched out 100 years previously at the 1st Battalion Hallowe'en dinner in France in 1918, as the Great War drew to a close. In typical pipe band fashion, Air Force Colonel and Taipei Military Attaché Li-Chiang Yuan attended the dinner, not as a distinguished guest of the top table, but as the guest of Piper Hume, once again demonstrating the international and political reach of members of the Pipes and Drums.

During remembrance weekend in this most special of years, the Pipes and Drums of the Tayforth Universities Officers' Training Corps once again renewed their links with the London Scottish. 9 November saw a massed band travel to Richmond Athletic Ground to perform at the London Scottish RFC versus Richmond RFC rugby match which included a centenary armistice commemoration before the kick-off. Both bands then massed with the London Irish to lead the London Regiment at the Lord Mayor's Show on 10 November before a joint band of 33 led the London Scottish regimental family, quite fittingly on Armistice Day itself, 11 November, on the annual regimental church parade. As the parade marched the long miles to St Columba's Church, the sound of the Pipes and Drums announced the regiment's presence:

> Passers-by clapped, children skipped and ran alongside us, people waved from buses, pubs full of veterans emptied and cheered us on, old soldiers with faded berets and blazers full of medals stood smartly to attention and saluted us; our predecessors would have certainly been 'weel pleased' with London's shouting tribute.[89]

---

89   *London Scottish Regimental Gazette* (2018), p.27.

The internal band competition evening took place on 28 February 2019 with Drum Major Rab McCutcheon, late of the 1st Battalion, Scots Guards, judging the drumming and Pipe Major Richard Grisdale, late of the Royal Regiment of Scotland and celebrating his first day as Sovereign's Piper, judging the piping. The MacLeod Medal was won by Piper Callum Young, with the Attwooll Trophy being won by Drummer Lowe. The Macpherson Quaich for Veterans Piping was awarded to Piper Gibb and Drummer Paul Scott took the Alderson Trophy for the most improved drummer. The Worshipful Company of Distillers Trophy for the best mini-band was taken by Pipe Major McLucas, Pipers Callum Young and Hume and Drummers McDonald and Lowe.

On 10 March, the London Scottish Regiment, including serving company, association, cadets, wider family and the Pipes and Drums, attended the unveiling ceremony of the London Scottish memorial stone at the National Memorial Arboretum in Staffordshire. Despite a howling gale, the ceremony went off without a hitch, with Pipe Major McLucas playing the lament, before the assembled regimental family 'retreated to the relative shelter afforded by the building line at Heroes Square, where the 20 strong Pipes and Drums struck up a superb set culminating with the Regimental March.'[90]

Links with ANZAC Day were re-established in April with a request from the Gallipoli Association for a piper to attend their remembrance service at St Paul's Cathedral. Piper Brenton Johnston, who had served in the Australian Army, volunteered for the ceremony, with Chairman of the Gallipoli Association, Brigadier James Stopford writing to the London Scottish Regimental Colonel to state that: 'Having an Australian piper in Scottish uniform at a service to commemorate the bravery and sacrifice of those who served in the 1915 campaign was very powerful. The High Commissioner of Australia was especially impressed.'[91] Once again, the diversity within the band had proved highly beneficial.

The following day a mini-band travelled to Scotland to play at the Glasgow branch of the London Scottish Regimental Association's annual lunch and, a few days later, Piper Callum Young and Drummer Garikayi travelled to Uzbekistan. 3 May saw another performance by the Pipes and Drums at the Royal Caledonian Ball, and 7-8 June saw the Pipes and Drums back at Beating Retreat on Horse Guards Parade having taken a year off in 2018 for the Italy tour. On this occasion, they were joined by the Military Band of the Royal Regiment of Scotland, the Royal Guard of Oman Pipes and Drums and the Combined Scottish Cadet Force Pipes and Drums. A week later, the London Scottish Pipes and Drums were reviewed by the Director of Army Bagpipe Music, Major Gordon Rowan, at the Regimental Colonel's annual cocktail party at regimental headquarters, for their continued suitability to perform ceremonial and state duties. They passed with flying colours.

Major Ian Johnson, Director of Music, Scots Guards, invited the band to support the Scots Guards at their summer concert at Kneller Hall, the home of British military music, on 26 June. This was the last opportunity for the Pipes and Drums to perform at this iconic venue as the Ministry of Defence later sold the building and grounds for development and moved the Royal Military School of Music to Portsmouth. Three days later the band travelled to Aberdeen for the National Army Day parade and, after landing back in London, the Pipes and Drums performed at the Ministry of Defence, Operations Directorate summer party at Wellington Barracks. Three days after that, on 7 July, the London Scottish Pipes and Drums supported the Military Band of The Princess of Wales's Royal Regiment at Herstmonceux Castle in East Sussex to Beat Retreat at a Tattoo in aid of ABF – The Soldiers' Charity. A week later, five pipers and drummers left for Bath to take part in an ITV periodic dramatisation of the Duchess of Richmond's famous Waterloo

---

90 *London Scottish Regimental Gazette* (2019), p.39.
91 *London Scottish Regimental Gazette* (2019), p.18.

Ball, where they performed as Napoleonic era Gordon Highlanders. On 25 July, the Pipes and Drums then played at the Honourable Artillery Company headquarters in the City of London to round off an extremely hectic, but also relatively standard, few months.

The five-yearly regimental pilgrimage to Messines and Ypres took place over the weekend of 5-7 October and included 25 members of the Pipes and Drums, which had continued its steady growth throughout 2018 and 2019. New recruits joined the band at a pace, and not only from the Scottish university officer training units. Drummers Robin Ling and Callum Sinclair joined in 2019, along with Pipers Adam Gudgeon, Peter Candy and Caroline Hicks, the first female piper to play regularly with the band. At the Last Post Ceremony at the Menin Gate on 5 October, Piper Hicks carried the bagpipes of her grandfather, Piper Alan Withey, which he had played there with the London Scottish 35 years previously. The remainder of the weekend was extremely wet, with the traditional regimental parade to the London Scottish Memorial on Messines Ridge having to be cut slightly short due to a thunderous downpour.

Hallowe'en dinner in 2019 came 100 years after the Great After War Reunion dinner of 1919 at which hundreds of London Scots had sat down together to remember their shared experiences during the First World War. A change to the traditional table layout a century later meant that the Pipes and Drums were able to play in the centre of the London Scottish drill hall during the dinner for the first time. On 7 November, the full band played before Her Royal Highness, The Countess of Wessex at the Heropreneurs Awards at the Plasterers' Hall, London. Remembrance weekend once again saw the combined London Regiment Pipes and Drums join the London Regiment in forming the guard of honour at the Lord Mayor's Show and, along with the Military Band of the Welsh Guards, lead the entire parade. Church parade came the following day with a band of 14 pipers, nine drummers and the Drum Major marching the regimental family through the streets of Westminster and Chelsea, followed by another Armistice Day parade at the Cenotaph on 11 November with the Western Front Association.

A mini-band performance at the Drapers Hall for Her Majesty, Queen Margrethe II of Denmark, took place on 4 December, before the year concluded with Piper Hain and Pipe Major McLucas, wearing the Personal Banner of His Royal Highness, The Earl of Wessex, performing at an ABF – The Soldiers' Charity concert at the Royal Hospital, Chelsea in the presence of Her Royal Highness, The Countess of Wessex. The London Scottish Pipes and Drums had completed over 60 full, mini-band and solo piping engagements over the course of the year.

The Pipes and Drums entered 2020 and their 160th anniversary year in rude health. Band membership had swollen to 23 pipers and 13 drummers, with a list of high-profile regimental, ceremonial and private engagements, including tours of Canada and the USA, lined-up for later in the year reflecting the continued growth in both the quality and reputation of the band. However, events would not turn out quite as planned.

After a hectic Burn's Night season for the pipers, the internal band competitions took place on 27 February, judged once again by Pipe Major Grisdale, the Sovereign's Piper, and leading tip, Drummer Hill. The McLeod Medal was won by Piper Candy, who also took the Macpherson Quaich, with the Attwooll Trophy won by Drummer Paul Connelly. The MacDougal-William Novice Piper award went to Piper Joseph Yu, a serving military musician with the Corps of Army Music, and the Alderson Trophy for Most Improved Drummer went to Drummer Scott. The Distillers mini-band competition was won by Pipers Nicholson, Callum Young, Arthur Montagu and Drummers Garikayi, Connelly and Sinclair.

Weeks later, after a promising start to the band's year and with much to look forward to, COVID-19 struck worldwide, and the country entered lockdown. The best laid plans for the 160th anniversary year were now trashed. While rehearsals and events could no longer take place, the Pipes and Drums, in true London Scottish fashion, continued to practise online with weekly Thursday virtual 'Zoom' meetings regularly attracting upwards of 25 members and going on long into the night. In addition, Pipe Sergeant Parsons, with a 'dram to hand' organised weekly military quizzes via the London Scottish Pipes and Drums Facebook page which began with questions specifically about the Pipes and Drums but, as his audience widened greatly, encompassed all military matters, included guest quiz masters and ran to over 50 episodes. The good humour and dedication of band members, alongside excellent leadership from both Pipe Major McLucas (now the longest serving pipe major in regimental history) and Drum Major Foulis (now also the longest serving drum major), not only ensured that the London Scottish Pipes and Drums emerged from 'Lockdown' in the best of health but also ensured that the band would take up from where it left off.

Lockdown also helped sow the seeds for a successful social media presence for the band, which was overseen by Piper Nicholson. The number of views of post information and videos of the band that he put together on Facebook, Instagram and You Tube grew from the thousands, into tens of thousands and into the hundreds of thousands, giving the Pipes and Drums a broader reach whilst also always promoting A (London Scottish) Company and the wider British Army.

Whilst the 75th Anniversary commemorations of VE Day and Beating Retreat were both cancelled in June, Pipe Major McLucas, Piper Hain and Piper Nicholson were given permission to perform on 12 June at the Queen Mother's Steps on The Mall, to commemorate the 80th anniversary of the capture of the Highland Division at St. Valery, whilst defending the Dunkirk evacuations during the Second World War.

After a number of false starts, the band were finally able to begin practising again in person (whilst still social distancing), and in earnest, during February 2021. Despite this, a number of events, including the annual in-house competitions in February, band supper in April and Beating Retreat on Horse Guards Parade in June were planned and then promptly cancelled. Funeral arrangements for His Royal Highness, Prince Philip, The Duke of Edinburgh, were also heavily curtailed following his death on 9 April, as images of Her Majesty, The Queen, mourning in dignified isolation during the service at St. George's Chapel, Windsor Castle on 17 April so eloquently portrayed. Instead of a full state funeral, Prince Philip, at his own request, was given a royal ceremonial funeral with 'minimal fuss' which meant that the services of a massed pipes and drums, including the London Scottish, were not required. The only piper in attendance was the Pipe Major of the 4th Battalion, Royal Regiment of Scotland, who played the lament during the service.

However, a return to ceremonial duties came in July with a specially arranged 'Military Musical Spectacular', 'The Sword and Crowd', showcasing the Massed Bands of the Household Division to the public for the first time since June 2019. The event included the Massed Bands of the Foot Guards, the Corps of Drums of the Grenadier Guards, the Drum Horse and Mounted Trumpeters of the Household Cavalry, the Corps of Drums of the Honourable Artillery Company and the London Scottish Pipes and Drums, who invited the pipe band from Aberdeen Universities OTC to join them in a massed band. The event, which ran from 20-22 July, was a tremendous success, with Her Royal Highness, The Princess Royal taking the salute as guest of honour on the final parade. It was a fitting occasion to mark the band's first full performances after the long months of national restrictions and lockdowns.

On 19 September, the Pipes and Drums performed at the Goodwood Revival festival for the first time in four years and on 23 September performed at a regimental open day at 95 Horseferry Road, as the regiment met for the first time as a family in over 18 months. Many of the drummers were in isolation or away on business and so Drummer Paul Scott held the entire performance together as the only side drummer.

The following month, on 9 October, the Pipes and Drums proudly supported the final 'official' regimental ceremony of the Gordon Highlanders at the unveiling and dedication of their memorial stone at the National Memorial Arboretum in Staffordshire. Nearly 300 Gordon Highlander veterans, headed by Regimental Colonel Lieutenant General Sir Peter Graham, attended the event, which concluded with the London Scottish Beating Retreat in honour of the Gordons, with whom they had been official associated for such a long portion of their history.

A mini band performed at the Cavalry and Guards Club, Piccadilly, on 25 October in support of a NATO function and playing for the first time in Hodden Grey was new recruit, Drummer Harry McGuire. Six days later, the annual regimental Hallowe'en dinner took place for the first time since 2019 and the Pipes and Drums were finally able to perform the new set they had begun learning for the 2020 dinner. Over 200 guests listened intently to a flawless performance, which was to be expected after 18 months of rehearsal. During the dinner, Pipe Major McLucas was presented with a special award for honourable service by the Regimental Colonel.

The Pipes and Drums were once again at The Cenotaph, Whitehall, on 11 November to commemorate the national observance with the Western Front Association, before leading the regimental family on Remembrance Sunday on their church parade march to and from St. Columba's Kirk in Knightsbridge, as they had done since the 1880s. Whilst the band were not involved in a scaled-back Lord Mayor's Show, the reappearance of these annual events was a sure sign that everyday life was beginning to return to normal, despite the refreshed Covid outbreak due to the omicron variant.

Regimental life, however, was about to be stood on its head once again with the publication on 25 November 2021 of *Future Soldier*, the British Government's guide to the reorganisation and redeployment of the British Army. *Future Soldier* summarises the outcome of the recommendations of the defence command paper, which was part of the Integrated Defence Review published on 16 March 2021 that promised the most radical overhaul of the British Army in 20 years. The publication stated:

> Future Soldier is about delivering a modern British Army that is fit for the challenges of the future. To become more lethal, agile and expeditionary; an army able to fight and win wars and to compete successfully in the grey-zone between peace and war.[92]

Page 93 of the guide, deep amongst the myriad of changes detailed for virtually every element of the British Army and listed amongst the changes for the London District, outlines the future for the London Regiment and 'A' (London Scottish) Company. It states that the London Regiment is to officially become the reserve battalion of the Foot Guards, restructured by February 2024 and officially redesignated 'The 1st Battalion, The London Guards.' Further details relating to the final structure for this new battalion are expected to be thrashed out over the next two years but at present it has been agreed that each regular battalion of Foot Guards will have an associated reserve company, with the London Scottish becoming 'G' (MESSINES) Company of the Scots Guards. Serving pipers and drummers from the London Scottish will wear the uniform of the Scots Guards, closing a circle that began in 1860 when pipers from the Scots (Fusilier) Guards helped to establish the London Scottish Regiment Pipes and Drums wearing, with the permission of their commanding officer, London Scottish uniform. It is envisaged that a 1st Battalion, London Guards Pipes and Drums Platoon will be created for serving pipers and drummers whilst the London Scottish Pipes and Drums will continue in their current voluntary role of providing musical support to the London Scottish, London Guards, London District and the Brigade of Guards. Funding for the band will come from multiple sources, including the Regimental Association, London District and the Army School of Bagpipe Music and Highland Drumming. It is envisaged that the band's military musical commitments will become greatly expanded under the terms of this new assignment.

---

92 *Future Soldier Guide* <http.publishing.service.gov.uk>

As if to highlight this increased level of responsibility and to emphasise that they are up to the task, a mini band from the London Scottish Pipes and Drums attended the British Army Piping and Drumming Championships at the Army School of Bagpipe Music and Highland Drumming, Edinburgh from 21-27 February 2022. Competing against regular and reserve pipe bands of the British Army, the London Scottish placed 2nd in the Medley and 3rd in the MSR, whilst Piper Candy placed 1st in Veterans March, 1st in Veterans Strathspey and Reel and 2nd in Piobaireachd. A creditable achievement and testament to the dedication of both serving and voluntary members of the band.

With the reincarnation of 'A' (London Scottish) Company into 'G' (Messines) Company and its associated changes, the London Scottish Pipes and Drums will once again continue to keep alive the cap badge, Hodden Grey uniform and battle honours of this proud regiment, as they had during the 25 years of the regiment's existence as 'G' (London Scottish) Company, 51st Highland Volunteers. The future status of the London Scottish Regiment remains unclear but whatever the future holds for the London Scottish family, the Pipes and Drums of the London Scottish Regiment will carry on with the skill, commitment and dedication to duty that has underlined the existence of the band and their antecedents for more than two centuries.

This volume serves, then, as confirmation that the history of the Pipes and Drums of the London Scottish Regiment is truly unique and of major historical importance. For 225 years they and their predecessors have played an important role in shaping regimental, military and pipe band history. Through war and peace, they have served their regiment and their country with distinction and have shown, time and again, the importance of a first-rate pipes and drums to the traditions, *esprit de corps* and fighting performance of this most unique of Scottish regiments and also within a wider context, to all Scottish regiments of the British Army and Scottish-related military units throughout the world. They have shaped pipe band history in a plethora of ways and earned the right to their senior position as one of the world's oldest and most influential pipe bands. As the ex-Regimental Colonel of the London Scottish, Brigadier Bruce of Crionaich once stated, no matter what the future holds:

The Pipes and Drums are our heartbeat and remain the best in the world![93]

STRIKE UP and STRIKE SURE

---

93   *London Scottish Regimental Gazette* (2015), p.92.

Appendix I

Pipe Majors of The London Scottish Regiment

1860 J. MacKenzie (Scots Fusilier Guards)
1861 A. Campbell
1873 R. Mackenzie (Scots Fusilier Guards)
1877 J.D. Mill
1880 N. MacGlashan
1881 J. Farquar
1885 R. Halley
1888 A.L. Reith
1902 R. Reith
1909 R. Robertson

FWW	1st Battalion:	2nd Battalion:	3rd Battalion:
1914	R. Robertson	R. Robertson	
1915	K. Grieg	D.C. Wills	R. Robertson
	A. Joss	J.A. McGilvray	
1916	H.F. Edgar		G. Shand
	W.P. Keith		
1918	R. Gordon	C. Oram	
1919	J.M. MacHattie	D.K. Pullar	
1920	R. Robertson		
1924	D.A. Smith		
1928	D.K. Pullar		
1936	T.K. Marshall		

SWW	1st Battalion:	2nd Battalion:	3rd Battalion:
1939	T.K. Marshall	A.C. Millar	W.D. Fielding
1940	C. Turnbull		W.D. Paterson
1943			(Sgt Piper J.H. Speirs)
1944		J. Bruce	
1945	J. Cheffins	R.M. Dunlop	J.H. Speirs
1946	J.H. Spiers		
	W. Smith		
	G.V. Lord		

1948	J.B. Robertson	
1949	E.B.H. Ledgett	
1954	L.V.N. de Laspee*	(1967 – 1975 Honorary Regimental Pipe Major)
1967	W. Ferguson	
1968	D. Duncan* (1975)	
1984	J.F.J. Spoore*	
1990	I.L. King*	
1999	C. Macpherson*	
2001	J. Bracken*	
2002	P.J. McLucas** (2012)	

Note
* Denotes appointment as Personal Piper to Her Majesty, Queen Elizabeth, The Queen Mother, Honorary Colonel-in-Chief of the London Scottish Regiment
** Denotes Appointment as Personal Piper to His Royal Highness, Prince Edward, Earl of Wessex and Royal Honorary Colonel, The London Regiment

The compilation of this list was started by the late Ian Bulpin, Curator of The London Scottish Museum, amended by Pipe Major John Spoore and subsequently revised and updated by Drummer Duncan de Silva.

Appendix II

Drum Majors of The London Scottish Regiment

1886	Albert J. Bertram
1887	Alfred Goodman
1903	Tommy Hodgson
1913–1914	Percy G.E. Cunningham

No Drum Major of 1st and 2nd Battalions serving overseas during the First World War

1914–1915	(Reserve Bn.) Walter McKinnon
1915	3 Bn Percy G.E. Cunningham
	3 Bn Edward G. 'Teddie' Hall
1923	Morris E. 'Morrie' Mills
1939–1940	Ian Thompson

No Drum Major of 1st, 2nd or 3rd Battalions during the Second World War

1956	Walter G. 'Jimmy' Riddell
1957	Edward G. 'Ted' Owens
1973	Bryan Alderson
1990	Michael 'Mickey' Powell
2000	Bryan Alderson
2001	David 'Nobby' Foulis

Bibliography

Archival Sources

Gordon Highlanders Museum, Aberdeen
Battalion diaries, library archives and service records and information relating to various officers and men et al

Hansards
Winston Churchill, 'We Shall Fight on the Beaches', speech, House of Commons, 4 June 1940 (Hansards, 1940, vol. 361 cc.787-78)

London Scottish Museum Archives, London
'1st Battalion Orders: August-September 1914'
Anon, 'Memoirs of the 'A' Troop Commander, 298 Battery, 3rd Battalion 1939-1946', unpublished manuscript
Anon., Unfinished letter from unknown London Scottish soldier who fought at Messines
Black, C., Lance Corporal, 'F' Company, unpublished diary, 1914
Bliss, Donald, Private, unpublished diary, September 1914 to July 1916
Cowper, J.B.F., Lance Corporal, 'F' Company, unpublished diary, 1914-1915
Davidson, Arthur G., Private, unpublished diary, August 1914 -September 1915
Dawnay, Captain Oliver, Private Secretary to H.M. The Queen Mother, Letter to Colonel R.J.L. Ogilby, 3 November 1953
Ferguson, John, 'Pioneer Commando – A Memoir of Special Service in Norway, The Mediterranean and North-West Europe, 1940-1945', unpublished manuscript
France, Bert, Private, 'F' Company, unpublished diary, 1914
Graham, James, unpublished diary, 1915-1918
Gibson, John, QMS, 'Army Book 152, Correspondence Book (Field Service) Sept. 1914 – Feb. 1915'
Hall, Lancelot Edey, Sergeant, 'F' Company, unpublished diary, 13 September 1914 to 9 April 1915
Hyslop, John L., Major, 'A Terrier in Flanders', unpublished diary written from notes by his son, Sam, 1914)
Hendry, Neil, Private, 'My Experiences with the London Scottish 1914-18', unpublished manuscript
Herbert C., unpublished diary, March to September 1915
Innes, A.G.S., unpublished diary, 1914-1915
Maben, Herbert C. unpublished diary, 1915
McIntyre, C.A., unpublished diary, 28 August 1942 to 28 April 1943
Moffat, Alex, Private, 'F' Company, unpublished diary, 1914 to 1915
Murray, Robert, 'My Adventures in the Great War: War Diary 1915-1919', unpublished manuscript, 1933
Petty, W.H., 'B' Company, 'The Lighter Side – 'Til We Went into Action', unpublished diary, 1914-1915
Smith, George Douglas, Corporal, unpublished diary, 25 August 1942-25 May 1945,

Tovey, Duncan, Sergeant, 'A' Company, unpublished diary, 1914-1915
Tovey, Duncan, Lieutenant, unpublished diary, 1916
Wilkins, E.M., 'A Brief Account of the Experiences of Private Eric Millward Wilkins on the 1st Battalion London Scottish During the Action of October 31st and November 1st, 1914, Near Messines Belgium', unpublished manuscript
Wilson, H.J., Lt. Col, OBE TD, unpublished Diary, 1914-18

London Scottish Museum Photography Archive, London
Multiple images relating to the Pipes and Drums

McMaster University, Hamilton, Canada
University Library Archives and Research Collection, F.5, Transfer Procedures, Box 9, WWI 1914-18 Official Documents, 2/14Bn London Scottish

The National Archives (TNA), Kew
HO 50/43: Home Department Papers, Highland Armed Association
HO 50/46: Home Department Papers, Highland Armed Association
HO 50/47: Home Department Papers, Highland Armed Association
HO 50/48: Home Department Papers, Highland Armed Association
HO 50/78: Home Department Papers, Loyal North Britons
HO 50/79: Home Department Papers, Loyal North Britons
HO 50/112: Home Department Papers, Loyal North Britons
HO 50/286: Home Department Papers, Loyal North Britons
Nottinghamshire Collection:
DD/P/6/12/40/1-25: Letters, Earl of Titchfield, Lord Lieutenant of Middlesex, re: Royal Highland Volunteers and Loyal North Britons
War Office:
WO 13/4456: Loyal North Britons
WO 95/1266/2-1: 1/14 Battalion London Regiment (London Scottish) War Diary, August 1914-September 1915
WO 95/1266/2-2: 1/14 Battalion London Regiment (London Scottish) War Diary, October 1915-January 1916
WO 95/2956/1-1: 1/14 Battalion London Regiment (London Scottish) War Diary, February 1916-May 1917
WO 95/2956/1-2: 1/14 Battalion London Regiment (London Scottish) War Diary, June 1917-November 1917
WO 95/2956/1-3: 1/14 Battalion London Regiment (London Scottish) War Diary, December 1917-August 1918
WO 95/2956/1-4: 1/14 Battalion London Regiment (London Scottish) War Diary, September 1918-May 1919
WO 95/3030/4: 2/14 Battalion London Regiment War Diaries, January 1915 to November 1916
WO 95/4928, 2/14 Battalion London Regiment War Diaries, 1 December 1916-30 June 1917
WO 95/4668: 2/14 Battalion London Regiment War Diaries, 1 July 1917-21 May 1918
WO 95/2340/2: 2/14 Battalion London Regiment War Diaries, 1 June 1918-31 August 1919
WO 329: War Office and Air Ministry, Service Medal and Award Rolls, First World War
WO 363: War Office, Soldiers' Documents, First World War 'Burnt Documents'
WO 364: War Office, Soldiers' Documents from Pension Claims, First World War
WO 372: War Office, Service Medal and Award Rolls Index, First World War
WO 373: War Office, Service Medal and Award Rolls Index, Second World War

National Army Museum, London
Various letters to Miss Nancy Morris from Robert Morris, Loyal North Britons 1803 – 1825: NAM 1988-09-71-1, NAM 1988-09-71-2, NAM 1988-09-71-4

National Library of Scotland, Edinburgh
Angus Family Letters, Account 7658,
Papers of Field-Marshal Sir Douglas Haig OM, KT, GCB, GCVO, 1st Earl Haig, Account 3155
Papers of the Highland Society of London, Acc. 10615, Deposit 268, Boxes 16, 22-26, 45

Scots Guards Archives, Wellington Barracks, London
Battalion Diaries, Library Resources, Service records of various pipe majors, drum majors, pipers and drummers et al

Audio & Video Interviews
Pipe Major Chris Macpherson, audio interview, 18 February 2010
Tenor Drummer Pat King, video interview, 30 June 2020
Drum Major Mickey Powell, video interview, 30 June 2020
Pipe Major Jim McLucas and Drum Major Nobby Foulis, joint audio interview, 1 July 2020

Newspapers & Journals
Aberdeen Evening Express
Aberdeen Journal
Aberdeen Weekly Journal
Aberdeen Press and Journal
The Advertiser
Arbroath Herald and Advertiser
Army and Navy Gazette: Journal of the Militia and Volunteer Forces, 1860-1921
The Belfast News-Letter
Belfast Telegraph
Birmingham Daily Post
Brechin Advertiser
Caledonian Mercury
Carlisle Journal
Carlisle Patriot
Chambers Journal
Chelsea News and General Advertiser
The City Press
Clerkenwell News and London Times
Colburn's United Service Magazine
The Cornishman
Croydon Advertiser
Daily Advertiser
Daily Graphic
Daily Mirror
Daily News
Daily Record
Dorking and Leatherhead Advertiser
Dumfries and Galloway Standard
Dundee Courier

Dundee Evening Telegraph
Dundee People's Journal
Ealing Gazette and West Middlesex Observer
Edinburgh Evening Courant
Eighth Army News
The Era
Evening News
The Evening Standard News
Evening Telegraph and Post
Freemans' Journal and Daily Commercial Advertiser
Fulham Chronicle
Glasgow Herald
The Globe
The Graphic
Hampshire Advertiser
Hobbies
Hull Daily Mail
Illustrated London News
The Inverness Courier
Jedburgh Gazette
Kentish Weekly Post
The Leeds Mercury
The Leisure Hour
Lloyds Weekly Newspaper
The London Gazette
London Scottish Regimental Gazette, 1896-2020
Maidstone and Kentish Journal
MacMillan's Magazine
Newcastle Journal
Morning Advertiser
Morning Chronicle
Morning Post
The Motherwell Times
Northern Whig
Pall Mall Gazette
Penny Illustrated Paper
The People
Piping Times
Piping Today
Portsmouth Times and Naval Gazette
Public Ledger
Punch
Reynolds Newspaper
The Scots Magazine and Edinburgh Literary Miscellany
The Scotsman
The Sportsman
Surrey Advertiser
Surrey Mirror
Tamworth Herald

Territorial Service Gazette
The Times
The Tomahawk
Trewman's Exeter Flying Post
The Volunteer Service Gazette, 1859 – 1903
The Volunteer Services and Imperial Yeomanry Chronicle, 1903-1908
Western Mail
West Middlesex Gazette

Published Sources

Anon., George Heriot's School, *Roll of Honour 1914-1919* (Edinburgh: War Memorial Committee, 1921)
Anon., *Presentation of Bagpipes to the London Scottish Rifle Volunteers in Westminster Hall, Wednesday 19th June, 1861* (London: Day and Son, 1861)
Anon., *Standing Regulations of the Highland Armed Association* (London, 1798)
Alderson, Bryan, *MacNamara's Band to Drum Major: A Drummers Anecdotes and Pictures* (London: self-published, 2009)
Baillie, George, *Narrative of the Mercantile Transactions of the Concerns of George Baillie and Co's Houses. From the Year 1793 to 1805 Inclusive* (London: 1805)
Barclay, C.N. (ed.), *The London Scottish in the Second World War 1939-1945* (London: William Clowes, 1952)
Barty-King, Hugh, *The Drum* (London: The Royal Tournament, 1988)
Berlyn, Philippa, *The Quiet Man* (Salisbury, Rhodesia: Collins, 1978)
Berry, Robert Potter, *A History of the Formation and Development of the Volunteer Infantry: From the Earliest Times* (Kent: Simpkins, Marshall, Hamilton, 1903)
Blanchard, Jerrold, *The Life of George Cruikshank: In Two Epochs, Vol. 1* (London: Chatto and Windus, 1882)
Blaser, Bernard, *Kilts Across the Jordan: Being Experiences and Impressions with the Second Battalion 'London Scottish' in Palestine* (London: H.F. and G. Witherby, 1926)
Calder, Julian and 'The Regiment' (eds.), *A Year in the Life of the London Regiment* (London: Calder Walker, 2001)
Campbell, Alistair, *Two Hundred Years: The Highland Society of London, 1778-1978* (London, The Highland Society, 1983)
Campbell, Jeannie, *Highland Bagpipe Makers* (Edinburgh: Magnus Orr, 2011)
—— *More Highland Bagpipe Makers* (Edinburgh: Magnus Orr, 2017)
Campsie, Alistair Keith, *The MacCrimmon Legend or The Madness of Angus MacKay* (Edinburgh: Cannongate, 1980)
Cannon, Roderick D., *The Highland Bagpipe and Its Music* (Edinburgh: Birlinn, 2004)
Cave, N. and Sheldon, J., *Ypres 1914: Messines* (Barnsley: Pen and Sword, 2015)
Chapman, Paul, *Menin Gate South: In Memory and In Mourning* (Barnsley: Pen and Sword, 2016)
Civilian on Trek, *On Trek with the Hodden Grey: Being an Illustrated Account of the Route March of the London Scottish from Aberdeen to Inverness, July 15th-26th, 1929* (Aberdeen: The Aberdeen Press and Journal, 1929)
Clemence, John (ed.), *Of No Military Importance: Cartoons, Drawings, Poems and Stories by Robert Louis Souter* (2014)
Corrigan, Gordon, *Mud, Blood and Poppycock* (London: Cassell Military, 2004)

Cunningham, Hugh, *The Volunteer Force: A Social and Political History, 1859-1908* (London: Routledge, 2020)

Dean, Colin and Turner, Gordon (eds.), *Sound the Trumpet, Beat the Drum: Military Music Through the Twentieth Century* (London: Parapress, 2002)

Dolden, Stuart A., *Cannonfodder: An Infantryman's Life on the Western Front, 1914-18* (Poole, Dorset: Blandford Press, 1980)

Elcho (Lord), *Speech of Lord Elcho M.P. at The Freemason's Tavern, July 4th* (London: J. Ridgway, 1859)

Ellis, John, *Eye-Deep in Hell: Life in the Trenches 1914-1918* (Glasgow: Fontana, 1976)

Farmer, Henry G., *The Rise and Development of Military Music* (London: W.M. Reeves, 1912)

Fraser, Alistair, Roberts, Steve, Robertshaw, Andrew, *Ghosts on the Somme: Filming the Battle June-July 1916* (London: Pen and Sword, 2009)

French, David, *Army, Empire, and Cold War: The British Army and Military Policy, 1945 – 1971* (Oxford: Oxford University Press, 2012)

Gibson, John G., *Traditional Gaelic Bagpiping 1745-1945* (Quebec: McGill-Queen's University Press, 1998)

Grierson, J.M., *Records of the Scottish Volunteer Force, 1859-1908* (Edinburgh: William Blackwood, 1909)

Harvey, J.M. Lee, *D-Day Dodgers* (London: William Kimber, 1979)

Herbert, S. and McKernan, L., *Who's Who of Victorian Cinema* (London: British Film Institute, 1996)

Herbert, Trevor (ed.), *The British Brass Band – A Musical and Social History* (London: Oxford University Press, 2000)

Holmes, Richard, *The World at War: The Landmark Oral History from the Classic TV Series* (London: Random House, 2011)

Hurrall, Andrew, *Popular Culture in London 1890-1918* (Manchester: Manchester University Press, 2001)

Keegan, J., *The Second World War* (London: Penguin, 1990)

Keir, David, *The Younger Centuries* (Edinburgh: William Younger, 1951)

Lindsay, J.H. (ed.), *The London Scottish in the Great War* (London: London Scottish Regiment Press, 1926)

Lloyd, Mark, *The London Scottish in the Great War* (London: Pen and Sword, 2001)

MacFarland, Paul (ed.), *Scots in Great War London: A Community at Home and on the Front Line 1914–1919* (Warwick: Helion and Co. Ltd., 2018)

MacKenzie, John T., *There Was a Piper, a Scottish Piper: Memoirs of Pipe Major John T. MacKenzie* (Toronto: National Heritage Books, 2001)

Macpherson, Ronald T.S. 'Tommy', *Behind Enemy Lines: The Autobiography of Britain's Most Decorated Living War Hero* (London: Mainstream Publishing, 2010)

Mackay, Angus, *The Book of Mackay* (Edinburgh: Norman MacLeod, 1906)

McNeil, Kenneth, *Scotland, Britain, Empire: Writing the Highlands, 1760-1860* (Columbus: Ohio State University Press, 2007)

Mair, C., *David Angus, The Life and Adventures of a Victorian Railway Engineer* (Stevenage: Strong Oak Press, 1989)

Malcolm, C.A., The *Piper in Peace and War* (London: John Murray, 1927)

Miller, Stephen M., *Volunteers in the Veld: Britain's Citizen Soldiers and the South Africa War, 1899-1902* (Norman, Oklahoma: University of Oklahoma Press, 2007)

Milligan, Spike, *Mussolini: His Part in My Downfall* (London: Penguin, 1980)

Moynihan, Michael (ed.), *Black Bread and Barbed Wire: Prisoners in the First World War* (London: Lee Cooper, 1978)

Murray, David, *Music of the Scottish Regiments* (Edinburgh: Mercat Press, 2001)

Nicholson, W., *London Types* (London: Heineman, 1898)
Palmer, Alan, *The Salient: Ypres, 1914-18* (London: Constable Press, 2007)
Pinkerton. Douglas R., *Ladies from Hell: With the London-Scottish Regiment During the First World War* (Driffield, Leonaur, 2011)
Pottinger, Ron, *A Soldier in the Cockpit: From Rifles to Typhoons in WWII* (Mechanicsburg, Pennsylvania, Stackpole Books, 2007)
Robson, J.O., *The Uniforms of The London Scottish 1859-1959* (London: Hadden, Best, 1960)
Robson, R.O., *London Scots of the Napoleonic Era* (Ipswich: Hadden, Best and Co, 1970)
Rowlandson, Thomas *The Illuminated School of Mars or Review of the Loyal Volunteer Corps of London and its Vicinity* (London: Rudolph Ackerman, 1798-99)
Sanderson, Adam, '150 Years of Proud History: Pipes and Drums of the London Scottish,' *Piping News*, March 2013
Sangar, Keith, 'Newspaper Report Could be the Earliest Evidence of Pipe Band Origin,' *Piping Times*, December 2003
Seton, Bruce and Grant, John (eds.), *Pipes of War: A Record of the Achievements of Pipers of Scottish and Overseas Regiments During the War 1914-1918* (Wakefield: E.P. Publishing, 1920)
Sinclair, John, *An Account of the Highland Society of London: From its Establishment in May 1778 to the Commencement of the Year 1813*, (London, 1813)
Spooner, Keith, *The Battalion*, (London: LSR Trust, 1979)
Stewart, Timothy J., *Toronto's Fighting 75th in the Great War 1915-1919: A Pre-History of the Toronto Scottish Regiment* (Waterloo, Ontario: Wilfrid Laurier Univ. Press, 2017)
Wilson, George, *Mobilised: Being the Record of Private George Wilson of F Company London Scottish. From the Call to Arms to his Return Wounded* (London: The Complete Press, n.d.)
Woollcombe, Robert, *All the Blue Bonnets: The History of the King's Own Scottish Borderers* (London: Arms and Armour Press, 1980)
Wright, A., Cannon, R. and Buis, F., *The MacArthur MacGregor Manuscripts of Piobaireachd, Music of Scotland Series, Vol. I* (Glasgow: Universities of Glasgow and Aberdeen Press, 2001)

Unpublished Theses

MacInnes, Iain I., 'The Highland Bagpipe: The Impact of The Highland Societies of London and Edinburgh 1781-1844', M.Litt. Thesis, University of Edinburgh, 1988
McCullough, Katie Louise, 'Building the Highland Empire: The Highland Society of London and the Formation of Charitable Networks in Great Britain and Canada, 1778-1857', PhD Thesis, University of Guelph, Canada, 2014

Music & Film

Books
Graham, P. and MacRae, B. (eds.), *The Gordon Highlanders Pipe Music Collection, Volume 1*, (UK: Hal Leonard, 2004)
Tovey, Duncan *The Big Drum Major* (London: Asherberg, Hopwood and Crew, 1901)

Film
Idle on Parade, Columbia Pictures, 1959
Tunes of Glory, United Artists, 1960
The Longest Day, 20th Century Fox, 1962

Vinyl

Corporal Piper Robert Reith, *The Barren Rocks of Aden*, Berliner 7700, London, 28 September 1898

Pipe Major A.L. Reith and Corporal Piper R. Reith, *Atholl Highlanders/The Lass*, Berliner 7701, London, 6 October 1898

Pipe Major A.L. Reith and Corporal Piper R. Reith, *Lord Lovat's March*, Berliner 7702, London, 6 October 1898

Pipe Major A.L. Reith and Corporal Piper R. Reith, *Cock o' the North*, Berliner 7705, London, 6 October 1898

Pipe Major A.L. Reith and Corporal Piper R. Reith, *March, Strathspey and Reel*, Berliner 7706, London, 6 October 1898

Pipe Major A.L. Reith and Corporal Piper R. Reith, *Tullochgorum/Reel of Tulloch*, Berliner 7707, London, 6 October 1898

Pipe Major A.L. Reith and Corporal Piper R. Reith, *Johnnie Cope/Brose and Butter*, Berliner 7708, London, 6 October 1898

Pipe Major A.L. Reith and Corporal Piper R. Reith, *Marquis of Huntley/Donal' Duncan*, Berliner 7709, London, 6 October 1898

Pipe Major A.L. Reith and Corporal Piper R. Reith, *March, Strathspey and Reel,* Berliner 8807x, London, 24 December 1898,

Pipe Major A.L. Reith and Corporal Piper R. Reith, *Highland Laddie March*, Berliner 7713, London, 24 December 1898

Pipe Major A.L. Reith and Corporal Piper R. Reith, *Back o' Benachie/The Campbells Are Coming*, Berliner 7714, London, 24 December 1898

Pipe Major A.L. Reith and Corporal Piper R. Reith, *The Barren Rocks of Aden*, HMV 12" Special, London, date unknown

The Sensational Alex Harvey Band, *Impossible Dream*, Vertigo Records, London (apple Studios), 1974

51st Highland Volunteers, *The Music of the 1st Battalion, The 51st Highland Volunteers*, Spec 5022, 1980

CD & Digital

The Pipes and Drums of the London Scottish Regiment, *Strike Sure*, Highland Classics, London, 2004

The Pipes and Drums of the London Scottish Regiment, *Tunes of Glory: Salute to the Scottish Regiments*, Highland Classics, London, 2007.

Index

Aberdeen Universities OTC, 346, 350, 352, 359
Aberdeen, 52, 94, 184, 258, 264, 267, 271, 276, 288, 299, 350, 352, 357
Afghanistan, 327, 331, 332, 335, 336, 337, 341, 344, 345
Alderson, Drum Major Bryan, 275, 281, 282, 289, 290, 291, 292, 293, 294, 298, 299, 300, 301, 304, 305, 308, 309, 310, 320, 321, 326, 327, 328, 330, 331, 335, 336, 340, 357, 358
Allenby, Field Marshal Sir Edmund, 164, 165, 167, 170, 186
Anderson, Piper Gary, 344, 345, 350
Angus, Piper Archibald, 111, 120-121
Anzio, 226, 238, 239-241, 247, 248, 264, 298, 312
Argentina, 111, 300, 309, 319
Argyll and Sutherland Highlanders, 71, 125, 185, 188, 250, 252, 253, 275, 280, 286, 317, 330, 343, 351
Argyll, Duke of, 106
Army School of Bagpipe Music and Highland Drumming, 298, 322, 326, 349, 360, 361
Army School of Music, Kneller Hall, 322, 343, 357
Arras, Battle of (1917), 143, 144, 146, 147, 295, 308
Attwooll Trophy, 184, 277, 333, 342, 345, 347, 349, 357, 358
Attwooll, Colonel Hugh, 184, 274, 275, 277, 280
Augustus Frederick, Prince (See Sussex, Duke of)

Bagpipe Music, First Recorded, 87-88
Baigrie, Piper Alexander, 293, 294, 295, 300, 301
Balfour, Colonel J.A., 103
Bari, 231, 244, 245, 246, 247, 319
Beating Retreat, 148, 152, 215, 244, 246, 264, 265, 276, 294, 298, 303, 321, 322, 333, 335, 336, 341, 344, 345, 349, 351, 352, 359, 360
Beersheba, 165, 167, 168, 177
Bennett, Drummer and Colonel Duncan, 144, 193, 200, 251, 267, 274, 277
Bennie, Piper John F., 123-124
Berliner Recordings (1898), 87-88
Bertram, Drum Major A.J., 78
Bethlehem, 169, 173
Big Blaw, 294, 298, 309, 322,

Bisley, National Rifle Centre, 106, 124, 187, 195, 262, 275, 311, 342
Black Watch of Canada, 299, 322
Black Watch, 23, 49, 51, 71, 125, 127, 135, 192, 223, 286, 287, 294, 299, 304, 309, 310, 328, 334
Blackledge, Piper Rob, 304, 333, 342, 347
Blake, Drummer Joe, 340, 345, 346
Boer War (1899-1902), 92-94, 95, 102, 104, 111
Bracken, Pipe Major John, 308, 321, 326, 327
British Broadcasting Corporation (BBC), 187, 199, 263, 268, 274, 275, 280-281, 291, 293, 336
British Military Tournament, 343, 344, 345, 346, 347
Brown, Rifleman James, 341
Bryden, Corporal Drummer John, 228
Buckingham Palace, 79, 80, 94, 109, 150, 200, 202, 269, 314, 316, 320, 327, 340, 348, 352, 353
Burley Camp, 201, 206

Cairns, Drummer John A., 125, 211
Cairns-Wilson, Piper Alfred, 110, 130, 139,
Caledonian Ball, 309, 316, 320, 329, 340, 342, 346, 347, 357
Caledonian Club, 345
Cambrai, Battle of (1917), 145,
Cambridge, Duke of, 46, 56, 63, 72, 73, 80, 89, 347
Cameron Highlanders, 23, 49, 125, 126, 127, 135, 138, 192, 198, 199, 254, 282, 286, 309
Campbell, Captain Lawrence Dundas, 16, 17
Campbell, Colin, Lord Clyde, 56, 58
Campbell, Pipe Major Alexander, 49, 53, 56, 58, 59, 62, 66
Campbell, Piper Simon, 144
Carey, Piper James, 113, 120
Caution, James C., 265, 268
Cavendish-Bentinck-Scot, Marquis of Titchfield, 16, 17
Cenotaph, Whitehall, The, 298, 337, 348, 349, 350, 351, 352, 358, 360
Centenary Anniversary Celebrations, 277-279, 322
Changing of the Guard, Buckingham Palace, 316, 320

373

Chapman, Piper Eric G., 121-122, 124
Chateau Balleroy, 314, 321
Cheffins, Pipe Major John, 213, 219, 226, 227, 251, 253
Chelsea Barracks, 81, 92, 337
Childers Reforms (1881), 71, 72, 198
City Imperial Volunteers (CIV), 93
Clarence House, 269, 270, 288, 299, 300, 309, 314, 321, 327
Clemence, Colonel John, 195, 311, 313, 314, 317, 347
Coldstream Guards, 46, 47, 115, 125, 315, 340
Connell, Piper Alexander A., 137, 139
Cooper, Drummer Alex, 350, 351
Cottam, Piper Haydn, 330, 332, 351, 353
COVID-19, 358, 360
Cowal Highland Gathering (World Pipe Band Championships), 180, 185, 186, 188, 189, 192, 193, 201, 275, 276, 279, 281, 289, 293, 327
Cowie, Drummer Douglas B., 211
Cowie, Piper William, 250, 257, 300, 301, 304
Crimean War, 23, 41, 71
Crowley, Drum Sergeant Mike, 268, 269, 277, 280, 283, 291, 294, 298, 300, 301, 304, 310, 327
Cruikshank, George, 38
Cruikshank, Private Robert, 171, 281
Cunningham, Drum Major Percy A.E., 106, 151

Dainville, 295, 356
de Laspée, Pipe Major Lesley V., 269, 270, 271, 274, 275, 276, 280, 281, 282, 283, 287, 288, 290, 295, 299, 300, 301
de Silva, Drummer Duncan, 330, 342
Dead-End Kids, 245, 247
Diamond Jubilee (1897), 83, 86-87
Dillon, Drummer and Medic Gary, 330, 331
Donaldson, Piper George, 213, 228, 229
'Drumfamily', 201, 206
Duke of York's Headquarters, 188, 200, 278, 312, 315, 317, 326
Duncan Drummer and CSM J.K., 252
Duncan, Pipe Major Davie, 282, 291, 293, 294, 295, 298, 299, 300, 301, 312,

Earl of Wessex, Prince Edward, 340, 344, 347, 348, 358
East Berlin, 299,
Edgar, Pipe Major Harry F., 133, 134, 135, 136, 138, 145
Edinburgh Castle, 276, 295, 298, 311, 322
Edinburgh, Duke of, 63, 73, 315, 344, 347, 359
Edward VII, 98, 278

Edward VIII, 199
Elcho, Lady, 52, 53, 62
Elcho, Lord, 39, 42, 42, 46, 47, 48, 49, 57, 58, 62, 64
Elizabeth II, 268, 309, 337, 344, 347, 351
Elizabeth Duchess of York, 193, 195, 199
Es Salt, 170

Farquhar, Pipe Major John, 68, 69, 77
Ferguson, Drummer Alfred, 157, 166, 167, 169
Ferguson, Pipe Major William, 277, 288, 290, 291, 292, 333
Ferguson, Piper Bill, 333, 337, 342
Ferguson, Piper Tom, 337
Fielding, Pipe Major W.D., 212
First live radio broadcast, 184
First live television broadcast, 263
First television broadcast, 199
First World War (1914-18), 115, 118-125, 127, 142, 143, 145, 149, 150, 156-57, 164-165, 170-72, 174, 177, 195, 293, 353
Forsyth, Pipe Major Henry, 98, 99, 185
Foulis, Drum Major Nobby, 328, 330, 336, 337, 341, 346, 348, 350, 351, 359
Freemason's Tavern, 42

Gair, Drummer Nick, 330, 341, 342, 343, 346, 347, 348
Gardiner, Piper Douglas, 313, 316, 317, 318, 346
Garikayi, Drummer Tafadzwa, 350, 357, 358
George III, HRH King, 26, 28, 30
George V, 104, 150, 153, 179, 195, 198
George VI, 199, 200, 204, 218, 329,
Ghillies, Pipe Major John, 99, 104
Gibbons, Piper and CQMS Roland, 258, 264, 270
Gibraltar, 111, 331, 332, 334, 335, 336, 340, 342-343
Gibson, Piper Ranald, 350, 352, 353
Gloucester, Duke of, 332
Golden Jubilee (1887), 79-80
Goodman, Drum Major Albert, 78, 81, 83, 86, 88, 95, 118, 294
Gordon Highlanders, 49, 71, 72, 77, 93, 94, 137, 149, 174, 195, 198, 200, 230, 236, 239, 240, 244, 264, 271, 278, 286, 300, 309, 311, 313, 337, 340, 352, 356, 359
Gordon, Pipe Major Ralston, 137, 147
Gosling, Drummer Frank A., 156
Gow, Drummer Sandy, 105, 106, 110, 161, 184
Gow, Drummer Thomas, 175
Greig of Eccles, Colonel, 99, 102, 152, 157,
Grenadier Guards, 80, 81, 93, 158, 315, 316, 335-336, 348, 359

Grieg, Pipe Major Kenneth, 98, 99, 122, 124, 125, 126, 127, 130, 132
Grosvenor House Hotel, 279, 304, 347
Guildhall, The, 93, 315, 336, 343, 347, 348, 351

Haig, Field Marshal Sir Douglas, 99, 174, 176, 177, 180, 186-187, 195
Hain, Piper Les, 345, 346, 349, 350, 353, 358, 359
Haldane Reforms, 99
Haldane, Richard, Secretary of State for War, 99
Halley, Pipe Major Ronald, 49, 50, 63, 66, 68, 69, 77, 78, 81
Hallowe'en Dinner, 63, 119, 134, 142, 157, 159, 177, 181, 186, 193, 200, 219, 251, 259, 271, 277, 279, 280, 283, 290, 291, 305, 308, 310, 311, 316, 317, 326, 336, 340, 348, 350, 356, 358, 360
Hamilton Lance Sergeant Drummer William I., 238
Harman, Drummer, Piper, Regimental Secretary Bob, 289, 313, 320, 337
Harrington, Lord, 28
Henderson, Piper and Colonel Lionel D., 105, 110, 184, 187, 188, 193, 194, 199-200, 211, 256
Henwood, Colonel Stephen, 328, 329, 330, 336
Hepburn, J.W., 138
Hepburn, Robert, 41
Hicks, Piper Caroline, 358
Highland Armed Association, 15-22
Highland Brigade, 23
Highland Light Infantry, 125, 132, 276, 288
Highland Society Piping Competition, 35, 36, 50
Highland Society, 15-16, 20-22, 26, 34-37, 41-42, 50
Highlanders (Seaforth, Gordons and Camerons), 313, 317
Hilden, 148
Hill, Drummer Stephen, 333, 342, 344, 345, 350, 358
Hodden Grey song, 278, 356
Hodden Grey, 46, 52, 56, 63, 64, 66, 77, 149, 150, 177, 180, 186, 234, 238, 241, 248, 253, 264, 278, 290, 293, 294, 302, 312, 330, 334, 340, 360, 361
Hodgson, Drum Major Tommy, 77, 95, 98, 105, 106, 184
Hogmanay, 142, 145, 160, 169, 173, 220, 222, 234, 235, 238, 252
Hollebone, Captain James C., 206, 250
Holyroodhouse, Palace of, 198, 277, 298
Honorable Artillery Company, 93, 215, 279, 315, 358, 359
Hope Grant, General Sir James, 63, 64, 66

Horse Guards Parade, 89, 150, 151, 199, 265, 266, 276, 293, 294, 303, 309, 318, 322, 335, 336, 340, 343, 344, 345, 349, 351, 352, 357, 359
Hume, Piper Stuart, 330, 332-333, 336, 352, 356, 357
Huskisson, William, 20
Hutchison, Drummer James, 236
Hyde Park, 26, 27, 38, 47, 48, 62, 98, 103, 105, 109, 179, 188, 198, 204, 268, 276, 293, 303, 295

Idle on Parade, 277
Imperial Yeomanry, 92-93
Iraq, 203, 219, 220, 226, 327, 331-332, 333, 335, 337, 341
Irish Guards, 158, 241, 265, 294, 308, 309, 329, 335, 345, 348, 351

Jerusalem, 165, 168, 169, 170, 195, 226, 353
Johnston, Piper Brenton, 352, 357
Johnston, Piper Tommy, 304, 316, 328, 342, 349, 350, 353
Joss, Pipe Major Alexander S., 125, 127, 130, 131, 132

Keith, Pipe Major William P., 134, 136, 137, 138, 144, 146, 147
Keith, Piper Alexander R., 89, 93-94, 111
Kent, Duke of, 318, 337
King, Drummer Patrick, 301, 309, 317, 332, 334, 340
King, Pipe Major Ian, 300, 301, 309, 310, 311, 312, 313, 315, 316, 317, 319, 320, 342, 345
King, Piper Russell, 321, 342
King's Own Scottish Borderers, 79, 102, 236, 268, 334
Kirkuk, 219, 220, 221

L'Arc de Triumphe, 289-290
Latham, Piper Harry G., 106, 114, 122-123, 124,
Lauder, Harry, 102
Ledgett, Pipe Major Bruce, 258, 259, 262, 263, 264, 265, 267, 268, 269, 270-271, 275, 289
Lloyd, Drummer Gordon, 328, 330
London Irish Rifles, 131, 138, 219, 220, 247, 253, 254, 263, 265, 277, 279, 310, 311, 312, 316, 317, 329, 334, 335, 336, 337, 347, 348, 356
London Regiment, The, 315, 316, 317, 319, 320, 326, 329, 331, 332, 333, 334, 335, 336, 340, 343, 344, 345, 347, 348, 353, 356, 358, 360
London Scottish Brass Band, (professional) 51, 57, 58, 63, 69, 78, 82, 83, 94-95
(amateur) 57, 78, 82
London Scottish Bugle Band, 69, 95, 104

London Scottish Children's Party, 189, 320, 337
London Scottish Golf Club, 308
London Scottish Memorial, 181, 352
London Scottish Piping Competitions, 59, 98, 99, 264
London Scottish Rugby Club, 258, 336, 356
London Scottish War Memorial Messines, 181
London to Brighton March, 106, 178-179
Longest Day, The, 281
Loos British Military Cemetery, 334, 343
Loos, Battle of (1915), 131, 133, 134
Lord Mayor's Show, 87, 199, 267, 316, 328, 335, 336, 344, 348, 351, 356, 358, 360
Loyal North Britons, 21, 22, 26-39
Ludlow, Colonel Mark, 331, 342
Lyall Grant, Piper and Colonel 'Dougie', 104, 110, 136, 176, 177, 178, 181, 184, 187, 188, 189, 193, 201, 215, 256, 257, 267, 276
Lyall-Grant Captain W., 88, 104

MacAdam, Drummer and Lieutenant Geoff, 301, 305
MacArthur, Charles, 35
MacFarlane, Lieutenant Colonel R., 17
Macglashan, Pipe Major Neil, 68, 69, 77
MacGregor, Malcolm, 36
MacGregor, Peter, 35, 37
MacGregor, Pipe Major John, 21, 35-37
MacHattie, Pipe Major John, 148
Machel-Varese, Piper Oscar, 111, 125, 153
MacInnes, Iain, 20, 35, 36
Mackay, Eric, Lord Reay, 22, 30, 38
Mackay, Piper Charles W.D., 120, 125, 127, 138,
MacKenzie John Ban, 50, 52
MacKenzie, Pipe Major John, 49, 50, 51, 52, 56, 57, 66, 68, 77, 98, 99
MacKenzie, Pipe Major Robert, 66, 68
MacKinnon, Piper and Drum Major Walter, 89, 110, 150, 151
MacLeod Medal, 184, 193, 201, 259, 265, 277, 298, 316, 321, 333, 342, 344, 349, 357
MacLeod, Drummer and Captain Archie, 201, 205, 245, 256, 258, 259, 265, 266, 293, 300
Macpherson, Colonel Ronald T.S., 281, 282, 349
Macpherson, Drummer Alexander, 146
Macpherson, Pipe Major Chris, 300, 301, 304, 305, 308, 314, 315, 320, 321, 326, 327, 328, 329, 330, 340, 342, 350, 357, 358
MacRae, Pipe Major Brian, 302, 313, 316, 317, 320, 327
MacTernan, Piper Chris, 321, 333
Malcolm, C.A., 23, 82
Malcolm, Colonel George A., 104, 115, 194

Mall, The, 79, 202, 300, 314, 359
Manic Street Preachers, 337
Mansion House, 277, 315, 347, 351
March Through Scotland, 88, 89, 94, 105, 184, 192, 199-200, 271
Marshall Pipe Major Tommy K., 198, 199, 200, 201, 207
Marshall, Piper Robert, 133, 134, 135, 137, 138, 142, 149
McDougall, Piper William K., 210, 238-239
McGilvray, Pipe Major John A., 152, 159, 166, 174
McIntyre-North, C.N., 49, 50, 62
McLelland, Colonel Peter, 335, 337, 340, 341, 356
McLucas, Pipe Major Jim, 313, 315, 317, 320, 321, 326, 327-328, 329, 330, 332, 333, 336, 337, 341, 342, 344, 345, 346, 347, 348, 349, 350, 353, 357, 358, 359, 360
McMillan, Piper and MSP Stuart, 330, 351
McNiven, Piper Kenneth, 102
Menin Gate, 124, 298, 301, 308, 333, 341, 343, 347, 352, 358
Mill, Pipe Major J.D., 68
Millar, Pipe Major Alec C., 198, 202, 204, 206, 211, 214, 223, 257
Milligan, Spike, 238
Mills, John, 280, 281
Mills, Piper and Drum Major Morrie, 142, 143, 144, 147, 148, 185, 188, 189, 201, 204, 256, 258, 275, 267
Moffat, Major, Presentation of Prize for Best Novice Piper, 264
Monte Camino, 237, 241
Monte Cassino , 237, 241, 298, 313, 317, 320
Morrison, John, Drumming Instructor, 77, 99, 103
Mules, Reaction to Pipe Band, 160
Muzzle Loaders Association, 342

Napoleon I, 15, 21, 38, 41
Napoleon III, 41
National Rifle Association, 56, 59, 63, 64, 65, 195, 275
Neikirk, Colonel Alan, 274, 275, 289, 291, 293
Newley, Anthony, 277
Nicholson, Piper Stuart, 347, 348, 349, 350, 352, 358, 358
Nicholson, Sir William, 88
Nicol, Piper Bertram, 119, 125, 178, 181
Norris, Robert, 21
Number 10 Downing Street, 320, 348
Number 59 Buckingham Gate, 79, 94, 99, 104, 108, 111, 149, 152, 178, 180, 189, 210-211, 256, 257, 262, 264, 266, 268, 277, 278, 280, 282, 286, 298, 300, 301, 302, 303, 305

INDEX

Ogilby, Colonel Robert J.S., 157, 165, 173, 195, 235, 264, 267, 269, 274,
Ogilvie, William, 15
Oram, Pipe Major Charles, 107, 119, 124, 160, 161, 173, 174, 177, 178, 181
Owens, Drum Major Ted, 274, 275-276, 280, 288, 290

Palestine, 109, 156, 164-165, 170-172, 174, 195, 226, 235, 268, 353
Parkyn, Piper Douglas R., 114, 120
Parsons, Pipe Sergeant Andrew, 303, 313, 317, 320, 321, 322, 326, 327, 328, 333, 336, 337, 340, 343, 345, 347, 349, 350, 352, 353, 356, 359
Paterson, Pipe Major William D., 204, 212, 215, 221, 258
Paton, Piper Andrew B., 144
Peddie, Colonel James, 201, 239, 244, 250
Personal Piper to, 268-270, 309, 320, 326, 327, 328, 329
Pert, Drummer Gunner W., 231, 234
Piave, Italy, 337, 340, 353
Piazza San Marco, 253, 340
Piazza Venezza, 250
Pinnington, Piper Donald, 111, 130, 131
Pipe Banners, 52, 53, 78, 103, 266, 267, 269, 278, 283, 287, 298, 313, 329, 344
PM and DM Plaid Brooches, 278
Pola, 248, 253
Porteous, Piper Robert, 106, 120, 125, 158
Porteous, Piper William, 106, 120, 124, 125
Powell, Drum Major Michael, 298, 299, 301, 305, 308, 310, 312, 313, 316, 318, 320, 321, 322, 326
Princes Anne, 341
Pullar, Pipe Major Davie, 173, 174, 181, 188, 189, 192, 194, 195, 198, 201, 207, 259,

Queen Mother, 268, 269, 270, 274, 278, 280, 282, 283, 287, 288, 291, 295, 298, 299, 300, 301, 302, 303, 305, 309, 311, 312, 314, 315, 318, 321-22, 344
Queen's Own Highlanders (Seaforth and Camerons), 313
Quilliams, Drummer and Corporal Peter, 234-235

Rankin-Hunt, Colonel David, 304, 308, 336, 340
Reay, 7th Lord. (See Mackay, Eric)
Redman, Drummer Charles, 289, 293, 300, 301
Regimental Pilgrimage, 181, 298, 301, 308, 310, 313, 321, 333, 340-341, 347, 358
Regiments
    42nd Highland Regiment (see Black Watch)
    4th London Regiment (Royal Fusiliers), 303

51st Highland Volunteers, 286, 287, 289, 292, 293, 294, 295, 298, 299, 300, 301, 302, 303, 304, 305, 308, 309, 310, 311, 312, 314, 319, 326, 361
79th Highland Regiment (See Cameron Highlanders)
8th Queen's Fusiliers, 312
91st Highland Regiment (See Argyll and Sutherland Highlanders)
92nd Highland Regiment (See Gordon Highlanders)
93rd Highland Regiment (See Sutherland Highlanders)
Reith, Pipe Major Alexander 'Sandie', 81, 82, 83, 86, 87, 95
Reith, Pipe Major Robert, 87, 95, 98, 102
Riddell, Drum Major Walter G., 201, 262, 265, 275
Rifle Associations, creation of, 41
Roberts, Field Marshall Frederick, 150
Robertson, Lord George of Port Ellen, 322, 332, 334
Robertson, Pipe Major James Blair, 259, 265, 266
Robertson, Pipe Major Robert, 102-103, 104, 105, 106, 110, 133, 151, 152, 158, 159, 176, 177, 180, 181, 184, 189, 195, 275
Robson, Corporal Drummer Tommy, 240
Rome, 238, 241, 250, 255, 264
Ross, Pipe Major William, 52, 56, 98, 99, 104
Royal Albert Hall, 184, 283, 291, 294, 320, 345
Royal Artillery, 80, 94, 204, 215, 238, 244, 245, 262, 276, 318, 322, 332, 334
Royal Caledonian Asylum, 53, 56, 59, 79
Royal Caledonian School, 179, 206, 278, 332
Royal Caledonian Society, 42, 66, 277, 278, 300, 342, 352
Royal Gibraltar Regiment, 331, 332, 343, 347
Royal Highland Volunteers, 17, 21, 22
Royal Hospital, Chelsea, 192, 204, 206, 321, 330, 342, 347, 356, 358
Royal Military Exhibition 1890, 81
Royal Military School of Music, 81, 343, 357
Royal Opera House, Covent Garden, 210
Royal Scots Dragoon Guards, 267, 300, 321, 330, 336, 349
Royal Tournament, 98, 193-194, 274, 299, 300, 337
Royal Volunteer Review, (1801) 18-19, (1803) 27-28, (1814) 38, (1860) 47-48, (1881) 73, (1887) 80, (1899) 89, (1905) 98, (1922) 179, (1937) 200, (1939) 204, (1977) 298
Ryan, Drummer and CQMS Jamie, 327, 331, 341

Salonika, 159, 161, 165
Sanger, Keith, 27
Second World War (1939-45), 203, 226, 235, 268
Scots Fusilier Guards, 43, 46, 47, 49-52, 66, 67, 70
Scots Guards, 20, 72, 79, 80, 92, 98-99, 104, 125, 126, 178, 179, 180, 185, 198, 253, 254, 258, 259, 274, 276, 300, 317, 318, 334, 336, 344-345, 349, 351, 357, 360
Scott, Drummer Paul, 357, 358, 359
Seaforth Highlanders of Canada, 99
Seaforth Highlanders, 34, 71, 110, 161, 192, 195, 198, 199, 200, 245, 286, 328,
Sensational Alex Harvey Band, The, 295
Shakespeare Tavern, 16, 22
Shand, Pipe and Drum Major George, 106, 151, 158, 172
Shaw, C.A. Drummer, 93
Sicily, 203, 218, 226, 227, 229, 230, 231, 237, 268, 350
Simmonds, Drummer Harold, 89, 92, 105, 114
Skilling, Pipe Sergeant Gordon, 301, 304, 310, 314, 315, 316, 319, 333, 340, 350
Smith Prime Minister Ian, 221
Smith, Drummer Chris, 330, 335, 336, 343, 344, 348
Smith, Pipe Major David, 179, 180, 181, 185, 187, 188
Somme, Battle of (1916), 127, 135, 136, 137, 139, 142, 145, 156, 158, 159, 308, 335, 351
Speirs, Iain, 342
Speirs, Pipe Major J., 221, 222, 231, 234, 244, 246, 247, 253, 342
Speirs, Tom, 342
Spence, Piper and Captain Donald R., 236-237
Spooner, Sergeant Keith, 203, 228, 251, 253, 254, 255
Spoore, Pipe Major John, 299, 300, 301, 302, 304, 305, 308, 309, 310, 312, 313, 320, 328, 331, 337, 340
St Clair, Isla, 321, 330, 331, 350, 351
St Columba's Church, 79, 103, 153, 180, 187, 195, 210, 235, 254, 257, 259, 274, 275, 279, 289, 329, 334, 336, 349, 351, 356, 360
St James's Palace, 63, 316, 341, 343
St Martin's Tavern, 50
St Paul's Cathedral, 31, 93, 150, 202, 337, 357
Stewart, Piper Davie, 330, 334, 347, 349
Stewart, Pipers Charles and James, 160, 164, 167
Stoddart, Drummer J.W.A., 89, 92, 94
Strike Sure, 332
Sudairi, Crown Prince Zeid, 300-301
Suez Canal, 164, 165, 166, 214, 223, 226, 230
Sussex, Duke of, 30, 31, 37, 38
Sutherland Highlanders, 23, 49, 71

Sutherland, Duke of, 30
Sutherland-Graeme, Piper Alan V., 107, 110

Tayforth UOTC, 350, 351, 356
Territorial Army (structure of), 99-102, 279, 282, 286, 292, 311-312, 313, 316, 319, 333, 334, 360
This is Your Life, 280-281
Tomkins, Drum Major Bert, 309
Toronto Scottish Regiment, 180, 189, 205, 212, 264, 278, 280, 282-283, 295, 299, 300, 301, 309, 322, 328, 333, 335, 340, 345, 346, 352, 353
Tovey, Drummer Percival, 114, 120, 125, 127, 131
Tovey, Duncan, 39, 62, 63, 95, 114, 118, 120, 126
Tower of London, 321
Trieste, 253, 254
Tuckey, Piper and WO2 Nick, 313, 315, 317, 318, 320, 331, 341, 342
Tunes of Glory (film), 280, 334
Tunes of Glory (play), 335
Tunes of Glory: Salute to the Scottish Regiments (CD), 334
Turkish Drums (liberated), 167, 169
Turnbull Gunner Piper William, 230
Turnbull, Pipe Major Charles, 207, 213, 219, 220, 226, 229, 230, 238-239, 250, 253
Turner, Drummer Hector, 156, 157, 160, 167, 169
Twickenham Stadium, 264, 274, 276
Tyne Cot Cemetery, 301, 313

Uniforms (Highland Armed Association), 15, 16-17, 20 (Loyal North Britons) 22, (London Scottish) 42, 43, 46, 48, 49, 50, 51, 63, 77, 102, 312, 278, 312
Uzbekistan, 344, 345, 351, 352, 353, 357

VE Day, (1945) 314, 359
Venice, 252, 253, 254, 340
Victoria, Queen, 46, 47, 51, 52, 56, 72, 78, 79, 80, 86, 95, 293
Vimy Ridge, 143, 146, 156, 343
Volunteer Movement, 41, 57
Volunteer Returns, 28-30, 31

Wallace, Drummer Walter M., 120, 125, 132
Watford Camp, 109, 112, 153
Wellington Barracks, 56, 62, 63, 68, 93, 204, 266, 294, 309, 329, 333, 337, 340, 345, 357
Welsh Air Training Corps (accident), 315
Westminster Abbey, 79, 104, 106, 150, 187, 200, 263, 329
Westminster Hall, Houses of Parliament, 47, 48, 52, 53, 64, 68, 329

Westminster, Duke of, 341
Westminster, Freedom of the City, 266
White City, 265, 266, 276
Wilkins, Drummer Frank, 125, 132
Wills, Pipe Major David C., 89, 151, 159
Wimbledon, 48, 56, 59, 63, 64, 65, 68, 80, 122, 136, 195, 275, 294, 308, 342
Windsor Castle, 46, 73, 77, 308, 337, 343, 359
Winifredian, S.S., 112, 135, 149
Winterbottom, John Bandmaster Royal Marines, 52
Withers, Drummer Andy, 341, 342, 344, 345, 346, 348, 350
Withers, Drummer Iain, 344, 347, 349
Withey, Piper Alan, 267, 280, 282, 290, 301, 358
Woodcock, Piper Henry J.R., 138

Worshipful Company of Distillers, 321, 345, 351, 357, 358

Xixon, Bagpipe Festival, 335, 340

York, Duke of, 27, 89, 198
Young, Major Stuart, 317, 331
Young, Piper and Sub Lieutenant Hamish, 349, 351
Young, Piper Callum, 349, 351, 357, 358
Younger, Ron, 334, 343, 356,
Ypres, 115, 123, 124, 144, 145, 181, 199, 298, 301, 308, 333, 341, 343, 347, 358

Zambra, Piper and Colonel William W., 134, 137, 142